D0027948

Iceland

Fran Parnell

Brandon Presser

HORNSTRANDIR (p192)
Explore lonely cliffs and coves on a life-changing hike across Hornstrandir

STRANDIR COAST (p194)
Take in the wild serenity of the Strandir coast, stopping at strange seductive Djúpavik before soaking in the waters at Krossnes

ÍSAFJÖRÐUR (p185)
Take in Iceland's most isolated town, set in the spectacular, rugged Westfjords

SNÆFELLSNES (p163)
Marvel at the Snæfellsjökull peak and glacier, the setting for *Journey to the Centre of the Earth*

GEYSIR & GULLFOSS (p126)
Don't miss Iceland's 'big two': a regularly exploding geyser and a majestic waterfall

REYKJAVÍK (p70)
Enjoy manic nightlife, great restaurants, museums and culture in this intimate capital

BLUE LAGOON (p117)
Bathe in the steaming blue waters of this famous thermal pool

LANDMANNALAUGAR (p285)
Relax among hot springs and colourful rhyolite hills

VESTMANNAEYJAR (p149)
Watch thousands of puffin chicks take flight from these spectacular islands every August

Arctic Circle

Denmark Strait

Hornstrandir

Bolungarvik
Suðureyri
Ísafjörður
Drangajökull

Norðurfjörður

Skagafjörður
76

Þingeyri

Húnaflói

Drangey

Skagaströnd
745

Bíldudalur

Hólmavík

Sauðárkrókur
74
Blönduós
75

Patreksfjörður

Brjánslækur

711

Hóp

Flatey

Hvammstangi

Breiðafjörður

35

Stykkishólmur

Búðardalur

Hellissandur-Rif
Ólafsvik
Grundarfjörður
Snæfellsnes

1

Eiríksjökull
(1675m)

Langjökull

54

Borgarnes

Faxaflói

ÞINGVELLIR NATIONAL PARK

Geysir

Gullfoss

Akranes

Reykjavík
REYKJAVÍK

Þingvallavatn

Keflavik
Hafnarfjörður
Kópavogur

30

Njarðvik

1

Hveragerði

Landmannalaugar

425

Selfoss

Grindavík
Þorlákshöfn
Hella

Selvogsgrunn

Mýrdalsjöku

Eyrarbakkabugur

Hvolsvöllur

Eyjafjallajökull
(1450m)

Skógar

NORTH

Heimaey
Heimaey

Vík

ATLANTIC

VESTMANNAEYJAR

OCEAN

Surtsey

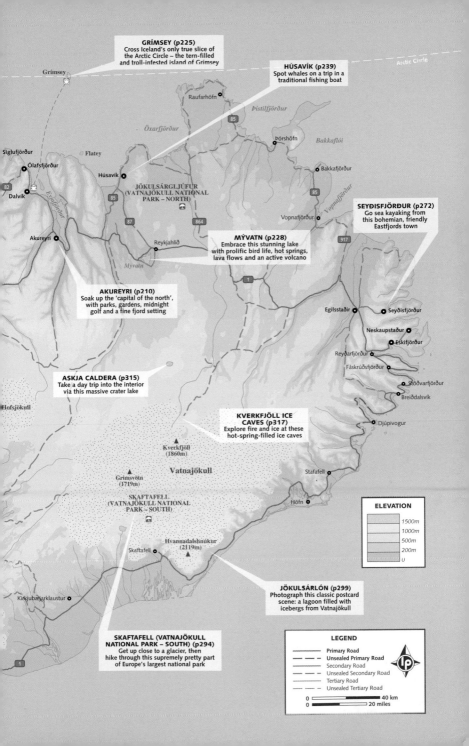

GRÍMSEY (p225)
Cross Iceland's only true slice of the Arctic Circle – the tern-filled and troll-infested island of Grímsey

HÚSAVÍK (p239)
Spot whales on a trip in a traditional fishing boat

SEYÐISFJÖRÐUR (p272)
Go sea kayaking from this bohemian, friendly Eastfjords town

MÝVATN (p228)
Embrace this stunning lake with prolific bird life, hot springs, lava flows and an active volcano

AKUREYRI (p210)
Soak up the 'capital of the north', with parks, gardens, midnight golf and a fine fjord setting

ASKJA CALDERA (p315)
Take a day trip into the interior via this massive crater lake

KVERKFJÖLL ICE CAVES (p317)
Explore fire and ice at these hot-spring-filled ice caves

JÖKULSÁRLÓN (p299)
Photograph this classic postcard scene: a lagoon filled with icebergs from Vatnajökull

SKAFTAFELL (VATNAJÖKULL NATIONAL PARK – SOUTH) (p294)
Get up close to a glacier, then hike through this supremely pretty part of Europe's largest national park

Grímsey

Arctic Circle

Raufarhöfn

Þistilfjörður

Öxarfjörður

Þórshöfn

Bakkaflói

Siglufjörður

Ólafsfjörður

Flatey

Bakkafjörður

Húsavík

JÖKULSÁRGLJÚFUR (VATNAJÖKULL NATIONAL PARK – NORTH)

82

Dalvík

Eyjafjörður

85

87

864

Vopnafjörður

Vopnafjörður

Akureyri

Reykjahlíð

917

Mývatn

1

Egilsstaðir

Seyðisfjörður

Neskaupstaður

Eskifjörður

Reyðarfjörður

Fáskrúðsfjörður

Stöðvarfjörður

Breiðdalsvík

Hofsjökull

Djúpivogur

Kverkfjöll (1860m)

Vatnajökull

Stafafell

Grímsvötn (1719m)

SKAFTAFELL (VATNAJÖKULL NATIONAL PARK – SOUTH)

Höfn

ELEVATION

1500m
1000m
500m
200m
0

Hvannadalshnúkur (2119m)

Skaftafell

Kirkjubæjarklaustur

LEGEND

Primary Road
Unsealed Primary Road
Secondary Road
Unsealed Secondary Road
Tertiary Road
Unsealed Tertiary Road

1

0 ——————— 40 km
0 ——————— 20 miles

On the Road

FRAN PARNELL Coordinating Author

I've been banging on about how marvellous Iceland is for years to anyone who will listen, including my long-suffering parents. So it was wonderful to finally persuade them to visit. We met up on the south coast and had a picnic on the banks of the glacial river Þjórsá in Þjórsárdalur (p129), before driving up to this incredible lookout. Such a gentle day – but it was magical to be standing on top of the world, dizzy with blue sky, clear water and distant Hekla, sharing my love of this country with my dear old mum and dad.

BRANDON PRESSER Breaks from the relentless research routine are few and far between when I'm on the road, but a chance to volunteer at the Arctic Fox Research Station (p188) was too good to pass up. After hiking and kayaking my way through Hornstrandir, I finally reached the survey camp at Hornbjarg, the reserve's ultimate Arctic edge. This photo was taken while I was 'on assignment'; I spent eight glorious hours on that mossy patch watching the foxes trot around their den while taking in the majesty of the snowcapped hills in the distance. It was a tough gig, but someone had to do it.

For full author biographies see p351

Iceland Highlights

Immense glaciers and wiggling fjords, unspoiled wilderness areas ripe for exploration, a clean and icy sea where humpback whales surface, roll and dive into the depths again – Iceland's cinematic beauty is overwhelming. Stir in a fascinating Viking past, tiny fishing villages, geothermal pools and hot pots, and a hint of magic in the air, and you've hit the holiday jackpot.

ANDERS BLOMQVIST

① WALLOWING IN THE BLUE LAGOON

My mum and I spent three hours at the Blue Lagoon (p117) on the way back home – and it was no-where near enough! It was so relaxing – I could go there every day and never get tired of it.

Catherine Parkes, Traveller, US

GRANT DIXON

A GLACIER WALK

One of my finest walks in Iceland was up the Svínafellsjökull glacier (p298) at Skaftafell (pictured below). We had perfect weather – that intoxicating combination of bright, warm sunshine and frosty air – and lovely people to walk with. Then there was the joy of striding across a normally treacherous surface, the entrancing holy blues of the ice, the gurgle of whirlpools, and every so often a mossy glacial mouse to stroke…cold, crisp memories that always make me smile.

Fran Parnell,
Lonely Planet Author, UK

2

LANDMANNALAUGAR

If you haven't time for a multiday hike to Land-mannalaugar (p285), a sightseeing flight over the highlands makes a fantastic alternative! The little eight-seater plane takes off from outside a kind of ranch in the middle of the sandur (sand delta) near Skaftafell – a surreal start to a journey that just gets weirder as you fly past the edge of the ice cap, over the massive Laki lava flow, and on to the rainbow-coloured mountains of Landmannalaugar.

Fran Parnell, Lonely Planet Author, UK

3

FRANS LEMM

ANDERS BLOMQV

4

HOT POT HOP

Iceland's unofficial pastime is splashing around in its surplus of geothermal water. There are 'hot pots' everywhere – from downtown Reykjavík to the isolated peninsular tips of the Westfjords – and not only are they incredibly relaxing, it's a great way to meet the locals!

Brandon Presser, Lonely Planet Author, Canada

SNÆFELLSNES PENINSULA

With its cache of wild sand-strewn beaches and crackling sulphur lava fields, the Snæfellsnes Peninsula (p163) is one of my favourite places to escape in all of Iceland. Jules Verne was definitely onto something when he used the area as his magical doorway to the centre of the earth. New Age types have flocked to the region to harness its natural power and energy. I'm not sure if I believe in the existence of 'earth chakras', but there's no doubt in my mind that there are greater forces at play along this stunning peninsula.

Brandon Presser, Lonely Planet Author, Canada

5

BRANDON PRESSER

WHALE WATCHING IN HÚSAVÍK

This is the real deal: beautiful old wooden fishing boats have been restored to take passengers whale watching. Húsavík (p239) is not only a hub for whale watching but it's also a whale research centre. It's not unusual to be on the boat with a team of scientists studying animal behaviour and trying to photo-identify the animals.

Jacob Kasper, Traveller, US

6

NICHOLAS PAVLOFF

GRAEME CORNWALLIS

7

HIKING IN SKAFTAFELL (VATNA-JÖKULL NATIONAL PARK – SOUTH)

Walking through Skaftafell (p294) – through the dwarf trees, over the springy turf and heather – is exhilarating. Once you've left the campsite behind, the sense of freshness and silence and spaciousness is indescribable. The quietness has an almost magical feel to it.

Pim Simmonds, Traveller

GRAEME CORNW

8 A BOAT TRIP TO HEIMAEY, VESTMANNAEYJAR

The first view of the Vestmannaeyjar (p149) from the ferry is what sticks with me: a grey arc of rocks in a grey sea, appearing and disappearing in the distance. When you reach Heimaey, the narrowness of the entrance to the harbour takes your breath away. And the proximity of the great lava mass to the town, the thought that underneath your feet are houses and streets and a settlement buried… Climb the crater or the cliffs, and it's right in front of your eyes. The time of the eruption is captured so vividly – you can see exactly where the disaster ended and the town continues.

Donald Stirling, Traveller, UK

ALAMY/HEIDA HELGADOT

9 THE COAST AT EYRARBAKKI

Although I love Iceland's dramatic landscapes and high-octane adventure, one of my great joys is to find an empty place and spend a few hours gaping into space. Quiet little Eyrarbakki (p135) is a good thinking spot, with its fresh sea air and a deserted beach looking out over endless grey ocean. There's no land between here and the Antarctic, a fact I like to swirl around in my mind while I watch the birds and listen to the waves.

Fran Parnell, Lonely Planet Author, UK

FRANS LEMMENS

MERTEN SNIJDERS

ÞINGVELLIR

I suggest you visit Þingvellir (p121), the site of the first parliament in the world. There you can see the rift between the North American and Eurasian plates, a truly unique geological experience.

travelguides, Traveller

11

10

STROKKUR'S ERUPTION

I stood at the edge of the roped-off area, counting down the five-minute interval between the geyser's eruptions. I removed my gloves despite the bitter cold (ouch!) to keep my camera steady, intently observing the water slosh about Strokkur's hole (p126), watching it swell just a tiny bit more each time, gathering momentum and inching closer to the inevitable gigantic climax. And then – boom! It startled me – a huge pent-up release of water shot out of the ground, carried by the wind towards where I stood, dangerously close to drenching me with 100°C water. Somehow in the split second that all this occurred I managed to press the shutter.

Eric V So, http://hello1newman.blogspot.com, US

ALAMY/MICHELE FALZONE

12

DYRHÓLAEY ROCK ARCH

At Dyrhólaey (p146) the colours and light were wonderful for photographing the black-sand beaches and towering cliffs.

Dr Paul Hirst, Traveller, US

LIVING THE SAGAS

Never have I been to a country whose history has been so perfectly and painstakingly documented. And the pages of Iceland's past are by no means typical – the sagas, as they're known, bring to life a mystical menagerie of adventurers, creatures and antiheroes. To some, the days of magic and mystique may feel long gone, but if you look closely you can still revel in the island's mysterious yesteryear through haunting sea stacks, ogre-faced stones and hidden cairns.

Brandon Presser, Lonely Planet Author, Canada

14

13 JÖKULSÁRLÓN

The Jökulsárlón lagoon (p299) is every bit as otherworldly and beautiful as expected. I've never seen so many shades of blue. Absolutely worth any detour.

CanadianGrrl, Traveller

15 SPACE

The vast open spaces of Iceland are a tonic for overcrowded city life. This is a country with a mere 300,000 inhabitants and where the biggest highway in the country turns to dirt in some parts. The further you get out of Reykjavík, the more isolated you will feel. Just be sure to have a full tank of petrol!

Stephanie A Yoder, http://twenty-somethingtravel.com, US

HIGHLANDS

A trip to Iceland is not complete without a trip to the wild interior highlands (p307). Some buses run on the two main cross-country routes, Sprengisandur and Kjölur, which provide access to the geothermal wonders of Kerlingarfjöll. The Askja-Kverkfjöll region, a mix of geothermal activity and glacial landscapes, is a gem that should not be missed.

James Barlow, Traveller, US

16

GRANT DIXON

REYKJAVÍK NIGHTLIFE

The city awakes from its slumberous state every Friday and Saturday night for what the locals call the *runtur* (pub crawl; p99). The 20-somethings of Reykjavík hop between the bars and discos of the city (pictured below) from midnight to 6am. Our favourite stop was a bar located on Klapparstigur. It was so hip it didn't need a name – just a sign showing a very serious man in a bowler hat.

**Katrina Bergmann Foster,
http://patrinadoestheglobe.blogspot.com, US**

17

JONATHAN SMITH

18 **NATIONAL PRIDE**

The Icelanders are really proud of their country. They always say things like 'we have the best lamb in the world' or 'this is the most beautiful mountain in the world' and they really mean it! You'll almost insult them if you dare ask if the water is drinkable. They'll say: 'Of course! We have the best water in the world!'

**Martina Pichrtová, Traveller,
Czech Republic**

MERTEN SNIJDERS

19 NORTHERN LIGHTS

DAVID TIPL

I was very lucky I guess…someone had warned me that if you see white smears in the daytime it might be a prelude to the northern lights. So I was very alert that day and evening. When I saw something funny from the window of my guest house (about 11.30pm) I took my camera, warm coat and hat, and walked as far as I could from the lights of the town, and then indeed there was a display of northern lights going on, lasting for about half an hour. I was very moved and it also felt like my eyes were playing tricks on me.

Cecilia, Traveller

BRANDON PRESS

20 HORNSTRANDIR PENINSULA

While most tourists are fighting the crowds along the Golden Circle, the real Icelandic wilderness experience can be found in Hornstrandir (p192). Accessible only by boat or multiday hike from the nearest road, Hornstrandir offers the best hiking and some of the most dramatic scenery in Iceland.

James Barlow, Traveller, US

Contents

Regional Map Contents

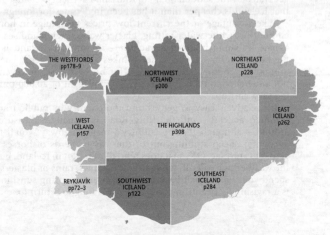

THE WESTFJORDS pp178–9

NORTHWEST ICELAND p200

NORTHEAST ICELAND p228

WEST ICELAND p157

THE HIGHLANDS p308

EAST ICELAND p262

REYKJAVÍK pp72–3

SOUTHWEST ICELAND p122

SOUTHEAST ICELAND p284

Destination Iceland

Few visitors can travel around Iceland without being deeply touched by the sheer beauty of it all; and few can leave the country without a pang and a fervent vow to return. It's that sort of place.

Perched on the edge of the Arctic, this wonderful little island contains some of the most impressive natural wonders in Europe. The continent's biggest waterfalls thunder down with such force that the ground trembles under your feet; the barren highlands form Europe's largest, loneliest desert; and the awesome ice cap Vatnajökull is the biggest outside the poles. Other spectacular phenomena include smouldering volcanoes, slow-flowing glaciers, extruding lava, gushing geysers, bubbling mudpots, soothing thermal pools and, in the darkness of winter, the magical northern lights.

Until about 20 years ago, Iceland's fantastic scenery, challenging hikes, friendly natives and eerily remote wilderness were a well-kept secret. Today the country is one of Europe's hottest travel destinations. As well as having awe-inspiring nature, it boasts the compact capital Reykjavík, a city filled with Viking history and renowned for its high-energy nightlife and kaleidoscopic music scene.

Some of this exuberance was knocked out of the country following the 2008 global financial crisis. Its three major banks went into receivership, the króna went into free fall, and relations between Iceland and Britain were strained as Gordon Brown used antiterrorist laws to freeze Icelandic assets. Violent protests forced the prime minister's resignation and a change of government in January 2009. EU membership is now on the cards – it's an unpopular move, but one that should stabilise the country's finances.

Although these recent horrors have shaken the country far harder than its biggest earthquakes ever do, and although national pride has been seriously dented, Icelanders are a tough, industrious and inventive bunch who have survived centuries of hardship. Their stoicism and black humour will no doubt help them weather the worst, as will the income generated by the sudden boom in tourism. Excellent exchange rates mean that Iceland is cheaper than it has been in decades for foreign visitors.

Take advantage of the current low prices to indulge in horse riding, elf hunting, white-water rafting, glacier walks, caving and sea kayaking. Whale watching is a big attraction – in summer Iceland is probably the best place in Europe to see minkes and humpbacks. The sea cliffs around the country are a paradise for birdwatchers, but even if you're not a twitcher you'll be blown away by the sight of 20,000 puffins nesting on a clifftop.

It's relatively easy to get around the country by public transport (in summer, at least), and the Ring Road is actually a pleasure to drive around – although it's the country's major highway, you'll frequently encounter sheep ambling out of the way or herds of horses galloping across the tarmac. OK, so it does tend to rain a lot in Iceland, but don't let the weather put you off. No matter if it snows, rains or blusters, or if you spend your whole visit basking in the sweetest spring sunshine, Iceland is a ravishingly beautiful place that you'll long to return to.

FAST FACTS

Population: 319,400

Unemployment precrash (2008): 2.3%; postcrash (2009): 6%

Number of foreign passengers passing through Keflavík International Airport (2007): 458,890

Percentage of Icelanders who use the internet: 93% (the world's highest)

Number of MacDonald's in Iceland: 0 (all three outlets closed in November 2009)

Most popular girl's name: Sara

Most popular boy's name: Jón

Total fish catch (2008): 1.3 million tonnes

Percentage of Icelanders who check the weather forecast daily: 70%

Getting Started

Nothing quite prepares you for a trip to Iceland. In the past, visitors have gone to experience a weekend of wild nightlife or a fortnight of pristine scenery, and have left again with expensive credit-card bills. These days, Iceland's become a top honeymoon destination, and is just waking up to the possibilities of adventure tourism, with skiing, white-water rafting, kayaking, snowmobiling and a host of other wild activities available. Reykjavík's Friday-night drinking and the Land of Fire and Ice cliché remain compelling drawcards, and the country's recent economic troubles mean that, for the time being at least, it's never been cheaper to visit.

A little planning is the best way to ensure you find the remote, stunningly beautiful fjords, waterfalls and geysers, dig out the best pubs and clubs, and uncover the country's hidden gems – from luxurious spas to ends-of-the-earth-style wilderness camping – all on whatever budget you can afford.

Iceland is a very seasonal destination, and planning ahead will mean you don't spend hours driving to see a puffin colony that migrated out to sea months previously, or get stuck waiting for a bus that never comes. Although the short summer season (June to August) offers the widest choice of activities and destinations, an off-season visit can be magical and gives you the benefit of having the top tourist attractions entirely to yourself.

WHEN TO GO

Iceland has a very distinct and short-lived tourist season, which runs from June to August. During this time you'll have the best weather, incredibly long days, the pick of tours and excursions, and the best choice of accommodation. On the downside, you'll also experience huge crowds at the biggest attractions, and at times the Ring Road will feel like a countrywide carousel where the fairground horses have been replaced by shiny grey hire cars.

See Climate Charts (p326) for more information.

September and May can be good months to travel, with generally good weather and far fewer tourists. Public transport will not be on a full schedule at these times, however; campsites will be closed; and, if you're hiking, snow may not clear from high passes until well into July.

Outside high season everything slows down. From late August rural attractions can start to close, by early September buses revert to a severely reduced winter schedule, and by the end of the month the days are getting noticeably shorter, tours are almost nonexistent and many museums,

---

IF YOU DON'T LIKE THE WEATHER NOW...

Although the Icelandic summer is short, the days are long and the climate is generally mild. Daytime temperatures hover around 12°C to 15°C, with lows of about 5°C overnight. May and June are the driest months, but coastal areas, particularly in the south and west, are prone to rain at any time. Thanks to the moderating effects of the Gulf Stream, winters are surprisingly mild, and it's often warmer in Reykjavík in midwinter than in New York or Zürich. Be prepared for fierce, wind-driven rain, gales and fog, however, and shrieking winds and icy blizzards in the highlands. The clearest and coldest winter weather is generally around Akureyri and Mývatn in the central north. You'll find a daily weather forecast in English at http://en.vedur.is, but if you're in any doubt just refer to the old local saying: 'If you don't like the weather now, wait five minutes – it'll probably get worse.'

DON'T LEAVE HOME WITHOUT...

■ A sleeping bag – even if you're not camping, you can save a packet by opting for a bed without linen at hostels, guest houses and some hotels. A blow-up pillow, pillow case and nonfitted sheet are also handy.

■ A large memory card or plenty of film for your camera – neither are cheap to buy locally.

■ Swimsuit and towel – for those glorious natural hot springs, geothermal pools and hot pots (outdoor hot tubs).

■ Rain gear and thermals – if you're planning to hike, cycle or hitch, don't dream of travelling without them.

■ A credit card – Icelanders wouldn't know what to do without plastic.

■ A sense of humour – for those days when fog and low cloud shrouds everything in your path or you're holed up in a hut while a summer blizzard rages outside.

---

attractions and guest houses outside Reykjavík and Akureyri have closed. Listings throughout the book give details of opening times, though, and despite reduced facilities it's well worth considering an off-season trip to see mighty waterfalls frozen still, experience the aurora borealis (see the boxed text, p59), ski, snowmobile or ice-fish, or just luxuriate in a steaming hot pool surrounded by snow. And everywhere you go you'll get an especially warm welcome from the locals. Another benefit is that accommodation costs drop substantially from about mid-September to mid-May, when you'll get up to 40% off the cost of a high-season hotel room and a 20% to 30% reduction in the rates of most guest houses. If you're planning to travel around the country in the low-season you'll need to hire a car, and you should check road conditions locally as rural roads and mountain passes can be closed due to snow.

HOW MUCH?

Guest-house accommodation d Ikr10,000–14,000

1L unleaded petrol Ikr185

Large glass of Egil's beer Ikr700

Whale-watching trip Ikr8000

Icelandic knitted jumper Ikr10,000

COSTS & MONEY

Iceland has traditionally been an expensive destination, but the recent financial crisis (see the boxed text, p35) has changed all that. At the time of writing, exchange rates were extremely favourable for tourists. But the economic situation is still up in the air, and of course those tourist-friendly rates could change at any time.

Iceland is an almost cashless society – Icelanders use their credit and debit cards for almost every transaction, so you don't need to make large cash withdrawals in order to get around.

The cheapest accommodation option in Iceland is camping, but if you don't fancy a night under canvas you can keep costs down by choosing sleeping-bag accommodation in guest houses. A bed in a guest house or farmhouse will cost roughly Ikr2500 to Ikr4000 for sleeping-bag accommodation and Ikr10,000 to 14,000 for a double room with made-up beds. Hotel room prices start at around Ikr14,000/18,000 for a single/double in high season, with prices dropping by up to 40% in low season. Families or groups can get cheaper deals by finding multiple-bed rooms or, in rural areas, stay in self-contained cottages or cabins. You can overnight in wonderful timber summer cabins (sleeping up to six people), with kitchen, lounge, bathroom, and barbecue deck and prices starting from around Ikr11,000 per cabin per night.

Eating out in Iceland can be expensive unless you're prepared for an overdose of fast food. Inexpensive, filling but largely unhealthy meals are available at the ubiquitous grill bars in petrol stations, where you'll get a burger or fried chicken, chips and a drink for about Ikr700. Alternatively, you can fill up in a fast-food pizza joint for around Ikr1400. To eat well you'll need to cook for yourself or be prepared to pay for the privilege. Fish and lamb are the main-course staples at most Icelandic restaurants, with fish dishes costing about Ikr1800 to Ikr2800 and lamb dishes anywhere from Ikr2500 to Ikr4000. For those on a budget, one helpful tip is to eat your main meal in the middle of the day, when lunchtime buffets or tourist menus can be great value.

Hiring a car gives you freedom to visit out-of-the-way attractions; sharing the hire with other travellers can keep expenses down and begin to rival the cost of bus passes. The cheapest hire cars cost around Ikr20,000 per day – book well ahead. Most hire cars are not insured to drive on the country's mountain F roads. If you want to access the highland interior, you'll need to hire a 4WD for around Ikr45,000 per day. It's also worth noting that air travel in Iceland is not much more expensive than bus travel. For more information, see p337.

For a true idea of how much a trip to Iceland will cost, you'll also need to factor in things such as nightlife (in Reykjavík and Akureyri at least), museum admission (usually Ik500 to Ikr800) and activities such as horse riding (Ikr3000 an hour), whale watching (Ikr8000) or a snowmobile tour (Ikr10,000). Budget travellers who camp regularly, self-cater and take the bus could scrape by on as little as Ikr3000 a day per person. Add in sleeping-bag or guest-house accommodation, a meal out, a bus tour and a shared hire car, and you're looking at about Ikr10,000 to Ikr16,000 a day. Those staying in average hotel accommodation, driving their own car, eating decent restaurant meals, and taking advantage of Iceland's tours and activities should budget for expenses of at least Ikr25,000 per day.

Our top tips for budget travellers:

- Bring a tent or use sleeping-bag accommodation in guest houses.
- Look for places where you can use a kitchen and cook for yourself.
- Become a member of Hostelling International (HI) before leaving home.
- Buy a bus pass if you're planning a round-Iceland trip.
- Choose a smaller area of the country to explore and plan to do plenty of walking.
- Travel outside high season.

TRAVELLING RESPONSIBLY

Iceland's reliance on geothermal and hydroelectric power gives the country an enviable environmental reputation. Iceland is suffering, however, from the rest of the world's reliance on fossil fuels – global warming is having a particularly devastating effect on the country's glaciers.

Short of avoiding the flight to Iceland in the first place, try to reduce your carbon footprint as much as possible. Consider using the bus service, which is not too bad in summer, particularly along the south coast.

WARNING: FLUCTUATING PRICES

This book contains prices researched in high season of 2009, but be warned that by the time you get there, the country's unstable financial situation might make prices look very different.

Many companies have begun listing prices in euros only, as it's a more stable currency; and now that Iceland has applied for EU membership, it's likely that Icelanders will abandon the króna altogether in favour of the euro around 2011.

ESSENTIAL VIEWING

Watch the black comedy *101 Reykjavík* before leaving home to understand Reykjavík's late-night hedonistic spirit. For a glimpse of teen angst in rural Iceland, try the quirky *Nói Albínói*, a touching coming-of-age movie with plenty of dark humour. The thriller *Jar City*, adapted from Arnaldur Indriðason's award-winning novel *Tainted Blood*, follows world-weary Detective Inspector Erlendur as he investigates a brutal murder and some dodgy doings at Iceland's Genetic Research Centre.

For more information on Icelandic films, see p46.

Recycling schemes are uncommon, although the youth hostelling association encourages travellers to separate their rubbish.

There's a growing Slow Food Movement – look out for restaurants participating in locally grown food schemes, and choose Icelandic lamb and reindeer dishes over those made from imported ingredients.

It isn't a crime to buy bottled water in Iceland – but it ought to be! Icelandic tap water generally comes from the nearest glacier, and is some of the purest you'll ever drink.

Although it looks huge, harsh and eternal, the Icelandic landscape is surprisingly fragile. If you've hired a 4WD vehicle, you must stick to marked trails. Off-road driving is illegal due to the irreversible damage it causes. See the boxed text, p67, for tips on low-impact camping and hiking.

TRAVEL LITERATURE

For a gritty glimpse of the Icelandic soul, Halldór Laxness's humorous, heart-breaking, deep-minded work *Independent People* is an absolute must. Follow it up with the dark humour and turbulent times of Einar Kárason's *Devil's Island*, a look at life in Reykjavík in the 1950s and 1960s, or some crime fiction by Iceland's best-selling author Arnaldur Indriðason – six of his novels have been translated into English, including the award-winning *Tainted Blood* (also known as *Jar City*). For more information on Icelandic literature, see p41.

For an irreverent look at the country from a traveller's point of view, try *Letters from Iceland* by WH Auden and Louis MacNeice, an amusing and unconventional travelogue written by the two poets in 1936. In contrast, Alan Boucher's *The Iceland Traveller – A Hundred Years of Adventure* is full of 18th- and 19th-century romance, history and drama. For a warts-and-all view of contemporary Icelandic travel, Tim Moore's *Frost on My Moustache* lays bare the realities of overambitious cycle trips and eating hot dogs for every meal.

INTERNET RESOURCES

You'll find a wealth of information online. The following sites are particularly useful for planning your trip:

BSÍ (www.bsi.is) Information on bus travel around Iceland from the bus companies' consortium.

Gisting (www.accommodation.is) Comprehensive list of accommodation options in Iceland laid out on relevant street maps.

Iceland Review (www.icelandreview.com) Excellent daily news digest from Iceland with current affairs, entertainment, culture and more.

Icelandic Tourist Board (www.visiticeland.com; www.icetourist.is; www.goiceland.org) The official sites of the Icelandic Tourist Board.

Lonely Planet (www.lonelyplanet.com) Information on travel in Iceland and plenty of traveller tips on the Thorn Tree forum.

Nordic Adventure Travel (www.nat.is) Practical information and planning tips, plus the low-down on lots of rural towns.

TOP PICKS

Reykjavík ICELAND

FESTIVALS & EVENTS

Icelanders love to party, and you'll find celebrations of music, culture, history or the changing of the seasons happening year-round. The following are our favourites; for more, see p22.

- Þorrablót (Viking midwinter feast; p22) – nationwide, February.

- Independence Day (p22) – nationwide, June.

- Sjómannadagurinn (Sailors' Day; p22) – coastal towns, June.

- Midsummer (p23) – nationwide, June.

- Listasumar Akureyri, (Akureyri Arts Festival; p217) – Akureyri, June to August.

- Bræðislan music festival (p270) – Borgarfjörður Eystri, July.

- Menningarnott (Culture Night; p87) – Reykjavík, August.

- Þjóðhátíð Vestmannaeyjar (National Festival; p153) – Heimaey Island, August.

- Herring festival (p210) – Siglufjörður, August.

- Iceland Airwaves music festival (p88) – Reykjavík, October.

EXPLOSIVE SIGHTS

Serene, majestic scenery belies Iceland's fiery heart. Vast explosions have shaped the land and forged the resilient spirits of its residents. Don't miss the volcanoes, craters, geysers and fiery light displays.

- Laki (p292) – marvel at a mountainous volcano and the still-volatile Lakagígar crater row.

- Leirhnjúkur (p239) – Iceland's best example of smouldering earth and smoking vents.

- Northern lights (p59) – lucky visitors may catch the eerie colour bursts and light storms.

- Heimaey (p149) – in the House Graveyard a third of the town lies buried under lava after the entire island blew up in 1973.

- Strokkur & the Great Geysir (p126) – Strokkur blasts steaming water into the air every six minutes, and the Great Geysir itself blows several times a day.

- Hekla (p139) – active and due to erupt any time. Dare you climb its ashy slopes?

- Menningarnott (p23) – fabulous fireworks light up the heavens at the end of Reykjavík's lively cultural festival.

ECCENTRIC ICELAND

Ever since Björk's astounding voice first made the world turn and stare, the words 'Iceland' and 'eccentric' have never been too far apart. Isolation, long days of darkness, an unpredictable landscape and brennivín (the local schnapps) have helped create a nation of quiet oddness.

- Blue Lagoon (p117) – Iceland's number one tourist attraction is an extremely weird idea: where else do you queue to go swimming inside a geothermal power station?

- 'Hidden People' – there's widespread respect for the supernatural creatures that are said to dwell throughout the country.

- Museum of Icelandic Sorcery & Witchcraft (p195) – 17th-century runes, riddles and the gruesome 'necropants' show that Westfjords weirdness is not a modern phenomenon.

- Quirky Gifts (p102) – fish-skin handbags, bowls made from radishes and boxes made from pigs' bladders…

- Víti Crater (p316) – skinny-dipping in this water-filled volcanic crater is a favourite Icelandic activity on highland trips.

- Singed sheep's head (p98) – sample the Icelandic delicacy of svið in traditional eateries.

- Icelandic Phallological Museum (p241) – an oddball museum, this place flashes a collection of 300+ penises at its visitors.

Events Calendar

True to their Viking roots, Icelanders love to party in raucous style. The country's main events tend to be based in Reykjavík, but all kinds of small, enthusiastic, and very often slightly unhinged celebrations are held countrywide.

JANUARY–MARCH

ÞORRABLÓT 18 Jan-16 Feb
The Viking midwinter feast is marked nationwide with stomach-churning treats such as *hákarl* (putrid shark meat) and *svið* (singed sheep's head).

BOLLUDAGUR Mon before Shrove Tuesday
In preparation for Lent, Bun Day sees children encouraged to beat their elders with coloured sticks in order to extract vast numbers of *bollur* (cream buns) from them.

SPRENGIDAGUR Shrove Tuesday
Bursting Day is another pre-Lenten celebration. The aim is to stuff yourself with *saltkjöt og baunir* (salted meat and split peas) until you burst.

ÖSKUDAGUR Ash Wednesday
Another excuse for children to menace adults, this time by collecting money for goodies and tying small sacks of ash on their backs.

WINTER LIGHTS mid- or late Feb
Reykjavík hosts a celebration of light and darkness to celebrate the end of winter, with cultural events, a mini food festival and illuminated buildings (www.vetrarhatid.is).

BEER DAY 1 Mar
Beer was illegal in Iceland for 75 years. On 1 March Icelanders celebrate the marvellous day in 1989 when the prohibition was overturned.

APRIL

ORKUGANGAN Mar or Apr
This popular cross-country skiing event sees participants race the 60km between Krafla and Húsavík in northern Iceland.

SUMARDAGURINN FYRSTI 1st Thu after 18 Apr
Icelanders celebrate the first day of summer with carnival-type celebrations and street parades, particularly in Reykjavík.

EASTER
The usual Easter-egg hunts, followed by smoked lamb for dinner.

SKÍÐAVIKAN & ALDREI FÓR ÉG SUÐUR around Easter
Snow permitting, Skiing Week (www.skidavikan.is) takes place at Ísafjörður in the Westfjords around Easter. The week ends with the free two-day music festival Aldrei Fór Ég Suður ('I Never Went South'; www.aldrei.is).

MAY

FOSSAVATN SKI MARATHON early May
Ísafjörður in the Westfjords hosts this 50km cross-country ski marathon (www.fossavatn.com).

LISTAHÁTÍÐ Í REYKJAVÍK mid-May
Reykjavík Arts Festival, Iceland's premier cultural festival, showcases two weeks of local and international theatre performances, film, dance, music and visual art. See www.listahatid.is/en for the program.

MÝVATN MARATHON late May
The annual Mývatn Marathon follows a circuit around the region's lovely lake (p232).

JUNE

SJÓMANNADAGURINN 1st Sun in Jun
Fishing is still a vital part of the Icelandic soul, and Sailors' Day is the biggest festival of the year in fishing villages. The Seamen's Union sponsors a party in each coastal town, with drinking, rowing and swimming contests, tugs-of-war and mock sea rescues.

HAFNARFJÖRÐUR VIKING FESTIVAL mid-Jun
The peace is shattered as Viking hordes invade this tiny seaside town near Reykjavík for a six-day festival.

INDEPENDENCE DAY 17 Jun
The country's largest festival commemorates the founding of the Republic of Iceland in 1944 with parades and general merriness. Tradition has it that the sun isn't supposed to shine. And it usually doesn't!

DJASSHÁTÍÐ EGILSSTAÐA 3rd weekend in Jun
In eastern Iceland, Egilsstaðir's annual jazz festival (www.jea.is) takes place at various venues in the area.

MIDSUMMER around 24 Jun
The longest day of the year is celebrated with solstice parties, although the Icelandic midsummer isn't as major an event as in the rest of Scandinavia. Some superstitious souls roll naked in the midsummer dew for its magical healing powers.

Á SEYÐI mid-Jun–mid-Aug
Seyðisfjörður's cultural festival teems with exhibitions, workshops and gigs. Its renowned Wednesday-evening concerts are held in the distinctive Blue Church (p274).

LISTASUMAR AKUREYRI late Jun-late Aug
The northern capital of Akureyri's 10-week annual arts festival attracts artists and musicians from around Iceland, with concerts, theatre performances, street parties and a parade (p217).

JULY

DÝRAFJARÐARDAGAR 1st weekend in Jul
This festival celebrates the area's Viking heritage and the saga of local man Gísli Súrsson (p183).

HUMARHÁTÍÐ early Jul
Höfn in southeast Iceland honours the lobster each year with a funfair, flea markets, dancing, music and lots of alcohol.

**SUMARTÓNLEIKAR Í
SKÁLHOLTSKIRKJU** Jul-early Aug
This free, five-week classical-music festival draws international musicians to the church at Skálholt, in southwest Iceland (p128).

ÞJÓÐLAGAHÁTÍÐ Á SIGLUFIRÐI mid-Jul
The tiny but perfect five-day folk-music festival (http://festival.fjallabyggd.is) in Siglufjörður welcomes Icelandic and foreign musicians.

EISTNAFLUG 2nd weekend in Jul
Punk and metal festival, held in the eastern-fjord town of Neskaupstaður (p279).

BRÆÐISLAN 3rd weekend in Jul
The Bræðislan pop/rock festival is earning itself a quality reputation, with big names coming to play in out-of-the-way Borgarfjörður Eystri (p270).

AUGUST

VERSLUNARMANNAHELGI 1st weekend in Aug
A bank-holiday long weekend when Icelanders flock to rural festivals, family barbecues, rock concerts and wild campsite parties.

**ÞJÓÐHÁTÍÐ
VESTMANNAEYJAR** 1st weekend in Aug
This earth-shaking event occurs in Heimaey on the August bank holiday, commemorating the day in 1874 when foul weather prevented the islanders partying when Iceland's constitution was established. More than 11,000 people descend to watch bands and fireworks, and drink gallons of alcohol.

HERRING FESTIVAL 1st weekend in Aug
On the August bank holiday, one of Iceland's most enjoyable local festivals takes place, celebrating Siglufjörður's former days of glory with dancing, feasting, drinking and fish cleaning.

**SKAGASTRÖND COUNTRY-MUSIC
FESTIVAL** 3rd weekend in Aug
A two-day country music festival in Skagaströnd, organised by Hallbjörn Hjartarson, the eccentric self-styled Icelandic Cowboy (p204).

MENNINGARNOTT mid-Aug
On Culture Night Reykjavík turns out in force for a day and night of art, music, dance and fireworks (www.menningarnott.is; p87).

REYKJAVÍK MARATHON mid-Aug
This race takes place on the same day as Culture Night, with full and half-marathons for the fabulously fit, as well as children's runs and fun runs. See www.marathon.is for application details and a route map.

REYKJAVÍK JAZZ FESTIVAL mid-Aug
This five-day festival (www.reykjavikjazz.is) attracts international names as well as Iceland's leading jazz musicians (p87).

GAY PRIDE 3rd weekend of Aug
Merriment and wild costumes as thousands parade carnival-style through the streets of Reykjavík to an open-air stage show featuring live music and entertainment (www.gaypride.is).

DANSKIR DAGAR 3rd weekend of Aug
Stykkishólmur celebrates its Danish roots with bridge dancing and live bands at the Danish Days festival.

SEPTEMBER

NIGHT OF LIGHTS   early Sep

Keflavík's Ljósanótt í Reykjanesbæ festival (www
.ljosanott.is) has a particularly lovely finale, when
waterfalls of fireworks pour over the local sea cliffs.

RÉTTIR   Sep

Farmers ride into the highlands to round up their
sheep for winter. The annual ritual is accompanied by
rural celebrations when the sheep are safely home.

**REYKJAVÍK INTERNATIONAL FILM
FESTIVAL**   late Sep/early Oct

This 10-day event features the hottest new international films as well as seminars and workshops
(www.riff.is; p87).

OCTOBER

FYRSTI VETRARDAGUR   3rd Sat of Oct

Families get together at Fyrsti Vetrardagur (First
Day of Winter) to mourn the passing of summer. As
you might expect, it's generally a low-key affair.

ICELAND AIRWAVES   mid-late Oct

Reykjavík is home to the cutting-edge Iceland
Airwaves music festival, staged at the end of the
month. It features five days packed with top DJs,
international live music and hard-core partying –
check out www.icelandairwaves.is for past and
present line-ups.

NOVEMBER

DAGAR MYRKURS   early Nov

Egilsstaðir (in eastern Iceland) perversely celebrates the onset of winter over 10 days, with
dark dances, ghost stories, star walks and torch-lit
processions during its unusual Days of Darkness
festival.

DECEMBER

NEW YEAR'S EVE   31 December

Festivities aplenty with dinners, bonfires, fireworks, parties and clubbing till the early hours
of New Year's Day to celebrate the arrival of a
brand-new year.

Itineraries
CLASSIC ROUTES

REYKJAVÍK & THE GOLDEN CIRCLE
Four days / Reykjavík to the Blue Lagoon (via the Golden Circle & south coast)

Arrive in **Reykjavík** (p70) on Friday to catch the *runtur* pub crawl (p99). Next morning, sober up in the fantastic geothermal swimming pool at Laugardalur (p83), before sweeping up the steeple of **Hallgrímskirkja** (p75), ingesting Viking history at the **National Museum** (p77) and admiring modern creations at **Hafnarhúsið** (p77) art gallery. Join a **whale-watching trip** (p84), then indulge in an afternoon's weird and wonderful shopping (p101).

Next up, the Golden Circle: start at **Þingvellir National Park** (p121), cradle of the nation, before heading to **Geysir** (p126) to watch the Strokkur geyser gush. Saddle up and horse-ride to thundering **Gullfoss** (p127), one of Iceland's most impressive waterfalls. Now head for tiny fishing village **Stokkseyri** (p136) to kayak on a tranquil lagoon or scare yourself silly at the Ghost Centre. The more sober attractions at neighbouring **Eyrarbakki** (p135) include the wonderful museum Húsið. Dine at a top-notch seafood restaurant, **Við Fjöruborðið** (p137) or **Hafið Bláa** (p136), between Eyrarbakki and Þorlákshöfn.

Stop at the idyllic **Blue Lagoon** (p117) on the way back to the airport.

A 300km route perfect for those with little time to spare. Once you've explored Reykjavík's charms, catch a glimpse of what lies in the vast beyond outside Iceland's only real city: waterfalls, geysers, lava formations, ghosts and trolls, tiny fishing villages and steaming geothermal pools.

ROADS LESS TRAVELLED

WESTFJORDS CIRCUIT   Seven days to three weeks / Stykkishólmur to Krossnes

Arrive in the Westfjords in style: take the ferry from pretty **Stykkishólmur** (p164) and stop off midroute at the quaint island of **Flatey** (p168), with its colourful houses and population of five. Once you've landed in the Westfjords, head straight for Iceland's most western point, the cliffs at **Látrabjarg** (p180), teeming with bird life. Wiggle your way north along the next big fjord to beautiful **Ketildalir** and **Selárdalur** (Kettle Valley; p183), where you'll find the weather-worn sculptures of Samúel Jónsson. Spend at least two days in remote, raven-filled **Ísafjörður** (p185) to take advantage of the kayaking, birdwatching and boat trips available from the town. Those with time to spare can branch off into true wilderness on a lonely multiday hike across the deserted **Hornstrandir Peninsula** (p192). Rte 61 out of town leads you to **Súðavík** (p190) and the newly opened Arctic Fox Center, before slowly shimmying its way round empty fjords and over mountains back to the mainland. Not you, though – instead, take Rte 643 up the eastern **Strandir Coast** (p194), a gloriously serene stretch of jagged crags. Drop in to **Hólmavík** (p195) to check out the necropants in the Museum of Icelandic Sorcery & Witchcraft. Go on to soak in the seaside geothermal hot pots at **Drangsnes** (p196). For even more exclusive bathing, head for the open-air geothermal swimming pool, on the edge of the world at **Krossnes** (p198).

Too many people shunt round the Ring Road and miss the wild and lovely Westfjords. This 560km route takes you to some of the emptiest, strangest and most spectacular parts of Iceland – places that will seem like a dream when you're safely back home.

THE EMPTY EAST   Three days to one week / Seyðisfjörður to Papey Island

Ferry passengers from Denmark have the good fortune to land in bohemian **Seyðisfjörður** (p272). Treat yourself to a kayak tour (p274) in the pretty fjord, or head to the isolated farm and nature reserve **Skálanes** (p275) for prime birdwatching. Head over the mountain and north to **Borgarfjörður Eystri** (p269) for quiet contemplation...or wild celebration, if you happen to catch the Bræðislan music festival (p23) in July.

Returning south, head for **Mjóifjörður** (p191), where an abandoned whaling station and ruined lighthouse enhance the sense of isolation; there's enough good hiking for a two-day stay.

Rte 92 takes you through **Reyðarfjörður** (p276) and **Eskifjörður** (p276), a pair of sleepy fishing villages enveloped by looming, emerald-green basalt mountains. From there the road climbs up and over Iceland's highest mountain pass, before dropping down to **Neskaupstaður** (p278), where Frú Lú Lú is one of the most fun places in the Eastfjords to hang out.

Return to Reyðarfjörður and head east along Rte 96, which undulates along the coast past the tiny villages of **Fáskúðfjörður** (p280), **Stoðvarfjörður** (p280) and **Breiðdalsvík** (p281). At Stoðvarfjörður, don't miss mineral collection of octogenarian Petra Sveinsdóttir, lovingly collected over a lifetime. Rejoin the Ring Road and follow the coast to the last fjord town **Djúpivogur** (p281), the harbour for boat trips to the beautiful nature reserve **Papey Island** (p282).

The Eastfjords are less showy than their western counterparts, but filled with quirky oddments and stunning blasts of nature. On this 500km route, swoop down vertical mountainsides to see how life is lived in Iceland's remote fishing villages.

TAILORED TRIPS

SEEKING THE VIKINGS & THEIR STORIES

Most of the stories that have survived about the Vikings were written down in the medieval sagas. Start your quest in Reykjavík at the **Culture House** (p77), where the original saga manuscripts are kept. To flesh out the stories, visit the **National Museum** (p77) which has a floor dedicated to the Vikings; the inventive **Reykjavík 871 +/-2** (p77) exhibition, based around an original Viking longhouse; and the larger-than-life **Saga Museum** (p76). Hafnarfjörður holds an annual Viking Festival (p109) in mid-June.

The excellent Settlement Centre at **Borgarnes** (p160) focuses on the Vikings' discovery of Iceland, and the bloodthirsty anti-hero of *Egil's Saga*. Scholar and schemer Snorri Sturluson probably wrote the latter – visit the museum dedicated to him at **Reykholt** (p162). In the 1960s a Viking grave was discovered at solitary **Skarðsvík** (p172), a stunning spot to sit and contemplate life. Check out the reconstruction of Eiríkur Rauðe's (Erik the Red) house at **Eiríksstaðir** (p175), deep in *Laxdæla Saga* country. Tragic hero Grettir the Strong met his death on the atmospheric island of **Drangey** (p207). There's a pleasant 10km marked walking trail from **Aðalból** (p269) in east Iceland, following the main sites featured in *Hrafnkell's Saga. Njál's Saga* is set around **Hvolsvöllur** (p140). For two different views of an early Norse farm, head for **Þjórsárdalur** (p129).

SWIMMING POOLS, SPAS & HOT SPRINGS

The swimming pool is sacred in Iceland, and the hot tub is the social hub of every village and town. No trip to Iceland would be complete without a visit to the **Blue Lagoon** (p117). Reykjavík has some fine swimming pools, including the Olympic-sized pool and spa at **Laugardalur** (p83), and its own little geothermal beach (p83). The river runs warm in Reykjadalur, near **Hveragerði** (p131) – bring your swimsuit. Friendly **Laugarvatn** (p125) has hot springs that feed a natural steam bath. In the highlands the pool at **Landmannalaugar** (p285) is a pleasure for muscle-weary walkers; delightful **Þórsmörk** (p143) has a large manmade outdoor hot tub; and the chance to swim in the

turquoise water inside the Víti volcanic crater at **Askja** (p315) presents a unique opportunity. The town of **Höfn** (p302) has just got a super new swimming pool, which seems almost miraculous after the long drive through nothingness on either side of town. The 'Blue Lagoon of the North' can be found at **Mývatn** (p232) – smaller, quieter, but just as relaxing as its famous forefather. If you're a connoisseur of open-air swimming pools in strange places, try **Þjórsárdalslaug** (p130), made from the leftovers of nearby Búrfell hydroelectricity plant; **Seljavallalaug** (p145), built straight into a hillside and filled by a natural hot spring; and **Krossnes** (p197), a pool perched on a lonely black-pebble beach.

History

Geologically young, staunchly independent and frequently rocked by natural (and recently financial) disaster, Iceland has a turbulent and absorbing history of Norse settlement, literary genius, bitter feuding and foreign oppression. Life in this harsh and unforgiving landscape was never going to be easy, but the everyday challenges and hardships have cultivated a modern Icelandic spirit that's highly aware of its stormy past yet remarkably resilient, fiercely individualistic, quietly innovative and justifiably proud.

EARLY TRAVELLERS & IRISH MONKS

A veritable baby in geological terms, Iceland was created around 17 million years ago. It was only around 330 BC, when the Greek explorer Pytheas wrote about the island of Ultima Thule, six days' sailing north of Britain, that Europe became aware of a landmass beyond the confines of their maps, lurking in a sea 'congealed into a viscous jelly'.

History of Iceland, by Jon R Hjalmarsson, is a lively and absorbing account of the nation from settlement to the present day, looking at Iceland's people, places, history and issues.

For many years rumour, myth and fantastic tales of fierce storms, howling winds and barbaric dog-headed people kept explorers away from the great northern ocean, *oceanus innavigabilis*. Irish monks were probably the first to stumble upon Iceland: they regularly sailed to the Faeroes looking for solitude and seclusion. The Irish monk Dicuil wrote in AD 825 of a land where there was no daylight in winter, but on summer nights 'whatever task a man wishes to perform, even picking lice from his shirt, he can manage as well as in clear daylight.' This almost certainly describes Iceland and its midnight sun.

It's thought that Irish *papar* (fathers) settled in Iceland around the year 700 but fled when the Norsemen began to arrive in the early 9th century.

THE VIKINGS ARE COMING!

After the Irish monks, Iceland's first permanent settlers came from Norway. The Age of Settlement is traditionally defined as the period between 870 and 930, when political strife on the Scandinavian mainland caused many to flee. Most North Atlantic Norse settlers were ordinary Scandinavian citizens: farmers, herders and merchants who settled right across Western Europe, marrying Britons, Westmen (Irish) and Scots.

The word Viking is derived from *vik*, which means bay or cove in old Norse and probably referred to Viking anchorages during raids.

It's likely that the Norse accidentally discovered Iceland after being blown off course en route to the Faeroes. The first arrival, the Swede Naddoddur, landed on the east coast around 850 and named the place Snæland (Snow Land) before backtracking to his original destination.

Iceland's second visitor, Garðar Svavarsson, circumnavigated the island and then settled in for the winter at Húsavík on the north coast. When he

Pet dogs were illegal in Reykjavík until 1988.

TIMELINE

AD 600–700	850–930	871
Irish monks voyage to uninhabited Iceland, becoming the first (temporary) settlers. There is no archaeological evidence, although the element *'papar'* (fathers) crops up in certain place names.	Norse settlers from Norway and Sweden arrive, call the island Snæland (Snow Land), then Garðarshólmi (Garðar's Island), and finally Ísland (Iceland). Scattered farmsteads rapidly cover the country.	Norwegian Viking Ingólfur Arnarson, credited as the country's first permanent inhabitant, sails to the southwest coast and makes his home in a promising-looking bay that he names Reykjavík (Smoky Bay).

left in the spring some of his crew remained, or were left behind, thereby becoming the island's first residents.

Around 860 the Norwegian Flóki Vilgerðarson uprooted his farm and family and headed for Snæland. He navigated with ravens, which, after

THE VIKINGS

Scandinavia's greatest impact on world history probably occurred during the Viking Age. In the 8th century, an increase in the numbers of restless, landless young men in western Norway coincided with advances in technology, as Nordic shipbuilders developed fast, manoeuvrable boats sturdy enough for ocean crossings.

Norwegian farmers had peacefully settled in Orkney and the Shetlands as early as the 780s, but the Viking Age officially began in bloodshed in the year 793, when Norsemen plundered St Cuthbert's monastery on the island of Lindisfarne, off Britain's Northumberland coast.

The Vikings quickly realised that monasteries were places of wealth, where a speedy raid could result in handsome rewards. They destroyed Christian communities and slaughtered the monks of Britain and Ireland, who could only wonder what sin they had committed to invite the heathen hordes. Despite this apparent predilection for warfare, the Vikings' barbarism was probably no greater than the standard of the day – it was the success and extent of the raids that led to their fearsome reputation.

In the following years Viking raiders returned with great fleets, terrorising, murdering, enslaving, assimilating or displacing the local population, and capturing many coastal and inland regions of Britain, Ireland, France and Russia. The Vikings travelled as far as Moorish Spain (Seville was raided in 844) and the Middle East (they even reached Baghdad). Constantinople was attacked six times but never yielded, and ultimately Vikings served as mercenaries with the forces of the Holy Roman Empire.

Icelandic tradition officially credits the Norse settlement of Iceland to a single mainland phenomenon. From the mid- to late 9th century the tyrannical Harald Haarfager (Harald Finehair, or Fairhair), the king of Vestfold district of southeastern Norway, was taken with expansionist aspirations. In 890 he won a significant naval victory at Hafrsfjord (Stavanger), and the deposed chieftains and landowners chose to flee rather than submit. Many wound up in Iceland and the Faeroes.

While Viking raids continued in Europe, Eiríkur Rauðe (Erik the Red), having been exiled from Iceland, headed west with around 500 others to found the first permanent European colony in Greenland in 987. Eiríkur's son, Leif the Lucky, went on to explore the coastline of northeast America in the year 1000. He called at Helluland (literally 'land of flat stones', probably Baffin Island), Markland ('land of woods', most likely Newfoundland or Labrador) and Vinland ('land of wine', probably somewhere between Newfoundland and New Jersey) – but permanent settlement was thwarted by the *skrælings* (Native Americans), who were anything but welcoming.

Viking raids petered out over the 11th century. The end of the Viking Age was marked by the death of King Harald Harðráði, the last of the great Viking kings, who died at the battle of Stamford Bridge in England in 1066.

930	1000	1100–1200
The world's oldest existing parliament, the Alþing, is founded at Þingvellir. The Icelanders' law code is memorised by an elected law speaker, who helps to settle legal matters at the annual parliamentary gatherings.	Iceland officially converts to Christianity under pressure from the Norwegian king, though pagan beliefs and rituals remain. Leif the Lucky lands in Newfoundland, the first European to reach America.	Iceland's literary Golden Age, during which the Old Norse sagas are written. Several are attributed to Snorri Sturluson – historian, poet and the shrewdest, most renowned political operator of this era.

some trial and error, led him to his destination and provided his nickname, Hrafna-Flóki (Raven-Flóki). Hrafna-Flóki sailed to Vatnsfjörður on the west coast but became disenchanted on seeing icebergs floating in the fjord. He renamed the country Ísland (Ice Land), and returned to Norway; although he did eventually come back to Iceland, settling in the Skagafjörður district on the north coast.

Credit for the first intentional settlement, according to the *Íslendingabók* (see p32), goes to Ingólfur Arnarson, who fled Norway with his blood brother Hjörleifur. He landed at Ingólfshöfði (southeast Iceland) in 871, then continued around the coast and set up house at a place he called Reykjavík (Smoky Bay), after the steam from thermal springs there. Hjörleifur settled near the present town of Vík but was murdered by his slaves shortly thereafter.

As for Ingólfur, he was led to Reykjavík by a fascinating pagan ritual. It was traditional for Viking settlers to toss their high-seat pillars (a symbol of authority and part of a chieftain's paraphernalia) into the sea as they approached land. Wherever the gods brought the pillars ashore was the settler's new home – a practice followed by waves of settlers who followed from the Norwegian mainland.

Iceland's 1100 Years: The History of a Marginal Society, by Gunnar Karlsson, provides an insightful, contemporary history of Iceland from settlement to the present.

ASSEMBLING THE ALÞING

By the time Ingólfur's son Þorsteinn reached adulthood, the whole island was scattered with farms, and people began to feel the need for some sort of government. Iceland's landowners gathered first at regional assemblies to trade and settle disputes, but it became apparent that a national assembly was needed. A national government was a completely novel idea at the time, but Icelanders reasoned that it must be an improvement on the oppressive system they had experienced under the Nordic monarchy.

The Alþing, established in 930, is the oldest continuous parliamentary democracy in the world.

In the early 10th century Þorsteinn Ingólfsson held Iceland's first large-scale district assembly near Reykjavík, and in the 920s the self-styled lawyer Úlfljótur was sent to study Norway's law codes and prepare something similar that would be suitable for Iceland.

At the same time Grímur Geitskör was commissioned to find a location for the Alþing (National Assembly). Bláskógar, near the eastern boundary of Ingólfur's estate, with its beautiful lake and wooded plain, seemed ideal. Along one side of the plain was a long cliff with an elevated base (the Mid-Atlantic Ridge) from where speakers and representatives could preside over people gathered below.

In 930 Bláskógar was renamed Þingvellir (Assembly Plains). Þorsteinn Ingólfsson was given the honorary title *allsherjargoði* (supreme chieftain) and Úlfljótur was designated the first *lögsögumaður* (law speaker), who was required to memorise and annually recite the entire law of the land. It was he, along with the 48 *goðar* (chieftains), who held the actual legislative power.

The Althing at Thingvellir, by Helmut Lugmayr, explains the role and history of the oldest parliament in the world and includes a section on Þingvellir's unique geology.

1200	1300, 1341 & 1389	1397
Iceland descends into anarchy during the Sturlung Age. The government dissolves and, in 1281, Iceland is absorbed by Norway.	Hekla erupts, causing death and destruction. The first eruption is the second largest since settlement began, with tephra covering a 30,000 sq km area; the second causes widespread livestock deaths and starvation.	On 17 June the Kalmar Union is signed in Sweden, uniting the countries of Norway, Sweden and Denmark under one king. As part of this treaty, Iceland comes under Danish control.

Although squabbles arose over the choice of leaders and allegiances were continually questioned, the new parliamentary system was a success. At the annual convention of the year 1000, the assembled crowd was bitterly divided between pagans and Christians, but eventually a decree was agreed and Iceland accepted the new religion and converted to Christianity. This decision gave the formerly divided groups a semblance of national unity, and soon the first bishoprics were set up at Skálholt in the southwest and Hólar in the north.

Over the following years the two-week national assembly at Þingvellir became the social event of the year. All free men could attend. Single people came looking for partners, marriages were contracted and solemnised, business deals were finalised, duels and executions were held, and the Appeals Court handed down judgments on matters that couldn't be resolved in lower courts.

ANARCHY & THE STURLUNG AGE

The late 12th century kicked off the Saga Age, when epic tales of early settlement, family struggles, romance and tragic characters were recorded by historians and writers. Much of our knowledge of this time comes from two weighty tomes, the *Íslendingabók*, a historical narrative from the settlement era written by 12th-century scholar Ari Þorgilsson (Ari the Learned), and the detailed *Landnámabók*, a comprehensive account of the settlement.

Despite the advances in such cultural pursuits, Icelandic society was beginning to deteriorate. By the early 13th century the enlightened period of peace that had lasted 200 years was waning. Constant power struggles between rival chieftains led to violent feuds and a flourishing of Viking-like private armies who raided farms across the country. This dark hour in Iceland's history was known as the Sturlung Age, its tragic events and brutal history graphically recounted in the three-volume *Sturlunga Saga*.

As Iceland descended into chaos, the Norwegian king Hákon Hákonarson pressured chieftains, priests and the new breed of wealthy aristocrats to accept his authority. The Icelanders, who saw no alternative, dissolved all but a superficial shell of their government and swore their allegiance to the king. An agreement of confederacy was made in 1262. In 1281 a new code of law, the Jónsbók, was introduced by the king, and Iceland was absorbed into Norwegian rule.

Norway immediately set about appointing Norwegian bishops to Hólar and Skálholt and imposed excessive taxes. Contention flared as former chieftains quibbled over high offices, particularly that of *járl* (earl), an honour that fell to the ruthless Gissur Þorvaldsson, who in 1241 murdered Snorri Sturluson, Iceland's best-known historian and writer (see the boxed text, p163).

Meanwhile, the volcano Hekla erupted three times, covering a third of the country in ash; a mini-ice age followed, and severe winters wiped out livestock and crops. The Black Death arrived, killing half the population, and the once indomitable spirit of the people seemed broken.

1402–04	1550	1602
The Black Death sweeps across Iceland, 50 years after first spreading across mainland Europe, and kills around half of the population.	King Christian III's attempts to impose Lutheranism finally succeed after the Catholic bishop Jón Árason is captured in battle and beheaded at Skálholt along with two of his sons.	Denmark imposes a crippling trade monopoly, giving Danish and Swedish firms exclusive trading rights in Iceland. This leads to unrestrained profiteering by Danish merchants and Iceland's slow impoverishment.

ENTER THE DANES

Iceland's fate was now in the hands of the highest Norwegian bidder, who could lease the governorship of the country on a three-year basis. In 1397 the Kalmar Union of Norway, Sweden and Denmark brought Iceland under Danish rule. After disputes between church and state, the Danish government seized church property and imposed Lutheranism in the Reformation of 1550. When the stubborn Catholic bishop of Hólar, Jón Arason, resisted and gained a following, he and his two sons were taken to Skálholt and beheaded.

In 1602 the Danish king imposed a crippling trade monopoly whereby Swedish and Danish firms were given exclusive trading rights in Iceland for 12-year periods. This resulted in large-scale extortion, importation of spoilt or inferior goods and yet more suffering that would last another 250 years.

RETURN TO INDEPENDENCE

Fed up with five centuries of oppressive foreign rule and conscious of a growing sense of liberalisation across Europe, Icelandic nationalism began to flourish in the 19th century. By 1855 Jón Sigurðsson, an Icelandic scholar, had successfully lobbied for restoration of free trade, and by 1874 Iceland had drafted a constitution and regained control of its domestic affairs.

Iceland's first political parties were formed during this period, and urban development began in this most rural of countries. By 1918 Iceland had signed the Act of Union, which effectively released the country from Danish rule, making it an independent state within the Kingdom of Denmark.

Iceland prospered during WWI as wool, meat and fish exports gained high prices. When WWII loomed, however, Iceland declared neutrality in the hope of maintaining their important trade links with both Britain and Germany.

On 9 April 1940 Denmark was occupied by Germany, prompting the Alþing to take control of Iceland's foreign affairs once more. A year later, on 17 May 1941, the Icelanders requested complete independence. The formal establishment of the Republic of Iceland finally took place at Þingvellir on 17 June 1944 – now celebrated as Independence Day.

Until 1903 Iceland's coat of arms was a silver stockfish (split, dried cod) topped by a golden crown.

WWII & THE USA MOVES IN

Iceland's total lack of military force worried the Allied powers and so in May 1940 Britain, most vulnerable to a German-controlled Iceland, sent in forces to occupy the island. Iceland had little choice but to accept the situation, but the country's economy profited from British construction projects and spending.

When the British troops withdrew in 1941 the government allowed American troops to move in, on the understanding that they would move out at the end of the war. Although the US military left in 1946, it retained the right to reestablish a base at Keflavík should war threaten. After the war, and back under their own control, Icelanders were reluctant to submit to any foreign power. When the government was pressured into becoming a founding

Iceland has the highest density of mobile-phone use in the world – there are more mobiles in use than there are people.

1627	**1783–84**	**1855–90**
The 'Turkish Abductions' take place: Barbary pirates raid the east of Iceland and the Vestmannaeyjar, taking hundreds prisoner and killing all who resist.	The Laki crater row erupts, pouring out poisonous gas clouds that kill 25% of the population and more than 50% of livestock. The haze covers Europe, leading to freak weather conditions, flooding and famine.	Iceland moves towards independence, with the restoration of free trade and a draft constitution. Not everyone sticks around to see it: during this period, many emigrate to start life afresh in North America.

member of NATO in 1949, riots broke out in Reykjavík. The government agreed to the proposition on the conditions that Iceland would never take part in offensive action and that no foreign military troops would be based in the country during peacetime.

These conditions were soon broken. War with Korea broke out in 1950, and in 1951 at NATO's request the US, jumpy about the Soviet threat, once again took responsibility for the island's defence. US military personnel and technology at the Keflavík base continued to increase over the next four decades, as Iceland served as an important Cold War monitoring station. The controversial US military presence in Iceland only ended in September 2006, when the base at Keflavík finally closed.

In 2002 scientists discovered the world's second-smallest creature, *Nanoarchaeum equitans*, living in near-boiling water in a hydrothermal vent off the north coast of Iceland.

MODERN ICELAND

Following the Cold War, Iceland went through a period of growth, rebuilding and modernisation. The Ring Road was completed in 1974 – opening up transport links to the remote southeast – and projects such as the Krafla power station in the northeast and the Svartsengi power plant near Reykjavík were developed. A boom in the fishing industry saw Iceland extend its fishing limit in the 1970s to 200 miles (322km), precipitating the 'cod war' with Britain.

The fishing industry has always been vital to Iceland, although it's had its ups and downs – quotas were reduced in the 1990s so stocks could regenerate after overfishing. The industry went into recession, leading to an unemployment rate of 3% (a previously unheard-of level in Iceland) and a sharp drop in the króna. The country slowly began a period of economic regeneration as the fishing industry stabilised. Today the industry still accounts for about half of the country's GDP, with the total catch valued at around 100 billion krónur in 2009.

In 2003 Iceland resumed whaling as part of a scientific research program, despite a global moratorium on hunts. In 2006 Iceland resumed commercial whaling, in spite of condemnation from around the globe. It's likely that this will be one of the major issues when its EU membership application, lodged in 2009, is formally considered.

See the 'Icelanders are Not Terrorists' website, www.indefence.is, for a typically Icelandic response to Gordon Brown's use of antiterrorist laws.

Iceland's huge dependence on its fishing industry and on imported goods means that the country has always had relatively high prices and a vulnerable economy prone to fluctuation. Exactly how vulnerable was brought into focus in September 2008, when the global economic crisis hit the country with a sledgehammer blow: see the boxed text, opposite.

Iceland has a tradition of coalition government, and is a democratic republic with a peaceful reputation. In late 2008, however, the capital Reykjavík was rocked by months of fierce protests outside the Icelandic Parliament, as the then-government's popularity evaporated along with the country's wealth. In January 2009, Prime Minister Geir Haarde resigned, citing ill health as his reason. His replacement, Jóhanna Sigurðardóttir, hit international headlines as the world's first openly gay prime minister. Her major act to date was to

1918	1940–41	1944
Denmark's grip on Iceland gradually loosens. Following Home Rule in 1904, the Act of Union is signed on 1 December 1918, making Iceland an independent state within the Kingdom of Denmark.	After the Nazi occupation of Denmark, the UK sends British troops to invade and occupy neutral Iceland, concerned that Germany might acquire a military presence there; a US base is later established at Keflavík.	A majority of Icelanders vote for independence from Denmark, and the Republic of Iceland is formally established on 17 June. King Christian X telegrams his congratulations.

ICELAND'S ECONOMIC MELTDOWN

Everything was looking so rosy: in early 2008 Iceland was full of confidence and riding high. Much of the country's wealth, however, was built over a black hole of debt – its banks' liabilities were more than 10 times its annual GDP. The ripples of the worldwide financial crisis became a tidal wave by the time they reached Icelandic shores, washing away the country's entire economy.

By October 2008 the Icelandic stock market had crashed; the króna plummeted, losing almost half its value overnight; all three national banks went into receivership; and the country teetered on the brink of bankruptcy.

Relations between Iceland and the UK were strained following the collapse of Icesave (a subsidiary of Iceland's national bank Landsbanki), in which 300,000 British customers had invested their savings. UK prime minister Gordon Brown invoked antiterrorist laws to freeze Icelandic assets; this was seen by many Icelanders as heavy-handed and the main cause of Kaupþing bank's collapse.

Help came in November 2008 with a US$2.1 billion International Monetary Fund (IMF) loan and a US$3 billion bailout from Scandinavian neighbours. Nevertheless, spiralling inflation, wage cuts and redundancies meant that Icelanders' incomes fell by a quarter in real terms, and national pride took a severe kicking. At home, protestors rioted in Reykjavík, furious with a government they felt had betrayed them; Prime Minister Geir Haarde resigned in January 2009.

One of the new government's first steps was to apply for EU membership, with a view to changing their currency from the króna, which has always been prone to fluctuation, to the more stable euro around 2011.

The crash has been a terrible blow to Icelanders, and the short-term situation is still uncertain. It's thought that Iceland's economy will continue to suffer until 2011 when it's hoped the economic situation will begin to right itself. In the meantime, the weak króna has made Iceland cheaper for foreign visitors than it has been for decades – so at least the country's tourists have something to smile about.

submit the government's application for EU membership on 17 July 2009. It's thought that membership and the adoption of the euro as the country's currency will soothe Iceland's economic troubles, although it's not a universally popular solution – a Gallup poll taken in September 2009 suggested that only 33% of the population support EU membership.

Despite the recent economic horrors, Iceland is one of Europe's most developed countries, with extremely high literacy levels, consistently high standards of living, and one of the highest levels of computer and mobile-phone use in Europe. State education and health-care facilities are so good that there is no demand for private facilities, crime levels are extremely low and life expectancy high.

For Icelanders today the most pressing questions centre around the country's money troubles. Environmental issues surrounding new hydroelectric power plants and aluminium smelters in east Iceland (see p62) have taken something of a back seat.

In 2009 the executives of the bankrupt Icelandic banks were awarded the Ig-Nobel prize for Economics.

2006	**2008**	**2009**
The controversial US military base at Keflavík closes down after 45 years in service; the government also approves resumption of commercial whaling.	The worldwide financial downturn hits Iceland particularly hard, precipitating the worst national banking crisis ever when all three of the country's major banks collapse.	Jóhanna Sigurðardóttir is appointed prime minister, becoming the world's first openly gay leader. Her coalition government applies for EU membership on 17 July.

The Culture

THE NATIONAL PSYCHE

Centuries of isolation and hardship, and a small, homogenous population have instilled particular character traits in Icelanders. This is a tight-knit nation of just over 300,000 souls, where everyone seems to know each other or to be distantly related: family ties are overridingly important.

Naturally enough for people living on a remote island in a harsh environment, Icelanders are self-reliant individualists who don't like being told what to do. The current whaling debate is a prime example. Although most Icelanders wouldn't dream of eating whale meat, a majority are in support of hunting – a silent sticking-up of two fingers at the disapproving outside world.

Icelanders have a reputation as tough, hardy, elemental types, and it's true that rural communities are mainly involved in the fishing or farming industries. But don't think they're badly educated bumpkins. Iceland has always had a rich cultural heritage and an incredibly high literacy rate, and its people have a passion for all things artistic. This artistic enthusiasm is true of the whole country, but it's particularly noticeable in downtown Reykjavík. Although people adopt an attitude of cool fatalism, get them talking about something they enjoy and the pessimism falls away. Most young Icelanders play in a band, dabble in art, or write poetry or prose – they're positively bursting with creative impulses.

This buoyant, confident, have-a-go attitude took a serious knock with the recent economic crisis (see the boxed text, p35). Many young Reykjavík-dwellers used to grumble that there was nothing for them in Iceland: the country was too small, they'd tried everything there was to try, the only option was to emigrate. The financial meltdown has made this gripe a reality – during 2009 there was a 1.6% rise in emigration, with a significant number of younger people leaving to find work in Norway.

But don't be fooled – their pride might have taken a knock, but Icelanders are quietly, rightfully patriotic. Icelanders who achieve international success (singer Björk, the band Sigur Rós, novelist Halldór Laxness, footballer Eiður Gudjohnsson), winning honour and prestige for their homeland, become heroes. And it's no coincidence that Icelandair wishes a heartfelt 'Welcome home!' to its passengers when the plane touches down at Keflavík.

Town layouts, the former US military base, the popularity of TV programs such as *Desperate Housewives, Lost* and *The Wire,* and the prevalence of hot dogs and Coca-Cola point to a heavy US influence, but Icelanders consider their relationship with the rest of Scandinavia to be more important.

Indeed, they have much in common, although Icelanders are not as aloof as their Scandinavian counterparts in Sweden, Norway and Finland. They're curious about visitors and eager to know what outsiders think of them. 'How do you like Iceland?' is invariably an early question. While most Icelanders speak English very well, they're extremely proud of their language, and to greet them with a little carefully pronounced Icelandic will result in a look of mild surprise (bordering on shock) followed by a broad smile.

While Icelanders are generally quite reserved and stoical, an incredible transformation comes over them when they party. On Friday and Saturday nights inhibitions are let down, and conversations flow as fast as the alcohol!

Xenophobe's Guide to the Icelanders, by Richard Sale, is a compact, humorous look at the Icelandic character and foibles – everything from customs and driving habits to obsession with material possessions.

Homer Simpson's friend and nuclear-plant colleague Carl Carlson was born in Iceland.

SOCIAL ETIQUETTE

Although Icelanders don't often stand on ceremony, there are a few simple rules that will pave the way for a smooth trip. It's important to take your shoes off as soon as you enter a house, and if you've been lucky enough to be invited for dinner, it's a good idea to bring a gift for your host – a bottle of foreign wine is usually welcomed. To make a toast you should say 'Skál!', and at the end of the meal 'Takk fyrir mig' shows your appreciation to your host.

LIFESTYLE

In the last century the Icelandic lifestyle has shifted from isolated family communities living on scattered farms and in coastal villages to a more urban-based society with the majority of people living in the southwestern corner around Reykjavík. Despite this more outward-looking change, family connections are still very strong in Iceland, but young people growing up in rural Iceland are more likely to move to Reykjavík to study and work.

Icelanders work hard – the retirement age is 70 – and have enjoyed a very high standard of living in the late 20th and early 21st centuries. But keeping up with the Jónssons and Jónsdóttirs has come at a horrific price. For decades, Icelanders straight out of university have begun borrowing money to buy houses or 4WDs and spent the rest of their days paying off loans and living on credit. The recent economic crash means that it's now payback time for all of that national debt. Most Icelanders have always had at least two jobs (for example, it's common to find teachers spending their summer holiday leading treks and running tours), and so working themselves out of this financial black hole is going to be tough.

The Icelandic addiction to grafting is counterbalanced by their excessive idea of recreation. The bingeing in Reykjavík on Friday and Saturday nights is relaxation gone mad. So too are the hundreds of summer houses you'll see when you're driving round the Golden Circle, and the exceptional number of swimming pools, which form the social hub of Icelandic life.

The social care system is so good here that young Icelandic women have few worries about the financial implications of raising a child alone, and there's no stigma attached to unmarried mothers. You'll see pushchairs with contented-looking mums behind them rather than haggard or harried faces.

Crime is notable for its absence. We can't think of a safer city than Reykjavík.

POPULATION

The population of Iceland was a shade under 320,000 in 2009. A whopping 37% of all Icelanders live in Reykjavík, and the number is growing steadily as more people migrate from the country to the city – around 4000 people drift into town every year.

The Icelandic birth rate has been very high over the last few years, although it dropped a little to 1.24% in 2008 – that's around one baby popping out every two hours. The little nippers can expect to live long in a pleasantly empty land: Iceland has one of the world's highest life expectancies – 79.6 years for men and 83.0 years for women – and the lowest population density in Europe, with only 2.9 people per sq km.

Icelanders discovered fairly recently that much of their genetic make-up is Celtic, suggesting that far more of the Viking settlers had children by their slaves than originally thought. Even though they speak the nearest thing to Viking in existence, Iceland is actually the least purely Scandinavian of all the Nordic countries.

Iceland's population has tripled in the last 100 years.

WHAT'S IN A NAME?

Icelanders' names are constructed from a combination of their first name and their father's (or, more rarely, mother's) first name. Girls add the suffix *dóttir* (daughter) to the patronymic and boys add *son*. Therefore, Jón, the son of Einar, would be Jón Einarsson. Guðrun, the daughter of Einar, would be Guðrun Einarsdóttir.

Because Icelandic surnames only tell people what your dad's called, Icelanders don't bother with 'Mr Einarsson' or 'Mrs Einarsdóttir'. Instead they use first names, even when addressing strangers. It makes for a wonderfully democratic society when you're expected to address your president or top police commissioner as Oliver or Harold!

About 10% of Icelanders have family names (most dating back to early settlement times), but they're rarely used. In an attempt to homogenise the system, government legislation forbids anyone to take on a new family name or adopt the family name of their spouse.

There's also an official list of names that Icelanders are permitted to call their children. Any additions to this list have to be approved by the Icelandic Naming Committee before you can apply them to your child – so there are no Moon Units, Lourdeses or Apples running round here! Interestingly, there's a lingering superstition around naming newborns: the baby's name isn't usually revealed until the christening, which can take place several months after the child is born.

Immigration laws were strict until the rules changed on 1 May 2006, encouraging foreign workers to come to Iceland. The incomers were mostly blue-collar workers in construction, fisheries and maintenance, with Polish people forming the largest group, followed by Danes. The number of immigrants peaked at around 9000 in 2007. As you might guess, Icelandic unemployment rates soared following the 2008 crash; jobs are now scarce, and the number of foreign workers entering the country fell to around 3000 in 2009.

Until recently, foreign immigrants had to give themselves Icelandic names before they could become citizens: the naming committee has now relaxed this rather stringent requirement!

SPORT

Football (soccer) is a national passion for both spectators and players. Although Iceland doesn't win a lot of international games, several Icelandic players have made it on to top European and English premier-league teams. The biggest national venue is the 14,000-seat Laugardalsvöllur stadium in Reykjavík, and matches are keenly followed.

The next most popular team sport is handball, a game played by two teams of seven. Internationally, Iceland has had some success with the game, finishing eighth in the 2007 world championships. You can see handball matches at sports halls around the country – Reykjavík, Hafnarfjörður and Akureyri are good places.

Iceland's most traditional sport is *glíma* (Icelandic wrestling), a unique national sport with a history dating back to Viking settlement in the 9th century. Icelanders still practise the sport, but it's not common on a competitive level and you're most likely to see it as a demonstration at a traditional festival.

MEDIA
Newspapers & Magazines

Iceland's main daily newspapers are published only in Icelandic. The biggest-selling, *Morgunblaðið*, is moderately right wing, but Icelanders generally take journalists little more seriously than they do their politicians.

For snippets of Icelandic news, the *Iceland Review* website (www.icelandreview.com) has a free daily news digest (which you can have delivered to your email inbox), and its glossy quarterly magazine has some entertaining, light articles about Icelandic people, culture, history and nature.

An excellent read for Icelandic news, views, reviews and what's hot in Reykjavík is the new *Grapevine* magazine, a fortnightly newsprint magazine distributed free in summer. The editors are not afraid to write at length about big issues in Iceland, but it's done with humour and a deft writing style. It's available at the tourist office, hotels and bars in Reykjavík.

TV & Radio
Until 1988 Iceland had only one state-run TV station – which went off air on Thursdays so that citizens could do something healthier instead. (It's said that most children born before 1988 were conceived on a Thursday…) Today there are three stations and they broadcast on a Thursday. So, now you have a choice.

TV and radio are more for entertainment than enlightenment, although the Ríkisútvarpið (RÚV; Icelandic National Broadcasting Service) evening news is the country's second-most-watched program. If you're near a TV on Saturday night, check out Iceland's favourite show – the unfathomable current-affairs satire *Spaugstofan,* which has been running for 20 years and is watched by over half the country. Much of the programming, particularly in the evenings, comes from the USA and the UK – in English, with Icelandic subtitles.

An award-winning Icelandic TV show that you might already have seen, particularly if you have children, is the violently colourful *Latibær* (Lazy Town), starring Sportacus, Stephanie, Robbie Rotten and some shudderingly ugly puppets.

RELIGION
Norse
The original religion in Iceland at the time of the Settlement was Ásatrú, which means 'faith in the Aesir (the old Norse gods)'. It was the ancient religion of most Germanic peoples and also appears as far away as India. The

---

ICELANDIC ANCESTRY & GENETIC RESEARCH

Thanks to Ári the Learned's painstaking 12th-century works, Icelanders can trace their family trees right back to the 9th century through two books – the *Landnámabók* and the *Íslendingabók,* which is all very interesting for history buffs. But add this well-documented genealogical material to Iceland's unusually homogenous population and you end up with something potentially quite sinister – a unique country-sized genetic laboratory.

In 1998 the Icelandic government controversially voted to allow the creation of a single database containing all Icelanders' genealogical, genetic and medical records. Even more controversially, in 2000 the government then allowed American biotech company deCODE access to it all.

The decision sparked public outrage in Iceland and arguments across the globe about its implications for human rights and medical ethics. The chief questions it raised were: should a government be able to sell off its citizens' medical records? And is it acceptable for a private corporation to use such records for profit? The company claimed that its encryption methods meant that individuals could not be identified by researchers (but read *Tainted Blood* by Arnaldur Indriðason for a cynical take on this statement).

The biotech company set to work, using the database to trace inheritable diseases and pinpoint the genes that cause them. The database was declared unconstitutional in 2004, and deCODE had to change its procedure, but it has still succeeded in isolating 15 genes linked to heart attacks, strokes and asthma. This information will be used to develop new drugs to combat the diseases. As a kind of pay-off, deCODE have promised that any drugs created through its research will be free to Icelanders.

SWIMMING-POOL SENSE

Icelanders are a relaxed bunch with a live-and-let-live attitude, but there is a sure-fire way of unwittingly causing offence. The one time we've seen Icelanders get visibly angry, disgusted and upset is when talking about tourists abusing their swimming pools. It's vital to conform to Icelandic etiquette by washing thoroughly without a swimsuit before hopping into the water. (It makes good hygiene sense, as Icelandic swimming pools don't contain chemical cleaners.)

medieval Icelandic text, the *Galdrabók*, reveals that people were calling upon the Aesir long after Christianity was adopted across northern Europe.

There were many gods in the pantheon, but Þór (Thor), Óðinn and Freyr were the major trinity worshipped across Scandinavia. The religion is also closely linked to a reverence for the natural world.

Óðinn, the god of war and poetry, was the highest-ranking deity, chief of the gods, and a brooding and intimidating presence. He influenced the sway of battle and handed out literary talent to those deemed worthy.

Free from warfare, in Iceland most people were devoted to Þór (and there are still plenty of Icelandic people with names such as Þórir, Þórdís and Þóra). This giant, rowdy god of the common people controlled thunder, wind, storm and natural disaster, so he was a vital deity for farmers and fishermen to have on their side. He was depicted as a burly, red-haired, red-bearded dolt, who rumbled through the heavens in a goat-drawn chariot.

Freyr and his twin sister Freyja, the children of the sea god Njörður, served as the god and goddess of fertility and sexuality. Freyr was the one who brought springtime, with its romantic implications, to both the human and the animal world and was in charge of the perpetuation of all species.

Icelanders peacefully converted to Christianity more than 1000 years ago, but the old gods are being revived. The Ásatrú religion evolved in the 1970s, almost simultaneously in Iceland, the US and the UK. Farmer-poet and high priest Sveinbjörn Beinteinsson managed to get the Íslenska Ásatrúarfélagið (www.asatru.is) recognised by the Icelandic government as early as 1973.

The two main rituals of Ásatrú are *blót* (sacrifice) and *sumbel* (toast). Nowadays sacrifices, which take place on the winter and summer solstices, on the first day of winter and summer, and at Þorrablót (see the boxed text, p50), are usually libations made with mead, beer or cider. The *sumbel* is a ritualised three-part toast: the first is made to the god Óðinn (it's also wise to pour a few drops for Loki, the trickster, to ward off nasty surprises); the second round is to the ancestors and honourable dead, and the third round is to whomever one wishes to honour.

Whereas membership of other religions in Iceland has remained fairly constant, Ásatrúarfélagið is growing and now has 1270 registered members and eight priests (five of whom can perform marriage ceremonies). It's Iceland's largest non-Christian religious organisation. In early 2008 the society bought a plot of land at Öskjuhlíð in Reykjavík, where it planned to build its first temple, but the financial crash later that year has put these plans temporarily on ice.

Christianity

Traditionally, the date of the decree that officially converted Iceland to Christianity has been given as 1000, but research has determined that it probably occurred in 999. What is known is that the changeover of religions was a political decision. In the Icelandic Alþing (National Assembly), Christians and pagans had been polarising into two radically opposite factions, threatening to divide the country. Þorgeir, the *lögsögumaður* (law speaker), appealed for moderation on both sides, and eventually it was agreed that Christianity would officially become the new religion, although pagans were still allowed to practise in private.

Today, as in mainland Scandinavia, most Icelanders (around 79%) belong to the Protestant Lutheran Church.

ARTS
Literature

Bloody, black and powerful, the late 12th- and 13th-century sagas are without doubt Iceland's greatest cultural achievement. Written in terse Old Norse, these epics continue to entertain Icelanders and provide them with a rich sense of heritage.

But Icelanders are never ones to rest on their literary laurels, and today the country produces the most writers and literary translations per capita of any country in the world.

THE SAGAS

Iceland's medieval family sagas have often been called the world's first novels. They're certainly some of the most imaginative and enduring works of early literature – epic and brutal tales that suddenly flower with words of wisdom, elegy or love.

Written down during the late 12th to late 13th centuries, sagas generally look to earlier times – they're tales of bloodthirsty disputes, doomed romances and the larger-than-life characters who lived during the Settlement Era. Most were written anonymously, though *Egil's Saga* has been attributed to Snorri Sturluson (see the boxed text, p163).

Betra er berfættum en bókarlausum að vera.
(It's better to be barefoot than bookless.)

SUPERNATURAL ICELAND: GHOSTS, TROLLS & HIDDEN PEOPLE

Once you've seen some of the lava fields, eerie natural formations and isolated farms that characterise much of the Icelandic landscape, it will come as no surprise that many Icelanders believe their country is populated by *huldufólk* (hidden people) and ghosts.

In the lava are *jarðvergar* (gnomes), *álfar* (elves), *ljósálfar* (fairies), *dvergar* (dwarves), *ljúflingar* (lovelings), *tívar* (mountain spirits), and *englar* (angels). Stories about them have been handed down through generations, and many modern Icelanders claim to have seen them…or to at least know someone who has.

As in Ireland, there are stories about projects going wrong when workers try to build roads through *huldufólk* homes: the weather turns bad, machinery breaks down, labourers fall ill – until the construction company decides to build around the fey folk's rock or hill and all goes smoothly once more. In fact, the town council at Hafnarfjörður contains three people who can mediate with elves during building projects.

As for Icelandic ghosts, they're not like the wafting shadows found elsewhere in Europe but are strangely substantial beings. Írafell-Móri (*móri* and *skotta* are used for male and female ghosts respectively) needed to eat supper every night, and one of the country's most famous spooks, Sel-Móri, got seasick when he stowed away in a boat. Even more strangely, two ghosts haunting the same area often join forces to double their trouble. And Icelandic ghosts can even age – one rather sad *skotta* claimed she was becoming so decrepit that she had to haul herself about on her knees.

Many folk stories explain away rock stacks and weird lava formations by saying that they're trolls, caught out at sunrise and turned forever to stone. But we don't know anyone who claims to have seen a troll – they're more the stuff of children's stories.

A quick word of warning – you might not be surprised to hear that many Icelanders get sick of visitors asking them whether they believe in supernatural beings. Their pride bristles at the 'Those cute Icelanders! They all believe in pixies!' attitude…and even if they don't entirely disbelieve, they're unlikely to admit it to a stranger!

HALLDÓR LAXNESS – ICELAND'S FINEST AUTHOR

It's frightening how we miss out on literary masterpieces from other countries, simply because no one bothers to translate them. Halldór Laxness (1902–98) is Iceland's most celebrated author of the 20th century, and his genius was recognised when he won the Nobel Prize for Literature in 1955. Despite this, his greatest work took years to appear in English, and only a portion of his 51 novels and countless short stories, articles, plays and poems are currently available in translation.

The author was born as Halldór Guðjónsson, but he took the name of his family's farm Laxnes (with an extra 's') as his nom de plume. Laxness, a restless, inquisitive, prolific soul, had work published from the age of 14 and began travelling at the age of 17, wandering and writing around Scandinavia. Three years later he joined a monastery in Luxembourg and converted to Catholicism, studying Latin, praying fervently and writing his first proper novel, *Undir Helgahnúk (Under the Holy Mountain)*. However, he soon became disillusioned with monastic life. After briefly returning to Iceland he went to Italy, where he wrote of his disaffection with the church and his increasingly leftist leanings in *Vefarinn Mikli frá Kasmír* (The Great Weaver from Kashmir). Laxness then set off for America to try his luck in the fledgling Hollywood film industry. There he wrote one of his best-known works, *Salka Valka*, as a screenplay. It was during this stay in America during the Great Depression of the 1930s that he became a communist sympathiser. Quickly finding himself facing deportation from the USA, he bought a ticket to Germany.

Laxness became so absorbed with the Communist Party that he attended the 1937 purge trials in Moscow and deliberately misrepresented them in his writings (by his own later admission) lest he in any way defame the system in which he had placed all hope and trust. Most of Laxness' work during his communist days reflects everyday life in Iceland, often with thinly disguised autobiographical details. *Independent People* describes the harsh conditions under which the average Icelander lived in the early 20th century, focusing on the heartbreakingly bloody-minded farmer Bjartur of Summerhouses, one of the most perfectly drawn characters in world literature. His other major novels include *Iceland's Bell* and *The Atom Station*. The former is a three-part work, a sagalike portrait of extreme poverty and skewed justice. Set in an Iceland subjugated by Danish rule, it revolves around the interweaving fates of destitute farmer and possible murderer Jón Hreggviðsson, and the stoical beauty Snæfríður, sister-in-law of the bishop of Skálholt. The second book, written prophetically in 1948, is a slim, droll volume about the American military presence in Iceland, nuclear proliferation and the socialist struggle for state welfare provision. His other works currently available in translation are *World Light, The Fish Can Sing, Paradise Reclaimed* and *Under the Glacier*.

All of Laxness's works are masterpieces of irony; his characters, however misguided, are drawn with sympathy; and seams of the blackest humour run through them all. Whatever you think of his works, it's impossible not to be affected by them. At the time they were written, they were very controversial – quite a few Icelanders disputed his observations, although their complaints were often motivated by national pride and reluctance to publicise Iceland's relative backwardness. When Laxness won the Nobel Prize for Literature in 1955, however, in true Icelandic style he became a hero of the people.

By 1962 Laxness had settled in Reykjavík for good (his home at Laxnes, near the suburb of Mosfellsbær, has now been turned into a museum – see p110). Apparently mellowed by his experiences with extremism at both ends of the spectrum, he wrote *A Poet's Time,* which recanted everything he'd ever written in praise of the Communist Party.

The sagas provided not just entertainment but a strong sense of cultural heritage, as they were written, over the long desperate centuries of Norwegian and Danish subjugation, when Icelanders had very little else. On winter nights, people would gather in farmhouses for the *kvöldvaka* (evening vigil), a time of socialising and storytelling. While the men twisted horsehair ropes and women spun wool or knitted, a family member would read the sagas and recite *rímur* (verse reworkings of the sagas).

And the sagas are very much alive today. Modern Icelandic has scarcely changed since Viking times, which means Icelanders of all ages can (and do) read the sagas in Old Norse, the language in which they were written 800 years ago. Most people can quote chunks from them, know the farms where the characters lived and died, and flock to cinemas to see the latest film versions of these eternal tales.

One of the best known, *Egil's Saga*, revolves around the complex, devious Egill Skallagrímsson. A renowned poet and skilled lawyer, he was also the grandson of a werewolf and a murderous drunk. Other favourite works include *Grettir's Saga*, about a superhuman but doomed outlaw, Grettir the Strong; *Laxdæla Saga*, the tragic account of a family in northwest Iceland; and *Njál's Saga* (see the boxed text, p141), another tragedy about two warring families, whose heroic characters make it one of the most popular sagas of all.

You can admire the original saga manuscripts in Reykjavík's Culture House (Þjóðmenningarhúsið; p77).

EDDIC & SKALDIC POETRY

The first settlers probably brought their oral poetic tradition with them from mainland Scandinavia; however, this ancient poetry wasn't written down until the 12th-century Saga Age.

Eddic poems are subdivided into three classes – the Mythical, the Gnomic and the Heroic – and were composed in free, variable metres with a structure very similar to that of early Germanic poetry. Mythical poetry was based on the antics of the Norse gods and was probably promoted as an intended affront to growing Christian sentiments in Norway. Gnomic poetry consists of one major work, the *Hávamál*, which extols the virtues of the common life. The Heroic Eddic poems are similar in form, subject matter and even characters to early Germanic works such as the *Nibelungenlied*.

Skaldic poetry was developed and composed by *skalds* (Norwegian court poets) in veneration of heroic deeds by the Scandinavian kings, but other themes were introduced as the genre grew in popularity. The most renowned *skald* was Egill Skallagrímsson – he of *Egil's Saga* – who amid his other exploits ran afoul of Eirík Blood-Axe, king of Jorvík (modern-day York), in 948. After being captured and sentenced to death, on the night before his execution Egill composed an ode to Eirík. The flattered monarch released Egill unharmed, and the poem is now known as the *Höfuðlausn* (Head Ransom).

Skaldic poems are mainly praise-poems, with lots of description packed into tightly structured lines. As well as having fiercely rigid alliteration, syllable counts and stresses, they're made more complex by *kennings*, a kind of compact word-riddle. Blood, for instance, is 'wound dew'; an arm might be described as a 'hawk's perch'; and battle is often referred to as 'the Valkyries' glorious song'.

20TH-CENTURY LITERATURE

Nobel prize–winner Halldór Laxness is Iceland's undoubted literary genius. His work is magnificent – for more details, see the boxed text, opposite.

Other authors you may come across are the early-20th-century children's writer Reverend Jón Sveinsson (nicknamed Nonni), who grew up in Akureyri. Although he mostly wrote in German, his old-fashioned tales of derring-do have a rich Icelandic flavour, and they were translated into 40 languages. *At Skipalón* is the only one readily available in English. Just after him, Jóhann Sigurjónsson wrote *Eyvind of the Hills*, a biography of the 18th-century outlaw Fjalla-Eyvindur, which was later made into a film. Two other masters

If you read nothing else, at least read Halldór Laxness's dark, funny, painful masterpiece *Independent People* – it's fantastic, and you'll marvel all the more at Iceland's progress in the last 70 years.

Iceland publishes the greatest number of books per capita in the world, and the literacy rate is a perfect 100%.

of Icelandic literature are Gunnar Gunnarsson (1889–1975) and Þórbergur Þórðarson (1888–1974), who was beaten to the Nobel prize by Laxness. You'll have to look out for their work in secondhand bookshops.

For more up-to-date and easily available fare, try Einar Kárason's outstanding *Devil's Island*, about Reykjavík life in the 1950s; it's the first of a trilogy, but unfortunately the other two haven't been translated into English. *101 Reykjavík*, by Hallgrímur Helgason, is the book on which the cult film was based. It's a dark comedy following the torpid life and fertile imagination of out-of-work Hlynur, who lives in downtown Reykjavík with his mother. Even more black, with flashes of humour, is the strange *Angels of the Universe*, by Einar Már Gudmundsson, about a schizophrenic man's spells in a psychiatric hospital.

Currently surfing a tidal wave of success is Arnaldur Indriðason, whose Reykjavík-based crime fiction permanently tops the bestsellers list. Six of his novels are available in English, including *Voices*, the award-winning *Silence of the Grave*, and our favourite, *Tainted Blood* (also published as *Jar City*).

Music

POP

Internationally famous Icelandic musicians include (of course) Björk. In Reykjavík, look out for the bestselling *Gling Gló*, a collection of Björk-sung jazz standards and traditional Icelandic songs that's quite difficult to find outside the country. Sigur Rós are following Björk to stardom with their strange, ethereal sound; their biggest-selling album *Takk* (2005) garnered rave reviews around the world. It was followed by the more accessible *Með suð í eyrum við spilum endalaust* (2007); and the band were just wrapping up a sixth studio album at the time of writing, due to be released in 2010. You may also be familiar with Emiliana Torrini, the Icelandic-Italian singer who sang the spooky *Gollum's Song* in the Lord of the Rings film *The Two Towers*.

Back home, Reykjavík's music scene continues to flourish – at times it seems the whole city acts as a dizzying music-producing machine, with everyone under 30 playing an instrument or singing in a band. (Something to do on those long, dark nights?) A swirling maelstrom of musicians play gigs, record albums, go solo and re-form – see www.icelandmusic.is for an idea of the variety.

This constantly changing line-up of new bands and sounds makes it hard to pin the scene down. Currently popular are FM Belfast (who set up their own recording label to release their first album *How to Make Friends*); Singapore Sling (their fourth neo-psychedelic album, the cheerfully entitled *Perversity, Desperation and Death*, was released in 2009); Leaves (called 'the new Radiohead' by NME); Trabant (who describe themselves as 'Monty Python meets Thomas Dolby'); Mugison (introspective but tuneful songs from one man and his guitar); Múm (electronica mixed with real instruments); Mínus (whose thrashy guitars have supported Foo Fighters and Metallica); Hafdís Huld (spiky female popstress); Cynic Guru (perky pop encompassing lots of different styles); and Benni Hemm Hemm (highly rated guitar strumming with blasts of brass). Also watch for *My Summer as a Salvation Soldier*, poignant acoustic songs from singer Þórir.

Several of these bands were brought to a wider audience by the music documentary *Screaming Masterpiece* (2005), which contains moments of toe-curling pretentiousness but is worth watching to grasp the sheer diversity of Icelandic music.

Reykjavík's music venues are ever-changing, but at the time of writing, NASA, Batteríið and Sódóma (p101) were the three major places for seeing live bands. Check the free paper *Grapevine* for current news. As computer-mad

---

You might think *Icelandic Folktales*, translated by Alan Boucher, is just a collection of children's tales, but these light-hearted little gems encompass Icelandic history, humour and belief; they're the stories the country has been telling itself for hundreds of years.

---

www.musik.is – this useful website contains links to the websites and MySpace pages of most of the underground bands currently rocking Reykjavík.

AROUND THE RING ROAD IN 16 TUNES

The contributors of this playlist are Arngrímur Arnarson and Ármann Guðmundsson, two members of the hit Icelandic band Ljótu Hálfvitarnir. The two admit that this playlist probably says more about them than the music scene in Iceland in general. It's possible to contact them, to criticise their taste, sell them insurance or have a friendly chat, through their website www.ljotuhalfvitarnir.is.

■ **Before you set off** – 'Keyrum yfir Ísland' by Sprengjuhöllin. The first song on Sprengjuhöllin´s debut album, *Tímarnir okkar,* is about a road trip around Iceland. An energetic and joyful song that should get you in the mood.

■ **Akranes** – 'Sautjándi júní' by Dúmbó & Steini. This song by a popular '60s band is about Iceland's Independence Day, and is a sort of national anthem for kids.

■ **Ísafjörður** – 'The Question' by Mysterious Marta. The victor of the music competition The Cod War 2009, Marta won a record deal and also 10kg of cod. Marta took up her stage name while living in Ísafjörður, where she felt she appeared mysterious to the local people.

■ **Súðavík** – 'Murr Murr' by Mugison. Currently living in Súðavík, Mugison is one of Iceland's most talented singer-songwriters.

■ **Skagaströnd** – 'Kántrýbær' by Hallbjörn Hjartarson. The king of country music in Iceland, Hallbjörn has been running a restaurant and radio station in Skagaströnd for decades.

■ **Skagaströnd** – 'Gullfallega útgáfa af forljótum náunga' by Bróðir Svartúlfs. Winners of the 2009 Battle of the Bands in Iceland, Bróðir Svartúlfs sound like nothing else.

■ **Siglufjörður** – 'Stolt siglir fleyið mitt' by Gylfi Ægisson. An old-timer who grew up in Siglufjörður and has written several hits through the decades.

■ **Hraundrangi, Öxnadalur** – 'Inní mér syngur vitleysingur' by Sigur Rós. This spectacular place in the northwest was one of the locations chosen by Sigur Rós for their Heima tour. Stop by, put 'Inní mér syngur vitleysingur' on and see what happens. Welcome to Iceland.

■ **Akureyri/Hvanndalur**– 'Maístjarnan' by Hvanndalsbræður. A folk-rock group claiming to be brothers from the abandoned valley Hvanndalur. They all live in Akureyri, though. This is a classical Icelandic lullaby in a rock arrangement: lyrics by the country's only Nobel-prize winner, Halldór Laxness, melody by composer Jón Ásgeirsson.

■ **Húsavík** – 'Bjór, meiri bjór' by Ljótu Hálfvitarnir. The band's name (Ugly Idiots) really says it all. Nine guys from Húsavík formed this folk-punk-pop band in 2006. They change instruments after each song, and quite often there's not a single beer left in the house when the evening is over (hence the name of this song, 'Beer, more beer').

■ **Vestmannaeyjar** – 'Love Song' by Foreign Monkeys. From the Vestmannaeyjar comes this young and promising stoner rock band, who released their first album in 2009.

■ **Selfoss** – 'Bahama' by Ingó & Veðurguðirnir. This Selfoss-based quartet became one of the country's most popular bands with their 2009 debut album.

■ **Keflavík** – 'Það sýnir sig' by Hjálmar. The kings of Icelandic reggae. Two key members of the band come from Keflavík. This song, along with the rest of their fourth album, was actually recorded in Jamaica.

■ **Garðabær** – 'Breaking the Waves' by Dikta. Formed in a garage in Garðabær, Dikta has become one of Iceland's biggest rock bands. This song is from their second album, *Hunting for Happiness*.

■ **Reykjavík** – 'Suitcase Man' by Hjaltalín. A band with an unusual instrumental set-up; one of the most popular Icelandic bands since their formation in 2007.

■ **Reykjavík** – 'Reykjavíkurnætur' by Megas. The undisputed lyrical master of Icelandic pop history has been releasing albums since the early '70s. In 'Reykjavíkurnætur' (Reykjavík Nights), some of the Sugarcubes perform with him, including Björk (and her sister Inga).

internet fiends, a lot of Icelanders spread their music via sites such as MySpace.

The best music festival in Iceland is Airwaves (held in Reykjavík in October), which showcases the cream of Iceland's talent along with international acts.

TRADITIONAL MUSIC

Until rock and roll arrived in the 20th century, Iceland was a land practically devoid of musical instruments. The Vikings brought the *fiðla* and the *langspil* with them from Scandinavia – both a kind of two-stringed box that rested on the player's knee and was played with a bow. They were never solo instruments but merely served to accompany singers, as did the few church organs that appeared in the 19th century.

It's not really surprising, in a country permanently on the verge of starvation, that instruments were an unheard-of luxury, and that singing was the sole music. The most famous song styles are the *rímur*, poetry or stories from the sagas performed in a low, eerie chant (Sigur Rós have dabbled with the form), and *fimmundasöngur*, sung by two people in harmony. Cut off from other influences, the Icelandic singing style barely changed from the 14th century to the 20th; it also managed to retain harmonies that were banned by the church across the rest of Europe for being the work of the devil!

Iceland has hundreds of traditional ditties that most Icelanders learn before school age and are still singing with relish in their old age. They're dredged up whenever an occasion brings the generations together: family parties, outings, camping. The two favourites (which you'll hear exhaustively) are *Á Sprengisandi*, a cowboy song about sheep herders and outlaws in the desert highlands, and a tear-jerking lullaby based on a legend about outlaw Fjalla-Eyvindur's wife, who threw her starving baby into a waterfall. Several collections of traditional Icelandic music are available from Reykjavík music shops and souvenir shops around the country.

Cinema

Iceland's film industry is young – regular production started around the early 1980s – but it's thrown out some distinctive work to date. Icelandic short films in particular have received all kinds of international awards. Full-length features are rarer, but they often contain the same quirky, dark subject matter and superb cinematography, using Iceland's powerful landscape as a backdrop.

In 1992 the film world first took notice of Iceland when *Children of Nature* was nominated for an Academy Award for Best Foreign Film. In the film, an elderly couple forced into a retirement home in Reykjavík make a break for the countryside. The film's director, Friðrik Þór

---

CONVERSATION ABOUT AN OLD ICELANDIC INSTRUMENT

Author: I'd love to hear how a *langspil* sounds – do you know where I could listen to one?
Museum curator: No, sorry, I don't.
A: Do any folk groups use them in their music?
MC: No, I can't think of any.
A: So not many people play them these days?
MC: No, not many.
A: Why's that, then?
MC: Well...they sound awful.

Friðriksson, is something of a legend in Icelandic cinema circles, although some of his films are definitely better than others. *Cold Fever* (1994), *Angels of the Universe* (2000) and *The Sunshine Boy* (2009) are three that are well worth watching.

Massive acclaim at home doesn't necessarily translate into international fame. Certain films have been storming successes in Iceland, but aren't well known outside the country. These include *Íslenski Draumurinn* (Icelandic Dream; 2000), a comic drama about a man whose life revolves around football, juggling current and former girlfriends, and peddling imported cigarettes; *Mávahlátur* (Seagull's Laughter; 2001), which follows the lives of a group of women in a 1950s fishing village; and *Þetta er ekkert mál* (2006), a biography of Jón Pál Sigmarsson.

If one film *has* put Iceland, and especially Reykjavík, on the cinematic stage, it's *101 Reykjavík* (2000), directed by Baltasar Kormákur and based on the novel by Hallgrímur Helgason. This dark comedy explores sex, drugs and the life of a loafer in downtown Reykjavík. Kormákur's later films have met with less success, although *Jar City* (2006) received an international release and good reviews. It stars the ever-watchable Ingvar E Sigurðsson as Iceland's favourite detective, Inspector Erlendur, and is definitely one to look out for.

www.icelandicfilmcenter. is – catch up on the latest in the Iceland film industry.

Another Icelandic director who has achieved international success is Dagur Kári, whose films include *Nói Albinói* (2003), about a restless adolescent in a snowed-in northern fjord town; and the English-language *The Good Heart* (2009), which received a standing ovation at its premiere at the 2009 Toronto International Film Festival. Also look out for Hilmar Oddsson's *Kaldaljós* (Cold Light; 2004), a slow-moving, poignant film about life in an isolated fjord, with a stunning performance from the little boy on whom it centres.

Iceland's immense beauty and the government's 20% production rebate for film-makers have encouraged Hollywood directors to make movies here. Try to spot the Icelandic scenery in blockbusters such as *The Fifth Element* (1997), *Tomb Raider* (2001), *Die Another Day* (2002), *Batman Begins* (2005), *Flags of Our Fathers* (2006), *Stardust* (2007) and *Journey to the Centre of the Earth* (2008).

Architecture

People who come to Iceland expecting to see Viking longhouses will be disappointed, as the turf-and-wood buildings haven't stood up to the ravages of time. At best you'll see grassed-over foundations. These materials, however, were used right up until the 19th century, and several later turf-roofed buildings around the country have been preserved as folk museums – there are good examples at Keldur (p142) and Skógar (p144) in southwest Iceland, and Glaumbær (p205) in north Iceland.

For information on architecture in Reykjavík, see the boxed text, p82.

A Guide to Icelandic Architecture (Association of Icelandic Architects) looks at 250 Icelandic buildings and designs.

Painting & Sculpture

Iceland's most successful artists have traditionally studied abroad (in Copenhagen, London, Oslo or elsewhere in Europe), before returning home to wrestle with Iceland's enigmatic soul. The result is a European-influenced style but with Icelandic landscapes and saga-related scenes as key subjects.

The first great Icelandic landscape painter was the prolific Ásgrímur Jónsson (1876–1958), who was attracted to Impressionism while studying in Italy. He produced a startling number of oils and watercolours depicting Icelandic landscapes and folk tales. You can see his work at Reykjavík's National Gallery (p82).

One of Ásgrímur's students was Johannes Kjarval (1885–1972), Iceland's most enduringly popular artist, who lived in the remote east Iceland village of Borgarfjörður Eystri as a child. His first commissioned works were, rather poignantly, drawings of farms for people who were emigrating, but he's most famous for his early charcoal sketches of people from the village and for his surreal landscapes.

www.statice.is – the Statistics Iceland site has thousands of fascinating facts and figures about Iceland.

Contemporary artists to look out for include pop-art icon Erró (Guðmundur Guðmundsson), who has donated his entire collection to Reykjavík Art Museum's Hafnarhúsið (p81); mural and glass artist Sjofn Har; and Tryggvi Ólafsson (p278), whose strikingly colourful abstracts depicting Icelandic scenes hang in national galleries in Reykjavík, Sweden and Denmark.

Sculpture is very well represented in Iceland, with works dotting parks, gardens and galleries across the country, and its most famous sculptors all have museums dedicated to them in Reykjavík. Notable exponents include Einar Jónsson (1874–1954; p80), whose mystical works dwell on death and resurrection; Ásmundur Sveinsson (1893–1982; p81), whose tactile work is very wide-ranging but tends to celebrate Iceland, its stories and its people; and Sigurjón Ólafsson (1908-92; p82), who specialised in busts but also dabbled in abstract forms.

Reykjavík heaves with modern-art showrooms full of love-'em-or-hate-'em installations – ask the tourist office for a full list of galleries, and also see p80.

Food & Drink

For much of its history, Iceland was a poverty-stricken hinterland where food was solely about survival. Its traditional dishes reflect a 'waste not, want not' frugality and are viewed by foreigners less as sustenance and more as body parts from a slasher movie (see p50).

Icelandic farmer-fishermen had a hard time: sparse soil and long, harsh winters meant crop growing was limited, and those who lived by the coast wrested a dangerous living from the sea and shore. Sheep, fish and sea birds and their eggs were common foods, and every part of every creature was eaten – fresh, or preserved by drying, salting, smoking, pickling in whey or even burying underground, in the case of shark meat.

In terms of staples, little has changed over the centuries: fish, seafood, lamb, bread and simple vegetables, such as potatoes, are the basis of a typical Icelandic diet. The way in which these ingredients are prepared, however, has changed drastically over the last 25 years. It's now a source of national pride to serve up traditional food as tastily and imaginatively as possible, using methods borrowed from fashionable culinary traditions around the world.

There's no denying that dining out in Iceland is expensive, but it's worth spending a little extra to try some of the nation's top restaurants. If you're being determinedly frugal, you'll almost certainly be eating French fries, hot dogs, hamburgers and pizzas.

STAPLES & SPECIALITIES
Fish & Seafood

Fish has always been the mainstay of the Icelandic diet. Fish served in restaurants or on sale in markets is always fresh, and when cooked it usually comes boiled, pan-fried, baked or grilled.

In the past, Icelanders merely kept the cheeks and tongues of *þorskur* (cod) – something of a delicacy – and exported the rest; but today you'll commonly find cod fillets on the menu, along with *ýsa* (haddock), *bleikja* (Arctic char) and popular meaty-textured *skötuselur* (monkfish). Other fish include *lúða* (halibut), *steinbítur* (catfish), *sandhverfa* (turbot; not an indigenous fish), *síld* (herring), *skarkoli* (plaice) and *skata* (skate). During the summer you can sometimes get *silungur* (freshwater trout) and *lax* (salmon). Wild salmon is called *villtur* and farmed salmon is *eldislax*.

Harðfiskur, a popular snack eaten with butter, is found in supermarkets and at market stalls. To make it, haddock is cleaned and dried in the open air until it has become dehydrated and brittle, then it's torn into strips.

Shrimp, oysters and mussels are caught in Icelandic waters – mussels are at their prime during both the very beginning and the end of summer. *Leturhumar* are a real treat. These are what the Icelanders call 'lobster', although the rest of us know them as langoustine. Höfn, in southeast Iceland, is particularly well known for them and even has an annual lobster festival (see p303).

Meat

Icelandic lamb is hard to beat. During summer, sheep roam free to munch on chemical-free grasses and herbs in the highlands and valleys, before being rounded up in the September *réttir* and corralled for the winter. The result of this relative life of luxury is very tender lamb with a slightly gamey flavour. You'll find lamb fillets, pan-fried lamb or smoked lamb on most restaurant menus.

During the filming of *Dancer in the Dark*, director Lars von Trier was supposedly so brutal to singer Björk that he drove her to the brink of sanity – she apparently ate her own cardigan.

Check out *50 Crazy Things To Eat in Iceland*, by Snæfroður Ingadóttir and Þorvaldur Örn Kristinundsson, for a few fun pictorials of Iceland's traditional eats.

Saltfish (wind-dried, salted fillets of cod) was so important to the Icelanders that it once appeared in the centre of the country's flag.

THE TRADITIONAL ICELANDIC KITCHEN: A HALL OF HORRORS!

Eyeball a plate of old-fashioned Icelandic food, and chances are it will eyeball you back. In the past nothing was wasted, and some traditional specialities look more like horror-film props than food. You won't be faced with these dishes on many menus, though – they're generally only eaten at the Þorrablót winter feast.

Þorrablót specials:

- *Svið* – singed sheep's head (complete with eyes) sawn in two, boiled and eaten fresh or pickled
- *Sviðasulta* (head cheese) – made from bits of *svið* pressed into gelatinous loaves and pickled in whey
- *Slátur* – a mishmash of sheep intestines, liver and lard tied up in a sheep's stomach and cooked (kind of like haggis)
- *Blóðmör* – similar to *slátur*, with added blood and bound by rye
- *Súrsaðir hrútspungar* – rams' testicles pickled in whey and pressed into a cake
- *Hákarl* – Iceland's most famous stomach churner. *Hákarl* is Greenland shark, an animal so inedible that it has to rot away underground for six months before humans can even digest it. Most foreigners find the stench (a cross between ammonia and week-old roadkill) too much to bear, but it tastes better than it smells… It's the aftertaste that really hurts. A shot of *brennivín* (schnapps) is traditionally administered as an antidote.

Other (more palatable) Icelandic snacks:

- *Brennivín* – sledgehammer schnapps made from potatoes and flavoured with caraway
- *Hverabrauð* – a rich, dark rye bread baked underground using geothermal heat; try it at Mývatn
- *Lundi* – puffin; this cute little sea bird looks and tastes like calf liver
- *Skyr* – delicious concoction made of pasteurised skimmed milk and a bacteria culture similar to yoghurt, sweetened with sugar and berries
- *Hangikjöt* – hung meat, usually smoked lamb, served in thin slices
- *Harðfiskur* – brittle pieces of wind-dried haddock, usually eaten with butter

---

Beef steaks are also excellent but are not as widely available and are consequently more expensive. Horse is still eaten in Iceland, although it's regarded as something of a delicacy – so if you see 'foal fillets' on the menu, you're not imagining things.

In eastern Iceland wild reindeer roam the highlands, and reindeer steaks are a feature of local menus. Reindeer season starts in late July and runs well into September.

Birds have always been part of the Icelandic diet. You'll often come across *lundi* (puffin), that sociable little sea bird, which appears smoked or broiled in liverlike lumps on many dinner plates. Another sea bird is *svartfugl*; it's commonly translated as blackbird on English-language menus, but what you'll actually get is guillemot *(langvía)*. High-class restaurants favouring seasonal ingredients often have succulent roasted *heiðagæs* (pink-footed goose) in autumn.

Like a turkey dinner is to American Thanksgiving, *rjúpa* (ptarmigan), a plump but tough bird related to the grouse, is the centrepiece of celebrations during the Icelandic holiday season. The bird is officially protected and you won't find it served in restaurants, but *rjúpa* hunting is still a popular pastime.

Sweets & Desserts

Don't miss out on *skyr*, a delicious yoghurtlike concoction made from pasteurised skimmed milk. Despite its rich and decadent flavour, it's actually low in fat and is often mixed with sugar, fruit flavours (such as blueberry) and cream to give it a wonderful taste and texture. *Skyr* can be found in any supermarket (it's a great snack for kids) and as a dessert in restaurants.

Icelandic *pönnukökur* (pancakes) are thin, sweet and cinnamon flavoured. Icelandic *kleinur* (doughnuts) are a chewy treat, along with their offspring *ástar pungur* (love balls), deep-fried, spiced balls of dough. You'll find these desserts in bakeries, along with an amazing array of fantastic pastries and cakes – one of the few sweet legacies of the Danish occupation.

Recently, homemade ice cream has become the *it* craze. Local dairy farms are churning out scrumptious scoops by the gallon – they're often featured on the menus of nearby restaurants. You can visit certain creameries for sample-filled tours (see the boxed text, p176).

DRINKS
Nonalcoholic

Life without *kaffi* (coffee) is unthinkable. Cafes and petrol stations will usually have an urn full of filter coffee by the counter, and some shops offer complimentary cups to customers. A coffee costs anywhere from Ikr200 to Ikr350, but normally you'll get at least one free refill. European-style cafes, where you can get espresso, latte, cappuccino, mocha and imported coffee, are quite popular in Reykjavík and Akureyri. Tea is available but clearly doesn't offer the caffeine fix Icelanders need.

And they really are caffeine addicts. Besides all that coffee, Icelanders drink more Coca-Cola per capita than any other country. Another very popular soft drink is Egils Appelsín (confusingly not apple but orange soda) and the home-grown Egils Malt Extrakt, which tastes like sugar-saturated beer.

Bottled water is widely available, but tap water is delicious and free.

Alcoholic

Icelanders generally don't drink alcohol to savour the taste – getting trollied is the aim of the game. Particularly in Reykjavík, it's the done thing to go out at the weekend and drink till you drop (see p99 and p221). Nevertheless, you might be surprised to learn that drinking during the week hasn't been culturally acceptable in the past. It's becoming more common but, if you order a midweek pint in the countryside, people may assume you have an alcohol problem!

You must be at least 20 years old to buy beer, wine or spirits, and alcohol is only available from licensed bars, restaurants and the government-run Vín Búð liquor stores (www.vinbud.is). There are roughly 50 shops around the country; most towns with more than two streets have one; the greater Reykjavík area has about a dozen. In larger towns and cities, the opening hours are usually from 11am to 6pm Monday to Thursday and on Saturdays, and 11am to 7pm on Fridays (closed Sundays). In small communities the liquor

Clink your steins and say '*skál!*' – the Icelandic version of 'cheers' or 'good health'.

Kaldi, Iceland's only microbrewed beer (and our personal fave), offers tours of their production plant, just north of Akureyri.

WOULD YOU BELIEVE...

...that beer was illegal in Iceland until just over 20 years ago? In an attempt to circumvent the law, several Reykjavík pubs began serving nonalcoholic beer mixed with vodka, until this too was banned in 1985. The nation gathered in protest, held mock funerals and sang dirges for the swill that had become a national staple. Suddenly, in 1988 a vote was taken to legalise real beer, and on 1 March 1989 the amber fluid began to flow. Reykjavíkurs have never looked back!

ICELAND'S UNOFFICIAL FOODIE TOUR

Inspired by a visit to Italy, master chef Friðrik and his wife Adda opened Friðrik V in Akureyri – a restaurant dedicated to Slow Food and locally sourced products. Friðrik's staunch insistence on purely Icelandic meals has earned him a great deal of respect throughout the nation and abroad.

While nibbling on a couple of his signature dishes (we could write a love poem to his *skyr brulée*) Friðrik gave us the skinny on where to fatten up. And thus the 'Unofficial Foodie Tour' was born, which rings around Iceland much like our destination chapters:

Reykjavík, the logical starting point, is a culinary treasure trove, so go ahead and peruse the eating section (p93) to see what tickles your fancy. We will, however, give **Dill** (☎ 552 1522; Sturlugata 5; ☼ 11.30am-2pm & 7-10pm), at Alvar Aalto's Nordic House, a special shout out for it's fresher-than-fresh daily specials.

From Reykjavík, head north to the town of Borgarnes in west Iceland. In general, museums don't usually have stellar food, but the on-site restaurant at the must-see **Settlement Centre** (p161) continues the sensory journey back through time. The selection of traditional eats – such as the buttery fish stew – goes well with the animated retelling of *Egil's Saga*.

There are plenty of tasty treats in the Westfjords, especially in Ísafjörður. It seems that these days most tourists are eating at the atmospheric Tjöruhisið (Tar House), but **Potturinn** (p189), the restaurant in Hótel Ísafjörður, has some of the best food around town, in spite of its 'I went to IKEA' decor. The fish comes in fresh from the docks every afternoon, and their puffin is exquisite.

Back on the Ring Road, you'll find Skagafjörður, a region known for its horse breeding. Over the last few years, the Slow Food Movement has really gained some momentum here, and, as weird as it may seem, you won't find better foal anywhere else in the country. The restaurant in **Hótel Varmahlíð** (p205) is your best bet. Nay-sayers (wink!) can try the lamb – the hotel manager also runs a sheep farm, so you'll be sampling some of her stock.

Then, go straight to **Friðrik V** (p220) in Akureyri, where you'll visit local farms and collect fresh produce with the owners during one of their gourmet safaris.

Hótel Norðurljós (p249), in oft-ignored Raufarhöfn, is a true hidden gem. The owner has a real knack for expanding the definition of local food – ask about his seaweed pesto made from scurvywort plant!

On the south side, don't forget to stop in **Höfn** (p301), Iceland's lobster capital. Drive-through service is available if you're in a rush – you'll find tasty langoustines in designer bento boxes.

And finally, as you make your way back to Reykjavík, take a slight dessert detour at **Lindin** (p125) – home to the best chocolate mousse in the world!

stores are only open for an hour or two in the late afternoon. Expect queues around 5pm on a Friday. You can pick up a bottle of imported wine for around Ikr1200 (and up), and beer costs about a third of what you'll pay in a bar.

Petrol stations and supermarkets sell the weak and watery 2.2% brew known as pilsner, but most Icelanders would sooner not drink it at all.

The three main brands of Icelandic beer – Egil's, Thule and Viking – are all fairly standard lager or pils brews; you can also get imported beers such as Carlsberg and (in Irish bars) Guinness. A pint of beer in a pub costs about Ikr700; a glass of house wine or a shot of spirits in a restaurant costs Ikr600 to Ikr1000.

The traditional Icelandic alcoholic brew is *brennivín* (literally 'burnt wine'), a potent schnapps made from potatoes and caraway seeds, with the foreboding nickname *svarti dauði* (black death).

WHERE TO EAT & DRINK
Restaurants

Most of Iceland's best restaurants are in Reykjavík (p93), but there are several magnificent finds popping up beyond the capital. Bear in mind that the price difference between an exceptional restaurant and an average one is often small, so it can be well worth going upmarket. Often, though, in rural Iceland you may not have a choice – the town's only eating place will probably be the restaurant in the local hotel (or the grill in the petrol station – see below).

Lunch usually costs between Ikr1000 and Ikr2500, and dinner between Ikr1800 and Ikr5500, depending on where you are and what you order. Á la carte menus usually offer at least one fish dish, one vegie choice (invariably pasta) and several meat mains. Lots of restaurants also have a menu of lighter, cheaper meals such as hamburgers, sandwiches and pizzas. In Reykjavík, and to a lesser extent Akureyri, there are an increasing number of ethnic restaurants, including Thai, Japanese, Italian, Mexican, Indian and Chinese.

Opening hours for restaurants are usually 11.30am to 2.30pm and 6pm to 10pm daily.

Cafes & Pubs

Downtown Reykjavík has a great range of bohemian cafe-bars where you can happily while away the hours sipping coffee, gossiping, people-watching, scribbling in your diary, or tinkering with your laptop. Menus range from simple soups and sandwiches to fish dishes and designer burgers. Cafe-bars offer some of the best bargain meals in Iceland (mains cost from about Ikr800).

Most of Reykjavík's cafes metamorphose into wild drinking dens in the evenings (Fridays and Saturdays mostly). Suddenly DJs appear, beer is swilled, and merry people dance, screech and stagger around until somewhere between 3am and 6am.

Skagafjörður in northwest Iceland, has developed a 'culinary tourism' infrastructure – menus in the area's restaurants have a fork-and-knife symbol next to items made solely from locally sourced produce.

Quick Eats
KIOSKS
Icelanders love fast food, and you'll soon discover that a cheap way to stave off hunger until dinner is to have a *pýlsur* (hot dog).

PETROL-STATION GRILLS
Outside Reykjavík, many large petrol stations have good, cheap grills and cafeterias attached to them – often the busiest eating place in town. They generally serve sandwiches and fast food from around 11am to 9pm or 10pm. Some also offer hearty set meals at lunchtime, such as meat soup, fish of the day or plates of lamb.

BAKERIES
We can't praise the wonderful Icelandic *bakari* (bakeries) enough. Every town has one, generally open from 7am or 8am until 5pm on weekdays (sometimes also Saturdays). They sell all sorts of inexpensive fresh bread, buns, cakes, sandwiches and coffee, and usually provide chairs and tables.

Self-Catering
Every town and village has at least one small supermarket. The most expensive are 10-11 and 11-11. Bónus (easily recognised by its drunk-looking

---

ICELANDIC PÝLSUR

Along with copious amounts of coffee, the *pýlsur* (hot dog) is the fuel of modern Iceland. Hot dogs are for sale (for around Ikr250) in every petrol station and fast-food kiosk. You can choose between toppings of raw onion, crunchy deep-fried onion, ketchup, mustard and tangy remoulade, or just ask for *'ein með öllu'* (one with everything – our favourite).

yellow-and-pink piggy-bank sign) is the country's budget supermarket chain. Others include Krónan, Kasko, Samkaup-Strax and Samkaup-Úrval. Opening times vary greatly; in Reykjavík most are open from 9am to 11pm daily, but outside the capital hours are always shorter.

Iceland imports most of its groceries, so prices are exorbitant – roughly twice or three times what you'd pay in North America, Australia or Europe. Fish (tinned or smoked) and dairy products represent the best value and are surprisingly cheap. Some fruit and vegetables are grown locally, and these tend to be fresh and tasty, but imported vegetables usually look tragic by the time they hit the supermarket shelves.

> Stop by a small-town bakery around 5pm – sweet treats are usually marked down by 50% before being thrown out at the end of the day.

VEGETARIANS & VEGANS

You'll have no problem in Reykjavík – there are several excellent meat-free, organic cafe-restaurants in the city, and many more eateries offer vegetarians plenty of choice. Outside the capital most restaurants have at least one vegie item on the menu – although as this is routinely cheese-and-tomato pasta or cheese-and-pepper-and-onion pizza, you could get very bored. Vegans will have to self-cater.

It's unlikely that you'll ever have to explain yourself in Icelandic but, just in case, *'Ég er grænmetisæta'* means 'I'm a vegetarian' and *'Ég borða ekki kjöt'* means 'I don't eat meat'.

HABITS & CUSTOMS

Icelandic eating habits are similar to elsewhere in northern Europe and Scandinavia. Breakfast is usually light (often just coffee), as is lunch (soup and bread or a snack). Dinner is the main meal of the day.

Three strange little foodie festivals follow the bloody Þorrablót feast in February (see the boxed text, p50). First off is Bolludagur (Bun Day; Monday before Shrove Tuesday), when Icelanders gorge themselves sick on puff-pastry cream buns. Kids get up early to 'beat' the buns out of their parents with a *bolluvöndur* (literally 'bun wand'). The following day is Sprengidagur (Bursting Day; Shrove Tuesday), when the aim is to stuff yourself with *saltkjöt og baunir* (salted meat and split peas) until you burst. Both are Lenten traditions. Continuing the excess, Beer Day (1 March) is a less traditional celebration. It dates back to the glorious day in 1989 when beer was legalised in Iceland. As you'd expect, Reykjavík's clubs and bars get particularly wild.

On Christmas Day, *hangikjöt* (hung meat) – which is normally smoked lamb – is served, as well as *flatkökur* (unleavened bread, or pancakes, charred on a grill or griddle without fat).

EAT YOUR WORDS

See p347 for pronunciation guidelines.

Food Glossary
STAPLES & CONDIMENTS

brauð	bread
(soðið) egg	(boiled) egg
flatkökur	rye pancakes
hrísgrjón	rice
hunang	honey
krydd	seasoning
marmelaði	marmalade
morgunkorn	cereal
ostur	cheese

pípar	pepper
salt	salt
sinnep	mustard
smjör	butter
sulta	jam
sykur	sugar
tómatsósa	tomato sauce (ketchup)

FISH

bleikja	Arctic char
fiskur	fish
harðfiskur	dried haddock
humar	lobster
lax	salmon
lúða	halibut
reyktur	smoked salmon
rækja	shrimp
sandhverfa	turbot
sild	herring
silungur	freshwater trout
skata	skate
skötuselur	monkfish
steinbítur	catfish
villtur	wild salmon
ýsa	haddock
þorskur	cod

Rabarbarasulta (rhubarb jam) – made locally and found in most small-town shops – doesn't require refrigeration before opening, thus making a tasty souvenir to stash in your suitcase.

MEAT

bjúgu	smoked minced-meat sausage
hangikjöt	smoked lamb
hreindýrakjöt	reindeer
kjúklingur	chicken
kjöt	meat
kjötsúpa	lamb, rice and vegetable soup
lambakjöt	lamb
lundi	puffin
nautakjöt	beef
pýlsa	hot dog, sausage
saltkjöt	salted lamb or mutton
skinka	ham
svínakjöt	pork

VEGETABLES

blómkál	cauliflower
græn paprika	green pepper
grænar baunir	green peas
grænmeti	vegetables
gulrætur	carrots
gúrka	cucumber
hvítkál	cabbage
hvítlaukur	garlic
kartöflur	potatoes
laukur	onion
salat	lettuce
sveppir	mushrooms

FRUIT

ananas	pineapple
appelsínur	oranges
aprikósur	apricots
ávextir	fruit
bananar	bananas
bláber	blueberries
epli	apples
ferskjur	peaches
jarðarber	strawberries
krækiber	crowberries
perur	pears
sítróna	lemon
vínber	grapes

SWEETS & DESSERTS

ávaxtagrautur	stewed fruit
bolla	cream bun
búðingur	pudding
ís	ice cream
kaka	cake
kex	biscuits
kleinur	doughnuts
pönnukökur	thin, sweet, cinnamon-dusted pancakes
rjómaís	ice cream
skyr	thick yoghurtlike concoction made from skimmed milk and bacteria culture
smákökur	biscuits
súkkulaði	chocolate

DRINKS

appelsínsafi	orange juice
ávaxtasafi	fruit juice
bjór	beer
brennivín	literally 'burnt wine'; caraway-flavoured schnapps
drykkir	drinks
G-mjólk	longlife milk
gosdrykkir	soft drinks
hvítvín	white wine
jógúrt	yoghurt
kaffi (með mjólk/svart)	(white/black) coffee
mjólk	milk
rauðvín	red wine
súrmjólk	sour milk
te	tea
vatn	water
whisky	whisky

In the depths of winter the sun doesn't rise above Iceland's steepest fjords. On the day it finally reappears, villagers gather to celebrate Sólarkaffi (Sun Coffee) with a stack of pancakes and generous amounts of Iceland's favourite brown beverage.

MEALS

hádegismat	lunch
kvöldmat	dinner
morgunmat	breakfast

Environment

It's difficult to remain unmoved by the amazing diversity of the Icelandic landscape. Contrary to popular opinion, it's not an island completely covered in ice, nor is it a barren lunar landscape of congealed lava flows and windswept tundra. Both of these habitats exist, but so too do steep-sided fjords sweeping down to the sea, lush farmland, rolling hills, glacier-carved valleys, steaming fields, bubbling mudpots and vast, desertlike wasteland. It is this rich mix of scenery and the possibility of experiencing such extremes, so close together, that attract, surprise and enthral anyone who has been lucky enough to visit the country.

THE LAND

Plonked firmly on the Mid-Atlantic Ridge, a massive 18,000km-long rift between two of the earth's major tectonic plates, Iceland is a shifting, steaming lesson in schoolroom geology. Suddenly you'll be racking your brains to remember long-forgotten homework on how volcanoes work, how glacial moraines are formed, and why lava and magma aren't quite the same thing. With 22 active volcanoes, 250 geothermal areas, 780 hot springs and the world's third-largest ice cap (after Antarctica and Greenland), it's a vast reserve of information for scientists and a stunning playground for the rest of us.

Iceland is roughly equal in size to England, but with only 319,400 people (compared to England's 51 million) scattered around its coast. Beyond the sliver of habitable land along its shores, an inhospitable desert covers half the country, and another 15% is taken up by ice caps. Add on some lava fields and a few sandar (glacial sand plains), sprinkle generously with geysers, fumaroles and hot springs, and you've pretty much covered the island.

Iceland isn't truly an Arctic country, though – the northernmost point of the mainland falls short of the Arctic Circle by a few kilometres. To cross that imaginary boundary you'll need to travel to the island of Grímsey (p225), Iceland's only true piece of Arctic territory.

For a bit of background information about the country's diverse landscape, check out *Iceland – Classical Geology*, by Þor Þordarson & Armann Hoskuldsson.

Geology

A mere baby in geological terms, Iceland is the youngest country in Europe, formed by underwater volcanic eruptions along the joint of the North American and Eurasian plates 17 to 20 million years ago. These two massive tectonic plates create a fault line across the centre of Iceland and right down the Atlantic Ocean.

GEOLOGICALLY SPEAKING

Everywhere you go in Iceland you'll be bombarded with geological jargon to describe the landscape. The terms below will let you one-up the other geological neophytes.

Basalt – the most common type of solidified lava. This hard, dark, dense volcanic rock often solidifies into columns.

Igneous – a rock formed by solidifying lava or magma.

Moraine – a ridge of boulders, clay and sand carried and deposited by a glacier.

Obsidian – black, glassy rock formed by the rapid solidification of lava without crystallisation.

Rhyolite – light-coloured, fine-grained volcanic rock similar to granite in composition.

Scoria – porous volcanic gravel that has cooled rapidly while moving, creating a glassy surface with iron-rich crystals that give it a glittery appearance.

Tephra – solid matter ejected into the air by an erupting volcano.

GEOLOGICAL MAP OF ICELAND

The earth's crust in Iceland is only a third of its normal thickness, and magma (molten rock) continues to rise from deep within, forcing the two plates apart. The result is clearly visible at Þingvellir (p121), where the great rift Almannagjá broadens by between 1mm and 18mm per year, and at Námafjall (p237), where a series of steaming vents mark the ridge.

Along with the dramatic steaming vents, bubbling mudpots, weird rock formations and lava fields that draw in valuable tourist currency, Iceland's unique position on top of a highly active fault line brings other benefits. Turn on any Icelandic shower and you'll have piping hot water instantly (but try to brush your teeth and you'll have to wait a minute for the cold water to filter through). Iceland has a surplus of superheated steam and hot water that is used to produce cheap electricity, heat buildings and swimming pools, and even keep the pavements of Reykjavík clear of snow in winter.

Iceland's use of geothermal power is one of the most creative in the world, and the country's energy experts are now advising both Chinese and Indian industries on possible ways to harness geothermal sources. Iceland is also hoping to reduce its dependency on imported fossil fuels, and it has begun to invest in hydrogen-fuel research with the aim of phasing out petrol- and diesel-powered cars by midcentury.

> Icelanders used to believe that if a pregnant woman stared at the aurora borealis her child would be born cross-eyed.

Glaciers & Ice Caps

Glaciers and ice caps cover about 15% of Iceland, many of which are remnants of a cool period that began 2500 years ago. Ice caps are formed as snow piles up over millennia in an area where it's never warm enough to melt. The weight of the snow causes it to slowly compress into ice, eventually crushing the land beneath the ice cap and allowing the ice around the edges to flow downward in glaciers.

These slow-moving rivers of ice have carved out and shaped much of the Icelandic landscape since its creation, forming the glacial valleys and fjords that make those picture-postcard photos today.

Iceland's largest ice cap, Vatnajökull in the southeast, covers almost 13% of the country and is the third-largest in the world. Other major ice caps are Mýrdalsjökull in the southwest, and Langjökull and Hofsjökull in the highlands.

There are more Icelandic horses in Germany than in Iceland.

WILDLIFE
Animals
Apart from sheep, cows and horses, you'll be very lucky to have any casual sightings of animals in Iceland. The only indigenous land mammal is the elusive arctic fox, and although polar bears occasionally drift across from Greenland on ice floes, armed farmers make sure they don't last long.

Your best bet for spotting the arctic fox is in remote Hornstrandir, in the Westfjords – wildlife enthusiasts can push pause on their holiday and monitor these precious creatures while volunteering at the Arctic Fox Centre (see the boxed text, p188 for details). In east Iceland, herds of reindeer can sometimes be spotted from the road. The deer were introduced from Norway in the 18th century and now roam the mountains.

Bird life, however, is prolific, at least from May to August. On coastal cliffs and islands around the country you can see a mind-boggling array of sea birds, often in massive colonies. Most impressive for their sheer numbers are gannets, guillemots, razorbills, kittiwakes, fulmars and puffins. Less numerous birds include wood sandpipers, arctic terns, skuas, Manx shearwaters, golden plovers, storm petrels and Leach's petrels. In addition, there are many species of ducks, ptarmigans, whooping swans, redwings, divers and gyrfalcons, and two species of owl. For information on where to see the birds, turn to p64.

Another drawcard is the rich marine life, particularly whales. On whale-watching tours from Húsavík in northern Iceland (among other places), you'll have an excellent chance of seeing minke, humpback, sperm, fin, sei, pilot and blue whales. Orcas (killer whales), dolphins, porpoises and seals can also be spotted. For more information on Iceland's whales, see p242. Try p69 for additional info on whale watching. Seals can be seen in the Eastfjords, on the Vatnsnes Peninsula in northwest Iceland, in the Mýrar region on the southeast coast (including at Jökulsárlón), in Breiðafjörður in the west, and in the Westfjords.

Arctic terns possess kamikaze instincts and have no qualms about crashing into you if you tread on their land (or worse, near their nest). When hiking in tern territory, raise your hand above your head (as if to ask a question) or carry a long stick. Terns go for the highest appendage when they swoop for a peck.

Plants
Although ostensibly barren in places, the vegetation in Iceland is surprisingly varied – you just need to get close to see it. Most vegetation is low growing,

---

AURORA BOREALIS

The Inuit thought they were the souls of the dead; Scandinavian folklore described them as the spirits of unmarried women; and the Japanese believed that a child conceived under the dancing rays would be fortunate in life. Modern science, however, has a much different take on the aurora borealis.

The magical curtains of colour that streak across the northern night sky are the result of solar wind – a stream of particles from the sun that collides with oxygen, nitrogen and hydrogen in the upper atmosphere. These collisions produce the haunting greens and magentas as the earth's magnetic field draws the wind toward the polar regions.

LITTLE NORTHERN BROTHERS

Cute, clumsy and endearingly comic, the puffin (*Fratercula arctica*, or *lundi* as they're called in Icelandic) is one of Iceland's best-loved birds. Although known for goofy antics, crash landings and frantic fluttering, the bird is surprisingly graceful underwater and was once thought to be a bird-fish hybrid.

The puffin is a member of the auk family and spends most of its year at sea. For four or five months it comes to land to breed, generally keeping the same mate and burrow (a multiroom apartment!) from year to year. Sixty percent of the world's population of puffins breed in Iceland, and from late May to August you'll see them in huge numbers around the island. The best places to see them are Borgarfjörður Eystri (p269), Grímsey (p225), Lundey (see the boxed text, p244), and the Vestmannaeyjar (p149). Then, at the end of summer they suddenly take to the sea as though they have their departure date marked in a calendar!

---

staying close to the ground and spreading as much as possible to get a better grip on the easily eroded soil. Even the trees, where there are any, are stunted. As the old joke goes, if you're lost in an Icelandic forest, just stand up.

If you're visiting in summer, you'll be treated to incredible displays of wildflowers blooming right across the country. Most of Iceland's 440 flowering plants are introduced species – especially the noxious purple lupin you'll see out the window after arriving at Keflavík airport (see opposite for details). Throughout Iceland you'll see the bright-pink flowers of the tall arctic fireweed around riverbeds; the distinctive, graceful bell shape of the purple arctic harebell; and several varieties of colourful saxifrage and daisies lining every trail. In grassy lowlands look out for the pale and dainty northern green orchid, and in upland areas the white heads of arctic cotton, the soft yellow petals of the upright primrose and the small, pretty flowers of the mountain heath. Coastal areas are generally characterised by low grasses, bogs and marshlands, while at higher elevations hard or soft tundra covers the ground.

Marimo balls (golf-ball-sized spheres of algae) are found naturally in only two places in the world: Lake Akan in Japan and Iceland's Mývatn (p228).

Another common sight when walking just about anywhere in Iceland is the profusion of fungi. There are about 1500 types of fungi growing in Iceland, and you'll see everything from pale white mushrooms to bright orange flat caps as you walk along trails, by roadsides or through fields.

In southern and eastern Iceland new lava flows are first colonised by mosses, which create a velvety green cloak across the rough rocks. Older lava flows in the east and those at higher elevations are generally first colonised by lichens.

NATIONAL PARKS & RESERVES

Iceland has three national parks and more than 80 nature reserves, natural monuments, country parks and wildlife reserves. **Umhverfisstofnun** (Environment & Food Agency; http://english.ust.is) is responsible for protecting many of these sites. Their website contains a comprehensive section on each national park. Green thumbs can volunteer on a number of their conservation projects; see p333 for details.

A Guide to the Flowering Plants and Ferns of Iceland, by Hörður Kristinsson, is the best all-round field guide to Icelandic flowers.

Þingvellir (www.thingvellir.is), Iceland's oldest national park, protects a scenic 84 sq km lake, the geologically significant Almannagjá rift, and is the site of the original Alþing (National Assembly). The park is administered directly by the prime minister's office and is a Unesco World Heritage Site. See p121 for more.

Snæfellsjökull (http://english.ust.is/Snaefellsjokullnationalpark) in west Iceland was established in June 2001. The park protects the Snæfellsjökull glacier (made famous by Jules Verne), the surrounding lava fields and coast; see p171.

Vatnajökull (www.vatnajokulsthjodgardur.is) is the largest national park in all of Europe and covers roughly 11% of Iceland. It was founded in 2008 by uniting two previously established national parks: Skaftafell (p294), in southeast Iceland, and Jökulsárgljúfur (p245) further north. The park protects the entirety of the Vatnajökull glacier, Dettifoss (the strongest waterfall in Europe) and sundry geological anomalies.

ENVIRONMENTAL ISSUES

Iceland's small population, pristine wilderness, lack of heavy industry and high use of geothermal and hydroelectric power give it an enviable environmental reputation. Recycling programs are expanding, and many small-business owners are signing up for various eco-conscious certifications such as National Geographic's Geotourism program (www.nationalgeographic.com/travel/sustainable/about_geotourism.html) or the Green Globe initiative (www.greenglobe.org).

Nevertheless, pressing environmental concerns have forced a realisation among Icelanders that the continued existence of their pristine backyard is not an absolute birthright.

Check out the following websites for the latest updates:

Greenpeace (www.greenpeace.org)
Iceland Nature Conservation Association (www.inca.is)
International Fund for Animal Welfare (IFAW) (www.ifaw.org)
International Whaling Commission (www.iwcoffice.org)
Kárahnjúkar Hydroelectric Project (www.karahnjukar.is)
Nature Watch (www.natturuvaktin.com/english.htm)
Ocean Alliance www.oceanalliance.org)
Saving Iceland (www.savingiceland.org)
WWF (www.panda.org/arctic)

Whaling

Whale hunting has been a hot topic ever since the Icelandic government ignored the International Whaling Commission's worldwide ban on commercial whaling in 1986. International pressure and direct action by conservationists forced Iceland to call a halt to its whaling activities in 1989. But by 2003 the country resumed whaling under the auspices of a scientific research program despite the global moratorium. In 2006 Iceland announced plans to resume commercial whaling, much to the consternation of environmentalists and conservationists worldwide. Members of Iceland's tourism board were also strong objectors, stating that Iceland's whale-watching industry generates significantly more money than whale hunting. Despite the surge in recent protests, sentiments about the whaling industry are not unanimous. Many believe that whaling is intrinsically linked to Iceland's national identity; others remember when jobs at the whaling station put food on the dinner table. Sigursteinn Másson, Iceland's spokesperson for IFAW, gives us his take on the whaling dilemma, p62.

Soil Erosion

One of Iceland's most enduring environmental issues is soil erosion caused by high winds and overgrazing of sheep. Iceland was most likely deforested by overgrazing shortly after settlement, and today the sheep continue to chew vegetation down to the roots and expose the underlying soil to the forces of water and fierce winds. In parts of the country, particularly around Mývatn lake, results are dramatic, with formerly vegetated land reduced to barren wastes.

One measure used to tackle the problem was the introduction of the Nootka lupin (a purple-flowered plant from the west coast of North America)

If hiring a 4WD vehicle, stick to marked trails; off-roading is illegal and causes irreparable damage to the delicate landscape.

Plants and Animals of Iceland, by Benny Génsböl and Jon Feilberg, is an illustrated guide to all of Iceland's flora and fauna, including birds, marine mammals and 220 species of plants.

Björk added 'investment banker' to her resume in early 2009 when she started the Björk Fund as a way of helping Iceland invest in green technology. She founded Nattura in 2008 to help support grassroots industries.

WHALE TALES

At the start of summer in 2009, we had the opportunity to tag along with Sigursteinn Másson, spokesperson for IFAW (International Fund for Animal Welfare) in Iceland, as he documented the late-night return of the season's first successful whale hunt. Tied to the side of the boat were two dead fin whales being taken to the high-security station in Hvalfjörður for processing. Here's what Sigursteinn had to say:

'When asked "why is Iceland whaling?" there is no short answer. According to a Gallup poll in 2006, only 1.1% of Icelanders eats whale meat regularly, there are no foreign markets interested in purchasing significant amounts of minke meat, and no one imports fin whale meat, thus the industry is not a profitable one. Whaling damages our flourishing whale-watching industry, not to mention the nation's image. So, one would think that it would be an easy task for the government to stop such a business – but not here in Iceland!

Not everyone supports the antiwhaling movement. Whaling seems to have become part of our national pride – we have a long tradition of not letting others dictate our actions. And in light of the economic downturn, we seem to be having a bit of an identity crisis (so it's no surprise that the summer of 2009 was a bloody one for whales). Local politicians and journalists – who worked at Hvalfjörd's whaling station some 40 years ago – bolster the notion of a lucrative whaling tradition and the 'wonderful times of yore'. It is interesting to note, however, that Norwegians operated most of the early whaling stations in Iceland – Icelanders used to complain, citing bad smells and heavy pollution.

In October 2009, 26 nations – including the US, UK, Australia, France, Sweden, Spain and Germany – organised a formal diplomatic demarche against whaling in Iceland. (These are some of the countries that import many of our products, but Icelanders didn't seem to make the connection.) An ad was placed in Iceland's biggest journal with photos of individuals from all 26 countries urging people to re-think the issue. Supporters in Iceland (including myself) tried to organise a similar demonstration using Icelanders, but we couldn't get enough local people to speak up against whaling.

In a way, protesting whaling in Iceland is like coming out of the closet. Most people try not to think about our whaling practices, focusing instead on the fallacy that the industry must be profitable since it continues to exist. Asking Icelanders whether or not they support whaling can often feel like asking a local whether or not they support Iceland.

When I see a dead whale I cannot help but think that Iceland is disrespecting nature by not stopping the killings. These are the second largest animals in the world; they've been swimming through the seas for millions of years. As I watch the hunters drag the mighty beasts into the station I am left utterly perplexed. Why is this happening?

Just 3kg of minke whale was exported by the end of the whaling season in 2009 – the rest remains virtually unused, locked away in massive freezers. I don't understand.'

to help anchor and add nitrogen to the soil. The project has been a victim of its own success, however, revegetating vast tracts of land but now also affecting Iceland's biodiversity. The lupin's bitter taste means that grazing sheep will not feed on it, so it continues to spread its relatively tall foliage, blocking light for indigenous mosses, lichens and shrubs.

Harnessing Natural Energy

Thanks to an abundance of green energy and a special allowance under the Kyoto protocol, Iceland attracts multinationals in search of cheap energy, and the Icelandic government seems keen to help out. Environmental campaigners foresee catastrophic environmental damage, while politicians and corporate big shots peddle promises of untold economic benefits and jobs for all (pretty appealing considering the current economic conditions!).

The most controversial scheme up to now is the Kárahnjúkar hydroelectric project in the Eastfjords. The project was the brainchild of Alcoa, the American aluminium smelter, and involved (and continues to involve) the construction of a network of dams, a vast reservoir, tunnels, a power station and high-tension lines to power their local smelter. According to Alcoa, it is cheaper to harness the power generated by damming the two rivers than it is to generate power by conventional methods. (Although it's not cheaper than recycling existing aluminium products, which requires 5% of the energy it takes to produce new aluminium.) It's the biggest construction project in Iceland's history; Alcoa was named one of the top sustainable corporations at the World Economic Forum in Davos, Switzerland, and the promise of development has meant a surge in lucrative contracts to local support services. Construction, however, has devastated the starkly beautiful landscape and some marvellous natural phenomena that are found nowhere else on earth.

Many locals identify Kárahnjúkar as one of the major triggers of the currency crash in October 2008. Foreign loans flooded the country during construction and contractors created housing for thousands upon thousands of projected workers who ultimately never came.

The dam and smelter are a dramatic illustration of the dilemma Iceland now faces with the currency currently in the doldrums. How will Icelanders earn their living in the future – through tourism and thriving cultural industries, or by opening up vast tracts of their wilderness to industrial megaprojects?

While the Kárahnjúkar project steals most of the headlines, many other areas of Iceland are subject to proposed dam projects, aluminium plants and smelters. In east Iceland, Eyjabakkar, the country's second-largest highland wetlands, has been partially submerged as a result of the extensive Kárahnjúkar damming; Kerlingarfjöll, southwest of Hofsjökull, is to be harnessed for its geothermal energy; north Iceland's Skálfandafljót, with its magnificent waterfalls Aldeyjarfoss and Goðafoss, sits directly in the path of the Bakki smelter and has been targeted as a possible site for future damming; the glacial rivers of Skagafjörður and Jökulsá á Fjöllum are potential power sources; on the serene northwestern tip of Reykjanes Peninsula construction of a new smelter has started; and Langisjór, at the western edge of Vatnajökull, is set to receive the redirected water flows from the Skafta and Tungnaá Rivers, transforming the lake into a reservoir-like expanse.

Many Icelanders understand the value of their virgin lands and government legislation is regularly enacted to help protect it. In 2008 the Vatnajökull National Park was created by combining the previous parks at Skaftafell and Jökulsárgljúfur. The ultimate goal is to completely encase the Vatnajökull glacier and all of its glacial run-off under one long strand of enviro-friendly red tape. Smaller-scale conservation projects are underway throughout the country as well.

During the 1950s and '60s it was considered patriotic to pick up a free bag of Nootka lupin seedlings at the local store and sprinkle them on flowerless tracts of land.

Activities

Iceland's dramatic scenery, pristine wilderness and abundance of tour operators mean that it's easy to get into the great outdoors and enjoy the country at its best. Whether you're a weather-beaten adrenalin junkie looking for the next high, or a more laid-back adventurer content with some leisurely walking and great photo opportunities, Iceland has something for you. This chapter will give you an overview of what's on offer; you'll find information on local trails, operators and activities listed in the destination chapters. Also check out our activities colour-spread (p253) for a bit of inspiration.

BIRDWATCHING

Get a bird's perspective on popular 'flight-seeing' plane ride tours – see www.ernir.is for tours in the south, and www.myflug.is for flights over Mývatn and the nearby highlands.

On coastal cliffs right around the country you can see huge numbers of sea birds, often in massive colonies. The best time for birdwatching is between June and mid-August, when gannets, guillemots, razorbills, kittiwakes and fulmars can be seen. Puffins are spotted from the end of April until mid-August, when they suddenly take to the sea en masse. Some of the best spots for birdwatching include Hornstrandir (p192), the Látrabjarg Peninsula (p180) and Grímsey (p225) in the Westfjords; Drangey and Málmey Islands (p207) in northwest Iceland; Mývatn (p228), Lundey (p244) and the Langanes Peninsula (p250) in northeast Iceland; Borgarfjörður Eystri (p269) and Skálanes (p275) in east Iceland; and Breiðamerkursandur (p299) in southeast Iceland.

For more comprehensive information on the bird species in Iceland, see p59.

BOATING

Many of Iceland's long, scenic fjords can be explored on scenic boat tours. While some local operators offer whale watching (p69) or sea angling (p66), other trips simply involve enjoying the beautiful surrounds. Many tours also take in adorable offshore islands such as those in Breiðafjörður (p167), or at Papey (p282), Grímsey (p225), Lundey and Flatey (p244) and Vigur (p191). Figure between Ikr3000 and Ikr6500 for an afternoon boat ride.

CAVING

Iceland's ice caves were formed by geothermal run-off water.

Caving and potholing are relatively new sports in Iceland and only a couple of operators run tours. Lava caves dating back more than 10,000 years are the most common types of cave and can be toured with minimum caving gear and experience. Organised tours are operated by **Ultima Thula** (www.ute.is), **Iceland Excursions** (www.icelandexcursions.is) and **Iceland Total** (www.icelandtotal.com). Experienced cavers in search of something more challenging should contact regional tourism boards for assistance in organising a caving expedition and advice on which caves to visit. Iceland's spectacular ice caves are extremely challenging and require professional equipment and knowledge. Iceland's most famous ice caves are at Kverkfjöll (p317).

CYCLING

For information on Iceland's mountain-bike club, check out www.fjallahjolaklubburinn.is.

Iceland is a great place for cycling independently or as part of a group. See p337 for more details.

DIVING

Little known but incredibly rewarding, diving in Iceland is becoming increasingly popular. The clear water (100m visibility!), great wildlife, spectacular lava ravines, wrecks and thermal chimneys make it a dive destination like no other. The best dive sites are Silfra at Þingvellir and the thermal cones in Eyjafjörður. There are only four local operators, but between them they offer day and multiday tours as well as training. For everything you need to know about diving in Iceland, check out p217, or contact **Dive.is** (☎ 663 2858; www.dive .is; Keflavík), **Strytan Divecenter** (☎ 862 2949; www.strytan.is; Akureyri), **IsDive** (☎ 694 1006; www. isdive.is; Vestmannaeyjar), or **Dive Iceland** (☎ 699 3000; www.kafarinn.is; Hafnarfjörður). **Iceland Excursions** (www.icelandexcursions.is) can also organise day trips. Scuba virgins can enrol in a PADI course with Dive.is; everyone else should have 10 or more dives under their belt and understand the basics of diving with a drysuit.

Visit www.strytan.is for inspirational photos taken on local scuba trips.

DOG SLEDDING

Dog sledding, where you're pulled along behind Greenlandic huskies, is another typically Arctic experience organised for tourists on the Mýrdalsjökull glacier on the southwest coast. A one-hour tour costs around Ikr15,000 with **Dogsledding.is** (☎ 487 7747; www.dogsledding.is). Longer expeditions can be arranged with sufficient numbers.

HIKING

The opportunities for hiking in Iceland are virtually endless, from leisurely half-day walks to multiday wilderness treks. However, the unpredictable weather is always a consideration, and rain, fog and mist can turn an uplifting hike into a miserable trudge. Come prepared with good rain gear and strong boots, and if you're planning anything other than a short hike, carry good maps, as many trails are unmarked. You'll also need to ford rivers on many trails (see p68), and look out for fissures, which can be hundreds of metres deep.

Visit www.outdoors.is for good information on hiking in Iceland.

In the highlands the best months for walking are July and August, since late or early snow is a real possibility; in some places it never melts. May to September is a good time throughout the rest of the country, and popular hiking routes may be less crowded late or early in the season. Weather conditions can change in minutes at any time of year, so always be prepared.

For more information on hiking and mountaineering, contact the Iceland Touring Association, **Ferðafélag Íslands** (☎ 568 2533; www.fi.is; Mörkin 6, IS-108 Reykjavík).

HORSE RIDING

Horses are an integral part of Icelandic life and you'll see them all over the country. Riding is a popular activity and the naturally gentle breed is ideal for even inexperienced riders.

You can hire horses and take riding tours in every part of the country; however, Skagafjörður (p204) and Eyjafjörður (p223), both in northwest

---

THE ICELANDIC HORSE

Pure-bred, sturdy and short, the Icelandic horse (*Equus scandinavicus*) is a mild-mannered breed widely used on farms and recreationally. Horses first arrived in Iceland with the early Norse settlers, and since no other horses have been imported recently, the breeding stock remains pure.

Standing about 1.3m high, the Icelandic horse is a photogenic creature but a tough breed perfectly suited to the rough Icelandic conditions. Like some Mongolian breeds, they have five gaits: *fet* (walk), *brokk* (trot), *stökk* (gallop), *skeið* (pace) and the famous *tölt* (running walk), which is so smooth and steady that the rider scarcely notices any motion.

Today the horses are mostly used during the autumn sheep roundup, but in the early days horse fights were organised as entertainment and the meat was consumed as a staple and used in pagan rituals.

Iceland, have proud horse-riding traditions and several excellent stables. On longer trips you'll often venture into wild and otherwise inaccessible corners of the landscape (check the destination chapters for details of operators). Expect to pay around Ikr4000/12,000 per hour/day trip. Longer tours, including tent or hut accommodation, guides and meals, are usually priced in euros and cost around €125 per day. In September you can also volunteer for the *réttir* (sheep roundup): contact local tourist offices to make arrangements.

Horse fanatics might be interested in the **Landsmót** (National Horse Festival; www.landsmot.is/en), which takes place every two years (2010 and 2012) in Skagafjörður in the north of Iceland.

Note that foreign riding clothing or equipment (saddles, bridles etc) must be disinfected upon entry into the country.

ICE CLIMBING

Iceland offers some excellent opportunities for ice climbing, with plenty of unclimbed routes and lots of ice virtually free of other climbers. Most routes are close to main roads and can be climbed between November and mid-April. Possibly the best time to visit is in February, when the Icelandic Alpine Club holds their annual ice-climbing festival.

Some of the most popular ice-climbing areas are in the west of the country. They include Múlafjall on the southern side of Hvalfjörður, and Glymsgil on Iceland's highest waterfall Glymur – these routes are best from December to February. There's also Haukadalur on Rte 586 near Eiríksstaðir; Kaldakinn in Skjálfanda near Björg on Rte 851 northeast of Akureyri; the crags across the bay from Húsavík; and Öræfasveit, one of the most varied but inaccessible ice-climbing areas of the country, about an hour from Höfn. For more information, contact regional offices or mountaineering clubs (see below).

Beginners can try ice climbing with experienced guides at the glacier Svínafellsjökull (see p298 for more information) near the Skaftafell section of the Vatnajökull National Park in Southeast Iceland.

MOUNTAINEERING & ICE TREKKING

Unfortunately for rock climbers, Iceland's young and crumbly rock formations don't lend themselves well to technical rock climbing, but experienced mountaineers will find lots of scope for adventure. Anywhere on the ice, however, dangerous crevasses may lurk beneath snow bridges, and even innocent-looking snowfields may overlay rock and ice fissures, so technical expertise and equipment are essential. Crampons, ropes and ice axes are needed for any walk on glacial ice, and clothing must be able to withstand extreme conditions, especially on alpine climbs.

Unless you're proficient, experienced and well prepared, the best way to get involved in mountaineering is with a locally organised expedition. For more information try the Iceland Touring Association **Ferðafélag Íslands** (☎ 568 2533; www.fi.is) or the commercial outfit **Mountain Guides** (☎ 587 9999; www.mountainguide.is). For information on routes and conditions, visit www .outdoors.is/mountaineering.

SEA ANGLING & FISHING

These days it seems like every fjord has a local sea-angling outfitter who will take you for an afternoon out on the waves. You'll find exceptional sea angling along the central peninsulas of the Westfjords and in Iceland's northeast corner.

Iceland's salmon fly-fishing is world renowned, but try it on the most popular lakes and rivers and it could be some of the most expensive fishing

Check out www.golf .is for all of your putting needs. Midnight golf is especially thrilling!

Check out www.ksi.is – the official site of the Football Association of Iceland.

TAKE A HIKE! RESPONSIBLE TREKKING TIPS IN ICELAND

Before embarking on a walking trip, consider the following points to ensure a safe and enjoyable experience that minimises your impact on the environment:

- Obtain reliable local information about conditions along your intended route.
- Be aware of local regulations about wildlife and the environment.
- Walk only in regions, and on trails, within your realm of experience.
- Check weather forecasts before setting out, and be prepared for dramatic changes in temperature and outlook. Icelandic weather is very fickle and conditions can deteriorate quickly.
- Stick to existing trails and avoid short cuts. Hillsides and mountain slopes, especially at high altitudes, are prone to erosion; walk through, rather than around, muddy patches so as not to increase the size of the patch. Avoid removing the plant life that keeps topsoils in place.
- Do not light camp fires. Bring a stove for cooking.
- Carry out all your rubbish.
- Where there is a toilet, use it. Where there is none, bury your waste in a hole 15cm (6in) deep and at least 100m (320ft) from any watercourse. Cover the waste with soil and a rock. In snow, dig down to the soil.
- Use biodegradable soaps, detergents or toothpastes and wash at least 50m (160ft) away from any watercourse. Disperse the waste water widely to allow the soil to filter it fully. Wash cooking utensils 50m (160ft) from watercourses using a scourer, sand or snow instead of detergent.
- Don't feed the wildlife, and keep food and gear out of reach of animals.

you'll ever do. One-day licences can cost up to Ikr250,000 on the Laxá river near Mývatn, and that's before you pay for gear hire, a guide or transport. The good news is that with all the celebrity fishers in the one place, you can safely avoid them by heading for some of the country's cheaper rivers, where day licences cost a more reasonable Ikr20,000 per day (book in advance). The salmon-fishing season runs from early June to mid-September.

From April to mid-September you can also fish for rainbow trout, sea trout and Arctic char on a more reasonably priced voucher system. Ice fishing is also possible in some areas in winter.

For further information, contact the **National Angling Association** (☎ 553 1510; www.angling.is).

SEA KAYAKING

Kayaking is gaining popularity, particularly in the calm, accessible waters of the Eastfjords and the rugged Westfjords. The best place in Iceland to go sea kayaking is around the Hornstrandir Reserve – see p187 for details. In the Eastfjords, you can go out on guided kayaking trips in Seyðisfjörður (p274) and Neskaupstaður (p278). Further south, try the lagoons of Stokkseyri (p137). A number of Reykjavík-based adventure-tour operators include kayaking in their programs (see p86).

SKIING

Iceland has some enjoyable, little-known slopes offering pleasant, no-frills skiing. In winter cross-country skiing is possible throughout the country, and in the highland areas it continues until early July. The main drawback is the limited winter transport and the bitter winds.

Akureyri (p210) and the surrounding hills along Eyjafjörður (p223) have the best downhill skiing in the country. Hlíðarfjall is the top spot to swish

CROSSING RIVERS

While trekking or driving in Iceland's highlands you'll undoubtedly face unbridged rivers that must be crossed – a frightening prospect for the uninitiated. Don't panic – there are a few simple rules to follow.

Melting snow and ice cause water levels to rise, so the best time to cross is early in the morning before the day warms up, and preferably no sooner than 24 hours after a rainstorm. Avoid narrow stretches, which are likely to be deep – the widest ford will likely be shallowest. The swiftest, strongest current is found near the centre of straight stretches and at the outside of bends. Choose a spot with as much slack water as possible.

Never try to cross just above a waterfall and avoid crossing streams in flood (identifiable by dirty, smooth-running water carrying lots of debris and vegetation). A smooth surface suggests that the river is too deep to be crossed on foot. Anything more than thigh deep isn't crossable without experience and extra equipment.

Before attempting to cross deep or swift-running streams, be sure that you can jettison your pack in midstream if necessary. Unhitch the waist belt and loosen shoulder straps, and remove long trousers and any bulky clothing that will inhibit swimming. Lone hikers should use a hiking staff to probe the river bottom for the best route and to steady themselves in the current.

Never try to cross a stream barefoot – slicing your feet open on sharp rocks will really spoil your holiday. Consider bringing a pair of wetsuit boots or sandals if you want to keep your hiking boots dry. While crossing, face upstream and avoid looking down or you may risk getting dizzy and losing your balance. Two hikers can steady each other by resting their arms on each other's shoulders.

If you do fall while crossing, don't try to stand up. Remove your pack (but don't let go of it), roll over onto your back, and point your feet downstream, then try to work your way to a shallow eddy or to the shore.

Crossing glacial rivers can be very dangerous in a vehicle. It's best to wade across your intended route first, as described above, to check the depth. Work with the water – drive diagonally across in the direction of the current, making sure you're in a low gear. Try to drive steadily, just slightly faster than the water is flowing (too slow and you risk getting stuck, or letting water up the exhaust). If you're not travelling in convoy, consider waiting for other traffic.

across the snow, although the slopes at nearby Ólafsfjörður, Siglufjörður and Dalvík are comparatively good as well. Further afield, you'll find basic resorts in Ísafjörður (p185), Húsavík (p239) and Eskifjörður (p276).

Reykjavík also has downhill resorts with ski rental and instructors, though Bláfjöll and Skálafell (see the boxed text, p85), the two closest to Reykjavík, get very busy.

Expect to pay anywhere between Ikr800 and Ikr2000 for combination day and evening lift tickets.

SNOWBOARDING & SNOWKITING

Snowboarding is slowly becoming more popular, and dedicated trails and terrain parks can be found at Bláfjöll near Reykjavík and in Akureyri.

Snowkiting (high-adrenalin snowboarding with a kite) is also taking off in Iceland. For more information or to organise a trip, contact **Vindsport** (http://snowkiter.co.uk).

SNOWMOBILING

Tearing around an ice cap on a snowmobile can be exhilarating, but for most travellers an hour or two is more then enough. For glacier tours the best places are Snæfellsjökull (p172), Mýrdalsjökull, Vatnajökull and Langjökull, and the cost is about Ikr6000 to Ikr12,000 per hour, including transport and gear.

While high-altitude glacier tours run from April to August, from January to May there are possibilities for snowmobiling in other parts of Iceland. Adventure-tour operators in Reykjavík and Akureyri can organise trips. The northern coastal highlands, such as Ólafsfjörður, provide excellent opportunities. See the destination chapters for details.

SWIMMING & SPAS

Thanks to Iceland's abundance of geothermal heat, swimming is a national institution, and nearly every town has at least one *sundlaug* (heated swimming pool). Most pools also offer hot pots (small outdoor heated pools), saunas and jacuzzis. Admission is usually around Ikr300/150 per adult/child.

Icelandic swimming pools have a strict hygiene regimen, which involves a thorough shower without swimsuit *before* you enter the swimming area. Watch what Icelanders do and observe signs and instructions. There are also plenty of glorious natural hot springs; see the destination chapters for details. If swimming in natural springs, remove all jewellery before entering the water as the minerals can sometimes discolour the metal.

Check out http://hot -springs.org for a map of all the natural springs in the country. It's in Icelandic; see the boxed text (p182) for help with navigating the site.

WHALE WATCHING

Iceland is one of the best places in the world to see whales and dolphins, and tours on quiet oak-hulled boats minimise disruption so you can get astonishingly close. The most common sightings are of minke whales, but you can also spot humpback, fin, sei and blue whales, among others. The best place in Iceland to see whales is Húsavík (p240). There are also trips departing from Dalvík (p224), Reykjavík (p84) and the Vestmannaeyjar (p153). Figure around €50 for a three-hour tour. Sailings run from May to October, with the best chances of success from mid-June to August. To learn more about whales see p242. For more information about Iceland's whaling industry, see p61.

WHITE-WATER RAFTING

With glacial rivers flowing off ice caps and thundering towards the coast, white-water rafting (often advertised as river rafting) can be an exhilarating Icelandic experience. Some of the best rafting rivers and most established operators are in north Iceland. **Hestasport Activity Tours** (☎ 453 8383; www.rafting .is) in Varmahlíð (p204) offers day trips or multiday safaris of the east and west glacial rivers, while **Arctic Rafting** (☎ 562 7000; www.adventures.Is) has trips on the Hvítá, Þjórsá, Markarfljót and Hólmsá rivers. **Mountaineers of Iceland** (☎ 580 9900; www.mountaineers.is) offer rafting trips all year upon request.

Rafting trips include guides, equipment and refreshments, and overnight trips usually include transport, accommodation (tents or huts) and food. Expect to pay Ikr6000 to Ikr10,000 for a day trip.

Reykjavík

The world's most northerly capital combines colourful buildings, quirky people, a wild night-life and a capricious soul to devastating effect. Most visitors fall helplessly in love, returning home already saving to come back.

The city's charm lies in its many peculiar contrasts, which, like tectonic plates clashing against one another, create an earthquake of energy. Reykjavík offers a bewitching combina-tion of village innocence and big-city zeal. It's populated by darkly cynical citizens (a quality brought very much to the fore by the country's recent near-bankruptcy), who are, in spite of everything, filled with unstoppable creativity and enduring spirit. In summer the streets are washed by 22 hours of daylight; in winter they're scoured by blizzards and doused in never-ending night. Reykjavík is a city that treasures its Viking past but wants the future – the very best of it – now!

You'll find all the cultural trappings of a large 21st-century European city here: cosy cafes, world-class restaurants, fine museums and galleries, and state-of-the-art geothermal pools. Reykjavík has also become infamous for its kicking music scene and its excessive Friday-night *runtur*, a wild pub crawl round the small, superstylish clubs and bars.

Add to this a backdrop of snow-topped mountains, an ocean that wets the very toes of the town, air as cold and clean as frozen diamonds, and incredible volcanic surroundings, and you'll agree that there's no better city in the world.

HIGHLIGHTS

- Swig coffee in a quirky **cafe** (p96), or treat yourself to some top-quality **Icelandic sea-food** (p95)
- Join the **runtur** (p99), a wild pub crawl through Reykjavík's tiny but oh-so-cool bars and clubs
- Enjoy the geothermal pools at **Laugardals-laug** (p84), **Nauthólsvík Beach** (p83) and, of course, the otherworldly **Blue Lagoon** (p117)
- Immerse yourself in Icelandic history at the **National Museum** (p77) and the high-tech exhibition **Reykjavík 871 +/-2** (p77)
- Survey the city from the heights of **Hall-grímskirkja's** steeple (p75)

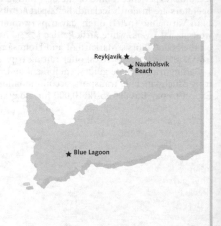

Reykjavík ★
★ Nauthólsvík Beach

★ Blue Lagoon

■ POPULATION: 118,700

HISTORY

Ingólfur Arnarson, a Norwegian fugitive, became the first official Icelander in AD 871. Myth has it that he tossed his *öndvegissúlur* (high-seat pillars) overboard, settling where the gods washed them ashore. This was at Reykjavík (Smoky Bay), which he named after steam rising from geothermal vents. According to 12th-century sources, Ingólfur built his farm on Aðalstræti, and excavations have unearthed a Viking longhouse there – see p77.

Reykjavík remained just a simple collection of farm buildings for centuries to follow. In 1225 an important Augustinian monastery was founded on the offshore island of Viðey (p105), although this was destroyed during the 16th-century Reformation.

In the early 17th century the Danish king imposed a crippling trade monopoly on Iceland, leaving the country starving and destitute. In a bid to bypass the embargo, local sheriff Skúli Magnússon, the 'Father of Reykjavík', created weaving, tanning and wool-dyeing factories – the foundations of the city – in the 1750s.

Reykjavík really boomed during WWII, when it serviced British and US troops stationed at Keflavík. The city grew, fast and frenetic, until recently when it took a slamming after the global credit crisis of 2008 (see p34). Angry protests outside Parliament eventually led to the resignation of Prime Minister Geir Haarde in February 2009.

ORIENTATION

The city is spread out along a small peninsula, with Reykjavík Domestic Airport and the long-distance bus terminal BSÍ in the southern half, and the picturesque city centre and harbour occupying the northern half. The international airport is 48km away at Keflavík (a special airport bus provides connections to the centre of Reykjavík).

The city centre is very compact, and contains most of Reykjavík's attractions. The main street is Laugavegur. At its eastern end is Hlemmur bus terminal, one of the two main city bus stations. Moving westwards, this narrow, one-way lane blossoms with Reykjavík's flashiest clothes shops, bars and eateries. It changes its name to Bankastræti, then Austurstræti as it runs across the centre. Running uphill off Bankastræti at a jaunty diagonal, the artists' street Skólavörðustígur ends at the spectacular modernist church Hallgrímskirkja.

Two-laned Lækjargata cuts straight across Bankastræti/Austurstræti. To its west are the old town squares Austurvöllur and Ingólfstorg. At the northern end is Lækjartorg bus terminal, the other important city bus stand. To the northwest lies Reykjavík's working harbour. Tjörnin lake and the domestic airport are to the south.

Maps

The tourist information centres are on the ball, and will provide you with a free city plan with your route marked on it probably while you're still pondering where you want to go. Most plans contain city bus maps.

You'll find the largest selection of road and hiking maps is available from the bookshops listed in the following Information section, or from the specialist Ferðakort map department at **Iðnú bookshop** (Map pp72-3; ☎ 562 3376; www.ferdakort.is; Brautarholt 8; ☒ 10am-5pm Mon-Thu, to 4pm Fri).

INFORMATION
Bookshops

Reykjavík's two biggest central bookshop branches have a superb choice of English-language books, newspapers, magazines and maps, and both contain great cafes.

Eymundsson Austurstræti (Map pp78-9; ☎ 540 2130; Austurstræti 18; ☒ 9am-10pm Mon-Fri, 10am-10pm Sat & Sun); Skólavörðustígur (Map pp78-9; ☎ 515 2500; Skólavörðustígur 11; ☒ 9am-10pm Mon-Fri, 10am-10pm Sat & Sun)

Also try the following bookshops:

Bókin ehf (Map pp78-9; ☎ 552 1710; Klapparstígur 25-27; ☒ 11am-6pm Mon-Fri, noon-5pm Sat) Great secondhand bookshop run by exactly the right kind of eccentric!

Bóksala Stúdenta (Map pp78-9; ☎ 570 0777; www .boksala.is; Hringbraut; ☒ 9am-6pm Mon-Fri, to 5pm in Jul & Aug) University bookshop.

Iða (Map pp78-9; ☎ 511 5001; Lækjargata 2a; ☒ 9am-10pm) Tourist shop and bookshop combined.

Cultural Centres

A-Hús Intercultural Centre (Alþjóðahús; Map pp78-9; ☎ 530 9300; www.ahus.is; Laugavegur 37) Advice bureau for immigrants.

Alliance Française (Map pp78-9; ☎ 552 3870; www .af.is; 2nd fl, Tryggvagata 8) Book and video library, and regular program of films, lectures etc.

REYKJAVÍK

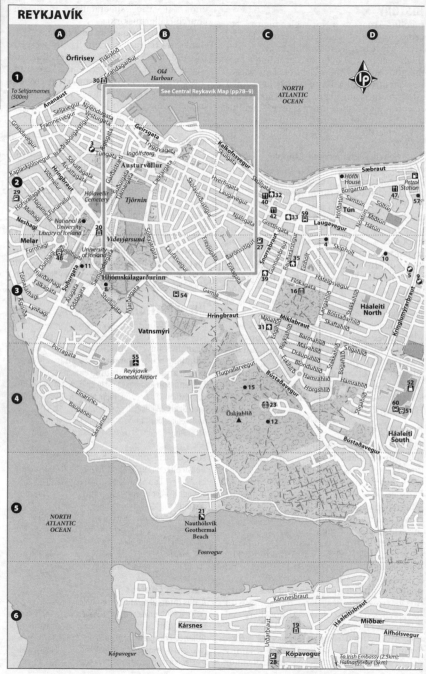

REYKJAVÍK

Örfirisey

Old Harbour

See Central Reykavík Map (pp78–9)

NORTH ATLANTIC OCEAN

To Seltjarnanes (500m)

Ananaust

Austurvöllur

Tjörnin

Hólavellir Cemetery

National & University Library of Iceland

Melar

Neshagi

Videyjarsund

University of Iceland

Hljómskálagarðurinn

Höfði House

Borgartún

Petrol Station

Sæbraut

Tún

Laugavegur

Háaleiti North

Vatnsmýri

Reykjavík Domestic Airport

Hringbraut

Miklabraut

Flugvallarvegur

Öskjuhlíð

Bústaðavegur

Bústaðavegur

Háaleiti South

NORTH ATLANTIC OCEAN

Nauthólsvík Geothermal Beach

Fossvogur

Kársnesbraut

Kársnes

Kópavogur

Kópavogur

Miðbær

Álfhólsvegur

To Irish Embassy (2.5km); Hafnarfjörður (5km)

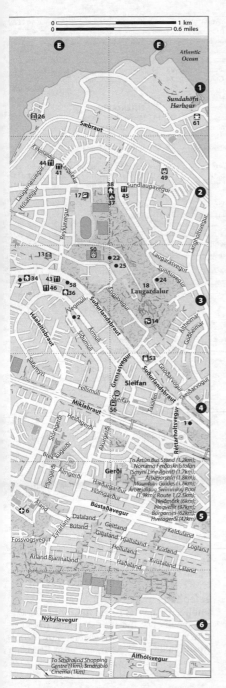

Norræna Húsið (Nordic House; Map pp72-3; ☎ 551 7030; www.nordichouse.is; Sturlugata 5; ✆ noon-5pm) Scandinavian cultural centre, with exhibitions, library, cafe and restaurant.

Discount Cards

The **Reykjavík Welcome Card** (24/48/72hr Ikr1400/1900/2400) is available at various outlets including the tourist office. The card gives you free travel on the city's buses and on the ferry to Viðey; free admission to Reykjavík's seven swimming pools, and to various galleries and museums (Árbæjarsafn, Ásmundarsafn, Culture House, Hafnarhús, Kjarvalsstaðir, Maritime Museum, National Museum, Reykjavík 871 +/-2, Reykjavík Zoo and Sigurjón Ólafsson Museum); and free internet access at the main tourist office. It's worth it if you make use of the buses and swimming pools but might not be good value if you're just visiting museums and galleries.

Emergency

For an ambulance, the fire brigade or the police, dial ☎ 112.

Landspítali University Hospital (Map pp72-3; ☎ 543 2000; Fossvogur) Has a 24-hour casualty department.

Internet Access

The cheapest internet places are Reykjavík's libraries (see below). Many hotels and guest houses have free internet access; the private tourist offices have rather overpriced services. If you've brought your laptop with you, lots of cafes have free wi-fi access where you can tap away for the price of a coffee.

G-Zero (Map pp78-9; ☎ 562 7776; Vallarstræti 4; per 15/35/60min Ikr250/350/550; ✆ 11am-1am Mon-Fri, noon-1am Sat & Sun) Reykjavík's only dedicated internet cafe, full of game-playing teenagers.

Libraries

The following offer books, novels and periodicals in English, French and other languages, and internet access for Ikr200 per hour.

Aðalbókasafn (Map pp78-9; ☎ 411 6100; www.bor garbokasafn.is; Tryggvagata 15; ✆ 10am-7pm Mon-Thu, 11am-7pm Fri, 1-5pm Sat & Sun) Excellent main library, in the heart of Reykjavík.

Kringlusafn (Map pp72-3; ☎ 580 6200; www.bor garbokasafn.is; cnr Borgarleikhús & Listabraut; ✆ 10am-7pm Mon-Thu, 11am-7pm Fri, 1-5pm Sat & Sun) Branch by the Kringlan shopping centre.

Medical Services

Dentist on duty (☎ 575 0505)
Health Centre (Map pp78-9; ☎ 585 2600; Vesturgata 7; doctor's appointment for European visitors Ikr2600, non-Europeans Ikr8000)
Læknavaktin (☎ 1770) Non-emergency telephone medical advice between 5pm and 11.30pm.
Lyfja (Map pp78-9; ☎ 552 4045; Laugavegur 16; 🕑 9am-6pm Mon-Fri, 11am-4pm Sat) Central pharmacy.
Lyfja Apótek (Map pp72-3; ☎ 533 2300; Lágmúli 5; 🕑 7am-1am) Late-night pharmacy, near the Hilton Reykjavík Nordica hotel. Buses S2, 15, 17 and 19.

Money

Beware of changing currency at hotels or private exchange offices in the city; commissions can reach 8.75% and exchange rates may be poor. There are central branches, with ATMs, of all three major Icelandic banks.

Landsbanki Íslands (Map pp78-9; ☎ 410 4000; www .landsbanki.is; Austurstræti 11)
Íslandsbanki (Map pp78-9; ☎ 440 4000; www .islandsbanki.is; Lækjargata 12)
Kaupþing (Map pp78-9; ☎ 444 7000; www.kaup thing.com; Austurstræti 5)

Post

Main post office (Map pp78-9; ☎ 580 1200; Pósthússtræti 5; 🕑 9am-6pm Mon-Fri) With an efficient parcel service, philatelic desk (www.stamps.is) and poste restante service.

Telephone

Public phones are rare in mobile-crazy Reykjavík. Try the tourist office, the post office, by the southwestern corner of Austurvöllur, on Lækjargata, or at Kringlan shopping centre.

At the city hostels you can buy an Atlas telephone card to make cheap international calls.

Tourist Information

Reykjavík has a very good main tourist office and an increasing number of private centres. Besides providing information, they can make accommodation, bus-tour and entertainment bookings.

Pick up the free booklets *Reykjavík This Month* and *What's On in Reykjavík* for events in the capital. The excellent English-language newspaper *Grapevine*, widely distributed, has the lowdown on what's new in town.

Main Tourist Office (Upplýsingamiðstöð Ferðamanna; Map pp78-9; ☎ 590 1550; www.visitreykjavik.is; Aðalstræti 2; ⊙ 8.30am-7pm daily Jun–mid-Sep, 9am-6pm Mon-Fri, to 4pm Sat & to 2pm Sun mid-Sep–May) Staff are friendly, and there are mountains of free brochures and leaflets, plus some maps for sale. Internet access costs Ikr350/500 per 30/60 minutes (free with the Reykjavík Welcome Card).

BSÍ bus terminal tourist desk (Map pp72-3; Vatnsmýrarvegur 10) Information leaflets.

Raðhús Tourist Information Desk (Map pp78-9; ☎ 411 1000; Tjarnargata 11; ⊙ 8.20am-4.30pm Mon-Fri, noon-4pm Sat & Sun mid-May–mid-Sep, closed Sun mid-Sep–mid-May) Small tourist desk inside the city hall.

Nordic Visitor (Map pp78-9; ☎ 511 2442; www.icelandvisitor.com; Lækjargata 2; ⊙ 9am-6pm Mon-Fri, 10am-4pm Sat Jun-Aug, 10am-6pm Mon-Fri Sep-May) Private office.

Icelandic Travel Market (Map pp78-9; ☎ 552 4979; www.icelandictravelmarket.is; Bankastræti 2; ⊙ 8am-9pm May-Aug, to 7pm Sep-Apr) Private office.

Travel Agencies

Numerous travel agents and tour companies in Reykjavík specialise in trips around Iceland by bus or plane. A few agents can also arrange international travel. Also see p342.

Ferðaþjónusta Bænda (Icelandic Farm Holidays; Map pp72-3; ☎ 570 2700; www.farmholidays.is) Arranges farm holidays and self-drive tours around Iceland.

Gavia Travel (☎ 511 3939; www.gaviatravel.com; Alfaheidi 44) Small local agency specialising in nature and birdwatching tours.

IcelandTotal (☎ 585 4300; www.icelandtotal.com; Skútuvogur 13A) Can organise coach tours, car hire and complete holiday packages.

Norræna Ferðaskrifstofan (☎ 570 8600; info@smyril-line.is; Stangarhyl 1) The local agent for Smyril Line, which runs ferries to the Faeroes and Denmark.

Úrval Útsýn (Map pp72-3; ☎ 585 4000; www.urvalutsyn.is; Lágmúli 4) Mainstream travel agency specialising in international travel.

Útivist (Map pp72-3; ☎ 562 1000; www.utivist.is; Laugavegur 178) Owns several mountain huts, including some at Þórsmörk and Landmannalaugar, and runs guided hikes.

Worldwide Friends (☎ 552 5214; www.veraldarvinir.is; Einarsnes 56) Non-profit agency specialising in the arrangement of volunteer programs in Iceland.

DANGERS & ANNOYANCES

If you find a safer city, let us know! Accidental injury at the hands of drunken revellers is a possibility, although considering how many beers are sunk at the weekend, it's surprising there isn't more trouble.

SIGHTS
Hallgrímskirkja

Reykjavík's most attention-seeking building is the immense concrete church **Hallgrímskirkja** (Map pp78-9; ☎ 510 1000; www.hallgrimskirkja.is; Skólavörðuholt; ⊙ 9am-8pm Mon-Sat, to 5pm Sun Jul & Aug, 9am-5pm daily Sep-Jun), star of a thousand postcards and visible from 20km away. However, in a scandal that has shaken the city, it was recently discovered that the original builders cut corners by skimping on quality materials, and that Reykjavík's iconic symbol is falling apart. The whole thing is covered in scaffolding and under repair until at least 2010. You can still get an unmissable view of the city by taking an elevator trip up the 75m-high **tower** (adult/7-14yr Ikr400/100), but the sound of drilling and hammering is something of a distraction.

In contrast to the high drama outside, the church's interior is puritanically plain. The most startling feature is the vast 5275-pipe **organ**, which has a strangely weapon-like appearance. From July to mid-August you can hear this mighty beast in action in Sunday-night **concerts** (admission Ikr1500; ⊙ 5pm).

The church's radical design caused huge controversy, and its architect, Guðjón Samúelsson, never lived to see its completion – it took a painstaking 34 years (1940–74) to build. Those sweeping columns on either side of the tower represent volcanic basalt – a favourite motif of Icelandic nationalists. Hallgrímskirkja was named after the poet Reverend Hallgrímur Pétursson, who wrote Iceland's most popular hymn book.

REYKJAVÍK IN TWO DAYS

Day One

Early risers should visit the bustling **working harbour** to watch the fishing boats come in. It's backed by stunning views of the peak **Esja**, across the fjord in southwest Iceland. Afterwards, head for breakfast at **Grái Kötturinn** (p97), a tiny eccentric cafe serving bacon, eggs and hunks of fresh bread.

Next, meander up arty **Skólavörðustígur**, poking your nose into its crafty little galleries. At the top of the hill is the immense concrete church **Hallgrímskirkja** (p75), Reykjavík's most dramatic building. For a perfect view of the city, take an elevator trip up the tower.

Once you've plumped back down to earth, pop across the road to the **Einar Jónsson Museum** (p80). You'll get a free glimpse of this gloomy sculptor's weird works in the garden round the back; if you like what you see, there are plenty more fantastical sculptures inside.

For further research into the Icelandic mind, head to the **National Gallery of Iceland** (p82). Here, paintings by the country's most treasured artists include hallucinogenic landscapes and eerie depictions of folk-tale monsters.

Pop into cosy **Café Paris** (p96) for a light lunch – it's a prime people-watching spot. Then, if you're here at the weekend, make **Kolaportið** (p101) your next stop – rummaging through foreign flea markets is always enlightening! You can also buy cubes of infamous *hákarl* (rotten shark meat) from the fish market – it might look innocuous, but find a quiet bin to stand by...

Next, catch bus 18 from Lækjartorg bus station to **Perlan** (below). There are two excitements here: first is the superb **Saga Museum**, which brings Iceland's early history to life with fantastically realistic models and a soundtrack of horrible screams – we think the Vikings would approve. Second is the hexagonal **viewing deck and cafe**, where you'll get tremendous views. For dinner,

---

Gazing proudly into the distance outside is a **statue** of the Viking Leifur Eiríksson, the first European to stumble across America. It was a present from the USA on the 1000th anniversary of the Alþing (p83).

Perlan & the Saga Museum

Looking like half of Barbarella's bra, **Perlan** (Map pp72-3; ☎ 562 0200; www.perlan.is; 🕐 10am-10pm) is a complex based around the huge hot-water tanks on Öskjuhlíð hill. It's about 2km from the city centre (take bus 18 from Hlemmur).

The main attraction is the endearingly bloodthirsty **Saga Museum** (Map pp72-3; ☎ 511 1517; www.sagamuseum.is; adult/child/concession Ikr1500/800/1000; 🕐 10am-6pm Apr-Sep, noon-5pm Oct-Mar), where Icelandic history is brought to life by eerie silicon models and a soundtrack of thudding axes and hair-raising screams. Don't be surprised if you see some of the characters wandering around town, as moulds were taken from Reykjavík residents (the museum's owner is Ingólfur Arnarson, and his daughters are the Irish princess and the little slave gnawing a fish!).

The hexagonal **viewing deck** offers a tremendous 360-degree panorama of Reykjavík and the mountains: multilingual recordings explain the scenery. There's a busy **cafe** (🕐 10am-9pm) on the same level, so if it's brass-monkey weather, you can admire the same beautiful views over coffee and crêpes. The mirrored dome on top of the tanks contains one of the city's finer restaurants, Perlan (p94).

Two **artificial geysers** will keep small children absolutely enthralled: the one inside blasts off every few minutes, while the outside geyser comes on in the afternoon. There are numerous **walking and cycling trails** on the hillside, including a path to Nauthólsvík hot beach (p83).

Volcano Show

Eccentric eruption-chaser Villi Knudsen is the photographer, owner and presenter of the fascinating **Volcano Show** (Map pp78-9; ☎ 845 9548; vknudsen2000@yahoo.com; Red Rock Cinema, Hellusund 6a; adult/child 1hr show Ikr1300/free, 2hr show Ikr1800/free; 🕐 in English 11am, 3pm & 8pm daily, in German 6pm daily, in French 1pm Sat Jul & Aug, in English 3pm & 8pm daily Sep & Apr-Jun, 8pm Oct-Mar), a film show that captures 50 years of Icelandic volcanoes. Although some of the footage is a bit old and wobbly, you're still left reeling by images of the town Heimaey (p149) being crushed by molten lava, or the island Surtsey (p155) boiling its way out of the sea.

make sure you've booked a table at one of the capital's excellent seafood restaurants, such as **Við Tjörnina** (p95). Once the bill's been settled, head back to your hotel for a kip and a freshen-up: you're going to need some energy to get you through the **runtur** (p99), Reykjavík's notorious Bacchanalian pub crawl, which starts around midnight and carries on until 5am. Rather than cosying down in one venue, it's the done thing to cruise from bar to bar. To get you started, try perennial favourites **Kaffibarinn** (p98), **Kaffi Sólon** (p98) and **Thorvaldsen Bar** (p98).

Day Two

After the night you've just had, start the recovery slowly with brunch at **Café Oliver** (p98).

At 12.30pm we recommend taking the 'express' version of the **Golden Circle tour**. OK, so it's a bit of a rush – maybe next time you'll book more than two days in lovely Iceland! At least you get to see some of the Icelandic countryside and marvel over two of its natural wonders – the tumbling waterfall **Gullfoss** (p127) and the spouting hot springs at **Geysir** (p126).

Tired but happy, you'll get back to Reykjavík in the early evening just in time for dinner. For a dash of spice, why not try an Indian meal made with Icelandic ingredients? Go for succulent tandoori salmon at **Austur Indía Félagið** (p93), or try the unique guillemot dish at **Indian Mango** (p93). Round off the evening at the **Volcano Show** (opposite), an explosive introduction to Iceland's violent geography.

'What about the **Blue Lagoon** (p117)?' we hear you ask. Well, here's the clever part – you can visit Iceland's number-one attraction on your way back to the airport tomorrow. Wallowing in its warm, sapphire-blue waters is certainly a fantastic last memory to take home.

Museums

Displays at the **National Museum** (Þjóðminjasafn; Map pp72-3; ☎ 530 2200; www.natmus.is; Suðurgata 41; adult/under 18yr/concession Ikr800/free/400, free Wed; ☼ 10am-5pm daily May-mid-Sep, 11am-5pm Tue-Sun mid-Sep–Apr) are well thought out and give an excellent overview of Iceland's history and culture. The strongest section delves into the Settlement Era, with swords, silver hoards and a great little bronze **model of Thor** on display. However, the most treasured artefact in the museum is a beautiful 13th-century **church door**, carved with the touching story of a knight and his faithful lion! Upstairs, you really get a sense of the country's poverty over the following 600 years. Simple, homey artefacts utilise every scrap: check out the **gaming pieces** made from cod ear bones, and the **wooden doll** that doubled as a kitchen utensil.

The city's newest exhibition, **Reykjavík 871 +/-2** (Settlement Exhibition; Map pp78-9; ☎ 411 6370; www.reykjavik871.is; Aðalstræti 16; adult/13-18yr Ikr600/300; ☼ 10am-5pm), is based around a single 10th-century Viking house but shows what miracles can be achieved when technology, archaeology and imagination meet. Through 21st-century wizardry, a fire leaps from the hearth, while around the walls ghostly settlers

materialise to tend crops, hunt, launch a boat, and bury their dead. Go and marvel!

Creeping into the darkened rooms of the **Culture House** (Þjóðmenningarhúsið; Map pp78-9; ☎ 545 1400; www.thjodmenning.is; Hverfisgata 15; adult/under 16yr/concession Ikr300/free/200, free Wed; ☼ 11am-5pm) is a true thrill for saga lovers. A permanent exhibition covers saga history: from a Who's Who of Norse gods to a fascinating account of Árni Magnússon, who devoted his life to saving Icelandic manuscripts, and died of a broken heart when his Copenhagen library went up in flames. Two hushed display rooms contain the original vellums; if you're interested in seeing more, contact the **Árni Magnússon Institute** (Map pp72-3; ☎ 525 4010; www.arnastofnun.is; Suðurgata).

Quaint old buildings have been uprooted from their original sites and rebuilt at the open-air **Árbæjarsafn** (off Map pp72-3; ☎ 411 6300; www.arbae jarsafn.is; Kistuhylur 4; adult/under 18yr Ikr600/free, free Fri in summer; ☼ 10am-5pm daily Jun-Aug, by tour only 1pm Mon, Wed & Fri Sep-May), a kind of zoo for houses, 4km from the city centre. Alongside the 19th-century homes are a turf-roofed church, and various stables, smithies, barns and boathouses – all very picturesque. There are summer arts-and-crafts demonstrations, and it's a great place for kids to let off steam. Take bus 12.

CENTRAL REYKJAVÍK

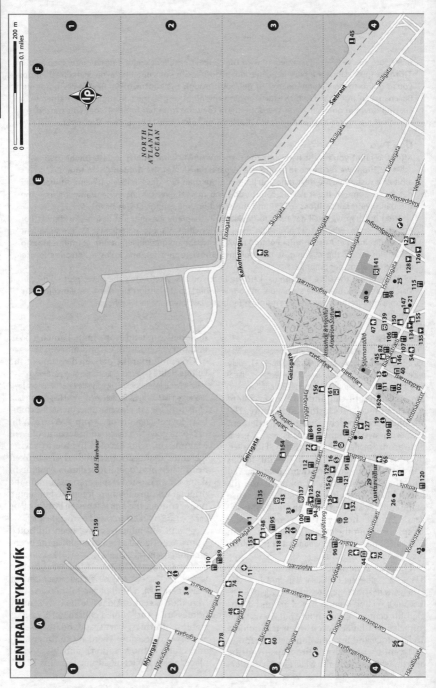

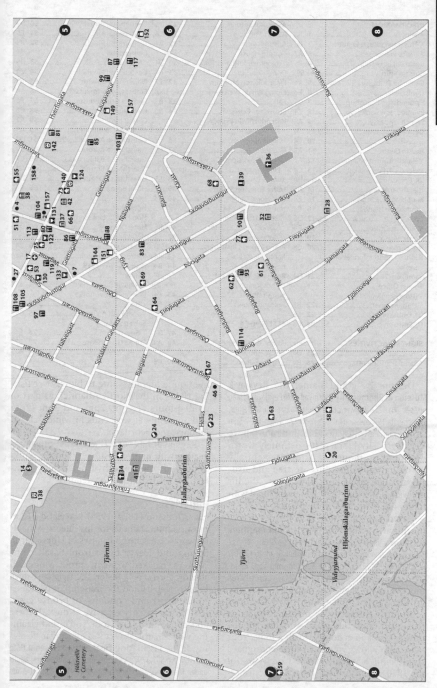

Despite its grand name, the **Reykjavík Museum of Photography** (Ljósmyndasafn Reykjavíkur; Map pp78-9; ☎ 411 6390; www.photomuseum.is; 6th fl, Grófarhús, Tryggvagata 15; admission free; ⊙ noon-7pm Mon-Fri, 1-5pm Sat & Sun) is really just an exhibition room above Reykjavík City Library. It's definitely worth dropping in, though – its quintessentially Scandinavian exhibitions are free and usually thought-provoking. If you take the lift up, walk down the stairs, which are lined with funny old black-and-white photos.

Based appropriately in a former freezing plant for fish, the small **Víkin Maritime Museum** (Víkin Sjóminjasafnið; Map pp72-3; ☎ 517 9400; www.sjominjasafn.is; Grandagarður 8; adult/13-18yr Ikr700/500; ⊙ 11am-5pm Tue-Sun Jun–mid-Sep, 11am-5pm Tue-Fri, 1-5pm Sat & Sun mid-Sep–May) celebrates the country's seafaring heritage, focusing on the trawlers that transformed Iceland's economy. Much of the information is in Icelandic only, but silent film footage of trawler crews in action is worth a look. Your ticket also allows you aboard the coastguard ship *Óðinn*, a veteran of the Cod Wars (of the 1970s when British and Icelandic fisher-

men quite literally came to blows over fishing rights in the North Atlantic), as part of guided tours at 1pm, 2pm and 3pm (2pm and 3pm only at weekends in winter, closed January and February).

Reykjavík has several specialist museums dealing with natural history, medicine, banknotes and coins, and hydroelectricity; contact the tourist office for details.

Galleries

Einar Jónsson (1874–1954) is Iceland's foremost sculptor, famous for his intense symbolist works. Chiselled allegories of Hope, Earth, Spring and Death burst from basalt cliffs, weep over naked women, sprout wings and slay dragons. For a taster, the **sculpture garden** (admission free), behind the museum, is dedicated to the artist and contains 26 bronze casts; they're particularly effective at dusk. If these appeal to your inner Goth, you'll find gleaming white-marble sculptures on similar themes inside the fascinating **Einar Jónsson Museum** (Map pp78-9; ☎ 551 3797; www.skulptur.is; Njarðargata; adult/under 16yr/concession Ikr500/free/300; ⊙ 2-5pm Tue-Sun

Jun–mid-Sep, 2-5pm Sat & Sun mid-Sep–Nov & Feb-May). The building itself was designed by the artist and contains his austere penthouse flat, with unusual views over the city.

The excellent **Reykjavík Art Museum** (Listasafn Reykjavíkur; www.listasafnreykjavikur.is; admission free) is split over three sites: Ásmundarsafn, Hafnarhúsið and Kjarvalsstaðir.

There's something immensely tactile about Ásmundur Sveinsson's monumental concrete creations – see for yourself in the **garden** outside the rounded, white **Ásmundarsafn** (Ásmundur Sveinsson Museum; Map pp72-3; ☎ 553 2155; Sigtún; ⊙ 10am-4pm May-Sep, 1-4pm Oct-Apr). Duck inside the museum for smaller, spikier works in wood, clay and metals, exploring themes as diverse as folklore and physics. Ásmundur (1893–1982) designed the building himself; getting into the spirit of things, the council later added an igloo-shaped bus stop in front. Buses 14, 15, 17, 19 and S2 pass close by.

Hafnarhúsið (Map pp78-9; ☎ 590 1200; Tryggvagata 17; ⊙ 10am-5pm Fri-Wed, to 10pm Thu) is a former warehouse now converted into a severe steel-and-concrete exhibition space. Pride of place is usually given to the distinctive, disturbing comic-book paintings of Erró (Guðmundur Guðmundsson; 1932–), a political artist who has donated several thousand works to the gallery. The rest of the industrial interior holds temporary modern-art installations: for example, fluorescent paintings of moss, a kaleidoscopic coffin and works by Japanese Pop artist Yoshitomo Nara have appeared over the last few years. The cafe has great harbour views.

Jóhannes Kjarval (1885–1972) was a fisherman until his crew paid for him to study at the Academy of Fine Arts in Copenhagen. He's one of Iceland's most popular artists, and his unearthly landscapes can be seen inside the angular glass-and-wood **Kjarvalsstaðir** (Map pp72-3; ☎ 517 1290; Flókagata; ⊙ 10am-5pm), alongside changing installations.

Surreal mud-purple landscapes are intermingled with visions of trolls, giants and dead men walking at the **National Gallery of**

REYKJAVÍK

REYKJAVÍK'S ARCHITECTURE

The old town's mid-18th-century houses demonstrate the Icelandic talent for adaptation. In a country devoid of many building materials, most are made from driftwood (which floated from Siberia and South America) and covered in sheets of corrugated tin to protect them from the elements. Even churches, such as the **Fríkirkjan í Reykjavík** (1899; Map pp78–9), were made the same way. By happy chance, this light construction method also makes the buildings pretty earthquake-proof.

Building houses from scraps didn't mean that artistic impulses were squashed – check out **A-Hús** (Map pp78–9), from 1906, one of the city's finest examples of wood-and-tin architecture. Its tall turrets are topped by swirling arabesques, and the wooden struts supporting the balconies are carved with whales.

As the country rallied from almost 700 years of deprivation, a new pride worked its way into Iceland's public architecture. Basalt became a nationalist symbol – the country's parliament building, the **Alþingi** (opposite), is built from blocks of the stuff, and **Hallgrímskirkja** (p75) has sweeping concrete representations of basalt columns that make it Reykjavík's most iconic building. The recent economic crash put a halt to Reykjavík's modern building boom, but city-dwellers still have hopes that the avant-garde harbourside concert hall will be completed by 2011. This structure is another that makes use of lava-inspired hexagonal shapes in its design.

Reykjavík Tours (☎ 821 9880, 862 7812; www.reykjaviktours.is; Laufásvegur 7; tour Ikr1500; ☼ 10.30am Mon, Tue, Thu & Fri, 11am Sun) runs a two-hour 'Historic Houses' walking tour around the centre for those interested in learning more. It departs from outside the main tourist office.

Iceland (Listasafn Íslands; Map pp78-9; ☎ 515 9600; www .listasafn.is; Fríkirkjuvegur 7; admission free; ☼ 11am-5pm Tue-Sun). Iceland's main art gallery, overlooking Tjörnin, certainly gives an interesting glimpse into the nation's psyche. As well as a huge collection of 19th- and 20th-century paintings by Iceland's favourite sons and daughters (including Ásgrímur Jónsson, Jóhannes Kjarval and Nína Sæmundsson), there are works by Picasso and Munch.

The **Sigurjón Ólafsson Museum** (Map pp72-3; ☎ 553 2906; www.lso.is; Laugarnestangi 70; adult/under 18yr Ikr300/free; ☼ 2-5pm Tue-Sun Jun–mid Sep, 2-5pm Sat & Sun mid-Sep–Nov & mid-Feb–May) is a peaceful little place showcasing the varied works – portrait busts, driftwood totem poles and abstract football players – of sculptor Sigurjón Ólafsson (1908–82). A salty ocean breeze blows through the wooden rooms, which also contain Reykjavík's only shoreside cafe. On Tuesday from early July to August there are classical concerts at 8.30pm. Buses 12 and S5 pass close by.

Close to Reykjavík University, **Norræna Húsið** (Nordic House; Map pp72-3; ☎ 551 7030; www.nordichouse. is; Sturlugata 5; ☼ noon-5pm) is a Scandinavian cultural centre with an **exhibition gallery** (adult/under 15yr/concession Ikr300/free/150, free Wed; ☼ noon-5pm Tue-Sun), a library of Scandinavian literature, a pleasant cafe and restaurant, and regular Nordic-themed concerts, lectures and films.

Reykjavík has many small contemporary art galleries. Try the Icelandic Labour Union's collection, housed in the **ASÍ Art Museum** (Map pp78-9; ☎ 511 5353; Klapparstígur 33; admission free; ☼ 1-5pm Tue-Sun), which often has interesting installations; **i8** (Map pp78-9; ☎ 551 3666; www.i8.is; Tryggvagata 16; ☼ 11am-5pm Tue-Fri, 1-5pm Sat), which represents some of the country's favourite modern artists; **Lost Horse Gallery** (Map pp78-9; ☎ 861 9887; Skólastræti 1; www.this.is/sub aqua/newshow; ☼ 1-7pm Sat & Sun), with its eclectic mix of photography, paintings and design; young artists' exhibition space **Kling & Bang** (Map pp78-9; ☎ 696 2209; http://this.is/klingogbang; Hverfisgata 42; ☼ 2-6pm Thu-Sun); and **Nýlistasafnið** (The Living Museum; Map pp78-9; ☎ 551 4350; www .nylo.is; Laugavegur 26; ☼ 10-5pm Mon-Fri, noon-5pm Sat), with its entrance on Grettisgata.

Parks & Gardens

Reykjavík Botanic Gardens (Map pp72-3; ☎ 411 8650; www.grasagardur.is; Skúlatún 2; admission free; ☼ greenhouse 10am-10pm Apr-Sep, to 5pm Oct-Mar) contains over 5000 varieties of subarctic plant species, colourful seasonal flowers, a summer cafe serving coffee and waffles, and lots of bird life (particularly grey geese and their fluffy little goslings).

Laugardalur (Map pp72–3) was once the main source of Reykjavík's hot-water supply – the name translates as 'Hot-Springs Valley'. Just north of the botanic garden you'll find the **old wash house** (Map pp72–3) – sadly, rather graffitied – where washerwomen once scrubbed the city's dirty laundry in sulphurous pools. A small open-air exhibition of old photos brings the past to life.

Reykjavík's Family Fun Park & Zoo (see p84) is also based in the valley, along with most of the city's sport and recreational facilities. Buses 14, 15, 17, 19 and S2 pass within a few hundred metres of Laugardalur.

At the heart of the city, grassy **Austurvöllur** (Map pp78–9) was once part of first settler Ingólfur Arnarson's hay fields. Today it's a favourite spot for lunchtime picnics and summer sunbathing, and is sometimes used for open-air concerts and political demonstrations. The statue in the centre is of Jón Sigurðsson, who led the campaign for Icelandic independence.

The parks around the lake Tjörnin (see the following section) are great for strolling.

Buildings & Monuments

Tjörnin (The Pond; Map pp78–9) is the placid lake at the centre of the city. It echoes with the honks, squawks and screeches of over 40 species of visiting birds, including swans, geese and artic terns; feeding the ducks is a popular pastime for the under-fives. Pretty sculpture-dotted parks line the southern shores, and their lacing paths are much used by cyclists and joggers. In winter, hardy souls strap on ice skates and turn the lake into an outdoor rink.

Reykjavík's waterside **Ráðhús** (City Hall; Map pp78–9; ☎ 563 2005; Vonarstræti; admission free; 8am-7pm Mon-Fri, noon-6pm Sat & Sun) is a postmodern construction that divides all who see it into 'hate-its' or 'love-its'. Concrete stilts, tinted windows and mossy walls make it look like a half-bird, half-building rising from Tjörnin. Inside there's a fabulous 3D map of Iceland – all mountains and volcanoes, with flecks of nothing-towns disappearing between the peaks. There's also a pleasant cafe, with free internet access for customers and an intimate view of the ducks.

Compared to the sky-scraping hulk of Hallgrímskirkja (p75), Iceland's main cathedral, **Dómkirkja** (Map pp78–9; ☎ 520 9700; www.dom kirkjan.is; Lækjargata 14a; admission free; 10am-5pm Mon-Fri) is a modest affair, but it played a vital role in the country's conversion to Lutheranism. The current building (from 1848) is small

but perfectly proportioned; its plain wooden interior is animated by glints of gold.

Iceland's first parliament, the Alþingi, was created at Þingvellir in AD 930. After losing its independence in the 13th century, the country gradually won back its autonomy, and the modern **Alþingi** (Map pp78-9; ☎ 563 0500; www.althingi .is; Túngata) moved into the current basalt building in 1881; a stylish glass-and-stone annexe was completed in 2002. You're welcome to attend **sessions** (4 times weekly Oct-May) when parliament is sitting.

Popular with skateboarders, the stone square **Ingólfstorg** is notable for its billowing **steam vent**, where pent-up geothermal energy finds a release. Some of the city's oldest houses line the square. **Fálkahús** (Map pp78-9; Hafnarstræti 1) has a particularly interesting history – it's where Icelandic falcons were kept before being shipped off to Europe's noblemen.

Reykjavík is littered with fascinating statues and abstract monuments, but it's Jón Gunnar Árnason's shiplike **Sun-Craft** (Map pp78–9) sculpture that seems to catch visitors' imaginations. Its situation – facing the sea and snow-capped Esja – may have something to do with it.

ACTIVITIES
Geothermal Pools & Spas

Reykjavík's pools (and beach) are the heart of the city's social life: children play, teenagers flirt, business deals are made, and everyone catches up on the latest gossip. Volcanic water keeps the temperature at a mellow 29°C, and most of the baths have *heitir pottar* (hot pots), Jacuzzi-like pools kept at a toasting 37°C to 42°C. Admission usually costs Ikr360/110 for adults/children aged six to 15 years, and towels and swimsuits can be rented for Ikr350 each. For further information, see www.spacity.is.

Reykjavíkurs get very upset by dirty tourists in their nice, clean pools (for good reason – the city's pools are free of chemicals). To avoid causing huge offence, visitors *must* wash thoroughly without a swimsuit before hopping in.

The dinky Blue-Flag **Nautholsvík Geothermal Beach** (Ylströndin; Map pp72-3; ☎ 511 6630; 10am-8pm mid-May–mid-Aug), on the edge of the Atlantic, is packed with happy bathers in summer, thanks to golden sand imported all the way from Morocco and an artificial hot spring that keeps the water at a pleasant 18°C to 20°C. There are sociable hot pots on shore and in the sea, a snack bar, changing rooms (Ikr200), and **canoes and rowing boats** (hire per hr Ikr600; ☾ 4-7pm Wed & Thu). Get there on bus 19.

Laugardalslaug (Map pp72-3; ☎ 411 5100; Sundlaugavegur 30a; ☾ 6.30am-10.30pm Mon-Fri year-round, plus 8am-10pm Sat & Sun Apr-Oct, 8am-8pm Sat & Sun Nov-Mar) is the largest pool in Iceland, with the best facilities: an Olympic-size indoor pool, an outdoor pool, four hot pots and a whirlpool, a steam bath, and a curling 86m water slide. Take bus 14.

The five-star **Laugar spa** (Map pp72-3; ☎ 553 0000; www.laugarspa.is; spa admission Ikr4620; ☾ spa 6.30am-10.30pm Mon-Fri year-round, plus 8am-10pm Sat & Sun Apr-Oct, 8am-8pm Sat & Sun Nov-Mar; beauty & massage salons 9am-9pm Mon-Fri, 11am-5pm Sat) is attached to Laugardalslaug (above), and offers delicious ways to pamper yourself. There are six themed saunas and steam rooms, a vast and well-equipped gym, and beauty and massage clinics with soothing treatments (detox wraps, facials and hot-stone therapies).

It's a step out of town, but the slickly designed **Árbæjarlaug** (off Map pp72-3; ☎ 411 5200; Fylkisvegur, Elliðaárdalur; ☾ 6.30am-10.30pm Mon-Fri year-round, plus 8am-10pm Sat & Sun Apr-Sep, 8am-8.30pm Sat & Sun Oct-Mar; ♿) is well known as the best family pool: it's half inside and half outside, and there are lots of watery amusements (slides, waterfalls and massage jets) to keep the kids entertained. Take bus 19.

Other central pools include the following two:

Sundhöllin (Map pp72-3; ☎ 551 4059; Barónsstígur 16; ☾ 6.30am-9.30pm Mon-Fri, 8am-7pm Sat & Sun) Reykjavík's oldest swimming pool (with a definite 'municipal baths' feel to it) is close to the Hlemmur bus station and is the only indoor pool within the city.

Vesturbæjarlaug (Map pp72-3; ☎ 551 5004; Hofsvallagata; ☾ 6.30am-9.30pm Mon-Fri, 8am-7pm Sat & Sun) Also within walking distance of the centre (or take bus 11 or 15), Vesturbæjarlaug has a basic 25m pool and three hot pots.

Whale Watching

Iceland is a fantastic place for whale watching – its waters hold over 20 species of cetacean. In Faxaflói bay you'll most commonly come across white-beaked dolphins, harbour porpoises and minkes; migratory humpbacks are also spotted from time to time.

Between April and October, **Elding Whale Watching** (Map pp78-9; ☎ 555 3565; www.elding.is; adult/7-15yr Ikr8000/3500) runs three-hour trips from Reykjavík's old harbour, at 9am and

1pm (1pm only in October; also at 5pm June to August). There's also an interesting floating nature centre, with whale models and films. In breeding season (mid-May to mid-August), the whale-watching boats spin around Akurey or Lundey islands, offshore from Reykjavík, to look at the **puffins**.

Puffin Watching

Around 50,000 of these wonderful little birds (see the boxed text, p60) nest on Lundey and Akurey, two islands just offshore from Reykjavík. Between May and late August you can visit them on the one-hour **Puffin Express boat trips** (Map pp78-9; ☎ 892 0099; www.puffin express.is; adult/under 12yr Ikr3000/1500), which sail from Reykjavík harbour at 8.30am, 10.30am, 2.30pm and 4.30pm daily.

Also see Whale Watching, left.

Horse Riding

Trotting through lava fields under the midnight sun is an unforgettable experience. Horse farms around Reykjavík offer tours for all ages and experiences, and can collect you from your hotel. Most operate at least some of their trips year-round.

Several long-established companies offer everything from 1½- to two-hour outings (Ikr6000 to Ikr10,000), to nine-day tours into the wilderness, including riding and rafting/whale-watching/Blue Lagoon combinations (Ikr9800 to Ikr20,000):

Eldhestar (☎ 480 4800; www.eldhestar.is; Vellir) Near Hveragerði.

Íshestar (☎ 555 7000; www.ishestar.is; Sörlaskeið 26, Hafnarfjörður)

Laxnes (☎ 566 6179; www.laxnes.is; Mosfellsbær)

Cycling

See p104 for information.

REYKJAVÍK FOR CHILDREN

Icelanders love their kids, but they're treated as small adults rather than as a separate species; consequently, there are only a handful of attractions aimed specifically at children. However, kids get discount rates at the theatre and cinema, and can travel free or at discount rates on many excursions.

The **Family Fun Park & Zoo** (Fjölskyldu-og húsdýragarðsins; Map pp72-3; ☎ 575 7800; www.mu.is; Laugardalur; adult/5-12yr Ikr600/500, 1-/10-/20-ride tickets Ikr200/1800/3400; ☾ 10am-6pm mid-May–mid-Aug, to 5pm mid-Aug–mid-May) is the city's only attrac-

REYKJAVÍK IN WINTER

It's bitterly cold and the sun barely rises, but there are *some* advantages to wintery Iceland. The major joy, of course, is watching the unearthly glory of the **northern lights** (see p59).

The **Reykjavík Skating Hall** (Map pp72-3; ☎ 588 9705; www.skautaholl.is; Múlavegur 1, Laugardalur; adult/child Ikr700/500, skate hire Ikr300; ☾ noon-3pm Mon-Wed, to 3pm & 5-7.30pm Thu, 1-8pm Fri, 1-6pm Sat & Sun Sep-Apr) throws open its doors in winter. Some people also skate on **Tjörnin** (p83) when it freezes.

The **skiing** season runs from November to April, depending on snowfall. The three ski areas close to Reykjavík (Bláfjöll, Hengill and Skálafell) are managed by the organisation **Skíðasvæði** (☎ 530 3000; www.skidasvaedi.is; Pósthússtræti 3-5, IS-101 Reykjavík). Iceland's premier ski slopes are at 84-sq-km **Bláfjöll** (☎ 561 8400; ☾ 2-9pm Mon-Fri, 10am-5pm Sat & Sun), which has 14 lifts and downhill, cross-country and snowboarding facilities – and gets swamped by eager city dwellers when the snow begins to fall. Passes cost Ikr2000/550 per adult/child six to 16 years, and you can hire skis, poles, boots and other gear at reasonable rates. The resort is located about 25km southeast of Reykjavík on Rte 417, just off Rte 1. A shuttle bus leaves from the Mjódd bus stand southeast of town once per day in season – check with Skíðasvæði for departure times.

More **bus tours** (p86) operate in winter than you might imagine, offering a startling vision of familiar places: a white and frozen Gullfoss, caves full of icicles, and snow-covered mountains.

---

tion especially for (youngish) children. Don't expect lions and tigers; think seals, foxes and farm animals with slightly dismal enclosures, and tanks of cold-water fish. The family park section is jolly, with a mini-racetrack, child-size bulldozers, a giant trampoline, boats and kids' fairground rides. The Family Fun Park is in the middle of a large park area, so buses don't go directly to the door, but buses S2, 14, 15, 17 and 19 pass within a few hundred metres.

Water babies will have a splashingly good time in Reykjavík's wonderful geothermal **swimming pools** (p83), particularly Laugardalslaug and Árbæjarlaug. **Icelandic horse-riding** (opposite) is a great confidence-booster for novice riders – the horses have calm temperaments and aren't too high off the ground. The 18-lane bowling-hall **Keiluhöllin** (Map pp72-3; ☎ 511 5300; www.keiluhol lin.is; Öskjuhlíð; disco bowling ½/1/2hr Ikr2300/4600/9200, other evening & weekend times ½/1/2hr Ikr1900/3800/7600, cheaper weekdays; ☾ 11am-midnight Sun-Thu, to 2am Fri & Sat) has arcade games and pool tables; its weekend **disco-bowling sessions** (☾ noon-3pm Sat & Sun) may appeal to teenyboppers. To get there take bus 19. In winter, **skating** (above) is a popular family activity. Buses S2, 14, 15, 17 and 19 pass within a few hundred metres.

The best museums for children are the open-air **Árbæjarsafn** (p77), where they can zoom around in a safe green space; and the **Saga Museum** (p76), which will appeal to Viking fans (although may be too scary

for very young children). Take bus 19 for Árbæjarsafn and bus 18 or 19 for the Saga Museum. The **National Museum** (p77) has dressing-up clothes, and puzzles and games relating to the museum's collections.

TOURS
Walking Tours

Reykjavík is perfect for exploring under your own steam, but if you'd like a little guidance, the tourist office has free themed brochures. They're easy to follow; the 'City Centre Walk' is probably the most interesting, followed by 'The City Parks' and 'The City Statues'.

Whatever the weather, a two-hour **city walking tour** (www.goecco.com; ☾ May–mid-Sep), which explores the old town's history, leaves at 1pm from outside the main tourist office on Aðalstræti. The walk is free, although tips are encouraged.

The 1½- to two-hour **Reykjavík Haunted Walk** (☎ 843 6666; www.goecco.com; adult/under 12yr Ikr2500/ free; ☾ 8pm May–mid-Sep), also departing from the main tourist office, combines ghost stories – gruesome, sad or just plain strange – with Viking history. The tour finishes, as all ghost walks should, in a twilight graveyard.

In a similar vein is the **Reykjavík Hidden World Walk** (☎ 843 6666; www.goecco.com; adult/ under 12yr Ikr2500/free; ☾ 3pm Wed, Sat & Sun May–mid-Sep), which wends round sites in the old town where the 'hidden people' are said to live, merging folklore with modern Icelandic environmentalism.

REYKJAVÍK

SUGGESTED TOURS FROM REYKJAVÍK

Destination/Activity	Price	Season
Diving/snorkelling at Þingvallavatn	€199/99	year-round
Geysir & Gullfoss, plus horse riding	Ikr15,500	year-round
Glacier walks	Ikr17,900	year-round
Golden Circle (Þingvellir, Geysir, Gullfoss)	Ikr8600-9800	year-round
Ice-climbing	Ikr15,990	Jun-Aug
Landmannalaugar geothermal area	Ikr17,000	Jul–mid-Sep
Lava tunnel exploration	Ikr11,000	year-round
Northern Lights spotting	Ikr4700-5500	Oct-Mar
Rafting on the Hvítá river	Ikr9990-11,990	May–mid-Sep
Reykjanes Peninsula & Blue Lagoon	Ikr8000-12,500	year-round
Snowmobiling	Ikr26,700-35,000	year-round
Snæfellsnes coast	Ikr17,300-19,000	Jun-Aug
Snæfellsnes coast & boat ride	Ikr19,700-25,500	Jun-Aug
South coast	Ikr15,000-16,500	year-round
Quad biking	Ikr12,990-15,500	year-round
Þórsmörk nature reserve	Ikr10,400-16,500	mid-Jun–mid-Sep

A more cultural exploration of the city can be had on the free **Reykjavík in Literature tour** (☯5pm Thu Jul & Aug). This 1½-hour stroll through the city is an introduction to ancient and modern Icelandic authors – Snorri Sturluson, Halldór Laxness, Arnaldur Indriðason, Hallgrímur Helgason et al – and an exploration of the Reykjavík settings that inspired them. It departs, appropriately, from the city library.

Bicycle Tours

An ingenious idea, the **Reykjavík Bike Tour** (☎ 694 8956; www.icelandbike.com; ☯10am & 8pm Jun-Aug, 10am Sep-May) is a two-hour guided ride around the city. Make a reservation, and the guides will come and pick you up – they'll even bring you a bike if you don't have one of your own. The tour is free – but tip what you think it's worth at the end.

Bus & Activity Tours

A day-long bus tour from Reykjavík is one of the best ways to see some of the country's spectacular natural wonders, particularly if you're not here for long. They're also good if you want to combine sightseeing with snowmobiling, horse riding, kayaking, rafting and other exhilarating activities.

Tours need to be booked in advance (either at the tourist office, at your hotel or hostel, or directly with the company) and they may be cancelled if there are insufficient numbers or if the weather turns rancid. Young children generally can travel free or at discounted rates.

Every year more tour operators pop up, but here are some of the better-established ones:
Arctic Adventures (Map pp78-9; ☎ 562 7000; www .adventures.is; Laugavegur 11) With young and enthusiastic staff, this company specialises in action-filled tours – rafting, horse riding, quad bike tours, glacier walks etc.
Guðmundur Jónasson Travel (Map pp72-3; ☎ 511 1515; www.gjtravel.is; Borgartún 34) Offers day excursions along the Ring Road and into the highlands, and can arrange super-Jeep trips, self-drive holidays and group travel.
Iceland Excursions (Gray Line Iceland; Map pp78-9; ☎ 540 1313; www.grayline.is; Hafnarstræti 20) A bus-tour operator with comprehensive day trips plus horse riding, whale watching, underground explorations, diving, and self-drive holidays. Book online for the best prices.
Reykjavík Excursions (Kynnisferðir; Map pp72-3; ☎ 580 5400; www.re.is; BSÍ bus terminal, Vatnsmýrarvegur 10) The most popular bus-tour operator has summer and winter programs. Extras include horse riding, snowmobiling and themed tours tying in with festivals.

See the boxed text (above) for examples of places to visit and things to try, with approximate prices and seasonal availability. See p64 for a rundown on major activities available in Iceland.

Super-Jeep & Supertruck Tours

If you fancy bigger wheels and a little more exclusivity, you can go sightseeing by super-Jeep or supertruck instead of by bus. Most of the places and activities listed in the previous section are on offer (prices are at least double).

Activity Group (☎ 580 9900; www.activity.is) Super-Jeep and supertruck activity and sightseeing tours.
Atours (☎ 517 4455; www.atours.is) Super-Jeep trips to the Golden Circle, Landmannalaugar, Þórsmörk and the south coast, plus the option of adding on outdoor activities.

Air Tours

Iceland is surprisingly large, and driving distances to beauty spots outside Reykjavík can be daunting if you're only here for a short time. One solution is an air tour: **Eagle Air Iceland** (Map pp72-3; ☎ 562 4200; www.eagleair.is; Reykjavík Domestic Airport) offer sightseeing flights over volcanoes and glaciers from €120 per 30 minutes.

FESTIVALS & EVENTS

Also see the list of festivals (p22), many of which are celebrated with gleeful enthusiasm in Reykjavík. For forthcoming live music, see www.musik.is.

February

Winter Lights (www.vetrarhatid.is) In mid- or late February Reykjavík celebrates the end of winter with cultural events, a mini food festival and lots of illuminated buildings.

May

Listahátíð í Reykjavík (Reykjavík Arts Festival; www.listahatid.is/en) Held from mid-May every year, this popular two-week event features films, dance, theatre, concerts and art exhibitions from Iceland and around the world.

August

Gay Pride (www.gaypride.is) This is Iceland's second-biggest festival – thousands of people parade carnival-style through the streets of Reykjavík on the second weekend of the month, with open-air concerts in the city centre.
Reykjavík Marathon (www.marathon.is) Held on a Saturday in mid-August, with shorter distances and fun runs for those who like to grit their teeth less.
Menningarnott (Culture Night; www.menningarnott .is) Iceland's biggest festival takes place mid-August; this evening of cultural events follows the marathon – more than a third of Iceland's population attends. It includes musicians on every street corner, citywide cultural and artistic performances, much drunkenness and a massive fireworks display.
Tango on ICEland (www.tango.is) Tango has really gripped the Icelandic soul. This three-day annual event at the end of August is composed of dance workshops and performances.
Reykjavík Jazz Festival (www.reykjavikjazz.is) The five-day Reykjavík Jazz Festival (Jazzhátíð Reykjavíkur) celebrated its 20th anniversary in 2009, and attracts a range of local and international talent. It has moved around the calendar a lot in recent years: check the website for dates.

September

Reykjavík International Film Festival (www.riff. is) This is a 10-day celebration of art-house films, with screenings across the city and talks by Icelandic and international directors – for example, 2009's star guest was Oscar-winner Milos Forman, director of *One Flew Over the Cuckoo's Nest*.

GAY & LESBIAN REYKJAVÍK

Reykjavík is a very tolerant place; its bar and club scene is so integrated that segregated gay bars close down almost before they've opened.

The gay and lesbian organisation **Samtökin '78** (Map pp78-9; ☎ 552 7878; www.samtokin78.is; 4th fl, Laugavegur 3; ☽ office 1-5pm Mon-Fri) provides information during office hours and doubles as an informal gay **community centre** (☽ 8-11pm Mon & Thu year-round, sometimes also 1-5pm Sat late Jul–Aug).

Created especially for gay, lesbian and bisexual visitors to Iceland, www.gayice.is is an English-language website with great information and upcoming events.

Q Bar (Map pp78-9; ☎ 578 7868; Ingólfsstræti 3; ☽ to 1am Sun-Thu, to 5am Fri & Sat) is one of the smallest bars in Reykjavík, a smart, stylish, minimalist place that transformed itself into a gay bar a couple of years ago. It bills itself as 'straight friendly' and certainly entertains a mixed clientele. **Barbara** (Map pp78-9; Laugavegur 22) is also a gay bar/club in theory, although in practice it attracts everyone in town who likes wild dancing. The only specifically gay club in Reykjavík is the men-only leather bar, **MSC Iceland** (Map pp78-9 ; ☎ 893 9552; basement, Laugavegur 28; ☽ from 11pm Fri & Sat).

There are several good gay-friendly guest houses close to the centre, such as Room with a View (p90). Reykjavík has a lively Gay Pride celebration – see above for more information.

October
Iceland Airwaves (www.icelandairwaves.com) This five-day event in mid-October is one of the world's coolest music festivals. Homegrown talent and international DJs and bands play their souls out in various intimate venues around the city; past acts have included Sigur Rós, Fat Boy Slim, the Flaming Lips and Hot Chip.

SLEEPING
Reykjavík has loads of accommodation choices, with midrange guest houses and business-class hotels predominating. In July and August accommodation fills up quickly; reservations are strongly advised. Most places open year-round apart from Christmas (we've noted where accommodation is summer only) and offer 20% to 45% discounts from October to April.

Budget
Reykjavík campsite (Map pp72-3; ☎ 568 6944; www.rey kjavikcampsite.is; Sundlaugavegur 32; sites per person Ikr1000; ☾ mid-May–mid-Sep) The only camping option in the city (right next door to the city hostel, 2km east of the centre in the Laugadalur valley) gets very busy in summer, but with space for 650 people in its three fields, you're likely to find a place. Facilities include free showers, bike hire, a kitchen and barbecue area, and a reception desk selling gas bottles and postcards; you can share the hostel's internet access and laundry room, but emphatically *not* its kitchens.

Reykjavík City Hostel (Map pp72-3; ☎ 553 8110; www.hostel.is; Sundlaugavegur 34; sb 6-bed dm with shared bathroom Ikr2100, sb 4- or 6-bed dm with bathroom Ikr3000, sb r with bathroom Ikr4300; P ⌨ ☏) Reykjavík's eco-friendly youth hostel sleeps 170 people and has excellent facilities. There are three guest kitchens, a library, four internet-linked computers, free wi-fi, a laundry room (Ikr300 per washer/dryer) and bike hire, as well as regular film shows, pancake nights and pub crawls. Its lovely staff can book trips and the airport bus. The downsides are that it's a good 2km out of town; and screaming school kids may well drive you to despair. The bus from the airport should drop you off here directly. Bus 14 (Ikr280, every 20 to 30 minutes) runs to Hlemmur and Lækjartorg in the city centre.

Salvation Army Guesthouse (Map pp78-9; ☎ 561 3203; www.herinn.is; Kirkjustræti 2; sb/s/d/tr/q Ikr3000/71 00/9900/14,000/17,500) This is the nearest thing Reykjavík has to a Japanese capsule hotel! The

tiny rooms at this Christian 'guest house' are highly functional and frill-free, but there's a bustling backpackery atmosphere, guest kitchen and lounging area. Step outside and the whole of Reykjavík is at your feet. Breakfast Ikr800.

Reykjavík Backpackers (Map pp78-9; ☎ 578 3700; www.reykjavikbackpackers.com; Laugavegur 28; sb 4- to 8-person dm Ikr3490, sb d Ikr10,990) Wait years for more backpacker accommodation in the city centre, and suddenly two budget places appear at once! This hostel, opened in June 2009, is a very nuts-and-bolts affair based in a former office block. Rigidly rectangular rooms are whitewash plain – double bunks to sleep in and lockers for your stuff are the only furniture – and only rooms on the 4th floor have access to a kitchen. But you can't argue with its A1 location, or the friendly staff.

Garður Inn (Map pp78-9; ☎ 562 4000, 551 5900; www.inns-of-iceland.com; Hringbraut; sb dm Ikr4000, s/d Ikr11,000/13,000; ☾ Jun-Aug; P) In summer, once the students have left, the university campus offers visitors utilitarian rooms with shared bathrooms. The cheapest sleeping-bag accommodation is in 16-person dorms. Single/double rates include breakfast.

Reykjavík Downtown Hostel (Map pp78-9; ☎ 553 8120; www.hostel.is; Vesturgata 17; sb 10-bed dm Ikr4400, sb 4-bed dm Ikr5200, sb d Ikr13,900; ⌨ ☏) A brand-new HI hostel opened in March 2009. Located on a quiet street, it has the same fine amenities as the City branch – but fall out of the door and you're in the heart of town. Thirty of its 70 beds are in 8- to 10-bed dormitories, while the rest are in doubles or family rooms. Higher prices repel backpackers and attract more couples and families than the original hostel.

Midrange

GUEST HOUSES

Reykjavík is packed with *gistiheimili* (guest houses) and there are new places opening every year. Most are in converted houses, so rooms often have shared bathrooms, kitchens and TV lounges. Some offer sleeping-bag accommodation.

Guesthouse Andrea (Map pp78–9; ☎ 899 1773; www.aurorahouse.is; Njarðargata 43; sb dm Ikr4000, s/d Ikr9000/12,000; ☷ mid-May–mid-Sep; ▣) Friendly Siggi runs this hidden place, tucked down a sidestreet in a tranquil residential area. Its five private rooms have smart wooden floors and are ideal for self-caterers: each has a sink, cooker, fridge and tiny two-seater table.

Snorri Guesthouse (Map pp72–3; ☎ 552 0598; www.guesthousereykjavik.com; Snorrabraut 61; sb d Ikr8000, s/d/tr from Ikr8500/10,700/16,300; ℗ ☏) On the corner of a big road intersection, this pebble-dashed building doesn't look too promising. However, its clean rooms in muted shades – particularly the more expensive 'family' variety, which have kettles, fridges and private bathrooms – make for a decent base. It's about a 20-minute walk into the city centre.

Guesthouse Butterfly (Map pp78–9; ☎ 894 1864; www.kvasir.is/butterfly; Ránargata 8a; s/d/apt €89/99/150; ☷ mid-May–Aug; ☏) On a quiet residential street within fluttering distance of the centre, Butterfly has neat, simply furnished rooms. There's a guest kitchen and wi-fi access, and the friendly Icelandic-Norwegian owners make you feel right at home. The top floor has two self-contained apartments with kitchen and balcony.

Álfhóll Guesthouse (Map pp78–9; ☎ 898 1838; www.islandia.is/alf; Ránargata 8; s/d/tr Ikr9000/12,500/16,000, 2- to 4-person apt 18,000–23,000; ☷ Jun-Aug) Almost identical in feel and facilities to Butterfly is this neighbouring guest house, run by a family of elf enthusiasts. Breakfast is a help-yourself affair in the home-away-from-home kitchen.

Guesthouse Aurora (Map pp78–9; Freyjugata 24; sb dm Ikr4000, s/d Ikr9000/12,000, apt from Ikr15,500; ☷ mid-May–mid-Sep; ▣ ☏) Just around the corner from the Andrea, this homely purple town house is also run by Siggi. Its 14 rooms are simple and clean, although there can be bathroom queues! The newly renovated apartments are the pick of the bunch here.

Alba Guesthouse (Map pp72–3; ☎ 552 9800; www.alba.is; Eskihlíð 3; s/d/tr Ikr9900/12,500/15,500; ℗ ▣ ☏) In a quiet residential area fairly close to Perlan, Alba is a peaceful choice. It has fresh, modern, attractive rooms (with shared bathrooms) and pleasant staff, with free wi-fi and breakfast included.

our pick **Sunna Guesthouse** (Map pp78–9; ☎ 511 5570; www.sunna.is; Þórsgata 26; s/d from Ikr10,100/12,800, apt Ikr16,100-32,000; ℗ ▣) Rooms at this guest house are simple and sunny with honey-coloured parquet floors. Nine have private bathrooms, and several at the front have good views of Hallgrímskirkja. Families are made to feel welcome; choose between neat studio apartments holding up to four people, or more spacious apartments with accommodation for up to eight. Breakfast – with home-baked bread – is included.

Galtafell Guesthouse (Map pp78–9; ☎ 551 4344; www.galtafell.com; Laufásvegur 46; s/d from Ikr10,100/12,800, 2-bed apt Ikr 19,900) In the quiet, well-to-do 'Embassy District', and within easy walking distance of town. The four spruce apartments here each contain a fully equipped kitchen, a cosy seating area and a separate bedroom, and there are three doubles with access to a guest kitchen. The only drawback is that they're basement rooms, so there are no views of anything but the pavement!

Gistiheimilið Ísafold (Map pp78–9; ☎ 561 2294; www.isafoldguesthouse.is; Bárugata 11; s/d from Ikr9900/13,200) This rambling old house (a former rehab centre/bakery/bookshop) lies in peaceful old Reykjavík. Sun-filled bedrooms contain washbasins and rustic beds; there are tea-making facilities in the lounge; and solemn Icelandic dolls keep an eye on diners in the attic breakfast room. At the nearby annexe (Bárugata 20), all accommodation comes with private bathrooms (around Ikr2000 extra).

Guesthouse 101 (Map pp72–3; ☎ 562 6101; www.iceland101.com; Laugavegur 101; s/tw/tr/q €65/89/100/115) Slightly cheaper than the 4th Floor Hotel on the floor above, these rooms in a converted office building are good value for such a central location. White is the dominant colour, with startling splashes of red here and there. All rooms have washbasins. Summer prices include a breakfast buffet; prices drop out of season, but you'll have to forage for your own food in town.

Domus Guesthouse (Map pp78–9; ☎ 561 1200; www.domusguesthouse.is; Hverfisgata 45; sb dm/d Ikr4500/11,000, s/d Ikr9900/13,900, apt Ikr21,900-26,900; ▣) A place where room types vary immensely. The main building was once the Norwegian embassy, and houses the better rooms. These have stately proportions, slightly battered but comfy-feeling furniture, TVs and fridges, and shared bathrooms. A second building contains plainer and darker rooms, most with bunk beds; a massive dormitory divided by curtains (which makes it feel kind of hospital-like); and three pleasant wood-panelled, maze-like apartments (one with Jacuzzi) on the upper floor. Breakfast is included in accommodation above sleeping-bag level, and there's a guest kitchen and laundry facilities.

ourpick **Guesthouse Baldursbrá** (Map pp78-9; ☎ 552 6646; baldursbra@centrum.is; Laufásvegur 41; s/d Ikr8900/14,000; 🖳 ⛶) This exceptional little guest house, on a quiet street close to Tjörnin and the BSÍ bus station, stands out thanks to the care and kindness of its owners. The decent-sized, comfy rooms all have washbasins, and the additional facilities are admirable – a sociable sitting room–TV lounge, wi-fi, and a private garden with a fab hot pot, sauna and barbecue. Rates include breakfast.

Guesthouse Óðinn (Map pp78-9; ☎ 561 3400; www .odinnreykjavik.com; Óðinnsgata 9; s/d/tr from €95/105/130; ⛶) This family-run guest house has simple white rooms with splashes of colourful artwork. An excellent buffet breakfast, included in the rates, is served in a handsome room with sea views. Some en-suite rooms are available.

4th Floor Hotel (Map pp72-3; ☎ 511 3030; www.4thfloorhotel.is; Laugavegur 101; s/d/tr without bathroom Ikr11,900/17,900/19,900, d/tr/ste with bathroom Ikr19,900/25,900/15,900, apt Ikr34,900-44,900; 🖳 ⛶) Close to Hlemmur bus station, the 24 rooms at this 'hotel' (really a guest house) are a mixed bag. All have desk, kettle, TV, washbasin, wi-fi access and duvets printed with zebra stripes(!). Economy rooms fit these accoutrements into a tiny space and have shared bathrooms, while more expensive en-suite rooms are larger: four have sea views and two have balconies. The smart studio apartments here are worth every króna.

APARTMENTS
Apartments in Reykjavík are often very good value.

Castle House & Embassy Apartments (Map pp78-9; ☎ 511 2166; http://hotelsiceland.net; Skálholtsstígur 2a & Garðastræti 40; 1-6 person apt Ikr11,600-39,900) Turn to these pleasant self-contained apartments for

satisfyingly central and commendably quiet accommodation. The two sets of apartments (located on opposite sides of Tjörnin) are much more personal than a hotel, but come with room service: fresh towels appear daily and washing-up seems to magically clean itself. Breakfast not included. The tariff changes depending on demand – cheapest rates are through the website.

Forsæla Guesthouse (Map pp78-9; ☎ 551 6046, 863 4643; www.apartmenthouse.is; Grettisgata 33b; d/tr Ikr14,400/17,400, 2-/3-/4-person apt Ikr19,200/23,200/27,200, house Ikr60,000) This is a really lovely option in Reykjavík's conservation area. Star of the show is the 100-year-old wood-and-tin house for four to eight people, which comes with all the old beams and tasteful mod-cons you could want. Three apartments have small but cosy bedrooms and sitting rooms, fully equipped kitchens and washing machines. There's a minimum three-night stay and the friendly owners prefer prebookings.

Three Sisters (Þrjár Systur; Map pp78-9; ☎ 565 2181; www.threesisters.is; Ránargata 16; 1-/2-person apt €82/108, family apt €133; ⛄ mid-May–Aug; 🖳 ⛶) A twinkly eyed former fisherman runs the Three Sisters, a lovely town house in old Reykjavík, now divided into eight studio apartments. Comfy counterpaned beds are flanked by old-fashioned easy chairs and state-of-the-art flat-screen TVs. Each room comes with a cute fully equipped kitchen (including fridge, microwave and two-ringed hob). A short stroll seawards is a second building with eight more apartments, and sleeping-bag accommodation in six-bed dorms (around Ikr3000).

Room With A View (Map pp78-9; ☎ 552 7262; www. roomwithaview.is; Laugavegur 18; 1-/2-/3-/4-bedroom apt around Ikr27,900/36,900/43,900/49,900; 🅿 ⛶) This ridiculously central apartment hotel offers one- to four-bedroom apartments, decorated in Scandinavian style and with private bathrooms, kitchenettes, CD players, TVs and washing machines. Half have those eponymous sea and city views, and most have access to a Jacuzzi. Rooms vary – check the website for a wealth of details. It has a bang-on-centre location; the downside is Friday- and Saturday-night street noise.

HOTELS
Many of Reykjavík's midrange hotels are places built for and favoured by business travellers, and the places can be pretty bland. Rooms have private bathrooms unless mentioned otherwise.

Metropolitan Hotel (Map pp78-9; ☎ 511 1155; www .metropolitan.is; Ránargata 4a; s/tw/tr lkr14,200/17,400/20,500; 🖳 🛜) In the peaceful old town, within a few blocks of the city's core, the Metropolitan received a top-to-toe makeover in 2004. This couldn't alter the small size of its 31 rooms, but they certainly look much better than they did! Facilities stretch to TVs, mini-fridges and wireless internet access, and a lift (elevator) – rare in Iceland in a hotel of this class! Essentially, a fairly basic place in a good location.

Hótel Leifur Eiríksson (Map pp78-9; ☎ 562 0800; www.hotelleifur.is; Skólavörðustígur 45; s/d/tr lkr15,200/18,400/21,500) This hotel glories in one of the best locations in Reykjavík: it's slap on the end of arty Skólavörðustígur, and more than half its 47 rooms have inspiring views of Hallgrímskirkja. They're fairly small and basic (with blue carpeting, narrow beds, TVs and phones), but you're paying for the hotel's coordinates rather than its interior design. There's no restaurant, but free tea and coffee are available in the lobby, and guests get reduced rates at the Indian Mango restaurant (p93).

Hótel Frón (Map pp78-9; ☎ 511 4666; www.hotelfron .is; Laugavegur 22a; s/d/studio/2-bed apt lkr15,900/18,900/1 9,900/29,900; 🖳 🛜) This bright blue hotel has lots in its favour – particularly its excellent location overlooking Laugavegur (although rooms at the front can be noisy at weekends), and the stylish apartments in the new wing. They come with TV, safe, hardwood floors, modern bathrooms and well-equipped kitchenettes (cooker, fridge and microwave) – try to bag one with a balcony. Older rooms are less inspiring. Room service comes from the Mexican restaurant below.

CenterHótel Plaza (Map pp78-9; ☎ 595 8550; www .plaza.is; Aðalstræti 4; s/d/tr from €70/80/130; 🅿 🖳 🛜) The 104-room Plaza has the feel of a smaller, family-run affair. Rooms have all mod-cons (digital TVs, kettles, bathrobes and free broadband connections) and come in two styles. Half are modern and business-like, with navy furnishings and clean-lined wooden furniture – most look onto bustling Ingólfstorg. Those in the new extension feature antique beams and a softer beige decor, although some are a little dark. The superior double on the 6th floor has superb views of the square, sea and mountains from its glassed-in balcony. Buffet breakfast is included.

CenterHotel Skjaldbreið (Map pp78-9; ☎ 595 8510; www.centerhotels.is; Laugavegur 16; s/d from €70/80; 🌙 closed 18-27 Dec; 🖳) In the same family-run CenterHotel group is this old town house, round the corner on Laugavegur, with grandma-style orange-and-green decor. The curved corner rooms are best. Rates include breakfast in a light and modern rooftop room.

CenterHotel Klöpp (Map pp78-9; ☎ 595 8520; www. centerhotels.is; Klapparstígur 26; s/d from €75/100; 🌙 closed 18-27 Dec) This mellow place has a boutique-hotel spirit. The foyer-breakfast area sets the tone, with gleaming hardwood floors, genial staff and lots of light pouring in. Rooms are modest in size with minimal furnishings, but warm woody tones, textured mauve textiles and stylish slate-floored bathrooms give them a modern yet cosy feel. All contain TV, fridge, radio, kettle and internet connection point, and you can just about see the sea and mountains from the 5th-floor rooms.

Park Inn Ísland (Map pp72-3; ☎ 595 7000; www.rey kjavik.rezidorparkinn.com; Ármúli 9; s/d from lkr22,000/25,000; 🖳 🛜) The standard-issue rooms here have good facilities, and some even manage to break free of the chain-hotel mould. Go for ones with kitchenettes, or stunning panoramic views of Reykjavík and the mountains. All have TV, telephone, minibar and tea-making kit. Guests (rather sweetly) get free admission to the city's swimming pools, and there's a filling hot-and-cold breakfast buffet, although you might have to fight for food with the many package tour groups that use the hotel.

Fosshótel Barón (Map pp72-3; ☎ 562 3204; www. fosshotel.is; Barónsstígur 2-4; standard s/d €185/200, 1-/2-bed apt €290/330; 🅿 🖳 🛜) The corporate chain-hotel Barón is fairly central, and its 4th- and 5th-floor front-facing rooms have marvellous views of the sea and Esja – worth the extra €40. There are 31 apartments of varying sizes, with cooking facilities. Laptop users have free wi-fi coverage, or there's internet access in the lobby.

Top End

All rooms in this category have bathroom, TV, phone and minibar; rates rarely include breakfast!

CenterHótel Arnarhvoll (Map pp78-9; ☎ 595 8540; www.centerhotels.com; Ingólfsstræti 1; s/d from €135/160; 🖳 🛜) A sleek new hotel on the waterfront, Arnarhvoll offers unimpeded views of the bay and Mt Esja in the distance. Cool, Scandinavian-designed rooms with clean lines and large windows let in all that lovely Nordic light: it's definitely worth paying extra and getting one with a sea view. Rooms are on the small side, but the extremely comfortable beds more than compensate for this common Icelandic shortcoming. A small sauna and steam room in the basement add novelty.

Radisson SAS 1919 Hotel (Map pp78-9; ☎ 599 1000; www.radissonblu.com; Pósthússtræti 2; standard/deluxe d €170/220; 🖳 🛜) Although this is part of a large chain, the catchily named Radisson SAS 1919 Hotel is a boutique place with plenty of style. Attractive rooms sport wooden floors, large beds, flatscreen TVs and wireless access. Keep walking up the carved iron stairwells to the 4th floor and you'll reach the large, comfy suites (rooms 414 and 412). Other bonuses include a fantastic location, a gym and the cool Gullfoss bar-restaurant.

CenterHótel Þingholt (Map pp78-9; ☎ 595 8530; www.centerhotels.com; Þingholtsstræti 3-5; s/d from €145/170; 🖳 🛜) Compact, quirky and full of character, Þingholt opened in 2006 and still retains a fresh, new feel. It was designed by architect Gulla Jónsdóttir, who used natural materials and some very Icelandic ideas to create one of Reykjavík's most distinctive boutique hotels. Rooms are compact, but feel cosy rather than cramped. This snuggly effect is heightened by moody lighting, stylish dark-grey flooring and black-leather headboards and furniture. A good breakfast buffet is included.

Hótel Reykjavík (Map pp72-3; ☎ 514 7000; www.hotelreykjavik.is; Rauðarárstígur 37; s/d/tr around €203/239/288; 🅿 🖳 🛜) In a commercial area close to the Hlemmur bus station, Hótel Reykjavík is a no-nonsense business hotel offering decent internet rates. Many of its respectably sized rooms were Ikea-ified in 2008, with hardwood floors, new beds, updated bathrooms and new fixtures (TVs, mini-fridges, phones, wireless internet access and tea-making facilities). A good buffet breakfast is included.

Hótel Holt (Map pp78-9; ☎ 552 5700; www.holt.is; Bergstaðastræti 37; s/d Ikr21,000/24,300; 🅿 🖳 🛜) Cross the threshold and enter a world of luxury. Original paintings, drawings and sculptures adorn the rooms here (Holt houses the largest private art collection in Iceland), set off by warm-toned decor and rose-coloured carpets. Downstairs is a handsome amber-hued library, a bar with flickering fire and a

huge selection of single-malt whiskys, and one of the country's best restaurants.

Hótel Óðinsvé (Map pp78-9; ☎ 511 6200; www.hotelodinsve.is; Þórsgata 1; s/d from Ikr18,900/25,900; 🖳) A boutique hotel with bags of personality, Óðinsvé contains 43 sun-drenched rooms with wooden floors, original artwork and classic furnishings. They're all very different – some are split-level, some have balconies and many have bathtubs – but only room 117 has a resident ghost! The hotel also owns some stunning apartments, which overlook the prison a short walk away on Skólavörðustígur.

Hótel Borg (Map pp78-9; ☎ 551 1440; www.hotelborg.is; Pósthússtræti 9-11; s/d €154/259; 🖳) The city's most historic hotel was completely overhauled in 2007. Super-smart beige, black and cream decor, parquet floors, leather headboards and flatscreen Bang & Olufsen TVs are now standard throughout, lending the hotel an elegant (if rather masculine) feel. It may have lost some of its art deco charm, but thankfully it's retained the enormous showerheads in its bathrooms! Quadruple-glazed windows cut down on drunken weekend street noise.

Hótel Reykjavík Centrum (Map pp78-9; ☎ 514 6000; www.hotelcentrum.is; Aðalstræti 16; s/d/tr €244/288/345; 🛜) This central hotel has striking architecture – mezzanines and a glass roof unite two buildings, giving the whole place a spry, light feel. Its 89 neatly proportioned rooms come in two styles: 'traditional', with patterned wallpaper and white-painted furniture; and 'deluxe', with leather seats and a more contemporary feel. Both have safes, minibars, pay TVs (with films to order), tea-making facilities and wi-fi internet access.

Hilton Reykjavík Nordica (Map pp72-3; ☎ 444 5000; www.hilton.com; Suðurlandsbraut 2; s/d from Ikr22,600/29,000; 🅿 🖳) Bring your autograph book to the Nordica – visiting celebs often stay here. Cool Scandinavian chic oozes from every part, with amenities such as 24-hour room service, gym, spa and the gourmet restaurant Vox (p94). Light-filled rooms with enormous beds are decorated in subtle shades of cream and mocha; those on the upper floors have super sea views. The hotel's about 2km from the city centre, but it runs a free city-centre shuttle service. Breakfast costs an extra Ikr2000, but is one of the best in Iceland.

101 Hotel (Map pp78-9; ☎ 580 0101; www.101hotel.is; Hverfisgata 10; s/d/ste from Ikr45,900/52,900/68,900;

🖳 📶) The 101 is devilishly divine. Its sensuous rooms – with yielding downy beds, iPod sound docks and Bose speakers, rich wooden floors and glass-walled showers – may mean you skip the bars and opt for a night in instead. A spa with masseurs, a small gym and a glitterati restaurant-bar add to the opulence. Some people have been underwhelmed by the service, but all in all this is one of the city's sexiest places to stay.

EATING

Reykjavík's eateries vary from hot-dog stands to world-class restaurants. Two things are consistent: high quality and high prices. For the types of eateries and opening hours, see p52. Reykjavík's dining places are found mainly along Laugavegur, Hverfisgata and also Austurstræti.

Restaurants

ASIAN

Krua Thai (Map pp78-9; ☎ 561 0039; www.kruathai.is; Tryggvagata 14; mains Ikr1100-1900; ☽ noon-9.30pm Mon-Sat, 6-9.30pm Sun) Look beyond the simple interior to the tasty food: here you'll find genuine recipes, popular with Thai residents of Reykjavík. The glossy photo-menu shows soups, spicy salads, curries and stir-fries; you order at the counter, and generous, freshly-cooked dishes appear looking just like they do in the snaps.

Ning's (Map pp72-3; ☎ 588 9899; Suðurlandsbraut 6; mains Ikr1200-1900; ☽ 11.30am-10pm) The mouth-watering smell of frying pork greets you at this Chinese fast-food restaurant, handy for the City Hostel. There's a good, cheap menu of noodles and stir-fries, and the cooking is MSG-free. The set lunch is very popular at lunchtime, or there's a takeaway counter.

INDIAN

Indian Mango (Map pp78-9; ☎ 551 7722; www.indianmango.is; cnr Frakkastígur & Grettisgata; mains Ikr2200-3400; ☽ from 5pm Mon-Sat) Indian Mango specialises in Goan food, serving beef, duck, fish and some vegie mains. Its chef – poached from a five-star restaurant – makes up light, spicy, delicious dishes. Its bestselling (seasonal) creation is an Icelandic-Indian hybrid completely unique to this restaurant – *svartfugl* (guillemot) marinaded in Indian spices.

our pick **Austur Indía Félagið** (Map pp78-9; ☎ 552 1630; Hverfisgata 56; mains Ikr2600-4000; ☽ from 6pm) The northernmost Indian restaurant in the

world is an upmarket experience, with a minimalist interior and a select choice of sublime dishes (a favourite is the tandoori salmon). One of its finest features, though, is its lack of pretension – the atmosphere is relaxed and the service warm. Apparently Harrison Ford likes it – and who dares argue with Indy?

ITALIAN

Hornið (Map pp78-9; ☎ 551 3340; Hafnarstræti 15; 9in pizza Ikr1360-2440; mains Ikr2300 4000; ☽ 11 30am-11pm) There's an easy-going air at this bright art deco cafe-restaurant, with its warm terracotta tiles, weeping-fig plants and decently spaced tables. Pizzas are freshly made before your eyes, the prettily presented pasta meals will set you up for the day, and you can sample traditional Icelandic fish dishes.

Basil & Lime (Map pp78-9; ☎ 555 3696; Klapparstígur 38; mains Ikr1850-3650; ☽ 11.30am-10pm Mon-Sat, 5-10pm Sun) Specialising in honest-to-blazes Italian food, this new restaurant makes its pasta from scratch daily – try the langoustine tagliatelle in a garlicky creamy sauce. The interior is rather nondescript and strangely dark, even in the daytime: pick good weather and devour the lunch special (a bargain) at one of the outdoor tables.

Ristorante Ítalía (Map pp78-9; ☎ 552 4630; www.italia.is; Laugavegur 11; pizzas Ikr2300, mains Ikr2200-4600; ☽ 11.30am-11.30pm) One of the better Italian options, this family-run place has a proper wood-fired pizza oven, and good pasta and *secondi piatti* (mains). It's a romantic option for a candle-lit dinner.

La Primavera (Map pp78-9; ☎ 561 8555; www.laprimavera.is; Austurstræti 9; mains Ikr3200-4500; ☽ noon-2pm & 6-10.30pm Tue-Fri, 6-10.30pm Sat) Pizza Hut it ain't. This is a cultivated eatery serving contemporary Italian dishes – the pastas, gnocchi and polenta are all homemade. The menu is select, with some imaginative combinations – for example, pan-fried scallops with pomegranate and lime.

STEAKHOUSES

Hereford Steakhouse (Map pp78-9; ☎ 511 3350; www.hereford.is; Laugavegur 53b; mains Ikr3300-5600; ☽ 5-10pm) This modern 1st-floor steakhouse grills up top-class steaks (of beef, lamb, turkey, veal and whale), priced by weight and cut. You can pick from fillets, T-bones, rib eyes and entrecôtes, and watch as they're cooked at the grilling station in the centre of the dining room. There's a good red-wine list.

Argentína (Map pp72-3; ☎ 551 9555; www.argen tina.is; Barónsstígur 11a; mains Ikr3850-5980; ☒ 6-10.30pm Sun-Thu, to 11.30pm Fri & Sat) This dark, fiery steakhouse rightly prides itself on its succulent locally raised beef – the best red meat you'll eat in Reykjavík. It also serves tender chargrilled salmon, reindeer, lamb, pork and chicken, with a wine list to complement whatever choice you make.

ICELANDIC

Many upmarket restaurants (including those in the city's top hotels) take great national pride in presenting Icelandic ingredients in their finest possible glory. Gourmet menus generally feature *bacalao* (salt cod), smoked lamb and seafood, and more unusual dishes such as guillemot, puffin and reindeer. Also see Seafood, opposite.

However, not all Icelandic food is found in gourmet settings: there is a growing movement to resurrect traditional 'Grandma's Kitchen' dishes – hearty fish stews and meat soups – now some of the cheapest meals to be found in Iceland.

Segurmo (Map pp78-9; ☎ 845 4549; Laugavegur 28b; mains Ikr1500; ☒ lunch & dinner Mon-Sat, dinner only Sun) This new restaurant is run by the people who owned the much-missed bar Sirkus, though it's a little more grown-up than that wacky club. Even so, the menu's emphasis on traditional Icelandic food still reveals a few unusual quirks. Minke whale with ratatouille, for example; or salt cod with banana and blue cheese sauce.

Lækjarbrekka (Map pp78-9; ☎ 551 4430; www.laek jarbrekka.is; Bankastræti 2; mains Ikr3220-5580; ☒ 11.30am-11pm) This top-notch restaurant has built up its reputation over more than 20 years, cooking traditional Icelandic dishes (game, lobster, juicy pepper steak and mountain lamb) with half an eye on the tourist dollar. From June to August it puts on a high-quality Icelandic buffet (Ikr5600) every evening from 6pm.

Einar Ben (Map pp78-9; ☎ 511 5090; www.einarben. is; Ingólfstorg; mains Ikr3400-4900; ☒ 6-10pm Mon-Thu, to 11pm Fri-Sun) One of the city's finest restaurants, Einar Ben is frequented by diplomats and is renowned for its top-class service and gastronomical marvels. Dishes are Icelandic with a continental twist – think puffin terrine, and lamb Dijon with blueberries and thyme.

Perlan (Map pp72-3; ☎ 562 0200; www.perlan.is; Öskjuhlíð; mains Ikr3900-5700; ☒ from 6.30pm) Perched on top of the city's water tanks is the revolving restaurant Perlan, which spins at one sedate revolution every two hours. The views are superb and, if you can tear your eyes away from the city-and-mountain vista, the grub (reindeer, lamb, flounder, guillemot) isn't bad either.

our pick **Vox** (Map pp72-3; ☎ 444 5050; www. voxrestaurant.com; Suðurlandsbraut 2; mains Ikr4100-6900; ☒ 6-10pm Tue-Sat) The Hilton's five-star restaurant serves up superb seasonal dishes – think pink-footed goose with caramelised apples – and there's usually a vegie option. The waiters sometimes bring out extra little treats for you to try – for example, their amazing 'invisible gazpacho'! The daytime bistro puts on a recommended Sunday-brunch hot buffet (Ikr2850/1425 for adults/children six to 12 years) – gorge on fruit, bread, prawns (shrimps), bacon, eggs, sausage and pancakes until you burst.

INTERNATIONAL

Tapas Barinn (Map pp78-9; ☎ 551 2344; www.tapas.is; Vesturgata 3b; tapas plates from Ikr690; ☒ 5-11.30pm Sun-Thu, to 1am Fri & Sat) Indecisive types will have a tough time at this outstanding tapas bar, with over 50 different dishes on the menu – a thousand possible combinations! Alongside familiar Spanish nibbles such as mixed olives and *patatas bravas*, you'll find Icelandic ingredients turned into tasty titbits – puffin with blueberries, saltfish, and pan-fried lobster tails. Expect to spend around Ikr3900 per person for a full meal.

Santa Maria (Map pp78-9; ☎ 552 7775; Laugavegur 22a; mains Ikr990; ☒ noon-10pm Mon-Sat, 5-10pm Sun) A genuine Mexican restaurant in the heart of town, Santa Maria is run by Ernesto, originally from Mexico City, who brought his mum to Iceland to train his chefs in cooking up authentic enchiladas, mole, chicken tortillas and the rest. Relaxed, and extraordinarily good value.

Askur Brasserie (Map pp72-3; ☎ 553 9700; www.askur .is; Suðurlandsbraut 4; mains Ikr2200-3800; ☒ 11.30am-10pm) Close to the big hotels on Suðurlandsbraut, this relaxed family restaurant is popular with tourists and locals alike. Despite its noncentral location, it's wise to book on Friday and Saturday. There's a long menu of burgers, steaks, pasta, lamb, fish and sizzling fajitas, many of which come with soup and a free visit to the salad bar (loosen your belts). The weekday lunchtime buffet is good value at Ikr1790.

Domo (Map pp78-9; ☎ 552 5588; Þinghóltsstræti 5; mains Ikr3700-5300; ☺ 6-10pm Tue, Wed & Sun, 6-11pm Thu, 6pm midnight Fri & Sat) Part of Hótel Þingholt, this fine fusion-food restaurant mixes Far-Eastern flavours with high-quality Icelandic ingredients and French cooking styles. Dishes such as fruit-filled lamb served with artichokes and sweet potatoes are backed up by an extensive wine list. The sushi and sashimi menu is also available to take away.

Fiskfélagið (Fish Company; Map pp78-9; ☎ 552 5300; www.fishcompany.is; Vesturgata 2a; mains Ikr3800-5000; ☺ 11.30am-2pm & 6-11.30pm) Built on top of part of the old harbour, this brand-new restaurant is one of the city's cosiest, with its hotchpotch seating, candles and copper lamps. The menu is a truly ambitious sampling of world cuisines (and in spite of the restaurant's name, the focus isn't really on fish): begin with slow-cooked Spanish *serrano* ham, travel to South America for skate with black-bean purée, and finish with Tahitian banana and coconut cake!

SEAFOOD

Sægreifinn (Map pp78-9; ☎ 553 1500; Verbúð 8, small-boat harbour; mains Ikr990-2500; ☺ 11am-10pm) Eccentric Sægreifinn serves up fresh seafood in what looks almost like a 1950s English chip shop… except for the stuffed seal. The owner is a sprightly old gent who buys and cooks all the fish himself – lobster soup and fish kebabs are specialities. He only speaks Icelandic, so make sure you know what you're asking for!

Icelandic Fish & Chips (Map pp78-9; ☎ 511 1118; www.fishandchips.is; Tryggvagata 8; mains around Ikr1700; ☺ noon-9pm) A reader-recommended restaurant serving hearty portions of…well, have a guess! It's good-value fare (for Iceland, at least), and the owners have put their own singular slant on it with a range of 'Skyronnaises' – *skyr*-based sauces (eg rosemary and green apple) that add an unusual zing to this most traditional of dishes.

Lauga-Ás (Map pp72-3; ☎ 553 1620; www.laugaas.is; Laugarásvegur; mains Ikr2300-3800; ☺ 11am-9pm Mon-Fri, 5-9pm Sat & Sun) For about 30 years this small, friendly restaurant, close to the City Hostel, has been quietly cooking up some great-tasting grub. It's particularly well known for its seafood soup and lobster but it also serves deceptively large portions of pasta, steaks and lighter meals. The room itself is a little draughty, but the food is worth wearing a sweater for! Book ahead on Friday and Saturday night.

Við Tjörnina (Map pp78-9; ☎ 551 8666; www.vidtjornina.is; Templarasund 3; Ikr2200-5900; ☺ from 6pm) People return again and again to this famed seafood establishment, tucked away near Tjörnin. It serves up beautifully presented Icelandic feasts such as guillemot with port, garlic langoustine, or the house speciality marinated cod chins (far more delicious than they sound!). The restaurant itself is wonderfully distinctive – it feels like a quirky upper-class 1950s drawing room.

Þrír Frakkar (Map pp78-9; ☎ 552 3939; www.3frakkar. com; Baldursgata 14; mains Ikr3000-5300; ☺ noon-2.30pm & 6-10pm Mon-Fri, 6-11pm Sat & Sun) Owner-chef Úlfar Eysteinsson has built up an excellent reputation at this snug little restaurant – apparently a favourite of Jamie Oliver's. Specialities include salt cod, anglerfish and *plokkfiskur* (fish stew) with black bread. You can also sample nonfish items, such as seal, puffin, reindeer and whale steaks.

Fiskmarkaðurinn (Map pp78-9; ☎ 578 8877; www.fiskmarkadurinn.is; Aðalstræti 12; dishes Ikr3700-5400; ☺ 11.30am-2pm & 6-11.30pm Mon-Fri, 6-11.30pm Sat & Sun) Don't let the weird dead-bony-fish logo put you off – this new restaurant excels in infusing Icelandic seafood with Far-Eastern flavours. Ingredients have a strong focus on local produce. For example, there's the 'Farmers' Market' menu, which takes specialities from around Iceland (lobsters from Höfn, salmon from the Þjórsá, halibut from Breiðafjörður) and introduces them to spicy chillis, papaya, mango, coconut, satay glazes and *ponzu* sauce.

Sjávarkjallarinn (Map pp78-9; ☎ 511 1212; www.sjavarkjallarinn.is; Aðalstræti 2; dishes Ikr3800-6200; ☺ 6-10.30pm Sun-Thu, 6-11.30pm Fri & Sat) This atmospheric subterranean restaurant was, until recently, the hottest eating place in town; the loss of its award-winning chef means that quality has slipped a little, although it still offers some exotic choices. Shimmering fish and succulent crustaceans are combined with the unexpected – pomegranate, coconut, lychee and chilli – and presented like miniature works of art.

Humarhúsið (Map pp78-9; www.humarhusid.is; ☎ 561 3303; Amtmannsstígur 1; mains Ikr4100-6500) Understated and utterly elegant, the Lobster House is justly celebrated for its succulent shellfish, langoustine and lobster. Although crustaceans feature in most dishes, you can also sample game, fish, lamb and beef, plus there's a vegetarian option.

VEGETARIAN

Grænn Kostur (Map pp78-9; ☎ 552 2028; www.graenn kostur.is; Skólavörðustígur 8; daily special Ikr1390; ☯ 11.30am-9pm Mon-Sat, 1-9pm Sun) Tucked away in a small shopping arcade off Skólavörðustígur, this friendly little cafe serves great-tasting vegie set meals, with a daily-changing menu. There are also lighter snacks such as pizza, pies and salads. The high round tables and bar stools aren't particularly relaxing, but it's worth sitting up straight for good food.

Á Næstu Grösum (First Vegetarian; Map pp78-9; www .anaestugrosum.is; ☎ 552 8410; Laugavegur 20b; daily special Ikr1490; ☯ 11.30am-10pm Mon-Sat, 5-10pm Sun) This first-rate vegie restaurant, in a cheerful orange room overlooking Laugavegur, offers several daily specials. It uses seasonal organic veg, and inventive dressings guaranteed to give even lettuce new appeal. Things get extra spicy on Indian nights (Friday and Saturday), and organic wine and beer are available.

Cafes

Reykjavík's cool and cosy cafes are one of the city's best features. Lingering is encouraged – many offer magazines and free wi-fi access. They're the best places to go for morning coffee and light, tasty lunches. As the evening wears on, most undergo a Jekyll-and-Hyde transformation – coffee becomes beer, DJs materialise in dark corners, and suddenly you're not in a cafe but a kick-ass bar! Magic. Because the dividing line is so blurred, also see Drinking, p98.

Babalú (Map pp78-9; ☎ 552 2278; Skólavörðustígur 22a) More inviting than your own living room, this first-floor cafe is ubercute. It only sells tea, coffee, hot chocolate and the odd crêpe, but once you've settled into one of its snug corners you won't want to move. A teeny wooden balcony gives you a great vantage point over Skólavörðustígur, and in summer there's occasional live music.

Kaffi Mokka (Map pp78-9; ☎ 552 1174; Skólavörðustígur 3a; ☯ 9am-6.30pm) Reykjavík's oldest coffee shop is an acquired taste. Its decor has changed little since the 1950s, and its original mosaic pillars and copper lights either look retro-cool or dead tatty, depending on your mood! It has a mixed clientele – from older folk to tourists to trendy young artists – and a selection of sandwiches, cakes and giant waffles.

Kofi Tómasar Frænda (Koffin; Map pp78-9; ☎ 551 1855; Laugavegur 2; snacks around Ikr600; ☯ 10am-1am Mon-Thu, to 5.30am Fri & Sat, 11am-1am Sun; ☜) Subterranean Koffin has a studenty feel. Relax with magazines and a snack (nachos, lasagne, sandwiches, cakes or chocolate-coated marzipan) and watch disconnected feet scurry along Laugavegur. At night the place turns into a candle-lit bar with DJs.

Café Paris (Map pp78-9; ☎ 551 1020; Austurstræti 14; snacks Ikr700-1500; ☯ 9am-1am Sun-Thu, to 5am Fri & Sat) An old favourite, Paris is one of the city's prime people-watching spots, particularly in summer when outdoor seating spills out onto Austurvöllur square; and at night, when the leather-upholstered interior fills with tunes and tinkling wine glasses. The selection of light meals, including sandwiches, crêpes, burgers, salads and tacos, is secondary to the socialising.

Café Konditori Copenhagen (Map pp72-3; ☎ 588 1550; www.konditori.is; Suðurlandsbraut 4a; ☯ 8am-6pm Mon-Fri, 9am-5pm Sat & Sun) For pure cake porn, head to this cafe near the City Hostel – Danish-influenced delicacies flaunt glazed strawberries, curls of chocolate and dribbled cream. It also does more prosaic sandwiches and good coffee, which you can consume from supercomfy leather seats. There's a branch at the Kringlan shopping centre.

Café Garðurinn (Map pp78-9; ☎ 561 2345; Klapparstígur 37; soup/mains Ikr800/1350; ☯ 11am-5pm Mon-Fri, noon-5pm Sat, closed Aug) This tiny but tasteful vegie cafe is based around seven tables and the hum of civilised conversation. Choice is limited, but the daily soup and main are always delicious and unusual (we can vouch for the weird-sounding Catalonian tofu balls!). Half portions are available.

Kaffitár (Map pp78-9; ☎ 511 4540; www.kaffitar.is; Bankastræti 8; ☯ 7.30am-6pm Mon-Sat, 10am-5pm Sun; ☜) A Starbucks-style cafe, Kaffitár has opted for barristas, flavoured syrups, merchandised mugs and Italian biscuits by the till. The service is personal and there's even a small play area for toddlers. There's a branch at the Kringlan shopping centre.

Kaffi Hljómalind (Map pp78-9; ☎ 517 1980; Laugavegur 23; www.kaffihljomalind.org; snacks Ikr890-1250; ☯ 9am-10pm Mon-Fri, 11am-10pm Sat, 11am-6pm Sun; ☜) This commendable organic and Fair Trade cafe is run on a not-for-profit basis and serves as a meeting-place for Reykjavík's radicals. The interior has been cobbled together in retro style, with wooden floors, 1970s orange-flowered wallpaper, sofas and armchairs, chintzy lampshades and a battered piano. The short menu is composed of burritos, lasagne, soup, bagels, and toast with hummus, and service is entirely erratic; you'll either get this place or you won't!

Nýlenduvöruverslun Hemma & Valda (Map pp78-9; ☎ 551 64 64; Laugavegur 21; ☯ 10am-11pm Sun-Thu, to 1am Fri & Sat) Hemmi and Valdi's Colonial Store is another mismatched, beat-up, heavy-on-the-irony cafe. This relaxed place was set up by a couple of young dads to sell coffee, beer and, erm, baby clothes. There are huge windows perfect for street-gaping, comforting pottery mugs, a warm welcome for kids and a short menu of coffees and cakes. At night, this transmutes into a great little bar selling some of the cheapest booze in Reykjavík.

our pick Svarta Kaffið (Map pp78-9; ☎ 551 2999; Laugavegur 54; snacks & light meals Ikr900-1750; ☯ 11am-1am Sun-Thu, to 3am Fri & Sat) Order the thick homemade soup (one meat and one veg option daily for Ikr1290) at this quirky cavelike cafe – it's served piping hot in fantastic bread bowls. Other light lunches include nachos, burritos, toasted sarnies and lasagne. It's also a whimsical nightspot, with African masks and dim lighting adding a certain frisson.

Vegamót (Map pp78-9; ☎ 511 3040; www.vegamot .is; Vegamótastígur 4; light meals Ikr1300-2500; ☯ 11am-1am Mon-Thu, 11am-5am Fri & Sat, noon-1am Sun) A long-running cafe-bar-club, but still a voguish place to eat, drink, see and be seen. There's a startling choice on the 'global' menu, including Mexican salad, seafood *quesadilla*, sesame-fried monkfish and blackened chicken, and the kitchen stays open until 11.30pm on Fridays and Saturdays. The attached takeaway charges 10% less.

b5 (Map pp78-9; ☎ 552 9600; www.b5.is; Bankastræti 5; light meals Ikr1500-2000; ☯ 11am-midnight Sun-Wed, to 1am Thu, to 2am Fri & Sat; ☏) With its barely-there name and super-sleek interior, this bistro-bar flirts with pretentiousness but is actually a very mellow place. Pop in for the comfy seating, light Scandinavian-style bistro meals, games consoles for the kids to borrow and funky tunes on Friday and Saturday nights.

Kaffi Sólon (Map pp78-9; ☎ 562 3232; www.solon.is; Bankastræti 7a; snacks/light meals Ikr950-3000; ☯ 11am-1am Mon-Thu, to 5am Fri & Sat, noon-midnight Sun; ☏) Decked out with white-leather seats and oversized artwork, this ultracool bistro (and nightspot) offers tasty international dishes at reasonable prices. Vegetarians should head here for the best quiche in town.

Grái Kötturinn (Map pp78-9; ☎ 551 1544; Hverfisgata 16a) This tiny six-table cafe looks like a cross between an eccentric bookshop and a lop-sided art gallery – quite charming! Opening hours are odd, but it serves breakfast from 7am weekdays and 8am weekends – toast, bagels, American pancakes, or bacon and eggs served on thick, buttery slabs of freshly baked bread.

Café Haiti (Map pp78-9; ☎ 551 8484; Tryggvagata 16; ☯ 8.30am-6pm Mon-Thu, 8.30am-7.30pm Fri, 10am-6pm Sat) If you're a coffee fan, this tiny cafe near the harbour is the place for you. Owner Elda buys her beans from her home country of Haiti, and roasts and grinds them on-site, producing what regulars swear are the best cups of coffee in the country.

Café Loki (Map pp78-9; ☎ 466 2828; Lokastígur 28; snacks Ikr350-880, Icelandic platters Ikr1490; ☯ 10am-6pm Mon-Fri, noon-6pm Sun) Ignore the garish signage slapped across the exterior of this cafe located close to Hallgrímskirkja, and you'll discover it has a tasteful interior. Café Loki serves up very traditional dishes, from light snacks such as eggs and herring on homemade rye bread to Icelandic platters of sheep's-head jelly and sharkmeat. The food is popular with curious tourists, and with the locals, too.

Quick Eats

Icelanders are utterly addicted to hot dogs, and they swear the best are those from **Bæjarins Beztu** (Map pp78-9; Tryggvagata; ☯ 10am-1am Sun-Thu, 11am-4am Fri & Sat), a van situated near the harbour that's patronised by Bill Clinton! Use the vital sentence *Eina með öllu* ('One with everything') to get one with mustard, tomato sauce (ketchup), rémoulade and crunchy onions.

Late-opening snack bars and kiosks include **Hlölla Bátar** (Map pp78-9; Ingólfstorg; ☯ 11am-2am Sun-Thu, 10am-7am Fri & Sat) and **Emmessís & Pylsar** (Map pp78-9; Ingólfstorg), selling ice cream and hot dogs (Ikr330 to Ikr790); and **Nonnabiti** (Map pp78-9; ☎ 551 2312; Hafnarstræti 9; snacks Ikr450-900; ☯ to 2am).

Reykjavík residents are devoted to the pizzeria **Eldsmiðjan** (Map pp78-9; ☎ 562 3838; www.eldsmidjan.is; Bragagata 38a; 10in pizzas Ikr900-1500; ☯ 11am-11pm), tucked away on a quiet residential street. Its fiercely busy takeaway serves the best pizzas in the city, baked in a brick oven fired by Icelandic birch – or you can sit down to devour.

Several canteens around town serve cheap, filling traditional grub.

Fljótt og Gott (Map pp72-3; ☎ 552 1288; Vatnsmýrarvegur 10; mains Ikr1300-2000; ☺ 7am-9pm) Inside the BSÍ bus terminal, this cafeteria serves burgers, sandwiches and 'food like Mum makes it': big roast dinners and Icelandic delicacies such as *svið* (singed sheep's head), *plokkfiskur* (creamy haddock and potato mash) and salt cod.

Múlakaffi (Map pp72-3; ☎ 533 7737; www.mulakaffi .is; Hallarmúli; canteen meals Ikr1300-2700; ☺ 7.30am-8pm Mon-Fri, 7.30am-2pm Sat, 11am-8pm Sun) Shining-white walls and brand-new tables can't disguise Múlakaffi's old-fashioned soul. Hearty local meals such as meatballs, salt cod, roast pork and rye bread are dished up from the hotplate.

Self-Catering
ALCOHOL
Alcohol is pricey in bars and restaurants. The only shops licensed to sell alcohol are the government-owned liquor stores **Vín Búð**, of which there are 13 branches across the Reykjavík area. The most central branch is on **Austurstræti** (Map pp78-9; ☎ 562 6511; Austurstræti 10a), with another on the way towards Laugardalur at **Borgartún** (Map pp72-3; ☎ 561 8001; Borgartún 26). There are also branches in **Kringlan** (Map pp72-3; ☎ 568 9060) and **Smáralind** (☎ 544 2112) shopping centres. All are open 11am to 6pm Monday to Thursday and Saturday, and 11am to 7pm Friday.

BAKERIES
Iceland has fantastic bakeries with good coffee, sandwiches, soup and drool-inducing cakes, and many have tables for eating them.

Kornið Hrísateigur (Map pp72-3; ☎ 568 0110; Hrísateigur 47; ☺ 7am-5pm Mon-Fri, 7.30am-4pm Sat, 8.30am-4pm Sun) Handy for the City Hostel and campsite; Lækjargata (Map pp78-9; ☎ 552 1808; Lækjargata 4; ☺ 7am-5.30pm Mon-Fri, 8am-6pm Sat & Sun) Central bakery.

Bakarí Sandholt (Map pp78-9; ☎ 551 3524; www .sandholt.is; Laugavegur 36; ☺ 7.30am-6.15pm Mon-Fri, 7.30am-5.30pm Sat, 8.30am-5pm Sun) An old favourite on Laugavegur.

SUPERMARKETS
Bónus Kringlan shopping centre (Map pp72-3); ☺ noon-6.30pm Mon-Thu, 10am-7.30pm Fri, 10am-6pm Sat, noon-6pm Sun); Laugavegur (Map pp78-9; Laugavegur 59; ☺ noon-6.30pm Mon-Thu, 10am-7.30pm Fri, 10am-6pm Sat) The cheapest supermarket.

10-11 Austurstræti (Map pp78-9; ☺ 24hr), Barónsstígur (Map pp72-3; ☺ 24hr), Borgartún (Map pp72-3; ☺ 24hr) and Laugalækur (Map pp72-3; ☺ 24hr) Has many branches in the city.

DRINKING
See the boxed text (opposite) for the lowdown on Reykjavík's infamous pub crawl. At night, many of the city's cafes turn the lights down, the volume up, and swap cappuccinos for cocktails – so see p96 for more funky drinking venues.

Bars
Café Oliver (Map pp78-9; ☎ 552 2300; www.cafeoliver. is; Laugavegur 20a; ☺ to 1am Sun-Thu, to 4.30am Fri & Sat) One of Reykjavík's newer cafe-bars, Oliver is the most in-vogue place for brunch, and for partying late in superstyle. DJs pump out the tunes on Thursday, Friday and Saturday, with long queues snaking back from the doors.

Kaffibarinn (Map pp78-9; ☎ 551 1588; Bergstaðastræti 1; 🛜) This old house, with the London Underground symbol over the door, contains one of Reykjavík's coolest bars; it even had a starring role in cult movie *101 Reykjavík* (2000). At weekends you'll need a famous face or a battering ram to get in. At other times it's a place for artistic types to chill with their Macs.

Vegamót (Map pp78-9; ☎ 511 3040; www.vegamot. is; Vegamótstígur 4; ☺ to 1am Sun-Thu, to 5am Fri & Sat) Vegamót is another smart cafe-by-day, club-by-night – wear your best togs if you want to fit in. The buzzy balcony is a fine place to watch the fashion-conscious flocks. There are usually top DJs and a thronging dance floor. The minimum age here is 22.

Thorvaldsen Bar (Map pp78-9; ☎ 511 1413; www. thorvaldsen.is; Austurstræti 8-10) This understated modernist bar is ultraposh, from the fusion-style food to the clientele. There are DJs from Thursday to Saturday – dress up well or you won't get in, and after midnight be prepared to queue…and queue. There's a tiny dance floor, and 'theme nights' on Asia de Cuba Wednesday and Mojito Thursday.

Kaffi Sólon (Map pp78-9; ☎ 562 3232; www.solon.is; Bankastræti 7a; ☺ to midnight Sun-Thu, to 1am Fri & Sat) This great bistro becomes a swish bar for a beautiful, martini-drinking set by night. There are long queues, in-demand DJs, moody lighting and a dance floor containing around 17 people per sq metre. There are usually DJs or live music on Thursday.

THE RUNTUR

Reykjavík is renowned for its Friday- and Saturday-night *runtur*, when industrious Icelanders abandon work and pub crawl with passion. Friday night is the big one; midweek drinking is not really done, although it's gradually becoming more common for people to go out on Thursday night, when many bars have DJs or live music.

Much of the partying happens in the city's cafes and bistros, which transform into raucous beer-soaked bars at the weekend; there are also dedicated pubs and clubs. But it's not the quantity of drinking dens that makes Reykjavík's nightlife special – it's the upbeat energy that pours from them!

Places usually open until 1am Sunday to Thursday and until 3am or later on Friday and Saturday. 'In' clubs have long queues at weekends.

Thanks to the high price of alcohol, things don't get going until late. Icelanders brave the melee at the alcohol store Vín Búð (see opposite), then toddle home for a prepub party. Once they're merry, people hit town around midnight, party until 5am, queue for a hot dog, then topple into bed or the gutter, whichever is more convenient. Considering the quantity of booze swilling around, the scene is pretty good-natured.

Rather than settling into one venue for the evening, Icelanders like to cruise from bar to bar, getting progressively louder and less inhibited as the evening goes on. Most of the action is concentrated on Laugavegur and Austurstræti. You'll pay around Ikr700 to Ikr800 per pint of beer, and some venues have cover charges (about Ikr1000) after midnight. Things change fast – check *Grapevine* for the latest listings. You should dress up in Reykjavík, although there are pub-style places with a more relaxed dress code. The minimum drinking age is 20.

101 Hotel Bar (Map pp78-9; ☎ 580 0101; www.101hotel.is; Hverfisgata 10) Frankly, we fear being ejected as riff-raff from this beautiful granite-and-white-leather cocktail bar. Based inside the ultracool 101 Hotel (p92), this long, thin, sleek, chic space is favoured by local glamourpusses and celebrities. Although it gets rammed to the rafters at weekends, it also closes early (at 1am on Friday and Saturday) – dress to the hilt, and get on down there.

Hressingarskálinn (Map pp78-9; ☎ 561 2240; www.hresso.is; Austurstræti 20; ☎) Known colloquially as Hressó, this large open-plan cafe-bar serves a diverse menu until 10pm daily (everything from porridge to *plokkfiskur*). At weekends, it loses its civilised veneer and concentrates on beer, bar and dancing; a garden out back provides fresh air. There's usually a DJ or live music on Thursday nights.

Boston (Map pp78-9; ☎ 517 7816; Laugavegur 28b) Boston is cool, arty – and easily missable. It's accessed through a doorway on Laugavegur that leads you upstairs to its laid-back lounge, decorated in cool black wallpaper grown over with silver leaves. Live music and DJs.

Gullfoss Lounge Bar (Map pp78-9; ☎ 599 1000; Pósthússtræti 2) A lustrous bar-restaurant attached to the Radisson SAS 1919 Hotel, Gullfoss is gloriously upmarket. It's all clean Scandinavian lines, low luxurious seats and soft purple-toned lighting. It's not a place to get falling-over drunk in, but one for early-evening cocktails or a glass or two of good wine.

Karamba (Map pp78-9; ☎ 552 7710; Laugavegur 22) Quiet during the day, colourful Karamba becomes a lively drinking spot at night. Newly opened in 2009, the bar has become an instant hit for its eclectic DJ sets and frequent (and often impromptu) live band performances. There's sometimes a cover charge if better-known musicians are playing.

Jacobsen (Map pp78-9; ☎ 895 0455; Austurstræti 9) Drum & bass and jungle are still going strong in Iceland. Breakbeat, the country's oldest club night, has recently transferred itself to this cellar bar. There are also regular bands, attracting a young, studenty crowd.

Pubs

The following are our picks for a more relaxed, less dressy night on the town.

Ölstofan (Map pp78-9; ☎ 552 4687; Vegamótastígur 4) Locals come to this no-nonsense bar specifically to avoid all that dancing rubbish, and the music is kept at a level where you can hear your neighbour speaking. Turn up, drink beer, chat, relax.

Prikið (Map pp78-9; ☎ 551 2866; Bankastræti 12) Prikið is one of the later-closing bars (5.30am), where dancers grind away to hip-hop on the jammed dance floor. If you survive the night, it's a popular place to indulge in a next-day 'hangover sandwich'.

Dillon (Map pp78-9; ☎ 578 2424; Laugavegur 30) Beer, beards and the odd flying bottle…atmospheric Dillon is a RRRRROCK pub, drawing lively crowds. There are frequent concerts on its tiny corner stage, a great beer garden, and an unusual DJ, the white-haired white-wine-and-rum-swilling 'rokkmamman' Andrea Jons, a kind of female Icelandic John Peel.

Grand Rokk (Map pp78-9; ☎ 551 5522; www.grand rokk.is; Smiðjustígur 6) This down-to-earth pub was once a great live-music venue, but a few years ago the owners installed large-screen TVs upstairs and turned it into a sports bar. There have been recent signs that bands are being welcomed back…keep your fingers crossed, and in the meantime, you know where to go to watch football.

If Víking beer isn't doing it for you, head for a pint of Guinness at one of Reykjavík's two Irish pubs: **Celtic Cross** (Map pp78-9; ☎ 511 3240; Hverfisgata 26; 🕑 to 1am Sun-Thu, to 5.30am Fri & Sat), done up like a funeral parlour and with bands in the basement at weekends; and **Dubliner** (Map pp78-9; ☎ 511 3233; Hafnarstræti 4), which also has live music at the weekends.

Nightclubs

The clubs below shut between 5am and 6am at the weekend.

Hverfisbarinn (Map pp78-9; ☎ 511 6700; www.hverfisbarinn.is; Hverfisgata 20; 🕑 to 1am Thu, to 5.30am Fri & Sat) This trendy bar and club attracts a young, dressy crowd and has long queues at weekends. It's done out in a cool modern-Scandinavian style, which adds to the spacious feel. There's live music on Thursday from 10pm, and DJs on Friday and Saturday.

NASA (Map pp78-9; ☎ 511 1313; nasa@nasa.is; Austurvöllur; admission Ikr1500-3500) The biggest nightclub in Reykjavík, NASA is a stripped-pine affair filled with Prada-clad crowds. It plays chart music and club anthems, and is the city's main live-music venue – email for upcoming gigs.

ENTERTAINMENT

For nightclubs, see above.

Cinemas

Cinemas in Reykjavík are mostly American-style multiplexes showing American block-busters. Movies are screened in their original language with Icelandic subtitles. Cinemas charge around Ikr1000/550 per adult/child under eight years, and films are usually shown at 5.45pm, 8pm and 10pm. The newspaper *Morgunblaðið* lists shows and times, or click on the 'Bíó' tab at www.kvikmyndir.is.

Háskólabíó (Map pp72-3; ☎ 525 5400; Hagatorg) At the university; sometimes shows arts films.

Laugarásbíó (Map pp72-3; ☎ 553 2075; Laugarás) Near the City Hostel.

Regnboginn (Map pp78-9; ☎ 551 9000; Hverfisgata 54) Central cinema, sometimes showing arts films, with the cheapest tickets.

Sambíóin (Map pp72-3; ☎ 575 8900; Kringlunni 4-6) In Kringlan shopping centre.

Smárabíó (off Map pp72-3; ☎ 564 0000; Kópavogur) Iceland's biggest cinema, in Smáralind shopping centre.

Cultural Activities

Reykjavík has several theatre groups, an opera house and a symphony orchestra. Information on current events can be found in *What's On in Reykjavík*, *Grapevine* or the daily papers.

Íslenska Óperan (Map pp78-9; ☎ box office 511 4200; www.opera.is; Ingólfstræti; 🕑 box office 2-6pm) The Icelandic Opera has a busy program of international operas, with tickets ranging from Ikr3100 to Ikr7500.

Iceland Symphony Orchestra (Map pp72-3; ☎ 545 2500; www.sinfonia.is; Háskólabíó, Hagatorg; tickets Ikr3300-3700; 🕑 box office 9am-5pm Mon-Fri, to 7.30pm on concert eves) The orchestra will eventually move to flashy new premises by the harbour, currently half built. The economic crisis has put a temporary halt to the construction work and planned relocation, so for now the orchestra will remain at Reykjavík University cinema. There are around 60 classical performances per season, normally on Thursday at 7.30pm.

National Theatre (Map pp78-9; ☎ 551 1200; www.leikhusid.is; Lindargata 7; tickets adult/under 16yr Ikr3400/2800; 🕑 box office 12.30-6pm, to 8pm on performance eves, theatre closed Jul & Aug) The most important of several venues in the city, the National Theatre has three separate stages and puts on around 12 plays, musicals and operas per year, from modern Icelandic works to Shakespeare.

Reykjavík City Theatre (Map pp72-3; ☎ 568 8000; www.borgarleikhus.is; Kringlan, Listabraut 3; adult/under 12yr from Ikr3950/free; 🕑 box office 10am-6pm Mon & Tue, 10am-8pm Wed-Fri, noon-8pm Sat & Sun, theatre closed Jul & Aug) The country's second-largest theatre, behind Kringlan shopping centre, stages at least six plays and musicals per year, showing at around 8pm from Thursday to Sunday. The **Icelandic Dance Company** (www.id.is) is in residence there.

Iðnó Theatre (Map pp78-9; ☎ 551 9181; www.light nights.com; Vonarstræti 3; tickets adult/7-16yr Ikr3500/2000; ⏰ 8.30pm Mon & Tue mid-Jul & Aug) In summer there are tourist performances at this lakeside venue: 'Light Nights' is a mixed bag of Icelandic history, dance, folk tales and ghost stories and a slide show.

Live Music

The Reykjavík live-music scene is chaotic, ever-changing and strangely organic, with exotic new venues mushrooming up over the stumps of the old. To catch up with the current state of Icelandic music, consult the free English-language paper *Grapevine* (widely available), or pop into one of the city's two independent music shops (see p102). There are frequent live performances at various bars, pubs and clubs, including **NASA** (opposite) and (currently) the two following venues:

Batteríið (Map pp78-9; ☎ 861 4521; Hafnarstræti 1-3) For a few years now, this place on the wrong side of Lækjargata has been one of Reykjavík's main live-music venues. When you know it holds just 300 people, you understand how cute and teeny the city's bar scene really is... Escape the crush in the fairy-lighted courtyard.

Sódóma (Map pp78-9; ☎ 860 2216; Tryggvagata 22) Just opened in 2009, Sódóma (named after a fictional bar from a famous Icelandic film) is a central venue rising from the ashes of former stalwart Gaukur á Stöng. It acts as a rougher rock bar, and its size gives it prominence as one of the city's main live-music venues.

Sport

The country's passion for football (soccer) is huge. However, the Icelandic league is on a tiny scale and matches are generally played at suburban sports grounds. One of Reykjavík's biggest teams is **KR** (www.kr.is), who play in the Newcastle United strip! Their home ground is KR-völlur. Cup and international matches are played at the **national stadium** (Laugardalsvöllur; Map pp72-3; ☎ 510 2914) in Laugardalur; see the sports sections of Reykjavík's newspapers for fixtures, and buy tickets directly from the venue.

The Reykjavík Marathon (see p87), held annually in August, is tremendously popular. Contact your local running club or see www.marathon.is for information on how to participate.

SHOPPING

Spending sprees in Reykjavík are now viable for visitors, ever since the country's terrible economic troubles began and the value of the króna plummeted through the floor. At the time of writing, just about every shop on the high street and in the shopping malls was plastered with signs reading 'Útsala 40%'; add to that your 15% tax-free shopping refund (see the boxed text, p327), and prices are now almost on a par with other destinations.

It's shocking for Iceland, but great news for visitors looking for unusual gifts. The city centre is full of tiny, tantalising shops – Icelanders seem genetically programmed with a talent for quirky design. Look out for well-made Icelandic sweaters, delicate jewellery, weird-and-wonderful clothing, CDs by the latest bands, bags of dried fish, chocolate-covered liquorice, and bottles of the Icelandic schnapps *brennivín*.

Austurstræti and Hafnarstræti contain tourist stores selling puffin mugs and troll trinkets; Skólavörðustígur sells arty-crafty one-offs; and Laugavegur is the main shopping street.

Antiques & Bric-a-Brac

Kolaportið Flea Market (Map pp78-9; Geirsgata; ⏰ 11am-5pm Sat & Sun) Held in a huge industrial building by the harbour, this weekend market is a Reykjavík institution and definitely worth a visit, particularly in these economically challenged times. Browse through piles of secondhand clothes, music, antiques and children's toys, or pick up Icelandic fish delicacies including cubes of *hákarl*.

Fríða Frænka (Map pp78-9; ☎ 551 4730; Vesturgata 3; ⏰ noon-6pm Mon-Fri, 10am-2pm Sat) This place is a two-storey treasure trove of everything from antique furniture to '60s plastic kitsch. Items are piled precariously in tiny side rooms – the art-installation effect adds to the experience.

Clothes

Reykjavíkurs are style crazy, although the credit crunch has slowed the rush of start-up boutiques that made clothes shopping in Iceland such a fascination. For international brand-name clothing, try the two big shopping centres (see p102).

66° North (Map pp78-9; ☎ 535 6680; www.66north. is; Bankastræti 5; ☺ 10am-6pm Mon-Fri, 10am-4pm Sat, 11am-4pm Sun) Iceland's outdoor-clothing company began by making all-weather wear for Arctic fishermen. This metamorphosed into weatherproof but fashionable streetwear – coats, fleeces, hats and gloves. The branch at Kringlan shopping centre stays open until 9pm on Thursdays.

ELM (Map pp78-9; ☎ 511 0991; www.elm.is; Laugavegur 1; ☺ 11am-6pm Mon-Fri, to 4pm Sat) Black-and-cream women's fashion – the designs are unmistakeably Icelandic, with sharp, eccentric but very flattering cuts.

Gaga (Map pp78-9; ☎ 551 2306; www.gaga.is; Vesturgata 4) Strange knitted goods from designer Gaga Skorrdal.

GuSt (Map pp78-9; ☎ 551 7151; www.gust.is; Banka stræti 11) Classy women's clothing, made from wool and fish leather and cut in that indefinable Icelandic style.

Handknitting Association of Iceland (Map pp78-9; ☎ 552 1890; www.handknit.is; Skólavörðustígur 19; ☺ 9am-6pm Mon-Sat, 11am-3pm Sun) Traditional handmade hats, socks and sweaters are sold at this knitting collective, or you can buy yarn and knitting patterns and do it yourself. There's a smaller branch (Map pp78-9; ☎ 562 1890; Laugavegur 64; ☺ 9am-7pm Mon-Fri, 10am-5pm Sat Jul & Aug, shorter hr winter), which sells made-up items only.

Naked Ape (Map pp78-9; ☎ 551 1415; www.dont benaked.com; Bankastræti 14; ☺ 11am-6pm Mon-Fri, to 4pm or 5pm Sat) Drop into this 2nd-floor boutique-gallery for ultracool T-shirts and hoodies, mostly in bright graffiti-like colours, designed by a bunch of artist-friends.

Jewellery
Various shops along Laugavegur specialise in Icelandic jewellery.

Aurum (Map pp78-9; ☎ 551 2770; Bankastræti 4; ☺ 10am-6pm Mon-Fri, 11am-4pm Sat) Guðbjörg at Aurum is one of the more interesting designers; her whisper-thin silver jewellery is sophisticated stuff, its shapes often inspired by leaves and flowers.

Guðbrandur Jósef Jezorski (Map pp78-9; ☎ 552 3485; Laugavegur 48; ☺ 10am-6pm Mon-Fri, to 1pm Sat) Tasteful silver and gold jewellery incorporating little lumps of lava and Icelandic stones.

Music
12 Tónar (Map pp78-9; ☎ 511 5656; www.12tonar. is; Skolavörðustígur 15; ☺ 10am-6pm Mon-Fri, to 2pm or 4pm Sat, plus 1-5pm Sun Jul & Aug) A very cool place to hang out is 12 Tónar, responsible for launching some of Iceland's favourite new bands. In the three-floor shop you can listen to CDs, drink coffee and maybe catch a live performance on Friday afternoons.

Skífan Kringlan shopping centre (Map pp72-3; ☎ 591 5320; ☺ 10am-6.30pm Mon-Wed, 10am-9pm Thu, 10am-7pm Fri, 10am-6pm Sat, 1-6pm Sun); Laugavegur (Map pp78-9; ☎ 591 5310; Laugavegur 26; ☺ noon-10pm) Reykjavík's biggest music chain store has lots of choice, bargain-bin offers, and listening headsets so you can try CDs before you buy.

Smekkleysa Plötubúð (Map pp78-9; ☎ 534 3730; www.smekkleysa.net; Laugavegur 35) Bad Taste records is the label that launched The Sugarcubes, and they're still producing new music. Their shop has moved around a lot in recent years, and had just reopened on Laugavegur at the time of writing.

Outdoor Equipment
Útilíf (Map pp72-3; ☎ 545 1500; www.utilif.is) Climbing, camping, cycling and fishing equipment and repairs are available from Útilíf, in Kringlan and Smáralind shopping centres and in the small Glæsibær arcade.

Quirky Design
Kirsuberjatréð (The Cherry Tree; Map pp78-9; ☎ 562 8990; www.kirs.is; Vesturgata 4; ☺ 10am-6pm Mon-Fri, 11am-3pm Sat) This women's art collective sells weird and wonderful fish-skin handbags, music boxes made from string and (our favourite) beautiful coloured bowls made from radish slices!

Kraum (Map pp78-9; ☎ 517 7797; www.kraum.is; Aðalstræti 10) Fish-skin clothing, silver jewellery, driftwood furniture and ceramic seabirds, much of it created by up-and-coming young Icelandic designers, fill two storeys of Reykjavík's oldest house.

Shopping Centres
Mallrats can choose between two large shopping centres. Both contain big-name clothing chains, home-furnishing outlets, a Vín Búð alcohol shop, banks, a food court and a cinema.

Kringlan (Map pp72-3; ☎ 588 788; www.kringlan. is; ☺ 10am-6.30pm Mon-Wed, 10am-9pm Thu, 10am-7pm Fri, 10am-6pm Sat, 1-6pm Sun) Reykjavík's biggest shopping centre, 1km from town, has 150 shops. Take bus S1-4, S6, 13 or 14.

Smáralind (off Map pp72-3; ☎ 528 8000; www.sma ralind.is; Hagasmári 1; ☺ 11am-7pm Mon-Fri, 11am-6pm Sat, 1-6pm Sun) A smaller centre 6km away in the suburb of Kópavogur. Take bus S2.

Souvenirs
Rammagerðin (Map pp78-9; ☎ 551 1122; http://ram magerdin.is; Hafnarstræti 19; ☺ 9am-6pm Mon-Fri, 10am-6pm Sat & Sun) This 60-year-old tourist shop is the oldest and biggest. Besides the usual trinkets (coffee-table books, souvenir mugs and plastic Viking helmets), it has a large range of knitwear and a handmade glass and ceramics section.

BUS SERVICES FROM REYKJAVÍK

Destination	Duration	Frequency	Price	Year-round
Akranes	80min	several daily	Ikr840	Yes
Akureyri	6hr	daily	Ikr9000	Yes (reduced in winter)
Blue Lagoon (incl lagoon admission)	45min	several daily	kr5000	Yes
Borgarnes	1¼hr	several daily	Ikr2000	Yes
Geysir/Gullfoss	2½hr	daily	return Ikr7000	Jun-Aug
Höfn	8½hr	daily	Ikr11,500	Yes (reduced in winter)
Hveragerði	35min	many daily	Ikr840	Yes
Keflavík	40min	several daily	Ikr1600	Yes
Kirkjubæjarklaustur	6hr	daily	Ikr6600	Yes (reduced in winter)
Landmannalaugar	5½hr	daily	Ikr6300	mid-Jun–Aug
Ólafsvík	3hr	several daily	Ikr5100	Yes
Þorlákshöfn (for the Vestmannaeyjar ferry)	1hr	2 daily	Ikr1400	Yes
Þórsmörk	3½hr	1 or 2 daily	Ikr5200	Jun–mid-Sep
Reykholt	2hr	Fri & Sun	Ikr2900	May-Aug
Selfoss	1hr	many daily	Ikr1120	Yes
Skaftafell (stops at Freysnes in winter)	7hr	daily	Ikr8200	Jun–mid-Sep
Vík í Mýrdal	5hr or 3¼hr	2 daily	Ikr4900	Yes (reduced in winter)

GETTING THERE & AWAY
Air
Reykjavík Domestic Airport (Innanlandsflug; Map pp72-3; www.reykjavikairport.is) is based just south of Tjörnin. From morning to evening, planes fly between Reykjavík and Akureyri (Ikr14,000 one way), Egilsstaðir (Ikr15,700) and Ísafjörður (Ikr14,000); as well as to Greenland and the Faeroes. Internal flight operator **Air Iceland** (Flugfélag Íslands; ☎ 570 3030; www.airiceland.is) has a desk at the airport, but you can usually save money if you book over the internet (a computer terminal is provided near the check-in desks).

International flights operate through **Keflavík International Airport** (☎ 425 0600, 425 6000; www.kefairport.is), 48km west of Reykjavík. The easiest way to get there is on the Flybus – see right. For international airlines, see p335.

Boat
For information on the Viðey ferry service, see p106.

Bus
Almost all long-distance buses use the **BSÍ bus terminal** (Map pp72-3; ☎ 562 1011; www.bsi.is; Vatnsmýrarvegur 10), near the domestic airport – the company name is pronounced *bee ess ee*. The desk here can book you onto bus services around Iceland. You can pick up

summer (June to August or mid-September) or winter (mid-September to May) bus time-tables, and there's also a rack of tourist information available. There's a good cafeteria, Fljótt og Gott (p98), with internet access.

In summer regular direct services include those listed in the table (see boxed text, above). There's reduced or no service the rest of the year.

For other destinations on the northern and eastern sides of the island (eg Egilsstaðir, Mývatn and Húsavík), you'll need to change buses in Höfn or Akureyri, which may involve an overnight stop.

Buses to Reykjanes, Snæfellsnes and the main towns on Rte 1 run year-round, with the exception of the section from Akureyri to Höfn. Services are less frequent on all routes between September and May.

Buses to the Westfjords (see p178) only run from June to August, and routes across the highlands also close down for winter.

GETTING AROUND
To/From the Airport
From Keflavík International Airport it's easy: the **Flybus** (☎ 580 5400; www.re.is) meets all international flights. One-way tickets cost Ikr1700/850 per adult/child 12 to 15 years, or Ikr2200/1100 if you want to be dropped off at your hotel. Buy tickets before you board from

the booth just inside the airport doors (credit cards accepted). The journey to Reykjavík takes around 50 minutes.

On the return journey the bus leaves the BSÍ bus terminal two hours before international departures.

Reykjavík City and Downtown hostels and the main hotels can arrange transfers to the bus station, if you let them know the night before you intend to travel.

The Flybus will also drop off and pick up in Garðabær and Hafnarfjörður, just south of Reykjavík, if you book in advance. Taxis to/from the airport cost at least Ikr9500 one way.

From the domestic airport terminal it's a 1km walk into town or there's a taxi rank outside. Bus 15 runs from here to Hlemmur bus station.

Bicycle

Reykjavík has a steadily improving network of well-lit cycle lanes – ask the tourist office for a map, or see www.rvk.is/paths (click on Footpaths and Cycle Paths in Reykjavík for the English version). At times, though, you will probably end up on busy roads. Be cautious, as drivers show little consideration for cyclists. Refreshingly, you are actually allowed to cycle on pavements as long as you act sensibly and don't cause pedestrians any problems.

Bicycles are available for hire from **Borgarhjól SF** (Map pp78-9; ☎ 551 5653; www.borgar hjol.net; Hverfisgata 50; 4/24hr Ikr2000/3600; ☘ 8am-6pm Mon-Fri, 10am-2pm Sat), and from Reykjavík City Hostel (p88) and the campsite (p88).

Bus

Reykjavík's excellent **Strætó city bus system** (☎ 540 2700; www.straeto.is/english) offers regular and easy transport around central Reykjavík and out to the suburbs of Seltjarnarnes, Kópavogur, Garðabær, Hafnarfjörður and Mosfellsbær.

For the most up-to-date information on bus numbers and routes, pick up a copy of the *Welcome to Reykjavík City Map*, which includes a very clear bus-route map. The map is widely available, including from tourist offices and bus stations.

Buses run from 7am until 11pm or midnight daily (from 10am on Sunday). Services depart at 20-minute or 30-minute intervals. A limited night-bus service runs until 2am on Friday and Saturday. Buses only stop at designated bus stops, marked with a yellow letter 'S'.

TICKETS & FARES

The fare is Ikr280/100 per adult/child six to 18 years (no change is given). Books of 11 tickets (Ikr2500), and one-/three-day passes (Ikr600/1500) can be bought from the two bus stations, Kringlan and Smáralind shopping malls and the bigger swimming pools. If you need to take two buses to reach your destination, *skiptimiði* (transfer tickets) are available from the driver – you have a limited time (usually 45 minutes) in which to use them.

The Reykjavík Welcome Card (see p73) also acts as a free Strætó bus pass.

BUS STATIONS

The two central terminals are **Hlemmur** (Map pp72-3), at the far end of the main shopping street Laugavegur; and **Lækjartorg** (Map pp78-9), right in the centre of town. Check your route carefully, as not all buses stop at both.

Big suburban bus stands include Grensás (Map pp72-3), Hamraborg in Kópavogur, Fjörður in Hafnarfjörður (Map p108), Háholt in Mosfellsbær, Ártún in the suburb of Höfðar and Mjódd in the suburb of Breiðholt.

Useful routes:

14 Lækjartorg bus station, National Museum, BSÍ bus terminal, hospital, Hlemmur bus station, Laugardalur (for swimming pool, City Hostel and campsite).

15 Domestic airport terminal, BSÍ bus terminal, hospital, Hlemmur bus station, Laugardalur, Háholt bus station (Mosfellsbær).

S1 Hlemmur bus station, Lækjartorg bus station, National Museum, BSÍ bus terminal, hospital, Hamraborg bus station (Kópavogur), Fjörður bus station (Hafnarfjörður).

Car & Motorcycle

A car is fairly unnecessary in the city, because it's so easy to travel round on foot and by bus. However, if you want to get into the countryside and don't fancy the bus tours (see p86), it's worth hiring a car.

The capital's drivers can be inconsiderate: beware of people yattering into mobile phones (illegal, in case you're wondering), drifting across lanes or cutting corners at junctions.

PARKING

The City Hostel, campsite and top-end hotels have private parking for guests; at other guest houses and hotels, you'll have to scrum for spaces. In central Reykjavík, metered street parking and municipal car parks are divided into zones – P1 is the most expensive, then P2 and P3. An hour's city-centre parking costs about Ikr200; parking is free on Sunday and in the evening.

GETTING OUT OF TOWN

Getting out of town is easy – follow the signs for Rte 1. Getting back into Reykjavík can be more confusing, as there are dozens of exits from the highway and road signs are marked with abbreviations rather than full street names. To help you, the main road into Reykjavík is Vesturlandsvegur, which turns into Miklabraut and then Hringbraut. Exit by the Kringlan shopping centre for the Laugardalur area; at Snorrabraut for the Hallgrímskirkja area; and at Suðurgata for the town centre.

Taxi

Taxi prices are high. Flagfall starts at around Ikr500, with a minimum journey cost of around Ikr1800. Tipping is not required.

There are usually taxis outside the bus stations, domestic airport, and pubs and bars on weekend nights (you'll find there are huuuuge queues for the latter). Alternatively, call **Borgarbílastöðin** (☎ 552 2440), **BSH** (☎ 555 0888), **BSR** (☎ 561 0000) or **Hreyfill-Bæjarleiðir** (☎ 588 5522).

Walking

Reykjavík's compact layout means that it's very easily walkable. Most restaurants, bars, hotels and attractions are clustered within a 1.5-sq-km area.

AROUND REYKJAVÍK

One of the fantastic things about Reykjavík is the sea that practically surrounds it. Get closer to the ocean by visiting the island Viðey, a nugget of nature just a few minutes offshore, or the stony beaches at Seltjarnarnes, on the western tip of the Reykjavík Peninsula.

Several nearby towns have been sucked into Reykjavík's sprawl and are now part of its suburbs. Kópavogur, Garðabær, Hafnarfjörður and Mosfellsbær, which are of varying degrees of interest to visitors, can all be easily reached by city bus.

VIÐEY

If the weather's fine, the tiny uninhabited island of Viðey makes a wonderful day trip.

It's just 1km north of Reykjavík's Sundahöfn Harbour, but it feels like another world. Strange modern artworks, an abandoned village and shipwreck sites add to its melancholy spell. Here, life slows right down – the only sounds are the wind, the waves, and golden bumblebees buzzing among the tufted vetch and hawkweed.

History

Viðey had an explosive beginning – it's actually the tip of a long-extinct volcano. Despite its tiny size, the island has played a prominent part in Iceland's history. Its main roles were as a pilgrimage place and religious battleground.

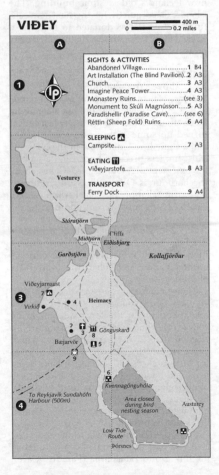

VIÐEY

0 ————— 400 m
0 ————— 0.2 miles

SIGHTS & ACTIVITIES
Abandoned Village.........................1 B4
Art Installation (The Blind Pavilion)..2 A3
Church...3 A3
Imagine Peace Tower......................4 A3
Monastery Ruins........................(see 3)
Monument to Skúli Magnússon.....5 A3
Paradíshellir (Paradise Cave).......(see 6)
Réttin (Sheep Fold) Ruins.............6 A4

SLEEPING 🏕
Campsite......................................7 A3

EATING 🍴
Viðeyjarstofa...............................8 A3

TRANSPORT
Ferry Dock....................................9 A4

In 1225 a wealthy Augustinian monastery was founded here; it kept the coffers full by imposing a cheese tax on a massive area of land surrounding it. During the 16th-century Reformation, the monastery was sacked by Danish Lutherans and all its riches taken. Incensed by this cultural and religious outrage, Iceland's last Catholic bishop, Jón Arason, made a stand. He seized the island in 1550 and built the fort Virkið (no longer visible) to protect it, but he was captured and then beheaded in November that year.

Skúli Magnússon, the founder of the modern city of Reykjavík, built the fine mansion Viðeyjarstofa here in 1751–5. It's now Iceland's oldest stone building. The island existed quietly for the next few centuries before it was donated to the city of Reykjavík in 1986, on the 200th anniversary of its municipal charter.

Sights

Just above the harbour, you'll find Viðeyjarstofa, an 18th-century wooden **church**, and a small **monument to Skúli Magnússon**. Excavations of the old **monastery foundations** turned up some 15th-century wax tablets and a runic love letter, now in the National Museum; less precious finds can be seen in the basement of Viðeyjarstofa. Higher above the harbour is Ólafur Elíasson's interesting art installation **The Blind Pavilion** (2003). Nearby is the most recent addition to the island's artworks, Yoko Ono's **Imagine Peace Tower** (2007), a 'wishing well' that blasts a dazzling column of light into the sky every night between 9 October (John Lennon's birthday) and 8 December (the anniversary of his death).

The whole island is crisscrossed with **walking paths**. Some you can cycle (there are free bikes available at the ferry stop, or bring your own), while others are more precarious. A good map at the harbour shows which paths are which. The whole island is great for birdwatchers (30 species of **birds** breed here) and budding botanists (over one-third of all Icelandic **plants** grow on the island). In August, some Reykjavík inhabitants come here to pick **wild caraway**, originally planted by Skúli Magnússon.

From the harbour, trails to the southeast lead you past the natural sheep fold **Réttin**, the tiny grotto **Paradíshellir** (Paradise Cave), and then to the old **abandoned fishing village** at Sundbakki. Most of the south coast is a protected area for birds and is closed to visitors from May to June.

Trails leading to the northwest take you past low ponds, monuments to several shipwrecks, the low cliffs of Eiðisbjarg and **basalt columns** at Vesturey at the northern tip of the island. Richard Serra's **artwork**, made from huge pairs of basalt pillars, rings this part of the island.

Eating

Viðeyjarstofa (☎ 660 7886; ◷ 11.30am-5pm mid-May–Sep) Soup, salad, sandwiches, waffles and coffee are served in this lovely restored mansion.

Getting There & Away

The summer-only **Viðey ferry** (☎ 533 5055) takes a mere five minutes to skip across to the island from Reykjavík. It operates from Sundahöfn (Map pp72–3) from mid-May to the end of September, leaving at 11.15am, 12.15pm, 1.15pm, 2.15pm, 3.15pm, 4.15pm, 5.15pm and 7.15pm, returning 15 minutes later. In winter, there's a reduced weekends-only service. A boat also sails from Reykjavík harbour from June to early September, leaving at noon and returning at 3.30pm. The return fare is Ikr1000/500 per adult/child aged 6 to 18 years.

SELTJARNARNES
pop 4400

Visiting the coast at Seltjarnarnes is a strange feeling. Head 1.5km west from the bustle of Lækjartorg, and you reach a red-and-white **lighthouse**, a strip of **lava-strewn beach** and a windswept **golf course**. Waves rush in, the air has that salt-sea tang, fish-drying racks sit by the shore, and arctic terns scream overhead – it all feels a million miles away from Reykjavík.

Seltjarnarnes is a haven for **birdwatching** – 106 visiting species have been recorded here. The offshore island **Grótta**, where the lighthouse stands, is accessible at low tide but closed from May to July due to nesting birds. Across the water of the fjord there are super **views of Esja** (909m).

One of the nicest ways to get here is along the good coastal path, popular with walkers, joggers and cyclists. You can also take bus 11 from Hlemmur or Lækjartorg bus stations.

KÓPAVOGUR

pop 30,000

Kópavogur, the first suburb south of Reykjavík, is just a short bus ride away – but it feels far from the tourist trail. There are a few culture-vulture attractions in the complex next door to the distinctive arched church.

Sights

The cultural complex **Menningarmiðstöð Kópavogs** (Map pp72–3) contains Kópavogur's **Natural History Museum** (Náttúrufræðistofa Kópavogs; ☎ 570 0430; www.natkop.is; Hamraborg 6a; admission free; ☼ 10am-8pm Mon-Thu, 11am-5pm Fri, 1-5pm Sat & Sun), which explores Iceland's unique geology and wildlife. There's an orca skeleton, a good collection of stuffed animals and geological specimens, and a fish tank housing some of Mývatn lake's weird *Marimo* balls.

You'll also find Iceland's first specially designed concert hall here, built entirely from Icelandic materials (driftwood, spruce and crushed stone). **Salurinn** (☎ 570 0400; www.salurinn.is; Hamraborg 6) has fantastic acoustics – see the website for details of its (mostly classical) concert program. Tickets cost from Ikr1800 to Ikr3000 depending on the concert.

Next door, there are changing modern-art exhibitions in the beautifully designed **Gerðarsafn Art Museum** (Map pp72-3; ☎ 554 4501; www.gerdarsafn.is; Hamraborg 4; ☼ 11am-5pm Tue-Sun). Its small cafe has mountain views.

If you're testing out the city's geothermal pools, try the Olympic-sized **Sundlaug Kópavogs** (Map pp72-3; ☎ 570 0470; Borgarholtsbraut 17; adult/child Ikr280/120; ☼ 6.30am-10pm Mon-Fri, plus 8am-7pm Sat & Sun Apr-Sep & 8am-6pm Sat & Sun Oct-Mar), popular with families, with a children's pool, slide, sauna and hot pots.

Getting There & Away

Buses S1 and S2 leave every few minutes from Hlemmur or Lækjartorg in central Reykjavík, stopping at the Hamraborg stop in Kópavogur (look out for the church). The journey takes about 10 minutes.

HAFNARFJÖRÐUR

pop 25,900

The 'Town in the Lava' rests on a 7000-year-old flow and hides a parallel elfin universe, according to locals. Its old tin-clad houses and lava caves are worth a visit on a sunny summer's day, but in winter, unless the Christmas market is on, tumbleweeds roll.

Hafnarfjörður was once a major trading centre, monopolised by the British in the early 15th century, the Germans in the 16th and the Danes in the 17th. Many of the finest houses in town once belonged to rich merchants. Today the town is spreading like spilt milk, but the endless new-building estates east of the harbour hold nothing of interest for visitors.

Information

The **tourist office** (☎ 585 5500; www.visithafnarfjordur.is; Strandgata 6; ☼ 8am-5pm Mon-Thu, 9am-5pm Fri) is in the town hall (Raðhús). At weekends from June to August, there's tourist help at Pakkhúsið from 11am to 5pm.

Internet access is available at the super **library** (☎ 585 5690; Strandgata 1; ☼ 10am-7pm Mon-Wed, 9am-7pm Thu, 11am-7pm Fri year-round, plus 11am-3pm Sat Oct-May) for Ikr200 per hour.

There are banks with foreign-exchange desks and ATMs at the Fjörður shopping centre, right by the bus station.

Sights

Hafnarfjörður Museum (Byggðasafn Hafnarfjarðar; ☎ 585 5780; admission free) is divided over several buildings. **Pakkhúsið** (Vesturgata 8; ☼ 11am-5pm daily Jun-Aug, 11am-5pm Sat & Sun Sep-May) is the main section, with three storeys of exhibits. The ground floor may interest English visitors. It deals with the British invasion of (neutral) Iceland in WWII – how many of us were taught that in history lessons?! Upstairs, there are displays on the history of Hafnarfjörður, and a small toy museum in the attic.

Next door, **Sívertsen's Hús** (Vesturgata 6; ☼ 11am-5pm Jun-Aug) is a beautiful 19th-century home belonging to merchant Bjarni Sívertsen, once the most important man in Hafnarfjörður. It's decked out with period pieces – a piano, rich drapes, woven wallpaper, mahogany furniture, delicate crockery and silver spoons.

To take on board the huge contrast between Bjarni's lifestyle and the typical impoverished Icelander's, you can visit another home from the same period – the tiny restored fishing hut **Siggubær** (Sigga's House; Kirkjuvegur 10; ☼ 11am-5pm Sat & Sun Jun-Aug), next to the park at Hellisgerði.

New additions to the museum are **Beggubúð** (Begga's Shop; Vesturgata 6; ☼ 11am-5pm Jun-Aug), a shop laid out as it was in 1906; and **Bookless Bungalow** (Vesturgata 32; ☼ 11am-5pm daily Jun-Aug, 11am-5pm Sat & Sun Sep-May), once the home of two Scottish brothers heavily involved in

REYKJAVÍK

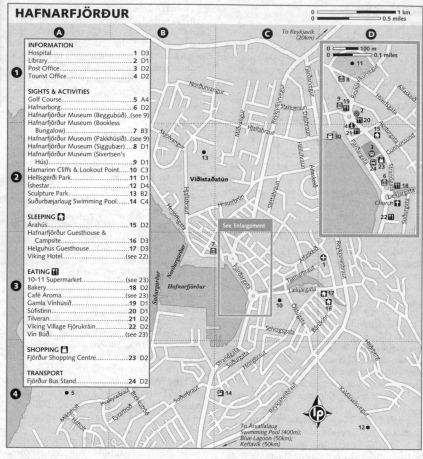

HAFNARFJÖRÐUR

Hafnarfjörður's fishing industry, and now containing an exhibition on fishing.

Well worth a look, the upbeat modern-art gallery **Hafnarborg** (☎ 555 0080; www.hafnarborg.is; Strandgata 34; free admission; ☼ 11am-5pm Wed, Fri-Mon, to 9pm Thu) has two floors of regularly changing exhibitions, and occasional musical concerts.

On a fine day, muse over the 12 large-scale works making up the town's **sculpture park** (Víðistaðatún) or visit **Hellisgerði** (Reykjavíkurvegur), a peaceful park filled with lava grottoes and apparently one of the favourite places of the hidden people. Another pleasant stroll is to the home of elfish royalty, **Hamarinn Cliffs**, where there's a lookout and view disc.

Activities & Tours

From April to October, **Sjósigling** (☎ 562 5700; www.sjosigling.is; adult/6-12yr €45/22) runs three-hour whale-watching trips into Faxaflói bay on the wooden ship *Númi*.

Find out if you have second sight on a 45-minute **Hidden Worlds tour** (☎ 694 2785; www.alfar.is; per person Ikr3300; ☼ 2.30pm Tue & Fri Jun-Aug), a guided storytelling walk around the homes of the hidden people, departing from the tourist office. It's rather pricey, although a copy of the *Hidden Worlds* map is included in the cost, marking the Hafnarfjörður homes of elves, fairies, hermits and dwarves.

Inland there are loads of **walking trails** in the tree plantations around lake Hvaleyrarvatn and on the slopes of the mini-mountain

Helgafell (338m) – shown on the free map *Ratleikur*, available from the tourist office.

There are three good swimming pools in town, including the spanking brand-new indoor **Ásvallalaug** (☎ 512 4050; Ásvellir 2; adult/child Ikr300/100; ☼ 6am-10pm Mon-Fri, 8am-8pm Sat & Sun) and old-time outdoor favourite **Suðurbæjarlaug** (☎ 565 3080; Hringbraut 77; adult/child Ikr300/100; ☼ 6.30am-9.30pm Mon-Fri, 8am-6.30pm Sat, 8am-5.30pm Sun). There's also a **golf course** (☎ 565 3360; www. keilir.is; Steinholt 1), built on a lava field and edged by the ocean.

If you fancy a trot, the horse farm Íshestar (see p84) is based in Hafnarfjörður.

The diving company **Diveiceland.com** (☎ 699 3000; www.diveiceland.com) is also based in Hafnarfjörður. They run dive trips to þingvellir, Akureyri and the Vestmannaeyjar – see the website for upcoming tours.

Festivals

In mid-June the peace is shattered as Viking hordes invade town for the six-day **Viking festival**. Its staged fights and traditional craft demonstrations are centred on the Fjörukráin hotel.

Sleeping

Hafnarfjörður Guesthouse & Campsite (☎ 565 0900, 895 0906; www.hafnarfjordurguesthouse.is; Hjallabraut 51; sb dm/s/d Ikr2000/4000/5000, linen per stay Ikr1000, camping per adult/14-18yr Ikr900/450; ☼ mid-May–mid-Sep; 🖳) Overlooking the strange sculptures of the Víðistaðatún park, this 'guest house', run by the Icelandic Scouts, offers basic hostel-style accommodation in a stylish decking, glass and concrete building. Good facilities include kitchen, washing machine and internet access. The campsite is sheltered by a bushy row of trees; campers can use the guest house kitchen, and also have their own smart new toilet and laundry block. The future of this

place was looking uncertain at the time of writing: phone first.

Árahús (☎ 555 1770; Strandgata 21; s/d Ikr6000/8000; ☼ Jun-Aug) The owner, Smári, keeps up appearances at this very central option on the pedestrian main street. Always fresh and neat, Árahús has a homey feel, with bookshelves, paintings, leather settees in the sitting room, and two good guest kitchens. It becomes a student house from September, but there may still be room for guests – call to check.

Helguhús Guesthouse (☎ 555 2842; www.helguhus. is; Lækjarkinn 8; s/d/tr Ikr5900/8900/11,500) Close to a small lake a 10-minute walk out of town, Helguhús is a well-turned-out town house with cosy, cream-coloured rooms (all with shared bathrooms). Breakfast is included.

Viking Hotel (☎ 565 1213; www.fjorukrain.is; Strandgata 55; s/d Jun-Aug Ikr14,900/16,500, Sep-May Ikr11,300/13,800; 🖳) The over the-top Viking Village complex Fjörukráin also offers 42 hotel rooms. Rather than being stuffed full of swords and battle-axes, they're surprisingly smart modern rooms, with TV, tea-making kit, phone and bathroom. There's also a hot tub and sauna for guests. Breakfast is included.

Eating

Café Aroma (☎ 555 6996; www.aroma.is; Fjörður, Fjarðargata; snacks Ikr750-1700; ☼ 10am-midnight Mon-Wed, to 1am Thu, to 3am Fri & Sat, 1pm-midnight Sun) A satisfying surprise awaits on the upper floor of the shopping centre – this smart cafe has huge windows with stunning sea views. There's a very popular salad bar (Ikr1290). It becomes a bar later on.

Súfistinn (☎ 565 3740; Strandgata 9; snacks Ikr800-1500; ☼ 8.15am-11.30pm Mon-Fri, 10am-11.30pm Sat, 11am-11.30pm Sun) This great cafe-bar is the most cheerful place to eat in town – ladies lunch, readers read, kids play chess, and half

---

HIDDEN WORLDS

Many Icelanders believe that their country is populated by hidden races of little folk – *jarðvergar* (gnomes), *álfar* (elves), *ljósálfar* (fairies), *dvergar* (dwarves), *ljúflingar* (lovelings), *tívar* (mountain spirits), *englar* (angels) and *huldufólk* (hidden people).

Although most Icelanders are embarrassed to say they believe, around 90% of them refuse to say hand-on-heart that they *don't* believe. Many Icelandic gardens feature small wooden cut-outs of *álfhól* (elf houses) to house the little people in case the myths are true.

Hafnarfjörður is believed to lie at the confluence of several strong ley lines (mystical lines of energy) and seems to be particularly rife with these twilight creatures. In fact, construction of roads and homes in Hafnarfjörður is only permitted if the site in question is free from little folk.

of Hafnarfjörður gathers to gossip about the other half. There's a satisfying selection of salads, sarnies, burritos, crêpes, quiches and coffee on offer, and an all-new outside deckng area.

Tilveran (☎ 565 5250; Linnetsstigur 1; mains Ikr2100-3700; ☒ 11.30am-2pm & 6-9pm Mon-Fri, 6-10pm Sat & Sun) On the main pedestrian street, this unassuming little restaurant specialises in seafood, with dishes such as tagliatelle with lobster. Lunch specials are good value, with soup, main and coffee/tea for Ikr1790.

Viking Village Fjörukráin (☎ 565 1213; www.vikingvillage.is; Strandgata 50a & 55; mains Ikr2500-5600; ☒ from 6pm) The tacky but strangely endearing restaurant Fjörukráin is housed in a totally outrageous reconstruction of a Viking long-house, complete with carved pillars and dragons on the roof. It offers Viking feasts (*hákarl*, dried fish, braised lamb, fish soup and *skyr*), served up by singing Vikings. If you're going to be a spoil sport, you can order Icelandic specialities from the Viking-free Fjaran restaurant in the same complex.

Gamla Vínhúsið (☎ 565 1130; Vesturgata 4; pizzas from Ikr1500, mains Ikr3200-4800; ☒ 11am-2pm & 6-9.30pm Mon-Fri, 6-10.30pm Sat & Sun) Essentially a pizzeria, Gamla Vínhúsið has a no-frills dining room. It also serves mains of fish, beef, lamb and lobster.

For self-caterers, there's a tiny **bakery** (☒ 7.45am-5.30pm Mon-Fri, 9am-4pm Sat & Sun) on the main street; or the Fjörður shopping centre has a 10-11 supermarket, a bakery and a Vín Búð liquor store.

Getting There & Around

It's an easy 15-minute bus ride from Reykjavík to the Fjörður bus stand at Hafnarfjörður – bus S1 (Ikr280) leaves every 10 minutes from Hlemmur or Lækjartorg.

If you book ahead, the **Flybus** (☎ 562 1011) to Keflavík airport will stop in Hafnarfjörður; confirm the exact location of the bus stop on booking.

Hafnarfjörður is small and it's easy to get around on foot. **A-Stöðin/Airport Taxis** (☎ 520 1212; www.airporttaxi.is) have taxis standing outside the Fjörður shopping centre.

MOSFELLSBÆR
pop 8200

Fast-growing Mosfellsbær (www.mos fellsbaer.is) has more or less become another of Reykjavík's suburbs, although it's 15km

from the city centre. There's some good **walking** in the surrounding hills, including long day hikes to Þingvellir (p121) and the geo-thermal field at Nesjavellir (p124) – see the pamphlet *Útivist í Mosfellsbæ*, available from the town library.

Nobel Prize–winning author Halldór Laxness lived in Mosfellsbær all his life. His home is now the **Gljúfrasteinn Laxness Museum** (☎ 586 8066; www.gljufrasteinn.is; Mosfellsbær; adult/6-16yr Ikr500/250; ☒ 9am-5pm daily Jun-Aug, 10am-5pm Tue-Sun Sep-May), just outside the suburban centre on the road to Þingvellir, a superb example of an upper-class 1950s house, complete with original furniture and Laxness' fine-art collection. A guided audio-tour leads you round; highlights in-clude the study where Laxness wrote his de-fining works and his beloved Jaguar parked outside.

Near to the museum are two **horse-riding farms** (see p84). If you're in need of retail therapy, the factory outlet shop **Álafoss** (☎ 566 6303; Álafossvegur 23; ☒ 9am-6pm Mon-Fri, to 4pm Sat) sells woollen goods that are slightly cheaper than at the city's tourist shops.

The town **campsite** (☎ 566 8121; sites per person Ikr700; ☒ Jun-Aug) is next to the river Varmá and has toilets, sinks and showers. **Fitjar** (☎ 565 6474; www.fitjarguesthouse.com; s/d without bath-room Ikr6000/9000, with bathroom Ikr7000/10,000), 4km north of Mosfellsbær off Rte 1, is a stylish modern house. Some rooms (three en suite, three with shared bathroom) have views towards Reykjavík and the house is sur-rounded by wonderful countryside. There's a guest kitchen and a laundry.

REYKJANES PENINSULA

As the first bit of the country that most visitors see, the Reykjanes Peninsula might lead you to wonder why you chose Iceland for your holidays. From the air, or from the bus between Keflavík airport and Reykjavík, it can look like the most blighted and dis-heartening place on earth. But cast off your doubts! Nestling among the grey-black lava fields is Iceland's most famous attrac-tion, the Blue Lagoon; and there are plenty of other marvels hiding in this forbidding landscape. Give it time, and the grey waves, smoking earth and bleak, mournful beauty will mesmerise you.

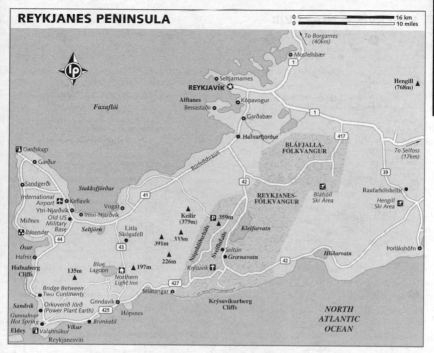

REYKJANES PENINSULA

Most towns – Keflavík, Njarðvík, Vogar – are squeezed into Miðnes, a small spur on the northern coast of the peninsula; the rest is wilderness. Northwest of the international airport are the wave-lashed fishing villages of Garður and Sandgerði, lost places where you can watch migrating birds while the wind blows all your thoughts away. A back road runs south from Keflavík along the rugged coast to Reykjanestá, a wonderful spot full of battered cliffs and strange lava formations.

The only town on the south coast is Grindavík, home to the Saltfish Museum. Northeast lies the Reykjanesfólkvangur wilderness reserve, full of wild lava landscapes and geothermal springs.

Public transport to Keflavík, Grindavík and the Blue Lagoon is fast and frequent, but you'll need private transport to reach more remote parts of the peninsula. Buses within Reykjanes are provided by **SBK** (☎ 420 6000; www.sbk.is). **Blue Line** (☎ 421 1515) runs a service from Reykjanesbær to the Blue Lagoon and Grindavík.

Several tour companies offer guided trips to this melancholy area:

Arctic Horses (☎ 696 1919; Hestabrekka 2; ❦ Jun–mid-Sep) Explore the region on horseback with this company, based 2km east of Grindavík.

ATV Adventures (☎ 857 3001; www.atv-adventures. com; Tangasund 1, Grindavík; from Ikr9900 per person) One-hour quad bike tours around Reykjanes, with pick-up from Keflavík or Reykjavík. Driving licence needed.

Salty Tours (☎ 820 5750, www.saltytours.com; Ikr11,500; ❦ 9am daily) Nine-hour tours of Reykjanes covering Krýsuvík (p119), the Saltfish Museum (p118), Víkingaheimar (Viking World; p113) and the Blue Lagoon (p117).

Volcano Tours (☎ 426 8822; www.volcanotours. is; Víkurbraut 2, Grindavík; 5–6hr tour Ikr17,000) Offers guided walks around Krýsuvík (see p119), stopping to explore lava tunnels and caves before soaking tired muscles in the Blue Lagoon.

KEFLAVÍK & NJARÐVÍK (REYKJANESBÆR)

pop 12,900 (combined)

The twin towns of Keflavík and Njarðvík, on the coast about 50km west of Reykjavík, are a rather ugly mush of suburban boxes and fast-food outlets. Together they're known simply as 'Reykjanesbær'. Although they

REYKJAVÍK

KEFLAVÍK & NJARÐVÍK

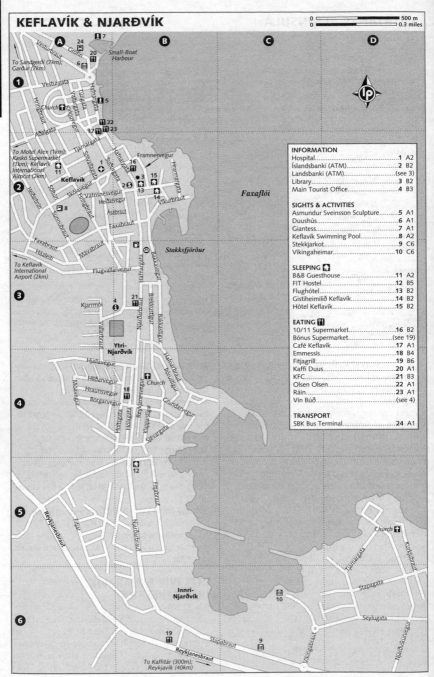

0 ____ 500 m
0 ____ 0.3 miles

INFORMATION
Hospital.....................................1 A2
Íslandsbanki (ATM)...................2 B2
Landsbanki (ATM)................(see 3)
Library.......................................3 B2
Main Tourist Office..................4 B3

SIGHTS & ACTIVITIES
Asmundur Sveinsson Sculpture..........5 A1
Duushús....................................6 A1
Giantess....................................7 A1
Keflavík Swimming Pool............8 A2
Stekkjarkot...............................9 C6
Víkingaheimar........................10 C6

SLEEPING
B&B Guesthouse....................11 A2
FIT Hostel...............................12 B5
Flughótel................................13 B2
Gistiheimilið Keflavík..............14 B2
Hótel Keflavík........................15 B2

EATING
10/11 Supermarket.................16 B2
Bónus Supermarket...........(see 19)
Café Keflavík.........................17 A1
Emmessís...............................18 B4
Fitjagrill.................................19 B6
Kaffi Duus..............................20 A1
KFC...21 B3
Olsen Olsen...........................22 A1
Ráin..23 A1
Vín Búð.............................(see 4)

TRANSPORT
SBK Bus Terminal...................24 A1

REYKJAVIK

aren't somewhere you'd want to spend a massive amount of time, they're the largest settlement on the peninsula and make a good base for exploring the area. If you've an early flight they're handy for the airport.

If you're around at the beginning of September, the well-attended **Night of Lights** (Ljósanótt í Reykjanesbæ; www.ljosanott.is) festival is worth seeing, particularly its grand finale, when waterfalls of fireworks pour over the Bergið cliffs.

Orientation

Keflavík is the biggest of the settlements, with the best visitor facilities. To its east are the suburbs of Ytri-Njarðvík (Outer Njarðvík), which has a youth hostel and a swimming pool, and forlorn little Innri-Njarðvík (Inner Njarðvík).

Information

There's a small **tourist information desk** (☎ 425 0330; www.reykjanes.is; ☺ 6am-8pm Mon-Fri, noon-5pm Sat & Sun) at Keflavík International Airport. At the time of writing, the area's **main tourist office** (☎ 421 3520; www.reykjanes.is; Krossmói 4; ☺ 9am-5pm Mon-Fri, 10am-2pm Sat) had just moved from its central location to a couple of kilometres out of town. Net access is available for Ikr250 per hour. Ask for a free Reykjanes map and the booklet 'Reykjanes Peninsula'.

ATMs and foreign-exchange desks are located at Íslandsbanki and Landsbanki on Hafnargata.

Sights

KEFLAVÍK

In a long red warehouse by the harbour, **Duushús** (☎ 421 3796; Grófin; admission free; ☺ 11am-5pm Mon-Fri, 1-5pm Sat & Sun) is Keflavík's historic cultural centre. There's a permanent exhibition of around 60 of Grímur Karlsson's many hundreds of miniature ships, made compulsively over a lifetime; a gallery where seven international art exhibitions are held each year; and a changing local-history display.

The area around Duushús is the prettiest part of Keflavík; just to the east on the seashore is an impressive **Ásmundur Sveinsson sculpture**, used as a climbing frame by the local kids. To the north, the larger-than-life **Giantess** (Gróf small boat harbour; admission free; ☺ 1-5pm Sat & Sun), a character from Herdís Egilsdóttir's children's books brought to life by a local art collective, sits in a rock-

ing chair in her black cave. There are two interesting artworks in front of the terminal building at **Keflavík International Airport** – Magnús Tómasson's *Þotuhreiður* (Jet Nest) resembles a Concorde emerging from an egg, while Rúrí's *Regnbogi* (Rainbow) is a glittering arch of steel and coloured glass.

Keflavík has started its own Hollywood Blvd – Clint Eastwood, fresh from filming *Flags of Our Fathers* (2006), gamely left his **hand print** outside the theatre on the main street!

NJARÐVÍK

Close to the Bónus supermarket at Innri-Njarðvík is the turf farmhouse **Stekkjarkot** (☎ 894 6725; admission free; ☺ 1-5pm Thu-Sun Jun-Aug), which was abandoned in 1924, and has been refurbished as a tiny folk museum.

A short distance away by the sea shore is the brand-new **Víkingaheimar** (Viking World; ☎ 422 2000; www.vikingaheimar.com; Víkingabraut 1; adult/child Ikr1500/free; ☺ 11am-6pm), an exhibition focusing on Norse exploration. The centrepiece is the 23m-long *Íslendingur*, a curvaceous reconstruction of the Viking Age *Gokstad* longship. It was built almost singlehandedly by Gunnar Marel Eggertsson, who then sailed it from Iceland to New York in 2000 to commemorate the 1000th anniversary of Leif the Lucky's journey to America. The ship is a lovely piece of engineering, shown off to great advantage in the slick new 'Viking Wave' building... but the admission price may leave you pale and breathless.

Activities

Keflavík and Njarðvík both have pools, but the 25m outdoor **swimming pool** (☎ 421 1500; Sunnubraut; adult/child Ikr250/free; ☺ 6.45am-9pm Mon-Fri, 8am-5pm Sat, 9am-4pm Sun) in Keflavík is the better one.

Sleeping

All the sleeping options listed provide a free airport transfer.

KEFLAVÍK

Motel Alex (☎ 421 2800; www.alex.is; Aðalgata 60; sites per person Ikr800, sb dm/tw/hut Ikr2200/12,000/15,900; ☐) A mere two-minute drive from the airport, Alex offers a range of basic accommodation. There's a small campsite for campers; a 14-person dormitory for hostellers; simple bedrooms for guest housers; and small wooden chalets

---

GOODBYE TO THE MILITARY BASE

Keflavík owed a great deal of its former prosperity to the former American military base, which closed down in September 2006.

In 1951 a fear of Reds under the bed led the US to establish a military presence in Iceland, which was a handy submarine fuelling stop between America and Russia. Over the years various passionate protests were made demanding that the troops leave, but all came to nothing. It was only as submarines became more advanced and the Cold War ended that US operations in Iceland were scaled back.

America eventually made tentative noises about a complete closure. Contrarily, this time many Icelanders demanded that the soldiers stay – the jobs that the base provided and the money it brought into the economy were too valuable to lose; and how could Iceland defend itself without an army of its own?

But the units drifted home and the base powered down, until on 30 September 2006 a simple ceremony took place – the US flag was lowered, and the Icelandic flag was raised in its place, ending 55 years of occupation.

Keflavík is sorely missing its soldiers: the town now has the highest unemployment rate in Iceland. There are no cohesive plans for the enormous military zone on Reykjanes. The Lego-like barracks are being used as accommodation for Reykjavík University students, but the shooting ranges, warehouses and miles of razor wire all lie abandoned. It's estimated that it will cost the Icelandic government Ikr4 billion to clean up toxic areas and demolish unwanted buildings…but after the recent economic crisis, it's unlikely to be a priority for some time.

---

for Swiss yodellers (open in summer only). Extras include a guest lounge and kitchen, free luggage storage, and bike and car rental. It's 1.5km from the town centre. The motel is closed from December to mid-April.

B&B Guesthouse (☎ 421 8989, 867 4434; Hringbraut 92; s/d/tr Ikr6500/8700/10,200; ☐) This green-and-yellow guest house above a fresh-fish shop is neat as a pin inside. Rooms are all parqueted and non-idiosyncratic, but there are some quirky touches in the common areas – like the peacock tapestry over the stairs and the cosy curvy settee in the TV room. Prices include free internet and breakfast, and there's a guest kitchen.

Gistiheimilið Keflavík (☎ 420 7000; www.hotel keflavik.is; Vatnsnesvegur 9; s/d Ikr10,800/12,800) Run by Hótel Keflavík, this is a pricey option with slightly old-fashioned rooms (all with shared bathroom and TV), but you do have use of the hotel's four-star facilities. There's also a guest kitchen, and a continental breakfast is included in the price.

Flughótel (☎ 421 5222; www.icehotel.is; Hafnargata 57; r Ikr17,600-20,800; ☐ ☜) The green-and-cream rooms at this typical Icelandair property are clean and modern. Standard rooms are just as comfortable as the deluxe, so don't pay extra unless you really want a kettle and a bathrobe. There's a hot pot, sauna, restaurant and free internet access. Breakfast costs Ikr1200.

Hótel Keflavík (☎ 420 7000; www.hotelkeflavik.is; Vatnsnesvegur 12-14; s/d Ikr22,800/27,800; ☐) Almost next door to Flughótel is the friendly family-run Hótel Keflavík, with its smell of clean laundry and coffee as you enter, and a lobby thrumming with activity. Its rooms are comfy if chintzy, but the place has good facilities – there's a glass-walled restaurant, free internet access, and a large fitness centre with solarium and sauna. Deluxe rooms (with CD player, large TV and bath) are worth the extra Ikr2000. Prices include breakfast.

NJARÐVÍK

FIT Hostel (☎ 421 8889; www.fithostel.is; Fitjabraut 6a; sb/s/d Ikr2200/3800/5200; ☐ ☜) In an industrial estate off busy Rte 41, this hostel has an unfortunate location but decent facilities – good, clean rooms (holding up to seven people), left luggage (Ikr250), internet access (Ikr600 per hour) and free wi-fi, laundry (Ikr600) and a hot tub. You can catch buses to Reykjavík and Keflavík in front of the hostel, but a car or a love of walking through concrete suburbs would be helpful here. Breakfast (Ikr1000) is available mid-May to August.

Eating

KEFLAVÍK

There are enough drive-through snack bars and greasy grills in Keflavík to give you an instant burger-induced coronary. For more civilised fare, there are several places along the main street; plus the two hotels have high-quality restaurants.

Olsen Olsen (☎ 421 4457; Hafnargata 17; snacks Ikr700-1000; ☺ 11am-10pm) In the 1950s, thanks to rock and roll, Keflavík was the coolest place in Iceland. This American-style diner transports locals back to the glory days, with shiny silver tables, red plastic seats and pictures of Elvis on the walls. There's a gigantic range of hoagies, as well as sandwiches, burgers and a kids' meal.

Café Keflavík (☎ 421 4919; Hafnargata 26; ☺ noon-10pm Mon-Thu, noon-midnight Fri & Sat) Above a tattoo shop on the main street, this chilled-out cafe-bar has a long coffee menu, including quirky alcoholic drinks such as 'Lilly Loves Cinnamon' and 'Nutty Icelander'. Vegans and those with dairy allergies have a choice of soya-based beverages, and there are bagels and cakes to nibble.

Kaffi Duus (☎ 421 7080; Duusgata 10; mains Ikr2900-3700; ☺ kitchen noon-10pm, bar to 1am Fri & 2am Sat) This friendly nautical-themed cafe-restaurant-bar, decorated with whale vertebrae and giant crabs, overlooks the small-boat harbour and cliffs. It serves generous platefuls of fish, fish, fish, fresh out of the sea, with a few pasta dishes, salads and burgers thrown in. It's a popular evening hangout with occasional live bands.

Ráin (☎ 421 4601; www.rain.is; Hafnargata 19a; mains Ikr2950-4100; ☺ kitchen 11am-3pm & 6-10pm, bar to 1am Sun-Thu, to 3am Fri & Sat) If you visit on a day like we did, Ráin's renowned panoramic views of sea, mountains and distant Reykjavik will be nothing but mist! Keflavík's finest restaurant is large but friendly and serves a familiar menu of Icelandic fish, lobster, lamb and beef.

Self-caterers have plenty of supermarkets to choose from, including the 24-hour **10-11** (Hafnargata 53-55) and a Kaskó close to Motel Alex. There's also a **Vín Búð** (☎ 421 5699; Krossmói; ☺ 11am-6pm Mon-Thu, to 7pm Fri, to 4pm Sat) on the same out-of-town lot as the tourist office.

NJARÐVÍK

Unless you love drive-throughs and supermarkets, you're going to go hungry in Njarðvík. Choose from the car-friendly **Emmessís**, **KFC** or **Fitjagrill**; or the **Bónus supermarket** (Fitjum; ☺ noon-6.30pm Mon-Thu, 10am-7.30pm Fri, 10am-6pm Sat, noon-6pm Sun) or **Kaffitár** (☎ 420 2710; www.kaffitar.ls; Stapabraut 7; ☺ 9am-5pm Mon-Fri, 11am-4pm Sat) off Rte 41.

Getting There & Around
TO/FROM THE AIRPORT

Most of Reykjanesbær's accommodation options offer free airport transfers for guests. A taxi will cost about Ikr2500 – call **Airport Taxi** (☎ 420 1212; www.airporttaxi.is) or **Hreyfill-Bæjarleiðir** (☎ 588 5522; www.hreyfill.is). For information on the Flybus between the airport and Reykjavík, see p103.

AIR

Apart from flights to Greenland and the Faeroes, all of Iceland's international flights use Keflavík International Airport. For more information, see p335.

BUS

SBK (☎ 420 6000; www.sbk.is) runs seven daily buses between Reykjanesbær and the BSÍ bus station in Reykjavík from Monday to Friday, and three on Saturday and Sunday. The fare is Ikr1600/800/1150 per adult/child four to 11 years/12 to 18 years. A couple of buses run on weekdays from Keflavík to Sandgerði and Garður – see below for details.

The **Blue Line** (Bláa Línan; ☎ 420 6000, 425 0381) service operates three or four buses per day between Keflavík airport, Reykjanesbær and the Blue Lagoon. A one-way ticket costs Ikr1150.

CAR

Four car-rental companies have stands at the international airport: **Avis** (☎ 491 4000; www.avis.is), **Bílaleiga Akureyrar/National** (☎ 425 0300, 840 6042; www.holdur.is), **Budget** (☎ 521 5551, 562 6060; www.budget.is) and **Hertz** (☎ 522 4430, 505 0600; www.hertz.is); prices cost around Ikr18,000 for a day's hire in summer.

NORTHWESTERN REYKJANES

The western edge of the Reykjanes Peninsula is rugged and exposed – perfect if you love wild rain-lashed cliffs and beaches! There are several fishing villages and some quirky sights to be seen among the lava fields.

GETTING THERE & AWAY

On weekdays, **SBK** (☎ 420 6000; www.sbk.is) has two buses (Ikr570/285/350 per adult/child four to 11 years/12 to 18 years) from Keflavík to Sandgerði (10 minutes) and Garður (15 minutes), with one bus on Saturday and Sunday. Heading back to Keflavík, you should book with SBK.

Garðskagi

From Keflavík, if you follow Rte 41 for 9km, on through the village of Garður, you'll reach the beautiful wind-battered Garðskagi **headland**, one of the best places in Iceland for bird spotting – it's a big breeding ground for sea birds, and it's often the place where migratory species first touch down. It's also possible to see seals, and maybe whales, from here.

Two splendid **lighthouses**, one old and one new, add drama – you can get near-360-degree sea views from the old lighthouse. There's also a small **folk museum** (☎ 422 7220; www.svgardur.is; admission free; ⊙ 1-5pm Apr-Oct), filled with a pleasing mishmash of fishing boats, birds' eggs and sewing machines. It contains the balconied **Flösin Cafeteria** (☎ 422 7214; ⊙ 1-5pm daily Apr-Dec, 1-5pm Fri, Sat & Sun Jan-Mar, later in Jul & Aug), with superb views over the ocean to Snæfellsjökull.

There's a tranquil, free camping area by the lighthouse, with toilets and fresh water.

Sandgerði

Five kilometres south of Garður, it's worth stopping at this industrious fishing village to see the classroom-like but interesting **Fræðasetrið nature centre** (☎ 423 7551; Gerðavegur 1; adult/child Ikr400/300; ⊙ 9am-noon & 1-5pm Mon-Fri, 1-5pm Sat & Sun year-round), where there are stuffed Icelandic creatures (including a monstrous moth-eaten walrus), jars of pickled things (look out for the freaky Gorgonocephalus), and a small aquarium with sea squirts, crabs and anemones.

There are some quite nice **beaches** on the coast south of Sandgerði, and the surrounding marshes are frequented by more than 170 species of **birds**. About 7km south, you can walk to the ruins of the fishing village **Básendar**, which was destroyed by a giant tidal wave in 1799.

SOUTHWESTERN REYKJANES

The vast lava flows at Reykjanesviti were spewed out by a series of small shield volcanoes. The area is crisscrossed by walking tracks that are marked on the *Reykjanes* map, available from most tourist offices, including those in Keflavík and at the international airport. However, the terrain is tough and not all the paths are clearly marked.

GETTING THERE & AWAY

There are no public bus routes in this area. If you're driving, you'll need enough petrol to last you from Keflavík to Grindavík.

Keflavík to Reykjanesviti

If you turn off Rte 41 onto Rte 44 just outside Keflavík, you'll first pass the deserted barracks, barbed-wire fences and tank ranges of the **old US military base** (see the boxed text, p114).

After several kilometres the road zooms past the fading fishing village of **Hafnir**. There's nothing much to see here – just humps and bumps in a field, thought to be a 9th-century longhouse belonging to Ingólfur Arnarson's foster brother, and the anchor of the 'ghost ship' *Jamestown*, which drifted ashore mysteriously in 1870 with a full cargo of timber but no crew.

About 8km south, a 30-minute walk from the road will take you to the sea cliffs of **Hafnaberg**, an important bird-nesting area and a good lookout point for whales.

A little further south, just off the main road, is the so-called **Bridge Between Two Continents**. It's basically a photo stop – a bridge spanning a sand-filled gulf between the North American and European plates.

In the far southwest of the peninsula the landscape breaks down into wild volcanic crags and sea cliffs. The black beaches near Sandvíkur stood in for Iwo Jima in Clint Eastwood's WWII epic *Flags of Our Fathers* (2006). Several bizarre-looking **factories** here exploit geothermal heat to produce salt from sea water and to provide electricity for the national grid. **Orkuverið Jörð** (Power Plant Earth; ☎ 422 5200; www.powerplantearth.is; adult/child Ikr1000/600; ⊙ 11.30am-3.30pm May-Oct, 11.30am-3.30pm Thu-Sun Nov-Apr), based inside one of these factories, is an interesting interactive exhibition about the world's energy supplies. You also get a glimpse into the vast, spotless turbine hall, and can meander along a concrete culvert down to the seashore afterwards to watch 67°C waste water steaming into the cold waves. (It's much more exciting than that sentence sounds!)

One of the most wild and wonderful spots is **Valahnúkur**, where a dirt track leads off the main road through 13th-century lava fields down to the most desolate cliffs imaginable. You can clamber up to the ruins of the oldest lighthouse (1878) in Iceland, destroyed by a devastating earthquake, and contemplate the fragility of life and the futility of everything. From here you can see the flat-topped rocky crag of **Eldey**, 14km out to sea, which is home to the world's largest gannet colony. Some claim the last great auk was killed and eaten here, though this is disputed by Faeroe islanders, who insist that the event occurred at Stóra Dímun. Today Eldey is a protected bird reserve.

Back towards the main road is a steaming multicoloured **geothermal area**. This includes the hot spring **Gunnuhver**, named after the witch Gunna, who was trapped by magic and dragged into the boiling water to her death.

Pick a bleak and blasted day to appreciate the last natural wonder before reaching Grindavík. About 7km east of Gunnuhver, slabs of cracked black lava are battered by grey breakers and waves spray up inside the churning, cauldron-shaped hole **Brimketil**.

BLUE LAGOON

As the Eiffel Tower is to Paris, as Disney World is to Florida, so the **Blue Lagoon** (Bláa Lónið; ☎ 420 8800; www.bluelagoon.com; adult/12-15yr €23/7, towel/swimsuit/robe hire €4/4/7; ☟ 8am-9pm Jun-Aug, 10am-8pm Sep-May; ☍) is to Iceland...with all the positive and negative connotations that implies. Those who say it's too expensive, too clinical, too crowded are kind of right, but you'll be missing something special if you don't go.

Set in a tortured black lava field, just off the road between Keflavík and Grindavík, the milky-blue spa is fed by water (at a perfect 38°C) from the futuristic Svartsengi geothermal plant. The silver towers of the plant provide an off-the-planet scene-setter for your swim; add roiling clouds of steam and people daubed in blue-white silica mud, and you're in another world.

The lagoon has been imaginatively landscaped with hot pots, wooden decks and a piping-hot waterfall that delivers a powerful hydraulic massage – it's like being pummelled by a troll. There are also two steam rooms and a sauna.

The superheated sea water is rich in blue-green algae, mineral salts and fine silica mud, which condition and exfoliate the skin – sounds like advertising-speak, but you really do come out as soft as a baby's bum. The water is always hottest near the vents where it emerges, and the surface is several degrees warmer than the bottom.

For extra relaxation, you can lie on a floating lilo and have a masseuse knead out your knots (€13/26/35/66 per 10/20/30/60 minutes); be aware, though – you need to book spa treatments sometimes days in advance. The complex also includes a cafe, restaurant and shop selling Blue Lagoon products.

Three warnings: the Blue Lagoon requires the same thorough naked prepool showering that applies in all Icelandic swimming pools; the water can corrode silver and gold, so leave watches and jewellery in your locker; you'll also need bucketfuls of conditioner afterwards – all that briny water plays havoc with your hair.

Many people make the lagoon a stop on the way to/from the airport. If you travel with Reykjavík Excursions, luggage storage is free; otherwise, queue at the hut outside the complex to leave your bags (Ikr500 for up to three pieces of luggage).

Sleeping & Eating

Northern Light Inn (☎ 426 8650; www.northernlightinn .is; s/d/tr €140/190/235; ☍) Nearby, and with similarly unearthly views, this recently enlarged bungalow hotel now has 32 spacious en-suite rooms with phone and satellite TV. There's a sunny sitting room with free tea and coffee, and free transfers are provided to the international airport and the lagoon (although the latter is easily walkable).

Blue Lagoon – Clinic (☎ 420 8806; www.bluelagoon .com; s/d €150/220; ☍ ☞ ☎) Guests don't have to be undergoing treatment to stay at the Blue Lagoon clinic, a 10-minute walk across the lava field from Iceland's most famous attraction. Rooms are soothing and modern, with heated-floor bathrooms, and each has a small porch from where you can regard the surrounding moonscape. Rates include breakfast and entry to the lagoon.

Kristjana's Kitchen (mains Ikr1700-3200; ☟ 11.30am-1pm & 6-9pm; ☞) The Northern Light Inn's fab panoramic restaurant serves 'hearty Nordic soul food' – this means herring platters, fish dumplings, smoked lamb and other Icelandic favourites; plus there's a choice of vegie dishes.

Getting There & Away

The lagoon is 50km southwest of Reykjavík, but there are plenty of bus services that run there year-round. You'll need to book in advance.

The cheapest is the **Blue Lagoon Bus Service** (☎ 511 2600; www.bustravel.is), which leaves six times daily from the BSÍ bus terminal in Reykjavík, or you can arrange to be picked up from certain hotels. You can return to the city, or three services continue to the international airport. The return journey (or journey there and then onward to the airport) is a bargain – Ikr5000, including lagoon admission.

Alternatively, **Reykjavík Excursions** (☎ 580 5400; www.re.is) runs slightly more frequently, at a cost of Ikr5900 including lagoon admission.

GRINDAVÍK
pop 2850

Grindavík (www.grindavik.is), the only settlement on the south coast of Reykjanes, is one of Iceland's most important fishing centres. If this were an English seaside town, its waterfront would be full of B&Bs, pubs and shops selling sticks of rock; here, all flimflam is rejected in favour of working jetties, cranes and warehouses. The busy harbour and tourist-free town are actually quite refreshing.

Sights & Activities

The main attraction here is **Saltfisksetur Íslands** (Saltfish Museum; ☎ 420 1190; www.saltfisksetur.is; Hafnargata 12a; adult/under 8yr/8-16yr Ikr500/free/250; 11am-6pm), a pretty well done museum dedicated to explaining the fish-salting industry. An audioguide (English, German or French) leads you over wooden piers to tableaux showing various stages of the process. It's probably not for everyone, but if you're interested in Icelandic history, an understanding of the saltfish industry is vital – after all, it was so important that the country's coat-of-arms was a filleted cod until 1904. The museum also serves as a **tourist information desk** (11am 6pm).

There's a good modern **swimming pool** (☎ 426 7555; Austurvegur 1; adult/under 16yr Ikr300/free; 7am-9pm Mon-Fri, 10am-5pm Sat & Sun summer, to 3pm Sat & Sun winter), with a rather litter-strewn, graffitied reconstruction of a **Viking temple** outside.

Sleeping & Eating

The town **campsite** (☎ 660 7323; Austurvegur 26; per person Ikr750; Jun–mid-Sep), near the swimming pool, has just undergone a massive facelift and is now one of the country's flashiest.

Heimagisting Borg (☎ 895 8686, 896 8685; bjorksv@hive.is; Borgarhraun 2; s/d Ikr6500/9000;) This wonderfully clean and congenial guest house is one of the best-value places to stay in Reykjanes. Mellow creamy-pink rooms have big squishy beds, there's a TV lounge with English satellite channels, internet computer, washing

machine and kitchen, and prices include a great little serve-yourself breakfast. This is definitely a place you'd come back to.

Besides the usual petrol-station grills and snack bars, Grindavík has several good eating options.

Lukku Láki (☎ 426 9999; Hafnargata 6; dishes Ikr900-2500; 6-9pm Tue-Thu & Sun, to 3am Fri & Sat) The Lucky Luke sports bar-bistro is a crazy mixed-up place – African masks, big-screen football, a bar made from old five-aurar pieces, fairy lights and blues on the stereo all compete for your attention. But the confusion somehow makes for a great atmosphere. Add free internet access, beer and huge portions of well-priced bar meals (salmon, burgers, chips, chicken nuggets) and you're on to a winner.

Veitingahúsið Brim (☎ 426 8570; www.brimveitingar.is; Hafnargata 9; mains Ikr1800-3400; lunch & dinner summer, lunch only winter) This fish restaurant, just opposite the museum, offers a taste of saltfish – with spinach and tomatoes in white-wine sauce – so you can see what the fuss is about. You can also sample lamb, beef and chicken mains, or go for a lighter burger (including one for vegetarians), soup or sandwich snack.

Salthúsið (☎ 426 9700; www.salthusid.is; Stamphólsvegur 2; dishes Ikr2300-4500; 5-10pm Mon & Wed-Fri, 12.30pm-midnight Sat, 12.30-10pm Sun) The classy wooden Salthúsið is the first dedicated saltfish restaurant in Iceland. The *baccalao* is prepared in different ways (with ginger, chilli, olives and garlic; au gratin; as nibbly nuggets; or with mushrooms, red onion and capers), so there's plenty of variety. If the idea of saltfish doesn't grab you, fall back on perfectly prepared lobster, chicken or lamb.

Getting There & Away

Three scheduled daily buses travel between Reykjavík and Grindavík (Ikr1400, one hour), past the Blue Lagoon.

REYKJANESFÓLKVANGUR

For a taste of Iceland's weird and empty countryside, you could visit this 300-sq-km wilderness reserve, a mere 40km from Reykjavík. Its three showpieces are **Kleifarvatn**, a deep grey lake with submerged hot springs and black-sand beaches; the spitting, bubbling geothermal zone at **Seltún**; and the southwest's largest bird cliffs, the epic **Krýsuvíkurberg**.

The reserve was established in 1975 to protect the elaborate lava formations created by the Reykjanes ridge volcanoes. The whole area is crossed by dozens of **walking trails**, which mostly follow old paths between abandoned farms. They're detailed in the good pamphlet map *Walking & Hiking in Krýsuvík* (in English), available from the tourist offices at Keflavík or Hafnarfjörður. There are parking places at the beginnings of most of the popular walks, including the loop around Kleifarvatn, and the tracks along the craggy Sveifluháls and Núpshlíðarháls ridges.

GETTING THERE & AWAY

There's no public transport to the park, but you could get here on an organised bus trip. Reykjavík Excursions and other tour agents offer six-hour tours through the Reykjanes Peninsula (see p86).

Otherwise, you'll need a bike or hire car. Follow unsurfaced Rte 42 from Hafnarfjörður, which continues eastwards through lava fields to Þorlákshöfn, passing more dramatic volcanic scenery. Rte 427 from Grindavík will also get you to the reserve.

Kleifarvatn

This deep and creepy lake sits in a volcanic fissure, surrounded by wind-warped lava cliffs and black-sand shores. Legend has it that a worm-like monster the size of a whale lurks below the surface – but the poor creature is running out of room, as the lake has been shrinking ever since two major earthquakes shook the area in 2000. For a macabre fictional slant on this event, seek out Arnaldur

Indríðason's thriller *The Draining Lake* (2007). A walking trail runs right around the water's edge, offering dramatic views and the crunch of volcanic cinders underfoot.

Krýsuvík & Seltún

The volatile **geothermal field** Austurengjar, about 2km south of Kleifarvatn, is often called Krýsuvík after the nearby abandoned farm. Even by Icelandic standards, this area is prone to geological tantrums. The temperature below the surface is 200°C and the water is boiling as it emerges from the ground. A borehole was sunk here to provide energy for Hafnarfjörður during the 1990s, but it exploded without warning in 1999 and the project was abandoned.

At Seltún, boardwalks meander round a cluster of **hot springs**. The steaming vents, mud pots and solfataras (volcanic vents) shimmer with rainbow colours from the strange minerals in the earth, and the provocative eggy stench will make a lasting impression.

Nearby is the lake **Grænavatn**, an old explosion crater filled with weirdly green water – caused by a combination of minerals and warmth-loving algae.

Krýsuvíkurberg

South of Seltún, about half a kilometre past Krýsuvík church, a dirt track leads down to the coast at **Krýsuvíkurberg**. These bleak black cliffs stretch for 4km and are packed with puffins, guillemots and other sea birds in summer. A walking path runs along their length.

Southwest Iceland

SOUTHWEST ICELAND

Geysers spout, waterfalls topple, black beaches stretch into the distance, and brooding volcanoes and glittering ice caps line the horizon. The beautiful southwest contains many of Iceland's most famous natural wonders – and is consequently a relatively crowded corner of the country. But get off the Ring Road (Rte 1) and there are plenty of quiet valleys and splashing streams you can have all to yourself.

Almost everyone who comes to Iceland visits the Golden Circle, east of Reykjavík. Here you'll find the gorgeous national park Þingvellir, a Unesco World Heritage Site; the bubbling springs and spouting geysers at Geysir; and one of the country's most dazzling rainbow-tinged waterfalls, Gullfoss.

On the coast, you can visit the entertaining little fishing villages Eyrarbakki and Stokkseyri, or walk the black beaches at drop-dead beautiful Vík. Just offshore, the charming Vestmannaeyjar are filled with fearless puffins and friendly people. Inland you'll find one of Iceland's best museums at Skógar; important saga-age ruins in the Þjórsárdalur valley; or wonderful walking at Þórsmörk. And, if you want more of an adrenalin rush, try snowmobiling or dog sledding on the Mýrdalsjökull ice cap.

HIGHLIGHTS

- Wait for water to shoot skywards at **Geysir** (p126), or watch it tumbling down at **Gullfoss** (p127)
- Go dog sledding or snowmobiling on **Mýrdalsjökull ice cap** (p146)
- Scream at the **Stokkseyri Ghost Centre** (p137), or enjoy a dose of culture at the brilliant **Skógar Folk Museum** (p145)
- Fall in love with puffins, volcanoes and teetering cliffs on the wonderful **Vestmannaeyjar** (p149)
- Stroll black-sand beaches at **Vík** (p147) and **Reynisfjara** (p147), and watch otherworldly ocean sunsets from nearby **Dyrhólaey** (p146)

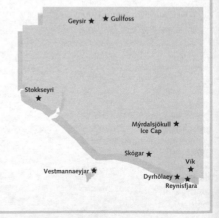

Getting There & Around

For information on bus routes and schedules in the southwest, see the Getting There & Away sections for individual destinations or contact the **BSÍ bus station** (☎ 562 1011; www.bsi.is), or bus companies **Reykjavík Excursions** (☎ 580 5400; www.re.is) or **Trex** (☎ 551 1166; www.bogf.is).

Frequent organised tours visit this area (see p86 for ideas). Hiring a car can work out cheaper; most southwestern roads are suitable for 2WDs.

THE GOLDEN CIRCLE

Gullfoss, Geysir and Þingvellir are unique sites commonly referred to as the Golden Circle. These sites make up Iceland's major tourist destinations, offering visitors the opportunity to see a wild, roaring waterfall, spouting hot springs and the country's most important historical area in one condensed, doable-in-a-day tour. Although they're mobbed by coach parties year-round, they're still worth visiting for their undeniable natural beauty.

Hiring a car will mean you'll be able to enjoy other nearby highlights. Nesjavellir is great for its surreal other-planet landscape; on clear days, the active volcano Hekla is a sublime sight; and there are interesting Viking ruins in the scenic Þjórsárdalur valley.

ÞINGVELLIR

This **national park**, 23km east of Reykjavík, is Iceland's most important historical site and a place of lonely beauty. The country's first national park, it was finally made a Unesco World Heritage Site in 2004.

The Vikings established the world's first democratic parliament, the Alþing, here in AD 930. As with many saga sites, there aren't many Viking remains to be seen, but the park has a superb natural setting, inside an immense rift valley caused by the separating North American and Eurasian tectonic plates. Its undulating mossy lava flows are scarred by streams and rocky fissures. It's particularly awesome in autumn, when the dwarf birch forests glow with brilliant red, orange and yellow hues.

History

Many of Iceland's first settlers had run-ins with royalty back in mainland Scandinavia.

These chancers and outlaws decided that they could live happily without kings in the new country, instead creating district *þings* (assemblies) where justice could be served.

Eventually, a nationwide *þing* became necessary. One man was dispatched to Norway to study law, while his foster brother travelled the country looking for a suitable site. Bláskógur – now Þingvellir (Parliament Fields) – lay at a crossroads by a huge fish-filled lake. It had plenty of firewood and a setting that would make even the most tedious orator dramatic, so it fitted the bill perfectly. Every important decision affecting Iceland was argued out on this plain – new laws were passed, marriage contracts were made, and even the country's religion was decided here. The annual parliament was also a great social occasion, thronging with traders and entertainers.

Over the following centuries, escalating violence between Iceland's most powerful men led to the breakdown of law and order. Governance was surrendered to the Norwegian crown and the Alþing was stripped of its legislative powers in 1271. It functioned solely as a courtroom until 1798, before being dissolved entirely. When it regained its powers in 1843, members voted to move the meeting place to Reykjavík.

Information

On Rte 36, the **Park Service Centre** (þjónustumiðstöð; ☎ 482 2660; www.thingvellir.is) contains a cafe (open every day between February and mid-November, weekends only November, December and January, and a seasonal tourist desk, with books and maps for sale (open from 8.30am to 8pm Monday to Friday, till 10pm Saturday & Sunday May to mid-September).

Above the park, on top of the Almannagjá rift, is an interesting **multimedia centre** (admission free; ☺ 9am-7pm daily Jun-Aug, 9am-5pm daily Apr, May, Sep & Oct, 9am-5pm weekends Nov-Mar) exploring the area's nature and history.

Sights & Activities
THE ALÞING

The Alþing used to convene annually at the **Lögberg** (Law Rock), between the Flosagjá and Nikulásargjá fissures. This was where the *lögsögumaður* (law speaker) recited the law to the assembled parliament each year. After Iceland's conversion to Christianity, the site shifted to the foot of Almannagjá cliffs, which acted as a natural amplifier, broadcasting the

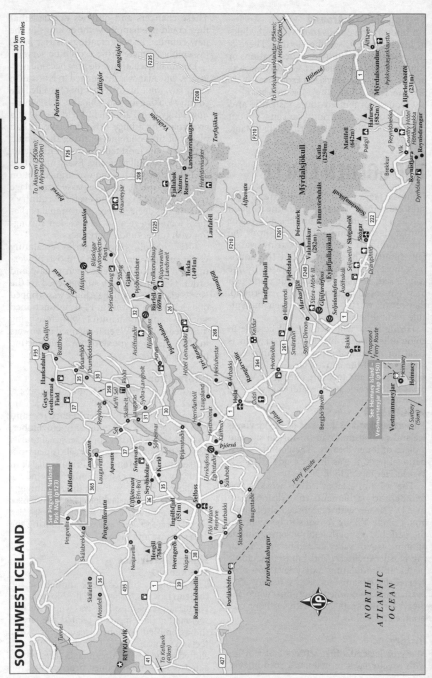

SOUTHWEST ICELAND

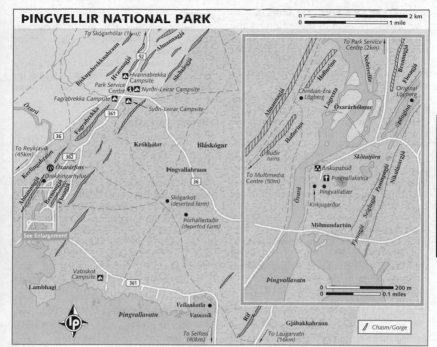

ÞINGVELLIR NATIONAL PARK

voices of the speakers across the assembled crowds. The site is marked by a flagpole, and a path leads down to it from the multimedia centre at the top of Almannagjá.

Decisions were reached by the Lögrétta (Law Council), made up of 146 men (48 voting members, 96 advisers and two bishops) who are thought to have assembled at **Neðrivellir** (Low Fields), the flat area in front of the cliffs.

FISSURES & WATERFALLS

The Þingvellir plain is precariously situated on a tectonic plate boundary – here, North America and Europe are tearing away from each other at a rate of 1mm to 18mm per year. As a result, the plain is scarred by a series of dramatic fissures, including the great rift **Almannagjá**. A broad track follows the fault from the multimedia centre on top of the cliffs to the plain below.

The river Öxará cuts across the rift, tumbling towards the lake in a series of pretty cascades. The most impressive is **Öxarárfoss**, hidden away behind the eastern lip of the fault. The pool **Drekkingarhylur** was used to drown women found guilty of infanticide, adultery or other serious crimes.

There are other smaller fissures on the eastern edge of the plain. During the 17th century nine men accused of witchcraft were burnt at the stake in **Brennugjá** (Burning Chasm). Nearby are the fissures of **Flosagjá** (named after a slave who jumped his way to freedom) and **Nikulásargjá** (after a drunken sheriff discovered dead in the water). The southern end of Nikulásargjá is known as **Peningagjá** (Chasm of Coins) for the thousands of coins tossed into it by visitors, a tradition started by the Danish king Frederick VIII in 1907.

BÚÐIR

On the left of the path as you walk down Almannagjá are the ruins of various *búðir* (booths). These small stone-and-turf shelters were where parliament-goers camped; and they also acted like stalls at today's music festivals, selling beer, food and vellum to the assembled crowds. Most of the remains date from the 17th and 18th centuries; the largest, and one of the oldest, is **Biskupabúð**, which belonged to the bishops of Iceland and is located north of the church.

SOUTHWEST ICELAND

ÞINGVALLABÆR & ÞINGVALLAKIRKJA

The little farmhouse in the bottom of the rift, **Þingvallabær** wass built for the 1000th anniversary of the Alþing in 1930 by the state architect Guðjón Samúelsson. It's now used as the park warden's office and prime minister's summer house.

Behind the farmhouse, **Þingvallakirkja** (☼ 9am-7.30pm mid-May–Aug) is one of Iceland's first churches. The original was consecrated in the 11th century, but the current wooden building only dates from 1859. Inside are several bells from earlier churches, a 17th-century wooden pulpit, and a painted altarpiece from 1834. The Independence-era poets Jónas Hallgrímsson and Einar Benediktsson are interred in the small cemetery behind the church.

ÞINGVALLAVATN

At a whopping 84 sq km, **Þingvallavatn** is Iceland's largest lake. Pure glacial water from Langjökull glacier filters through bedrock for 40km before emerging here. It's joined by the hot spring Vellankatla, which spouts from beneath the lava field on the northeastern shore.

Þingvallavatn is an important refuelling stop for **migrating birds** (including the great northern diver, barrow's golden-eye and harlequin duck). Weirdly, its waters are full of *bleikja* (Arctic char) that have been isolated for so long that they've evolved into four subspecies.

An unforgettable way of exploring the lake is by **scuba diving** (see p64) in the fissure Silfra, where the visibility is stunning.

WALKS AROUND ÞINGVELLIR

Well-marked trails criss-cross the national park, shown in the Icelandic leaflet *Gönguleiðir í Þingvellir* (Ikr500) sold at the Park Service Centre. Serious walkers might think of investing in the topographical map sheets 1613 I *Þingvellir* and 1613 II *Hengill*, both on a scale of 1:50,000. Most trails converge on the abandoned farm at Skógarkot. Southeast lie the ruins of another farm, Þórhallastaðir, where ale was brewed and served to 13th-century Alþing participants. The 5km walk from Þingvellir to the western rim of the continental rift takes a few hours.

Walking trails at the southern end of Lake Þingvallavatn cut south across the slopes of the volcano Hengill (768m) to Hveragerði and the Hengill ski area, just off Rte 1. See p132 for more information.

Tours

Various companies offer Golden Circle tours to Þingvellir, Geysir and Gullfoss from around Ikr8600 (see p86).

Within the park, there are free one-hour English **guided tours** (☼ departures 10am & 3pm Mon-Fri Jun-Aug) in summer, setting off from the church.

Sleeping & Eating

Unfortunately, the 111-year-old Hótel Valhöll, the only hotel within Þingvellir National Park, burned to the ground in July 2009. In these troubled economic times there are no signs of a rush to rebuild, so for now the five **Þingvellir campsites** (☎ 482 2660; sites per person Ikr800; ☼ Jun–mid-Sep), overseen by the Park Service Centre, are the only place to stay at Þingvellir. The best are the two at Leirar, near the cafe – Syðri-Leirar is the biggest and Nyrðri-Leirar has laundry facilities. Fagrabrekka and Hvannabrekka are for campers only (no cars). The fifth campsite, Vatnskot, is down by the lake side.

Getting There & Away

The easiest way to get here is on a Golden Circle tour (p86) or in a hire car.

From mid-June to August the daily **Reykajvík Excursions** (☎ 580 5400; www.re.is) bus service 6/6A runs at 8.30am from Reykjavík to Þingvellir, stopping for 45 minutes at the Park Service Centre before continuing to Geysir, Gullfoss and back to Reykjavík (return trip Ikr7000).

There's no public transport to the southern end of Þingvallavatn.

AROUND ÞINGVELLIR
Nesjavellir

Whenever you step into that pongy shower in Reykjavík, think of the weird shining **Nesjavellir geothermal plant**, southwest of Þingvallavatn. It's here that boreholes plunge 2km into the earth, bringing up water heated to 380°C by toasting-hot bedrock. It drives a series of huge turbines that produce the city's electricity. Hot water is also channelled off to Reykjavík, 23km away. The whole system is explained at the **visitor centre** (☎ 516 7508; www.or.is; ☼ 9am-6pm Jun-Aug), where you can admire the immaculate-looking machinery; and there are **hot rivers** and **steaming vents** all around (stick to paths). The visitor centre also has leaflets showing walking trails in the area.

Icelandair's sleek new **Hótel Hengill** (☎ 482 3415; hengill@icehotels.is; s/d Ikr15,500/18,700; 💻 🛜), just off Rte 360, perches on the toes of the volcano Hengill, overlooking the gleaming geothermal plant and its steaming, eggy-smelling surroundings, and lake Þingvallavatn. It offers a serene setting; smart, comfortable rooms with flatscreen TVs, kettles, leather sofas and striking forged-iron artwork on the walls; a good restaurant; a gym and sauna – and hot pots, of course! Breakfast costs an extra Ikr1200.

Iceland Excursions (Gray Line Iceland; ☎ 540 1313; www.icelandexcursions.is, www.grayline.is) has a Golden Circle Classic day tour (Ikr11,000) that visits Nesjavellir, Þingvellir, Gullfoss, Geysir and Hveragerði (although in winter, access to the geothermal plant may not be possible).

You can also walk to Nesjavellir from Hveragerði via the volcano Hengill (see p132).

Laugarvatn
pop 200

Laugarvatn (Hot Springs Lake) wasn't named this way for nothing – this agreeable body of water is fed not only by streams running from the misty fells behind it but by the hot spring Vígðalaug, famous since medieval times. A village, also called Laugarvatn, sits on the lake's western shore, and it is one of the best places to base yourself in the Golden Circle area. Naturally, there's a swimming pool here.

SIGHTS & ACTIVITIES

Down by the shore is **Vígðalaug**, used for early Christian baptisms. Rather more gruesomely, the bodies of Jón Arason (Iceland's last Catholic bishop) and his sons were dug up a year after they were executed in 1550, and brought here to be washed and blessed; the bier stones **Líkasteinar** are where they were laid.

Near Vígðalaug, you can hire **kayaks, paddleboats** and **rowing boats** (☎ 897 8988, 899 5409; kayaks & paddleboats per 30/60 min Ikr700/1200, rowing boats Ikr1000/1500; ☽ 1-5pm Jun-Aug) to take onto the lake if the weather is good.

You'll also find the natural **geothermal swimming pool & steam bath** (Gufubað; ☎ 486 1251; Lindarbraut 1; adult/under 12yr Ikr350/200; ☽ 10am-10pm Mon-Fri, 10am-6pm Sat & Sun Jun–mid-Aug, 5-8pm Mon-Fri, 1-5pm Sat & Sun mid-Aug–May) there, with three hot pots. A **geothermal beach** is also planned.

Laugarvatn Adventure (☎ 862 5614; www.caving.is; Laugarvatn campsite; Ikr4900-5900) runs two- to three-hour caving trips in the hills around town. The company provides boiler suits, but bring a pair of gloves for crawling and scrambling through lava tunnels and up rocky slopes.

Many short hikes are possible from Laugarvatn, including one up to the viewpoint Hringsjá, north of the village.

SLEEPING & EATING

Laugarvatn campsite (☎ 486 1155; sites per person Ikr800; ☽ May-Sep) By the highway just outside the village, this is a major Icelandic party venue on summer weekends. If you want quiet, stay elsewhere! Good facilities include showers and a washing machine.

Laugarvatn Youth Hostel (☎ 486 1215, 899 5409; laugarvatn@hostel.is; sb dm/s/d/tr/q Ikr2100/4500/5800/7150 /9250, 💻) This large year-round hostel, spread over three sites across town, is a great place to stay. The 'little house' is just as it sounds, and is the most homey. The large main building rises up three floors, and has plenty of kitchen space (with great lake views while you're washing up), a hot tub and an internet connection. The third building, near the lake, doubles as a sports and community centre and has a huge industrial kitchen available to guests. Breakfast costs Ikr1100. The hostel also rents out boats.

Edda hotels (☎ 444 4000; www.hoteledda.is; s/d without bathroom Ikr8000/10,000, with bathroom Ikr12,900/16,900; ☽ mid-Jun–mid-Aug) Laugarvatn's two big schools become hotels in summer. ML Laugarvatn has the usual serviceable Edda rooms that will have you reminiscing about your college days (sleeping-bag option available from Ikr2300), and a rather draughty basement restaurant. ÍKÍ Laugarvatn is swankier by far: its 28 rooms (singles/doubles Ikr14,600/18,300) all have private bathrooms, half with beautiful panoramic lake views.

Lindin (☎ 486 1262; Lindarbraut 2; mains Ikr3000-5500; ☽ 11.30am-9pm Mon-Fri, 11.30am-9.30pm Sat & Sun May-Sep) Lindin is the best restaurant for miles. Its menu uses local and seasonal ingredients – fresh char from the lake, reindeer, goose and guillemot – and quiet jazz and candlelight create a relaxing atmosphere. Its French dark chocolate mousse, with raspberry purée and watermelon pieces, is allegedly the best in the world – and, having tasted it, we won't argue!

GETTING THERE & AWAY

There's a year-round bus service to Laugarvatn. From June to August the bus leaves at 8.30am daily from Reykjavík, calling at Laugarvatn (Ikr1700, 1¾ hours), continuing on to Gullfoss and Geysir, and then returning to Reykjavík. From September to May the bus leaves at 3pm Monday to Thursday, 2pm Friday and at 5pm at weekends but does not stop at Gullfoss and Geysir.

In summer a dirt road called Gjábakkavegur (Rte 365) provides a short-cut between Laugarvatn and Þingvellir. It's impassable in winter – you'll have to drive south almost to Selfoss, before heading north on Rte 36 to Þingvellir. In the other direction, Rte 37 heads east to Gullfoss and Geysir.

GEYSIR

One of Iceland's most famous tourist attractions, Geysir (pronounced GAY-zeer) is the original blasting **hot-water spout** after which all other geysers around the world are named. The Great Geysir once gushed water up to 80m into the air but, sadly, it became clogged in the 1950s when tourists threw rocks into the spring in an attempt to set it off. Large earthquakes in 2000 seem to have shifted some blockage – it now erupts two or three times daily, although not to its former height.

Luckily for visitors, the world's most reliable geyser, **Strokkur**, is right next door. You rarely have to wait more than six minutes for the water to swirl and vanish down what looks like an enormous plughole, before bursting upwards in an impressive 15m to 30m plume. Don't stand downwind unless you want a shower.

Geysers are formed when geothermally heated water becomes trapped in narrow fissures. The water at the surface cools, whereas the water below the ground becomes superheated, eventually turning into steam and blasting out the cooler water above it.

Geysir and Strokkur are surrounded by smaller colourful springs, bubbling milky pools and steam vents, where water emerges from the ground at 100°C. The geothermal area is free (it was only ever a paying venue when an Englishman owned it in 1894).

Sights & Activities
GEYSIR CENTER

Across the road from the geysers you'll find this **tourist complex** (☎ 480 6800; www.geysircenter

.com; ☯ 9am-7pm, to 10pm in summer). It contains a petrol station, cafe, huge souvenir shop and **Geysisstofa** (☎ 480 6800; www.geysircenter.com; adult/concessions Ikr1000/800; ☯ 10am-7pm Jun-Aug, noon-5pm Sep-May), an audiovisual exhibition on geysers and volcanoes, with an earthquake simulator and some folk-museum pieces upstairs. It might provide 20 minutes' distraction, but really the geysers themselves are far more fun.

HAUKADALUR

A pleasant 2km stroll north of the steaming springs is Haukadalur, a major centre of learning in Viking times. As with many saga sites, there isn't a lot to see now, but it's a picturesque walk. The Icelandic Forestry Commission (yes, there really is one!) has planted thousands of trees in the area.

HORSE RIDING

It's possible to rent horses from Hótel Geysir. Rates start at Ikr4000 for a one-hour horse trek. Experienced riders can do a day trip to Gullfoss (Ikr12,000 including lunch).

Sleeping & Eating

Geysir campsite (sites per person Ikr900; ☯ May-Sep) Stay at this campsite and you'll get to marvel at the spouting springs before the coach parties arrive. Pay at Hótel Geysir, where you can use the hot tub and pool for free.

Hótel Geysir (☎ 480 6800; www.geysircenter. com; s/d from Ikr12,100/17,500; ☯ closed Jan; P ☒) Accommodation is in spick, span and tasteful alpine-style cabins; there's a geothermal pool (open mid-April to August) and two hot pots, and the hotel can arrange horse rides (see above). Some of the newer 'luxury' rooms overlook the geyser field. The hotel restaurant (mains Ikr2200 to Ikr4000) already has a prime view of the geysers, and serves good meaty dishes such as reindeer steak with truffle gravy.

There's a reasonable **cafe** (snacks Ikr300-1200; ☯ 9am-7pm) inside the Geysir Centre.

Getting There & Away

From June to August, scheduled **Trex** (☎ 551 1166; www.bogf.is) bus 2/2a runs from the BSÍ bus station in Reykjavík to Geysir and Gullfoss (at 8.30am, plus also at 11am in July and August; Ikr3300 one way) and back, a circuit of around 8½ hours.

Also from mid-June to August, the **Reykjavík Excursions** (☎ 580 5400; www.re.is) daily bus 6/6a

RAFTING IN SOUTHWEST ICELAND

The great glacial rivers of southwest Iceland provide some wonderful opportunities for white-water rafting. **Arctic Rafting** (☎ 562 7000; www.arcticrafting.is; ⊙ Jun–early Sep) offers something to suit everyone, from an easy 3½-hour River Fun trip (Ikr6990, with pick-up Ikr9990) to the experienced-rafters-only adrenalin rush down the Hólmsá (Ikr9990, with pick-up Ikr14,990). You have to be at least 12 years old for most of the trips. It's best to book ahead – and bring a swimsuit.

The company can pick you up from Reykjavík and hotels on the southwest coast, but if you want to save on the pick-up cost, you can drive there yourself. The Arctic Rafting HQ is at Drumboddsstaðir; head 7km north from Reykholt on Rte 358 (a minor road running parallel to Rte 35), then take the signposted right turn – it's about 2.5km further along on a bone-shaking dirt track.

(8.30am, return Ikr7000) stops at Þingvellir, Geysir and Gullfoss for at least 45 minutes each, before returning to Reykjavík.

Very popular Golden Circle tours run year-round from Reykjavík (see p86).

GULLFOSS

Iceland's most famous waterfall, Gullfoss is a spectacular double cascade. It drops 32m, kicking up a sheer wall of spray before thundering away down a narrow ravine. On sunny days the spray creates shimmering rainbows, and it's also magical in winter when the falls glitter with ice. On grey, drizzly days, mist can envelop the second drop, making Gullfoss slightly underwhelming.

The falls came within a hair's breadth of destruction during the 1920s, when a team of foreign investors wanted to dam the Hvitá river for a hydroelectric project. The land-owner, Tómas Tómasson, refused to sell to them, but the developers went behind his back and obtained permission directly from the government. Tómasson's daughter, Sigríður, walked to Reykjavík to protest, even threatening to throw herself into the waterfall if the development went ahead. Thankfully, the investors failed to pay the lease, the agreement was nullitied and the falls escaped destruction. Gullfoss was donated to the nation in 1975 and has been a nature reserve ever since.

Above Gullfoss is a small visitor centre and **cafe** (☎ 486 6500; snacks Ikr800-1300; ⊙ 9am-9.30pm Jun-Aug, 9am-6pm Mon-Fri, 9am-7pm Sat & Sun Sep-May), whose speciality is lamb soup (Ikr1290). A tarmac path suitable for wheelchairs leads to a lookout over the falls, and a set of steps continues to the water.

With a 4WD it's possible to continue from Gullfoss to the glacier at Langjökull and other parts of the interior via mountain road F35.

There's accommodation a few kilometres before the falls at **Hótel Gullfoss** (☎ 486 8979; www .hotelgullfoss.is; s/d/tr Ikr15,000/18,500/25,000; ⊙ mid-May-Sep, bookings necessary Oct–mid-May), a large, modern bungalow hotel. Its en suite rooms, overlooking the moors, are modest-sized and businesslike, and there are two hot pots and a restaurant. Breakfast is included.

See opposite for bus info for Gullfoss.

GULLFOSS TO SELFOSS

From Gullfoss there are several possible routes back to the Ring Road, passing through an agricultural region dotted with farms, ham-lets…and countless summer houses. There isn't too much to see in this area, but there are plenty of possible bases for exploring the Golden Circle.

Most people follow surfaced Rte 35, which passes the turn-off to the Arctic Rafting HQ (see the boxed text, above), continues through Reykholt, then meets the Ring Road about 2km west of Selfoss. You can detour off Rte 35 to Skálholt, once Iceland's religious powerhouse.

Alternatively, you could follow Rte 30, which is intermittently surfaced and passes through Flúðir, meeting Rte 1 about 15km east of Selfoss. An interesting detour from this road is through the scenic Þjórsárdalur valley, along Rte 32. From here you can follow Rte 26 past the foothills of the Hekla volcano, emerging on Rte 1 about 6km west of Hella.

Reykholt
pop 190

The rural township of Reykholt – one of several Reykholts around the country – is centred on the hot spring Reykjahver. Several local farms have greenhouses heated by the springs, and there's the inevitable **swimming pool** (☎ 486 8807; adult/5-16yr Ikr300/150;

10am-10pm Mon-Thu, 10am-7pm Fri-Sun). Services include a petrol station and grill, a shop, a post office and a bank.

Friendly **Húsið** (☎ 486 8680, 897 5728; husid@ best.is; Bjarkarbraut 26; sb/linen Ikr3200/4500) has B&B and sleeping-bag accommodation in a quiet cul-de-sac; there's a hot tub and a barbecue. Camping (☎ 897 5728) is also available.

Kaffi Klettur (☎ 486 1310; mains Ikr1300-4500; noon-9pm daily Jun-Aug, Sat & Sun Sep-May) is decorated in mock-old-fashioned style, with tapestries, old coffee mills and horse bridles. It has a wide selection of pizzas, burgers, crêpes, pasta and traditional fish and meat mains. It's housed in a wooden lodge in a large garden with children's swings.

There's also the **petrol-station grill** (9am-6pm Mon-Fri, 11am-6pm Sat & Sun).

See right for details on how to get there.

Skálholt & Laugarás

The name of Skálholt (population 184) resounds through Iceland's history. This hugely important religious centre was one of two bishoprics (the other was Hólar in the north) that ruled Iceland's souls from the 11th to the 18th centuries.

Skálholt rose to prominence under Gissur the White, the driving force behind the Christianisation of Iceland. The Catholic bishopric lasted until the Reformation in 1550, when Bishop Jón Arason and his two sons were executed by order of the Danish king. Skalhólt continued as a Lutheran centre until 1797, when the bishopric shifted to Reykjavík.

Unfortunately, the great cathedral that once stood here was destroyed by a major earthquake in the 18th century. Today there's just a modern theological centre and a church with a tiny basement **museum** (admission Ikr100; 9am-7pm except during services or concerts) containing the stone sarcophagus of Bishop Páll Jónsson (bishop from 1196 to 1211). According to *Páls Saga*, the earth was wracked by storms and earthquakes when he died; and, spookily, a huge storm broke at the exact moment that his coffin was re-opened in 1956.

Given that Skálholt played such a major role in Iceland's history, the modern settlement is rather a letdown, although its inhabitants have done their best to make the post accessible with the nicely put-together leaflet 'Historical trail in Skálholt', outlining a 2km walking tour

around the hamlet. Literature lovers should read the brilliant *Iceland's Bell* by Halldór Laxness for a vivid picture of Skálholt's wealth and power in the 17th century.

There's an important free classical-music festival, **Sumartónleikar í Skálholtskirkju** (☎ 562 1028; www.sumartonleikar.is), at Skálholt for five weeks from July to early August, featuring composers and musicians from all over Iceland and Europe.

Just 1.5km from Skálholt is the village of Laugarás (population 144), mainly known for its greenhouses. If you've got young children, you could pop into the little family park, **Dýragarðurinn í Slakka** (☎ 868 7626; www.slakki.is; adult/2-16yr Ikr700/400; 11am-6pm Jun–mid-Sep). Its beguilements include minigolf, farm animals, parrots and ice cream.

SLEEPING & EATING

Hótel Hvítá (☎ 486 8600; hotelhvita@simnet.is; sites per person Ikr600, sb from Ikr3200, s/d/tr Ikr10,000/14,700/19,800; May-Sep;) In a great location beside the suspension bridge in Laugarás, this basic hotel offers sleeping-bag bunk beds and simple parquet-floored guest-house rooms, and also caters for campers. There's a grill-style restaurant, with a splendid view over the Hvítá river.

Skálholtsskóli (☎ 486 7088; www.skalholt.is; sb Ikr3700, s/d Ikr8500/12,000) The Lutheran theological centre at Skálholt is open to guests. It's often booked out by visiting church groups, but if you're seeking clean, plain, twin-bedded en suite rooms in a peaceful hamlet, it's worth calling. A separate building contains cheaper sleeping-bag accommodation, and there's a restaurant. Breakfast is Ikr1100.

GETTING THERE & AWAY

From June to August, scheduled **Trex** (☎ 551 1166; www.bogf.is) bus 2/2a does an 8½-hour circuit from Reykjavík to Geysir and Gullfoss, calling at Reykholt (Ikr2600) and Skálholt/Laugarás (Ikr2500). The bus leaves the city at 8.30am. Outside those months, Skálholt/Laugarás is a request stop only.

To drive to Skálholt, take Rte 35 from Selfoss. After around 30km, turn right onto Rte 31; the settlement is a couple of kilometres further along.

Kerið & Seyðishólar

Around 10km further southwest of Skálholt and Laugarás, Rte 35 passes Kerið, a 6500-

year-old explosion crater containing a spooky-looking green lake. Björk once performed a concert from a floating raft in the middle; and it's said that some joker has introduced fish to the water.

About 3km northeast across the road is the bright-red Seyðishólar crater group, which produced most of the surrounding lava field.

FLÚÐIR

pop 380

Flúðir's mainly known for its mushrooms, grown in geothermal greenhouses, and for its many summer house, where hardworking Reykjavíkurs come to throw off big-city cares. This peaceful green settlement is the largest in this area; it has all necessary services and makes an alternative base for exploring the Golden Circle (it's around 25km south of Gullfoss and Geysir).

There's a **swimming pool** (☎ 486 6790; adult/6-15yr Ikr300/150; ☼ 4-9pm Mon-Fri, 10am-6pm Sat, 1-6pm Sun), a small folk museum containing farming equipment at the farm **Gróf** (☎ 486 6634; ☼ by arrangement), a bank with ATM and a post office. **Horse riding** is available at Syðra-Langholt – see below.

Sleeping & Eating

Tjaldmiðstöðin Flúðum (☎ 618 5005; siters per person Ikr850; ☼ Easter-Sep; ☎) Flúðir's new campsite, on the banks of the Litla Laxá stream, has a well-equipped service centre, with kitchen, washing machine and dryer, TV and wireless internet access. Flúðir's popularity with city-dwellers newly released into the countryside can make this an extremely crowded and noisy site in summer.

Syðra-Langholt (☎ 486 6574, 861 6652; sydralangholt@emax.is; sites per person Ikr800, sb Ikr3500, s/d/tr Ikr6500/10,000/12,500) Ten kilometres southwest of Flúðir on Rte 340 is this big white farmhouse. The owners are a lively bunch and the house has all mod cons, including a hot pot. Room prices include breakfast; evening meals are a possibility if booked in advance. Horse riding (☎ 894 8974) is available for Ikr3800/5000 per hour/two hours.

Hótel Flúðir (☎ 486 6630; fludir@icehotels.is; Vesturbrún 1; s/d Ikr20,100/23,600; ☼ early Jan-late Dec; ☐) Icelandair owns this stylish chaletlike bungalow, which has much more warmth than other hotels in the chain. Comfortable rooms have parquet floors, brown leafy bed

covers, and soothing prints of fruit and flowers. They all have bathroom, TV, phone and minibar, and there's a good restaurant that opens for dinner daily.

Kaffi Sel (☎ 486 6454; Efra-Sel; pizzas Ikr1000, snacks Ikr1000-1800; ☼ 8am-9pm May-Sep) We recommend this comical option, 3km northwest of Flúðir – the local golf clubhouse! It's strange but satisfying to sit among golf trophies while you eat your lunch, watching people thwack balls around on the green. There's a good menu of homemade soup, burgers, pizzas and Mexican dishes, and sociable staff.

Flúðir has a **Samkaup-Strax supermarket** (☼ 9am-7pm Mon-Fri, 10am-7pm Sat, 10am-5pm Sun), and a pizzeria, **Útlaginn** (☎ 486 6425; www.utlaginn.is; pizzas Ikr900-2000).

Getting There & Away

From June to mid-September, Trex bus service 8/8a from Reykjavík to Flúðir (Ikr2800, 1½ hours) runs at 8.30am and 5pm daily, returning at 10.30am and 5pm. Outside those months, the service runs from Reykjavík at 3pm Monday to Thursday, and at 2pm and 5pm Friday and Sunday, returning at 7.25am Monday to Friday, and at 5pm Friday and Sunday, and 2pm Sunday. Most Flúðir buses run via Árnes (Ikr2700, one hour 20 minutes), and pass 5km from Syðra-Langholt.

ÞJÓRSÁRDALUR

The Þjórsá is Iceland's longest river, a fast-flowing, churning mass of milky glacial water that runs 230km from Vatnajökull and Hofsjökull to the Atlantic. With its tributaries, it accounts for almost one third of Iceland's hydroelectric power.

You can follow it upstream awhile via Rte 32, along a valley of Saga Age farms, past the hydroelectric plants Búrfell and Bláskógar, and through the lava fields of Hekla. Rte 32 eventually meets up with mountain road F26, which continues across the highlands; if you don't have a 4WD you can turn back towards the coast here along Rte 26.

Árnes

The tiny settlement of Árnes, near the junction of Rtes 30 and 32, is a possible base for exploring Þjórsárdalur. **Árnes HI Hostel** (☎ 486 6048; arnes@hostel.is; sites per tent Ikr1000, sb d Ikr5500; ☼ mid-Apr–mid-Sep) isn't the cosiest place on earth, but its twin rooms and dorm are adequate, plus there's a guest kitchen, a licensed restaurant (open June to August) and small octagonal **pool** (☎ 486 6117; ☯ 2-10pm Mon-Fri, 11am-10pm Sat, 11am-6pm Sun Jun-Aug).

Most buses between Reykjavík and Flúðir go via Árnes – see p129.

Stöng & Þjóðveldisbær

Heading along Rte 32 from Árnes towards Stöng and Þjóðveldisbær, take a short (2km) detour along a signposted track to the delightful waterfall **Hjálparfoss**, which tumbles in two chutes over a scarp formed from twisted basalt columns.

Perhaps the most strangely situated swimming pool in Iceland is the open-air **Þjórsárdalslaug** (☎ 661 2503; adult/child Ikr350/200; ☯ noon-6pm Thu & Sun, noon-8pm Fri & Sat Jun-Aug). It was built from concrete left over from the construction of the Búrfell hydroelectricity plant.

The **ancient farm** at Stöng was buried by white volcanic ash in 1104 during one of Hekla's eruptions. It once belonged to Gaukur Trandilsson, a 10th-century Viking who lived a tempestuous life. Unfortunately, the centuries have destroyed all traces of his saga; brief mentions in some 12th-century graffiti in Orkney, in *Njál's Saga* and in a scurrilous medieval rhyme hint that he had a fling with the housewife at the nearby farm Steinastöðum and was killed over the affair in an axe duel.

Stöng was excavated in 1939 – Iceland's first proper archaeological dig – and is an important site, used to help date Viking houses elsewhere. The farm ruins are covered over by a large wooden shelter at the end of a bad, bumpy dirt road that branches off Rte 32 about 20km beyond Árnes. You can still see stone-lined fire pits and door lintels made from octagonal basalt columns, and the surrounding lava landscape is impressively desolate. A **walking path** behind the farm takes you a couple of kilometres to a strange and lovely little valley, Gjáin, full of twisting lava and waterfalls.

We happen to think it's an atmospheric spot, but **Þjóðveldisbærinn** (☎ 488 7713; www.thjodveldisbaer.is; adult/under 13yr Ikr500/free; ☯ 10am-noon & 1-6pm Jun-Aug), a reconstructed Viking-era farm, is more photogenic. The farm exactly reproduces the layout of Stöng and its neighbouring church. The two farms are like a cosmetic surgeon's 'before' and 'after' photos.

South of the reconstructed farm is the **Búrfell hydroelectricity plant**, decorated by one of Sigurjón Ólafsson's largest sculptures.

From Stöng you can walk 10km northeast along a 4WD track to Iceland's second-highest waterfall, **Háifoss**, which plunges 122m off the edge of a plateau. You can also get most of the way there by 4WD.

SLEEPING

From mid-May to September you can camp in a plantation of fir trees at **Sandártunga** (☎ 893 8889; sites per person Ikr600), about 7km before Búrfell.

Hólaskógur (☎ 661 2503; www.icesafari.is; sites per person Ikr800, sb Ikr2500) Offers the most remote accommodation in Þjórsárdalur, on the edge of the highlands. It's effectively a mountain hut, big enough for 80 sleeping-baggers, with camping places outside and a great sauna (Ikr500). The company offers quad-bike (ATV) tours.

GETTING THERE & AWAY

Reykjavík Excursions (☎ 580 5400; www.re.is) runs a 12-hour tour (Ikr17,000) from Reykjavík to Landmannalaugar that stops at the reconstructed Viking farm Þjóðveldisbærinn. The tour runs at 8am daily from July to mid-September. **Iceland Excursions** (☎ 540 1313; www.grayline.is) has a 10-hour tour (Ikr18,000) from Reykjavík to Landmannalaugar that visits Hjálparfoss waterfall. For tours focusing just on Þjórsárdalur, contact **Gaukur Travel** (☎ 557 1113, 897 1112; www.gaukur-travel.is), which runs 4WD (Ikr15,000) and bus (Ikr10,000) tours to the valley from Reykjavík.

THE SOUTHWEST COAST

Coming from Reykjavík, this is one of the most exciting bits of the southern coast, simply because of the suspense. Rte 1 trundles through a flat, wide coastal plain, full of horse farms and greenhouses, before the landscape suddenly begins to spasm and grow jagged. Mountains thrust upwards on the inland side of the road and the first of the awesome glaciers appears.

Public transport isn't bad along the Ring Road, which is studded with interesting settlements: Hveragerði, famous for its geothermal fields and hot springs; Hvolsvöllur, the leaping-off point for Þórsmörk, one of Iceland's most popular hiking destinations; Skógar, further east, home to one of Iceland's best folk museums; and Vík, surrounded by glaciers, vertiginous cliffs and black beaches, which will leave you giddy with love.

Treats lying off the Ring Road include the tiny fishing villages of Stokkseyri and Eyrarbakki; brooding volcano Hekla (a possible gateway to hell!); the Mýrdalsjökull ice cap, where you can go dog sledding or snowmobiling; and farms and valleys rich with saga heritage.

HVERAGERÐI
pop 2320
At first glance, you might write Hveragerði off as a dull grid of boxy buildings. However, spend longer than half an hour here and your ominous muttering should fade away. This friendly town has soul, and lots of small, strange things to see and do.

Hveragerði sits on top of a highly active geothermal field, which provides heat for hundreds of greenhouses. Nationally, the town is famous for its horticultural college

and naturopathic clinic. There are also some fantastic hikes in the area, so it makes a good walking base.

Information
Hveragerði contains the regional tourist office for the whole south coast, **Upplýsingamiðstöð Suðurlands** (☎ 483 4601; www.southiceland.is; Sunnumörk 2-4; ⏱ 9am-5pm Mon-Fri, 10am-2pm Sat mid-May–mid-Sep, 9am-4.30pm Mon-Fri mid-Sep–mid-May), which shares its premises with the post office, inside the shopping centre. It can book accommodation for a Ikr300 fee. When the office is closed, one of the new 'Look & Book Iceland' information terminals is located just outside the door.

A tiny room with three internet computers (Ikr150 per half-hour) can be accessed from both the tourist office and the friendly **library** (☎ 483 4531; Sunnumörk 2; ⏱ 1-7pm Mon & Wed-Fri, to 9pm Tue, 11am-2pm Sat). While you're here (yes, inside the building!), look down by your feet for the rift, discovered during the construction of the shopping centre.

There's a Kaupþing bank on Breiðamörk and an ATM in the shopping-centre entrance.

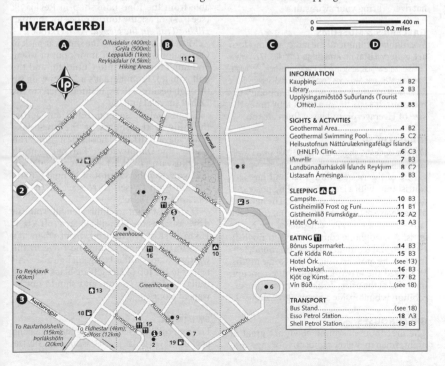

HVERAGERÐI

0 ———— 400 m
0 ———— 0.2 miles

INFORMATION
Kaupþing...................................1 B2
Library.......................................2 B3
Upplýsingamiðstöð Suðurlands (Tourist Office)..............................3 B3

SIGHTS & ACTIVITIES
Geothermal Area..........................4 B2
Geothermal Swimming Pool.............5 C2
Heilsustofnun Náttúrulækningafélags Íslands (HNLFÍ) Clinic.....................6 C3
Ilaavellir...................................7 B3
Landbúnaðarháskóli Íslands Reykjum 8 C2
Listasafn Árnesinga......................9 B3

SLEEPING
Campsite..................................10 B3
Gistiheimilið Frost og Funi.............11 B1
Gistiheimilið Frumskógar...............12 A2
Hótel Örk..................................13 A3

EATING
Bónus Supermarket......................14 B3
Café Kidda Rót............................15 B3
Hotel Örk..............................(see 13)
Hverabakarí...............................16 B3
Kjöt og Kúnst.............................17 B2
Vín Búð.................................(see 18)

TRANSPORT
Bus Stand............................(see 18)
Esso Petrol Station.......................18 A3
Shell Petrol Station......................19 B3

To Reykjavík (40km)

To Raufarhólshellir (15km); Þorlákshöfn (20km)

To Eldhestar (4km); Selfoss (12km)

Ölfusdalur (400m); Grýla (500m); Leppalúði (1km); Reykjadalur (4.5km); Hiking Areas

Greenhouse

Greenhouse

Sights

GEOTHERMAL FIELDS

There's a small **geothermal area** (☎ 483 4601; Hveramörk; admission free; ☺ 10.30am-6pm Mon-Fri, noon-4pm Sat & Sun Jun–mid-Sep) in the centre of town, with baked earth, small mudpots and several hot springs and pools. They're a little tame, but the information sheet contains some great stories – read all about the hot-spring spider *Pirata piraticus*, the burping Garbage Spring, and the murderous mudpot. In summer there's a small cafe where you can buy eggs (Ikr50) and bread (Ikr150) boiled and baked in the area. Out of season, ask the tourist office to unlock the gates.

For something a little more explosive, head up Breiðamörk and on out of town. This valley is **Ölfusdalur**, site of several mudpots, steaming vents and the geyser **Grýla** (on the left), which erupts 12m several times daily. There's also an artificial borehole, **Leppalúði**, on the right by the bridge near the golf-course road, which gushes continually. If you keep going a further 1.5km, you'll reach a car park; from here, it's a 3km walk to unmissable **Reykjadalur**, a delightful geothermal valley where there's a bathable **hot river** – bring your swimsuit.

GALLERIES & MUSEUMS

We highly recommend the large, airy modern art gallery **Listasafn Árnesinga** (☎ 483 1727; www.listasafnarnesinga.is; Austurmörk 21; admission free; ☺ noon-6pm daily May–mid-Sep, noon-6pm Thu-Sun mid-Sep–mid-Dec & mid-Jan–Apr), which puts on great temporary exhibitions. It's worthy of a town four times the size of Hveragerði, and has a fine cafe too.

IÐAVELLIR

Iðavellir (Norse Mythology Centre; ☎ 483 0000; www.idavellir.is; Austurmörk 25; ☺ 9am-9pm Jun-Aug, 9am-7pm Sep-May) is one of the nearest things Iceland has to a tourist trap, with a large shop selling postcards and woollen goods, and a canteen. The new **Well of the Norns exhibition** (Ikr1200) is a mazelike area stuffed full of cartoony cut-outs of the Norse gods. A headphone commentary (in English, German and Icelandic) guides you round, telling you the most exciting of the Norse myths. We loved the artwork, enjoyed the concept, quivered at the price, disliked the heat (the exhibition is built inside a former greenhouse).

GREENHOUSES

The greenhouses around town are great at night, when they glow radioactive orange, and

several nurseries are open to the public. It's also fine to amble into the **Landbúnaðarháskóli Íslands Reykjum** (Agricultural University of Iceland; ☎ 433 5000; www.lbhi.is; Reykir; ☺ 9am-5pm, closed Jul) to look at the plants.

HNLFÍ CLINIC

Iceland's most famous clinic, **Heilsustofnun Náttúrulækningafélags Íslands** (HNLFÍ; ☎ 483 0300; www.hnlfi.is; Grænumörk 10; adult/concession/under 12yr Ikr600/300/300; ☺ 8am-4pm Mon-Fri), has mainly treated prescription-only patients in the past. However, it's now keen to throw open its doors to visitors seeking relaxing massages (Ikr5300 to Ikr8600) and deep-heat mud baths (Ikr4700). HNLFÍ has excellent facilities, including indoor and outdoor pools, hot pots, a sauna, a steam bath and a relaxation room. Treatments are available year-round – book ahead.

Activities

HIKING

There are loads of interesting walks around Hveragerði. Bring the Ferðakort topographical map sheet 1613 II *Hengill* 1:50,000, available from the Iðnú bookshop in Reykjavík (see p71), or ask the tourist office for the map *Hiking Trails in the Hengill Area* (Ikr600).

Most trails begin from the small car park in Ölfusdalur (follow Breiðamörk out of town, and don't turn right into Gufudalur and the golf course). From here it's a 3.5km walk up through beautiful Reykjadalur (see left) to the Dalsel survival hut.

From Dalsel, several trails cut across the hills to the shores of the great lake Þingvallavatn (p124). The shortest routes run northeast to Úlfljótsvatn (13km) or due north to Ölfusvatn (13.5km). A longer route will take you over the summit of Hengill (768m; 11.7km from Dalsel) to Nesjavellir (p124), 18.7km from Dalsel.

If you just want to climb Hengill, you can drive as far as the Hengill ski area (off Rte 1, 16km west of Hveragerði), from where it's 7km to the summit along the ridge to the west, or 6km via the Hengladalir valley. All routes to the top of Hengill are black walking trails – officially 'tough, and should not be walked alone'.

SWIMMING

Hveragerði's open-air **geothermal swimming pool** (☎ 483 4113; Laugaskarði; adult/child Ikr310/120;

⊙ 6.45am-9.15pm Mon-Fri, 10am-6.30pm Sat & Sun Jun-Aug, 6.45am-9.15pm Mon-Fri, 10am-5.30pm Sat & Sun Sep-May), beside the Varmá river just north of town, is among Iceland's favourites. Goodies include a massaging hot pot and a steam room built directly over a natural hot spring.

HORSE RIDING
A few kilometres east of Hveragerði, the horse farm **Eldhestar** (☎ 480 4800; www.eldhestar.is; Vellir) has all kinds of riding tours, from one-hour trots (around Ikr5000) in the surrounding area to multiday tours into the highlands (contact Eldhestar for prices).

Sleeping
Campsite (☎ 483 4601, 483 4605; Reykjamörk 1; sites per person Ikr850) This excellent modern campsite is just east of the centre, and has toilets, showers, a cooking area and a laundry.

Gistiheimilið Frumskógar (☎ 896 2780; www.frum skogar.is; Frumskógar 3; s/d/apt Ikr5000/7000/12,000; ▯) Clean, good-value rooms are offered at this cosy suburban guest house. They all come with comfy beds, thick duvets, TVs, washbasins and dressing gowns. A yummy breakfast (Ikr1000) can be ordered, and there's a hot pot in the garden. Self-catering apartments at the back have TV, bathroom and kitchen.

Gistiheimilið Frost og Funi (Frost & Fire Guest House; ☎ 483 4959, 893 4959; www.frostandfire.is; Hverhamar; s/d Ikr12,000/16,900; ▯ ⊒) This is a romantic option, with access to a private pool, an idyllic riverbank hot pot and a natural steam sauna. The 14 rooms are simple but tasteful, with large beds, TVs, en-suite bathrooms and modern Icelandic artwork on the walls. Breakfast is included.

Hótel Örk (☎ 483 4700; www.hotel-ork.is; Breiðamörk 1; s/tw/tr Ikr15,500/18,900/21,100; ▯ ⊒) Although the rooms in this big custom-built building are staid and slightly old-fashioned, unusually for Iceland they all have bathtubs. The hotel itself has excellent facilities, particularly for families – saunas, tennis courts, a nine-hole golf course, a ping-pong table and an excellent swimming pool with slide, hot tubs and a children's pool. Breakfast is included.

Eating
Hverabakarí (☎ 483 4879; Breiðamörk 10; ⊙ 8.30am-6pm Mon-Fri, 9am-6pm Sat & Sun) An unusual cake maker works at this little bakery – look out for the marzipan chessboard and buns pulling horrible faces. There are plenty of tables, and

good coffee and snacks, including hot-spring bread baked using geothermals. There's another bakery in the town's shopping centre, but it's not as much fun.

Kjöt og Kúnst (☎ 483 5010; Breiðamörk 21; ⊙ 11.30am-9pm Mon-Sat Jun-Aug, shorter hrs rest of year) This deli serves delicious nibbly things for picnics – mouth-watering salads, cakes, roast chicken, slices of meat and fish. You can also eat in (lunch available until 1.30pm, evening meals from 5pm) – choose from various different hotplate courses, then take your plate to be weighed. Dishes are cooked using steam from nearby hot springs.

Café Kidda Rót (☎ 552 8002; Sunnumörk 2; mains Ikr1100-3000; ⊙ 11am-10pm Sun-Thu, to 11.30pm Fri & Sat) In the shopping centre, the town's cafe-bar sells good coffee and a diverse menu of pizzas, burgers, Chinese meals and cheap (although not hugely flavoursome) wild trout. It doubles as a kind of art gallery, and old men come in to watch the news on a giant-screen TV.

Hótel Örk (☎ 483 4700; Breiðamörk 1; mains Ikr3000-4000) The restaurant at Hótel Örk is the poshest place in town, and it serves a small menu of Icelandic specialities such as *hangikjöt* (smoked lamb) and *bacalao* (salt cod), plus burgers, beef steaks and seafood kebabs.

There's a **Bónus** (☎ 482 1818; Sunnumörk 2; ⊙ noon-6.30pm Mon-Thu, 10am-7.30pm Fri, 10am-6pm Sat, noon-6pm Sun) supermarket, and the **Vín Búð** (☎ 481 3932; Breiðamörk 1; ⊙ noon-6pm Mon-Thu, 11am-7pm Fri, 11am-4pm Sat) is inside the N1 garage.

Getting There & Away
The bus stop is at the N1 petrol station on the main road into town. All buses from Reykjavík to Selfoss and places further east stop in Hveragerði (Ikr840, 35 minutes).

AROUND HVERAGERÐI
Route 38 runs south from Hveragerði to Þorlákshöfn (20km), from where the ferry to the Vestmannaeyjar departs (see the boxed text, p155, for alterations to the route).

Raufarhólshellir
This 11th-century lava tube is over 1km long, and contains some wonderful (protected) lava columns. You'll need a torch and sturdy boots to explore; the going underfoot can be quite treacherous from earlier cave-ins. In winter, cold air is funnelled down and trapped inside, producing amazing ice formations.

You'll find the tube southwest of Hveragerði off the Reykjavík–Þorlákshöfn route (Rte 39), which passes right over the tunnel. It's about 1km north of the junction where Rtes 38, 39 and 427 meet.

Þorlákshöfn
pop 1580

In the past, most people came to this fishing town, 20km south of Hveragerði, to catch the ferry to the Vestmannaeyjar; however, the ferry route is due to change in 2010 – see the boxed text, p155. There's a **campsite** (☎ 483 3807, 863 9690; olfus@olfus.is; sites per person Ikr750; ⏰ mid-May–Aug) next to the swimming pool if you need to stay over.

The bus service from Reykjavík to Þorlákshöfn currently connects with the ferry – see p155. A new bus service will operate from Reykjavík to Bakki once the new harbour there is built – ask at the BSÍ bus station in Reykjavík for timetables.

Just outside Þorlákshöfn, Rte 38 runs to Hveragerði, Rte 39 runs to Reykjavík, and unsurfaced Rte 427 runs west along the bottom of the Reykjanes Peninsula to Krýsuvík.

SELFOSS
pop 6570

Selfoss is the largest town in southern Iceland, an important trade and industry centre, and witlessly ugly. Iceland's Ring Road is its main shopping street – as a pedestrian, you're in constant danger of ending up as road jam.

The main reason to come here is to buy groceries before heading into the highlands; to establish a base to explore the Flói Nature Reserve (p136) or the lovely fishing villages of Eyrarbakki (opposite) and Stokkseyri (p136); or if you're desperate to go to the cinema. The nicest part is the winding river Ölfusá.

Information

The **tourist information desk** (☎ 480 1990; http://tourinfo.arborg.is; Austurvegur 2; ⏰ 10am-7pm Mon-Fri, 11am-2pm Sat mid-May–Aug), inside the town library and close to the roundabout on the main road, is staffed in summer; at other times, leaflets are available. The library offers internet access for Ikr300 per hour.

Landsbanki Íslands, Kaupþing and Íslandsbanki all have branches with ATMs on Austurvegur.

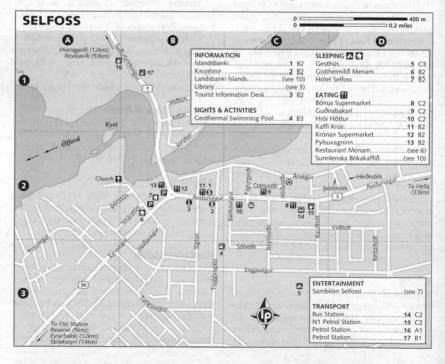

SELFOSS

0 / 400 m
0 / 0.2 miles

INFORMATION
Íslandsbanki.............................1 B2
Kaupþing.................................2 B2
Landsbanki Íslands...............(see 10)
Library....................................(see 3)
Tourist Information Desk..........3 B2

SIGHTS & ACTIVITIES
Geothermal Swimming Pool....4 B3

SLEEPING
Gesthús...................................5 C3
Gistiheimilið Menam.................6 B2
Hótel Selfoss............................7 B2

EATING
Bónus Supermarket..................8 C2
Guðnabakarí.............................9 C2
Hrói Höttur............................10 C2
Kaffi Krús...............................11 B2
Krónan Supermarket...............12 B2
Pylsuvagninn..........................13 B2
Restaurant Menam...............(see 6)
Sunnlenska Bókakaffið.........(see 10)

ENTERTAINMENT
Sambíóin Selfossi..................(see 7)

TRANSPORT
Bus Station............................14 C2
N1 Petrol Station...................15 C2
Petrol Station.........................16 A1
Petrol Station.........................17 B1

Activities

Selfoss has a fine **geothermal swimming pool** (☎ 480 1960; Bankavegur; adult/under 18yr Ikr370/free; ☻ 6.45am-9.30pm Mon-Fri, 9am-8pm Sat & Sun), with hot pots, water slides and a kids' play pool.

Sleeping

Gesthús (☎ 482 3585; www.gesthus.is; Engjavegur 56; sites per person Ikr800, sb/s/d/tr Ikr3000/9000/11,500/13,500; ☻ sites mid-May–mid-Sep, cabins year-round; ♿) For a choice of accommodation – sleeping-bag/camping/made-up beds in wooden cabins – try this friendly place by the park. There's a sociable kitchen hut and a laundry for campers, and the two- to four-bed cabins are nicely equipped with desks, kitchenettes and TVs. There are two hot pots for guests.

Gistiheimilið Menam (☎ 482 4099; www.menam.is; Eyravegur 8; d Ikr9900) This small guest house above a Thai restaurant has four rooms based around a central sitting room. The guest house has recently been revamped with cream walls, dark furniture and many buddhas – it's pleasant, although we found that the newly parqueted flooring caused a lot of sound to carry from the restaurant downstairs. Bathrooms are shared.

Hótel Selfoss (☎ 480 2500; www.hotelselfoss.is; Eyravegur 2; s/d from Ikr20,300/23,700; 🖳 🛜) This is a 99-room behemoth near the bridge, with four-star business-style hotel rooms and great facilities. Make sure you get a room overlooking the broad and lovely river Ölfusá, rather than the car park. There's a good restaurant, and a spa, beauty salon and fitness centre were added in 2007.

Eating

Guðnabakarí (☎ 482 1755; Austurvegur 31b; snacks Ikr600-800; ☻ 8am-5.30pm Mon-Fri, to 4pm Sat, 9.30am-4pm Sun) The sweet people in this busy bakery-cafe have a small menu of crêpes, soup and pasta, as well as buns and sandwiches.

Hrói Höttur (☎ 482 2899; Austurvegur 22; pizzas Ikr800-1400; ☻ 11.30am-10pm daily summer, shorter hrs winter) This pizzeria and takeaway fairly heaves with families and gangs of teens on a Friday and Saturday night.

Restaurant Menam (☎ 482 4099; Eyravegur 8; mains Ikr1400-3000; ☻ 11.30am-2pm & 5-10pm) For a break from grills and fish and chips, head for this authentic Thai place on the road to Stokkseyri. There's a big choice of beef, lamb, chicken and pork dishes, as well as a small international menu, although there's not much of interest for vegetarians.

Kaffi Krús (☎ 482 1672; www.kaffikrus.is; Austurvegur 7; snacks Ikr500-1500, mains Ikr1800-2700; ☻ 10am-midnight Sun-Thu, to 2am Fri & Sat) Krús is a cafe-bar based in a fantastic old house, with beams and creaking floorboards. There's a varied menu of coffees and light meals – salads, sandwiches, burgers, nachos, felafel and more substantial fish-of-the-day mains.

Sunnlenska Bókakaffið (☎ 482 3079; Austurvegur 22; ☻ 10am-10pm summer, shorter hrs winter; 🛜) This small, friendly independent bookshop (selling both new and secondhand books) also sells coffee and cake, and has free wireless access plus an internet-linked computer.

Self-caterers have a choice between the **Bónus** (☎ 481 3710; Austurvegur 42; ☻ noon-6.30pm Mon-Thu, 10am-7.30pm Fri, 10am-6pm Sat, noon-6pm Sun) and **Krónan** (☎ 585 7195; Tryggvatorg; ☻ 10am-8pm Mon-Fri, 10am-7pm Sat & Sun) supermarkets on the main road. For fast food, try the drive-through hot-dog stand **Pylsuvagninn** (hot dogs Ikr400-900; ☻ 10am-10pm) on the edge of the hotel car park.

Entertainment

There aren't many cinemas on the south coast – catch up with Hollywood at **Sambíóin Selfossi** (☎ 575 8900; www.sambioin.is; adult/child Ikr1100/900), a shiny cinema inside Hótel Selfoss.

Getting There & Away

All buses between Reykjavík and Höfn, Skaftafell, Fjallabak, Þórsmörk, Flúðir, Gullfoss, Laugarvatn and Vík pass through Selfoss; there are numerous options daily. The hour-long journey from Reykjavík costs Ikr1120.

EYRARBAKKI

pop 590

It's hard to believe, but tiny Eyrarbakki was Iceland's main port and a thriving trading town well into the 20th century. Farmers from all over the south once rode here to barter for supplies at the general store – the crowds were so huge it could take three days to get served!

Eyrarbakki is as bleak as can be in winter, when you'll slither down its only street without seeing a soul, but there are some interesting summer sights.

Sights

One of Iceland's oldest houses, built by Danish traders in 1765, **Húsið á Eyrarbakka** (☎ 483 1504; www.husid.com; Hafnarbrú 3; admission to both museums Ikr500; 11am-6pm mid-May–mid-Sep) has glass display cabinets explaining the town's history, rooms restored with original furniture, a bird-egg collection, a gallery of naive artwork, and CCTV footage of the destruction caused by the earthquake that hit the region in 2008. Also look out for Ólöf Sveinsdóttir's shawl, hat and cuffs, knitted from her own hair.

Just behind Húsið is a small maritime museum, **Sjóminjasafnið á Eyrarbakka** (483 1082; Túngata 59; admission to both museums Ikr500; 11am-6pm mid-May–mid-Sep), with displays on the local fishing community. Its main exhibit is the beautiful, tar-smelling, 12-oared fishing boat, *Farsæll*.

The wild, sandy coastline is a fine place to observe migrating **birds**, and you'll often see **seals** loafing about on the rocks.

Another of Eyrarbakki's claims to fame is that it's the birthplace of Bjarní Herjólfsson, who made a great sea voyage in AD 985 and was probably the first European to see America. Unfortunately, Bjarní turned back and sold his boat to Leifur Eiríksson, who went on to discover Vinland and ended up with all the glory.

The large fenced building to the east of the village is Iceland's largest prison, Litla-Hraun.

Sleeping & Eating

There's a rudimentary **campsite** (661 7002; sites per person Ikr500) on a patch of scrub at the western end of the village, with toilets and tap water.

Rein (693 3543; www.rein-guesthouse.is; Þykkvaflöt 4; s/d Ikr10,000/14,000; year-round, bookings necessary in low season) This calm, quiet guest house has three rooms in its wooden walled attic. Although the creaking timbers and shabby-chic furniture give the house an ancient feel, it was actually only built in 1997! Guests can use the hot tub in the garden, and breakfast is included.

Eyrarbakki Hostel (483 1280, 842 2550; www.gonholl.is; Eyrargata 51-53; apt Ikr16,000 plus laundry hire per person Ikr1000;) Although this place falls under the aegis of the Icelandic hostelling association, it's unlike any hostel we've ever seen. It's composed of four lovely apartments, all with warm peach-toned walls, wooden floors, fully equipped kitchens (including dishwashers and washing machines) and cosy sitting rooms. At the time of research, it was possible to pay for sleeping-bag ac-

commodation here if the apartments weren't rented out. However, there were also plans to open a dorm.

Gónhóll (483 1280, 842 2550; www.gonholl.is; Eyrargata 51-53; snacks & light meals Ikr800-3000; 1-5pm Fri-Mon May-Sep) Next door to (and owned by) the hostel keepers, this long, low building is an odd combination of craft market, secondhand shop, farm shop and cafe.

Rauða Húsið (483 3330; www.raudahusid.is; Búðarstíg 4; mains Ikr1900-3500; 11.30am-9pm Sun-Thu, to 10pm Fri & Sat) Arch-rival of the lobster restaurant in Stokkseyri, this place operates in an old red house, with cheery staff and great fresh seafood. *Bacalao* and grilled lobster are specialities, and it gets the prize for best dessert name – 'Þjórsá lava', a cracked chocolate muffin.

Hafið Bláa (483 1000; www.hafidblaa.is; mains Ikr1900-4200; noon-9pm summer) Halfway between Eyrarbakki and Þorlákshöfn, this superb seafood restaurant has a small menu based on the catch of the day, supplemented by trout, salmon and lobsters. The beautifully designed building is like an upturned boat, with Arctic terns and gannets diving from the ceiling. Even if you don't get a table overlooking the ocean, the sweeping estuary views on the opposite side are equally impressive.

Getting There & Away

There are eight buses between Selfoss and Eyrarbakki/Stokkseyri on weekdays only, the first leaving at 6.50am and the last at 10.55pm.

FLÓI NATURE RESERVE

Birdwatchers should head for the estuarine **Flói Nature Reserve**, an important marshland on the eastern bank of the Ölfusá. It's visited by many wetland birds – common species include red-throated divers and various kinds of ducks and geese – with the biggest numbers appearing during the nesting season (May to July). There's a 2km circular hiking trail through the marshes. For more information, contact the **Icelandic Society for the Protection of Birds** (562 0477; www.fuglavernd.is).

The reserve is 3km northwest of Eyrarbakki – you'll need your own transport.

STOKKSEYRI

pop 490

Eyrarbakki's twin lies east along the shore. It's another small fishing village, with a tourist emphasis less on museums and more on family fun. Again, winter is not the time to visit, but come in summer and you could easily spend a day enjoying the two villages' attractions.

Sights & Activities

For spooky (if pricey) fun, the first port of call should be **Draugasetrið** (Ghost Centre; ☎ 483 1202; www.draugasetrid.is; Hafnargata 9; adult/12-16yr Ikr1500/990; ☼ 1-6pm Jun-Aug), on the top floor of a huge warehouse in the village centre. A 40-minute CD-guide (in English, French or German) tells you blood-curdling ghost stories in each of the 24 dark, dry-ice-filled rooms. The ghost centre recommends itself to over-12s; it certainly scared our pants off. Round the corner, and run by the same people, is the **Icelandic Wonders** (☎ 483 1202; www .draugasetrid.is; Hafnargata 9; adult/12-16yr Ikr1500/990; ☼ 1-6pm Jun-Aug) centre, which is in a similar vein but walks you into a world of trolls and elves.

Tots will love the supercute family park **Töfragarðurinn Stokkseyri** (☎ 896 5716; v/ Stjörnusteina; adult/2-12yr Ikr700/500; ☼ 11am-6pm May-Aug), signposted from the centre. Sweet baby animals – Arctic foxes, puppies, piglets, rabbits, lambs and goats – frolic in ridiculously green enclosures. There's also a big climbing frame, a bouncy castle and a cafe. It's only titchy, but it's infinitely nicer than Reykjavík's zoo (p84).

Kajakferðir Stokkseyri (☎ 896 5716; www. kajak.is; Heiðarbrún 24; ☼ Apr-Oct) offers guided kayaking on the nearby lagoon (Ikr3750 per hour), or out on the sea (two hours Ikr6800, over 14 years only). You can also choose to wander off on a 'Robinson Crusoe' – guideless but with a 'treasure map' to follow (adult/child six to 14 years Ikr3850/1000). Prices include admission to Stokkseyri's swimming pool.

Sundlaug Stokkseyrar (☎ 480 3260; adult/under 18yr Ikr370/free; ☼ 1-9pm Mon-Fri, 10am-5pm Sat & Sun Jun–mid-Aug, 5-9pm Mon-Fri, 10am-3pm Sat & Sun mid-Aug–May) is a fine example of the swimming-pool genre, with water slide and hot tubs.

About 6km east of Stokkseyri is **Rjómabúið á Baugsstöðum** (Baugsstaðir Creamery; ☎ 486 3369; adult/child Ikr300/free; ☼ 1-6pm Sat & Sun Jul & Aug), an old dairy cooperative (1905–52) that still has its original machinery. Interestingly, most of its produce was sold to England – so some readers' grandparents may have eaten butter from here!

Sleeping & Eating

Campsite (☎ 661 7002; per person Ikr500) There's a grassy little camping ground off Dvergasteinar, with toilets and running water.

Gaulverjaskóli Hostel (☎ 551 0654, 865 2121; gaulver jaskoli@hostel.is; s/d/tr/q Ikr4000/5800/7150/9250; ☼ Feb-mid-Nov) A brand-new hostel, opened in 2009. Its current keepers have poured their energy into renovating this former school into a clean, quiet hostel with a spacious separate kitchen block. It's based in a tiny hamlet marooned in a vast expanse of flat agricultural land, 10km from Stokkseyri along the coastal road.

Guesthouse South Coast (☎ 695 0495; www.stokk seyri.com; Eyjasel 2; s/d/tr Ikr4200/7300/8650) Another new sleeping choice, Guesthouse South Coast is owned by stained-glass artist Ella Rósinkrans. Its rooms are easy on the wallet, and for budget travellers without a car, it's more conveniently located than the hostel.

Kvöldstjarnan (Evening Star; ☎ 483 1800; www.kvold stjarnan.com; Stjörnusteinum 7; s/d Ikr5900/9100) Opened in September 2007, this family-run guest house still has that fresh-out-of-the-box feel. Its five bright, white rooms come with washbasins and fluffy feathery duvets, and there's a small lounge area and sparkling kitchen. The owner's father has created an impressive garden, in spite of strong ocean breezes and salt-laden air. Breakfast is Ikr1000.

Við Fjöruborðið (☎ 483 1550; www.fjorubordid.is; Eyrabraut 3a; mains Ikr1900-4700; ☼ noon-10pm daily Jun-Aug, 6-9pm Mon-Thu, 5-9pm Fri, noon-10pm Sat, noon-9pm Sun Sep-May) This upmarket seafood restaurant on the shore has a reputation for serving the best lobster in Iceland. The legendary lobster soup costs Ikr1820 and is worth every penny. The decor is quite distinctive – old flagstones, fishermen's glass floats, black tablecloths – and in summer you can dine on the patio out back. Reservations strongly recommended.

For cheap meals, there's a grill at the Shell petrol station.

Getting There & Away

For bus info, see Eyrarbakki (opposite).

HELLA
pop 810

This small agricultural community sits on the banks of the pretty Ytri-Rangá river in an important horse breeding area. It's also the nearest village to the hulking, shadow-wreathed volcano Hekla (p139), 35km north up Rtes 264 then 268.

THE EDDAS

The medieval monastery at Oddi was the source of the Norse Eddas, the most important surviving books of Viking poetry. The *Prose Edda* was written by the poet and historian Snorri Sturluson around 1222. It was intended to be a textbook for poets, with detailed descriptions of the language and metres used by the Norse *skalds* (court poets). It also includes the epic poem *Gylfaginning*, which describes the visit of Gylfi, the king of Sweden, to Ásgard, the citadel of the gods. In the process, the poem reveals Norse creation myths, stories about the gods, and the fate in store for men at Ragnarök, when this world ends.

The *Poetic Edda* was written later in the 13th century by Sæmundur Sigfússon. It's a compilation of works by unknown Viking poets, some predating the settlement of Iceland. The first poem, *Voluspá (Sibyl's Prophecy)*, is like a Norse version of Genesis and Revelations: it covers the beginning and end of the world. Later poems deal with the story of how Óðinn discovered the power of runes, and the legend of Siegfried and the Nibelungs, recounted in Wagner's *Ring Cycle*. The most popular poem is probably *Þrymskviða*, about the giant Thrym, who stole Þór's hammer and demanded the goddess Freyja in marriage in exchange for its return. To get his hammer back, Þór disguised himself as the bride-to-be and went to the wedding in her place. Much of the poem is devoted to his appalling table manners at the wedding feast, during which he consumes an entire ox, eight salmon and three skins of mead.

The handicrafts cooperative **Hekla Handverkshús** (☎ 487 1373; Þrúðvangur 35; ☼ 9am-12.30pm & 4-8.30pm Mon-Fri, 1-5pm Sat & Sun summer, weekends only winter) doubles as a tourist information desk. Pick up the free guide map *Power and Purity*, which covers the region from Hella to Skógar.

Sights & Activities

With its many **horse farms**, dramatic volcanic backdrop and proximity to the highlands, Hella is a good place for hacks into the wilderness on horseback. Most places offer trips for more experienced riders – unguided horse hire and longer tours into the highlands. Some local horse farms:

Hekluhestar (☎ 487 6598; www.hekluhestar.is; Austvaðsholt) Rtes 271 then 272, 9km northeast of Hella. Six- to eight-day tours to Landmannalaugar/Fjallabak from mid-June to mid-August.

Herriðarhóll (☎ 487 5252; www.herridarholl.is) Off Rte 284, 15km northwest of Hella. Week-long stays at the farm in July and August, with daily rides.

Hestheimar (☎ 487 6666; www.hestheimar.is) Near Rte 281, 7km northwest of Hella. Horse rental.

Kálfholt (☎ 487 5176; www.kalfholt.is; Ásahreppi) Rte 288, 17km west of Hella (eastern bank of the Þjórsá). Horse rental, plus two- to five-day rides from June to August.

Leirubakki (☎ 487 8700; www.leirubakki.is) Rte 26, 30km northeast of Hella (near Hekla). Horse rental.

Of course, Hella has a good **geothermal swimming pool** (☎ 487 5334; ☼ 7am-9pm Mon-Fri, 10am-7pm Sat & Sun Jun–mid-Aug, 4-9pm Mon-Fri, 1-6pm Sat & Sun mid-Aug–May), with hot pots and sauna.

Oddi (about 8km south of town on unsurfaced Rte 266) was once the site of an important Saga Age monastery – see the boxed text, above. There's nothing much to see here today, though; you'll get a better sense of Viking history from reading the Eddas themselves.

Sleeping & Eating

Árhús (☎ 487 5577; www.arhus.is; Rangárbakkar; sites per person Ikr700, sb d with/without bathroom Ikr8000/6500, self-catering cabins Ikr6500-13,300; ☼ cafe 11.30am-10pm summer, noon-9pm winter) Right on the riverbank south of Rte 1, Árhús offers a well-equipped campsite and 28 wooden cabins with kitchenettes that sleep three to four people. Most have bathrooms, but the seven cheapest share the campers' toilet block. There's also a cafe selling so-so light meals (Ikr900 to Ikr2500) – but it's worth stopping to enjoy the lovely river views from the outside balcony. Breakfast is Ikr1000.

Gistiheimilið Brenna (☎ 487 5532; www.mmedia.is/toppbrenna; Þrúðvangur 37; sb/linen Ikr2300/3100) Down by the river north of Rte 1, this pink guest house has the most beautiful window boxes, and offers hostel-style accommodation. There are three family and three double rooms, plus a cute little kitchen and a guest sitting room. Walls are quite thin, so you'll have to tiptoe on those laminated floors.

SOUTHWEST ICELAND

Fosshótel Mosfell (☎ 487 5828; bokun@fosshotel. is; Þrúðvangur 6; s/d with washbasin Ikr9500/11,500, with bathroom Ikr20,900/22,900; 🖵) Facilities are limited, but the staff here are really charming! Most of the 53 rooms are en suite, with neat if unremarkable green decor; however, upstairs rooms are half-price because they're tiny and bathroomless. The hotel has plenty of big communal spaces, plus there's internet access in the lobby.

Hótel Rangá (☎ 487 5700; www.hotelranga.is; Suðurlandsvegur; d from €234; 🖵 🛜) Midway between Hella and Hvolsvöllur, Rangá is a kind of luxurious ranch. It has cosy wood-panelled rooms (all with verandahs, bathtubs and the extras you'd expect from a top hotel), three outdoor hot pots and a superior restaurant. If you can afford it, go for one of the seven fantastically decorated 'World Pavilion' suites (€750). They're so distinctive that it's hard to choose a favourite, although Africa – with its ostrich-egg lightshades and grass roof – is pretty magical. Prices include breakfast.

The cheapest place to eat is the grill at the Olís petrol station. Alternatively, there's **Kanslarinn** (☎ 487 5100; Dynskálum 10c; meals Ikr1200-3000) on the main road or the bar-restaurant **Kristján X** (☎ 487 5484; Þrúðvangur 34; meals Ikr800-2900). Both serve the usual burgers, fish, grills and pizzas.

There's a **Kjarval supermarket** (☎ 585 7585; Suðurlandsvegur 1; 🕒 9am-8pm Mon-Fri, 11am-9pm Sat, noon-6pm Sun).

Getting There & Away

Reykjavík Excursions (RE; ☎ 580 5400; www.re.is) and **Trex** (☎ 551 1166; www.bogf.is) both run numerous services between Reykjavík and Skaftafell, Landmannalaugar, Þórsmörk, Vík and Höfn that stop at Hella (and also Hvolsvöllur, with the exception of the Landmannalaugar buses). The RE buses run from mid-June to mid-September only, but in winter a reduced schedule is operated by Trex. The fare from Reykjavík is Ikr2500.

HEKLA

The name of Iceland's most famous and active volcano means Hooded One, as its 1491m-high summit is almost always shrouded in ominous-looking cloud. Hekla has vented its fury numerous times throughout history, and was once believed to be the gateway to hell.

The volcano is due to blow its top again in around 2010. Several walking trails lead up to the summit, but many people are happy just to see Hekla at a distance.

History

Viking-era settlers built farms on the rich volcanic soils around Hekla, only to be wiped out by the eruption of 1104, which buried everything within a radius of 50km. Since then there have been 15 major eruptions – the 1300 eruption covered more than 83,000 sq km in ash.

By the 16th century, Europe had decided that Hekla was the entrance to hell. Contemporary literature reported that the black skies overhead were filled with vultures and ravens, and that you could hear the howling of the damned.

In 1947, after more than 100 years of inactivity, Hekla belched a mushroom cloud of ash more than 27km into the air. This was followed by another huge eruption in 1970. Since then Hekla has gone off at roughly 10-year intervals, with short but powerful outbursts in 1980, 1991 and 2000. The main danger comes from the ash, whose high fluorine content has poisoned thousands of sheep; although, unexpectedly, the 2000 eruption produced a small pyroclastic flow (a high-speed and highly destructive torrent of rock particles and gas, which typically travels at over 130km per hour and can reach temperatures of 800°C).

Sights & Activities

HEKLA CENTER

The **Hekla Center** (☎ 487 8700; adult/child Ikr700/350; 🕒 9am-11pm summer), a small exhibition devoted to the volcano, can be seen at Leirubakki farm (see p140).

CLIMBING HEKLA

You can climb Hekla, but remember that it's still an active volcano. There's never much warning before eruptions, which are usually indicated by multiple small earthquakes 30 to 80 minutes before it blows! Stick to days when the summit is free from heavy cloud, and carry plenty of water – the volcanic ash makes you thirsty.

There's a small car park where mountain road F225 branches off Rte 26 (about 18km northeast of Leirubakki, or 45km northeast of Hella). Most hire cars aren't insured for F roads and will need to be parked here, but it's a long and dusty walk (16km) to the foot of the volcano (or you could try your luck at hitching).

With a 4WD you can continue along F225 to the bottom of Hekla. From here, a well-marked walking track climbs steadily up to the ridge on the northeastern flank of the mountain and then southwest to the summit crater. Although the peak is often covered in snow, the floor of the crater is still hot. From the bottom of the volcano, the return trip takes about four hours.

SNOWCAR TOURS

In winter you can take a snowcar tour to the summit of Hekla with **Toppferðir** (☎ 487 5530, 861 1662; www.mmedia.is/toppbrenna) – call for prices.

Sleeping & Eating

Rjúpnavellir í Landsveit (☎ 892 0409; http://rjupnavel lir.123.is; sb/linen Ikr2400/3500) The closest accommodation to the Rte 26–F225 junction are these two large wooden cabins, with sleeping-bag space for 44 people and cooking facilities. There's also a five-person hut for hire.

Hótel Leirubakki (☎ 487 6591; www.leirubakki.is; sites per person Ikr800, sb Ikr4200, s/d without bathroom Ikr10,900/15,200, with bathroom Ikr17,500/20,800) This exceptionally appealing historical farm (18km from the Rte 26–F225 junction) has accommodation for everyone: a quiet campsite by the old churchyard; an 11-room guest house with shared bathrooms and kitchen, and sleeping-bag accommodation in the basement; and a hotel with bright parquet-floored rooms and volcano views. Facilities include hot tubs and a 'Viking pool'; an information and exhibition centre; horse hire (Ikr4000 per hour) and petrol pump. Its 1st-class restaurant (mains Ikr2700 to Ikr4600) serves trout and lamb prepared in the farm's smokehouse, from noon to 5pm and 6pm to 9pm daily, June to early September; phone for times rest of the year.

Getting There & Away

From mid-June to mid-September, **Reykjavík Excursions** (☎ 580 5400; www.re.is) has a daily bus at 8.30am from Reykjavík to Landmannalaugar, which passes Leirubakki (Ikr3500, 2¼ hours) at 10.45am. The return trip passes Leirubakki at 4.45pm.

HVOLSVÖLLUR
pop 850

The countryside surrounding Hvolsvöllur is soaked with history. Its farms were the setting for the bloody events of *Njál's Saga* (see the boxed text, opposite), one of Iceland's favourites; today, though, the saga sites exist mainly as place names, peaceful grassed-over ruins or modern agricultural buildings.

Hvolsvöllur itself is a small village dominated by a huge petrol station at either end. It's a jumping-off point for Þórsmörk, and the last place where you can stock up on supplies.

Sögusetrið (see Sights & Activities, below) also doubles as a seasonal tourist information centre.

Sights & Activities

As you might expect, **Sögusetrið** (Saga Centre; ☎ 487 8781; njala@njala.is; Hliðarvegur; adult/under 16yr Ikr700/free; ⏰ 9am-6pm daily mid-May–mid-Sep, 11am-5pm Sat & Sun mid-Sep–mid-May) is devoted to the events of *Njál's Saga*, which took place in the surrounding hills. Written boards explain the most dramatic parts of the story (in Icelandic, English and German). It's OK if you just want a potted version of the saga, but you're probably better off reading the real thing (books are on sale in the attached souvenir shop).

The town has a good outdoor **swimming pool** (☎ 488 4295; Vallarbraut 16; adult/12-16yr Ikr300/150; ⏰ 7am-9pm Mon-Fri, 10am-3pm Sat & Sun) with a baby pool and two hot pots.

Ask the tourist office about local **horse riding**.

Sleeping & Eating

Campsite (☎ 487 8078, 895 9160; www.hvolsvollur.is, in Icelandic; sites per person Ikr850; ⏰ Jun-Aug) There's a site opposite the Shell station on Austurvegur; pay for your pitch at the tourist office.

Ásgarður (☎ 487 1440; www.asgardurinn.is; Stórólfshvol; sb/s/d Ikr3500/4500/8000) Accommodation here is in trim one- or two-bed rooms inside small wooden cabins in a peaceful garden. All have a shower room, fridge and kettle. You can hire the whole cabin or individual rooms, and use your own sleeping-bag for a reduced rate. There's also a full kitchen and a lounge in the main building. Ásgarður is 500m off the Ring Road, signposted up Rte 261.

Vestri-Garðsauki (☎ 487 8078; www.gardsauki.is; s/d Ikr5000/8000) This summer guest house just off Rte 1 is run by a friendly Icelandic-German farming family. The four neat, plain rooms are all in the basement but are surprisingly bright; they share two bathrooms. There's also a kitchen for guest use. Breakfast can be ordered for Ikr800.

NJÁL'S SAGA

One of Iceland's best-loved sagas deals with two friends, Gunnar Hámundarson and Njál Þorgeirsson, destined by fate to become bitter enemies. A petty squabble between their wives kicks off a bloodthirsty feud, which escalates until practically everyone in the saga is dead. Written in the 13th century, it recounts 11th-century events that took place in the hills around Hvolsvöllur.

The saga's doomed hero is Gunnar of Hlíðarendi (near Fljótsdalur), who falls for and marries the beautiful, hot-tempered Hallgerður, who has long legs but – ominously – a 'thief's eyes'. Hallgerður has a falling-out with Bergþóra, wife of Njál. Things become increasingly strained between Gunnar and Njál as Hallgerður and Bergþóra begin murdering each other's servants.

In one important episode, Hallgerður sends a servant to burgle food from a man named Otkell. When Gunnar comes home and sees Hallgerður's stolen feast, his temper snaps. 'It's bad news indeed if I've become a thief's accomplice', he says, and slaps his wife – an act that later comes back to haunt him.

Through more unfortunate circumstances, Gunnar ends up killing Otkell and is eventually outlawed and sentenced to exile. As he rides away from home, his horse stumbles. Fatally, he takes one last glance back at his beloved farm Hlíðarendi and is unable to leave the valley. His enemies gather their forces and lay siege to the farm, but Gunnar manages to hold off the attackers until his bowstring breaks. When he asks Hallgerður for a lock of her hair to repair it, she refuses, reminding him of the slap she received years earlier – and Gunnar is killed.

The feud continues as Gunnar and Njál's clan members try to avenge their slaughtered kin. Njál himself acts as a peace broker, forming treaties between the two families, but in the end it all comes to nothing. Njál and his wife are besieged in their farm. Tucking themselves up in bed with their little grandson between them, the couple allow themselves to be burnt alive.

The only survivor of the fire is Njál's son-in-law Kári, who launches a legal case against the arsonists, commits a bit of extrajudicial killing himself and is finally reconciled with his arch-enemy, Flosi, who ordered the burning of the Njál family. The story is incredibly convoluted and it can be hard to keep track of who is murdering whom, but it's certainly epic.

Hótel Hvolsvöllur (☎ 487 8050; www.hotelhvolsvol lur.is; Hlíðarvegur 7; s/d Ikr14,400/18,200; 🖳 🛜) This large business-class hotel has 54 comfortable, green-shaded rooms. Twenty-six of these are new, although they're smaller than the older rooms, their deep turquoise carpets and dark-wood fittings give them a smarter air. The bar-restaurant, which specialises in fish dishes, is open for dinner year-round; there are also two rooftop hot tubs.

Galleri Pizza (☎ 487 8440; Hvolsvegur 29; meals Ikr1300-2300; ☽ noon-9pm Sun-Thu, noon-10pm Fri & Sat) The town pizzeria, one street back from the main road, is a busy, beery place with a cheery atmosphere. It also sells burgers, sandwiches and grills.

Café Eldstó (☎ 487 1011; Austurvegur 2; soup & bread Ikr890, lamb soup Ikr1590; ☽ noon-7pm Tue-Sun May-Sep) This posh little cafe serves light meals (soup, salad and sandwiches) on its own handmade crockery. Opera plays in the background, the scent of coffee wafts…nice, although the service can be a little brusque.

There are **grills** (☽ to 9pm) at both the N1 and Shell petrol stations; the N1 garage also has a **Vín Búð** (☎ 487 7797; ☽ 11am-6pm Mon-Thu, 11am-7pm Fri, 11am-4pm Sat Jun-Aug, 7-6pm Mon-Thu, 2-7pm Fri, 11am-2pm Sat Sep-May). Pick up self-catering supplies at the Kjarval supermarket.

Getting There & Away

Buses stop at the N1 petrol station on the main road. Public transport to Hvolsvöllur is identical to that going to Selfoss or Hella; the fare from Reykjavík is Ikr2900.

From mid-June to mid-September, Reykjavík Excursion's scheduled buses to Þórsmörk (Ikr3000, 1½ hours) leave Hvolsvöllur at 10.15am daily, returning at 4pm. From 15 June to 31 August, a second service leaves Hvolsvöllur at 5.50pm. In the reverse direction, it leaves Þórsmörk at 8.30am.

Charter flights to Heimaey (see p155) leave from the airstrip at Bakki, about 27km south of Hvolsvöllur. From 2010, the ferry will also leave from here – see the boxed text, p155.

AROUND HVOLSVÖLLUR

Keldur

About 5km west of Hvolsvöllur, unsurfaced Rte 264 winds north along the Rangárvellir valley to the **medieval turf-roofed farm** (☎ 487 8452) at Keldur. This historic settlement once belonged to Ingjaldur Höskuldsson, a character in *Njál's Saga*. The interior was closed to visitors in 2000 after earthquake damage, but it's still worth visiting to see these Saga Age buildings. There's no public transport along Rte 264, but the 12km walk to Keldur is pleasant enough.

Bergþórshvoll

Down by the coast, Bergþórshvoll was Njál's farm (although there's not too much to see today). *Njál's Saga* relates that this is where he and his wife and grandchild were burnt to death in their bed in 1011; interestingly, an archaeological excavation in 1951 did find traces of a burnt-out building here. About 4km east of Hvolsvöllur, Rtes 255 and then 252 will take you there (21km).

Hvolsvöllur to Fljótsdalur

At the edge of Hvolsvöllur, Rte 261 turns east off the Ring Road. It follows the edge of the Fljótshlíð hills, offering great views over the flood plain of the Markarfljót river and the Eyjafjallajökull glacier. There are several B&Bs along the surfaced section of the road, which ends near the farm and church at **Hlíðarendi**, once the home of Gunnar Hámundarson from *Njál's Saga*. Although it seems tantalisingly close, Þórsmörk can be reached only by 4WD via mountain road F249, on the far side of the Markarfljót bridge on Rte 1.

About 8km after the tarmac ends, Rte 261 passes the turf-roofed youth hostel at **Fljótsdalur**. This is a very popular place to stay, and there are great walks in the surrounding countryside, including the 10km hike northeast to the ice cap at **Tindfjallajökull** (1462m). With a 4WD you can continue along mountain road F261 towards Landmannalaugar or up to the glacier Mýrdalsjökull.

SLEEPING & EATING

Kaffi Langbrók (☎ 487 8333; Kirkjulækur III; sites per person Ikr700; ☺ May-Aug; ☐) This wooden ranch-style building 10km from Hvolsvöllur has a peaceful campsite on its grounds. There's also a cafe with internet access – and, more importantly, homemade waffles and cream!

Fljótsdalur Youth Hostel (☎ 487 8498; www.hostel.is; Fljótshlíð; sb Ikr2000; ☺ Easter-Oct) It's very basic and not to everyone's taste, but if you're looking for a simple but peaceful base for highland walks, with knowledgeable staff, a beautiful garden, a homey kitchen, a cosy sitting room, an excellent library and mountain views that make your knees tremble, then you'll find it at Fljótsdalur. Advance booking is recommended, as space is limited – there's one seven-mattress attic and two four-bed rooms. The nearest shop is 27km away at Hvolsvöllur, so bring in all supplies.

Smáratun (☎ 487 8471; www.smaratun.is; sites per person Ikr900, sb Ikr3000, guest house d Ikr9000, hotel d Ikr15,400, summer house Ikr9000-17,000) This attractive white farm with a blue tin roof has four- to six-person summer houses for hire (three with their own hot pots, eight without). There are also smart hotel-style rooms, cheaper guest house rooms (with shared bathrooms), sleeping-bag places, and spaces to pitch a tent, plus a general hot tub open to everyone, and horse hire. It's about 13km from Hvolsvöllur.

Hvolsvöllur to Þórsmörk

The road to Þórsmörk (Rte 249/F249) begins just east of the Markarfljót river on Rte 1. Although it quickly turns into a 4WD-only road, there are some interesting sights at the start of the road that can be reached by car.

From the highway you can see the beautiful high falls at **Seljalandsfoss**, which tumble over a rocky scarp into a deep, green pool. It's perfect for romantics who dream of walking behind waterfalls – a (slippery) path runs round the back. Buses on the Höfn–Reykjavík route often wait here for the Þórsmörk bus, giving passengers time for a few quick photos.

A few hundred metres further down the Þórsmörk road, in the grounds of the farm Hamragarðar, is the spooky waterfall **Gljúfurárfoss**, which gushes into a hidden canyon. To see the falls, you have to wade into the stream beside the farm.

You can camp at the farm **Hamragarðar** (☎ 487 8920; sites per person Ikr700; ☺ Jun-Aug), right next to the hidden waterfall at Gljúfurárfoss.

About 5km closer to Þórsmörk (still on Rte 249), the historical **Stóra-Mörk III** (☎ 487 8903; storamork@isl.is; sb/linen Ikr2000/2800) farmhouse (mentioned, of course, in *Njál's Saga*) offers rooms with or without bathroom, a guest kitchen, and a good breakfast spread. There are lovely views of the Eyjafjallajökull glacier from the farm's conservatory.

ÞÓRSMÖRK

One of the most beautiful places in Iceland is Þórsmörk, a stunning valley full of weird rock formations, twisting gorges, a singing cave, mountain flowers and icy streams. Three glaciers (Tindfjallajökull, Eyjafjallajökull and Mýrdalsjökull) shelter it from harsher weather and provide a dramatic backdrop. Way back in 1921, the loveliness of Þórsmörk was officially recognised when it was given national reserve status.

Be warned, though: Þórsmörk's ravishing appearance and proximity to Reykjavík (130km) make it an extremely popular spot in summer. It gets particularly crowded in July, when students from around Iceland descend to party.

The main accommodation area is at Húsadalur (Map p287), where the Reykjavík Excursions bus from Reykjavík terminates. The large, artificial hot pool **Þórslaug** is a welcome feature – perfect for easing tired muscles after a long walk. On the hill behind the hut is the cave **Sönghellir** (one of several singing caves in Iceland), from where a maze of walking trails leads through scrubby dwarf birch forests to the Þórsmörk hut, about 3km further up the valley. The summit of **Valahnúkur** (458m), immediately west of Þórsmörk hut, has a view disc that identifies all the surrounding mountains. Allow about an hour to get there from either Húsadalur or Þórsmörk.

The higher reaches of the valley are known as **Goðaland** (Land of the Gods) and are full of bizarre hoodoo formations. There's a mountain hut at **Básar** (Map p287), on the far bank of the Krossá river, which marks the start of the popular hike over Fimmvörðuháls Pass to Skógar. The trail passes right between Eyjafjallajökull and Mýrdalsjökull, and the pass itself makes an easy day hike from either Þórsmörk or Básar. To get to Básar from further down the valley, you must cross the pedestrian bridge over the Krossá, just downstream from the Þórsmörk hut. It's one of Iceland's more dangerous rivers for 4WDs – only attempt to cross, in a high-clearance 4WD vehicle, if you know what you're doing.

Accommodation at Þórsmörk is open from May to September, although the plentiful scheduled buses and tours generally only run between mid-June and mid-September.

Activities

Myriad hikes are possible in the mountains around Þórsmörk, and most can be undertaken

independently. The relevant topographic sheet is *Þórsmörk/Landmannalaugar* 1:100,000. As well as local hikes, you can continue inland to Landmannalaugar (see p285). Alternatively, you could head down to the coast at Skógar via Fimmvörðuháls Pass – see below.

SHORT HIKES

From Rte F249, you can easily hike up to **Steinholtsjökull**, a tongue of ice extending off the north side of Eyjafjallajökull. The ice has carved a sheer-sided, 100m-deep gorge, and the short river Stakksholtsá flows out from under it and winds down to Markarfljót. Further west the larger glacier **Gígjökull** descends into a small lagoon right beside Rte F249, filling it with carved icebergs. To explore the main ice caps at Eyjafjallajökull and Mýrdalsjökull you'll need special equipment – including ropes, crampons and ice axes – and ideally a GPS device.

ÞÓRSMÖRK TO SKÓGAR HIKE

The dramatic and popular hike from Þórsmörk to Skógar passes right between the glaciers of Eyjafjallajökull and Mýrdalsjökull. The hike can be done in a long day, but it's more enjoyable to break the journey at Fimmvörðuháls Pass (1093m), which has a mountain hut run by Útivist (see below). Although the glaciers seem close enough to touch, this walk is fairly easy and you won't need any special gear. It's best attempted from mid-July to early September, but always keep an eye on the weather – it can change rapidly up here.

The hike starts about 1.5km east of the Básar hut at Goðaland and then climbs steadily to **Morinsheiði**, which has dramatic views over Mýrdalsjökull, and Eyjafjallajökull. From here, you face a steep ascent to the ridge at **Heljarkambur**. The next stage takes you across tundra and snowfields to **Fimmvörðuháls Pass** itself, with Mýrdalsjökull on the left and Eyjafjallajökull on the right. The Fimmvörðuskáli mountain hut is a short walk off the main track, near a small lake.

The following day, you can begin the hike down to Skógar. The main trail is clear and well trodden, but an interesting alternative is to leave the track at the footbridge and follow the stream down to the waterfall **Skógafoss**, about 1km west of Skógar village.

Útivist (☎ 562 1000; www.utivist.is) and **Ferðafélag Íslands** (☎ 568 2533; www.fi.is) both run guided hikes from Skógar over Fimmvörðuháls to Þórsmörk from around Ikr24,000; contact

SOUTHWEST ICELAND

them for details. The **Icelandic Mountain Guides** (☎ 587 9999; www.mountainguides.is) run similar trips, although their prices are much higher.

Sleeping

There are three huts in the Þórsmörk area – at Þórsmörk, Básar and Húsadalur – and another at the top of the Fimmvörðuháls Pass. All have cooking facilities, showers and running water, but they tend to get packed out, particularly at weekends. Bring your own food and sleeping bag; a stove is also a good idea, to avoid waiting for the crowded facilities.

Wild camping is prohibited, but the three Þórsmörk huts have tent sites around them; the hut at Fimmvörðuháls Pass doesn't, as the ground is too rocky.

To book spaces at the huts (strongly advised), contact the organisations listed in the following reviews.

HÚSADALUR

The **Húsadalur cabins and huts** (☎ 894 1506 May-Sep; sites per person Ikr800, sb dm/d Ikr2800/6800, 5-person hut Ikr10,500), along with the cafe, kitchen and shower block, hot pool and sauna, almost form a tourist village of their own. They're now being run by **Hostelling International Iceland** (☎ 552 8300; thorsmork@thorsmork.is, www.hostels.is).

ÞÓRSMÖRK HUT

The Þórsmörk hut **Skagfjörðsskáli** (☎ 854 1191 mid-May–Sep; sites per person Ikr900, sb Ikr3300) can sleep 75. Book through **Ferðafélag Íslands** (☎ 568 2533; www.fi.is; Mörkin 6, IS-108 Reykjavík). This organisation can also take bookings for huts along the Landmannalaugar–Þórsmörk track.

BÁSAR HUT & FIMMVÖRÐUHÁLS PASS

There's space for 80 people in the hut at **Básar** (sites per person Ikr800, sb Ikr2300), booked through **Útivist** (☎ 562 1000; www.utivist.is; Laugavegur 178, IS-101 Reykjavík).

The comfortable 23-bed hut at **Fimmvörðuskáli** (sb Ikr2300), on the pass between Eyjafjallajökull and Mýrdalsjökull, is also Útivist's. It lies 600m west of the main trail and is easy to miss in poor weather (GPS ref N 63°37.320', W 19°27.093'). Útivist tour groups have priority here, so it's often booked out. There's no campsite.

Getting There & Away

BUS

Reykjavík Excursions (☎ 580 5400; www.re.is) run scheduled services from mid-June to mid-September. Buses run between Reykjavík and Húsadalur (over the hill from Þórsmörk) at 8.30am daily (Ikr5200, 3¼ hours), reaching Húsadalur around noon and returning at 4pm. From 15 June to 31 August, a second service runs daily from Reykjavík at 4pm; in the reverse direction, the extra bus leaves Þórsmörk at 8.30am.

From mid-June to mid-September, there's a 'sightseeing' bus that runs at 1pm from Húsadalur to Básar, returning at 2pm.

Several companies run day trips from Reykjavík in summer for around Ikr14,000 – see p86.

CAR & BICYCLE

Even though Þórsmörk seems almost touchable from the Ring Road (only 30km along F249), you *cannot* drive there without a 4WD with decent clearance. The gravel road surface eventually turns into boulders, and even a 4WD car probably won't make it over the bumps. Even experienced 4WD drivers sometimes get into difficulty at the river sections on this route.

Plenty of cyclists fight their way up to Þórsmörk, but it's a hard slog. You can shave off a few kilometres by leaving Rte 1 near the farm Vorsabær and taking the old bridge over the Markarfljót, which is now closed to cars.

HIKING

You can walk to Þórsmörk from Landmannalaugar (four days), Skógar (one or two days) or along Rtes 249 and F249 from Seljaland (one long day). The Skógar hike is covered in more detail on p143, and the Landmannalaugar to Þórsmörk hike is covered in the boxed text, p288.

SKÓGAR & AROUND
pop 20

You begin to enter the south coast's realm of ice at Skógar, which nestles under the Eyjafjallajökull ice cap about 1km off Rte 1. This tiny settlement offers two corking attractions. At its western edge, the dizzyingly high Skógafoss waterfall tumbles down a mossy cliff. On the eastern side you'll find the fantastic folk museum, open year-round for your delectation.

The village is also the start – or the end – of the hike over the Fimmvörðuháls Pass to Þórsmörk (see p143).

At the time of writing, a small summer-only branch of the **Icelandic Travel Market** (☎ 894 2956; www.itm.is; ◷ 8.30am-6.30pm Jun-Aug) was operating from the Fossbúð restaurant building (next to the youth hostel).

Sights

The highlight of Skógar – indeed of this whole stretch of coast – is the wonderful **Skógar Folk Museum** (☎ 487 8845; www.skogasafn.is; adult/12-15yr Ikr1000/500; ◷ museum 9am-6.30pm Jun-Aug, 10am-5pm May & Sep, 11am-4pm Oct-May, cafe 10am-5pm Jun-Aug, 11am-4pm May & Sep), which covers all aspects of Icelandic life. The vast collection was put together by 88-year-old Þórður Tómasson, who has been amassing items for 74 years. You might be lucky enough to meet Þórður in person – he often comes in to play traditional songs for visitors on an old church organ. There are also various restored buildings (church, turf-roofed farmhouse, cowsheds etc) in the grounds, and a hangarlike building at the back houses an interesting transport museum, plus a cafe and souvenir shop.

The 62m-high **waterfall** of Skógafoss topples over a rocky cliff at the western edge of Skógar in dramatic style. Climb the steep staircase alongside for giddying views downwards; or walk to the foot of the falls, shrouded in sheets of mist and rainbows. Legend has it that a settler named Þrasi hid a chest of gold behind Skógafoss; sometimes you can almost see it glittering…

Activities

The most popular walk in the area is the two-day **hike** (see p143) over Fimmvörðuháls Pass to Þórsmörk. However, you can also take a morning hike up to the pass and return to Skógar the same day. The trail starts on the 4WD track to Skógarheiði behind the village. The return trip should take about seven hours. For the past two summers, a small shop has been operating from inside the Fossbúð restaurant building, where you can stock up on drinks and snacks.

Built into a hillside at Seljavellir, 7km west of Skógar, **Seljavallalaug** is a historical old concrete pool filled by a natural hot spring. Park by the farm and follow the path upwards.

Horse riding can be arranged through the farm **Skálakot** (☎ 487 8953; www.skalakot.com; sh Ikr2000), 15km west of Skógar. Short rides cost Ikr2600 per hour; you can wander up by the glacier on four-hour trips (Ikr6000) or

plan an all-inclusive riding holiday (around Ikr18,000 per day). Skálakot also has rather strange sleeping-bag accommodation, in a dorm that looks straight into the stables!

Sleeping & Eating

SKÓGAR

Skógar campsite (☎ 487 8801, 899 5955; sites per person Ikr850; ◷ Jun–mid-Sep) This place has a great location, right by Skógafoss; the sound of falling water makes a soothing lullaby. There's a small toilet block with fresh water (showers Ikr200).

Skógar Youth Hostel (☎ 487 8801; skogar@hostel .is; sb/d/tr Ikr2100/5800/7150; ◷ 25 May–15 Sep) In an old school, this 30-bed hostel is very close to the waterfall…but, unfortunately, you can't quite see it from the building! Never mind – a minute's walk and you're there. There's a guest kitchen and a laundry.

Edda Hotel (☎ 444 4000; www.hoteledda.is; sb/s/d Ikr2000/8000/10,000; ◷ mid-Jun–mid-Aug) This modern and comfortable summer hotel close to the museum is split over two buildings. Sleeping-bag spaces are in the gym, or choose simple rooms with shared bathrooms. The Edda Hotel has a licensed restaurant and a hot pot.

Hótel Skógar (☎ 487 4880; www.hotelskogar.is; s/d from €167/222; ◷ May–mid-Sep; ▯) Breaking the IKEA mould, this architecturally interesting hotel has unusual but quite romantic rooms, all with en suites, embroidered curtains and bedspreads, and wooden animals dotted about. There's a decent restaurant, a hot tub and sauna in the garden, a computer for internet access, and a bad bird-eating cat.

Fossbúð (◷ 11am-8pm Jun-Aug) Advertised as a restaurant, Fossbúð is really more a place for quick snacks – soup, salad, hamburgers and pizzas. It opens inside the local community centre in high season only.

WEST OF SKÓGAR

There are several places to stay at Ásólfsskáli, around 15km west of Skógar; and at Lambafell/Raufarfell, about 6km west of Skógar.

Gistihúsið Edinborg (☎ 846 1384; www.islandia .is/thorn; Lambafell; s/d Ikr10,500/15,200, cottage Ikr16,400; ⬥) Formerly named Hotel Edinborg (and still signposted as such from the main road), this is actually farmhouse accommodation with few facilities! However, this tall tin-clad house does have inviting wooden-floored en suite rooms with comfy beds, and an attic seating area with glacier views. There are also two snug cottages for hire. The nearest place for an evening meal is 5km away. Breakfast is Ikr1200.

Drangshlíð I (☎ 487 8868; drangshlid@drangshlid.is; Raufarfell; s/d Ikr8700/17,000; ☾ advance bookings necessary Oct-May) At the foot of a green cliff full of nesting birds, this modern white farmhouse has large guest rooms, all with private bathroom, and a big, bright dining room for meals. Look out for the barns built into caves in the surrounding fields.

Country Hotel Anna (☎ 487 8950; www.hotelanna.is; Ásólfsskáli; s/d Ikr14,500/19,800; ▯) Ooh, this place is nice! Its seven en suite rooms are furnished with antiques, embroidered bedspreads settle over big, comfy beds, and facilities include minifridges, kettles and satellite TV. The hotel has a Green Globe award for environmental goodness. Prices include breakfast, and evening meals at the whitewashed cafe (open 2pm to 8.30pm mid-June to August) are possible if prebooked.

Getting There & Away

Buses from Reykjavík to Skaftafell, Vík and Höfn stop at the Edda Hotel in Skógar (Ikr4900, three hours).

SKÓGAR TO VÍK Í MÝRDAL
Sólheimajökull

One of the easiest glacial tongues to reach is Sólheimajökull, which unfurls from the main Mýrdalsjökull ice cap. A 5km bumpy dirt track (Rte 222) leads off the Ring Road to a small car park; from there, the ice is approximately 800m away. You can scramble up onto the glacier, but keep an eye out for fissures and crevasses. The sand and gravel deposited by the rivulets running out of the end of the glacier are a definite no-go area because of quicksand.

Much better than slithering in normal shoes, you can strap on crampons and go for a proper walk up Sólheimajökull with the **Icelandic Mountain Guides** (Reykjavik office ☎ 587 9999, seasonal Skógar office Jun-Aug 894 2956; www.mountainguide.is). Their Blue Ice Adventure (adult/8-15yr Ikr5500/3900, 1½ hours, five trips per day between 9am and 4.30pm; minimum age eight) or longer Sólheimajökull Exploration (Ikr8200 per person, 3½ hours, 11.30am; minimum age 10) leave from the car park between June and August (less frequently late May and early September). It's best to book ahead. The guides also do trips on Svínafellsjökull at Skaftafell – see p298.

Mýrdalsjökull

The gorgeous glacier Mýrdalsjökull is Iceland's fourth-largest ice cap, covering 700 sq km and reaching a thickness of almost 750m in places. The volcano Katla snoozes beneath, periodically blasting up through the ice to drown the coastal plain in a deluge of meltwater, sand and tephra.

ACTIVITIES

With the right equipment, hikes are possible on the main ice cap and on the fingerlike projection Sólheimajökull, close to Skógar (see left). You can also walk to the ice cap from the lovely Þakgil campsite (p148).

For 4WD, snowmobile and dog-sled tours, turn off the Ring Road and head 10km up Rte 222 to the mountain hut Sólheimaskli. Here you'll find **Arcanum** (☎ 487 1500; www.snow.is), which can take you bouncing over the glacier on one-hour snowmobiling trips (€170/230 with one person/two people aboard), or on a super-Jeep tour over the ice. If you don't have a vehicle, it can pick you up from Vík (€200), Skógar (€110) or just off Rte 1 (€65).

Although they have similar frostproof ears and thick furry coats, the dogs that pull the sleds at **Dogsledding.is** (☎ 487 7747, 863 8864; www.dogsledding.is; adult/under 12yr Ikr14,900/7500) are Greenland dogs, not huskies! At times when the glacier isn't safe, the one-hour dog-sled rides take place on the black-sand beach 9km east of Skógar. Bookings necessary.

TOURS

Various tour companies (see p86) offer trips from Reykjavík to Mýrdalsjökull.

Dyrhólaey

One of the south coast's most recognisable natural formations is the rocky plateau and huge stone sea arch at Dyrhólaey (10km west of Vík), which rises dramatically from the surrounding plain. The promontory is a nature reserve and is particularly rich in bird life, including puffins; however, it's closed to visitors during the nesting season. At other times you can visit its crashing black beaches and get the most awesome views from the top of the archway (best seen in its entirety from Reynisfjara – see opposite).

SOUTHWEST ICELAND

KATLA ERUPTION

Of all the volcanoes in Iceland, it will probably be Katla that causes the most trouble to Icelanders over the next few years. This highly active 30km-long volcano, buried deep under the Mýrdalsjökull glacier, has erupted roughly twice per century in the past. Since the last eruption was in 1918, it's now several decades overdue.

It's expected that when Katla does blow, days of poisonous ashfall, tephra clouds and lightning strikes will follow the initial explosion, with flash floods due to the sudden melting of glacial ice. The geological record shows that past eruptions have created tidal waves, which have boomeranged off the Vestmannaeyjar and deluged the area where the town of Vík stands today.

Local residents receive regular evacuation training for the day when Katla erupts. After receiving mobile phone alerts, farmers must hang a notice on their front doors to show that they have evacuated, before unplugging their electric fences, opening cattle sheds so that their animals can flee to higher ground, and heading for one of the evacuation centres in Hella, Hvolsvöllur or Skógar.

The national TV station RÚV has a webcam close to Vík, set up to film the floods when Katla erupts (www.ruv.is/katla).

You can take a tour through the arch in an amphibious vehicle with **Dyrhólaeyjarferðir** (☎ 487 8500; www.dyrholaey.com; tours adult/6-14yr Ikr4500/3500).

According to *Njál's Saga*, Kári – the only survivor of the fire that wiped out Njál's clan – had his farm here. Another Viking Age connection is the cave **Loftsalahellir**, reached by a track just before the causeway to Dyrhólaey, which was used for council meetings in saga times.

Camping is prohibited on Dyrhólaey. There's accommodation available at **Hótel Dyrhólaey** (☎ 487 1333; dyrholaey@islandia.is; s/d Ikr15,900/19,900; ☎), about 9km west of Vík at the farm Brekkur I. This large green guest house has the big rooms typical of modern bungalow motel-style hotels in Iceland; some have great views of the coast. There's also a restaurant (open 11.30am to 2pm and 7pm to 9pm April to September).

Reynisfjara

On the west side of Reynisfjall, the high ridge above Vík, a dirt road leads down to the black volcanic beach at Reynisfjara, which is backed by an incredible stack of **basalt columns**, which look like a giant church organ. The surrounding cliffs are full of caves formed from twisted and tortured basalt, and puffin chicks belly-flop off the cliffs here every summer. Immediately offshore are the sea stacks of **Reynisdrangur**. There are fabulous views west along the beach to the rock arch at Dyrhólaey.

VÍK Í MÝRDAL
pop 300
One of our favourite places in Iceland, Vík is a tiny strip of green wedged between the looming glacier Mýrdalsjökull and a battered beach of black sand and pebbles. It's a welcoming little community surrounded by natural wonders. The village started life as a fishing outpost, but a cooperative society was formed here in 1906 and is still Vík's biggest employer.

Information
The **tourist office** (☎ 487 1395; http://brydebud .vik.is; Víkurbraut 28; ⌚ 10am-1.30pm & 2.30-5pm Jun-Aug) is housed in the historic trading house Brydebúð. Kaupþing has an ATM and foreign-exchange desk. The post office has internet access (Ikr700 per hour).

Sights & Activities
Vík's most famous sight is the cluster of sea stacks at **Reynisdrangur**, which rise from the ocean at the western end of the **black-sand beach** like sinister rocky fingers. The highest stack is 66m tall. The nearby cliffs are good for puffin watching. A highly recommended **walk** (upwards from the western end of Vík) takes you to the top of the ridge **Reynisfjall** (340m), which offers superb views along the coast.

The tin-clad house **Brydebúð** was built in Vestmannaeyjar in 1831 and moved to Vík in 1895. Today it houses the tourist office, Halldórskaffi and a small **museum/exhibition centre** (adult/under 16yr Ikr500/free; ⌚ 10am-1.30pm & 2.30-5pm Jun-Aug), with displays on fishing, what it's like to live under the volcano Katla, and locally made church vestments.

Vík's **church** has some unusual red-and-white stained-glass windows in spiky geometrical shapes. The big souvenir shop **Víkurprjón** (☎ 487

1250; www.vikwool.is; Rte 1) is a coach-tour hit – you can watch woolly jumpers being made here.

Vík has a small open-air **swimming pool** (☎ 487 1174; Mánabraut 3; adult/5-15yr Ikr300/150; ⊙ 7am-9pm Mon-Fri, 10am-7pm Sat & Sun Jun-Aug, shorter hrs winter).

Sleeping & Eating

Vík campsite (☎ 487 1345, 899 2406; sites per person Ikr800, cottages Ikr6000; ⊙ Jun-Aug) The campsite sits under a grassy ridge at the eastern end of the village, just beyond the Edda Hótel. There's an octagonal building with cooking facilities, washing machine, toilets and free showers. Six-person farmhouse-style cottages are also available.

Norður-Vík Youth Hostel (☎ 487 1106; www.hostel.is; Suðurvíkurvegur; sb m/d Ikr2100/5800; ⊙ Apr-Oct) Vík's friendly hostel is this old beige house on the hill behind the village. Good facilities include guest lounge, kitchen, breakfast (Ikr1000) and bike hire (per half-day/day Ikr1300/1800). It's usually booked out in summer.

Gistihús Ársalir (☎ 487 1400; simon@ismennt.is; Austurvegur 7; sb/s/d Ikr2400/5000/8000) There are spacious rooms with shared bathrooms (some with balconies) at this white house on the outskirts of the village, plus a kitchen and mountain-bike hire.

Guesthouse Puffin (Víkurbraut 24a; sb Ikr2900) This place has very thin bedroom walls but a great old guest kitchen (check out the diagonally opening drawers) and a possibly haunted lounge. The guest house is attached to Hótel Lundi.

Hótel Lundi (☎ 487 1212; www.hotelpuffin.is; Víkurbraut 24-26; s/d/tr Ikr12,650/17,250/21,400; 🖥 🛜) This small old-fashioned family-run hotel has rooms with telephones and bathrooms, and a respectable restaurant; prices include breakfast.

Edda Hótel Vík í Mýrdal (☎ 444 4000; www.hoteledda .is; s/d Ikr14,600/18,300; ⊙ May–mid-Sep; 🖥) One of the three-star Edda Plus hotels, this serviceable modern place has good, clean rooms with phone, TV and en suite bathroom. There's a restaurant with ocean views, and free internet in the dining room.

Halldórskaffi (☎ 487 1202; Víkurbraut 28; mains Ikr400-1800; ⊙ 11am-11pm Sun-Fri, to 2am Sat Jun-Aug, 6-11pm Fri, to 2am Sat Sep-May) In the same building as the tourist office, this place serves pizzas, burgers, sandwiches, fish mains and beer in an old-world wooden dining room.

There are restaurants at the Edda Hótel and Hótel Lundi. The N1 petrol station contains

the **Ströndin Bistro** (☎ 487 1230; ⊙ 3-10pm); or for cheaper eats with a view of Reynisdrangur, there's the restaurant-grill **Víkurskáli** (☎ 487 1230; snacks Ikr790-1800; ⊙ to 9pm). For alcohol, there's a **Vín Búð** (⊙ 5-6pm Mon-Thu, 4-6pm Fri), and self-caterers can make use of the large **Kjarval supermarket** (☎ 487 1325; Víkurbraut 4; ⊙ 9am-6pm Mon-Fri, 11am-1pm Sat) near Brydebúð.

Getting There & Away

Vík lies on the main bus route between Höfn and Reykjavík, and buses stop at the N1 petrol station. From June to mid-September, the bus from Reykjavík leaves at 8.30am, stopping at places of interest, and returns from Vík at 3pm (one-way Ikr4900, five hours). A second bus leaves at 5pm, returning at 9am: this one is faster, with a journey time of 3¼ hours.

In winter, the bus runs from Reykjavík at 3pm on Tuesday, and 2pm Friday and Sunday.

EAST OF VÍK
Mælifell

On the edge of the glacier, this 642m-high **ridge** and the countryside around it are just spectacular. The simple but idyllic campsite at **Þakgil** (☎ 853 4889; www.thakgil.is; sites per person Ikr850, cabins Ikr12,000; ⊙ Jun & Jul), a green bowl among stark mountains, makes a convenient base from which to explore. You can walk up Mælifell, or even get up onto the glacier – a path leads to the nunatak (hill or mountain completely surrounded by a glacier) Huldufjöll. You can drive to Þakgil, 14km along a rough dirt road (Rte 214) that branches off Rte 1 about 5km east of Vík, or there are two walking paths from Vík.

At the start of Rte 214, **Country Hótel Höfðabrekka** (☎ 487 1208; www.hofdabrekka.is; s/d Ikr14,100/19,300; 🖥) is a large and reputedly haunted hotel! It offers tasteful wood-panelled rooms with en suites, four hot tubs, a guest kitchen and a good restaurant (open from 6pm to 10pm; bookings necessary in winter). Internet access costs Ikr300 per 20 minutes.

Mýrdalssandur

The vast black-lava sand flats of Mýrdalssandur, just east of Vík, are formed from material washed out from underneath the glacier Mýrdalsjökull. This 700 sq km area of sand is bleak and desolate, and apparently lifeless, but arctic foxes (which have a black coat in summer) and sea birds are common sights here. To the south of Rte 1, the small peak of **Hjörleifshöfði** (231m) rises above the sands and offers good views towards Vestmannaeyjar. On the other side of Rte 1, the green hill of **Hafursey** (582m) is another possible destination for walks from Vík. As you head east towards Höfn, look out for stone cairns constructed by early travellers to mark safe routes across the sands.

VESTMANNAEYJAR

Black and brooding, the Vestmannaeyjar form 15 eye-catching silhouettes off the southern shore. The islands were formed by submarine volcanoes around 11,000 years ago, except for sulky-looking Surtsey, the archipelago's newest addition, which rose from the waves in 1963. Surtsey was made a Unesco World Heritage Site in 2008, but its unique scientific status means that it is not possible to land there.

Heimaey is the only inhabited island. Its little town and sheltered harbour lie between dramatic *klettur* (escarpments) and two ominous volcanoes – blood-red Eldfell and conical Helgafell. Heimaey is famous for its puffins – around 10 million birds come here to breed – and for Þjóðhátíð, Iceland's biggest outdoor festival, held in August.

At the time of writing, the ferry *Herjólfur* provided daily connections to Þorlákshöfn on the mainland. It carries cars, but Heimaey is small enough to explore on foot. See the boxed text (p155) for planned changes to the ferry route. There are also flights here from Reykjavík and Bakki (near Hvolsvöllur).

HEIMAEY
pop 4090

Heimaey enjoys a spectacular setting, squeezed between dramatic cliffs to the west and the two looming volcanic cones to the east.

History

The island has had a turbulent and bloody history. The *Landnámabók* recounts that Ingólfur Arnarson originally came to Iceland with his blood-brother Hjörleifur, who was murdered by his Irish slaves (Westmen) shortly after landing. The slaves then fled to Heimaey, but Ingólfur hunted them down and killed them all.

Over the centuries the island was a marauders' favourite. The English raided Heimaey throughout the 15th century, building the stone fort Skansinn as their HQ. In 1627 Heimaey suffered the most awful attack by Algerian pirates, who went on a killing spree around the island, murdering 36 islanders and kidnapping 242 more (almost three-quarters of the population). The rest managed to escape by abseiling down cliffs or hiding in caves along the west coast. Those who were kidnapped were taken as slaves to north Africa; years later, 27 islanders had their freedom bought for them…and had a long walk home.

The volcanoes that formed Heimaey have come close to destroying the island on several occasions. The most famous eruption in modern times began unexpectedly at 1.45am on 23 January 1973, when a vast fissure burst open, gradually mutating into the volcano Eldfell, and prompting the island's evacuation (see the boxed text, p153).

Information

The summer **tourist office** (Map p151; ☎ 481 3322; www.visitwestmanislands.com; Heiðarvegur; ⊗ 10am-6pm daily mid-May–mid-Sep) moved to the main street in 2008 but may move back to the library again.

There are **Sparisjóðurinn** (Map p151; ☎ 488 2100; Bárustigur 15) and **Íslandsbanki** (Map p151; ☎ 440 4000; Kirkjuvegur 23) banks with ATMs near the post office.

Internet access is available for Ikr200 per hour at the **library** (Map p151; ☎ 488 2040; Ráðhústræti; ⊗ 10am-6pm Mon-Thu, to 5pm Fri year-round, plus 11am-2pm Sat Oct-Apr).

Sights
FISKA-OG NÁTTÚRUGRIPASAFN

The **Aquarium & Natural History Museum** (Map p151; ☎ 481 1997; Heiðarvegur 12; adult/6-13yr Ikr400/200; ⊗ 11am-5pm mid-May–mid-Sep, 3-5pm Sun mid-Sep–mid-May) has an interesting collection of stuffed birds and animals, plus fish tanks of hideous Icelandic fish and a live video link to a puffin colony. The museum acts as a hospital for puffin chicks.

BYGGÐASAFN

Housed in Heimaey library, this **folk museum** (Byggðasafn; Map p151; ☎ 488 2040; Ráðhústræti; adult/6-13yr Ikr400/200; ⊗ 11am-5pm mid-May–mid-Sep, by arrangement at other times) has loads of local-history displays, including fascinating photos

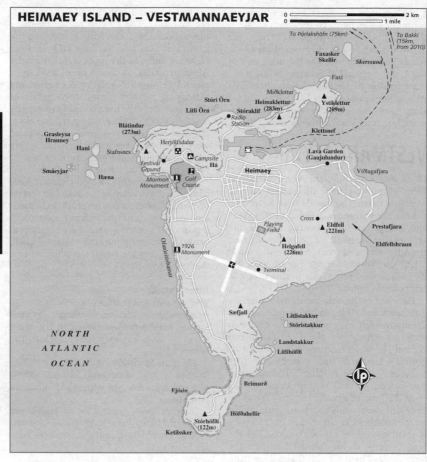

HEIMAEY ISLAND – VESTMANNAEYJAR

of Heimaey's 1973 evacuation. Note the cabinet of Nazi regalia, from Vestmannaeyjar's short-lived branch of the Nazi Party. The items on display were deposited anonymously at the museum in the middle of the night!

A combined ticket to both museums costs Ikr750/350 per adult/child six to 13 years.

VOLCANIC FILM SHOW

The explosive hour-long **show** (Map p151; ☎ 481 1045; Heiðarvegur; admission Ikr700; ⌚ 11am & 3.30pm mid-May–mid-Sep, plus 2pm & 9pm mid-Jun–Aug, by request rest of year) plays at the local cinema, and includes footage of Surtsey, the 1973 eruption and puffin rappelling. The film quality is naturally rather old and snowy, but it's fascinating stuff.

In the foyer there's some useful information about walking trails.

SKANSINN

This lovely green area by the sea has several unique historical sights. The oldest structure on the island was **Skansinn** (Map p151), a 15th-century fort built to defend the harbour (not too successfully – when Algerian pirates arrived in 1627, they simply landed on the other side of the island). Its walls were swallowed up by the 1973 lava, but some have been rebuilt. Above them, you can see the remains of the town's **old water tanks**, also crushed by molten rock.

A shocking 80% of Heimaey's babies once died at birth, until in the 1840s an island woman, Sólveig, was sent abroad to be trained as a midwife. The tiny wooden house **Landlyst** (Map p151; adult/child Ikr400/200; 11am-5pm Jun-Aug, by arrangement other times) was Sólveig's maternity hospital, and today contains a small display of her blood-letting equipment and other 19th-century medical paraphernalia.

Bitumen-coated **Stafkirkjan** (Map p151; admission free; 11am-5pm Jun-Aug) is a reconstruction of a medieval wooden stave church. It was presented by the Norwegian government in 2000 to celebrate 1000 years of Christianity. Deafen yourself by ringing the bell on your way out.

HOUSE GRAVEYARD & POMPEI OF THE NORTH

Four hundred buildings lie buried under the 1973 lava. On the edge of the flow is an eerie graveyard (Map p151) where beloved homes rest in peace. **'Pompei of the North'** (off Map p151; www.pompeinordursins.is) is a modern 'archaeological' excavation in which 10 houses are being dug up. So far, the crumpled concrete remains of four houses have been unearthed along what was formerly Suðurvegur.

STÓRAKLIF

The top of the craggy precipice **Stóraklif** (Map p150) is a treacherous 30-minute climb from behind the petrol station at the harbour. The trail starts on the obvious 4WD track; as it gets steeper you're 'assisted' by ropes and chains (don't trust them completely), but it's worth the terror for the outstanding views.

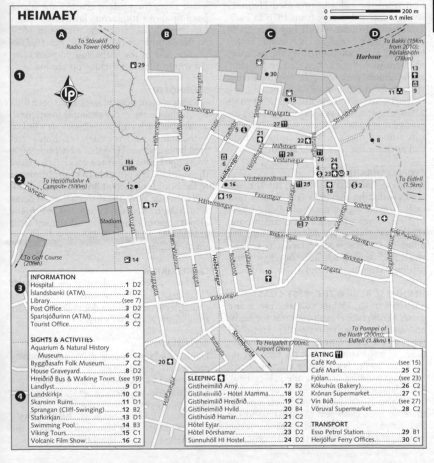

HEIMAEY

0 ————— 200 m
0 ————— 0.1 miles

SOUTHWEST ICELAND

SOUTHWEST ICELAND

PUFFIN FOR TEA?

These tiny, colourful birds have been an important source of food in the Vestmannaeyjar since Viking times. Puffins are still hunted here in the traditional way: either by climbing the cliffs or by fishing them out of the air with a long net called a *hafur*. They end up on restaurant menus, either roasted or smoked.

Of course, not all the locals regard puffins as free lunch. Every August, Heimaey is bombarded by puffin chicks attempting to fly for the first time. They're supposed to be heading out to sea, but some get confused by the lights and end up round the harbour. Many locals gather up the chicks and release them by hand at the water's edge.

For more on puffins, see the boxed text, p60.

ELDFELL & HELGAFELL

The 221m-high volcanic cone **Eldfell** (Map p150) appeared from nowhere in the early hours of 23 January 1973 (see the boxed text, opposite). Once the fireworks finished, heat from the volcano provided Heimaey with geothermal energy from 1976 to 1985. Today the ground is still hot enough in places to bake bread or char wood. Eldfell is an easy climb from town, up the collapsed northern wall of the crater; stick to the path, as the islanders are trying to save their latest volcano from erosion.

Neighbouring volcano **Helgafell** (Map p150; 226m) erupted 5000 years ago. Its cinders are grassed over today, and you can scramble up here without much difficulty from the football pitch on the road to the airport.

ELDFELLSHRAUN

Known as **Eldfellshraun** (Map p150), the new land created by the 1973 lava flow is now criss-crossed with a maze of hiking tracks that run down to the fort at Skansinn and the house graveyard, and all around the bulge of the raw, red eastern coast. Here you'll find small black-stone beaches, a lava garden (Gaujulundur) and a lighthouse.

HERJÓLFSDALUR & THE WEST COAST

Sheltered by an extinct volcano, green and grassy **Herjólfsdalur** (Map p150) was the home of Vestmannaeyjar's first settler, Herjólfur Barðursson. Excavations have revealed remains of a Norse house (not the bizarre construction in the bowl of the volcano, but a more unassuming site near the golf course). The island's campsite is also here.

On the cliffs west of the golf course, there's a little **monument** (Map p150) to the 200 people who converted to Mormonism and departed for Utah in the 19th century.

Several perilous tracks climb the steep slopes around Herjólfsdalur, running along the top of Norðklettur to **Stafsnes** (Map p150). The ascent is exhilarating, but there are some sheer drops. A gentler walk runs south along the western coast of the island, passing above numerous lava caves where local people hid from the pirates in 1627. At **Ofanleitishamar** (Map p150), hundreds of puffins nest in the cliffs, and you can often get within metres for close-up photos.

STÓRHÖFÐI

A windy meteorological station has been built on Stórhöfði, the rocky **peninsula** (Map p150) at the southern end of Heimaey. It's linked to the main island by a narrow isthmus (created by lava from Helgafell's eruption 5000 years ago), and there are good views from the summit. It's possible to scramble down to the boulder beach at **Brimurð** (Map p150) and continue along the cliffs on the east coast, returning by the main road just before the airport. From June to August the sea cliffs at **Lítlihöfði** (Map p150) are a good place to watch puffins.

LANDSKIRKJA

The lava stopped just short of the **Landskirkja** (Map p151) in the middle of town. The church's carved wooden doors feature scenes from Vestmannaeyjar's history.

Activities

Heimaey's large indoor saltwater **swimming pool** (Map p151; adult/child Ikr300/150; ☉ 6.15am-9pm Mon-Fri, 9am-6pm Sat & Sun Jun-Aug, 6.15am-8am, noon-1pm & 2.30-9pm Mon-Fri, 9am-5pm Sat & Sun Sep-May) has hot pots and a gym.

A new PADI company **IsDive** (☎ 694 1006; www.isdive.is) has just been set up in the Vestmannaeyjar – contact them for prices.

Golfers can hire clubs at the 18-hole **golf course** (Map p150; ☎ 481 2363; www.gvgolf.is) in the Herjólfsdalur valley; green fees are Ikr3500.

In summer you can see locals practising the ancient art of **sprangan** (cliff-swinging; Map p151) – an essential skill for egg-collectors and puffin-hunters – on the cliffs between the harbour and Herjólfsdalur.

Tours

From May to August, **Viking Tours** (Map p151; ☎ 488 4884; www.vikingtours.is; small boat harbour, off Ægisgata; adult/9-14yr €30/20) runs daily two-hour **boat tours**, leaving at 10.30am and 3.30pm. They bounce right around the island, slowing for the big bird-nesting sites on the south coast, and sailing into the sea-cave Klettshellir, where the boat driver gets to show off his saxophone skills! His wife, Unnur, runs recommended two-hour bus tours at 1pm in summer (possible out of season if prebooked). You can also arrange whale-watching and fishing trips, and 3½-hour boat rides around Surtsey (€60) on request. If nobody's about, track staff down in nearby Café Kró.

The friendly folk at Hreiðrið guest house run **walking tours** (Map p151) when there's a group, and two-hour **bus tours** (Ikr2900) of the island on Tuesday and Wednesday from June to August: you'll get to sample bread cooked in the still-smoking ash of Eldfell.

Festivals & Events

The country's biggest outdoor festival is the three-day **Þjóðhátíð** (National Festival; www.dalurinn.is; admission Ikr12,900), held at the festival ground at Herjólfsdalur over the first weekend in August. It involves music, dancing, fireworks, a big bonfire, gallons of alcohol and, as the night progresses, lots of drunken sex (it's something of a teen rite of passage), with upwards of 11,000 people attending. Extra flights are laid on from Reykjavík, but you should book transport and accommodation far in advance.

Historically, the festival was first celebrated when bad weather prevented Vestmannaeyjar people from joining the mainland celebrations of Iceland's first constitution (1 July 1874). The islanders held their own festival a month later, and it's been an annual tradition ever since.

Sleeping

Heimaey has a campsite, several hotels and loads of guest houses, but they fill up fast after the ferry arrives. Most places drop their rates by around 20% in winter.

BUDGET

Campsite (Map p150; ☎ 692 6952; sites per person Ikr700; ☼ Jun-Aug) Cupped in the bowl of an extinct volcano, this dandelion-dotted camping ground has hot showers, a laundry room and cooking facilities. The wind can get strong.

THE 1973 ERUPTION

Without warning, at 1.45am on 23 January 1973 a mighty explosion blasted through the winter's night as a 1.5km-long volcanic fissure split the eastern side of the island. The eruption area gradually became concentrated into a growing crater cone, which fountained lava and ash into the sky.

Normally the island's fishing boats would have been out at sea, but a force-12 gale had prevented them from sailing the previous afternoon. Now calm weather and a harbourful of boats allowed the island's 5200 inhabitants to be evacuated to the mainland. Incredibly, there was just a single fatality.

Over the next five months more than 30 million tonnes of lava poured over Heimaey, destroying 360 houses and creating a brand-new mountain, the red cinder cone Eldfell. One-third of the town was buried beneath the lava flow, and the island increased in size by 2.5 sq km.

As the eruption continued, advancing lava threatened to close the harbour and make the evacuation permanent – without a fishing industry, there would have been no point in returning. In an attempt to slow down the inexorable flow of molten rock, firefighters hosed the lava with over six million tonnes of cold sea water. The lava halted just 175m short of the harbour mouth – actually improving the harbour by creating extra shelter!

The islanders were billeted with friends and family on the mainland, watching the fireworks and waiting to see if they could ever go home. Finally, the eruption finished five months later at the end of June. Two-thirds of the islanders returned to face the mighty clean-up operation.

Sunnuhöll HI Hostel (Map p151; ☎ 481 2900; www .hotelvestmannaeyjar.is; Vestmannabraut 28b; sb dm/s/d Ikr2100/3700/5800) We have a soft spot for tiny, homely Sunnuhöll hostel, with its seven plain, neat rooms. The cheapest accommodation is in a mixed attic dorm. There's a guest kitchen and sitting room, and you can do laundry in Hótel Mamma across the road. Reception is at Hótel Þórshamar.

Gistiheimilið Hvíld (Map p151; ☎ 481 1230; www .simnet.is/hvild; Höfðavegur 16; sb Ikr2500, s/d Ikr4000/7500) A friendly family owns this large green house, which has smallish guest rooms with shared bathroom, a TV lounge and a peaceful garden. There's no breakfast, but there is a guest kitchen where you can prepare your own.

Gistiheimilið Hreiðrið (Map p151; ☎ 481 1045, 699 8945; http://tourist.eyjar.is; Faxastígur 33; sb/s/d Ikr2500/4600/8900) Run by the helpful volcano-show people, Ruth and Sigurgeir, this winning guest house has a family feel. Features include wall-to-wall puffins, a well-stocked kitchen, a cosy TV lounge and bike hire. Breakfast (Ikr1000) is available year-round. They also run walking and bus tours in summer, and can run you to the far end of the island for Ikr800.

Gistiheimilið Árný (Map p151; ☎ /fax 481 2082; Illugagata 7; sb/s/d Ikr4000/7000/12,000) A charming couple runs this neat suburban house, which also offers guests a kitchen and washing machine, and packed lunches by arrangement. Upstairs rooms have epic views, and the owner prays for a sound sleep for all her guests!

Gistiheimilið-Hótel Mamma (Map p151; ☎ 481 2900; www.hotelvestmannaeyjar.is; Vestmannabraut 25; s/ d/tr Ikr6000/8500/11,300) This is a cheery, peaceful Hótel Þórshamar–owned guest house with spacious rooms, all with TV and shared bathroom. There are two guest kitchens and a laundry in the basement. The attic steps are extremely small and steep – avoid if you're at all clumsy.

Gistihúsið Hamar (Map p151; ☎ 481 2900; www .hotelvestmannaeyjar.is; Herjólfsgata 4; d/tr Ikr10,700/13,900; ☼ Jun-Aug; ☲ ☜) Also owned by Þórshamar, this place has large, modern en suite rooms and wireless internet access. Reception for both Hamar and Mamma is at Þórshamar.

MIDRANGE

Hótel Eyjar (Map p151; ☎ 481 3636; www.hoteleyjar.eyjar .is; Bárustígur 2; s Ikr9500-12,000, d Ikr12,000-16,000) This hotel, on the corner of Strandvegur, offers huge and comfortable apartment-style rooms

with bathrooms, kitchens and lounges – basically they're suites at room prices! Breakfast is an extra Ikr1300.

Hótel Þórshamar (Map p151; ☎ 481 2900; www. hotelvestmannaeyjar.is; Vestmannabraut 28; s/d/ste Ikr11,000/16,100/21,500; ☲) Iceland's first cinema is now a hotel, with pale, pleasant rooms and facilities including a sauna, hot tubs and a snooker room. Of the older rooms, 209 is best, tucked in the corner with its own balcony; otherwise, go for the three stylish new suites. Breakfast included.

Eating

Kökuhús (Map p151; Bárustígur 7; ☼ 7.30am-5.30pm Mon-Fri, 8.30am-4pm Sat, 10am-4pm Sun) This is a great sit-down cafe-bakery, with a constant flow of people through the doors. It sells hot soup, buns and sandwiches (which can be made to order).

Café Kró (Map p151; ☎ 488 4884; Harbour; mains Ikr1500-3000; ☼ 11am-9pm Jun-Aug, shorter hrs May & Sep; ☜) This little harbourside cafe recently underwent an unlikely transformation and turned itself into a pizzeria and Chinese restaurant in addition to a caffeine cave. There are tourist information leaflets available and free wi-fi.

Café Maria (Map p151; ☎ 481 3160; Skólavegur 1; mains Ikr1900-3500; ☼ 11.30am-11.30pm Sun-Thu, to 1am Fri & Sat) A stuffed gannet surveys proceedings at this pleasant cafe-restaurant, which is quiet during the day but busy at night. Pizzas, burgers, savoury crêpes, and fresh-fish and meat mains are served here – plus, yes, fresh puffin.

Fjólan (Map p151; ☎ 481 3663; Vestmannabraut 28; mains from Ikr2000; ☼ 7am-11pm year-round) Next door to Hótel Þórshamar, this high-ceilinged, gold-columned place is the only proper restaurant on the island. The buffet breakfast is open to all; it serves probably the best fish on Heimaey, and staff are friendly and accommodating.

Heimaey has several cheap petrol-station snack bars where you can get French fries, hot dogs and burgers for between Ikr500 and Ikr1000. For self-catering, there's the igloo-like **Vöruval supermarket** (Map p151; ☎ 481 3184; Vesturvegur 18; ☼ 9am-7pm), and two streets away is **Krónan supermarket** (Map p151; Strandvegur; ☼ 11am-7pm Mon-Fri, 11am-6pm Sat, 11am-4pm Sun). The local **Vín Búð** (Map p151; ☎ 481 1301; ☼ noon-6pm Mon-Thu, 11am-7pm Fri, 11am-2pm Sat) is also on Strandvegur.

Getting There & Away

AIR

The Vestmannaeyjar airport (Map p150) is about 3km from Heimaey – a **taxi** (☎ 698 2038) will cost about Ikr1300, or you could walk it in 20 minutes. Scheduled flights to Heimaey are offered by **Flugfélag Íslands** (☎ 570 3030; www .airiceland.is), which flies two or three times daily from Reykjavík's domestic airport. The flight lasts 25 minutes, and the fare is Ik9500 for a full-price one-way ticket.

Flugfélags Vestmannaeyja (☎ 481 3255; www .eyjaflug.is) runs charter flights from the small airstrip at Bakki (Ikr8000 round trip). Most flights require a minimum of five people.

BOAT

The ferry **Herjólfur** (Map p151; ☎ 481 2800; www .herjolfur.is) sails from Þorlákshöfn (on the mainland) at noon and 7.30pm, and returns from Heimaey at 8.15am and 4pm daily throughout the year. The boat can carry cars, but Heimaey is so small it's scarcely worth bringing one. The crossing takes 2¾ hours in good weather. The one-way fare per adult/child 12 to 15 years is Ikr2420/1210. Motorbikes/cars cost an additional Ikr1635/2420. However, the ferry route is due to change in 2010 – see the boxed text (right) for details.

If the sea looks rough, a Vestmannaeyjar tip is to book a cabin, dose yourself with seasickness tablets, and try to sleep your way through the trip.

The bus service between Reykjavík and Þorlákshöfn (Ikr1400, one hour) is run to connect with the *Herjólfur*. It leaves the city at 10.40am and 5.50pm daily, and it leaves Þorlákshöfn at 11.30am and 6.50pm.

Getting Around

The whole island can be comfortably explored on foot. If you need a taxi, call ☎ 698 2038.

SURTSEY

In November 1963, the crew on the fishing boat *Ísleifi II* noticed something odd – the sea south of Heimaey appeared to be on fire.

ALTERATION TO THE VESTMANNAEYJAR FERRY

At the time of writing, a new harbour was being built at Bakki, 27km south of Hvolsvöllur. This is to be the new terminal for the Vestmannaeyjar ferry (which currently departs from Þorlákshöfn) from 2010. Details on sailing times and connecting buses were still to be confirmed; contact any tourist centre, or the ferry company **Eimskip** (☎ 481 2800; www .eimskip.com) and the **BSÍ bus station** (☎ 562 1011; www.bsi.is) to check the latest transport details.

Rather than flee, the boat drew up for a closer look – and its crew were the first to set eyes on the world's newest island.

The incredible subsea eruption lasted for 4½ years, throwing up cinders and ash to form a 2.7 sq km piece of real estate (since eroded to 1.4 sq km). What else could it be called but Surtsey (Surtur's Island), after the Norse fire giant who will burn the world to ashes at Ragnarök.

It was decided that the sterile island would make a perfect laboratory, giving a unique insight into how plants and animals colonise new territory. Surtsey is therefore totally off limits to visitors (unless you're a scientist specialising in biocolonisation). Just so you know, though, in the race for the new land, the blue-green algae *Anabaena variabilis* got there first.

You can get a vicarious view of Surtsey's thunderous birth by visiting the Volcano Show (p76) in Reykjavík, or the Volcanic Film Show (p150) on Heimaey. You can also charter a flight over the islands with Flugfélags Vestmannaeyja (left), and Viking Tours (p153) run boat trips around it if chartered in advance.

And here's a little conundrum for you: what are fossils doing on this newly minted island?

West Iceland

Geographically close to Reykjavík yet miles and miles away in sentiment, west Iceland is in many ways a splendid microcosm of what the country has to offer beyond the capital. Yet surprisingly many tourists have somehow missed the memo, preferring instead to zoom around the Ring Road in search of other wonders. It's good news for you though – you're likely to have much of this under-appreciated region to yourself.

The long arm of the Snæfellsnes is west Iceland's star attraction. Capped by a glacial fist at its tip, the peninsula is a veritable artist's palette of sulphuric yellows, snowy whites, mossy greens, scorched charcoals, Caribbean blues and surprising beachy peach tones that all blend together to form something truly inspiring. New Age gurus believe that there are greater forces at play here – and Jules Verne agreed; his *Journey to the Centre of the Earth* starts at Snæfellsjökull's icy crown.

While tourists undoubtedly gravitate towards the natural highlights, Icelanders hold west Iceland in high regard for its canon of local sagas. Two of Iceland's best-known tales, the *Laxdæla* and *Egil's Sagas,* take place along the region's brooding waters. Snorri Sturluson, of *Prose Edda* fame lived and died in Borgarbyggð, while Viking Eiríkur Rauðe (Erik the Red) plotted missions to the end of the earth from his farmstead in little-visited Dalir. Today, only cairns and ruins remind us of this bygone era, but you can gain historical insights from a couple of must-see museums.

With nature and history as the region's two biggest drawcards, west Iceland comes up trumps because it offers a little bit of everything and proves that you don't have to travel long distances to uncover the real Iceland.

WEST ICELAND

HIGHLIGHTS

- Tramp through crunchy lava fields, then zip across windswept Snæfellsjökull, the icy heart of the magical **Snæfellsjökull National Park** (p171)

- Follow the green carpet of velvety moss through the striking crags between **Hellnar** (p172) and **Arnarstapi** (p173)

- Wander around charming **Stykkishólmur** (p164) and picturesque **Grundarfjörður** (p169), passing a whimsical world in between

- Sail past swooping puffins and ancient Viking hideouts on a breezy boat ride through the innumerable islands of **Breiðafjörður** (p167)

- Step back into Saga times at the impressive Settlement Centre in **Borgarnes** (p160)

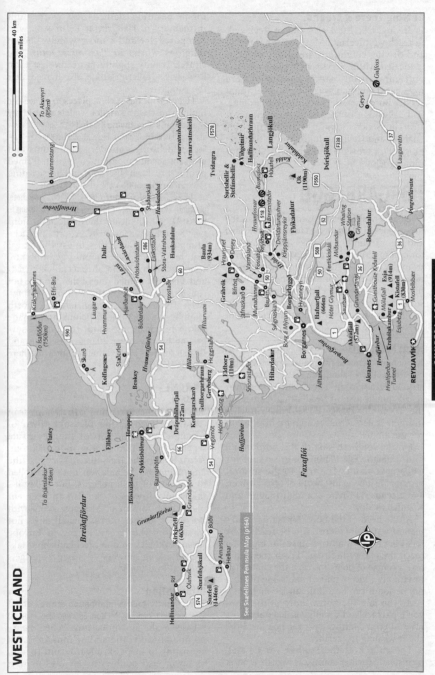

WEST ICELAND

WEST ICELAND

Getting There & Around

If driving, take Rte 1 west out of Reykjavík to reach west Iceland. Most roads are paved and driving conditions are good. Akranes is located within Reykjavík's public transport infrastructure, so the connections are frequent. Long-haul buses from the capital service Borgarnes, Reykholt and Búðardalur, and daily buses to the Snæfellsnes Peninsula stop in Stykkishólmur, Grundarfjörður, Ólafsvík and Hellissandur. If you're tight on time, follow the signs through the Hvalfjörður tunnel (below).

BORGARBYGGÐ

Decidedly positioned beyond Reyjavík's suburban sprawl, **Borgarbyggð** (www.borgarbyggd.is) and the surrounding area feels suddenly pastoral despite being a mere 30-minute drive from the capital. Although lacking the mystique and majesty of the Snæfellsnes Peninsula further on, the region's finger-like fjords and stone-strewn highlands offer plenty of day-trip fodder for those who need a quick fix of country living.

HVALFJÖRÐUR

If you have plenty of time (and a private vehicle) follow Rte 47 along the scenic 80km road around Hvalfjörður. Those with a need for speed should instead head straight through the 5.7km-long **tunnel** (Ikr800) that runs beneath its waters. Cyclists aren't permitted to use the tunnel.

On the southern side of the fjord you'll find dramatic **Esja** (914m), a great spot for wilderness hiking. The trail to the summit begins at Esjuberg, just north of Mosfellsbær, and ascends via Krehólakambur (850m) and Kistufell (830m).

At the head of the fjord, **Glymur**, Iceland's highest waterfall (198m), can be reached by following the turn-off to Botnsdalur until you reach the end of the road. From there, it'll take a couple of hours to reach the chute. Try to visit after heavy rain or snow-melt – in a dry period it can be a little underwhelming.

As you join the north shore of the fjord you'll pass Iceland's main **whaling station** – a place of great controversy – see p62 for more about whaling in Iceland.

The church at the **Saurbær** (☎ 433 8952) farmstead, further along, is worth a look

for its beautiful stained-glass work. Built in memory of Hallgrímur Pétursson, who composed Iceland's most widely known religious work, *50 Passion Hymns*, the church is only slightly more modest than Reykjavík's Hallgrímskirkja, also named after the composer.

Hvalfjörður has several places to spend the night. Those with smaller wallets should try the adorable **Guesthouse Kiðafell** (☎ 566 6096; www .dagfinnur.is/kidafell; sb/s/d Ikr2800/6000/9000; May-Sep), which offers modern bathrooms and pleasant accommodation covered in framed photos. Breakfast (Ikr1000) and horse riding (two hours Ikr6000) are also available.

ourpick **Hótel Glymur** (☎ 430 3100; www.hotel glymur.is; May-Oct s/d/ste €185/260/380, 15% discount in winter;), on the northern side of the fjord near Saurbær, is a favourite. A veritable cache of contemporary amenities, this stylish retreat features double-decker rooms, giant picture windows, heated floors, abstract knick-knacks and a hot pot named one of the 'top five hot tubs in the world' by the *New York Times*. Even if you aren't staying here, it's worth stopping by for some delicious homemade cake while learning about the fjord's surprising history (over 20,000 American and British soldiers parked their submarines here during WWII).

AKRANES
pop 5600

Set under the imposing concave plateau Akrafjall (572m), the pleasant town of Akranes lies at the tip of the peninsula separating Hvalfjörður from Borgarfjörður. According to the Icelandic history text the *Landnámabók*, the area was once controlled by a group of Irish hermits, but today it's the factory towers of the fish and cement plants that dominate. Akranes, along with Borgarnes further north, gets all of its hot water from the largest spring in Europe (near Reykholt), so don't feel bad about taking extra-long showers – unused water gets dumped into the sea.

Information

The friendly **tourist information centre** (☎ 431 5566; www.visitakranes.is; 10am-5pm mid-May–mid-Sep) is based at the museum centre. When there's no one on duty, the smiley museum staff are happy to help. Skrúðgarðurinn (p160), in town, also doubles as an information

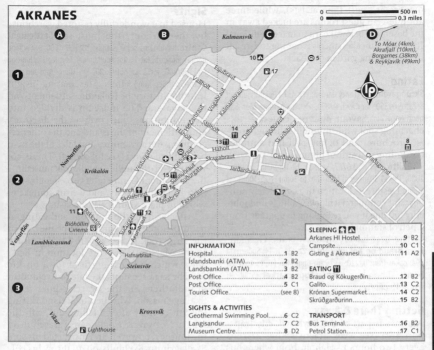

AKRANES

INFORMATION
Hospital................................1 B2
Íslandsbanki (ATM)................2 B2
Landsbankinn (ATM)..............3 B2
Post Office............................4 B2
Post Office............................5 C1
Tourist Office.................(see 8)

SIGHTS & ACTIVITIES
Geothermal Swimming Pool........6 C2
Langisandur..........................7 C2
Museum Centre......................8 D2

SLEEPING
Arkanes HI Hostel..................9 B2
Campsite.............................10 C1
Gisting á Akranesi................11 A2

EATING
Braud og Kökugerðin.............12 B2
Galito.................................13 C2
Krónan Supermarket..............14 B2
Skrúðgarðurinn....................15 B2

TRANSPORT
Bus Terminal........................16 B2
Petrol Station.......................17 C1

WEST ICELAND

point. You'll find the **post office** (☎ 431 1000; Kirkjubraut 37) and several banks with ATMs on Kirkjubraut, the main street.

Sights & Activities
The town's main attraction is the engaging **Museum Centre** (☎ 431 5566; www.museum.is; adult/under 16yr/senior Ikr500/free/300; ☺ 10am-5pm Jun-Aug, 1-5pm Sep-May), which is full of nautical relics, crystals, fossils and tales of local sporting heroes. The folk museum wing – housed in the '70s-style building – displays semi-interesting antiques like an old car and fishing apparel. Outside, there's a restored boathouse, a drying shed, a church and several fishing boats, including the cutter *Sigurfari*. The museum is about 1km east of the centre, just off Graðagrund.

Also worth a visit is the 1km-long sandy beach at **Langisandur**. It's perfect for a gentle walk, a game of football with the locals (watch out – they're good!), or a quick swim on a warm day. During inclement weather, the town's **geothermal swimming pool** (Jaðarsbakkar; ☎ 433 1100; Innesvegur; adult/under 14yr Ikr260/free; ☺ 6.15am-9pm Mon-Fri, 9am-6pm Sat & Sun) is a better option.

Sleeping
Campsite (☎ 864 5510; sites per person Ikr1000; ☺ mid-May–mid-Sep) The well-maintained town campsite is close to the shore and has sweeping views over the fjord to Snæfellsjökull on clear days. There are excellent washing and laundry facilities here.

Akranes HI Hostel (☎ 868 3332; www.hostel.is; Suðurgata 32; dm/d member Ikr2100/4100, nonmember Ikr2600/5100) Sparking after a recent renovation, this beautiful hostel sits along a quiet residential lane near the port. Look for the white house with 'Apotek' written across the facade – the building was once the local drugstore.

Móar (☎ 431 1389; sollajoh@simnet.is; sb/cottage Ikr3000/12,000) Although located out of town, this friendly, modern farmhouse is well worth seeking out for its spotless rooms and excellent service. Móar is just off Rte 1 near Akranesvegamót, 4km east of Akranes.

Gisting á Akranesi (☎ 695 6255; www.leopold.is/gisting; Bakkatún 20; s/d Ikr6000/9800) We just adore the friendly couple that runs this lively B&B. The living room is cluttered with quilts, watercolours and various works-in-progress (the owners are part-time artists), while three antique-clad guest rooms are tucked away in the basement below. Learn to make traditional Icelandic pancakes, then savour the end-result in the inviting garden out back.

Eating

Skrúðgarðurinn (Fancy Garden; ☎ 431 1780; Kirkjubraut 8; latte Ikr350, sandwich Ikr890; ☺ 10am-10pm Mon-Sat, noon-6pm Sun) Savour designer coffees at this charming spot while thumbing through tourist brochures and ogling polished antiques (including a beautiful phonograph!).

Galito (☎ 430 6767; Stillholt 16-18; mains Ikr1200-2000; ☺ 11.30am-9pm Mon-Thu, to 10pm Fri, 5-10pm Sat & Sun) Despite its location in a completely nondescript commercial block, Galito is undoubtedly top dog if you're looking to upgrade from a petrol station hot dog.

The best bakery in town is the German-run **Braud og Kökugerðin** (☎ 431 1644; Suðurgata 50a; cakes from Ikr220; ☺ 7am-6pm Mon-Fri, to 4pm Sat & Sun). There's a **Krónan supermarket** (Stillholt) for self-caterers.

Getting There & Away

Akranes is part of the Reykjavík city transport area (see www.straeto.is); bus 27 runs every two hours to Háholt, from where bus 57 runs to the city centre. The entire journey takes about 80 minutes and costs Ikr840 for a daypass.

BORGARNES
pop 1780

Unassuming Borgarnes guards its convenient position on the Ring Road near the brooding waters of Borgarfjörður. The buzzing petrol station signs may trick you into zooming straight through, but a quick trip into the old town will reveal a lovely bucolic vibe and one of Iceland's best museums.

Orientation & Information

Travellers arriving from Reykjavík will follow Rte 1 over the fjord bridge into town. After passing a cluster of plazas (containing petrol stations, ATMs and supermarkets), the road forks – head left to reach the town centre (and the Settlement Museum), or go right, continuing along Rte 1, to reach west Iceland's main **tourist information centre** (☎ 437 2214; www.west.is; Sólbakki 2; ☺ 9am-4.30pm Mon-Thu, noon-8pm Fri, 10am-3pm Sat & Sun Jun-Aug, reduced hours Sep-May; ☺).

Sights

Housed in a wonderfully restored warehouse by the harbour, the must-see **Settlement Centre** (Landnáms-setur Íslands; ☎ 437 1600; www.land nam.is; Brákarbraut 13-15; adult/under 14yr for 1 exhibition Ikr1100/800, for 2 Ikr1600/1100; ☺ 10am-7pm Jun-Aug, 11am-5pm Sep-May) offers a fascinating insight into the history of Icelandic settlement and the Saga era. The museum is divided into two exhibitions, one covering the discovery and settlement of the island and the other recounting the adventures and tales of the man behind *Egil's Saga* (see following). This is not your run-of-the-mill Icelandic folk museum – the Settlement Centre offers excellent insight into Iceland's history and a firm context in which to place your Icelandic visit.

After visiting the museum and eating at its top-notch restaurant (opposite), visit the large rock *(borg)* at **Borg á Mýrum** (Rock in the Marshes), the core location in *Egil's Saga*, which lies just north of town on Rte 54. The saga recounts the tale of Kveldúlfur, grandfather of the warrior-poet Egill Skallagrímsson, who fled to Iceland during the 9th century after a falling out with the king of Norway. Kveldúlfur grew gravely ill on the journey, however, and instructed his son, Skallagrímur Kveldúlfsson, to throw his coffin overboard after he died and build the family farm wherever it washed ashore – this just happened to be at Borg. Egill Skallagrímsson grew up to be a bloodthirsty individual who killed his first adversary at the age of seven and went on to carry out numerous raids on the coast of England.

The Settlement Museum has marked additional sites featured in *Egil's Saga*, including **Skallagrímsgarður** (Skallagrímsgata), the burial mound of the father and son of saga hero Egill Skallagrímsson.

Back in Borgarnes, up the street from the Settlement Museum, is **Brúðuheimar** (Puppet World; ☎ 551 1620; www.figurentheatre.is, www .vruduheimar.is; adult/child Ikr1400/800, evening shows Ikr3500; ☺ 10am-7pm Jun-Aug, 11am-5pm Sep-May). Situated in a series of restored homes from the 18th century, this brand-new museum features several hands-on exhibits. The puppets bring the Icelandic sagas to life during the popular evening recitals (visit the website for more details).

Beyond the puppet museum is **Bjössaróló**, a public playground made from a menagerie of previously discarded items.

Sleeping

The following options represent but a smattering of choices in the area. Stop by the information centre for a supplemental list, or try browsing the ubiquitous *Áning* guide. There's a **campsite** (sites per person Ikr750) on the main road (Borgarbraut) connecting the old town and the regional information centre – a ranger comes by in the morning to collect camping fees. Borgarnes is a haven for budgetarians – it isn't worth making the price leap into the midrange category.

Borgarnes HI Hostel (☎ 695 3366; www.hostel.is; Borgarbraut 9-13; sb member/nonmember Ikr2100/2600; ☜) One of the newer links in the HI chain, this no-frills sleeping spot across from the post office gets the job done, but we much prefer the hostel in nearby Akranes.

Hvití Bærinn (☎ 437 2000; http://hvitibaerinn.is; sb/ linen Ikr2500/4200) Set in a restored farmhouse above a golf club and small cafe (mains Ikr500 to Ikr2700), this hostel is a cosy, well-equipped place with a basic kitchen and a TV lounge. The hostel is about 5km north of town on Rte 1.

Bjarg (☎ 437 1925; bjarg@simnet.is; sb/s/d Ikr2000/5500/9800) One of the nicer places to stay in the area, this attractive farmhouse overlooking the fjord has warm, cosy rooms with tasteful wood panelling and crisp white linens. There's a shared guest kitchen, a BBQ, spotless bathrooms and an additional self-catering studio apartment sleeping four. Bjarg is about 1km north of the centre, just off Rte 1.

Venus Guesthouse (☎ 437 2345; motel@centrum.is; 311 Borgarnes; sites per tent Ikr1500, sb Ikr2700, s/d without bathroom Ikr5150/8300, d with bathroom Ikr10,800) Like something out of the American Midwest, this rather forlorn-looking motel (think Bates) on the far side of the fjord bridge has faded and dated rooms, but excellent views to the distant Snæfellsnes Peninsula. The on-site restaurant serves the usual assortment of pub grub (mains Ikr680 to Ikr1700). Room rates drop about 30% in winter.

Borgarnes B&B (☎ 842 5866; www.borgarnesbb.is; Skúlagata 21; s/d incl breakfast Ikr8900/11,400; ☐ ☜) Antique wooden doors, modern fixtures and generous coats of white paint put this charming guest house near the top of our list. Go for one of the two rooms on the ground floor (the rest are in the basement) – they have fab views of the bay out back. Included in the price is a gut-busting buffet-style breakfast of Icelandic faves.

Hótel Borgarnes (☎ 437 1117; www.hotelborgarnes.is; Egilsgata 12-14; s/d incl breakfast Ikr14,500/16,500; ☺ May-Sep; ☐ ☜) Large and characterless, Hótel Borgarnes has boring business-style rooms sprouting off the tired carpeted hallways.

Hotel Hamar (☎ 433 6600; www.icehotels.is; Golfvöllurinn; s/d incl breakfast Ikr16,700/21,100 May-Sep, Ikr11,000/14,700 Oct-Apr; ☐ ☜) We found the prefab exterior to be slightly off-putting, but surprisingly sleek decor and a cache of mod cons hide within. Hamar sits on a well-maintained golf course flanked by snowy peaks in the distance.

Eating

our pick **Búðarklettur** (☎ 437 1600; Brákarbraut 13; mains Ikr1100-2200; ☺ 10am-9pm) After reliving Egil's adventures, continue the sensorial journey back through time at the Settlement Centre's restaurant – Borgarnes' best bet for food. The large windows, stripped wood floors and modern furniture give it a wonderfully stylish vibe. Choose from an assortment of traditional Icelandic eats (lamb, fish stew etc) then flip to the back of the menu and read up on the history of the town's oldest buildings (including the one you're sitting in!).

Café des Amis (Vinakaffi; ☎ 437 1010; Hrafnakletti 1b; mains Ikr1450-2590; ☺ lunch & dinner) Perfect for a quick fish soup or roadside coffee break, Café des Amis sits in a small house on the Ring Road, just north of the old town.

For the usual array of burgers, fried chicken and doughy pizza, try the grill bar at the N1 petrol station. The puppet museum has healthier choices if you're looking for a light snack. Self-caterers should head to the **Bónus supermarket** (Borgarbraut 57) at the edge of the fjord bridge coming into town. There's a branch of **Vín Búð** (Hyrnu Torg centre) on the main road.

Getting There & Away

All buses between Reykjavík and Akureyri, Snæfellsnes and the Westfjords stop near the cluster of petrol stations at the fjord bridge. In winter, high winds rolling in off the Atlantic can close the southern approach to town. Borgarnes is one hour from Reykjavík.

UPPER BORGARFJÖRÐUR
Bifröst

Heading north from Borgarnes along Rte 1 you'll pass through a large lava field belched

WEST ICELAND

out by the 3000-year-old cinder cones of Grábrók and Grábrókarfell near the college complex at Bifröst. There are plenty of walking trails criss-crossing the area, and a well-worn track leads up through the moss, lichen and dwarf birch to the lip of **Grábrók** (173m), which offers great views over the surrounding lava flow but can be extremely windy.

Bifröst is a stop on the main Reykjavík–Akureyri bus route (bus 60/60a). Buses from Reykjavík *and* Akureyri leave at 8.30am. There is at least one daily bus passing through in both directions.

Reykholt

Laid-back, postcard pretty and incredibly unassuming, Reykholt is a sleepy kind of place that on first glance offers few clues to its bustling past as one of the most important medieval settlements in Iceland.

To get some insight into the significance of the area, visit the fascinating medieval study centre **Snorrastofa** (☎ 433 8000; www.reykholt.is, www.snorrastofa.is; admission Ikr600; ☉ 10am-6pm May-Sep, to 5pm Mon-Fri Oct-Apr), devoted to the celebrated medieval historian Snorri Sturluson. The displays here explain the laws, literature, society and way of life in medieval Iceland. Iceland's oldest documents, the 12th-century deeds to the original church, are also here.

The on-site **church** features beautiful stained glass, an early Lutheran baptismal font and a 600-year-old organ that was originally installed in Reykjavík's cathedral. If you're visiting in late July, look out for information on the annual classical-music festival.

Further on, you'll come to **Snorralaug** (Snorri's Pool), a circular, stone-lined pool fed by a hot spring. The stones at the base of the pool are original, and it is believed that this is where Snorri came to bathe. The wood-panelled tunnel beside the spring leads to the old farmhouse – the site of Snorri's gruesome murder.

The Reykholt area is also home to Europe's biggest hot spring, **Deildartunguhver**, where billowing clouds of steam rise up as scalding water bubbles up from the ground (180L per second!)

The only accommodation in Reykholt proper is **Fosshótel Reykholt** (☎ 435 1260, 562 4000; www.fosshotel.is; May-Sep s/d Ikr20,900/22,900, Oct-Apr Ikr12,000/14,000). Housed in a modern block behind the old church, this well-equipped link in the Fosshótel chain has businesslike rooms,

a couple of 'wellness' hot pots and interesting displays on Norse mythology. The hotel's restaurant (mains Ikr2000 to Ikr3000) is the only one around, although the nearby petrol station sells sandwiches in summer.

Refer to the handy *The Ideal Holiday* farmstay brochure for sleeping options scattered further afield, such as **Brennistaðir** (☎ 435 1193; brennist@islandia.is; sb/cottage/apt Ikr2500/9000/13,000), 16km down the valley, which offers three comely cabins along the ravine and a new apartment in the farm's converted lockhouse.

Mini-golf, playgrounds and stunning waterfall views make the family-oriented campsite at **Fossatún** (☎ 433 5800; www.fossatun.is; sites per adult/child Ikr900/400; ☉ Jun-Aug; 🖳 🛜) one of the best in the country. Fossatún is located on Rte 50 between Borgarnes and Reykholt.

Reykholt is 40km northeast of Borgarnes along Rte 518. Buses from Reykjavík leave at 5pm on Friday and Sunday. In the opposite direction the bus leaves Reykholt at 7.10pm.

Húsafell

Tucked between the river Kaldá and a desolate lava field, the campus of cottages at Húsafell is a popular outdoor retreat for Reykjavík residents. The leisure complex **Ferðaþjónustan Húsafelli** (☎ 435 1550; www.husafell.is; sites per person Ikr900, sb Ikr2500, cabins from Ikr8000) is a one-stop shop, with campsite, cabin accommodation, restaurant (mains from Ikr1200) and outdoor geothermal swimming pool (Ikr400/50 adult/child, open 10am to 10pm daily from June to September, weekends only in low season).

There's no public transport to Húsafell, but twice a week you can get as far as Reykholt from Reykjavík (see left). Hitch or organise a car share in advance on www.semferda.net from there to Húsafell.

Around Húsafell

HALLMUNDARHRAUN

East of Húsafell, along Rte 518, the vast, barren lava flows of Hallmundarhraun make up an eerie landscape dotted with gigantic lava tubes. These long, tunnel-like caves are formed by flows of molten lava beneath a solid lava crust, and they look as though they've been burrowed out by some hellish giant worm.

As Rte 518 begins to loop back around, a bright yellow sign marks the turn-off to Arnarvatnsheiði along Rte F578. Make the turn (2WDs can do it too – just take it slow) and follow the bumpy track for 7km until

SNORRI STURLUSON

The chieftain and historian Snorri Sturluson is one of the most important figures in medieval Norse history – partly because he wrote a lot of it down himself. Snorri was born at Hvammur near Búðardalur (further north), but he was raised and educated at the theological centre of Oddi near Hella and later married the heir to the farm Borg near Borgarnes. For reasons not fully revealed, he abandoned his family at Borg and retreated to the wealthy church estate at Reykholt. At the time Reykholt was home to 60,000 to 80,000 people and was an important trade centre at the crossroads of major routes across the country. Snorri composed many of his most famous works at Reykholt, including *Prose Edda* (a textbook to medieval Norse poetry) and *Heimskringla* (a history of the kings of Norway). Snorri is also widely believed to be the hand behind *Egil's Saga*, a family history of Viking *skald* (court poet) Egill Skallagrímsson (see p160).

At the age of 36 Snorri was appointed *lögsögumaður* (law speaker) of the Alþing (Icelandic parliament), but he endured heavy pressure from the Norwegian king to promote the king's private interests at the parliament. Instead Snorri busied himself with his writing and the unhappy Norwegian king Hákon issued a warrant for his capture – dead or alive. Snorri's political rival and former son-in-law Gissur Þorvaldsson saw his chance to impress the king and possibly snag the position of governor of Iceland in return. He arrived in Reykholt with 70 armed men on the night of 23 September 1241 and hacked the historian to death in the basement of his home.

you reach **Surtshellir**, a dramatic, 2km-long lava tube connected to **Stefánshellir**, a second tunnel about half the size. It is possible to explore Surtshellir on your own – you'll need good shoes and a torch. Keep an eye out for the cairn markings, or try the travel service at Húsafell (☎ 435 1550) for updates on possible tours. If you've got a 4WD it's possible to continue beyond Surtshellir along the 'L'-shaped Rte F578 through the lakes at **Arnarvatnsheiði** and on to Hvammstangi. Note that Rte F578 is usually only open for seven weeks each year; see www.vegagerdin.

A third lava tube, the 1.5km-long **Viðgelmir**, is on private property near the farmstead at Fljótstunga, and at the time of research it was off-limits to visitors. The owner, who lives in Borgarnes, used to offer tours – it's worth asking around if this has started up again.

KALDIDALUR
Southeast of Húsafell, the Kaldidalur valley skirts the edge of a series of glaciers offering incredible views of the Langjökull ice cap and, in clear weather, the snows of Eiríksjökull, Okjökull and Þórisjökull. Although there's no public transport along unsurfaced Rte 550, you can visit the area on a day trip from Reykjavík or drive south in a private vehicle to Þingvellir.

ELDBORG
From Borgarnes, it's a straight shot up to the stunning Snæfellsnes on Rte 54. Along the way you'll pass the prominent eggcup-shaped volcano **Eldborg** rising over 100m above the desolate Eldborgarhraun plain. It's a great place to stop and stretch your legs. Head to **Hótel Eldborg** (☎ 435 6602; www.hoteleldborg.is; sites per person Ikr800, sb Ikr2900, s/d Ikr7500/10,900; ⊙ Jun-Aug; 🛒 💻 🛜) and grab their informative leaflet about the area's geological anomalies, including the cave at **Gullborgarhraun**, and the stunning basalt towers at **Gerðuberg**. The equestrian-focused hotel offers very simple rooms (all with shared bathroom), but there's a good restaurant (mains Ikr1900 to Ikr3100) and a toasty geothermal pool. Horse-riding trips can be arranged for competent riders (from Ikr10,000).

Basic accommodation is also available at the horse farm **Snorrastaðir** (☎ 435 6628; www.snorrastadir.com; sites per tent Ikr1500, sb/6-person cabin Ikr3000/13,000).

There's no public transport to either Hótel Eldborg or Snorrastaðir, but buses between Reykjavík and Stykkishólmur can drop you at the junction on the main road.

SNÆFELLSNES

Lush fjords, haunting volcanic peaks, dramatic sea cliffs, sweeping golden beaches, and crooked crunchy lava flows make up the diverse and fascinating landscape of the 100km-long Snæfellsnes Peninsula. The area is crowned by the glistening ice

WEST ICELAND

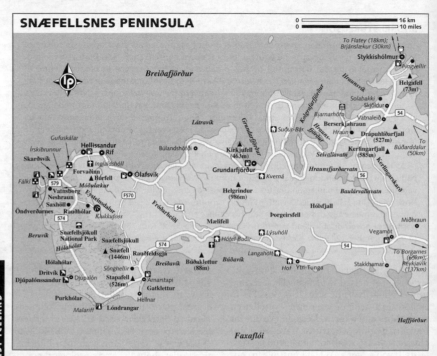

SNÆFELLSNES PENINSULA

WEST ICELAND

cap Snæfellsjökull, immortalised in Jules Verne's fantasy tale *Journey to the Centre of the Earth.* Good roads and regular buses mean that it's an easy trip from Reykjavík and ideal for a short break, offering a cross section of the best Iceland has to offer in a very compact region.

Orientation
Our Snæfellsnes section begins in Stykkishólmur on the populated northern coast. It's the region's largest town and a logical base for exploring the peninsula. From there we move west along the northern shoreline passing several smaller townships before circling around the glacier (the heart of Snæfellsjökull National Park) and returning along the quieter southern coast.

Getting There & Around
As with the rest of rural Iceland, the best way to explore the Snæfellsnes Peninsula is by private vehicle (see p337 if you plan to use some of the minor regional roads), but if funds are limited, there are bus services from Reykjavík to the Vatnaleið transport junction near

Stykkishólmur (where you'll find connections to the various townships on the peninsula). See p167 for detailed transport information. Both Iceland Excursions and Reykjavík Excursions offer day trips from Reykjavík to the Snæfellsnes Peninsula (around Ikr17,000; see p342). **TREX** (www.bogf.is) offers several bus passports through the region (starting at around Ikr13,800); SBA/Reykjavík Excursions does not.

STYKKISHÓLMUR
pop 1100
The charming town of Stykkishólmur, the largest on the Snæfellsnes Peninsula, is built up around a natural harbour protected by a dramatic basalt island. It's a picturesque place with a laid-back attitude and a sprinkling of brightly coloured buildings from the late 19th century. With a comparatively good choice of accommodation and restaurants, and convenient transport links, quaint Stykkishólmur makes an excellent base for exploring the region.

Information
The **tourist information centre** (☎ 433 8120; www.stykkisholmur.is; Borgarbraut 4; ☼ 10am-6pm Jun-Aug) is

located in the same recreational complex as the swimming pool (see p166). The friendly sports-centre staff can offer tourism tips when the information centre is closed. Internet connections are available for Ikr100 per 15 minutes at the tourist information office and at the **library** (☎ 438 8160; Hafnargata 3; ☿ 3-7pm Tue-Thu & 1-5pm Fri Jun-Aug, 2.30-6.30pm Mon-Thu & noon-5.30pm Fri Sep-May).

Sights & Activities

Stykkishólmur's quaint, maritime charm comes from the cluster of wooden warehouses, stores and homes orbiting the town's harbour. Most date back about 150 years and many are still in use. One of the most interesting buildings (and the oldest) is the **Norska Húsið** (Norwegian House; ☎ 438 1640; norkshus@ simnet.is; Hafnargata 5; admission Ikr500; ☿ 11am-5pm Jun-Aug), now the municipal museum. Built by trader Árni Þorlacius in 1832, the house has been skilfully restored and displays a wonderfully eclectic selection of local antiques. On the second floor you can see the typical layout of an upper-class home in 19th-century Iceland.

Looking decidedly out of place among the clutter of quaint maritime houses, Stykkishólmur's futuristic church, **Stykkishólmskirkja** (☎ 438 1560; ☿ 1-5pm) is a striking white structure with a sweeping bell tower that looks like a ship's vent or a giant vertebra. The interior features hundreds of suspended lights and a large painting of the Mother and Child floating in the night sky. Enthusiasts of oddball architecture will be glad to know that there are heaps of funky churches throughout Iceland (see p203).

For relaxing views of the town and the bay, head up the hill to the **Library of Water** (Vatnasafn; www.libraryofwater.is; Bókhlöðustígur 17; admission free; ☿ 1-6pm early May–Aug). Housed in the old municipal library, this hallowed space flooded by natural light features a permanent exhibit by noted American artist Roni Horn. Twenty-four glass pillars are scattered throughout the room, each one filled to the brim with locally sourced glacier water. Light is reflected and refracted through the aqueous tubes, and adjectives in both English and Icelandic are inscribed into the delicate floor. It's the perfect place to curl up with your journal or play a

WEST ICELAND

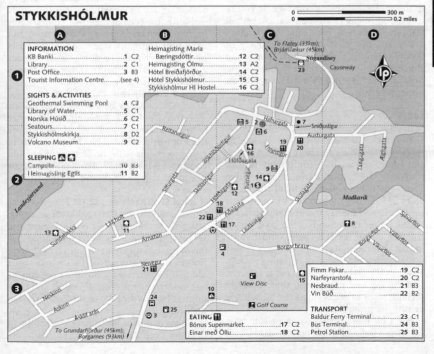

STYKKISHÓLMUR

0 _____ 300 m
0 _____ 0.2 miles

INFORMATION	
KB Banki	1 C2
Library	2 C1
Post Office	3 B3
Tourist Information Centre	(see 4)

SIGHTS & ACTIVITIES	
Geothermal Swimming Pool	4 C3
Library of Water	5 C1
Norska Húsið	6 C2
Seatours	7 C1
Stykkishólmskirkja	8 D2
Volcano Museum	9 C2

SLEEPING	
Campsite	10 B3
Heimagisting Egils	11 B2

Heimagisting María Bæringsdóttir	12 C2
Heimagisting Ölmu	13 A2
Hótel Breiðafjörður	14 C2
Hótel Stykkishólmur	15 C3
Stykkishólmur HI Hostel	16 C2

To Flatey (33km);
Brjánslækur (45km)
Súgandisey
Causeway

Hafnargata
Smiðjustígur
Austurgata
Reitarvegur
Nesvegur
Lágholt
Skólastígur
Aðalgata
Höfðagata
Þvervegur
Skúlagata
Madkavík
Laufásvegur
Borgarbraut
Silfurgata
Sundabakka
Arnafún
View Disc
Golf Course
Neskinn
Askinn
Ásklif arás

To Grundarfjörður (45km);
Borgarnes (93km)

EATING	
Bónus Supermarket	17 C2
Einar með Öllu	18 C2

Fimm Fiskar	19 C2
Narfeyrarstofa	20 C2
Nesbraud	21 B3
Vín Búð	22 B2

TRANSPORT	
Baldur Ferry Terminal	23 C1
Bus Terminal	24 B3
Petrol Station	25 B3

game of chess (provided); just don't forget to take off your shoes. Although the space is closed during the colder months, travellers can arrange a visit via email, or they can pick up the keys at the town library (p164).

Get the back story on the neighbouring lava flows at the newly built **Volcano Museum** (Eldfjallasafn; ☎ 433 8154; www.eldfjallasafn.is; admission Ikr600; ☒ 11am-5pm Jun–mid-Sep), housed in the town's old cinema. The brainchild of vulcan-ologist Haraldur Sigurðsson, the museum features art and artefacts relating to the study of eruptions and their devastating effects. Haraldur himself is usually hangin' around offering additional titbits from his 40 years in the field. Ask about the geologically themed day trips (eight hours; Ikr13,000), which circle the peninsula.

Also worth exploring is the basalt island of **Súgandisey**, which features a scenic lighthouse and offers grand views across Breiðafjörður. You can get to the island by walking across the stone causeway from the harbour.

Try the tangle of water slides or one of the soothing hot pots at the town's **geothermal swimming pool** (☎ 438 1372; adult/under 14yr Ikr380/150; ☒ 7.05am-10pm Mon-Fri, 10am-7pm Sat & Sun) located in the municipal sports complex. If you're lucky, you might catch the local basketball team (Iceland's best) practising their tricks.

Perhaps the most enjoyable activity in Stykkishólmur is a pleasant boat tour of the alluring islands that freckle the brooding Breiðafjörður (see following Tours section for more info).

Tours

Seatours (Sæferðir; ☎ 438 1450; www.seatours.is; Smiðjustígur 3; ☒ 8am-8pm mid-May–mid-Sep, 9am-5pm mid-Sep–mid-May) runs a variety of boat tours, and offers sea angling equipment rentals (Ikr6600). Our favourite trip is the 'Unique Tour' – a 2¼-hour boat ride (adult/under 16 years Ikr5950/free), which takes in postcard-worthy views of the bay and its myriad islands. Kodak moments abound as the boat passes colonies of puffins and eagles, and haunt-ing basalt formations (keep your ears peeled for the gruesome legend of 'hanging rock'!). Towards the end of the trip a net is lowered into the sea, and pretty soon there's wiggly shellfish ready to be devoured raw (absolutely delish – we promise).

For a bit more luxury, try a private boat tour (from Ikr95,000; four person max) – visit

the booking office for details. Seatours also operates the Baldur car ferry, which stops in lovely Flatey on the way to the Westfjords. Day trips and overnight stays on Flatey (p168) can be easily arranged at the Seatours bureau. Most activities run from mid-May to mid-September. At the time of research, Seatours' whale-watching trips (based in Ólafsvík) were not operating; however, this may change in the future.

Festivals & Events

If you're passing through the area during the third weekend in August, you'll be treated to festive bridge dancing and a bevy of live bands during Stykkishólmur's annual Danish Days ('*Danskir dagar*' in Icelandic) – an event which pays tribute to the town's Danish roots.

Sleeping

Campsite (☎ 438 1075; mostri@stykk.is; sites per person Ikr800, electricity Ikr400; ☒) Managed by the golf course nearby, this 'five-star' campsite is one of Iceland's swankiest spots to pitch a tent.

Stykkishólmar HI Hostel (Youth Hostel Sjónarhóll; ☎ 438 1095, 861 2517; stykkisholmur@hostel.is, www.hostel.is; Höfðagata 1; sb member/nonmember Ikr2100/2800, d Ikr5600; ☒ May-Sep) Situated in a wonderfully wobbly house (one of the town's oldest), this bastion of backpackers is a tad cramped, but has a great communal vibe – none of the doors have locks. There are dorms and doubles aplenty (no private bathrooms), and there's a handy kitchen for self-caterers.

Hótel Breiðafjörður (☎ 433 2200; www.hotel breidafjordur.is; Aðalgata 8; s/d Ikr9500/15,200 Jun-Aug, reduced rates Sep–May; ☒ ☒) Right in the centre of town, this small hotel – which looks more like a dowdy residential block – offers bright, spacious rooms with modern furniture and good views from the balconies. The decor is simple and neutral, and all the fittings are new.

Hótel Stykkishólmur (☎ 430 2100; www.hring hotels.is; Borgarbraut 8; s/d Ikr17,500/20,000, discounts in winter; ☒ ☒) Slightly out of the centre and set on a hill, this boxy hotel feels almost as out of place as the modern church next door. Rooms are spread across two wings – the old hall has the views, but the new annexe has modern furnishings. Free golf and tasty dinners (mains Ikr2900 to Ikr4500) sweeten the deal.

A slew of quaint B&Bs have popped up in the town's residential area:

Heimagisting Ölmu (☎ 438 1435, 848 9833; almdie@
simnet.is; Sundabakka 12; sb/s/d Ikr3200/6500/8000,
breakfast Ikr1000)
Heimagisting Egils (☎ 820 5408; Lágholt 11; s/d
Ikr7000/10,000; ☺ Jun-Aug)
Heimagisting María Bæringsdóttir (☎ 438
1258; fax 438 1245; Höfðagata 11; s/d incl breakfast
Ikr7500/9500) An old favourite.

Eating

Nesbraud (☎ 438-1830; Nesvegur 1; snacks from Ikr195;
☺ 8am-6pm) At the crossroads on the way out
of town, this small bakery is a good choice for
a budget-friendly breakfast or lunch. Stock up
on sugary confections like *kleinur* (traditional
twisty doughnuts) or *ástar-pungur* (literally
'love balls'; fried balls of dough and raisins).

Einar með Öllu (Aðalgata; mains from Ikr250 ☺ noon-
8pm Jun-Aug) Skip the greasy grill at the local
petrol station and swing by this friendly *pylsuvagninn* (wiener wagon) for the best hot dogs
in town. It's a great spot to up your caloric
intake, especially if you missed the ubiquitous
pýlsur stands in Reykjavík (see the boxed text,
p53). When you grab your grub to go, don't
forget to ask the cashier about the wagon's
punny name (it's a great li'l play on words!)

Narfeyrarstofa (☎ 438 1119; Aðalgata 3; mains from
Ikr1090; ☺ 11.30am-11pm) Well, the jig is up – everyone's figured out that this atmospheric joint is
the best place in town for a bite, including *all*
the tour groups. It's definitely worth sampling
the delicious assortment of cakes and burgers; just don't stop by during prime lunching
hours 'cause you won't get a table!

Fimm Fiskar (☎ 436 1600; Frúarstígur 1; mains Ikr1400-
4900; ☺ 11am-11pm) The Five Fishes is housed
in a chalet-style abode just up the street from
Narfeyrarstofa, it's main competition. New
management has kicked things up a notch,
offering a colourful assortment of fresh fish
from the pier. Dishes are on the small side, but
get decent reviews nonetheless.

Self-caterers will be sated at the **Bónus supermarket** (☺ noon-6pm Mon-Fri, 10.30am-6pm Sat & Sun)
near the swimming pool, although you can
also head down to the pier around 6pm to buy
the latest catch from the docking fishermen.
The local **Vín Búð** is located across the main
road from the Bónus.

Getting There & Away
BOAT
The car ferry **Baldur** (☎ 438 1450; www.seatours.
is) operates between Stykkishólmur and

Brjánslækur in the Westfjords (three hours),
via Flatey. From 10 June to 20 August there
are daily departures from Stykkishólmur at
9am and 3.30pm, returning from Brjánslækur
at 12.15pm and 6.45pm. During the rest of
the year, there is only one ferry per day,
leaving Stykkishólmur at 3pm (11am on
Saturdays), returning at 6pm, and often not
stopping in Flatey at all. See p168 if you plan
to stop on Flatey along the way. Adult fares
to Brjánslækur are Ikr3850; vehicles cost an
additional Ikr3850. A roundtrip ticket from
Stykkishólmur to Flatey costs Ikr5300. During
the summer/winter, children under 16 years
are free/50% off.

Buses in the Westfjords are scheduled for
relatively seamless connections with the ferry;
see p179 for details.

BUS
There are at least two daily buses running
to/from Reykjavík (2½ hours) from mid-
June to August. One daily bus continues
out of season except on Wednesday and
Saturday. To reach town, you must get off
at the Vatnaleið stop and switch to reach
Stykkishólmur. Buses also link Vatnaleið to
Grundarfjörður, Ólafsvík and Hellissandur.
Services from Vatnaleið don't always link
well with the *Baldur* ferry (left).

BREIÐAFJÖRÐUR
Stykkishólmur's jagged peninsula pushes
north into stunning Breiðafjörður, a gaping waterway ('breiðafjörður' means 'broad
fjord') separating the torpedo-shaped
Snæfellsnes from the looming cliffs of the
distant Westfjords.

According to local legend, there are
only two things in the world that cannot
be counted: the stars in the night sky and
the craggy islets in the bay. Despite the
numerical setback, those who visit beautiful Breiðafjörður *can* count on epic vistas –
idyllic tapestries of greens and blues – and
its menagerie of wild birds (puffins, eagles,
guillemots etc).

The Seatours office, which is based in
Stykkishólmur (see opposite), runs a vari-
ety of tours around the bay, and also dis-
penses several handy brochures that detail
the region's local bird life and its intriguing
Viking history. Travellers who are staying in
Grundarfjörður can enquire about trips at
Hótel Framnes (p170).

WISHING AT HELGAFELL

It is commonly believed that those who ascend humble Helgafell (below) will be granted three wishes, provided that the requests are made with a pure heart. However, it isn't as simple as merely climbing the hill and thinking happy thoughts. You must follow three important steps in order to make your wishes come true:

- Step 1: Start at the marked grave of Guðrún Ósvífursdóttir, heroine of an ancient local saga.
- Step 2: Walk up to the Tótt (the chapel ruins) never uttering a single word, and (like Orpheus leaving Hades), never looking back along the way.
- Step 3: Once at the chapel ruins, you must turn and face east while wishing. And remember – never tell your wishes to anyone or they won't come true.

Flatey

Of Breiðafjörður's innumerable islands, adorable Flatey (literally 'flat island') is the only one with year-round inhabitants: two families embroiled in an age-old feud that rivals the Capulets and Montagues. In the 11th century, Flatey was home to a literary monastery, and today the charming island is a popular layover for travellers heading to (or from) the Westfjords. Push the slo-mo button on life, and enjoy a windswept afternoon amid brightly coloured catalogue houses and swooping arctic terns.

If you are crossing Breiðafjörður aboard the *Baldur* ferry (p167) and would like to have a look around the island, you must take the first ferry of the day, disembark, and board the second daily ferry to your final destination (boats only pause on the island for around five minutes as they cross the fjord). For those travelling by car, it is possible to send your vehicle across the bay (at no additional charge) while staying behind in Flatey. Note that the twice-per-day ferry service only runs between 10 June and 20 August (in May and September you will have to spend the night, and in the colder months you may have to spend several days).

Sleeping on Flatey is a cinch. Both of the island's farms – **Krákuvör** (☎ 438 1451) and **Læknishús** (☎ 438 1476) – are about 300m to 400m from the pier and offer modest accommodation (around Ikr3000) in summer. You can also pitch a tent at Krákuvör (Ikr700) or sleep at **Hótel Flatey** (☎ 422 7610; info@hotelflatey. is; d from Ikr18,200; ☒ mid-Jun–mid-Sep), which has comfy rooms and great views over the fjord.

STYKKISHÓLMUR TO GRUNDARFJÖRÐUR

The scenic stretch of land between Stykkishólmur and Grundarfjörður is filled with myth and mystique. About 5km south of Stykkishólmur is the holy mountain **Helgafell** (73m), once venerated by worshippers of the god Þór. Although quite small, the mountain was so sacred in Saga times that elderly Icelanders would seek out the hill near the time of their death. Today, locals believe that wishes are granted to those who climb the mount (see the boxed text, above). In the late 10th century, Snorri Goði, a prominent Þor worshipper, converted to Christianity and built a church at the top of the hill. The church ruins are still prominent in the terrain. The nearby farm of the same name was where the conniving Guðrun Ósvífursdóttir of the *Laxdæla Saga* lived out her later years in isolation. Her grave marks the base of the mount.

About 15km west of the intersection of Rte 54 and Rte 58 (the road to Stykkishólmur) lies the sweeping lava field at **Berserkjahraun** (Berserkers' lava field). Crowned by looming mountains, this lunar landscape gets its name from the *Eyrbyggja Saga* – see opposite. Those with a little extra time on their hands will enjoy the winding drive along the 2WD-friendly Rte 558. Known as **Bersekjahraunsvegur** (try saying that three times fast!), this scenic stretch ambles through an endless expanse of charcoal blacks, sulphur yellows and mossy greens. Pick a flat patch and pitch a tent – not only is this a prime spot for **wilderness camping**, it's one of the region's best-kept secrets (until now!). If you're looking for a bit of comfort, there are a few lodging options in the area as well (see opposite).

On the northeastern edge of Berserkjahraun is the farmstead at **Bjarnarhöfn** (☎ 438 1581; www. bjarnarhofn.is; museum admission Ikr700; ☒ 9am-7pm) – a must for every traveller with a taste for adventure (literally). Smell that? Yup, it's rotting shark flesh – the farm is the region's leading producer of *hákarl* (putrid shark meat), a traditional Icelandic dish. The on-site museum details the fragrant history of this culinary curiosity by displaying restored shark fishing boats, harpooning tools, and explaining the fermenting process. Each visit to the museum comes with a complimentary nibble of the delicacy in question. Some say it tastes like a sponge dipped in ammonia; we thought it was somewhat similar to old cheese. Before you leave, ask about the drying house out back. If you're lucky you'll see hundreds of dangling shark slices being attacked by zealous flies (you'll be glad you tried the shark meat *before* visiting the drying house!). To reach the farm, follow the signposts down a series of 2WD-friendly gravel roads leading away from Rte 54.

GRUNDARFJÖRÐUR
pop 910

Spectacularly set on a dramatic bay, little Grundarfjörður is surrounded by sugar-loaf peaks often shrouded in wispy, cotton-puff fog. Preferring prefab to wooden construction, the town feels like a typical Icelandic fishing community, but the tourist facilities are good and the surrounding landscape can't be beat.

A tourist information office, cafe, internet point and heritage museum all rolled into one, the **Saga Centre** (Eyrbyggja Heritage Centre; ☎ 438 1881; www.grundarfjordur.is; Grundargata 35; ☒ 10am-6pm May-Sep; ☺) is a must for every visitor. Sip a fresh double latte while chatting with the friendly employees, update your blog (internet Ikr200 for 15 minutes), and check out the museum's detailed exhibits (museum Ikr500,

includes 20-minute tour) about the town's French-influenced history and the advent of the boat engine. The museum also features a life-sized model of a turn-of-the-century Icelandic home. You'll be shocked to learn that this bite-size abode would sleep around eight people. Icelandic films and photo slide-shows often play in the on-site screening room during high season.

In the summer months, it'll be hard to tear yourself away from Grundarfjörður without ascending the majestic **Kirkjufell** (463m), guardian of the town's northern vista. Ask the Saga Centre to hook you up with a guide (around Ikr5000 per guide) – three spots involving a rope climb make it dangerous to scale the mountain without assistance. The whole adventure should take no more than four hours. After your hike, rest your muscles in one of the soothing hot pots at the local **swimming pool** (adult Ikr380; ☒ 8am-8pm, closed for lunch).

Sleeping

Campsite (☎ 894 5309; tent Ikr400 plus per person Ikr200, caravan Ikr2000; ☒ Jun-Aug) This new campsite, backed by a scenic waterfall, currently shares showering facilities with the public pool nearby. Campers can pay at the Saga Centre, or wait for the ranger to swing by (usually three times a day).

Grundarfjörður HI Hostel (☎ 562 6533, 895 6533; Hlíðarvegur 15; grundarfjordur@hostel.is, www.hostel.is; sb member/nonmember Ikr2100/2500; s/d Ikr3400/5800, apt Ikr10,500–16,500; ☒ ☺) Although lacking the ramshackle backpacker charm of Stykkishólmur's hostel, Grundarfjörður's

---

GONE BERSERK

Long ago, according to the *Eyrbyggja Saga*, a farmer from Hraun grew weary from having to walk around the jagged lava flows to visit his brother at the farm in Bjarnarhöfn. Returning from a voyage to Norway, he brought back two berserkers – insanely violent fighters who were employed as hired thugs in Viking times – to work on his farm, but to his dismay one of the berserkers took a liking to his daughter. He turned to the local chieftain, Snorri Goði, for advice, but Snorri had his eye on the farmer's daughter as well and he recommended setting the berserker an impossible task. The farmer decided to promise the amorous berserker his daughter's hand in marriage if he was able to clear a passage through the troublesome lava field – surely impossible for a normal man.

To the shock and horror of both Snorri and the farmer, the two berserkers quickly set to work and managed to rip a passage straight through the treacherous moonscape. Rather than honouring his promise, the farmer trapped the berserkers in a sauna and murdered them, allowing Snorri to marry his daughter.

Today, a path through the 'Berserkjahraun' can still be seen, and recently a grave was discovered in the vicinity containing the remains of two large men.

contribution to the budget category features simple rooms spread across a couple of brightly coloured houses. Swankier digs can be found atop the fish factory along the harbour. Reception is in the red house, at the listed address. Ask the staff about bike rentals, day trips and in-house internet access (Ikr450 per day). Free linen and half-price wi-fi sweetens the deal during the winter months. Note that the hostel closes from 15 December to 15 January – the owners wanna do a little travelling too!

Hótel Framnes (☎ 438 6893; www.hotelframnes.is; Nesvegur 8; s/d incl breakfast Jun-Sep Ikr13,700/18,000, Oct-May reduced rates) Brand new management has breathed new life into this comfy dockside inn. The reception area is surprisingly modern and top-floor rooms are adorably nestled under eaved roofs. Fish-oriented dishes dominate the restaurant's menu (mains Ikr2300 to Ikr3700), or you can try to catch your own meal on a hotel-run boat trip in Breiðafjörður (two hours, Ikr3500).

The following accommodation options are located off Rte 54 between Stykkishólmur and Grundarfjörður.

Kverná (☎ 438 6813; www.simnet.is/kverna; sites per person Ikr7000, s/d Ikr6000/9000) Cosy farm just outside town offering cottage accommodation, horse riding and sightseeing tours.

Suður-Bár (☎ 438 6815; www.sudurbar.sveit.is; Eyrarsveit; s/d from Ikr8000/12,000) Friendly guest house 8km east of town with pleasant rooms, horse riding and golf. Note that it's best to access the Eyrarfjall area from the Grundarfjörður side; the dirt road along Kolgrafarfjörður is often too rutty for a 2WD.

Eating

Krákan (☎ 438 6999; Sæból 13; mains Ikr1500-3600; ☯ 7-1am) Stark and bright, with a cream-coloured piano in the corner, Krákan has a brand new look after it was damaged in a recent fire. Cheap burgers lure the masses – staff could slap on a smile though.

Kaffi 59 (☎ 438 6446; Grundargata 59; mains Ikr1800-3100; ☯ 10am-11pm Mon-Thu, to 1am Fri, 11am-1am Sat, 11am-11pm Sun; ☏) This well-worn joint is the place for pizza, sandwiches, ice-cream sundaes and beer, served up in a crumby (both meanings) diner-style building by the main road through town.

A small **supermarket** (☯ 9am-10pm Jun-Aug, to 9pm Sep-May) and an N1 petrol station – with the usual grill hut – are within eyeshot of the Saga Centre.

Getting There & Away

The Reykjavík–Hellissandur bus stops here once or twice a day in summer. A bus runs every day except Wednesday and Saturday out of season. The trip from Reykjavík takes 2¾ hours.

ÓLAFSVÍK

pop 990

Quiet, unassuming and well kept, workaday Ólafsvík won't win any hearts, but it's a pleasant place to pause and regroup after negotiating a few too many bumps in the road. Although it's the oldest trading town in the country (it was granted a trading licence in 1687), few of the original buildings survive. Ólafsvík is the largest settlement in Snæfellsbær district – the region's **tourist information centre** (☎ 433 9930; Kirkjútún 2; information@snb.is; ☯ 8am-6pm Mon-Fri, 10am-5pm Sat & Sun) is located in a drab white building behind the Old Packinghouse.

Sights & Activities

Gamla Pakkhúsið (Old Packinghouse; ☎ 436 1543; Ólafsbraut; adult/under 16yr Ikr300/free; ☯ 11am-5pm Jun–mid-Sep) is an interesting folk museum telling the story of the town's development as a trading centre. Towards the harbour, the small maritime museum **Sjávarsafnið Ólafsvík** (☎ 436 6926; admission free; ☯ 9am-6pm Jun–mid-Sep) displays black-and-white pictures detailing the local history.

At the time of research, whale-watching tours had been permanently cancelled due to soaring oil prices. Contact Seatours (p166) in Stykkishólmur for updates.

The local **swimming pool** (☎ 436 1199; adult/under 14yr Ikr350/200; ☯ 8am-9pm Mon-Fri, 1-5pm Sat & Sun) is on Ennisbraut.

Sleeping & Eating

Although not as convenient as Stykkishólmur and Grundarfjörður, Ólafsvík has a couple of passable sleeping options. If everything is full you can pitch a tent at the local **campsite** (☎ 436 1543, 430 8600; Dalbraut; sites per person Ikr500) or stop by the tourist office – they'll set you up with a room in a local home (Ikr4000 per person).

Hótel Ólafsvík (☎ 436 1650; www.hotelolafsvik.is; Ólafsbraut 20; s/d without bathroom €59/79, with bathroom incl breakfast €125/148, 20% discounts in winter; ☐ ☏) A mighty step up from camping, this large hotel has spacious, functional rooms with tiled floors, neutral decor and very little character. Rooms with shared bathroom are in an attached annexe – the accommodation with private facilities is noticeably nicer. The hotel restaurant (mains Ikr2800 to Ikr3500) is popular with tour groups and offers a range of Icelandic meals and pub-grub standards.

Hobbitinn (☎ 436 1362; Ólafsbraut; mains from Ikr310; ☷ 10am-11.30pm Mon-Fri, 11.30am-11.30pm Sat & Sun) Dressed up with a shop-window facade, Hobbitinn is merely a fast-food joint specialising in burgers, pizzas and hot dogs. Apparently the owner is quite small and hobbit-like.

There's also a grill at the Shell petrol station, a good **bakery** (Bakari; ☎ 436 1119; cakes from Ikr220; ☷ 7.30am-6pm Mon-Fri, 9am-4pm Sat) next to Hobbitinn, and a supermarket at the junction of Ennisbraut and Norðurtangi.

Getting There & Away

In summer, there are one or two daily links (bus 350/350a) between Reykjavík and Ólafsvík, passing through Vegamót (2¾ hours) and continuing on to Hellissandur (15 minutes). There is a bus every day except Wednesday and Saturday in winter. The buses drop off and pick up at the petrol station.

RIF & HELLISSANDUR
pop 140 & 390

A mere 6km after Ólafsvík is blink-and-you'll-miss-it Rif, a harbour village that makes Ólafsvík look like the big city. Swing by **Gamla Rif** (☎ 436 1001; Háarifi 3; cakes from Ikr500, fish soup from Ikr1500; ☷ noon-8pm Jun-Aug) for tasty coffee and cakes. The owners, two fishermen's wives, have perfected a variety of traditional snacks and dispense local travel tips with a smile. They make a mean fish soup (from their husbands' daily catch) if you're feeling extra-peckish. Scenic **Svöðufoss**, with its trickling chutes and dramatic hexagonal basalt, can be seen in the distance.

Hellissandur, next door, is the original fishing village in the area and has a few more amenities. Snæfellsjökull National Park (right) has a ranger office here, but the opening hours are infrequent and limited; tourists should head to Hellnar (p172) for park information, or download a trail brochure from www.ust.is.

The only artificial sight in the area is **Sjómannagarður** (☎ 436 6619; Útnesvegur; adult/child Ikr250/free; ☷ 9.30am-noon & 1-6pm Tue-Sun Jun-Aug), a small maritime museum with an adorable

turf house, loads of old photos and plenty of local memorabilia, including a set of lifting stones once used to test the strength of prospective fishermen.

About 2km inland from Hellissandur is the lonely church at **Ingjaldshóll**, the first concrete church in the world (built in 1903). Ingjaldshóll was the setting of the *Víglundar Saga*. If the church doors are open you can see a painting depicting Christopher Columbus' apparent visit to Iceland in 1477 (see the boxed text, p173 for more details).

The local **campsite** (☎ 436 1543, 430 8600) has basic facilities managed by the info centre in Ólafsvík. For far more comfort, check into the **Hótel Hellissandur** (☎ 430 8600; www.hotelhellissandur.is; Klettsbúd 7; s/d incl breakfast mid-May–Aug Ikr16,700/19,200, 20-30% discount Sep–mid-May; ☐ ☷), a well-run place offering bright, modern rooms with contemporary interiors and sparkling bathrooms. The only dining options in Hellissandur are the hotel restaurant (mains from Ikr2500) and the N1 petrol station (open 11am to 9pm).

All buses from Reykjavík to Ólafsvík continue to Hellissandur, stopping at the N1 petrol station.

SNÆFELLSJÖKULL NATIONAL PARK

Continuing west from Hellissandur, the scenic Rte 574 skirts the rugged slopes of Snæfellsjökull – the icy fist at the end of the long Snæfellsnes arm. Known as Undir-Jökli, this desolate area offers eerie views of lava spurs sticking straight up through the scree, and, on misty days, when the fog swirls among the peaks, you can easily see how the legends of cantankerous trolls came to life.

As haunting and isolated as this ethereal realm may feel, the looming ice cap was famous worldwide long before it was protected under a national park mandate in June 2001 – Jules Verne used the glacier as the setting for his famous *Journey to the Centre of the Earth*. In the book a German geologist and his nephew embark on an epic journey into the crater of Snæfells, guided by a 16th-century Icelandic text with the following advice:

Descend into the crater of Yocul of Sneffels, Which the shade of Scartaris caresses, Before the kalends of July, audacious traveller, And you will reach the centre of the earth. I did it.

Arne Saknussemm

WEST ICELAND

Snæfellsjökull

It's easy to see why Jules Verne selected Snæfell – the dramatic peak was torn apart when the volcano beneath the ice cap exploded and the volcano subsequently collapsed into its own magma chamber, forming a huge caldera. Among certain New Age groups, Snæfellsjökull is considered one of the world's great 'power centres', and it definitely has a brooding presence.

Today the crater is filled in with ice and makes a popular hiking destination in summer. The best way to reach the glacial summit is to approach the peak from the south side of Rte F570 and link up with a snowmobile tour in Arnarstapi (opposite). Route F570's northern approach (near Ólafsvík) is frustratingly rutty (4WD needed) and frequently closed due to weather-inflicted damage.

Contact the visitor centre at Hellnar (see right) for more information. Do not attempt an ascent without a proper briefing about road conditions and weather forecasts. Note that there is no mobile phone reception from Hellisandur to Lóndrangar.

Öndverðarnes

At the westernmost tip of Snæfellsnes, Rte 574 cuts south, while a tiny gravel track heads west across an ancient lava flow to the tip of the Öndverðarnes peninsula. As the road winds through charcoal lava cliffs you'll pass Skarðsvík, a perfect golden beach lapped by Caribbean blue waters. A Viking grave was discovered here in the 1960s and it's easy to see why this stunning spot in the middle of an otherwise desolate area would have been favoured as a final resting place.

After Skarðsvík the track gets much bumpier (still manageable for a 2WD though). Follow the turn-off (left side) through the craggy lava flows to the imposing volcanic crater Vatnsborg, or continue straight on until you hit the dramatic Svörtuloft bird cliffs at the end of the road. A bumpy track runs parallel to the sea connecting the area's two squat lighthouses. To reach the very tip of the peninsula, go right (north) until you reach the yellow lighthouse. From the informal parking area near the lighthouse, it's a mere 200m stroll to Fálki, an abandoned stone well which used to be the only source of fresh water in the area.

Back on Rte 54, southwest of the Öndverðarnes area, follow the marked turn-off to the roadside scoria crater Saxhóll. There's a driveable track leading straight to the base, from where it's a quick 300m climb for magnificent views over the Neshraun lava flows.

Dritvík & Djúpalón

Further along, Rte 572 leads down to the wild black-sand beach at Djúpalónssandur. It's a dramatic place to walk, with a series of rocky stacks emerging from the ocean. You can also still see four 'lifting stones' on the beach where fishing-boat crews would test the strength of aspiring fishermen. The smallest stone is Amloði (Bungler) at 23kg, followed by Hálfdrættingur (Weak) at 54kg, Hálfsterkur (Half-Strong) at 100kg, and the largest, Fullsterker (Fully Strong), at 154kg. Hálfdrættingur marked the frontier of wimphood, and any man who couldn't heft it was deemed unsuitable for a life at sea. Mysteriously, there now appear to be five stones.

If you tramp up over the craggy headland you'll reach the similar black-sand beach at Dritvík, where around 60 fishing boats were stationed from the 16th to the 19th century. The black sands are covered in pieces of rusted metal from the English trawler *Eding*, which was wrecked here in 1948. Several freshwater pools and the rocky arch Gatklettur are close to the car park.

About 2km south of Djúpalón a track leads down to the rocket-shaped lighthouse at Malariff, from where you can walk along the cliffs to the rock pillars at Lóndrangar, which surge up into the air like a frozen splash of lava. Locals say that elves use the lava formations as a church.

SOUTHERN SNÆFELLSNES

Beyond the glacier's frosty grip, the road smooths out to the south, passing the interesting sea-sculpted rock formations at Hellnar and Arnarstapi (see the boxed text, p174), then continuing east along the broad southern coastal plain, hugging the huge sandy bays at Breiðavík and Búðavík.

Hellnar

Bárður, the guardian spirit of Snæfells, chose Hellnar, a picturesque spot overlooking a rocky bay, as his home. Today Hellnar is a tiny fishing village where the shriek of sea birds fills the air and whales are regularly sighted. Down on the shore, the cave Baðstofa is chock-

HEY COLUMBUS, EAT YOUR HEART OUT!

Icelanders are very quick to point out that Christopher Columbus did not 'discover' America. In fact, it is commonly believed that Columbus visited the Snæfellsnes Peninsula in 1477 to learn about the earlier Viking conquests in the New World.

During his Icelandic foray, Columbus was surprised to discover that a woman, Guðríður Þorbjarnardóttir, was among Iceland's pantheon of celebrated explorers. Born in Hellnar before the year 1000 (a beautiful sculpture marks the site of her family's farm), Guðríður had a serious case of wanderlust. Not only was she one of the first Europeans to reach Vinland (most likely Canada's Newfoundland), she bore a child while visiting (the first European child born in North America)! After her son, Snorri, married and moved to Glaumbær (p205), Guðríður converted to Christianity and embarked on an epic pilgrimage to Rome. Upon arrival, she met with the pope and recounted her experiences at the edge of the earth.

For more information about Guðríður, read *The Far Traveler* by Nancy Marie Brown, or *The Sea Road* by Margaret Elphinstone.

a-block with nesting birds, and **Bárðarlaug**, up near the main road, was supposedly Bárður's bathing pool (sadly the pond is no longer hot). Ancient, velvety moss–cloaked lava flows tumble east, spilling down the nearby mountains and into the churning sea.

Travellers seeking information about the Snæfellsjökull National Park (p171) should stop at **Gestastofa** (☎ 436 6888; admission free; ☼ 10am-6pm 20 May-10 Sep). The building functions as an info office and museum, featuring displays on the local geology, history, people, customs and wildlife. Note that the park's ranger station in Hellissandur has unpredictable hours and is often closed to visitors.

Hótel Hellnar (☎ 435 6820; www.hellnar.is; s/d incl breakfast from €120/140; ☼ 10 May-10 Sep; ☎) is the area's choice sleeping option. The twin-bedded rooms are sun-filled and simple (cards with self-esteem mantras are inexplicably placed on the pillows in lieu of the usual chocolate). The restaurant (dinner mains Ikr2600 to Ikr3500) earns brownie points for its use of local organic produce.

It's well worth following the rickety stone path down to the ocean's edge for a meal at quaint **Fjöruhúsið** (☎ 435 6844; fish soup Ikr1650; ☼ 10am-10pm late Apr-early Oct). It's located at the trailhead of the scenic Hellnar–Arnarstapi path (see the boxed text, p174).

Arnarstapi

Linked to Hellnar by both the main road and a must-do coastal hike (p174), this hamlet of summer cottages is nestled between the churning arctic waters and the gnarled pillars of a neighbouring lava field. A recently erected **monument** pays tribute to Jules Verne

with a wooden information panel and comical signpost measuring distances to major cities through the core of the earth.

Arnarstapi is the best place to organise an ascent to the glacial crown. Snowmobile tours on the glacier are run by **Snjófell** (☎ 435 6783; www.snjofell.is). In summer snowcat tours of the glacier cost Ikr6500 per person (minimum of six people), or there's a snowmobile tour for Ikr10,500 per person/Ikr12,500 for a solo ski-do (minimum of two people). Trips run every two hours until midnight and last for around 1½ hours.

The tours start at the edge of the snowfield, so you'll have to drive along the bumpy Rte F570 towards the summit. Road conditions can be uncertain, so it's best to ask at Snjófell for details when purchasing your tour ticket. Taxis to the top can be negotiated if you don't have your own wheels or if the roads are damaged. Note that the summit should always be approached from the south (from Arnarstapi). The northern part of Rte F570 (near Ólafsvík) is often closed and never suitable for a 2WD (see the boxed text, p341, for vital information about F roads).

As you drive up from Arnarstapi you'll pass **Stapafell** (526m), the supposed home to the local little people – you'll see miniature house gables painted onto rocks in their honour. Further along you'll pass a collapsed crater, which has created a series of strange lava caves about 1.5km from the main road. The largest cave is **Sönghellir** (Song Cave), which is full of 18th-century graffiti and is rumoured to resound with the songs of dwarfs. Bring a torch or use the flash of your camera to read the various markings of

SAVE IT FOR A RAINY DAY!

Rainy days in Iceland? Oh yes, there are many. But don't let the drizzle make your holiday plans fizzle – there are several stunning landscapes that are even more dramatic in the rain, including the scenic 2.5km walk (around 40 minutes) between Hellnar and Arnarstapi (p173). This slender trail follows the jagged coastline, passing frozen lava flows and eroded stone caves. During bouts of tumultuous weather the waves pound through the rocky arches like water spraying out of a blowhole. After your jaunt, reward yourself with a hearty repast at one of the cleverly positioned restaurants plunked on either side of the trail. If you finish in Hellnar, savour a perfected recipe for fish soup at Fjöruhúsið (p173), while those who end up in Arnarstapi can treat themselves to the daily catch at Ferðaþjónustan Snjófell (p173).

Don't get us wrong however; this short walk is absolutely stunning on a sunny day as well!

passers-by and don't be shy about belting out your favourite melody.

Snjófell also offers accommodation and dining at **Ferðaþjónustan Snjófell** (☎ 435 6783; www.snjofell.is, www.hringhotels.is; tent Ikr1500, plus electricity Ikr500, sb/d Ikr2500/7000) in Arnarstapi. Travellers can pitch a tent on a grassy patch outside (sorry, no showers) or plop their sleeping bag down in the prefab guest house. The menu in the turf-roofed restaurant (meals Ikr1890 to Ikr3490) focuses on the delicious assortment of fish brought to shore at the harbour down the street.

Rauðfeldsgjá

Past Stapafell, a small track branches east off Rte 574 to **Rauðfeldsgjá**, a steep and narrow cleft that mysteriously disappears into the cliff wall. A stream runs along the bottom of the gorge, and you can slink between the sheer walls for quite a distance.

Breiðavík & Búðavík

East of Hellnar and Arnarstapi, Rte 574 skirts the edges of the long sandy bays at Breiðavík and Búðavík. These windswept beaches are covered in yellow-grey sand and are wonderfully peaceful places to walk. At Búðavík the abandoned fishing village of Búðir has a stunningly lonely church, and is now home to one of Iceland's best country hotels. From the hotel, a walking trail leads across the elf-infested Buðahraun lava field to the crater **Búðaklettur**. According to local legend a lava tube beneath Buðahraun, paved with gold and precious stones, leads all the way to Surtshellir (p163). It takes about three hours to walk to the crater and back.

Windswept, lonely and very romantic, ** our pick** **Hótel Búðir** (☎ 435 6700; www.budir.is; d incl breakfast Ikr26,000-36,000, ste Ikr44,500; 🖳 🛜) is a

sleek, stylish hotel with an understated-yet-regal design and not a hint of pretension. Expect elegant furnishings, DVD players and plasma TVs, and – if you're lucky enough to bag No 23 – a freestanding bath separated from the bedroom by a wooden screen. No 28 has the best views (and a teeny tiny balcony). The house chef grew up on the peninsula and knows his local ingredients better than anyone else in the region. Try the eight-course kitchen special (Ikr8100) or go for one of the perfected fish dishes. If you're going to splash out at any point on your trip, this is the place to do it.

Fed by a geothermic source, serene **Lýsuhóll** (☎ 435 6716; www.lysuholl.is; s/d/cottages Ikr10,000/15,000/10,500) sits inland, just a few kilometres beyond Búðir. Horse riding (90 minutes/two hours/day trip Ikr3500/5000/12,000), swimming and brand new cottage accommodation makes this a good choice.

The golf-centric **Gistihúsið Langaholt** (☎ 435 6789; www.langaholt.is; Görðum; sites per person Ikr750, s/d incl breakfast Ikr9500-16,000; 🛜) feels more like a motel, offering a long strip of tasteful rooms. Nine holes of golf costs Ikr2000 (clubs available for rent). Book ahead.

Further along, friendly **Gistiheimilið Hof** (☎ 435 6802; www.gistihof.is; d sb/linen Ikr8000/10,000) has a selection of turf-roofed apartment-style accommodation with shared kitchens, living rooms and bathrooms. Ask the owners about the local colony of barking seals and don't forget to take a dip in the relaxing hot pots.

DALIR

The scenic corridor between west Iceland and the Westfjords served as the setting for the *Laxdæla Saga*, the most popular of the Icelandic sagas. The story revolves around a love triangle between Guðrun Ósvífursdóttir, said to be the most beautiful woman in Iceland, and the foster brothers Kjartan Ólafsson and Bolli Þorleiksson. In typical saga fashion, Guðrun had both men wrapped around her little finger and schemed and connived until both of them were dead – Kjartan at the hands of Bolli, and Bolli at the hands of Kjartan's brothers. Most Icelanders know the stories and characters by heart and hold the area in which the story took place in great historic esteem.

It's worth picking up a free copy of the excellent *Dalasýsla Heritage Map* available at the tourist information centre in Búðardalur or at the hotel in Laugar. Hikers should invest in the *Vestfirðir & Dalir £7* map (available at most regional information centres for a nominal fee).

EIRÍKSSTAÐIR

The farm Eiríksstaðir, across the Haukadalsá from Stóra-Vatnshorn's church, was the home of Eiríkur Rauðe (Erik the Red), father of Leifur Eiríksson, believed to be the first European to visit America. Although only a faint outline of the original farm remains, an impressive **reconstruction of the farm** (☎ 434 1118; www.leif.is; adult/under 12yr Ikr800/free; ☼ 9am-6pm Jun-Sep) has been built using only the tools and materials available at the time. Enthusiastic period-dressed guides show visitors around, brandish weapons, and tell the story of Erik the Red, who went on to found the first European settlement in Greenland.

You can stay at the nearby farmhouse **Stóra-Vatnshorn** (☎ 434 1342; storavatnshorn@islandia. is; Haukadalur; sb/linen/summer house Ikr2200/3500/6500; ☼ mid-May–mid-Sep), which has a selection of sun-drenched rooms sporting polished wooden floors and fresh coats of paint.

BÚÐARDALUR
pop 230

Founded as a cargo depot in Saga times, the pin-sized town now survives on fish processing and dairy farming, and it occupies a pleasant position looking out over Hvammsfjörður, at the mouth of the Laxá river.

There's a folk museum, tourist information centre and cafe all rolled into one at **Leifsbúð** (☎ 434 1441; www.dalir.is; ☼ 10am-6pm Mon-Fri, to 4pm Sat & Sun Jun-Aug) down by the harbour. Ask here about staying at the local **campsite** (☎ 434 1132; ☼ Jun-Aug). Alternatively, guest house **Bjarg**

(☎ 434 1644; www.aknet.is/bjarg; Dalbraut 2; sb/s/d Ikr2500/6000/7500) has simple rooms and an internet cafe in summer. The attached restaurant, **Villapizza** (mains Ikr850-1300; ☼ lunch & dinner), serves grilled meat and fish as well as pizza. You can also get fast food at the N1 petrol station – self-servers can stock up at the attached **Samkaup supermarket** (☼ 9am-10pm Sun-Fri, to 9pm Sat). A large corkboard in the supermarket offers information about other lodging options in the region.

Bus 37/37a runs between Reykjavík and Búðardalur (2¾ hours) daily except on Wednesday and Saturday. Service continues to Bjarkalundur in the Westfjords.

SAGA FARMS

Little remains of the original farms from Saga times, and although the region is central to many of the best-loved Icelandic sagas, you will need to use your imagination to make the connection.

About 4km up the Laxá river from Búðardalur, **Höskuldsstaðir** was the birthplace of Hallgerður Longlegs, wife of Gunnar of Hlíðarendi, who starred in *Njál's Saga*. Other important descendants of the family include Bolli and his foster brother Kjartan from *Laxdæla Saga*.

Across the river from Höskuldsstaðir is **Hjarðarholt**, the one-time home of Kjartan and his father, Ólafur Peacock. Their Viking farm was said to be one of the wonders of the Norse world, with scenes from the sagas carved into the walls and a huge dining hall that could seat 1100 guests. No trace of it remains today.

WILD CAMPING ON RTE 54

According to local law, wild camping (pitching a tent in a non-designated campsite) is perfectly legal so long as it is not done on private property without consent. So how does a keen camper know whether or not they are trespassing? Look for a bridge. Roads are considered public works, so when the government needs to build a bridge they buy up the surrounding land.

The quiet stretch of Rte 54, between the junctions with Rte 55 and Rte 60, is riddled with scenic ravines and their lonely bridges. Cars rarely come through, so pick a mossy patch and set up camp. It doesn't get much better than this…

DOUBLE DETOUR: ERPSSTAÐIR & RTE 590

When the peanut gallery starts moaning 'are we there yet?' you know it's time to pull off the road. **Erpsstaðir** (☎ 434 1357; www.erpsstadir.is; adult/child Ikr600/300; ☾ 1-5pm Sat & Sun) is the perfect place to stretch your legs – especially if you've got the brats in tow. Like a mirage for sweet-toothed wanderers, this dairy farm, on Rte 60 between Búðardalur and the Ring Road, specialises in delicious homemade ice cream. You can tour the farm, greet the buxom bovines, then gorge on your favourite flavour – we liked '*kjaftæði*' (which literally means 'mouth watering', but is best known as a euphemism for 'bullshit'). Erpsstaðir also offers accommodation (from Ikr13,000) if you're contemplating ice cream for breakfast...

For those of you who left the kids (or your inner-child) at home, a detour along scenic **Rte 590** will be decidedly more romantic. This 100km track (doable in a 2WD) follows the dramatic coastline of the oft-forgotten peninsula between the Snæfellsnes and Westfjords (look for the turn-off at Fellströnd along Rte 60). Windswept farmsteads lie frozen in time, and boulder-strewn hills roll skyward turning into flattened granite crowns – in the mist and midnight sun they look like impenetrable walls of a stone fortress. If you want to spend the night, there's a campsite at **Á** (☎ 434 1420), just before **Skarð** – a lonely farm that has remained in the hands of the same family for over 1000 years. If you're hungry for a bit of hiking, pick up the *Vestfirðir & Dalir £7* map (available at most regional tourist information centres for a nominal fee), which features a dozen trails on the shield-shaped peninsula.

Further north, follow the turn at Rte 590 to find the farm at **Hvammur**, which produced a whole line of prominent Icelanders, including Snorri Sturluson (p163) of *Prose Edda* fame. It was settled in around 895 by Auður the Deep-Minded, the wife of the Irish king Olaf Godfraidh, who has a bit part in the *Laxdæla Saga*. By coincidence, Árni Magnússon, who rescued most of the Icelandic sagas from the 1728 fire in Copenhagen, was also born at Hvammur.

Head past the turn-off for Rte 590 to find the geothermal village of **Laugar**, known throughout Iceland as the birthplace of *Laxdæla Saga* beauty Guðrun Ósvífursdóttir. Base yourself at the ultra-friendly **Hótel Edda** (☎ 444 4930; www.hoteledda.is; Sælingsdalur; sites per person Ikr700, sb Ikr1700, s/d without bathroom Ikr6800/8500, with bathroom Ikr12,400/15,000; ⌨ 🐾). There's a new wing with surprisingly modern rooms, an older hospital-style annexe with shared bathrooms, and sleeping-bag space is in converted classrooms. During the rest of the year, the complex is used as a boarding retreat for Icelandic teens. The restaurant (mains Ikr2200 to Ikr4900) gets good reviews – it serves the delicious ice cream from Erpsstaðir (see the boxed text, above). Local historians believe that they've found **Guðrun's bathing pool** in the hills nearby – ask at the hotel if it's open to the public.

The Westfjords

Like giant lobster claws snipping away at the Arctic Circle, the desolate Westfjords is one of Iceland's most spectacular regions. Sparsely populated, fantastically rugged, and isolated by its remote location and limited roads, the Westfjords is an outdoor adventurer's dream. The landscape here is truly humbling, ranging from soaring mountains and unfathomably deep and silent fjords to a tortuous coastline dotted with tiny fishing villages clinging doggedly to a traditional way of life.

To the north lies the uninhabited wilderness region of Hornstrandir, home to the 176-sq-km Drangajökull (925m), the last surviving ice cap in the region. Abandoned by the last villagers in the 1950s, Hornstrandir is now one of the country's premier hiking destinations. South of here lies the region's largest town, the cosmopolitan oasis of Ísafjörður. A friendly, happening mini-metropolis, it's the place to stock up and indulge before heading for the small villages that line the coast.

Unassuming, determined and often staunchly traditional, these smaller communities have suffered serious population decline in recent years. Many struggle to persuade their young people to stay and offer a warm welcome to the tourists who bring valuable income and energy to their quiet streets. Further south, nesting birds mob the cliffs at Látrabjarg, waves lash the golden sands at Breiðavík, and craggy inlets and precipitous peaks vie for your attention at every turn.

Give yourself plenty of time for a trip to the Westfjords. The roads around the coast weave in and out of fjords and over unpaved mountain passes pitted with giant potholes. The going is frustratingly slow at times, but the scenery is never short of breathtaking.

THE WESTFJORDS

HIGHLIGHTS

- Feel the breeze kiss your face as you rove around saw-toothed cliffs and lonely coves during a life-changing hike across **Hornstrandir** (p192)

- Take in the wild serenity of the **Strandir Coast** (p194), stopping at strangely seductive Djúpavík before soaking in the waters at Krossnes

- Pick wild rhubarb on the side of the highway, then gorge on piles of salted fish in **Ísafjörður** (p185), the Westfjords' surprisingly cosmopolitan capital

- Duel with an arctic tern on adorable off-shore Vigur, learn about the elusive arctic fox, or slink across silent fjordlings throughout beautiful **Ísafjarðardjúp** (p190)

- Watch chatty seabirds and clumsy puffins swoop around the crowded cliffs at **Látrabjarg** (p180)

★ Hornstrandir
★ Ísafjörður
★ Ísafjarðardjúp
★ Strandir Coast
★ Látrabjarg

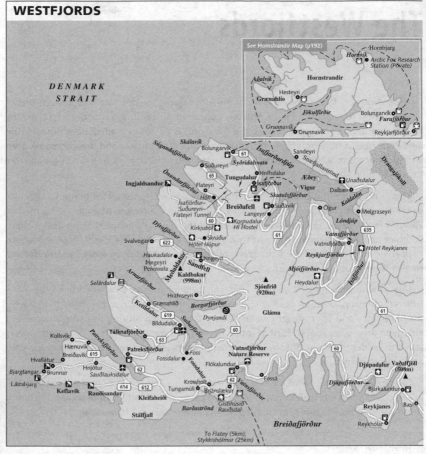

Getting There & Away

There are twice-daily flights between Reykjavík and Ísafjörður (p189) on Air Iceland, and additional summer flights on Eagle Air to Gjögur and Bíldudalur.

Roads in the Westfjords are, as one local pointed out, 'paved roads with unpaved tracks in between'. Quite a few of the region's roads are unsurfaced as they follow the deeply indented coastline and wind in and out of fjords and around headlands. Needless to say, the going can be very slow. Always keep an eye on the road – we've received accident reports every year about cars crashing over fjord edges. Public bus services are rather infrequent, running mostly from June to August.

On Monday, Wednesday and Saturday from June to August, buses run between Ísafjörður and Látrabjarg (Ikr4500, two hours), stopping in Patreksfjörður (Ikr4000) and Brjánslækur (Ikr3000) on the way. Note that the bus only stops in Látrabjarg if booked in advance; if no one has booked, the final stop is Patreksfjörður. You'll have a two-hour stop to admire the bird life before the bus turns around and heads back to Ísafjörður.

Coming from Reykjavík to Ísafjörður you'll need to change in Staðarskáli (further south, in northwest Iceland) and Hólmavík. Buses leave Reykjavík for Staðarskáli at 8.30am and 5pm (the 5pm service discontinues in winter), but they only connect with the Staðarskáli–Hólmavík service on Tuesday, Friday and

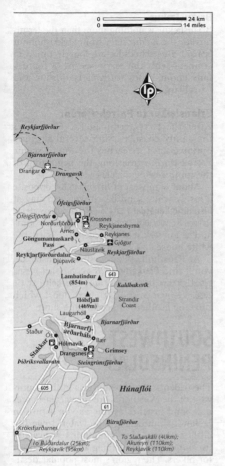

Sunday. The bus company **Stjörnubílar** (☎ 456 5518, 893 6356; www.stjornubilar.is) runs several buses around the region including the Hólmavík–Ísafjörður leg (Ikr5000) in cooperation with TREX on Tuesday, Friday and Sunday, calling in Súðvik along the way (Ikr4500).

The Westfjords can also be reached by the *Baldur* ferry, which departs at least once a day from Stykkishólmur on the Snæfellsnes Peninsula and lands at Brjánslækur on the south coast. See p167 for details. A system of buses link the ferry service to Ísafjörður and Reykjavík. However, the connections are not seamless – expect several hours of waiting.

If you want to travel between Ísafjörður and Akureyri, you'll also need to change in Hólmavík and Staðarskáli.

Ísafjörður is the best place to arrange a boat transfer to the remote Hornstrandir region, but ferries also run from Bolungarvík and the Strandir coast. Boats only run when the weather is calm between July and mid-August.

SOUTH COAST

The sparsely populated south coast of the Westfjords is the least dramatic of the region, and it's nowhere near as wild and wonderful as the peninsulas further north. However, the ferry connection to Stykkishólmur on the Snæfellsnes Peninsula is a handy route to the area. Although there are no towns on the south coast, you'll find a cluster of farms and guest houses near Brjánslækur, the landing point for the ferry.

DALIR TO DJÚPADALUR

Travellers who don't take the *Baldur* ferry will enter the Westfjords from the historic Dalir region in west Iceland (p174). If you have your sights set on the Strandir Coast (p194), follow the new concreted road to Hólmavík, which runs parallel to the rutty Rte 605.

Reykhólar

The little town of Reykhólar sits on the tip of the kidney-shaped Reykjanes Peninsula, a minor geothermal area. There's little to do here other than taking a dip in the **geothermal swimming pool** (☎ 434 7738; admission Ikr350; ☼ 10am-10pm mid-Jun–mid-Aug, reduced hr rest of year) or following informal walking paths through gurgling fields.

The local **tourist information centre** (☎ 892 2240; ☼ 11am-6pm Jun–mid-Aug) has a great map of the Westfjords (free!) and doubles as a tiny **folk museum** (admission Ikr500) covered in black-and-white photos of pioneers. There's an N1 petrol station next door.

Gistiheimilið Álftaland (Reykhólar HI Hostel; ☎ 434 7878; www.alftaland.is; sites per person Ikr1000, sb/s/d Ikr4000/7500/9900; ☞) meets all accommodation needs with clean and comfy rooms, a soothing hot pot, and a large kitchen available for guest use.

Bjarkalundur

On Rte 60, just beyond the turn-off to Reykhólar, is **Hótel Bjarkalundur** (☎ 434 7762,

THE WESTFJORDS

434 7863; www.bjarkalundur.is; sites per tent Ikr1000, s/d incl breakfast Ikr7000/9500; ☺ Easter-Sep, then weekends to New Year), a large farmhouse with a petrol station and a restaurant (sandwiches from Ikr750, pizzas from Ikr1090).

Buses run between Reykjavík and Bjarkalundur (3¾ hours), via Króksfjarðarnes in Dalir, every day except Wednesday and Saturday. There's no bus service between Bjarkalundur and Flókalundur or Brjánslækur.

Djúpadalur

Heading west, you'll come across the steaming waterfalls in the Djúpadalur geothermal field, 20km west of Bjarkalundur. There's an indoor **geothermal swimming pool** (☎ 434 7853; adult/under 14yr Ikr250/100; ☺ 8am-11pm) here and good accommodation at the welcoming nine-bed **Guesthouse Djúpadalur** (☎ 434 7853; sb/linen Ikr3000/3500).

FLÓKALUNDUR TO PATREKSFJÖRÐUR

After driving over a series of stunningly desolate fjords, you'll reach Flókalundur, the junction point between the road up to Ísafjörður and the bumpy route to the southwestern peninsulas.

Flókalundur

The two-house 'town' of Flókalundur was named after the Viking explorer Hrafna-Flóki Vilgerðarson (see p30), who gave Iceland its name in AD 860. Today, the most interesting thing in the area is the **Vatnsfjörður Nature Reserve**, established to protect the area around Lake Vatnsdalsvatn, a nesting site for harlequin ducks and great northern divers (loons). Various hiking trails run around the lake and into the hills beyond.

Pick up a Vatnsfjörður hiking brochure at **Hótel Flókalundur** (☎ 456 2011; www.flokalundur.is; sites per person Ikr750, s/d incl breakfast Ikr10,500/13,800; ☺ mid-May–mid-Sep), an ageing wooden bungalow-style hotel with small, wood-panelled rooms, a decent restaurant (mains Ikr850 to Ikr1920; open breakfast, lunch and dinner), a superette (open 9am to 11pm) selling wrapped sandwiches, and a petrol station. Down the road at Flókalaug is a **thermal swimming pool** (☎ 456 2011; adult/under 12yr Ikr100/50; ☺ 10am-noon & 4-7pm). At high tide, do as the locals do and jump in the frigid sea, then run back to the pool to warm up.

Brjánslækur

Brjánslækur is nothing more than the terminus for the *Baldur* ferry from Stykkishólmur (p167). Bus schedules are loosely timed to connect with the ferry; see p178 for details about buses to/from Ísafjörður and Látrabjarg.

Brjánslækur to Patreksfjörður

After the ferry terminal, Rte 62 follows the sandy coast, passing several sleeping options, until it reaches the top of scenic Patreksfjörður, marking the beginning of the southwest peninsulas.

About 8km west of Brjánslækur, opposite a lovely white-sand beach, you can stay at **Gistihúsið Rauðsdal** (☎ 456 2041; raudsdal@vortex.is; sb/linen Ikr2500/3000), which has decent rooms and a guest kitchen. Reception is in the white house.

At Krossholt, 14km west of Brjánslækur, you'll find **Bjarkarholt** (☎ 456 2025; torfi@vestur byggd.is; sb/apt Ikr3000/12,000) and **Arnarholt** (☎ 456 2080; silja@snerpa.is; sb Ikr3000) next door, which runs the geothermal pool on the shore.

SOUTHWEST PENINSULAS

The trident-shaped peninsulas in the southwest of the Westfjords are spectacularly scenic. Sand beaches as fine as you'll find in Iceland, shimmering blue water, towering cliffs and stunning mountains weave between the fjords, providing a fantastic retreat for hikers. The region's most popular destination is Látrabjarg, a 12km stretch of sea cliffs that is home to thousands of nesting sea birds in summer. The roads throughout this sparsely populated region are rough and driving is slow – take a deep breath, you'll get there!

LÁTRABJARG PENINSULA

Best known for its dramatic cliffs and abundant bird life, the Látrabjarg Peninsula also has wonderful deserted beaches and plenty of opportunities for long, leisurely walks.

Joining Rte 612 from Rte 62, you'll pass the rusting hulk of the fishing boat *Garðar* near the head of the fjord before passing the empty, golden beaches around the airstrip at Sauðlauksdalur. In **Hnjótur**, about 10km further on, it's worth stopping at the entertaining **Minjasafn Egils Ólafssonar** (☎ 456 1511; www.hnjotur.is; adult/under 14yr Ikr600/free; ☽ 10am-6pm mid-May–mid-Sep). The eclectic collection includes salvaged fishing boats, old aircraft and displays on the history of the region. There's a fantastic on-site cafe (snacks from Ikr180) specialising in local food, including razorbill eggs plucked from the cliffs. Jump online with wi-fi while you're there.

At **Breiðavík**, a stunning golden-sand beach is framed by rocky cliffs and the turquoise waters of the bay. It's an idyllic spot, certainly one of Iceland's best beaches and usually deserted. Should you find yourself with more company than you'd hoped for, head further on to **Hvallátur**, where there's another gorgeous golden-sand beach and excellent opportunities for wild camping.

Soon the Bjargtangar lighthouse, Europe's westernmost point (if you don't count the Azores), comes into view and nearby the renowned Látrabjarg **bird cliffs**. Extending for 12km along the coast and ranging from 40m to 400m, the dramatic cliffs are mobbed by nesting sea birds in summer and it's a fascinating place even for the most reluctant of twitchers. Unbelievable numbers of puffins, razorbills, guillemots, cormorants, fulmars, gulls and kittiwakes nest here from June to August. The puffins in particular are incredibly tame, and you can often get within a few feet of the birds. On calm days, seals are often seen basking on the skerries around the lighthouse.

East of the cliffs (about a 20km walk along the coast path from the lighthouse), the stunning **Rauðisandur** beach stretches out in shades of deep pink and red sands. Pounded by the surf and backed by a huge lagoon, it is an exceptionally beautiful and serene place. To get here by road you'll have to backtrack on Rte 612 towards the head of the fjord. Take a right turn onto Rte 614 soon after the airfield at Sauðlauksdalur and follow the bumpy track for about 10km.

Sleeping & Eating

Breiðavík (☎ 456 1575; www.breidavik.is; sites per tent from Ikr1000, sb/s/d without bathroom Ikr3500/7500/10,000, s/d with bathroom Ikr10,000/15,500; ☽ mid-May–mid-Sep) Set on a working farm by the incredible cream-coloured beach at Breiðavík, this guest house offers homey rooms with patchwork quilts and decent furniture. Evening meals are also served (Ikr2500 to Ikr3000).

Hótel Látrabjarg (☎ 456 1500; www.latrabjarg.com; s/d without bathroom €90/105, with bathroom €115/130; ☽ mid-May–mid-Sep) This former boarding school has been converted into a comfortable hotel with plain but tasteful rooms. There's a restaurant (three-course dinner Ikr3500). The hotel can also organise horse riding (Ikr2000 per hour) at the nearby farm Hestaleigan Vesturfari. To get to the hotel, turn right onto Rte 615 just after the museum at Hnjótur and continue for about 3km.

Getting There & Away

South of Patreksfjörður, Rte 62 cuts across the ridge at Kleifaheiði to the south coast, while Rte 612 runs west to the end of the Látrabjarg Peninsula.

On Monday, Wednesday and Saturday from June to August, buses from Ísafjörður route through Látrabjarg on their way to Brjánslækur, where you can pick up the *Baldur* ferry to Stykkishólmur (see p167). The buses stop at the cliffs for two hours, leaving you plenty of time to explore.

If you want to stay longer you'll have to camp overnight or hike back to the guest house at Breiðavík or Hótel Látrabjarg. You can also reach the cliffs by hiking 5km east from Hvallátur.

PATREKSFJÖRÐUR
pop 620

Although it's the largest village in this part of the Westfjords, unattractive Patreksfjörður is of very little interest to tourists. The town was named after St Patrick of Ireland, who was the spiritual guide of Örlygur Hrappson, the first settler in the area. The usual services can be found along the main road, including a **swimming pool** (☎ 456 1301; Eyrargata) beside the church.

There's a loosely marked campsite behind the N1 petrol station. **Stekkaból** (☎ 864 9675; stekkabol@snerpa.is; Stekkar 19; sb/linen Ikr2200/3500), up the hill, has sun-filled, simple rooms and a guest kitchen.

Þorpið (☎ 456 1295; Aðalstræti 73; mains Ikr900-2090; ☽ 9.15am-10pm Mon-Thu, to 11pm Fri, 10am-11pm Sat, to 10pm Sun) is your best bet for food, serving the usual assortment of grilled dishes. You can get snacks at **Albína** (☎ 456 1667; Aðalstræti 89), a superette with an ATM. The N1 petrol station on the main road has a **grill** (☽ 9am-10pm).

Buses connect Patreksfjörður to Brjánslækur (1¼ hours), Látrabjarg (two hours) and

---

HOT-POT HEAVEN

Put on those swimsuits – the Westfjords has more geothermal water than anywhere else in Iceland. And a soothing soak is definitely what the doctor ordered after a tiresome afternoon of negotiating the region's rutty roads. Here are some of our favourite hot pots in the Westfjords:

■ **Krossnes** (p198) A geothermal Valhalla at the edge of the world.

■ **Drangsnes** (p196) A well-kept secret hidden in a craggy sea wall.

■ **Reykjarfjörður** (p191) Skip the artificial pool and try the steamy ravine that feeds it!

For a complete list of the island's hot pockets, check out http://hot-springs.org. The site is in Icelandic – to find a map of naturally occurring pools, click '*Baðlaugaskrá*' then follow '*Nátturulegar baðlaugar*' to access the top swimming spots sorted by region.

Ísafjörður (two hours); see p178 for details. An 'airbus' runs by request from Patreksfjörður to meet flights into Bíldudalur. Call ☎ 893 2636 or ask the information centre in Tálknafjörður for details.

TÁLKNAFJÖRÐUR
pop 290

Set amid rolling green hills, rocky peaks and a wide fjord, Tálknafjörður is another soporific village surrounded by magnificent scenery. Fed by the geothermal field nearby, the local **swimming pool** (☎ 456 2639; adult/6-12yr Ikr300/180; 9am-9pm Mon-Fri & 11am-6pm Sat & Sun Jun-Aug, 4-9pm Sun-Fri & 1-5pm Sat Sep-May) is the main hangout spot in town. In summer, a friendly tourist office operates at the pool. Ask here for a detailed hiking map of the area, *Vestfirðir & Dalir #4* (try the gorgeous 10km cairn-marked hike to Bíldudalur); fjord fishing can also be arranged. Completely unknown to most tourists is the naturally occurring bathing pool at **Pollurinn**, 3.8km beyond the swimming pool along Rte 617. The spring is not marked, so you'll have to watch your odometer.

There's a **campsite** (☎ 456 2639; sites per person Ikr800; Jun-Aug) beside the swimming pool with laundry, cooking facilities and showers. You'll find accommodation at **Skrúðhamar** (☎ 456 0200; skrudhamar@visir.is; Strandgata 20; d Ikr5000; 🖳 🛜) and **Bjarmalandi** (☎ 891 8038; bjarmaland06@simnet.is; Bugatún 11; s/d Ikr5000/8000; 🛜).

Try the local fish recipes at **Hópið** (☎ 456 2777; Hrafnardalsvegur; mains from Ikr1000; noon-10pm Jun-Aug, 11am-8pm Sep-May), or **Kaffi Sælli** (☎ 456 2239; mains from Ikr1000; 11am-midnight Jun-Aug), which sometimes hosts live music.

The Patreksfjörður–Bíldudalur 'airbus' stops in Tálknafjörður along the way. Ask at the swimming pool for details, or call ☎ 893 2636. The bus only runs by request.

BÍLDUDALUR
pop 180

Set on a gloriously calm bay surrounded by towering peaks, the sleepy fishing village of **Bíldudalur** (www.bildudalur.is) has a beautiful fjord-side position. Arriving by road from either direction you're treated to some spectacular outlooks.

Bíldudalur was founded in the 16th century and today is a major supplier of prawns (shrimp). For tourists, attractions are limited to the small **Tónlistarsafn** (☎ 456 2186; Tjarnarbraut 5; admission Ikr400; 2-6pm Mon-Fri mid-Jun–Sep), a museum dedicated to Icelandic music from the '40s to the '60s, and the **Skrímslasetur Sea Monster Museum** (admission Ikr700; 11am-6pm) across from the church.

If you'd like to stay in Bíldudalur, there's a free campsite beside the golf course on the outskirts of town. For more comfort, try **Bíldudalur HI Hostel** (Gistiheimilið Kaupfélagið; ☎ 456 2100, 860 2100; www.hostel.is; Hafnarbraut 2; sb/s/d member Ikr2100/3700/5800, nonmember Ikr2600/4200/6800), in the heart of the harbour-front. The rooms are basic but squeaky clean.

Meals are limited to the petrol station or **Vegamót** (☎ 456 2232; mains Ikr800-2000; 🛜), which has a quaint pastoral vibe and stacks of journals for reading.

Eagle Air (☎ 562 4200; www.ernir.is; Reykjavík Domestic Airport, IS-101 Reykjavík) provides flights every day except Saturday to/from Reykjavík (45 minutes). The online fare for a one-way ticket is €115. Buses run on request to/from Patreksfjörður via Tálknafjörður to connect with flights. Call ☎ 893 2636 for details.

CENTRAL PENINSULAS

DYNJANDI

Tumbling in a broad sweep over a 100m-rocky scarp at the head of Dynjandivogur bay, Dynjandi (Fjallfoss) is the most dramatic waterfall in the Westfjords, and the perfect doormat to its central peninsulas. Coming from the car park you'll pass a series of smaller falls at the base of the main chute, but it's well worth following the path up to the base of the massive cascade that plunges over the mountain side. The thundering water and views out over the broad fjord below are spectacular.

The surrounding area is protected as a nature reserve, but there's a free (if noisy) campsite right by the falls. Dynjandi is well signposted off Rte 60. Buses between Brjánslækur and Ísafjörður take a 10-minute break here to appreciate the falls.

Beyond Dynjandi, Rte 60 cuts across the desolate moonscape of the **Gláma** moors, which are covered in coarse tundra vegetation and mirror-like pools of standing water. It's possible to hike across this bleak moorland up to the ridge at **Sjónfrið** (920m) in a long, damp day.

ÞINGEYRI PENINSULA

The Þingeyri Peninsula's dramatic northern peaks have been dubbed the 'Northwestern Alps', and the region offers some excellent remote hiking. The mountains are partly volcanic in origin, and the peaks are made up of rock and scree – a marked contrast to the green valleys elsewhere in the Westfjords. For detailed information on hiking in the area, visit www.thingeyri.is.

A dirt road runs northwest along the eastern edge of the peninsula to the scenic valley at **Haukadalur**, an important Viking site. If the road isn't blocked by landslides, you can continue right around the peninsula with a 4WD, passing cliffs where birds perch and the remote lighthouse at **Svalvogar**. Do not attempt this track with a 2WD – you will not make it. West Tours (p187), in Ísafjörður, runs popular horse-riding tours in beautiful **Meðadalur** nearby.

If you're visiting on the first weekend in July it's worth checking out the local **Dýrafjarðardagar Viking festival** (www.westvikings.info), held at a reconstructed stone circle in Haukadalur. The festival celebrates the area's Viking heritage and the saga of local man Gísli Súrsson.

Inland, the Westfjords' highest peak **Kaldbakur** (998m) is a good hiking spot. The steep trail to the summit begins from the road about 2km west of Þingeyri town.

Over on the southern side of the Þingeyri peninsula, **Hrafnseyri** was the birthplace of Jón Sigurðsson, the architect of Iceland's independence, which took place on 17 June 1811. The small and rather ugly **Hrafnseyri museum** (☎ 456 8260; www.hrafnseyri.is; adult/under 14yr Ikr500/free; ☼ 10am-8pm mid-Jun–Aug) outlines aspects of his life. There's also a wooden church here dating from 1886.

ÞINGEYRI

pop 300

This tiny village, on the north side of the peninsula, was the first trading station in the Westfjords, but these days the world seems to have passed Þingeyri by. Although there's little to see here, the surrounding hills offer excellent walking, including the short hike up to **Sandfell**, the 367m ridge behind the village, which begins just south of the village on Rte 60.

In summer there's a **tourist office** (☎ 456 8304; www.thingeyri.is; Hafnarstræti; ☼ 10am-6pm Mon-Fri, noon-4pm Sat & Sun Jun-Aug; ☎) and cafe on the main

---

DOUBLE DETOUR: KETILDALIR & SELÁRDALUR

Hidden beyond Bíldudalur along Rte 619 is beautiful Ketildalir (Kettle Valley) and a strange museum at the tip of the fjord. Local artist Samúel Jónsson lived out his remaining years at the remote farm in Selárdalur. He filled his days by creating a series of 'naïve', cartoon-like sculptures. Visitors can stop by and check out what remains. Currently there are four parts to the exhibition: a flamboyant house that looks somewhat like a birthday cake, a circle of lions (created from a postcard Samúel saw of the Alhambra), a church, and Samúel's home. (At the time of research the home was closed for renovations.) Of particular note, however, is the sculpture of a man and seal. If you look at them from the right (or wrong) angles they're placed in a rather unflattering pose…

road. The village also has an ubermodern **swimming pool** (☎ 456 8375; adult/under 16yr Ikr400/free; ☼ 8.15am-9pm Mon-Fri, 10am-6pm Sat & Sun Jun-Aug, 6-8am & 4-6pm Mon-Fri, noon-3pm Sat & Sun Sep-May).

If you'd like to stay, you'll find the **campsite** (☎ 456 8285; sites per tent/caravan Ikr1000/2000) behind the swimming pool. There are a few indoor options to spend the night in, but the friendly guest house **Við Fjörðinn** (☎ 456 8172; www.vidfjordinn.is; Aðalstræti 26; sb/d/apt Ikr2500/8000/15,000) is a great choice, with bright, cheerful rooms with simple decor and plain white linens. The sparkling bathrooms are shared, and there's a good guest kitchen and a TV lounge. The village has a small supermarket, and there's a snack bar at the modern N1 station.

Local **buses** (☎ 456 4258) run twice every weekday between Þingeyri and Ísafjörður (30 minutes). From June to August a daily bus runs to Brjánslækur, where you'll be able to catch the *Baldur* ferry to Stykkishólmur (see p167).

DÝRAFJÖRÐUR & ÖNUNDARFJÖRÐUR

Heading north from Þingeyri on the northern shore of Dýrafjörður are a series of gorgeous broad valleys. At the head of the valleys is a lovely weatherboard church and one of Iceland's oldest botanic gardens, **Skrúður** (admission free; ☼ 24hr), which was established as a teaching garden in 1905.

Beyond Skrúður, about 7km from Rte 60, is **Hotel Núpur** (☎ 456 8235; www.hotelnupur.is; sites Ikr1200, plus electricity Ikr200, sb/s/d without bathroom Ikr2500/5900/8400), a rather uninspiring place built in a converted schoolhouse. Another kilometre past the hotel, the friendly farmhouse **Alviðra** (☎ 456 8229; alvidra@snerpa.is; sb/s/d without bathroom Ikr2500/5500/9000, apt from Ikr10,000; ☼ Jun-Aug) has simple accommodation spread across three small buildings. Check out the quirky collection of tiny liquor bottles when checking in at the main house.

After Alviðra the road passes an abandoned farmhouse before swerving inland to head over the top of the rugged peninsula. It takes about 20 minutes to reach **Ingjaldsandur** at the mouth of Önundarfjörður. Set in a picturesque valley, this isolated beach is a fantastic spot to watch the midnight sun as it flirts with the sea before rising back up into the sky. Sæból, the lonely farm nearby, sells handicrafts in summer.

Back on Rte 60, near upper Önundarfjörður, you'll pass a marked turn-off for **Kirkjuból**

(☎ 456 7679; www.kirkjubol.is; s/d from Ikr5200/8500; ☼ Jun-Aug). The white-and-green exterior could use a little paint job, but the inside is squeaky clean, sporting several well-chosen antiques mixed in with a few mod cons.

A second turn-off further north (also marked Kirkjuból!) leads to the popular **Korpudalur HI Hostel** (Korpudalur Kirkjuból; ☎ 456 7808, 892 2030; www.korpudalur.is, www.hostel.is; tent site Ikr600, plus per person Ikr300, sb member/nonmember Ikr2600/3100; ☼ mid-Feb–mid-Sep; ☎). The adorable owners, stunning location, homemade breakfast bread and renovated rooms make this 100-year-old farmhouse well worth visiting. Hikers will find plenty of scenic spots to stomp around in the surrounding hills. Pick-ups can be arranged from Ísafjörður for a fee.

FLATEYRI
pop 300

Once a giant support base for Norwegian whalers, Flateyri is now a sleepy little place set on a striking gravel spit sticking out into broad Önundarfjörður. **Blossi** (☎ 456 7671; www.blossi.net; Drafnargata 6) runs sea angling trips, while two-hour to one-week sea-kayaking trips can be arranged through **Grænhöfði** (☎ 456 7762; jens@snerpa.is), which also offers apartment-style accommodation near the indoor-outdoor **swimming pool** (☎ 456 7738; adult/under 14yr Ikr300/180; ☼ 10am-9pm Mon-Fri, noon-4pm Sat & Sun Jun-Aug).

It's best to swing by the petrol station if you're looking for accommodation. There's a **campsite** (☎ 456 7738; sites per tent Ikr1000) out back and a corkboard inside lists a variety of cottages for rent around town.

Your top option for food is saloon-style **Vagninn** (☎ 456 7151; Hafnarstræti 19; mains Ikr900-2000; ☼ dinner), serving the usual selection of snacks and meat dishes. Alternatively, there's a **grill bar** (☎ 456 7878) at the N1 station with a few tables.

On weekdays there are three daily buses between Ísafjörður and Flateyri (30 minutes). To be picked up in Flateyri, call ahead (☎ 456 4258) – otherwise the bus might not drive into the village.

SUÐUREYRI
pop 350

Perched on the tip of 13km-long Súgandafjörður, the fishing community of Suðureyri was isolated for years by the forbidding mountains. Now connected with Ísafjörður by a 5km tunnel, the village has a new lease of life and warmly welcomes tourists into the community.

In many ways the village is staunchly traditional – all fishing is done by rod and hook, and the grand tourism plans being developed are all about preserving nature and sharing rather than changing this traditional way of life. It's the best place in Iceland to catch halibut, making the town a natural haven for angling.

Suðureyri gets all its energy and hot-water supplies from sustainable sources. In addition, the villagers' prime fishing grounds lie very close to shore, so little fuel is used to power boats, and traditional fishing methods mean that the natural balance of the fish stocks is not endangered. If there ever was a truly green destination, Suðureyri would be it.

There's no formal information centre; however, there are informative billboard-like posters at the beginning of town that offer insights into the town's history and recent attempts at creating an infrastructure for sustainable tourism.

Sights & Activities

The **Fisherman** (☎ 450 9000; www.fisherman.is) project allows visitors to join in the regular life of the village in order to understand the lifestyle of fishing families in rural Iceland. You can visit the local fish factory (Ikr1000), join a sea angling tour (two hours; Ikr20,000) or request to go out on a working fishing boat (Ikr15,000 for an afternoon). The project offers a unique insight into life in fishing communities and is the only one of its kind in the country. You can book activities online or at the Fisherman Hotel VEG (right). You can also hire fishing rods and buy bait at the petrol station to do your own cod fishing in the nearby lagoon. The trick to a successful catch is to first bounce a stone in the lagoon – then, when you feed them, some of the cod will actually jump out of the water to grab the food!

Those without the time (or money) for a seafaring adventure can swing by the harbour between 3pm and 5pm to watch the local fishermen bring in the daily catch.

If it all sounds too exciting you could just relax in the village's **geothermal swimming pool** (☎ 456 6121; Túngata 8; adult/under 14yr Ikr350/200; ☺ 10am-9pm Mon-Fri, to 7pm Sat & Sun Jun-Sep), sauna and hot pots.

Sleeping & Eating

There is a free, fully equipped **campsite** (☎ 450 9000) behind the N1 petrol station.

Fisherman Hotel VEG (☎ 450 9000; www.fisherman.is; Aðalgata 14; s/d/apt Ikr3750/7500/20,000; ☐ ☎) Customer focused, thoroughly modern and really comfy, this friendly guest house has bright rooms, crisp linens, pine furniture and informative cards about the area's fish.

ourpick Talisman (mains Ikr1900-2490; ☺ 8-10am & 6-10pm mid-May–mid-Sep) The Fisherman Hotel's on-site restaurant is a swish, contemporary-styled place with moleskin chairs, large windows, and place mats and menu covers made from fish skins. The menu features a wonderful array of locally sourced food – from sea creatures to lamb. A flatscreen TV shows a video describing a fisherman's life. If you don't have time to visit Suðureyri, you can order packs of their flash-frozen fish online.

Shopping

If you're thinking about buying any 66° North apparel, this is the place to do it. The founder was born in Suðureyri – conveniently located along the 66th parallel – and there's a poster in the hotel, which details the company's history.

Located across from the popular Talisman restaurant (above), **Á Milli Fjalla** (☎ 456 6163; Aðalgata; ☺ 1-6pm Mon-Fri, 1-4pm Sat & Sun) is an intriguing boutique selling a variety of locally crafted items like knits, ceramics, and unique trinkets made from horsehair. Apparently Björk likes to shop here.

Getting There & Away

From Monday to Friday there are three daily local buses between Ísafjörður and Suðureyri (20 minutes).

ÍSAFJÖRÐUR

pop 2540

Hub of activity in the Westfjords and by far the area's largest town, Ísafjörður is a pleasant and prosperous place and an excellent base for travellers. The town is set on a gravel spit that extends out into Skutulsfjörður, and is hemmed in on all sides by towering peaks and the eerily dark and still waters of the fjord.

The centre of Ísafjörður is littered with old timber and tin-clad buildings, many unchanged since the 18th century, when the harbour was full of tall ships and Norwegian

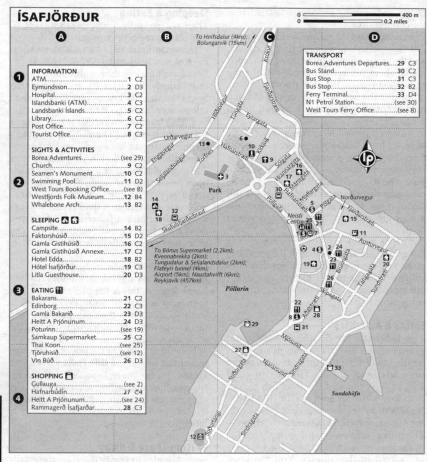

ÍSAFJÖRÐUR

To Hnifsdalur (4km);
Bolungarvík (15km)

INFORMATION
ATM...................................1 C2
Eymundsson........................2 D3
Hospital..............................3 C2
Islandsbanki (ATM)..............4 C3
Landsbanki Íslands..............5 C2
Library................................6 C2
Post Office..........................7 C2
Tourist Office......................8 C3

SIGHTS & ACTIVITIES
Borea Adventures................(see 29)
Church...............................9 C2
Seamen's Monument...........10 C2
Swimming Pool...................11 D2
West Tours Booking Office....(see 8)
Westfjords Folk Museum.......12 B4
Whalebone Arch.................13 B2

SLEEPING
Campsite...........................14 B2
Faktorshúsið.......................15 D2
Gamla Gistihúsið.................16 C2
Gamla Gistihúsið Annexe......17 C2
Hotel Edda.........................18 B2
Hótel Ísafjörður...................19 C3
Litla Guesthouse..................20 D3

EATING
Bakarans............................21 C2
Edinborg............................22 C3
Gamla Bakaríð....................23 D3
Heitt A Prjónunum...............24 D3
Poturinn............................(see 19)
Samkaup Supermarket..........25 C2
Thai Koon..........................(see 25)
Tjöruhisið..........................(see 12)
Vin Búð..............................26 D3

SHOPPING
Gullauga............................(see 2)
Hafnarbúðin........................27 C4
Heitt A Prjónunum...............(see 24)
Rammagerð Ísafjarðar..........28 C3

TRANSPORT
Borea Adventures Departures....29 C3
Bus Stand...........................30 C2
Bus Stop.............................31 C3
Bus Stop.............................32 B2
Ferry Terminal.....................33 D4
N1 Petrol Station..................(see 30)
West Tours Ferry Office..........(see 8)

Park

To Bónus Supermarket (2.2km);
Kvennabrekka (2km);
Tungudalur & Seljalandsdalur (2km);
Flateyri tunnel (4km);
Airport (5km); Naustahvilft (6km);
Reykjavík (457km)

Pöllurin

Sundahöfn

whaling crews. Today it is a surprisingly cosmopolitan place, and after some time spent travelling in the Westfjords, it'll feel like a bustling metropolis with its tempting cafes and fine choice of restaurants.

There's good hiking in the hills around the town, skiing in winter and regular summer boats to ferry hikers across to the remote Hornstrandir Peninsula. In fact, Ísafjörður's only downside is the long journey to get here. You'll either have to wind in and out of numerous fjords on bumpy roads or take a hair-raising flight into the tiny airstrip. Then again, it's the town's remote location and surprisingly urbane attitude that really give it its wonderful character.

History

The region to the west of Ísafjörður is geologically the oldest in the country, dating back about 20 million years. However, it was not until Norwegian and Icelandic traders arrived in the 16th century that the gravel spit in Skutulsfjörður saw human inhabitation. At first the camps were temporary, but soon German and English trading firms set up shop and a permanent post was established. The first mention of trading in the area dates back to 1569, when records show a Hanseatic League trading post here, but by 1602 the Danish Trade Monopoly had taken over business and begun developing Ísafjörður as a fishing and trading centre.

THE WESTFJORDS

In the following centuries Ísafjörður became a logistical centre for Norwegian whaling ships, although the local Icelanders only took up commercial whaling in the 1950s. In later years the town bore witness to some of the fierce battles between whalers and environmental campaigners that eventually led to the worldwide ban on commercial whaling in 1989.

In 1991 a tunnel was constructed to link Ísafjörður and the previously isolated communities of Suðureyri and Flateyri. The three towns and nearby Þingeyri were amalgamated into a single administrative unit called Ísafjarðarbær in 1996.

Information

The friendly **tourist information centre** (☎ 456 8060; www.isafjordur.is; Aðalstræti 7; ☺ 8.15am-6pm Mon-Fri, 11am-4pm Sat & Sun Jun-Aug, reduced hr Sep-May) is down by the harbour in the Edinborgarhús, built in 1781.

You'll find all the major banks along Hafnarstræti and the **post office** (☺ 9am-4pm) in the Neisti Centre at Hafnarstræti 9. Internet access is available at the town **library** (☎ 456 3296; Eyrartúni; ☺ 1-7pm Mon-Fri, 1-4pm Sat). The tourist office also has a single terminal that travellers can use for a free 10-minute session.

The bookshop **Eymundsson** (☎ 456 3123; Hafnarstræti 2; ☺ 9am-6pm Mon-Fri, 10am-4pm Sat) is well stocked and has maps, postcards, and coffee-table books in English. It also opens on Sundays when the cruise ships are in town.

Sights & Activities

Housed in a cluster of ancient wooden buildings by the harbour, the **Westfjords Folk Museum** (☎ 456 3293; Neðstíkaupstaður; adult/under 16yr/senior Ikr500/free/300; ☺ 10am-5pm Mon-Fri, 1-5pm Sat & Sun Jun, 10am-5pm daily Jul & Aug) is an atmospheric place full of relics. The dimly lit main building, the **Turnhús**, dates from 1784 and was originally used as a warehouse. Inside it's like stepping back in time, with every available surface covered by fishing and nautical exhibits, tools and equipment from the whaling days, and fascinating old photos depicting life in the town over the centuries. To the right of this building is the wooden **Tjöruhús** (1781), which now operates as a very pleasant cafe and seafood restaurant. Two other buildings on the site, the **Faktorhús**, built in 1765 to house the manager of the village shop, and the **Krambúd**

(1757), originally a storehouse, are now private residences.

Apart from the museum, Ísafjörður's formal attractions are pretty thin on the ground. There's a second Factor's House, or **Faktorhúsið**, in the centre of town. It's true heritage treasure and is one of the oldest catalogue buildings (an edifice made using IKEA-like instructions) in Iceland. Of minor interest is the **whalebone arch** made from a whale's jawbone in the park in the centre of town. Nearby are Ísafjörður's interesting **seamen's monument** and the modernist town **church**, which looks a lot like an old-fashioned press camera with a flash on top.

There are loads of **walking** trails around Ísafjörður, all of which are covered in the ultra-handy map series *Vestfirðir & Dalir*, available from the tourist office for a nominal fee. One of the more unusual and shorter walks is up to the truncated valley of **Naustahvilft** – about 1km above the airport – which offers fantastic views over the fjord. Several other trails start near the road bridge at the head of Skutulsfjörður, where the last wizards in Iceland were burned at the stake in 1656.

Although plain by Icelandic standards, the town **swimming pool** (☎ 456 3200; Austurvegur 9; adult/under 16yr Ikr300/180; ☺ 7am-9pm Mon-Fri, 10am-4pm Sat & Sun mid-Jun–Aug) makes a good retreat on a wet day.

In winter, the mountains around Ísafjörður are a popular destination for Icelandic skiers (see www.isafjordur.is/ski). The season runs from January to Easter, and there are daily flights from Reykjavík timed to fit in with the limited daylight hours. Snow permitting, there is a lively **ski festival** (www.skidavikan.is) here during the week after Easter. The week ends with a music festival attracting top bands. In May, cross-country skiers from around Iceland head to Ísafjörður for the 50km **Fossavatn Ski Marathon** (www.fossavatn.com), which has been running since 1935.

Tours

Housed in the same building as the tourist information centre, the popular and professional **West Tours** (Vesturferðir; ☎ 456 5111; www.vesturferdir.is) organises a mind-boggling array of trips in the area. There are trips to Vigur (from Ikr6100) and kayaking excursions (from Ikr11,385) all year. You can visit the abandoned village at Hesteyri (Ikr6200) on a day trip, or you can get a four-night package

THE WESTFJORDS

VOLUNTEERING AT THE ARCTIC FOX RESEARCH STATION

Trying to find an excuse to extend your Icelandic vacation? Look no further than the Arctic Fox Research Station, situated on the northern cliffs of the jaw-dropping Hornstrandir Peninsula (p192) – a photographer's Eden and naturalist's dream.

Although it's a private facility, the research station at Hornbjarg is quite informal – just a cluster of tents and a charming outhouse a few kilometres away. Each day the team of researchers/volunteers sets off for an eight-hour viewing session during which they monitor fox behaviours, interactions and changes in location. There's a lot of sitting and looking involved, but we can't think of a more stunning location to take in the views and the nature. In fact, we took a bit of time off from our research to hunker down on the mossy cliffs and help out. We lucked out with T-shirt weather – the temperatures are usually a bit more shivery…

There are no requirements for becoming a volunteer – just a love of the great outdoors! Preference is, however, given to those studying biology, conservation or tourism. Volunteers are asked to give at least one week of their time and should keep their departure date somewhat flexible (ferry service can be delayed by a day or two when the seas around Hornstrandir are particularly rough). You'll also need to have the usual trappings of an outdoor adventure: a tent, hiking boots, thermal sleeping bag and clothing appropriate for negative temperatures. The research centre will handle everything else (food, transport, additional equipment etc).

If the windswept wilderness isn't your cup of tea, you can also volunteer at the headquarters in cosy Suðavík, near Ísáfjörður. The Arctic Fox Center, as it's known, is affiliated with the University of Iceland in Reykjavík and features an exhibition space telling the story of the Arctic fox's lifestyle, biology, history and tumultuous relationship with fur-hunting humans. Volunteers working here may even have the opportunity to help train rescue dogs. Temporary room and board is provided.

See p190 for more information, or check out www.arcticfoxcenter.com.

(Ikr32,000) to explore Hornstrandir. Biking, birdwatching and cultural excursions are but a few of the other activities on offer. Visit the office when you're in town to learn more – we highly recommend this outfitter.

Borea Adventures (☎ 899 3817, 869 7557; www.boreaadventures.com; Hlíðarvegur 38) is a smaller local operation with a professional yet wonderfully laid-back staff. High-quality tours usually involve multiday trips aboard *Aurora*, a yacht built for the Clipper Round the World Race. The boat is beautifully outfitted and meals aboard will be some of the best you'll have during your visit to Iceland. A yearly voyage schedule is posted on the website and includes everything from out-of-this-world sea kayaking around Hornstrandir (six days, €1520) to exhilarating journeys to Greenland, Svalbard and Jan Mayen (around six to 10 days, €1750 to €2450). In winter Borea leads invigorating six-day skiing, glacier hiking, and northern lights trips around Jökulfirðir and the upper Hornstrandir (€1250). Try to book as early as possible – the fun-loving guides and kick-ass itineraries mean that these trips fill up very quickly.

Sleeping

Campers can pitch a tent at Hotel Edda's **campsite** (sites per person Ikr1000; ◯ Jun-Aug) or at the **campsite** (☎ 444 4960; Skutulsfjarðarbraut; sites per person Ikr700; ◯ mid-Jun–mid-Aug) further out of town near the scenic waterfall in Tungudalur. The last stop on the town bus will take you to within 1km of the site.

Gamla Gistihúsið (Old Guest House; ☎ 456 4146; www.gistihus.is; Mánagata 5; sb/d incl breakfast Ikr2600/7600; 🖳 ☎) Bright, cheerful and immaculately kept, this excellent guest house has simple but comfortable rooms with plenty of homey touches. The bathrooms are shared, but each double room has telephone, washbasin and bathrobes. An annexe just down the road has a guest kitchen and more modern, functional rooms.

Litla Guesthouse (☎ 474 1455; reginasc@simnet.is; Sundstræti 43; s/d Ikr700/10,000) Wooden floors, crisp white linen, fluffy towels and TVs are available in the high-quality rooms of Litla, another cosy guest house with tasteful decor. Two rooms share each bathroom, and there's a guest kitchen. Don't miss the jungle-like mural painted around the stairwell.

THE WESTFJORDS

Hotel Edda (☎ 444 4960; www.hoteledda.is; sb/s/d without bathroom from Ikr1700/8800/11,000, d with bathroom Ikr17,600; ⏰ Jun-Aug; 🖳 🛜) No-frills summer accommodation is available at the town's secondary school. You can choose from basic sleeping-bag accommodation in the classrooms, private rooms with shared bathrooms and doubles with private bathrooms. We actually liked the shared bathrooms more – the rooms with private facilities all had twin beds and felt a bit too like a hospital. Breakfast cots are Ikr1050. (On-site camping is available – with showers).

Hótel Ísafjörður (☎ 456 4111; www.hotelisafjordur. is; Silfurtorg 2; s/d incl breakfast from Ikr11,200/13,500; 🖳 🛜) Slap bang in the centre of the town, this business-class hotel offers spacious, international-style rooms with calm, neutral decor, good bathrooms and views over the sea or town square. Go for a deluxe room; it's only Ikr2000 more and you get a huge step up in quality.

Eating

Heitt A Prjónunum (☎ 456 3210; Aðalstræti; snacks Ikr200-600; ⏰ noon-6pm Mon-Fri, 11am-2pm Sat; 🛜) We weren't quite sure where to put this little treasure – it could be categorised as shopping, entertainment or even a sight. But we think it fits best under 'eating' because it's *the* place in town for some coffee, cake and afternoon gossip.

Thai Koon (☎ 456 0123; Neisti Centre, Hafnarstræti 9; mains Ikr990-1290; ⏰ 11.30am-9pm Mon-Sat, 5-9pm Sun) After a few weeks of limited choice for meals, this small Thai canteen seems decidedly exotic. Although there's no atmosphere here whatsoever, the food is excellent and served up in giant portions, making it incredible value for money.

Edinborg (☎ 456 8060; Aðalstræti 7; mains Ikr1290-2000; ⏰ lunch & dinner) In the same building as the info centre, this social space sees lots of tourist traffic and makes a convenient spot to grab a burger. The summer saltfish feasts are held here, and it's definitely worth trying to get a ticket (Ikr4500) and gorging on a variety of local recipes.

Poturinn (☎ 456 4111; Silfurtorg 2; mains Ikr1250-2650; ⏰ breakfast, lunch & dinner) Although the decor feels a bit too IKEA-ish, Hótel Ísafjörður's restaurant has an excellent selection of local cuisine. The windows offer great views over the fjord – you might even see your next meal getting hauled into the

harbour. Light lunches make it a better deal at midday than in the evening.

Tjöruhisið (Tar House; ☎ 456 3293; Neðstíkaupstaður; mains Ikr1500-3000; ⏰ 11am-10pm Jun-Sep) The atmospheric summer restaurant at the folk museum offers some of the best fish and seafood dishes in town at very reasonable prices.

For breakfast, lunch or a midmorning sugar fix, there's a clutch of tempting bakeries in town. At **Gamla Bakaríið** (☎ 456 3226; Aðalstræti; ⏰ 7am-6pm Mon-Fri, to 4pm Sat), a stampede of customers rush in at 5.30pm when the baked goods get marked down by 50%. **Bakarans** (☎ 456 4771; Hafnarstræti 14; ⏰ 7.30am-6pm Mon-Sat, 9am-4.30pm Sun) has a cosy seating area and a choice of savoury and sweet snacks to obliterate any diet.

There's a **Samkaup supermarket** (⏰ 9am-9pm Mon-Fri, 10am-9pm Sat, noon-9pm Sun) in the Neisti Centre on Hafnarstræti and a cheaper **Bónus supermarket** (⏰ 9am-6pm) on the main road into town (expect long lines – it's the only Bónus in the Westfjords). For alcohol, there's a **Vin Búð** (Aðalstræti 20).

Shopping

If you're heading for Hornstrandir you can buy outdoor clothing and camping equipment at **Hafnarbúdin** (☎ 456 3245; Suðurgata). Instead of buying an Icelandic sweater, why not knit your own? Stop by **Heitt A Prjónunum** (left) – it's a yarn shop, cafe and popular local hangout. **Rammagerð Ísafjarðar** (☎ 456 3041; Aðalstræti 16) sells quality glassware and other crafts, and **Gullauga** (☎ 456 3460; Hafnarstræti 4) is good for gold jewellery.

Getting There & Away
AIR
Air Iceland (☎ 456 3000; www.airiceland.is) is based at the airport and flies to/from Reykjavík two or three times daily. The cheapest online fare from Reykjavík is Ikr6500. Flights to Akureyri connect through Reykjavík.

A special bus service runs to the airport about 45 minutes before departures. It starts in Bolungarvík and stops near the Hótel Ísafjörður.

BUS & BOAT
All buses circling through the Westfjords stop in Ísafjörður; see p178 for details. Buses stop at the N1 petrol station on Hafnarstræti. Local council buses (☎ 456 4258) run twice daily Monday to Friday from Ísafjörður to

THE WESTFJORDS

Flateyri and Þingeyri and three times daily to Suðureyri and Bolungarvík.

In summer, ferries to Hornstrandir depart from the Sundahöfn docks on the eastern side of the isthmus – see p193 for details.

Getting Around

City buses operate from 7.30am to 6.30pm on weekdays (until 10.30pm in winter) and connect the town centre with Hnífsdalur and Tungudalur. Contact West Tours for bike rentals. For a taxi, call ☎ 456 3518.

BOLUNGARVÍK
pop 920

Bolungarvík is about as pretty as it sounds. Despite its stunningly dramatic position at the fjordhead, the town itself is sleepy and rundown. However, two local museums make it somewhat tempting, and it's a pleasant destination for hikers as well.

An informal **tourist information centre** (☎ 861 8415; Vistastíg 1; ☼ noon-6pm Mon-Fri, 2-5pm Sat mid-Jun–Aug) is set up in a dusty handicraft shop next to the Natural History Museum. Stop here for the latest details on local hikes and accommodation options.

Housed in a series of old turf-and-stone fishing shacks on the way into town, the interesting open-air **Ósvör Maritime Museum** (☎ 892 1616; adult/under 16yr Ikr600/400; ☼ 10am-5pm May-Aug) is well worth a visit. A guide in a typical sheepskin fisherman's outfit shows you round, explaining the history of the area and the traditional methods for salting fish. The cramped fishermen's hut is full of interesting relics. A traditional rowing boat and tug capstan are also on display. On a ridge across the road, a **view disc** describes the surrounding landscape.

In the town's main shopping arcade, the **Natural History Museum** (☎ 456 7507; www.naturugripasaen.is; Vistastíg 3; adult/under 16yr Ikr600/free; ☼ 9am-noon & 1-5pm Mon-Fri, 1-5pm Sat & Sun Jun-Sep) has a comprehensive collection of minerals and stuffed animals – including a polar bear shot by local fishermen while swimming off the Hornstrandir coast.

There are interesting **hikes** to the remote coastal valley at Skálavík, 12km from Bolungarvík along a steep mountain road. Afterwards, soak your muscles at the **swimming pool** (☎ 456 7381; admission Ikr390; ☼ 8am-8pm Mon & Fri, 1-8pm Tue-Thu, 10am-6pm Sat, 10am-4pm Sun).

Facilities for tourists are limited – you're better off basing yourself in Ísafjörður (p185). There's a basic **campsite** (☎ 456 7381; sites per person Ikr800, plus electricity Ikr200) with washing machines by the swimming pool, and fast food at the Shell station on the main street. Self-caterers will find a Samkaup supermarket nearby as well.

A surfaced road runs around the headlands from Ísafjörður to Bolungarvík, lined with tunnels and steel nets to catch falling debris from the steep slopes above.

From June to August there are three buses from Ísafjörður to Bolungarvík from Monday to Friday, and two in the opposite direction. A ferry service to Hornstrandir also leaves from town – see p193 for details.

ÍSAFJARÐARDJÚP

The largest of the fjords in the region, 75km-long Ísafjarðardjúp takes a massive swath out of the Westfjords' landmass. Circuitous Rte 61 winds in and out of a series of smaller fjords on the southern side, making the drive from Ísafjörður to Hólmavík like sliding along each tooth of a fine comb.

Súðavík
pop 200

Just east of Ísafjörður, the small fishing community of Súðavík commands an imposing view across the fjord to Hornstrandir. Although the township is nothing more than a string of bright, box-shaped houses, it is definitely worth stopping by to visit the brand new **Arctic Fox Center** (☎ 862 8219; www.arcticfoxcenter.com; admission Ikr800; ☼ 9am-6pm). The study of the adorable arctic fox has been underway on nearby Hornstrandir for several years, but the newly opened exhibition centre has taken things to the next level. Interesting exhibits detail the life of the local arctic fox and its relationship with humans and the surrounding nature. Don't forget to sign the beautiful fish-skin guestbook. The centre sits inside the renovated farmstead of Eyrardalur – one of the oldest buildings in the area. Even if foxes aren't your bag, the on-site cafe is a great place to break up the journey and hang out with welcoming locals.

The centre's friendly managers are always looking for enthusiastic volunteers to work in Súðavík and/or go on surveying missions in Hornstrandir – see the boxed text, p188, for details.

THE WESTFJORDS

Súðavík takes a stab at the all-American diner with **Amma Habbý** (☎ 587 7745; Rte 61; mains Ikr690-1590; ⏳ 11am-11pm). They've got the greasy grub down pat – burgers, 'birthday cake' and milkshakes – and there are Old Hollywood portraits decorating the walls. The restaurant also doubles as a candy shop if you're looking for a sugar boost before tackling another endless stretch of bumpy highway.

Let the rugrats run wild at **Raggagarður** (http://raggagardur.is) across the street. Constructed by volunteers, this recreation park is named after Raggi, a young local who was tragically killed in a car crash.

Contact **Isangling** (☎ 456 1540; www.isangling .is), one of the Westfjords' largest sea-angling outfits, for comfortable accommodation up the hill at No 15 – there's an immaculately kept campsite next door.

Daily from Monday to Saturday there's a private bus from Ísafjörður to Súðavík (20 minutes). The buses between Ísafjörður and Hólmavík also pass through town on Sunday, Tuesday and Friday.

Vigur

With one adorable farm and zillions of puffins, charming Vigur is a popular destination for day-trippers from Ísafjörður. The tiny island sits at the mouth of Hestfjörður, offering sweeping fjord views in every direction. There's not much to do on the island besides taking a stroll (grab a stick from the windmill and hold it over your head – the Arctic terns are fierce here!), visiting the eider ducks and savouring cakes at the cafe. Try 'marital bliss', a marzipan confection – it was either the most delicious thing we've ever eaten, or we were just insanely hungry, having worked up a monstrous appetite while kayaking all the way to the island. While you're sending some snail mail in the wee post office, don't forget to have a look at the interesting egg collection inside.

West Tours (☎ 456 5111; www.vesturferdir.is) in Ísafjörður runs excursions to Vigur (from Ikr6100) all year.

Mjóifjörður, Vatnsfjörður & Reykjarfjörður

Continuing on after Súðavík, Rte 61 wiggles along with the undulating, fjord-ridden coast. At the head of Mjóifjörður, 11km from the main road, the farm **ourpick Heydalur** (☎ 456 4824; www.heydalur.is; sites per adult Ikr700, sb/d from Ikr2500/10,800 Jun-Aug, Ikr7900/10,400 Sep-May) is a fantastic place to break up the journey. It's a peaceful spot, yet activities are aplenty – hiking, swimming, spa-ing, horse riding (Ikr3500 per hour) and guided Kayaking (Ikr5000 for 2½ hours), just to name a few. In winter you can go snowmobiling or link up with the excellent northern lights viewing trips (Ikr81,000, including transport to/from Keflavík).

Even if you don't have plans to stop for the night, Heydalur's **restaurant** (mains Ikr1500-3300; ⏳ breakfast, lunch & dinner) is a great place to unwind and stretch your legs. Say hello to the parrot (he'll say hello back!) while savouring excellent soups, homemade breads, organic vegies from the local garden, popular lamb fillets, and smoked puffin if you're inclined. The restaurant itself sits inside a restored barn. Don't forget to look up – the beautiful chandelier overhead is made from glass buoy balls once used to steady fishing traps.

Further on, at the end of tiny Reykjarfjörður, is the friendly but well-weathered **Hótel Reykjanes** (☎ 456 4844; www.rnes.is; sites Ikr1500, sb/s/d Ikr3000/4500/8500; 🖵 🛜), housed in the huge, white former district school. The rooms are compact and functional, but there's a randomly gigantic (50m) outdoor geothermal pool here, which is fed by a steamy spring just beyond. Reykjanes also has a restaurant (lunch/dinner from Ikr1200/1900), and campers have free access to all facilities.

Snæfjallaströnd

On the eastern shore of Ísafjarðardjúp the unsurfaced Rte 635 leads north to **Kaldalón**, a beautiful green valley running up to the receding Drangajökull ice cap. It's an easy walk up to the snow line, but watch out for dangerous crevasses if you venture out onto the ice. Further north, **Snæfjallaströnd** was abandoned in 1995, but adventurous hikers can walk from the church at Unaðsdalur along the coast to the bunkhouse at Grunnavík, from where you can catch boats to Ísafjörður and Hesteyri.

Just before the church at Unaðsdalur, **Félagsheimilið Dalbær** (☎ 456 2660; inkjar@eldhorn. is; sites per person Ikr700, sb Ikr2500; ⏳ mid-Jun–mid-Aug) is a good place to get a last meal and warm night's sleep before you head off into the wilderness.

THE WESTFJORDS

HORNSTRANDIR

Craggy mountains, precarious sea cliffs and plunging waterfalls ring the wonderful uninhabited Hornstrandir Peninsula at the northern end of the Westfjords. This is one of Europe's last true wilderness areas and covers some of the most extreme and inhospitable parts of the country. It's a fantastic destination for wilderness hiking, with challenging terrain and excellent opportunities for spotting arctic foxes, seals, whales and teeming bird life.

A handful of hardy farmers lived in Hornstrandir until the 1950s, but since 1975 the 580 sq km of tundra, fjord, glacier and alpine upland have been protected as a national monument and nature reserve. The area has some of the strictest preservation rules in Iceland, thanks to its incredibly rich, but fragile, vegetation.

There are no services available in Hornstrandir and hikers must be fully prepared to tackle all eventualities. The passes here are steep and you'll need to carry all your gear, so hiking can be slower than you might expect. In addition, most trails are unmarked, so it's essential to carry a good map (try *Vestfirðir & Dalir* #1) and carry a GPS.

The best time to visit is in July. Outside the summer season (late June to mid-August) there are few people around and the weather is very unpredictable. If travelling in the off season, it is essential to plan ahead and get local advice, as vast snow drifts with near-vertical faces can develop on the mountain passes. There are emergency huts with radios and heaters at various points in the park for use in case of sudden blizzards or storms.

TOURS

While unassisted hikes through Hornstrandir are a fantastic way of exploring the reserve, it isn't everyone's cup of tea. If you're an inexperienced hiker, or you're simply looking for something more convenient, then we highly recommend a tour with **West Tours** (☎ 456 5111; www.vesturferdir.is) or **Borea Adventures** (☎ 899 3817, 869 7557; www.boreaadventures.com). See p187 for complete details.

Also, the Icelandic hiking organisation **Ferðafélag Íslands** (☎ 568 2533; www.fi.is; Mörkin 6, IS-108 Reykjavík) offers a variety of guided Hornstrandir hikes several times each summer – check their regularly updated website for details.

SLEEPING

There are various accommodation options along the coast, accessible on foot or by boat from Ísafjörður or Norðurfjörður. Pitching a tent in the park campsites is free, but staying at private campsites costs between Ikr800 and Ikr1200. Expect to pay Ikr1500 to Ikr3500 for sleeping-bag space. All the following open in summer only and have guest kitchens.

On the east coast, camping and sleeping-bag accommodation is available at **Reykjarfjörður** (☎ 456 7215, 853 1615; reykjarfjordur@simnet.is) and **Bolungarvík** (☎ 456 7192, 852 8267). You can also

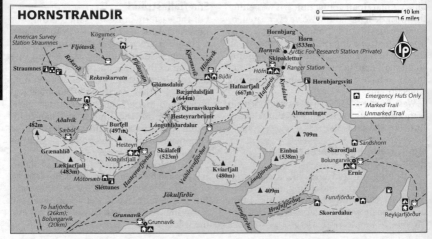

HIKING IN HORNSTRANDIR

The word 'Hornstrandir' is synonymous with stunning subarctic hiking, so how is one ever supposed to choose from the array of trails that zigzag across the peninsula like tangled shoelaces? To find the ultimate Hornstrandir hike, we thought it best to ask Jón Björnsson. No one knows the region better than him – he's the park ranger! Here's what he had to say:

Many types of adventures can be had in the Hornstrandir Nature Reserve, but the one I like the most is the comfortable four-to-five-day hike from Veiðileysufjörður to Hesteyri. This scenic hike gives a good picture of the region, and the itinerary can be easily modified if you run into bad weather. The trails on this route are clearly marked, but at the same time there are very few tourists, so it's a great opportunity to experience the desolate landscape.

On Day 1, sail from Ísafjörður to Veiðileysufjörður, one of the local *jökulfirðir* (glacier fjords). The hike begins on a street near the bottom of the fjord and follows a cairn-marked trail up the slope and through the mountain pass. From the pass you can descend the mountain on either side until you reach the campsite at Höfn in Hornvík. The hike from Veiðileysufjörður to Hornvík can take anywhere between four and eight hours. My ranger station is based at the campsite here, so feel free to stop by to get the latest weather forecast and information about trail conditions.

I recommend staying in Hornvík for two nights, and use Day 2 to visit Hornbjarg. Hornbjarg is an extremely beautiful bird cliff with diverse flora and fauna. Give yourself the entire day to explore the cliff – there's a lot to see.

On Day 3, hike from Hornvík to Hlöðuvík. The partly marked trail goes through a mountain pass and is relatively easy to find. Camping in Hlöðuvík is best by the Hlöðuvíkurós (the mouth of the Hlöðuvík river); there is a new campsite here. Like Hornvík, Hlöðuvík faces north – it's the perfect place to watch the spectacular midnight sun. Figure around six hours to reach Hlöðuvík.

On Day 4, hike through Kjarnsvíkurskarð (a mountain pass) and Hesteyrarbrúnir to Hesteyri (figure around eight hours). Hesteyri is an old village that was abandoned around the middle of the 20th century. There are still several well-kept houses here, amid the fields of angelica. Ruins of a turn-of-the-century whaling station are found near the village. The coffee shop in Hesteyri is a good place to visit at the end of your hike – you can get info about local trails and boats back to Ísafjörður. Boats from Hesteyri usually leave in the afternoon, so it's possible to plan your departure on the fourth day, but I advise hikers to spend one night in Hesteyri rather than having to race against the clock on the last day of hiking. Pitch your tent at the campsite just south of the village and spend Day 5 doing a series of short walks around the village while you wait for the ferry.

It is important that travellers take all their waste with them and leave no marks after their stay. If you carry driftwood or rocks back to your tent, please take them back before you leave. Fires are forbidden both on the beach and in vegetated land. Further information about the Hornstrandir Nature Reserve is available with the tourist information office in Ísafjörður (p187), which also houses West Tours' ticketing office.

stay at the lighthouse at **Hornbjargsviti** (☎ 566 6762; sites Ikr800, sb Ikr2200).

On the west coast, camping and sleeping-bag accommodation is provided at **Hesteyri** (☎ 456 1123, 853 5034, 845 5075; www.hesteyri.net; sb Ikr3500) and **Grunnavík** (☎ 852 4819; www.grunnavik. is; sites Ikr1200, sb Ikr3000; ☺ mid-Jun–mid-Aug).

GETTING THERE & AWAY

Getting to Hornstrandir requires a boat trip from Ísafjörður, from where there are regular services, or from Bolungarvík, Norðurfjörður or even Drangsnes from where boats run with less frequency and/or on request.

If you'd rather make the journey on foot, you can fly from Reykjavík to Gjögur (see p198) and walk in from there. Another possible access route for hikers is to take the Ísafjörður bus as far as the junction of Rtes 61 and 635 and then walk north along Rte 635 to the guest house at Dalbær (41km). From here, you can head up the Snæfjallaströnd coast to Grunnavík.

Scheduled boat services run from Ísafjörður from June to August providing there is a minimum of four passengers. Tickets can be booked directly with the boat companies or through the tour company **West Tours** (☎ 456 5111, 456 5122; www.vesturferdir.is).

THE WESTFJORDS

PUTTING THE 'COLD' BACK IN 'COLD WAR'

If you thought that the Cold War between the United States and the Soviet Union only involved space races and crafty KGB agents, then you are very, very wrong. The Cold War was the ultimate spy game spanning the circumference of the globe.

We sat down with James Barlow, a member of the US Navy who was stationed at Keflavík in southwest Iceland from 2003 until the base's closing in September 2006. Armed with a university degree in history, James developed a fascination with the American military presence in Iceland during the Cold War. Here's what he discovered:

Strategically located at the four corners of Iceland are the remains of four NATO radar sites that once protected Iceland's airspace from the Soviet Union. The most accessible is 'Rockville', or H-1, located near the town of Sandgerði on the Reykjanes Peninsula and the old NATO base at the airport. The Rockville buildings were used as a backdrop to the 2005 film *A Little Trip to Heaven*, directed by Icelandic director Baltasar Kormákur and starring Forest Whitaker and Julia Stiles. Rockville was torn down in 2006 in preparation for the closing of the Keflavík NATO base.

The next site, H-2, or 'Langanes', is located on the complete opposite side of the island outside the town of Þórshöfn in the northeast. To reach the site, follow Rte 869 out of town towards Skálar and Fontur. Just past the last inhabited farm at Hlið, head up the large mountain to the right (east). Almost nothing remains of the site today.

Site H-3 in southeast Iceland is also quite accessible, less than 5km along a dirt road leading off of the Ring Road. The Icelandic name for the site is 'Stokksnes', and it is the most complete of the four radar sites. The radar dome still stands today, and is used by the Icelandic government for aviation. You cannot approach the radar dome, as it is fenced off, but this location makes a great starting point for a hike around Vestrahorn.

The final and most remote of the radar sites is H-4, or 'Straumnes', in the Westfjords. H-4 is only accessible to hikers in Hornstrandir and makes a wonderful day hike from the base camp in Rekavík bak Látrar or Aðalvík. The easiest way to hike up to the old site is to start at the airstrip near Aðalvík (once used for ferrying supplies and personnel to the H-4 site) and follow the abandoned dirt road up to the windswept ruins. The road was cleared of rockfall debris in 2006 so that a vehicle could follow the veterans of H-4 as they hiked back to the place they had called home some 45 years earlier.

Despite the relative accessibility today, the journey to H-4 in the late 1950s was nothing short of harrowing. When a soldier arrived at the main base in Keflavík, he would immediately be flown on an Icelandic float-plane up to Ísafjörður (for a water landing – this was before the airport was built), then board a whaling vessel to distant Aðalvík where a flat-bottom landing craft would ferry him to shore. The lorries that shuttled the servicemen up the mount would often have mechanical problems due to the frigid temperatures, so the last part of the trip usually involved a gruelling hike through the unforgiving landscape. To learn more about the airmen who worked at the radar sites in the 1950s and 1960s, see www.usradarsitesiceland.org.

Sjóferðir (☎ 456 3879; www.sjoferdir.is) sails from Ísafjörður to Hesteyri (Ikr5200) five times a week, with one of these services continuing to Veiðileysufjörður. There is one weekly trip to Grunnavík (Ikr4800), which continues on to Hrafnfjörður. Two weekly trips head to Hornvík (Ikr9600) and Aðalvík Sæból (Ikr5700).

Bjarnarnes (☎ 892 3652, 853 0589; www.bjarnarnes. is) sails from Bolungarvík to Aðalvík and Hesteyri (Ikr4500) on a limited schedule; see p198 for info on boats from the Strandir coast.

STRANDIR COAST

Sparsely populated, magnificently peaceful and all but deserted by other travellers, the eastern coast of the Westfjords is one of the most dramatic places in all of Iceland. Indented by a series of bristle-like fjords and lined with jagged crags, the drive north of Hólmavík, the region's only sizeable settlement, is rough, wild and incredibly rewarding. South of here, gently rolling hills stretch along the isolated coastline as far as Staðarskáli, where the sudden rush of traffic

THE WESTFJORDS

tells you that you've returned to the Ring Road and the travelling masses.

There are buses along the coast as far as Hólmavík and Drangsnes, but you'll need your own vehicle and a sense of adventure to get further.

STAÐARSKÁLI TO HÓLMAVÍK

Although lacking the natural drama further north, the long drive from Staðarskáli (formerly Brú) to Hólmavík is pleasantly pastoral, with rolling hills dotted by small farmhouses and lonely churches. If counting sheep doesn't make you fall asleep, then stop by the small **Sheep Farming Museum** (☎ 451 3324; www.strandir. is/saudfjarsetur; adult/under 12yr Ikr700/free; ☯ 10am-6pm), which details the region's farming history through photos and artefacts. Chessboards and coffee may keep you around longer than expected. Nearby, sunbathing seals welcome visitors at **Kirkjuból** (☎ 451 3474; www.strandir.is/ kirkjubol; sb/s/d Ikr2900/4800/7200), about 12km south of Hólmavík. Rooms are fairly standard but there's a great guest kitchen and TV room. Two other lodging options – super-friendly **Snartartunga** (☎ 451 3362; snartartunga@bigfoot.com; sb Ikr3000, s/d incl breakfast Ikr6000/10,000; ☯ Jun–mid-Dec) and the retro starship–styled **Broddanes** (☎ 618 1830; www.broddanes.is; sb/linen Ikr3000/4000; ☜) – are positioned closer to Bitrufjörður along Rte 61.

HÓLMAVÍK
pop 420

The fishing village and service centre of Hólmavík offers sweeping views over the still waters of Steingrímsfjörður and has a quirky witchcraft museum. The town is a good place to stock up on supplies before venturing off into more rugged territory.

Information

The **tourist information centre** (☎ 451 3111; www. holmavik.is/info; Norðurtún 1; ☯ 9am-5pm mid-Jun–Aug) is beside the new swimming complex in the modern community centre – the N1 petrol station is across the street. You can access the internet here (Ikr200 for 30 minutes) and pick up copies of the extremely useful *Vestfirðir & Dalir* #3 & #6 hiking maps for a small fee. There's a post office and several banks with ATMs around Hafnarbraut, as well as a **Vík Garage** (☎ 451 3131; Hafnarbraut 14), which can fix car and tyre damage.

Sights & Activities

Hólmavík's main tourist attraction is the award-winning **Museum of Icelandic Sorcery & Witchcraft** (☎ 451 3525; www.galdrasyning.is; Höfðagata 8-10; adult/under 14yr Ikr700/free; ☯ 10am-6pm Jun–mid-Sep, ring the doorbell mid-Sep–May), by the central harbour. Unlike the widely known Salem witch trials in New England, almost all of Iceland's convicted witches were men. Most of their occult practices were simply old Viking traditions, but hidden *grimoires* (magic books) full of puzzling runic designs were proof enough for the local witch-hunters to burn around 20 souls at the stake. Several *grimoires* (some even used in the early 20th century!) are on display, as are kookier exhibits like 'the invisible boy' (you'll see), and the 'necropants' (see the boxed text, below). Additional displays can be found on the second floor, which doubles as a theatre.

There are two other sections of the museum along the Strandir coast – a turf-roofed 'sorcerer's cottage' in Bjarnarfjörður (p197) and a monument/cinema at Árnes, which was, at the time of research, in the early stages of construction.

THE WESTFJORDS

NECROPANTS...

Of all the strange displays at the Museum of Icelandic Sorcery & Witchcraft (above), perhaps the most bizarre is a plastic replica of the legendary 'necropants' – trousers made from the skin of a dead man's legs and groin. It was commonly believed that the necropants would spontaneously produce money when worn, so long as the donor made an honest verbal agreement that his corpse could be skinned upon his death. Once dead and buried, the donor corpse had to be unearthed at the dead of night, then a magic rune and a coin from a poor widow (the penniless widows *always* got picked on in Icelandic lore!) were placed in the dead man's scrotum.

The necropants brought incredible wealth to its wearer – anytime money was needed, one could reach down into the scrotal area and...voila! There was a catch, however; if you were to die wearing the necropants, your soul would be condemned to roam the earth until the end of time.

If you're heading northwest it's worth stopping off at the wooden church at **Staður**, 14km from Hólmavík, to see the 18th-century pulpit there.

Sleeping & Eating

Campsite (☎ 451 3560; sites per person Ikr800) The municipal campsite, beside the community centre, has toilets, showers and a laundry.

Gistiheimilið Borgarbraut (☎ 451 3136; www.borgarbraut4.is; Borgarbraut 4; sb/d Ikr3000/6000; 🛜) Set on the hill near the church, this welcoming guest house has well-kept rooms with great views. The smell of freshly baked bread often wafts through the air. There's also a guest kitchen and a TV lounge on each of the three floors, and free laundry facilities for all.

Steinhúsið (☎ 856 1911; www.steinhusid.is; Höfðagata 1; mid-May–mid-Sep s/d/apt Ikr6000/9000/15,000, mid-Sep–mid-May Ikr4500/7000/11,000; 🛜) A pleasant option across from the witch museum, Steinhúsið has a small collection of prim rooms and basement apartments. Breakfast is Ikr1400.

Galður (☎ 451 3525; Höfðagata 8-10; lunch Ikr900; 🕐 8am-6pm) A great place for a quick and cheap lunch, the witch museum's cafe serves up the usual soup lunches and an assortment of other light dishes. Be sure to stick around on Saturday afternoons – the museum's curator casts a few spells to keep the spirits at bay!

Café Riis (☎ 451 3567; Hafnarbraut 39; mains Ikr130-2990; 🕐 11.30am-9pm) The town's pub and restaurant is a popular place set in a historic wooden building with stripped floors and carved magic symbols on the bar. Roasted chicken breast, puffin and trout are the menu's biggest hits.

As always, there's a small grocery and cheap eats at the petrol station.

Shopping

Handverkshús Hafþórs (☎ 865 3713; Höfðagata 12; 🕐 9am-6pm Mon-Fri, 10am-6pm Sat & Sun Jun-Aug) Located in the red house beside the witchcraft museum is this immensely popular woodcarving studio and veritable sawdust blizzard. Hafþór, a local artisan, crafts adorable little birds (Ikr2000) by hand – they make great souvenirs.

Getting There & Away

From June to August, buses run between Staðarskáli and Hólmavík (two hours) on Tuesday, Friday and Sunday only. The same service continues from Hólmavík on to Drangsnes (30 minutes) on Friday. Buses from Ísafjörður to Hólmavík (Ikr4000 or Ikr5000, Sunday, Tuesday and Friday from June to August, four hours) are timed to connect with the service to Staðarskáli. You can connect to services to Reykjavík and Akureyri from Staðarskáli. During winter there is one bus a week (on Friday) from Reykjavík to Hólmavík via Staðarskáli.

Note that a concreted road connecting Hólmavík to Króksfjarðarnes (in the Dalir region) was being completed at the time of research. Public transport may start running here in the future.

DRANGSNES

pop 80

Across the fjord from Hólmavík, Drangsnes (pronounced *drowngs*-ness) is a remote little village with views across to north Iceland and the small uninhabited island of **Grímsey**. Guarding the shoreline is ominous rocky stack **Kerling**, the supposed remains of a petrified troll. **Uxi**, her bull, is the formation out at sea near Grímsey (see the boxed text, opposite).

As haunting as the bizarre sea stacks may be, a favourite attraction is the secreted set of free geothermal **hot pots** built into the sea wall along the main road. Even eagle eyes will have a hard time spotting these geometric Jacuzzis, so keep an eye out for the town's modern church instead – the little pools are directly across the street. During the colder months you'll often see bathrobe-clad locals driving up for a quick soak after work. There's also a town **swimming pool** (adult/child Ikr300/free; 🕐 10am-9pm mid-Jun–mid-Aug, 11am-6pm mid-Aug–mid-Jun) with two sparkling hot pots for when the weather's too tumultuous by the sea.

Next to the Kerling, **Malarhorn** (☎ 451 3238; www.malarhorn.is; Grundargata 17; s/d/cottage Ikr8900/12,000/28,000) is a peaceful row of crisp pine cabins that feel thoroughly modern yet remarkably cosy. There's no TV, no radio and definitely no internet here – it's the perfect place to escape.

Malarhorn also runs a variety of sailing, sea-angling and fishing trips (around Ikr3000). Visits to Grímsey (adult/child Ikr4000/2000) are on offer at 2pm on Thursday and Sunday. It may also be possible to charter a boat up to the Hornstrandir reserve – call for details about this and other trips.

Malarkaffi (mains from Ikr1300; 🕐 8am-9pm), across the gravel lot from Malarhorn, serves

---

THE GRÍMSEY TROLLS

According to legend the island of Grímsey, off the coast of Drangsnes, was created by evil trolls, now petrified into the stone stacks at Drangsnes. Intent on severing the Westfjords from the mainland, the trolls decided to dig a trench right across the peninsula. Unfortunately, they were so wrapped up in the job that they failed to notice the rising sun. As the first rays broke over the horizon, the two trolls at the trench's western end were transformed into standing stones at Kollafjörður. The female troll on the east side nearly escaped, but as she was turning to flee she realised that she had marooned her bull on the newly created island of Grímsey. Suddenly the sunbeams struck – she was promptly turned to stone forever, gazing back at her lost bull.

---

an array of traditionally prepared fish, whale and lamb on its second-storey verandah overlooking the fjord.

The Friday bus from Staðarskáli to Hólmavík continues to Drangsnes (30 minutes), returning the same day. No buses run north of Drangsnes, so you'll need a vehicle to reach Laugarhóll or anywhere further north.

BJARNARFJÖRÐUR

North of Drangsnes, a rough road winds around a series of gorgeous crumbling escarpments and dramatic fjords. There's no public transport and there are few services on this route, but if you've got your own vehicle, the utter tranquillity, incredible views and sheer sense of isolation are truly remarkable.

The first indent along the coast is **Bjarnarfjörður**, where you'll find the **Hótel Laugarhóll** (☎ 451 3380; d without/with bathroom Ikr10,000/12,500; 🖳), a large, modern building with spacious rooms and an in-house restaurant. At the time of writing, new managers were set to take over. The lovely **geothermal pool** (Ikr300) next door has some of the warmest water in Iceland.

Near the hotel is an ancient **artificial pool** that was blessed by a bishop in the 16th century and is now a national monument. The consecrated pool feeds the lovely geothermal pool nearby, so if you stop by for a dip you're essentially bathing in holy water (or so the locals say). Just a few steps away is the turf-roofed **Sorcerer's Cottage** (adult/child Ikr600/free), which is part of the witchcraft museum in Hólmavík (see p195). A collection of *grimoire* translations can be purchased in the gift shop – the author lives in the yellow house on the far side of the road.

North of Bjarnarfjörður the scenery becomes more rugged and there are fine views across to the Skagi Peninsula in north Iceland. This road often closes with the first snows in autumn and may not reopen until spring. If you're travelling late in the season, ask locally for up-to-date information on conditions.

At **Kaldbaksvík** the steep sides of a broad fjord sweep down to a small fishing lake that serenely reflects the surrounding mountains. Just beyond the lake, a 4km trail runs up to the summit of craggy Lambatindur (854m). You'll notice copious amounts of driftwood piled up along the shore on this coast – most of it has arrived from Siberia across the Arctic Ocean.

REYKJARFJÖRÐUR

Tucked in beneath a looming rock wall at Reykjarfjörður is the strangely enchanting factory at **Djúpavík**. Once a thriving centre for herring processing, the area was all but abandoned when the plant closed in 1950. The looming bulk of the deserted factory dominates the village, but for those travellers who make it here it's one of the most memorable locations of their trip.

ourpick **Hótel Djúpavík** (☎ 451 4037; www.djupavik. com; sb/s/d from Ikr2500/6700/8100; 🖳) is a charming bolt hole swathed in antiques and set in the former factory accommodation block. It's not the rooms that earn Djúpavík the 'our pick' symbol – it's the feeling of comfort and calm that washes over every visitor. When asked why visitors come back year after year, staff simply explain that Djúpavík is unforgettable and holds a special power over all who visit. There's an in-house restaurant serving fish fresh from the fjord, and at 2pm you can take a tour (Ikr500) of the abandoned factory.

NORÐURFJÖRÐUR

North of Djúpavík, there are two interesting churches at Árnes – one is a traditional wooden structure and the other is strangely and dramatically futuristic. Also worth a look is the small museum, **Kört** (☎ 451 4025; www.trekyl isvik.is; Árnes 2; admission Ikr500; 🕑 10am-6pm Jun-Aug), which sells handicrafts, offers info about the area and has displays on fishing, farming and collected knick-knacks. A second satellite of the witch museum in Hólmavík (see p195) was being constructed in Árnes at the time of writing. When completed, it will feature a large monument that doubles as a small cinema showing a 50-minute documentary about witchcraft. Nearby, **Kistan** (meaning 'the coffin') was the main site in the region for witch executions. It's marked on the main road, but easier to find if you ask for directions.

Clinging onto life at the end of the long bumpy road up the Strandir coast is the little fishing village of **Norðurfjörður**. Norðurfjörður has a cafe, a petrol station and a few guest houses, and it's the last place to stock up and indulge in some home comforts before heading off to Hornstrandir. About 2km beyond Norðurfjörður, at **Krossnes**, there's an open-air **geothermal swimming pool** (adult/under 14yr Ikr250/100) sitting at the edge of the universe on a wild black-pebble beach. It's an incredible place to watch the midnight sun flirt with the lapping waves.

Sleeping & Eating

Finnbogastaðaskóli (☎ 451 4013; sites per tent Ikr1500; sb/s/d Ikr1800/2700/4600; ☺ Jun-Aug) Recognisable by the rusted basketball net outside, this budget-friendly option is set in a converted primary school – there are arts and crafts adorning the walls, but everything's kept very clean. Walk-ins will find the manager at home in the field just beyond.

Gistiheimili Bergistanga (☎ 451 4003; gunnsteinn@ simnet.is; sb Ikr2500) On the hill overlooking the harbour, this friendly guest house has good sleeping-bag accommodation in comfortable rooms, and a guest kitchen.

Café Norðurfjörður (☎ 451 4034; mains from Ikr890; ☺ 11.30am-8.30pm) Located near the petrol station, this simple joint with excellent fjord views offers everything from waffles to lamb.

Getting There & Away

No buses run to Norðurfjörður, but **Eagle Air** (☎ 562 4200; www.ernir.is; Reykjavík Domestic Airport, IS-101 Reykjavík) pilots charter flights twice a week (Monday and Thursday) between Reykjavík and the airstrip at Gjögur, 16km southeast of Norðurfjörður. The online fare for a one-way ticket is €115 and the trip takes 50 minutes.

Freydís (☎ 852 9367; www.freydis.is) runs scheduled trips from Norðurfjörður to Hornvík and Reykjarfjörður (from Ikr6000) on Monday, Wednesday, Friday and Saturday between July and mid-August. Trips to other points in Hornstrandir can be arranged on request.

Northwest Iceland

Locals joke that the only tourists who stop in northwest Iceland are the ones who get pulled off the Ring Road for speeding. And is it true? Well, kinda. This is backdoor Iceland at its best – a region with three lonely peninsulas where each cairn has a story and each horse a name.

Much of northwest Iceland has an end-of-the-world feel to it. Little fishing villages cling tenaciously to life at the end of unsealed roads, their poignant history a constant reminder of Iceland's fickle fortunes. Quiet, remote Siglufjörður was once a thriving herring-fishing centre, Hofsós records the departure of thousands of Icelandic emigrants, and the bishopric at Hólar was once a beacon of medieval thought and culture.

Little Akureyri, with its surprising moments of big-city living, offers the only respite from the endless country vistas. Beyond this urban blip, you'll uncover barking seals on Vatnsnes, icy peaks in Tröllaskagi and windy pastures along Skagafjörður. Offshore in the fjords you'll find lonely islands with roaring colonies of sea birds and an impressive bunch of hardy locals.

To appreciate this area you've got to get off Rte 1, wind your way through the bays, fjords and braided river deltas that stretch north, and discover the spectacular scenery and quirky little towns that give this region its character. Tourists on tight schedules will pass straight through – those with extra time will go home saying they got to experience the Iceland that isn't always found in the tourist brochures.

HIGHLIGHTS

- Cross Iceland's only true slice of the Arctic Circle – the tern-filled and troll-infested island of **Grímsey** (p225)
- Grin quietly while relishing the undeniable splendour of **Goðafoss** (p223)
- Discover northern Iceland's version of city living during a spirited night out in **Akureyri** (p210)
- Experience the ultimate white-water thrills, spills and chills on a rafting trip from **Varmahlíð** (p204)
- Trot along serene **Skagafjörður** (p204) on horseback, taking in views of the Tröllaskagi peaks and lonely offshore islets

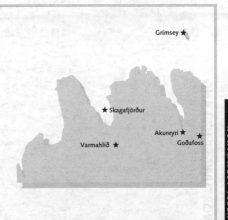

Grímsey ★

★ Skagafjörður

Akureyri ★ ★ Goðafoss

Varmahlíð ★

NORTHWEST ICELAND

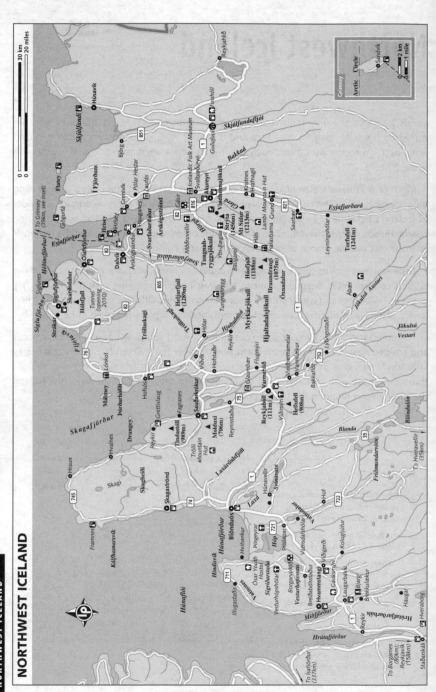

Getting There & Away

AIR

Air Iceland (☎ 570 3030; www.airiceland.is) has a minimum of five daily flights between Reykjavík and Akureyri (from Ikr5500 one way, 45 minutes).

BUS

From May to September two buses a day operate between Reykjavík and Akureyri (Ikr9900, 5¾ hours), via Staðarskáli (formerly Brú), Hvammstangi, Blönduós and Varmahlíð. They depart from Reykjavík *and* Akureyri at 8.30am and 5.30pm. There's a reduced service the rest of the year but still at least two buses daily. From mid-June to the end of August, Trex and SBA operate at least one daily service between Reykjavík and Akureyri along the highland Kjölur route (from Ikr9900, nine to 10 hours), leaving at 8am in both directions.

Heading east, there are daily buses from Akureyri to Mývatn (Ikr2200, 1½ hours), Húsavík (Ikr2300, one hour) and Egilsstaðir (Ikr5400, four hours).

Getting Around

Away from the Ring Road, getting around this area can be frustrating without your own transport. From May to August there are daily buses between Varmahlíð and Sauðárkrókur, and from June to August there's a service every day except Saturday between Sauðárkrókur and Siglufjörður. There's also a weekday bus from Akureyri to Ólafsfjörður, via Dalvík.

EASTERN HÚNAFLÓI

Although sparsely populated and scattered with only a handful of tiny settlements, Húnaflói is rich in wildlife. It's also known as Bear Bay – named after the many Greenland bears that have come ashore there. The scenery of the area is far gentler than that of the Westfjords, and the low, treeless hills provide nesting sites for wild swans, ptarmigans, divers and golden plovers. Add some neatly manicured towns, some barking seals, and a cluster of good museums, and there's plenty to keep you occupied en route to Akureyri.

It's worth stopping at an information point to pick up the *Húnavatnssýslur* booklet, which offers detailed info (including maps) about all there is to see and do in eastern Húnaflói. Try the *Ideal Holiday* guide too – there are heaps of homey farmstays in this neck of the woods.

HRÚTAFJÖRÐUR

Little Hrútafjörður cuts the divide between northwest Iceland and the Westfjords.

Staðarskáli

No more than a busy road junction with a huge N1 petrol station, Staðarskáli (once known as Brú) acts as a connection point for buses between Reykjavík, Akureyri and Ísafjörður.

There's no reason to stop here other than to change buses, fill up with petrol, grab a quick bite, stock up on maps and tourist brochures, or check your email (the station has a computer terminal and wi-fi). If you do want to stay, accommodation is available at **Staðarskáli** (☎ 451 1150; www.stadarskali.is; s/d incl breakfast Ikr8800/13,000; ☯ Jun-Aug; 🖳 🛜), 1km from the junction. The hotel has unmemorable but well-equipped rooms with bathroom, TV and wi-fi.

If you're up for a little adventure, follow the road past the hotel and park your car at the dead end. From here it's a 30-minute walk (keep an eye on your watch) to **Hveraborg**, a scenic geothermal spring that rarely sees any action.

Reykir

At Reykir, an active geothermal field 12km north of Staðarskáli, you'll find the **Byggðasafu museum** (☎ 451 0040; adult/under 12yr Ikr500/free; ☯ 10am-6pm Jun-Aug). This local folk exhibition features an array of household and agricultural implements from early Iceland, with an emphasis on the local black magic practised in early medieval times. Highlights include the well-reconstructed interior of a 19th-century homestead and the fantastic shark-fishing boat *Ófeigur*, built from driftwood in 1875 and used until 1915.

A few hundred metres from the folk museum at Reykir, the **Sæberg HI Hostel** (☎ 451 0015; saeberg@hostel.is; sites per tent Ikr1200, sb member/nonmember Ikr2300/2800; ☯ Jan-Nov) is a good place to break up the trip between Reykjavík and Akureyri. It's a cosy, well-equipped little hostel with a geothermally heated hot pot.

HVAMMSTANGI

pop 570

Six kilometres north of the Ring Road, slow-paced Hvammstangi's biggest (and pretty

NORTHWEST ICELAND

much only) attraction is the **Icelandic Seal Centre** (☎ 451 2345; www.selasetur.is; Brekkugata 2; adult/under 14yr/senior Ikr600/300/400; ☻ 9am-5pm Jun-Aug), where you can learn about seal conservation, historic seal products used in Iceland, and traditional folk tales involving seals. There's also a small tourist information point here.

At the time of research, there were no seal-watching tours in operation, but this may start up in the future – call ☎ 860 7252 for updates, and figure around Ikr3000 for a two-hour trip.

If you're looking for a place to crash, try **Hanna Sigga** (☎ 451 2407; www.simnet.is/gistihs; Garðavegur 26; sb/s/d Ikr2800/5600/7900) on a residential street back in the centre of town. Rooms are well kept, and there's a guest kitchen, but the real draw is the homemade breakfast (Ikr1000) served in a beautiful nook overlooking the town and harbour.

Rooms (sleeping bag/linen Ikr2500/3000) are also available in the back of **Sírop** (☎ 451 2266; Norðurbraut 1; mains Ikr890-2000; ☻ 11.30am-10pm Sat-Thu, to 3am Fri & Sat; ☐ 📶), Hvammstangi's main pub-grub-wielding haunt; or you can try the new **campsite** (☎ 869 3954; Kirkjuhvammur; sites per tent Ikr1600; ☻ mid-May–mid-Sep) up the hill near the old church. Rangers come by in the morning to collect the money. At the time of research, campers had free access to the local **swimming pool** (adult/under 17yr Ikr350/free; ☻ 7am-10pm Mon-Fri, 10am-8pm Sat & Sun) for showering.

There's a well-stocked supermarket and Vín Búð by the harbour.

VATNSNES PENINSULA
Poking out into Húnaflói, the stubby Vatnsnes Peninsula is a starkly beautiful place with wheat-strewn shores and a ridge of craggy hills that marches down its spine. On the west side there's a lonely cafe (open 3pm to 7pm from mid-June to August) and campsite at **Illugastaðir** (☎ 894 0695; sites per person Ikr750; mid-Jun–Aug), with wonderful views of dramatic peaks along the Strandir coast in the Westfjords. In the east you'll happen upon one of Iceland's largest accessible seal colonies at **Hindisvík**. A short walk from here, and accessible from a parking area near the road, is the bizarre 15m-high sea stack **Hvítserkur**. Legend has it that Hvítserkur was a troll caught by the sunrise while attempting to destroy the monastery at Þingeyrar.

About 10km further south is the charming **Ósar Youth Hostel** (☎ 862 2778; www.hostel.is; dm member/nonmember Ikr2100/2600; ☻ May-Sep), one of Iceland's nicest hostels, thanks to friendly management, good views and the nearby wildlife. The hostel is on a working dairy farm, and the owner indulges his hobby of building more rooms each year. Bring your own food as there are no shops nearby.

There is no public transport around the peninsula, but Rte 711, a rough gravel road, weaves along the coast. If you call ahead, the hostel can pick you up from the Ring Road (about Ikr2500).

VATNSDALUR
The cascade-filled stretch of highway from Hvammstangi to Blönduós is the aptly named Vatnsdalur – literally 'water valley' in Icelandic. Travellers, get those cameras ready!

Ecofriendly **our pick Gauksmýri** (☎ 451 2927; www.gauksmyri.is; s/d without bathroom Ikr7400/10,700, with bathroom Ikr11,200/15,000; ☐ 📶), near the Ring Road just beyond the turn-off to Hvammstangi, is a great place to overnight, especially if you're keen on horse riding. Other activities include birdwatching, dog sledding (in winter) and massage. There's even a small raven museum.

Speed demons will be happy to know that Gauksmýri marks the halfway point between Reykjavík and Akureyri along the Ring Road. Ask here for directions to **Kolugljúfur** – an enchanting canyon that was once home to a beautiful trolless. You can still see her bed.

Serious horse riders should book ahead with **Brekkulækur** (☎ 451 2938; www.geysir.com/brekkulaekur), 9km south from the Hvammstangi turn-off, which offers adventurous and highly acclaimed multiday trips (€1000 to €2500 for eight to 15 days).

Around 19km before you reach Blönduós, take a quick 6km detour along Rte 721 to find a precious stone church, **Þingeyrar**, sitting quietly on Hóp lagoon. The current structure was erected in the 1860s, but 800 years earlier the site hosted a district *þing* (assembly), and a prolific literary Benedictine monastery. Those who head south along Rte 722 will soon reach **Vatnsdalshólar**. Follow the staircase over the fence (you'll know what we mean when you arrive) to reach the bizarre **Kattarauga** (literally 'cat's eyes') – small tree-topped islets that mysteriously float around the crystalline lake.

BLÖNDUÓS
pop 940
A couple of museums and an unusual church – Blönduós is about as simple as that. There

---

THE FUNKY CHURCH HUNT

If you're driving straight from Reykjavík to Akureyri, you might be surprised to find yourself making a pit stop in Blönduós. Some tummies grumble at the sight of the big N1 station, other road-trippers get yanked off the highway for speeding (the cops are notorious here!) and a third subset of travellers slow down to utter a collective 'what the...?' when they pass the town's oddball church in the centre of town. If eccentric architecture is your thing, then you're in luck! Iceland's got a clutch of wonky worship houses that makes Blönduós' contribution seem remarkably staid. Here are three faves:

- Hallgrímskirkja (p75) in Reykjavík
- Stykkishólmskirkja (p165) on the Snæfellsnes Peninsula
- The 'New Church' at Arnes (p197) on the remote Strandir coast

---

isn't too much to woo you off the road, but it's a good place to break up the journey and refuel.

Orientation & Information

The churning Blanda river sharply separates the town in half. The N1 station marks the northern entrance into town, while the Olis station sits at the southern approach. Most food options can be scouted north of the Blanda and accommodation sits mostly south. The **tourist information centre** (☎ 820 1300; ferdamal @simnet.is; ☉ 8am-7.30pm Mon-Fri, 10am-4pm Sat Jun-Aug; ☉) is north of the river, just off the Ring Road – follow the signs for the campground.

The Blanda is an extremely dangerous river with fast currents and undertows. Keep all children and pets well away from the banks.

Sights & Activities

Set in an intriguing building (think 'turf-roof chic') on the north bank of the Blanda, the small **Textiles Museum** (Heimilisiðnaðarsafnið; ☎ 452 4067; www.simnet.is/textile; Árbraut 29; adult/under 16yr/ senior Ikr600/free/450; ☉ 10am-5pm Jun-Auq) displays local handicrafts and early Icelandic costumes. The small on-site cafe is a great place to relax with a hot coffee and enjoy the river views out the large picture windows.

Housed in the oldest timber merchant's house in Iceland, the **Sea Ice Exhibition Centre** (Hafíssetrið; ☎ 452 4848; www.blonduos.is/hafis; Blöndubyggð 2; adult/under 16yr Ikr500/free; ☉ 11am-5pm late May-Aug) looks at the formation and types of sea ice, weather patterns, early Icelandic settlers, and ice in nearby east Greenland. One display examines the possibility of an ice-free North Pole being used as a shipping lane, and another displays the polar bear that wreaked havoc in the region dur-

ing the summer of 2008 (don't worry –he's been stuffed).

The islet of **Hrútey**, just upstream from the Blanda Bridge, is a nature reserve and the site of a reforestation project. Access is via a footbridge 200m north of the campsite.

Keep an eye out for the town's new swimming pool – it was under construction when we passed through.

Sleeping & Eating

Occupying a lovely setting near the river, Blönduós' visitor information centre runs the neighbouring **campsite** (sites per tent Ikr1200) and **Glaðheimar cottages** (www.gladheimar.is; cabins Ikr10,000-17,000). Campers will find good washing facilities, while travellers opting for the large cabins will be treated to hot tubs and saunas within.

Hótel Blönduós (☎ 452 4205; www.hotelblonduos .is; Aðalgata 6; s/d incl breakfast Ikr15,900/19,900; ☐ ☉) The town's only hotel isn't anything to write home about, but it's popular with visiting anglers. The restaurant (mains from Ikr2700; open 6am to 10pm) could use a decorator's touch (dark wood and disco balls?), but the fish and lamb dishes are quite good. Nearby, the owners also run **Posthusið** (Blöndubyggð 10; s/d incl breakfast Ikr7900/9900), a faded, pistachio-toned guest house set in the former post office.

Við Árbakkann (☎ 452 4678; Húnabraut 2; mains Ikr1050-3000; ☉ 9am-5pm Mon-Fri, 10am-6pm Sat, 1-5pm Sun) This fine country-style cafe, set in a big blue house north of the river, serves a mixed bag of local faves and pub-grub staples.

Pottunrinn og Pannan (☎ 453 5060; Nordurlandsvegur 4; mains Ikr1200-3200; ☉ lunch & dinner) Set in a surprisingly modern dining room, 'Pots and Pans' has a great assortment of food and makes a pleasant step up from petrol-station

NORTHWEST ICELAND

ICELANDIC COWBOY

Hallbjörn Hjartarson, the 'Icelandic Cowboy', fell in love with country-and-western music while working on the American base at Keflavík in the 1960s. Even after moving back to the remote fishing community at Skagaströnd, he continued to indulge his passion for playing and recording country music. He released his first record in 1975 and organised Iceland's first country-music festival in Skagaströnd in 1984. The two-day event is held during the third weekend in August, and recently attracted about 3000 people!

eats. There's soup and salad all day, fantastic burgers, and a few delicious Indian dishes (the chef is from the Subcontinent).

A **Samkaup-úrval** (Húnabraut 4; 9am-7pm Mon-Fri, 10am-6pm Sat, 1-5pm Sun) fulfils self-caterers' needs.

Getting There & Away
Buses travelling from Reykjavík (Ikr6200, four hours)and from Akureyi (Ikr3800, two hours) stop off in Blönduós.

SKAGASTRÖND
pop 550
One of northern Iceland's oldest trading centres, Skagaströnd was first established in the 16th century, but today its main claim to fame is as the country-music capital of Iceland. Yes, you read it right. The main reason to venture the 22km north of the Ring Road is to pop into **Kántrýbær** (453 2829; www.kantry.is; Holanesvegur; 11.30am-10pm Sun-Thu, to 3am Fri & Sat Jun-Aug, lunch Sep-May), Iceland's only country-music bar. With its Wild West log-cabin atmosphere, bright murals, a gold bust of the owner (above) and the constant twang of country music, this place is truly a unique Icelandic experience. The menu has the usual pub grub (mains Ikr790 to Ikr2790), but also features lamb and pan-fried trout caught in the local lakes. Upstairs is a small **museum** (adult/child Ikr400/free) of country-music memorabilia and a working radio station (95.7FM in town, 100.7FM in Blönduós and 100.2FM in Sauðarkrókur).

Apart from the bar there's a bank, post office, Samkaup supermarket and small camp-site on the way into town.

SKAGAFJÖRÐUR
Renowned for its horse breeding and its wild landscapes, Skagafjörður is a little-visited region in Iceland's quiet northwest. Hit by recession, rough weather and lonely winters, the area is littered with abandoned farms and chilling reminders of how difficult life in isolated rural Iceland can be. For visitors, however, the bleak landscape, historic remains, abundant bird life and adrenalin-infused activities make it a rewarding destination. For more information, see www.visitskagafjordur.com.

VARMAHLÍÐ
pop 90
This bustling Ring Road service centre is slightly more than a road junction and yet not quite a town. Named after nearby geothermal sites, it's a busy place and a great base for rafting, hiking and horse riding.

Varmahlíð's **tourist information centre** (455 6161; www.visitskagafjordur.is; 9am-7pm mid-Jun–mid-Aug, 9am-5pm 1 Jun–14 Jun & 16 Aug–31 Aug, closed weekends Sep-May;) is in the little turf-roofed cottage near the N1 petrol station. It's a helpful place with local hiking maps, an internet terminal, wi-fi and coffee (all free!). The crafts sold in the centre are handmade by the wives of the local farmers. History buffs should enquire about saga-themed tours (Ikr3000) that have recently started up in this fable-rich region.

Activities
WHITE-WATER RAFTING
Between May and September the area around Varmahlíð offers the best white-water rafting in northern Iceland. **Hestasport Activity Tours** (453 8383; www.rafting.is) specialises in rafting trips on three local rivers. Options include a four-hour trip on the Jökulsá Vestari (West River; Ikr6500), with grade II+ rapids; a family-friendly three- to four-hour paddle on the Blanda (Ikr6500, one child per family free) with grade I+ rapids; and an exciting six-hour adventure on the Jökulsá Austari (East River; Ikr9800), where you can tackle grade IV+ rapids. Tours usually depart at 9am. The ultimate rafting adventure is the three-day, two-night 'River Rush' (Ikr59,800). There are usually three departures per summer – trips start on a Monday (see website for details).

NORTHWEST ICELAND

South along Rte 752 (11km from the Ring Road), the farm **Bakkaflöt** (☎ 453 8245; www.river rafting.com) also offers rafting on the Jökulsá Vestari and the Jökulsá Austari (Ikr6400 to Ikr9400 per person), departing at 10am and 2pm every day. The centre also has an uber-comfy guest house (sleeping bag/single/double Ikr3300/6500/10,000) with hot pots and a swimming pool.

HORSE RIDING & HORSE SHOWS

Hestasport Activity Tours (☎ 453 8383; www.riding.is) is one of Iceland's most respected riding outfits, offering one-hour horse rides for Ikr4000 and full-day rides for Ikr12,000. Longer trips (around €2000) are also available (book well in advance), including eight-day trips (five days in the saddle) along lesser-known routes through the untouched highlands. Winter riding trips (€1795) are available upon demand.

The farm **Lýtingsstaðir** (☎ 453 8064; www.lythorse .com), 19km south of Varmahlíð on Rte 752, offers a similar program of trips and hourly riding. They also feature a 'stop and ride' package that includes accommodation, breakfast, dinner and a two-hour ride for €110. Longer tours (from €860) are also available.

Regular horse shows are hosted by **Flugmýri** (☎ 453 8814; www.flugmyri.com; 1hr Ikr2200) and **Varmilækur** (☎ 898 7756; www.varmilaekur.is; 1hr Ikr2000). They showcase the five gaits of the Icelandic horse, and detail the breed's history. Both ranches also offer riding tours and are located within 10km of Varmahlíð. Ask at the tourist office for an up-to-date schedule of events.

SUPER-JEEP TOURS

Conveniently located near the doorway to the Icelandic 'Outback', Varmahlíð is also a fine place to join a 'super-Jeep' tour of the rugged highlands. Day trips visit the bubbling pools of Laugafell, while overnight adventures loop through the highlands connecting Laugafell, Askja, Herðubreið and Mývatn. Try **JSJ Tours** (☎ 453 8219; www.simnet.is/jeppaferdir; day trip/overnight Ikr7500/20,000) or ask at the information centre.

Sleeping & Eating

There are plenty of places to crash in the area – ask at the information centre or use the handy *Áning* guide or *Icelandic Farm Holidays* booklet. Campers can pitch a tent at **Lauftún** (sites per person Ikr500, dm Ikr1500) along the Ring Road opposite the service station. There's also a more secluded **camp-site** (sites per person Ikr1000) up the hill near the swimming pool.

Hestaport Cottages (☎ 453 8383; www.rafting .is; 2-person cottages Jun-Sep Ikr16,800, Oct-May Ikr9500) Perched on the hill above Varmahlíð (follow the gravel road past Hótel Varmahlíð), this group of self-contained timber cottages has good views, comfy rooms and a very inviting stone hot pool.

Hótel Varmahlíð (☎ 453 8170; www.hotelvarmahlid .is; s/d mid-Jun–Aug Ikr15,900/19,900, May–mid-Jun & Sep Ikr11,500/14,500, Oct-May Ikr8100/10,500; 🖵 🛜) This bland hotel dominates the area and has unmemorable but well-maintained rooms. Its restaurant (mains Ikr2500 to Ikr4100), however, is one of the best places in the region to try the local delicacy, foal, and the scrumptious lamb comes from the manager's own flock.

Getting There & Away

All buses from Reykjavík (4½ hours) and Akureyri (one hour) stop at the terminal between the tourist office and the supermarket. From May to August there are daily buses to Sauðárkrókur (30 minutes) and from there to Siglufjörður (daily except Saturday, 1¼ hours). The Trex Kjölur route comes out of the highlands at Varmahlíð.

VARMAHLÍÐ TO AKUREYRI (ÖXNADALUR)

If you haven't the time to explore scenic Skagafjörður, you'll pass instead through Öxnadalur, a narrow 30km-long valley on the Ring Road between Varmahlíð and Akureyri. Stunning peaks and thin pinnacles of rock flank the mountain pass – the imposing 1075m spire of **Hraundrangi** and the surrounding peaks of **Háafjall** are among the most dramatic in Iceland.

It's worth stopping for dinner at **Halastjarna** (☎ 461 2200; www.halastjarna.is; Háls; 3-course dinner around Ikr3000; 🕙 noon-10pm daily Jun-Aug, Sat & Sun Sep-Dec), near the summit of the pass. Hobbit-sized antiques abound and scrumptious locally sourced dishes (the menu changes daily) are served on mismatched dishware. Book ahead.

GLAUMBÆR

Following Rte 75 north from Varmahlíð towards Skagafjörður's marshy delta leads to the 18th-century **turf farm museum** (☎ 453 6173;

adult/under 16yr Ikr600/free; (◯ 9am-6pm Jun–mid-Sep) at **Glaumbær**. It's the best museum of its type in northern Iceland and well worth the easy 8km detour.

Stuffed full of period furniture, equipment and utensils, the 18th-and 19th- century buildings are now a beautifully restored collection of 12 turf houses that give a real insight into the cramped living conditions of that time.

Also on the site are two 19th-century timber houses, both examples of early wooden homes that replaced the turf dwellings. One house is now used as the gift shop while the other is home to **Áskaffi** (☎ 453 8855; (◯ 9am-6pm Jun-Aug), an impossibly quaint cafe with a roaring turf fire, old-world atmosphere and dollhouse dishware. Keep an eye out for the brochure explaining the history behind its tasty traditional Icelandic cakes. It's a perfect spot to while away some time sipping coffee and writing postcards.

Snorri Þorfinnsson, the first European born in North America (in 1004; see the boxed text, p173), is buried near the **church** at Glaumbær.

Buses between Varmahlíð and Sauðárkrókur pass Glaumbær daily in summer.

SAUÐÁRKRÓKUR
pop 2400

As the winding Jökulsá river collides with the marshy delta of upper Skagafjörður, you'll find scenic Sauðárkrókur sitting quietly at the edge of the windy waterway.

Economically, Sauðárkrókur is pretty well off, with fishing, tanning and trading keeping the community afloat and the population young and energetic. The community has all the services you'll need – a bank, a library, a laundry and a supermarket. There is, however, no information centre.

The town museum, **Minjahúsið** (☎ 453 6870; Aðalgata 16b; adult/under 16yr Ikr600/free; (◯ 1-6pm Jun-Aug), gives a great insight into local life in times past, with a series of restored workshops illustrating the day-to-day living conditions for local blacksmiths, carpenters, saddlers and watchmakers.

Sleeping

Campsite (☎ 453 8860) The free campsite beside the swimming pool has toilets, hot water and power. If the site is full, there is additional space by the church.

Gistiheimilið Mikligarður (☎ 453 6880; www.mikligardur.is; Kirkjutorgi 3; s/d without bathroom Ikr7800/11,300, with bathroom Ikr11,000/14,500; (◯) Absolutely adorable in every way possible, this welcoming spot near the church has comfortable, modern rooms with TV and tasteful decor. There's also a spacious guest kitchen and TV lounge. Sleeping bag accommodation (Ikr3500) is available in winter.

Hótel Mikligarður (☎ 891 9147; www.mikligardur.is; sb/s/d incl breakfast Ikr4000/14,000/18,000; (◯ Jun–Aug; 🖥 (◯) The district boarding school becomes a basic but rather characterless hotel in summer. This is where you'll end up when everything else is full.

Hótel Tindastóll (☎ 453 5002; www.hoteltindastoll.com; Lindargata 3; s/d incl breakfast Jun-Aug Ikr15,800/21,400, Sep-May Ikr8900/12,000; (🖥 (◯) Tucked away in this understated town, Hótel Tindastóll is a charming boutique hotel dating from 1884 (apparently making it Iceland's oldest hotel). The individually decorated rooms seamlessly blend period furniture and modern style. Outside there is an irresistible stone hot tub, and in the basement there's a cosy bar where you can while away your evenings. Legend has it that Marlene Dietrich stayed here in 1941.

Eating

Kaffi Krókur (☎ 453 6299; Aðalgata 16; mains Ikr900-3500; (◯ 11.30am-11pm Sun-Thu, to 3am Fri & Sat; (◯) The chef's motto is 'never trust a skinny cook' and we'd be keen on gaining a few kilos here! The menu covers everything from burgers, fish and lamb dishes to fillet of foal and authentic pasta.

Ólafshús (☎ 453 6454; Aðalgata 15; pizzas Ikr1020-3120, mains Ikr1290-3190; (◯ 11am-10.30pm Sun-Thu, to 11pm Fri & Sat) Almost across the road from Kaffi Krókur (and owned by the same people), this is a good choice for pizzas and Icelandic specialities such as fish and lamb. There's also some choice for vegetarians. The restaurant bar is open until 3am on Friday and Saturday.

There's a **supermarket** (Skagfirðingabraut) and a **Vín Búð** (Smáragrund 2).

Getting There & Away

In summer, two buses run daily between Varmahlíð and Sauðárkrókur, connecting with the Ring Road buses to Reykjavík and Akureyri. They leave from the shop opposite Hótel Tindastóll.

WESTERN SKAGAFJÖRÐUR

North of Sauðárkrókur, Skagafjörður's western coast is a stunningly silent place capped by scenic mountains that cast shadows over the islet-strewn sea.

Tindastóll

North of Sauðárkrókur, **Tindastóll** (989m) is a prominent Skagafjörður landmark, extending for 18km along the coast. The mountain and its caves are believed to be inhabited by an array of sea monsters, trolls and giants, one of which kidnapped the daughter of an early bishop of Hólar.

The summit of Tindastóll affords a spectacular view across all of Skagafjörður. The easiest way to the top is along the marked trail that starts from the high ground along Rte 745 west of the mountain. At the mountain's northern end is a geothermal area, Reykir, which was mentioned in *Grettir's Saga*. Grettir supposedly swam ashore from the island of Drangey (below), and soothed his aching bones in an inviting spring. Today, that very pool, **Grettislaug** (Grettir's Bath; adult/under 12yr Ikr300/free), is a popular spot with well-equipped camping facilities nearby.

From the farm Tunga, at the southwestern foot of Tindastóll, it's an 8km climb to the **Trölli mountain hut** at N 65°42.603', W 19°53.163'. The hut has 18 beds but no cooking facilities. To book, contact **Ferðafélags Skagafirðinga** (☎ 862 5907; www.ffs.is) or ask at the tourist office in Varmahlíð.

Drangey & Málmey

Guarding the mouth of Skagafjörður are the uninhabited islands of Drangey and Málmey, tranquil havens for nesting sea birds. Both are accessible on summer boat tours.

The tiny rocky islet of **Drangey** (*drowngay*), in the middle of Skagafjörður, is a dramatic flat-topped mass of tuff with 170m-high sheer cliff sides rising abruptly from the water. The cliffs serve as nesting sites for around a million sea birds, and have been used throughout Iceland's history as 'nature's grocery store'. *Grettir's Saga* recounts that both Grettir and his brother Illugi lived on the island for three years and were slain there.

The gentler 2.5-sq-km **Málmey** rises to just over 150m and is known mainly for its abundance of sea birds. Legend has it that no couple could live here for more than 20 years or

the wife would disappear. Málmey has been uninhabited since 1951.

Drangeyjarferðir (Jón Eiríksson; ☎ 847 9800, 453 6310; tours Ikr6000) is the only formal tour operator that visits Drangey, offering three-hour trips departing from Reykir (near Grettislaug; left), 16km north of Sauðárkrókur. **Málmeyarferðir** (☎ 894 2881; tours Ikr5000), based in Hólsos, runs boat trips to Málmey (minimum six people). Tours are in Icelandic, but informative brochures are available in English. The information centre in Varmahlíð (p204) can help you book either adventure.

HÓLAR Í HJALTADALUR

With its prominent red-sandstone church dwarfed by the looming Tröllskagi mountains, tiny **Hólar** (www.holar.is) makes an interesting historical detour from the Ring Rd. The bishopric of Hólar was the ecumenical and educational capital of northern Iceland between 1106 and the Reformation, and it continued as a religious centre and the home of the northern bishops until 1798, when the bishop's seat was abolished.

Hólar then became a vicarage until 1861, when the vicarage was shifted west to Viðvík. In 1882 the present agricultural school was established, and in 1952 the vicarage returned to Hólar.

Sights

Completed in 1763, Hólar's red-sandstone **cathedral** (☉ 10am-6pm Jun-Aug, Sun services 11am, evening prayer 6pm) was built from stone taken from looming Hólabyrða, and is the oldest stone church in Iceland. The church was financed by donations from Lutheran congregations all over Scandinavia and is brimming with historical works of art, including a baptismal font carved from a piece of soapstone that washed in from Greenland on an ice floe. The extraordinary carved altarpiece was made in Germany (or the Netherlands – no one knows for sure) around 1500 and was donated by the last Catholic bishop of Hólar, Jón Arason, in 1522. After he and his sons were executed at Skálholt for opposition to the Danish Reformation, his remains were brought to Hólar and entombed in the bell tower. The present church tower was built in 1950 as a memorial. It contains a mosaic of the good reverend, a chapel and his tomb.

You can pick up a church leaflet from the information desk in the accommodation block.

An informative historical-trail brochure (available at the info desk) guides you round some of the other buildings at Hólar and is well worth picking up. **Nýibær** is an historical turf farm dating from the mid-19th century and inhabited until 1945. Although the rooms here are unfurnished, a leaflet gives a good insight into how the buildings would have looked when in use.

Also worth seeing is **Auðunarstofa**, a replica of the 14th-century bishop's residence. Built using traditional techniques and tools, Auðunarstofa houses the current bishop's office and study room, and has an exhibition of 13th-century chalices, vestments and books in the basement.

At the time of research, a new building was being refurbished to house the **Icelandic Horse History Centre** (☎ 455 6300; www.sogusetur.is), which will feature a comprehensive permanent exhibit about Iceland's unique breed and its role in Iceland's history.

High on a hill behind the church is **Prestssæti**, a wonderful vantage point offering great views over the valley.

Ongoing archaeological digs in Hólar can be seen to the right of the road as you drive in – feel free to stop by and ask the friendly diggers about their research.

Sleeping & Eating

Ferðaþjónustan Holum Hjaltadal (☎ 455 6333; www .holar.is; sb/s/d Ikr3500/6900/7900; 🕑 Jun-Aug; 🖳 🖭) The college accommodation block offers summer stays in the vacant student apartments further afield. Alternatively, wooden cabins in the grounds sleep between two and 12 people and cost from Ikr11,900 per night. There's also a small campsite (Ikr700 per person) tucked away in the forest. Reception is open from 8am to 10pm. The on-site restaurant specialises in local foods (mains Ikr2850 to Ikr3200) and not-so-local pizza (Ikr1450), and there's a swimming pool (Ikr350/150 per adult/child under 12 years; open 10am to 8pm). Additional perks include an on-site ATM and an internet terminal (15 minutes for Ikr200).

Getting There & Away

Visiting Hólar is easiest by private vehicle. However, the buses between Siglufjörður and Sauðarkrókur (580 and 580a) do stop here. Buses run in summer every day (except Saturday)– it's 15 minutes from Sauðarkrókur and one hour from Siglufjörður.

EASTERN SKAGAFJÖRÐUR

The spectacular eastern coast of Skagafjörður lies along the rugged Tröllaskagi Peninsula. The dramatic scenery is more reminiscent of the Westfjords than the gentle hills that roll through most of northern Iceland. Craggy mountains and gushing rivers are ideal for hikers, and the views out the car window along Rte 76 are nothing short of breathtaking.

Hofsós
pop 180

The sleepy but attractive fishing village of Hofsós has been a trading centre since the 1500s. Today, several restored buildings along the harbour have been turned into the **Icelandic Emigration Center** (Vesturfarasafnið; ☎ 453 7935; www. hofsos.is; adult/under 12yr Ikr1000/free; 🕑 11am-6pm Jun-Aug), which explores the reasons behind Icelanders' emigration to the New World, their hopes for a new life, and the reality of conditions when they arrived. The main exhibition 'New Land, New Life' follows the lives of emigrating Icelanders through carefully curated photographs, letters and displays. It's an interesting place, even if you're not a descendant of Icelandic emigrants.

Also at the harbour is the historic, black-tarred **Pakkhúsið** (🕑 by arrangement), a log warehouse built in 1777 by the Danish Royal Greenland Company. It's one of the oldest timber buildings in Iceland.

American poet Bill Holm, of *Windows of Brimnes* fame, lived just across from the emigration centre until his death in 2009. Iceland's most famous religious poet, Hallgrímur Pétursson was born 3km south of the river at **Gröf**, which has an old turf-roofed church surrounded by a circular turf wall. Call ☎ 453 7460 to get in.

If you want to spend the night, the emigration center can handle your accommodation queries. You'll find sleeping-bag space (Ikr2500) at two simple cottages, Prestbakki and Kárastígur 9, in the village, and cosier digs at **Gistiheimilið Sunnuberg** (☎ 453 7310; gisting@hofsos.is; Sudurbraut 8; s/d Ikr6000/8500) opposite the petrol station.

Down at the small harbour among the museum buildings, **Sólvík** (☎ 453 7930; mains Ikr1390-3200; 🕑 11am-10pm Jun-Aug) is a pleasant country-style restaurant with an assortment of fish dishes and a large ice-cream bar. Enjoy a coffee or a beer on the welcoming summer verandah.

There's a bank, a post office and a petrol station here, and the Siglufjörður bus stops in town.

Lónkot

Battered by the wind and wonderfully blustery, **Lónkot** (☎ 453 7432; www.lonkot.is; 3-/4-course menu from Ikr5500/6500; ☺ May-Oct) is a gourmet pit stop sitting along the rugged coast between Hofsós and Siglufjörður. Smooth trumpet jazz fills the air as diners indulge in a 'safari' of finely tuned Icelandic recipes.

Lónkot also has pleasant accommodation (sleeping bag/linen Ikr4000/5500) in a traditional farmhouse with super sea views across to **Málmey** and the bizarre promontory **Þórðarhöfði**, which is tethered to the mainland by a delicate spit.

SIGLUFJÖRÐUR

pop 1280

The isolated fishing village of Siglufjörður sits precariously at the foot of a steep slope overlooking a beautiful fjord. Once one of Iceland's boom towns, it's now a quiet but endearing kind of place with a dramatic setting, plenty of historic buildings and a wonderful museum detailing the town's former glory as the herring-fishing capital of Iceland.

In its heyday Siglufjörður was home to 10,000 workers, and fishing boats crammed into the small harbour to unload their catch for the waiting women to gut and salt. After the herring abruptly disappeared from Iceland's north coast in the late 1960s, Siglufjörður abruptly declined and never fully recovered.

Information

There's a small but helpful **tourist point** (www .siglo.is) in the herring museum with a detailed map of the town and the surrounding hiking trails.

Sights

The main attraction in town is **Síldarminjasafnið** (Herring Era Museum; ☎ 467 1604; www.sild.is; Snorragata 15; adult/12-16yr Ikr800/400; ☺ 10am-6pm mid-Jun–late Aug, 1-5pm May–mid-Jun & late Aug-Sep, by appointment in winter), a re-creation of Siglufjörður's boom days between 1903 and 1968. Set in an old

Norwegian herring station, the museum brings the work and lives of the town's inhabitants vividly to life. In the first building, photographs, displays and 1930s film show the fishing and salting process, while the accommodation block is left much as it would have been when in use. Next door is a re-creation of the reducing plant, where the majority of herrings were separated into oil (a valuable commodity) and meal (used for fertiliser). The third and newest building is a re-creation of harbour life, with actual trawler boats and equipment based on life on the busy pier during the boom days.

If you're travelling in midsummer it's worth planning to visit on a Saturday when **herring-salting demonstrations** (admission Ikr600; ☺ 3pm Jul) are held, accompanied by lively concertina music and theatrical performances.

Thanks to its proximity to the bishopric in Hólar, music has always been of particular importance in Tröllaskagi, and Siglufjörður has a strong musical tradition. The **Icelandic Folk Music Centre** (☎ 467 2300; www.siglo.is/setur; Norðurgata 1; adult/under 14yr Ikr600/free; ☺ 10am-6pm Jul-Aug, 10am-5pm Jun) opened in 2006 and explores the history and development of Icelandic folk music. The collection is housed in the former home of Reverend Bjorn Thorsteinsson, who collected many of the instruments and recordings of traditional songs, nursery rhymes and chants on display.

Activities

Siglufjörður is a great base for hikers, with a series of interesting **walks** in the area. Seven of these routes are described in detail on the town website, www.siglo.is.

For a short hike you can walk north along the western shore of Siglufjörður to the abandoned herring factory, which was destroyed by an avalanche in 1919. Longer hikes will take you over the passes Hósarð and Hussarð to the wild, beautiful and uninhabited Héðinsfjörður, the next fjord to the east.

The most popular hike, however, is along the old road between Siglufjörður and Fljótavík. This allegedly haunted road was once the main route into town but was closed when an 800m-long tunnel was built. The route is prone to avalanches and only opens between early July and late August. It climbs up to the 630m Siglufjarðarskarð pass and then heads north along the ridge to Strákar, from where there are wonderful views over the fjord and out to sea.

NORTHWEST ICELAND

In winter a **ski lift** (day pass Ikr800) operates in Skarðsdalur above the head of the fjord. From there, it's a lovely day walk over Hólsfjall to the abandoned valley above Héðinsfjörður. In summer you can opt for a nine-hole round of golf at the Hóll sports centre.

Festivals & Events

Despite the utter demise of the herring industry, Siglufjörður remains nostalgic about the good old days and plays host to a lively **herring festival** on the bank holiday weekend in early August. It's one of Iceland's most enjoyable local festivals, with much singing, dancing, drinking, feasting and fish cleaning.

An annual Icelandic and foreign **folkmusic festival** (þjóðlagahátíð á Siglufirði; http://festival.fjallabyggd.is) is staged over five days in early July, with workshops and several concerts every evening.

Sleeping & Eating

Most sleeping and eating options can be scouted on Aðalgata – turn away from the looming church when you reach the town square.

Campsite (☎ 460 5600; sites per tent/caravan Ikr700/1000; ☼ Jun-Aug) Oddly placed right in the middle of town near the harbour and town square, this municipal campsite has a toilet block and showers. You'll find a second patch of grass beyond the city limits – follow Suðurgata out of town towards the tunnel to Ólafsfjörður.

Siglufjörður HI Hostel (Gistiheimilið Hvanneyri; ☎ 467 1378; alla@simnet.is; Aðalgata 10; sb/d Ikr2100/5800) Showing no signs of its former glory, Siglufjörður's best choice is a rather faded four-storey guest house caught in a decor time warp. There's a TV lounge, a huge dining room, a guest kitchen and a smattering of common bathrooms (the best one is on the third floor).

Aðalbakarí (☎ 467 1720; Aðalgata 36; ☼ 7am-5pm Mon-Sat) Ideal for breakfast or lunch, this bakery and cafe serves the usual selection of bread, cakes, pastries and filled rolls as well as the Icelandic speciality *ástar pungur* (love balls) – deep-fried spiced balls of dough.

Allinn (☎ 467 1111; Aðalgata 30; mains Ikr800-2000; ☼ 10am-1am Sun-Thu, to 3am Fri & Sat) This popular diner is the only genuine restaurant in town and serves good-value burgers, pizzas, fish and lamb dishes.

Pizza 67/Torgið (☎ 467 2323; Aðalgata; mains Ikr1500-2000; ☼ 11am-10pm Mon-Sat, 1-10pm Sun) Just down the road, this basic pizzeria is the only other dining option.

There's a **Samkaup-úrval supermarket** (☎ 467 1201; ☼ 9am-7pm Mon-Fri, 10am-7pm Sat, 11am-7pm Sun) across from the harbour, and fishmonger **Fiskbuð Siglufjörður** (☼ 8am-12.15pm & 2-6pm Mon-Fri, 10am-1pm Sat) is opposite Allinn. The Vín Búð is on Tungata near the intersection with Eyrargata.

Getting There & Away

From June to August there is a bus service that runs every day except Saturday (with two services on Tuesday and Friday) between Varmahlíð and Siglufjörður with a change in Sauðárkrókur.

A tunnel through the mountain will cut the journey between Siglufjörður and Ólafsfjörður (in Western Eyjafjörður; p224) to only 15km; it's expected to be finished in 2010. This is the quickest way to reach Akureyri from here. If the tunnel is not yet open, you can follow Rte 82 across the Tröllskagi Peninsula.

AKUREYRI

pop 17,500

Akureyri stands strong as Iceland's second city, but a Melbourne, Manchester or Montreal it is not. And how could it be? There are only 17,000 residents! It's a wonder the city (which would be 'town' in any other country) generates this much buzz. Expect bustling cafes, gourmet restaurants and a latenight bustle – a far cry from the other towns in rural Iceland.

Snowcapped peaks rise behind the town, and across the city flower boxes, trees and well-tended gardens belie the city's location just a stone's throw from the Arctic Circle. With a lively summer festival season, some of Iceland's best winter skiing, and a relaxed and easy attitude, it's the natural base for exploring Eyjafjörður.

HISTORY

The first permanent inhabitant of Eyjafjörður was Norse-Irish settler Helgi Magri (Helgi the Lean), who arrived in about 890. Although Helgi worshipped Þór and let the gods choose an auspicious site for him to settle by tossing his high-seat pillars overboard (they washed up 7km south of present-day Akureyri), he

AKUREYRI

0   700 m
0   0.4 miles

INFORMATION
Akureyri Hospital..................1 C3
Þvottahúsið Höfði..................2 C3

SIGHTS & ACTIVITIES
Akureyri Museum..................3 C4
Icelandic Aviation Museum..................4 D4
Jaðarsvöllur..................5 B4
Nonnahús..................6 C4

SLEEPING
Akureyri HI Hostel..................7 B1

EATING
Bónus Supermarket..................8 B1
Brynja..................9 C3
Café Brauðbúð Konditori........(see 8)
Netto Supermarket..................10 C1

DRINKING
Vélsmiðjan..................11 D2

TRANSPORT
Avis..................(see 12)
Budget..................12 D4
Dollar-Thrifty/Saga..................13 C1
Hertz..................(see 12)
National..................14 C1

hedged his bets by naming his farm Kristnes (Christ's Peninsula).

By 1602 a trading post had been established at present-day Akureyri. There were still no permanent dwellings, though, as all the settlers maintained rural farms and homesteads. By the late 18th century the town had accumulated a whopping 10 residents, all Danish traders, and was granted municipal status.

The town soon began to prosper and by 1900 Akureyri's population numbered 1370. The original cooperative, Gránufélagsins, had begun to decline and in 1906 it was replaced by Kaupfélagið Eyjafirðinga Akureyrar (KEA; the Akureyri Cooperative Society), whose ubiquitous insignia still graces many Akureyri businesses.

Today Akureyri is thriving. Its fishing company and shipyard are the largest in the country, and the city's university (established in 1987) gives the town a youthful exuberance.

ORIENTATION

Akureyri is small and easy to get around on foot, with a compact knot of cafes, bars, museums and shops just west of the busy commercial harbour. The town centre is concentrated around pedestrianised Hafnarstræti, with the small square Raðhústorg at its northern end. At the time of research, there were confirmed plans to move the information centre to the Hof near the harbour. This should happen sometime in 2010 once construction is complete.

LONG WEEKEND REMIX: THE NORTHERN TRIANGLE

Perfectly positioned in the cool Atlantic waters between North America and Europe, Iceland has become the *it* destination for a sexy weekend getaway. For the last decade, savvy jetsetters have hopped over in droves for a romp in happenin' Reykjavík, and tourist numbers spiked when the currency crashed in October 2008.

The constant stream of tourists has turned the three-day Reykjavík–Ring Road–Blue Lagoon trip into a well-worn circuit, so why not blaze a new trail and tackle Iceland's northern triangle of stunning attractions: Mývatn, Húsavík and Akureyri. It's a lot less legwork than you think – when you land at Keflavík airport, catch the Flybus to Reykjavík's domestic terminal, then hop on one of the many daily flights up to Akureyri (p221). And to make things even simpler, here's a handy li'l planner:

Day 1 – Akureyri

Jump-start your visit to the north with something quintessentially Icelandic: **horse riding** (p226). Trust us – these aren't your usual horses. Then, a half-day is plenty of time to bop around the charming streets in the city centre (start on pedestrian-friendly **Hafnarstræti**). Or for those who can withstand another plane ride, it's worth spending the afternoon on **Grimsey** (p225), Iceland's only slice of the Arctic Circle. For dinner, splurge on the ultimate Icelandic meal at **Friðrik V** (p220), then flex your drinking arm with a spirited night out on the town. It doesn't matter where you toss a few back 'cause you won't escape the wrath of the **runtur** (see the boxed text, p221).

Day 2 – Húsavík

In the morning, early risers can snoop around some of the region's hidden spots (see the boxed text, p241); hangover victims should head straight to Húsavík. First, swing by the **Húsavík Whale Museum** (p240) for a bit of background info, then hop aboard a **whale-watching tour** (p240). Get an eyeful of petrified manhood at the **Iceland Phallological Museum** (p241) before recounting your whale tales over dinner at **Gamli Baukur** (p244).

Day 3 – Mývatn

For those of you who have been drooling over the tantalising photos of Iceland's turquoise-tinted spa springs, fret not. Mývatn has its very own version of the Blue Lagoon! Known as the **Mývatn Nature Baths** (p232), it's smaller than its southern brother, but noticeably less touristy. After a leisurely soak, it's time to get the blood flowing again. Try the three-hour hike around **Eastern Mývatn** (p234), which takes in a veritable smorgasbord of geological anomalies. A stop at stinky **Hverir** (p238) is a must, and, if time permits, have a wander around the steam vents at **Krafla** (p238). Then make your way back to Akureyri to catch your flight, but not before visiting one last site – **Goðafoss** (p223) – a heavenly waterfall that looks like it's been ripped straight from an ad for shampoo.

INFORMATION

Bookshops

Fróði (Map p214; Kaupvangsstræti) Secondhand bookshop next to Café Karolína.

Eymundsson (Map p214; ☎ 461 5050; Hafnarstræti 91-93; ⊙ 9am-10pm) Excellent bookshop with souvenir books and DVDs in many languages. A great place to relax with a coffee and cookie, and thumb through gorgeous coffee-table hardbacks.

Emergency

Fire and ambulance (☎ 112, 462 2222)
Police (Map p214; ☎ 464 7700; Þórunnarstræti 138)

Internet Access

Akureyri is covered in a veritable blanket of wi-fi – most guest houses have connections, as do several cafes and museums. There are two internet terminals at the tourist information centre (opposite). The municipal library has computers and wi-fi as well (opposite).

Laundry

Most of Akureyri's accommodation offers laundry service for guests.

Þvottahúsið Höfði (Map p211; ☎ 462 2580; Hafnarstræti 34; loads up to 7kg Ikr2000; ⊙ 8am-noon & 3-5pm Mon-Fri) Service laundry.

NORTHWEST ICELAND

Libraries

Municipal Library of Akureyri (Amtsbókasafnið á Akureyri; Map p214; ☎ 460 1250; www.amtsbok.is; Brekkugata 17; 10am-7pm Mon-Fri Jun-Aug, 10am-7pm Mon-Fri, noon-5pm Sat Sep-May) One of the largest libraries in Iceland, this impressive complex holds a vast assortment of books and DVDs in both Icelandic and English. The welcoming cafe and internet kiosks often lure travellers.

Medical Services

Akureyri Hospital (Map p211; ☎ 463 0100; Eyrarlandsvegur)

Heilsugæslustöðin Health Care Centre (Map p214; ☎ 460 4600; Hafnarstræti 99) Doctors on call around the clock.

Money

All central bank branches (open 9am to 4pm) offer commission-free foreign exchange and have 24-hour ATMs. After hours, ask at Hótel KEA. Banks also distribute the all-important parking clocks (see p222).

Byr (Map p214; ☎ 575 4000; Skipagata 9)
Íslandsbanki (Map p214; ☎ 440 4000; Skipagata 14)
Kaupþing (Map p214; Geislagata 5)
Landsbanki (Map p214; ☎ 410 4162; Strandgata 1)

Post

Main Post Office (Map p214; ☎ 580 1000; Skipagata 10; 9am-4.30pm Mon-Fri)

Tourist Information

Tourist Information Centre (Map p214; ☎ 553 5999; www.visitakureyri.is; Hafnarstræti 82 or Hof; 7.30am-7pm mid-Jun–Aug, 8am-5pm Sep–mid-Jun) Friendly, efficient tourist office with internet access. The office is planning to move to Hof, the new Culture House (Map p214) by the harbour, in 2010. The info office sometimes opens on weekends in the colder months – this depends largely on government funding.

Travel Agencies

Domestic flights (including those to/from Grímsey) can be purchased online – travel agents don't offer any special deals. The tourist information centre (above) can help you with tour and travel bookings. It can also assist with booking accommodation in the area (and it will charge a phoning fee of Ikr500 if it takes a while to secure lodging). **Nonni Travel** (Map p214; ☎ 461 1841; www.nonnitravel.is; Brekkugata 5; 8am-6pm) is able to hook you up with just about any tour in the area.

SIGHTS
Churches

Dominating the town from high on a hill, **Akureyrarkirkja** (Map p214; Eyrarlandsvegur) was designed by Guðjón Samúelsson, the architect responsible for Reykjavík's Hallgrímskirkja. The church continues his geological theme, but is less blatantly 'basalt' and has a more traditional interior.

Built in 1940, Akureyrarkirkja contains a large and beautiful 3200-pipe organ and a series of rather untraditional reliefs of the life of Christ. There's also an unusual interpretation of the crucifixion and a suspended ship hanging from the ceiling. The ship reflects an old Nordic tradition of votive offerings for the protection of loved ones at sea. Perhaps the most striking feature, however, is the beautiful central window in the chancel, which originally graced Coventry Cathedral in England.

The **Catholic church** (Map p214; Eyrarlandsvegur 26) is an attractive old house built in 1912 and acquired by the church in 1952. On the nearby roundabout is Einar Jónsson's sculpture *Útlaginn* (The Outlaw).

Museums

Akureyri has several museums, and although it's laudable that the town celebrates its artists and authors, many of these institutions are of limited interest unless you have a particular admiration for a specific artist's work. If you have your own vehicle, consider visiting some of greater Eyjafjörður's museums flanking the eastern and western shores.

The **Akureyri Museum** (Minjasafnið á Akureyri; Map p211; ☎ 462 4162; www.minjasafnid.is; Aðalstræti 58; adult/under 16yr Ikr500/free; 10am-5pm daily Jun–mid-Sep, 2-4pm Sat mid-Sep–May) houses an interesting collection of art and historical items from the Settlement Era to the present. Among the displays are photographs, farming tools and re-creations of early Icelandic homes. An interesting exhibit details the life of early settlers along Eyjafjörður and displays artefacts from Gásir, one of Iceland's most fruitful archaeological digs. Plans are afoot to turn the site (near Árskógsströnd; p223) into an interactive historical attraction. Stay tuned for details. The **museum garden** became the first place in Iceland to cultivate trees when a nursery was established here in 1899.

Escape the bad weather with a little browse at the **Akureyri Art Museum** (Listasafnið á Akureyri; Map p214; ☎ 462 7610; www.listasafn.akureyri.is; Kaupvangsstræti

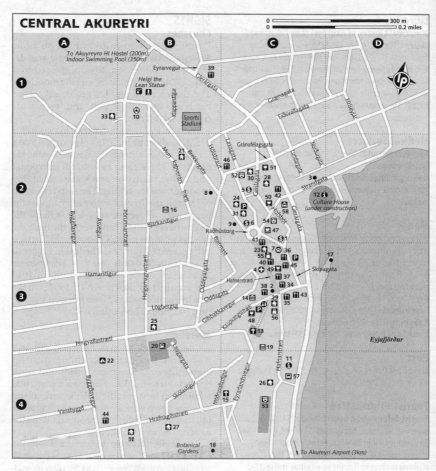

CENTRAL AKUREYRI

12; admission free; ☼ noon-5pm Tue-Sun). The emphasis is innovation, so expect sophisticated contributions from of a variety of local and international artists from Goya to Matthew Barney (Mr Björk).

In a hangar at Akureyri airport, the newly improved **Icelandic Aviation Museum** (Flugsafn Íslands; Map p211; ☎ 461 4400; www.flugsafn.is; admission lkr500; ☼ 1-5pm Jun-Aug, by appointment Sep-May) charts the history of aviation in Iceland, from the first flight in 1919 to the present. Several restored aircraft fill the exhibition space, including a coast-guard helicopter and the remains of a British war craft that crashed near Akureyri during WWII.

Celebrating 100 years of industry, the **Akureyri Industrial Museum** (Iðnaðarsafnið á Akureyri;

off Map p211; ☎ 462 3600; www.idnadarsafnid.is; Krókeyri; adult/under 16yr lkr500/free; ☼ 1-5pm Jun–mid-Sep, 2-4pm Sat mid-Sep–May) gives a bit of insight into Akureyri's past, with artefacts from more than 40 local companies.

The most interesting of the artists' homes, **Nonnahús** (Map p211; ☎ 462 3555; www.nonni.is; Aðalstræti 54; adult/under 16yr lkr500/free; ☼ 10am-5pm Jun-Aug) was once the childhood home of the renowned children's writer Reverend Jón Sveinsson (1857–1944), known to most as Nonni. The house dates from 1850; its cramped rooms and simple furnishings provide a poignant insight into life in 19th-century Iceland. A collection of old photographs and original books completes the display.

INFORMATION
- Byr ... 1 C2
- Eymundsson ... 2 C3
- Ferðafélag Akureyrar ... 3 C2
- Froði ... (see 48)
- Heilsugæslustöðin Health Care Centre ... 4 C3
- Íslandsbanki ... (see 45)
- Kaupþing ... 5 C2
- Landsbanki ... 6 C2
- Main Post Office ... 7 C3
- Municipal Library of Akureyri ... 8 B2
- Nonni Travel ... 9 C2
- Police Station ... 10 B1
- Tourist Information Centre ... 11 C4
- Tourist Information Centre (Proposed) ... 12 C2

SIGHTS & ACTIVITIES
- Akureyrarkirkja ... 13 C3
- Akureyri Art Museum ... 14 C3
- Catholic Church ... 15 C4
- Davíðshús ... 16 B2
- Haffarí ... 17 D3
- Húni II ... (see 17)
- Lystigarðurinn ... 18 B4
- Matthías Jochumsson Memorial Museum (Sigurhæðir) ... 19 C3
- Swimming Pool ... 20 B3

SLEEPING
- AkurInn ... 21 B2
- Campsite ... 22 A4
- Gistiheimili Akureyrar ... 23 C3
- Gula Villan ... 24 C2
- Gula Villan II ... 25 B3
- Hotel Akureyri ... 26 C4
- Hotel Edda ... 27 B4
- Hótel Harpa ... (see 29)
- Hotel Ibuðir ... 28 C2
- Hótel KEA ... 29 C3
- Hótel Norðurland ... 30 C2
- Hrafninn ... 31 C2
- Sólgarðar ... (see 24)
- Súlur ... 32 B4
- Súlur II ... 33 A1

EATING
- 1011 ... 34 C3
- Bautinn ... 35 C3
- Bryggjan ... 36 C3
- Cafe Páris (Blaá Kannan) ... 37 C3
- Friðrik V ... 38 C3
- Greifinn ... 39 B1
- Indian Curry Hut ... 40 C3
- Kristjáns Bakarí ... 41 C2
- Krua Siam ... 42 C2
- La Vita é Bella ... 43 C3
- Nætursalan ... (see 54)
- Rosagarðurinn ... (see 29)
- RUB 23 ... (see 48)
- Samkaup-Strax Supermarket ... 44 A4
- Strikið ... 45 C3
- Vín Búð ... 46 C2

DRINKING
- Café Amour ... 47 C2
- Café Karolína ... 48 C3
- Græni Hatturinn ... 49 C3
- Kaffi Akureyri ... 50 C2
- Sjallinn ... 51 C2

ENTERTAINMENT
- Borgabíó Cinema ... 52 C2
- Leikfélag Akureyrar ... 53 C4
- Nyja-Bíó Cinema ... 54 C2

SHOPPING
- Dogma ... 55 C3
- Fold-Anna ... 56 C3
- Viking ... (see 23)

TRANSPORT
- Bus Terminal ... 57 C4
- Taxi Stand ... 58 C2

Situated beside the Akureyrarkirkja stairs, the **Matthías Jochumsson Memorial Museum** (Sigurhæðir; Map p214; ☎ 466 2609; Hafnarstræti; www.listagil.akureyri.is; adult Ikr500; 3-5pm Mon-Fri Jun-Aug) honours the former Icelandic poet laureate and dramatist.

Northwest of the centre, **Davíðshús** (Map p214; ☎ 466 2609; Bjarkarstígur 6; admission Ikr200; 1-2.30pm Mon-Fri Jun-Aug) looks much like it did on the day that Icelandic poet laureate Davíð Stefánsson died in 1964. The lower floor serves as a writers' retreat.

Botanical Gardens

A host of exotic species from as far away as New Zealand, Spain and Tanzania flourish in Akureyri's botanical gardens, **Lystigarðurinn** (Map p214; ☎ 462 7487; Eyrarlandsholt; admission free; 8am-10pm Mon-Fri, 9am-10pm Sat & Sun Jun-Sep), thanks to the region's moderate microclimate. The wealth of plant life on display is truly astonishing considering the gardens' proximity to the Arctic Circle. You'll find examples of every species native to Iceland here, as well as an extensive collection of high-latitude and high-altitude plants from around the world, all meticulously labelled with scientific names and countries of origin.

Around the gardens are several interesting sculptures, including statues of poet Matthías Jochumsson and Margrethe Schiöth, who voluntarily managed the gardens for 30 years.

Kjarnaskógur

About 3km south of town is Iceland's most visited 'forest', the Kjarnaskógur woods (off Map p211). This bushland area has a 2km-long athletic course, walking tracks, picnic tables, an amusing children's playground and some novel fitness-testing devices. Check out the amusing log sundial designed by Icelandic Scouts.

ACTIVITIES

After church ogling, Akureyri has plenty of options to keep the blood flowing. In winter, skiing is the biggest draw, while summertime activities include golf, horse riding and hiking. For an experience you won't soon forgot, there's world-class diving in Akureyri's fjord, Eyjafjörður – see p217 for details.

Swimming

The superb **swimming pool** (Sundlaug Akureyrar; Map p214; ☎ 461 4455; Þingvallastræti 21; adult/6 15yr Ik410/150, sauna Ikr500; 7am-10pm Mon-Fri, 8am-6.30pm Sat & Sun), near the campsite, is one of Iceland's finest. It has three heated pools, hot pots, water slides, saunas, pummelling water jets and a solarium – perfect for a relaxing afternoon. If you're keen to hang with the locals rather than test out the water slides, there's an **indoor swimming pool** (Glerárlaug; ☎ 462 1539; Höfðahlíð; admission Ikr200) near the university campus.

Horse Riding

Horse tours and hire are available from a range of outlying farms; ask at the tourist office for a full list. **Pólar Hestar** (p226) offers by-the-hour trots and week-long wilderness trips in the surrounding mountains and valleys. **Norðanhestar** (off Map p211; ☎ 865 9165; nordan hestar@nordanhestar.is; Hamraborg; 2hr tour Ikr5000; ☺ May-Sep), located just beyond the campsite site at Hamrar, offers scenic riding trips, horse-wagon tours and short sightseeing excursions in Akureyri's old town district.

Boat Tours

Haffari (Map p214; ☎ 860 3890; www.haffari.is; ☺ Jun–mid-Sep) offers sightseeing and sea angling tours (three hours; adult/child Ikr3900/1950), departing from Akureyri's old port. Trips depart at 3.30pm and 8pm daily. It's also possible to take a tour on **Húni II** (☎ 848 4864; www.huni.muna .is). When the boat is docked, it turns into a **museum** (admission free; ☺ 1-5pm Jun-Aug); contact the Akureyri Industrial Museum for details.

Hiking

For information on hiking in the area, contact **Ferðafélag Akureyrar** (Map p214; ☎ 462 2720; www.ffa .is; Strandgata 23) and check out the helpful collection of Útivist & afþreying hiking maps (there are seven in the series – #1 and #2 focus on the Eyjafjörður area).

A pleasant but demanding day-hike leads up the Glerádalur valley to the summit of Mt Súlur (1144m). The trail begins on Súluvegur, a left turn off Þingvallastræti just before the Glerá bridge. Give yourself at least seven hours to complete the return journey.

With two days, you can continue up the valley to the beautifully situated Lambi mountain hut (at N 65°34.880', W 18°17.770'), which accommodates up to six people. Alternatively, from the Hlíðarfjall ski centre (right) there's a challenging but beautiful day hike up to the small glacier Vindheimajökull and the 1456m peak Strýta.

Golf

For anyone who loves to play golf, there's something strangely appealing about teeing off at midnight. At only a few degrees south of the Arctic Circle, Akureyri's **Jaðarsvöllur** (Map p211; ☎ 462 2974; gagolf@nett.is) basks in perpetual daylight from June to early August. In summer you can play golf here around the clock; just book ahead for the midnight tee-off. The par-71 course is home to the annual 36-hole Arctic Open, a golf tournament played overnight in late June. Contact the club for the latest information on green fees and club rentals.

Skiing

The **Hlíðarfjall ski centre** (off Map p211; ☎ 462 2280; www.hlidarfjall.is; 3hr/1-day/3-day pass Ikr1430/2200/5940), west of town 7km up Glerárdalur, is Iceland's premier downhill ski slope, with green and blue pistes suitable for beginner to upper-intermediate skiers. The longest run is 2.5km, with a vertical drop of about 500m. There's also 20km of cross-country ski routes and a terrain park for snowboarders.

The ski season usually runs between mid-December and the end of April, with the best conditions in February and March. In the long hours of winter darkness, the downhill runs are floodlit. The ski lodge has a restaurant, and a ski school offers individual and group instruction and equipment hire. In season, buses connect the site with Akureyri one time daily (Ikr500 round-trip), although it's best to ask at the information centre as this service is sometimes postponed.

TOURS

If you would like help booking tours, visit the tourism information centre (p213) or Nonni Travel (p213).

From June to September, SBA runs sightseeing tours to Mývatn (Ikr9500, nine hours), departing at around 8.15am daily from the airport and around 8.30am from the bus terminal/tourist information centre. These trips are linked with the early-morning arrival of the Reykjavík–Akureyri domestic flight, and if the flight is delayed, the tour is often delayed as well. There's a 10% discount for those with the overland highland bus pass.

Other summer tours include daily Akureyri city tours (Ikr2500), whale-watching at Húsavík (Ikr9500), Askja 'super-Jeep' tours (Ikr19,400), and self-guided trips by bus and ferry to Hrísey (Ikr3200). Rafting trips in Varmahlíð (Ikr9800) can also be organised from Akureyri, as can horse riding, and Arctic Circle flights (Ikr18,370, 10 June to 20 August). See p225 for information

DIVING IN EYJAFJÖRÐUR

Thoughts of scuba usually involve sun-kissed beaches and neon tropical fish, so perhaps it's surprising that some of the world's most fascinating diving lies within Iceland's frigid waters. Most bubble-blowers flock to crystalline Silfra (p124), but the real diving dynamo, known as 'strýtan', lurks beneath the lapping waves of Eyjafjörður. Strýtan, a giant cone (55m) soaring up from the ocean floor, commands a striking presence as it spews out gushing hot water. This conical structure – made from deposits of magnesium-silicate – is truly an anomaly. You see, the only other strýtan-like structures ever discovered were found at a depth of 5000m; strýtan's peak is a mere 15m below the surface.

We had the opportunity to grab a meal with the man who discovered strýtan – Erlendur Bogason – and over a hearty plate of home-cooked reindeer, he told us all about Eyjafjörður's other scuba superlatives.

In addition to majestic strýtan, there are smaller steam cones on the other side of the fjord. Known as Artnanesstrýtur (also dubbed 'French Gardens'), these smaller formations aren't as spectacular, but it's fun to bring down guillemot eggs and cook them over the vents. Actually, the water that bubbles up is completely devoid of salt, so you can put a thermos over any of the vents, bottle the boiling water, and use it to make hot chocolate when you get back to the surface!

Diving around the island of Grimsey is also a very memorable experience – it's one of the only places in the Arctic Circle where you can dive recreationally. The water is surprisingly clear here, but the main draw is the birdlife. (Yes, you read that correctly.) Bazaars of guillemots swoop down deep as they search for food. Swimming with birds is definitely a strange experience – when the visibility is particularly good it can feel like you're flying!

Interested in checking out these marvels and more? Drop Erlendur a line at his diving outfit, **Strytan Divecentre** (☎ 862 2949; www.strytan.is; 2-dive day trips from €199). If you're visiting in late spring, you can accompany Erlendur as he explores other fjords for whale graveyards, hidden wrecks, and other strýtan-like enigmas.

on getting to Grímsey. Sightseeing charter flights (p230) can be organised at the tourist information centre or at Nonni Travel. Day trips to Greenland can also be arranged from Akureyri, but it is easier and more cost-efficient to base yourself in Reykjavík for that trip.

FESTIVALS & EVENTS

Akureyri's annual **arts festival** runs for 10 weeks from late June to late August and attracts artists and musicians from around Iceland. There are special exhibitions, concerts, free jazz at 9.30pm on Thursdays, theatre performances and everything from clay-pigeon shooting to historical walks. It all culminates in a weekend street party and parade. For details on events and exhibitions, contact the tourist office or ☎ 462 7733.

SLEEPING

If there were ever a time to book ahead it's now. On chillier evenings (when it's too cold to pitch a tent) virtually every room along Eyjafjörður will be booked out.

Travellers with a private vehicle should be mindful of the strange 'parking clock' rules that apply in the city centre (see p222).

Budget & Midrange

Akureyri has a good selection of guest houses, but the best places get booked up fast, especially in summer. Most are open all year and offer substantial discounts in the colder months.

CENTRAL AKUREYRI

Campsite (Map p214; ☎ 462 3379; Þórunnarstræti; sites per person Ikr900; ☼ mid-Jun–Aug) This well-managed site across from the main swimming pool has a kitchen, toilets and showers; there's a laundry too.

Akureyri HI Hostel (Stórholt; Map p211; ☎ 462 3657, 894 4299; www.hostel.is; Stórholt 1; dm/s/d/tr from Ikr2100/3700/5900/7200) Well within the city limits though slightly removed from the action, this friendly, well-equipped and immaculately kept hostel is a 15-minute walk north of the city centre. There's a TV lounge, three kitchens, a barbecue deck and a laundry as well as two attractive summer houses sleeping up to seven people. Substantial discounts are available for a variety of local restaurants and activities (some people stay here just for the coupons!) Advance bookings are essential in summer. Check-in time (between 3pm and 10pm) is strictly enforced.

Sólgarðar (Map p214; ☎ 461 1133; solgardar@simnet.is; Brekkugata 6; sb/s/d Ikr4000/5500/7500) Clean and well kept but quite dated, this small, friendly guest house has three nicely furnished rooms and an ancient kitchen. Each room has a TV, but with paper-thin walls between rooms you may need earplugs for a good night's sleep.

Gula Villan (Map p214; ☎ 896 8464; www.gulavillan.is; Brekkugata 8; sb/s/d Ikr4800/6000/8600) Spotless rooms with simple but comfortable furnishings and friendly owners are available at this centrally located guest house. A second building, Gula Villan II (Map p214), on Þingvallastræti 14; open from June to August) is run by the same couple and offers extra space in summer. Both guest houses have guest kitchens and breakfast served on request (Ikr1000).

AkurInn (Map p214; ☎ 461 2500; www.akurinn.is; Brekkugata 27a; sb s/d Ikr5200/7700, s/d Ikr7200/10,000 Apr-Sep, reduced rates in winter) A cut above most of Akureyri's guest houses, this stately heritage home has a variety of rooms with high ceilings, wood floors and period charm. Crisp white linens, pale neutral colours and simple style give the rooms a very calm atmosphere.

Hotel Edda (Map p214; ☎ 444 4000; www.hoteledda .is; Hrafnagilsstræti; s/d without bathroom Ikr6800/8500, with bathroom from Ikr10,900/13,600; ☼ mid-Jun–late Aug) Bland but comfortable rooms are available at this vast summer hotel in the local school. There's a modern wing with surprising hotel-style accommodation, while the older annexe feels very dated. There's a cafe and large restaurant on site. The staff was rude and unhelpful when we were there; fortunately it's a different batch each summer.

Hrafninn (Map p214; ☎ 661 9050; www.hrafninn.is; Brekkugata 4; s/d mid-May–mid-Sep Ikr8900/12,900, mid-Sep–mid-May Ikr6900/9900; ☐ ☎) Priced below the competition yet delivering well above, beautiful Hrafninn (The Raven) feels like an elegant manor house without being pretentious or stuffy. The location is ideal and the owner is kind; the only possible downside is that there's barely any common space.

Hotel Akureyri (Map p214; ☎ 462 5600; www.hotel akureyri.is; Hafnarstræti 67; s/d Ikr14,900/18,900; ☐ ☎)

Compact rooms with simple decor, satellite TV, phone and minibar are on offer at this new hotel near the tourist office. All rooms have private bathrooms and, although comfortable, are lacking in any personal touch.

This list goes on:

Súlur (Map p214; ☎ 461 1160, 863 1400; sulur@islandia .is; Þórunnarstræti 93 & Klettastígur 6; sb/s/d/tr Ikr5000 /6000/8600/12,000; ☼ Jun-Aug) Sun-filled guest house with simple rooms and guest kitchen.

Gistiheimili Akureyrar (Map p214; s/d without bathroom Ikr6900/8900, with bathroom Ikr8900/10,400) Run by Hotel Akureyri, on busy Hafnarstræti.

Hotel Íbúðir (Map p214; ☎ 462 3727, 892 9838; www .hotelibudir.is; Geislagata 10; apt Ikr14,900-27,900) A choice of luxurious apartments sleeping two to eight guests.

BEYOND THE CITY LIMITS
Mere minutes by car from central Akureyri are some of the best lodging options in the area.

Hamrar campsite (off Map p211; ☎ 461 2264; hamrar@hamrar.is; Hamrar við Kjarnaskóg; sites per person Ikr900; ☼ Jun-Aug; ☐ ☎) This huge campsite, 1.5km south of town in a leafy setting, has newer facilities than the other site, and mountain views. There's a good kitchen and laundry room, ample shower rooms and internet access.

Lonsá (off Map p211; ☎ 462 5037, 895 1685; lonsa@ simnet.is; Hörárbyggð; sb/linen Ikr3300/4200) About 2km north of the city limits, this pleasant option sits in a well-tended garden full of colourful petals. Made-up beds are in a lovely annexe with an inviting living room and guest kitchen. Sleeping bags go in a separate building that feels older and much more dorm-like.

Pétursborg (off Map p211; ☎ 461 1811; www.peturs borg.com; s/d without bathroom Ikr5900/8500, with bathroom Ikr8400/11,800) A great retreat from the city, this pleasant farmhouse on the edge of the fjord has cosy, well-furnished rooms and a wooden summer house (Ikr10,000) sleeping six. There's an outdoor hot pot and a barbecue, a guest kitchen, and a large lounge and dining room. Breakfast is included. Pétursborg is 5km north of Akureyri, on Rte 817.

Öngulstaðir (off Map p211; ☎ 463 1380; www.on gulsstadir.is; Eyjafjarðarsveit; s/d/tr from Ikr6000/8000/10,000) This friendly farm, gallery and souvenir shop offers comfy accommodation in a range of rooms as well as an on-site restaurant if you don't want to head back into town to eat. Öngulstaðir is on Rte 829, 9km south of Akureyri (cross to the eastern side of the fjord before heading south).

Hotel Natur (off Map p211; ☎ 467 1070, 862 7711; www.hotelnatur.com; Þórisstaðir; s/d incl breakfast Jun-Aug Ikr14,500/20,700, Sep & May Ikr11,600/16,560, Oct-Apr Ikr8700/12,420; 🖳 🛜) A wonderfully restored farm, Hotel Natur's main accommodation is housed in the old cow barn (but you'd never guess!) Today the rooms are modern, with standard furnishings, and it's a truly inviting place to stay, with plentiful coffee-table books and agricultural bric-a-brac. Don't miss the seductive hot pot out back.

Additional options:

Smáratún (off Map p211; ☎ 462 5043, 893 6843; Smáratún 5, Svalbarðseyri; apt/cottage from Ikr8500/12,000) Comfy guest-house quarters 12km east of centre.

Leifsstaðir (off Map p211; ☎ 461 1610, 861 1610; www.leifsstadir.is; Eyjafjarðarsveit; s/d without bathroom Ikr8990/12,900, with bathroom from Ikr11,990/14,990; 🌜 14 Jun–27 Aug) Gorgeous country guest house with views of the fjord. Breakfast included. About 4km southeast of Akureyri.

Top End

Hótel Norðurland (Map p214; ☎ 462 2600; www.kea hotels.is; Geislagata 7; s/d Jun-Aug Ikr16,200/20,200, Sep-May Ikr11,400/14,500; 🖳 🛜) A business hotel from the KEA chain, this place is less appealing than its sister hotels; its big, bright rooms have tired furnishings and little atmosphere. All have private bathrooms and are comfortable enough, but we thought Harpa was a bit better.

Hótel Harpa (Map p214; ☎ 460 2000; www.keahotels .is; Hafnarstræti 83-85; s/d Jun-Aug Ikr16,200/20,200, Sep-May Ikr11,400/14,500; 🖳 🛜) A sister property of Hótel KEA, it has smaller rooms but, thanks to a recent renovation, they're brighter, smarter and altogether better value. Contemporary styling, parquet flooring and sparkling new bathrooms are on offer, but the reception and restaurant are shared with the KEA.

Hótel KEA (Map p214; ☎ 460 2000; www.keahotels .is; Hafnarstræti 87-89; s/d Jun-Aug Ikr18,600/23,900, Sep-May Ikr13,300/16,600; 🖳 🛜) KEA has spacious business-style rooms with a dated design and large bathrooms. There's little local character about it, but some rooms have balconies and good views over the fjord. There's a bar, a cafe and a swanky but soulless restaurant, Rosagardurinn.

EATING

You'll be spoilt for choice when it comes to eating out in Akureyri, with a large selection of cafes and restaurants serving everything from spicy noodles to authentic Icelandic cuisine. Locals love dipping their edibles in Béarnaise sauce – don't be shy to follow suit!

Restaurants & Cafes

BUDGET

Café Brauðbúd Konditori (Map p211; Undirhlíð) This excellent-value canteen at the Bónus supermarket serves the usual sandwiches, cakes and soup as well as hearty pasta, pizza and meat dishes from Ikr500. Despite the boxy facade, there's a tinge of character here.

Kristjáns Bakarí (Map p214; Hafnarstræti; 🌜 8am-5.30pm Mon-Fri, to 5pm Sat, 10am-5pm Sun) For a quick pit stop this small bakery and cafe on the main drag sells a bumper selection of fresh bread, cakes and pastries.

Café Paris (Blaá Kannan; Map p214; ☎ 461 4600; Hafnarstræti 96; lunches Ikr950; 🌜 9am-10.30pm Mon-Sat, 10am-10.30pm Sun) This old-style cafe with wooden interior and chilled atmosphere is a great spot for breakfast or lunch. The huge windows and outdoor tables provide prime locations to watch the world go by and the good-value lunches (often veggie) draw the crowds.

Indian Curry Hut (Map p214; ☎ 461 4242; Hafnarstræti 100B; mains from Ikr1395; 🌜 11.30am-1.30pm & 5-9pm Mon-Thu, to 10pm Fri & Sat, 5-9pm Sun) Add a little heat to your chilly Akureyri evening with a flavourful curry from this popular takeaway hut.

MIDRANGE

Krua Siam (Map p214; ☎ 466 3800; Strandgata 13; mains Ikr1200-2300; 🌜 lunch & dinner) Eating Thai noodles while staring out into a blizzard can be a bit strange, but Krua Siam does a darn good job of transporting tastebuds to the Land of Smiles, despite being a mere 40km from the Arctic Circle.

Bryggan (Map p214; ☎ 440 6600; Skipagata 12; pizza Ikr1295-2895; 🌜 11.30am-10pm) Enjoy this nod to Italy amid flashy plasma TVs and artsy B&W photos.

Bautinn (Map p214; ☎ 462 1818; Hafnarstræti 92; mains Ikr1300-3400) A local favourite, this friendly, relaxed place in the centre of town has an excellent all-you-can-eat soup and salad bar (Ikr1500) and an extensive menu featuring everything from pizza, fish and lamb to such Icelandic favourites as puffin, whale and horse meat.

La Vita é Bella (Map p214; ☎ 461 5858; Hafnarstræti 92; mains Ikr1770-3070; ⏰ 6-11pm) This Italian restaurant features a good-value selection of salads, risottos and pasta, including lasagne and ravioli, a good range of pizzas and excellent Mediterranean-inspired fish and meat dishes.

Greifinn (Map p214; ☎ 460 1600; www.greifinn.is; Glerárgata 20; burgers from Ikr1770, pizzas Ikr1380-3140; ⏰ 11.30am-11.30pm) Family-friendly and always buzzing, Greifinn is one of the most popular spots in town. The menu features plenty of comfort food, from juicy burgers and nachos dripping with cheese to good pizzas, salads and devilish desserts.

Strikið (Map p214; ☎ 462 7100; www.strikid.is; Skipagata 14; mains lunch Ikr890-2790, dinner Ikr1590-3150; ⏰ 11.30am-11pm) This slick, minimalist top-floor restaurant has great views over the harbour and an eclectic menu featuring everything from soup and burgers to Thai noodles, pasta, and meat and seafood dishes. Friendly waitresses serve Kaldi – Akureyri's microbrew.

TOP END

RUB 23 (Map p214; ☎ 462 2223, 461 2756; www.rub.is; Kaupvangsstræti 23; sushi from Ikr1950, fish from Ikr3750; ⏰ 6-10pm Sun-Thu, to 11pm Fri & Sat) Pulling off 'minimal chic', trendy RUB lets patrons create their own marinades (or 'rubs') for their fresh fish and lamb. If you're not so keen on turning your meal into a science project, then you can select from their sushi remix – Icelandic maki prepared with savoury Japanese ingredients. Then, for dessert (called 'sweet rubs') you can have a 'chocolate three-way'. Is the bark a little bit bigger than the bite? Perhaps. But you have to give the place credit for thinking outside the bento box.

our pick Friðrik V (Map p214; ☎ 461 5775; Kaupvangsstræti 6; small plates from Ikr600, 5-course meals from Ikr10,000; ⏰ 6-10pm Tue-Sun) If you're going to choose one place to splash out on a gourmet Icelandic meal, this is the right place to do it. Friðrik's eponymous master chef helped create our 'Unofficial Foodie Tour' – see the boxed text, p52 – and is known throughout the country for championing the Slow Food Movement. Each dish is a carefully prepared medley of locally sourced ingredients presented in a forward-thinking manner. There's skyr brulée, filet mignon carpaccio, rhubarb sorbet, langoustine with roasted veggies, skyr mozzarella caprese… the list goes on. In summer, the owners

organise a weekly 'food safari' (Ikr20,000) where they take visitors around Eyjafjörður to collect ingredients for their evening meal. Those who can't afford to splurge should at least stop by during the day and sample a few tapas treats at the in-house delicatessen.

Quick Eats

On the pedestrian shopping mall are several small kiosks selling hot dogs, chips, burgers, sandwiches and soft drinks.

Nætursalan (Map p214; Strandgata) Near the Nyja-Bíó cinema, this is the most popular fast-food place with the late-night crowd. It's open until at least 3am on Friday and Saturday night. Don't go here when you're sober – people will think you're weird.

Brynja (Map p211; Aðalstræti 3; ⏰ 9am-11.30pm) Slightly out of the centre but well worth the effort to get to, this legendary sweet shop is known across Iceland for the best ice cream in the country.

Self-Catering

Akureyri has a great choice of supermarkets. The biggest is the huge **Netto** (Map p211; Glerágata) in the Glerártorg shopping mall. **Samkaup-Strax** (Map p214; Byggðavegur) is near the campsite west of the centre, and there are two cut-price **Bónus** (Map p211; Undirhlíð) supermarkets, one of which is behind the youth hostel. There's also the handy **1011**.

Vín Búð (Map p214; ☎ 462 1655; Hólabraut 16; ⏰ 11am-6pm Mon-Thu, to 7pm Fri, to 4pm Sat), the government alcohol shop, is near the Borgabíó cinema.

DRINKING

Akureyri has some lively nightlife, but compared with Reykjavík it's all pretty tame. The following hangouts make up the best drinking dens in town. Make sure to try Kaldi, a local beer; tours of the microbrewery (the only one in Iceland) can be organised at the info centre.

Café Amour (Map p214; ☎ 461 3030; Ráðhústorg 9; ⏰ 11am-1am Sun-Thu, to 4am Fri & Sat) Stylish and sophisticated, Café Amour tries hard to lure in Akureyri's bright young things with its lengthy cocktail list and New World wines. The small club upstairs is pretty garish but draws the crowds at weekends.

Café Karolína (Map p214; ☎ 461 2755; Kaupvangsstræti 23; ⏰ 3pm-1am Sun-Thu, to 4am Fri & Sat; 📶) Self-

THE AKUREYRI RUNTUR

Bored, restless and keen to be seen, Akureyri's teenagers have developed their own brand of *runtur* (literally 'round tour'). While Reykjavík's world-famous equivalent demands a hard stomach and a disco nap (see p99), in Akureyri you just need to be old enough to borrow a car. From about 8pm on any night of the week (though usually Friday and Saturday), you'll see a procession of cars, bumper to bumper, driving round and round in circles along Skipagata, Strandgata and Glerárgata. The speed rarely rises above 5km/h, but horns blare and teenagers scream out to each other until the wee hours.

Runtur rowdiness is inversely proportional to a city's size, so if you think Akureyri's honk-fest is irksome then don't go to Húsavík – that town only has three streets!

consciously cool and a favoured hangout with the young and trendy, Karolina is a relaxed place serving a limited selection of coffee and cakes. The deep leather sofas and mellow music make it easy to while away a few hours here.

Kaffi Akureyri (Map p214; ☎ 461 3999; Strandgata 7; ☺ 3pm-1am Sun-Thu, to 4am Fri & Sat) This purple-striped cafe-bar is one of Akureyri's better live-music venues and gets packed on Friday and Saturday nights when bands play.

Sjallinn (Map p214; ☎ 461 2700; Geislagata 14; ☺ to 3am Fri & Sat) Perennially popular and always jammed, this bar, club and live-music venue has DJs playing everything from chart tunes to indie rock and live bands at weekends.

Græni Hatturinn (Green Hat: Map p214; ☎ 461 4646; Hafnarstræti 96) More traditional and usually less boisterous than Sjallinn, this popular British-style pub is down a lane behind Café Paris. This is the best place in town to see live music.

Vélsmiðjan (Map p211; ☎ 462 6020; Strandgata 53) Down by the harbour, Vélsmiðjan is the sort of pub you don't often see in Iceland. It's in a historical building (with reputedly the longest bar in Iceland), is popular with a mature drinking crowd and has regular karaoke.

ENTERTAINMENT

Leikfélag Akureyrar (Map p214; ☎ 462 0200; www.leikfelag.is; Hafnarstræti 57), Akureyri's main theatre venue hosts drama, musicals, dance and opera, with its main season running from September to June. Check the website for information on upcoming performances.

There are two cinemas in the town centre: **Borgabíó** (Map p214; ☎ 462 3599; Hólabraut 12), and **Nyja-Bíó** (Map p214; ☎ 461 4666; Strandgata 2), just around the corner from the town square. Both show original-version mainstream films with subtitles.

SHOPPING

Several shops on Hafnarstræti sell traditional woollen jumpers, books, knick-knacks and souvenirs under the tax-free scheme (see p327). Check out the quirky Christmas Garden (p226) for a bit of holiday cheer any time of year.

Viking (Map p214; ☎ 461 5551; Hafnarstræti 104) This hard-to-miss shop lures the masses with its giant Viking statue plunked out front. There's a good selection of Icelandic knitted jumpers and souvenir knick-knacks here. You can also rent bicycles for the day (p222).

Dogma (Map p214; ☎ 562 6600; Hafnarstræti 106) If you didn't pick up your 'I'm Huge In Iceland' T-shirt in the capital, then swing by the Akureyri branch of Reykjavik's quirky clothing mainstay.

Fold-Anna (Map p214; ☎ 461 1120; Hafnarstræti 85; ☺ 9am-6pm Mon-Fri, 10am-2pm Sat) Marginally cheaper woollen goods can be found at this factory outlet. Staff can be seen knitting behind the counter as you browse.

GETTING THERE & AWAY

Air

Iceland Express (☎ 550 0600; www.icelandexpress.com) runs one or two flights a week during summer from Akureyri to London (Gatwick) and Copenhagen.

Air Iceland (☎ 460 7000) runs flights up to seven times daily between Akureyri and Reykjavík (45 minutes), and from Akureyri to Grímsey (25 minutes), Vopnafjörður (45 minutes) and Þórshöfn (45 minutes). All other domestic (and international) flights are routed via Reykjavík. Prices start at Ikr4990 for all one-way domestic destinations.

Akureyri airport (Map p211; www.flugstodir.is) is located 3km south of the city centre.

Bus

Akureyri is the hub for bus travel in the north. To get the most up-to-date information on bus prices and schedules, it is well worth stopping by the city's helpful tourist information centre, or checking the timetables online. Both **SBA** (http://english.sba.is) and **Trex** (Bíar og fólk; www.bogf.is) are based at the tourist office at Hafnarstraeti 82. Note that the tourist office will move to the Hof along the waterfront when construction is completed – this will probably happen in 2010. At the time of research it had not been decided if the bus terminus would move to the Hof as well. Check locally for up-to-date information, or visit www.visitakureyri.is.

Buses run between Akureyri and Reykjavík twice daily from May to September (Ikr9900, 5¾ hours). There is at least one service daily during the rest of the year. From mid-June to the end of August an additional service runs to Reykjavík along the highland Kjölur route (from Ikr9900, 10 hours), leaving in the morning.

Heading east, there are daily summer buses that run from Akureyri to Egilsstaðir (Ikr6700, four hours), calling at Reykjahlíð and Skútustaðir, at Mývatn (Ikr2800, 1½ hours). In high season expect up to four additional bus connections to Mývatn. From June to August there are three daily services to Húsavík (Ikr2500, one hour), from where you can connect to Ásbyrgi and Þórshöfn on weekdays.

Car

After Reykjavik, Akureyri is Iceland's second transport hub – check out www.semferda.net for information about sharing rides with other travellers. There are several rental agencies in town – rates start at around Ikr17,500 per day for a small car with unlimited kilometres and insurance, to around Ikr27,000 per day for a small 4WD. For an extra fee of around Ikr10,000, most companies will let you pick up a car in Akureyri and drop it off in Reykjavík or vice versa.

Avis (Map p211; ☎ 824 4010, 461-2428, national reservations line 591 4000; www.avis.is; Akureyri airport)

Budget (Map p211; ☎ 660 0629; Akureyri airport)

Dollar Thrify/Saga (Map p211; ☎ 461 1005; Tryggvabraut 5)

Hertz (Map p211; ☎ 522 4440; www.hertz.is; opposite Akureyri airport)

National (Map p211; ☎ 461 6000; www.holdur.is/en; Akureyri Airport & Tryggvabraut 12)

GETTING AROUND

Central Akureyri is quite compact and easy to get around on foot. Take note of Akureyri's quirky parking policies (below) if you plan to leave your car in the city centre.

Bicycle

The **Viking Shop** (p221) offers bike rentals during the summer for around Ikr1800/2400 per half/full day. If they're out of bikes, try **Skíðaþjónustan** (☎ 462 1713; Fjölnisgata 4b), located northwest of the town centre. They primarily sell bikes, but sometimes have a few used cycles that they'll lend out for around Ikr2500 per day.

Bus

Akureyri is easy to get around on foot, but there's a free town bus service (running regularly from 6.25am to 11pm on weekdays and 12.15pm to 6pm on weekends). Unfortunately, it doesn't go to the airport.

Car

Akureyri has the most bizarre parking restrictions in the entirety of Iceland. When parking in the city centre, you must put a plastic parking disk, or 'clock', (available free from all shops and banks) – marking time you parked – on display in your car (preferably near your steering wheel so as to be seen through the windshield). Sheets of grided paper are often dispensed in lieu of the disks, so make sure you have a pen. Spaces are signposted with maximum parking times (between 15 minutes to two hours). And although you'll never have to actually pay for parking, you'll be slapped with a fine (Ikr1000 if you pay within three days, then it goes up to Ikr1500) if you're not back at your car before the time runs out. This is strictly enforced – we had a lovely little yellow slip waiting for us after 'researching' a tasty meal.

Taxi

The BSO **taxi stand** (Map p214; ☎ 461 1010) is on the corner of Strandgata and Hofsbót. Taxis may be booked 24 hours a day.

AROUND AKUREYRI (EYJAFJÖRÐUR)

If you have some extra time it's worth getting off the Ring Road and exploring the region around Akureyri's fjord, Eyjafjörður.

AKUREYRI TO MÝVATN (GOÐAFOSS)

Travellers heading from Akureyri to Mývatn (or Akureyri to Húsavík if you take a small detour) will happen across heavenly **Goðafoss** (Waterfall of the Gods), which rips straight through the Bárðardalur lava field along Rte 1. Although smaller and less powerful than some of Iceland's other chutes, it's definitely one of the most beautiful.

The falls play an important part in Icelandic history. At the Alþing in the year 1000, the *lögsögumaður* (law speaker), Þorgeir, was forced to make a decision on Iceland's religion. After 24 hours' meditation he declared the country a Christian nation. On his way home to Ljósavatn he passed the waterfall near his farm, Djúpá, and tossed in his pagan carvings of the Norse gods, thus bestowing the falls' present name.

If the sound of pounding water puts you to sleep then a night at **Fosshóll** (☎ 464 3108; www .nett.is/fossholl; s/d without bathroom Ikr12,500/17,800, with bathroom Ikr16,500/22,800), next to the falls, might be for you. Orbiting the inn is a restaurant – serving a few Icelandic delicacies such as *hákarl* (putrid shark meat) – a petrol station, money exchange and lovely souvenir shop.

WESTERN EYJAFJÖRÐUR

Árskógsströnd

The rich agricultural region known as Árskógsströnd runs north along the western shore of Eyjafjörður, from where there are dramatic views across the water to the mountains opposite. It's the main jumping-off point for those who want to explore little Hrísey offshore.

It's worth detouring to the village of **Hauganes** to climb aboard the former fishing boat **Niels Jonsson** (☎ 867 0000; www.niels.is; 3hr trips adult/under 15yr Ikr5000/free; ☼ Jun-Aug) for a fun-filled adventure that includes fishing and whale watching while taking in the bird-filled scenery. Hauganes is 2km off Rte 82, about 14km south of Dalvík.

Hrísey
pop 180

Iceland's second-largest offshore island (after Heimaey) is the peaceful, low-lying Hrísey, a thriving community easily reached from the mainland. Thrust out into the middle of Eyjafjörður, the island is especially noted as a breeding ground and protected area for ptarmigan, as well as being home to a flourishing population of eider duck and an enormous colony of Arctic terns.

Traditionally the island was a centre for fish processing and salting, but today most of its inhabitants are employed at the quarantine station for pets and livestock being imported to Iceland.

There's a small **information office** (☎ 695 0077; ☼ 1-6pm mid-Jun–Aug) in the Pearl Gallery by the harbour. You can pick up the handy Hrísey brochure here or in Akureyri. The island also has a bank and a post office on the main street of the village.

At the island's southern end is the picturesque **village** – a cluster of houses (with two mildly interesting museums) around the harbour linked by cobbled streets frequented by incredibly tame ptarmigan. From here, three marked **nature trails** loop around the southeastern part of the island and lead to some good clifftop viewpoints.

Most of the northern part of Hrísey is a private ptarmigan and eider-duck sanctuary, and visitors must obtain permission to pass through the area. The cliffs along the northeastern coast are indented by **sea caves** and the bush areas have reverted to a natural state, having been free of sheep for many years.

Not to be missed are the tons-of-fun **tractor trips** (☎ 695 0077; per person Ikr1000), which plough across the island, passing all the important sights.

While a leisurely half-day is enough to explore the island, it's worth staying overnight for a more authentic glimpse of island life. Try **Gistiheimilið Brekka** (☎ 466 1751; brekkahriseyelli@ sjallinn.is; Hólabraut; s/d Ikr5500/9000), Hrísey's one-stop shop for food and accommodation.

Or ask about homestays at the info centre or at Eyjabud, the village store, which also sells a variety of food and souvenirs. Campers can pitch a tent at the **campsite** (☎ 466 1769;

Skálavegur; sites per person Ikr800; (🕑 Jun–mid-Sep) near the community centre – wild-camping is prohibited.

The ferry **Sævar** (☎ 695 5544) runs between Árskógssandur and Hrísey (15 minutes) 11 times daily between 9am and 11.30pm during summer. A reduced service runs during the rest of the year. Buses from Akureyri connect with the ferries three times daily from Monday to Friday.

On Tuesday and Thursday throughout the year, the **Sæfari ferry** (☎ 458 8970; www.saefari.is) runs from Dalvík to Hrísey at 1.15pm (30 minutes), returning immediately after passengers and cargo are discharged and loaded.

Dalvík
pop 1400

Sleepy Dalvík found a snugly spot between breezy Eyjafjörður and the rolling hills of Svarfaðardalur. Most tourists come here to catch the Grímsey ferry (see opposite), but if you've got some time there's good hiking, an interesting museum and a lovely swimming pool nearby.

There's a tiny **tourist information point** (☎ 466 3233; www.dalvik.is) at the sparkling modern **swimming pool** (☎ 466 3233; adult/under 16yr Ikr450/free; 🕑 6am-8pm Mon-Fri, 10am-7pm Sat & Sun Jun-Aug, 6am-7pm Mon-Fri, 10am-7pm Sat & Sun Sep-May) on Svarfaðarbraut. Hot pots and waterslides abound, and there's 15 minutes' free internet access for visitors. Grab the useful Dalvíkbyggð fold-out map for details on local hiking routes, or ask Ferðafélag Akureyrar (p216) in Akureyri for additional hut and map info.

There are a bunch of oddball museums around Eyjafjörður and **Byggðasafnið Hvoll** (☎ 466 1497; www.dalvik.is/byggdasafn; Karlsbraut; adult/under 16yr Ikr500/100; 🕑 11am-6pm daily Jun-Aug) definitely qualifies as one of the strangest. Skip the usual taxidermic characters and find the room dedicated to local giant Jóhan Pétursson who, at 2.34m (almost 7ft 7in), was Iceland's tallest man. There are photos and personal effects, many from his days as a circus act. Another room is dedicated to another local, Kristjárn Eldjárn, who became president of Iceland.

Horse riding and hire can be organised through **Tvistur** (☎ 466 1679, 861 9631; ebu@ismennt.is; 1hr/2hr tours Ikr3000/4500), a farm about 3km from town along Rte 805 in the Svarfaðardalur valley.

Surely there can't be good rooms behind the hideous facade at **Foss Hótel** (☎ 466 3395; www.fosshotel.com; Skíðabraut 18; s/d without bathroom Ikr9500/11,500, with bathroom Ikr20,900/22,900), but there actually are! After a recent renovation, Dalvík's only hotel offers comfy accommodation in simple but tasteful rooms. There's a free campsite just behind.

There's a supermarket and several small restaurants in the small shopping complex between the main road and the harbour.

Dalvík is the jumping-off point for ferries to Grímsey – see opposite for details. The ferry-focused bus to/from Akureyri (one way Ikr400) is also available to travellers who aren't making the trip to the Arctic Circle. Two additional buses link Akureyri and Ólafsfjörður daily.

Ólafsfjörður
pop 850

Beautifully situated beneath snowcapped peaks, the fishing town of Ólafsfjörður makes a pleasant day trip from Akureyri. Locked in between the sheer mountain slopes and the dark waters of the fjord, the place has a real sense of rural isolation. You have to pass through a thin 3km tunnel just to make your way into town.

SIGHTS & ACTIVITIES

If you're looking for something indoors, try **Nátúrrugripsafnið** (☎ 466 2651; Aðalgata; admission Ikr500; 🕑 2-5pm Jun-Aug), a small bird-oriented museum above the post office, and Ólafsfjörður's only formal sight.

Ólafsfjörður receives good snow coverage in winter, when the downhill **ski slopes** above town lurch into action. Ask at Brimnes about organising snowmobiling and ice-fishing excursions in winter, or check out www.sporttours.is.

Ólafsfjörður competes with Siglufjörður for the title of Iceland's northernmost **golf course**. The nine-hole course is in a lush geothermal area just north of town.

SLEEPING & EATING

There's a basic **campsite** (☎ 466 2363) at the swimming pool.

Brimnes Hotel & Cabins (☎ 466 2400; www.brimnes.is; Bylgjubyggð 2; s/d/cabins incl breakfast Ikr12,000/16,000/15,000) This is the main place to stay in town. The real draws here are the cosy Scandinavian-style log cabins on the lake shore, with hot tubs built into the verandah and views over the water. The hotel restaurant (mains Ikr1520 to Ikr3000) is a bright, cheery place with good service and a decent menu of fish and lamb dishes as well as pizza and some superb homemade Icelandic desserts. The hotel can help organise such activities as horse rental, lake and sea fishing, rowing boats and winter snowmobile excursions.

Höllin (☎ 466 4000; Hafnargötu 16; pizzas Ikr800-2500; 11.30am-10pm Sun-Thu, to 2am Fri & Sat) Apart from Brimnes, your only other option for food is the local pizza joint that plays movies on the plasma and shows English football as frequently as possible.

GETTING THERE & AWAY
During our visit, the finishing touches were being put on the brand new Siglufjörður–Ólafsfjörður tunnel – it should be open by the time you read this. Three daily buses run between Ólafsfjörður and Akureyri during summer.

GRÍMSEY
pop 90
Best known as Iceland's only true piece of the Arctic Circle, the remote island of Grímsey, 41km from the mainland, is a lonely little place where birds outnumber people by about 1000 to one. Believe it or not, Grímsey has been inhabited by humans since the year 1200, and the graves of the first settlers are marked by a pile of stones on the side of the road between the airport and the village. According to legend, it was a Norse fisherman named Grimur who first arrived on the island after falling in love with the daughter of a local troll. Sadly, the troll swiftly met her maker after an accidental encounter with the midnight sun – her petrified remains lie frozen near the island's pencil-thin church. (The stones are so easily anthropomorphised that you'll instantly start believing in Iceland's 'hidden people'.)

Today, much of Grímsey's appeal remains mythic in nature. Tourists flock here to snap up their 'I visited the Arctic Circle' certificate and pose for a photo with the 'you're standing on the Arctic Circle' monument (which is actually around 20m south of the 'real' line). Afterwards, there's plenty of time to appreciate the wind swept setting. Scenic coastal cliffs and dramatic basalt formations make a popular home for 36 different species of sea birds, including the kamikaze Arctic tern. It's best to hold a stick overhead as you won't find a tree under which to hide – Grímsey doesn't have any!

If sleeping in the Arctic Circle sounds too adventurous to pass up, there are two places offering accommodation. Follow the stairs up through the trapdoor at **Gullsól** (☎ 467 3190; stellagella15@hotmail.is; sb/linen Ikr2000/2500) to find teeny tiny rooms perched above the island's gift shop (which opens in conjunction with ferry arrivals). The fully equipped kitchen (microwave, coffee maker etc) is handy for self-caterers. Things are a bit more upmarket at cream-coloured **Básar** (☎ 467 3103; gagga@sim net.is; sb/linen Ikr2000/3900) next to the airport. This is the island's original guest house, and it's still the only place to get a proper meal. Breakfast/lunch/dinner costs Ikr900/1500/2500. There's also a free camping ground at the community centre, or you can wild-camp anywhere outside the village. Be mindful of your rubbish as the winds are quite strong.

Getting There & Away
Despite its isolated location, getting to Grímsey is a cinch. From mid-June to late-August, **Air Iceland** (☎ 467 3148; www.airiceland.is) flies every day to/from Akureyri. From late March to mid-June and late August to October, flights operate on Tuesday, Thursday and Sunday only. The bumpy journey takes in the full

---

GRÍMSEY'S CHECKMATE

Although chess is no longer the sacred pastime it once was on Grímsey, the island is still known for its avid players. Historically, failure at chess was equated with failure in life on Grímsey, and the game was taken so seriously that a poor performance was often followed by a messy dive from the cliffs. This enthusiasm and dedication to the game attracted the attention of US millionaire journalist and chess champion Daniel Willard Fiske in the 1870s.

Although he never visited the island, he set himself up as its protector, sending badly needed firewood, financing the island library and bequeathing part of his estate to the community. Grímsey still celebrates Fiske's birthday on 11 November, and his portrait is on display in the library at the community centre. For more on Grímsey's unconventional benefactor, read Lawrence Millman's account of a visit to the island in his book *Last Places: A Journey in the North*.

length of Eyjafjörður and is an experience in itself. You'll find one-way fares from around Ikr6000 to Ikr10,000.

In summer the **Sæfari ferry** (☎ 458 8970, 853 2211; www.saefari.is) departs from Dalvík for Grímsey at 9am on Monday, Wednesday and Friday, returning from Grímsey at 4pm. If coming from Akureyri, a bus leaves from the information centre (at Hafnatstræti 82) around 8am to connect with the ferry and returns from Dalvík after the ferry docks around 7.30pm. A one-way journey (3¼ hours) costs Ikr2900, or Ikr5800 for the round-trip (free for children under 12 years; half-price for pensioners). Add an extra Ikr800 if you require the round-trip bus service between Akureyri and Dalvík. In winter, the departure service remains the same; however, the ship immediately returns to Dalvík once cargo has been discharged and loaded.

Grímsey can also be reached on one of North Sailing's three-day, two-night sailing expeditions (usually three or four trips per summer) – see p240 for details.

EASTERN EYJAFJÖRÐUR

Eyjafjörður's eastern shore is much quieter than its western counterpart, offering a few interesting places to pause among the long grassy vistas.

The **Icelandic Folk Art Museum** (Safnasafnið; ☎ 461 4066; www.safnasafnid.is; adult/under 16yr Ikr500/free; ☽ 1–5pm Jun–Aug, 2 5pm Sep–May), across the fjord from Akureyri, is a collector's dream. In Icelandic, the museum's name literally means 'the museum museum', a name coined because the curators display just about anything, as long as it was made with an earnest heart.

Further north, around 19km from Akureyri, you'll happen upon the turf roofs at **Laufás** (☎ 463 3196; adult/under 16yr Ikr500/free; ☽ 9am–6pm mid-May–mid-Sep), a preserved manor farm and vicarage giving wonderful insights into rural living in times past. Stop in the sun-filled restaurant and sample the homemade mountaingrass bread with smoked trout.

Pólar Hestar (☎ 463 3179; www.polarhestar.is; Grýtubakki 2), one of the best-known stables in northern Iceland, offers a great introduction to riding for the uninitiated, as well as acclaimed six- to eight-day horse-riding tours (five or six days in the saddle). The farm has over 100 horses and the owners' little boy has memorised all of their names. Complimentary pastries are served during breaks. Figure around Ikr4000/6000 for two-/four-hour tours and Ikr9000 for the day. Multiday trips range from €900 to €1500 and include accommodation and meals.

The road ends in **Grenivík** where you can link up with Fjörðungar, a local hiking operator, for multiday trips into **Í Fjörðum** further north. Visit Jónsabúð, Grenivík's shop (there's only one) to organise your adventure. Try the campsite near the pool if you want to stay the night.

UPPER EYJAFJÖRÐUR

Heading south from Akureyri, Rte 821 follows Eyjafjörður to its head, passing several sites of historical importance. If you're touring around in a private vehicle and have already explored eastern and western Eyjafjörður, then why not spend one more afternoon away from the Ring Road traffic? Hikers should pick up the handy *Útivist & afþreying* #2 map, which details the network of trails between the Eyjafjarðará river delta and the rugged highlands.

About 10km south of Akureyri, **Kristnes** was the site of Helgi the Lean's original settlement. His high-seat temple pillars washed up at Pollurinn, near the head of the fjord, and Helgi decided to settle here.

If you can handle the Christmas cheer out of season, then the nearby **Christmas Garden** (Jólagarðurinn; ☎ 463 1433; ☽ 10am–10pm Jun–Aug, 2–10pm Sep–Dec, 2–6pm Jan–May) has a lovely selection of locally made decorations, cards, sweets and traditional Icelandic Christmas foods. They also serve excellent lamb.

Another 2km south is **Hrafnagil**, which was the historic home of Bishop Jón Arason of Hólar (p207). The odd little onion-domed church at **Grund**, about 5km past Hrafnagil, was built by the farmer Magnús Sigurðsson in 1905. Its neo-Romanesque style seems anomalous in Iceland, but early in the 20th century it was one of the country's most impressive churches. Ask for a key at the farmhouse.

Saurbær farm, 28km south of Akureyri on Rte 821, has an interesting turf-and-stone church dating from 1838, now under national protection. It was constructed on the site of a church that had existed there since the 11th century.

The eccentric **Museum of Small Exhibits** (Smámunasafn Sverris Hermannssonar; ☎ 463 1261; www.smamunasafnid.is; admission Ikr500; ☽ 1–6pm mid-May–mid-Sep), at Sólgarður near Saurbær, is a mindboggling collection of watches, door knockers, bridle bits, electrical switches, kitchen equipment, tools, fishing gear and anything else you could possibly think of, all meticulously mounted and displayed.

Northeast Iceland

Shattered lava fields, epic waterfalls, snow-capped peaks and breaching whales – this is Iceland at its best. The region's brilliant sights are variations on one theme: a grumbling volcanically active earth. The violence and turbulence of the tortured land is undeniable and awe-inducing, but perhaps even more impressive is the fact that the area's diverse attractions are so neatly and conveniently clustered together.

Ethereal Mývatn, with its alien pseudocraters and haunting lava castles, is undoubtedly the region's darling destination. Not to be missed is rust-coloured Hverir next-door, with its gurgling vents and belching mudflaps. Further north you'll pass steamy Krafla before uncovering the geological smorgasbord at the Jökulsárgljúfur canyon in Vatnajökull National Park. Hikers will be treated to puzzling rock anomalies that surround Dettifoss – Europe's most powerful chute. To the northwest the stunning fishing village of Húsavík holds the much-coveted title of Iceland's whale-watching capital and, further on, the remote northeastern corner stretches to within a few kilometres of the Arctic Circle.

This remote peninsula to the northeast is a little-visited and sparsely populated area of desolate moors and wildly beautiful scenery. Bypassed by the tourist hordes who whiz around the Ring Road to the south, this forgotten region feels like the end of the earth, with a rugged and captivating character all of its own. Dotted with sleepy fishing villages and home to some of Iceland's hardiest souls, it makes a wonderful destination for wilderness hiking on the remote, uninhabited headlands that jut into the sea.

HIGHLIGHTS

- Wander around lava castles, alien pseudo-craters and hidden fissures at otherworldly **Mývatn** (p228) before soaking your aching muscles at the Nature Baths

- Hold your breath as gentle giants suddenly emerge from the deep on a whale-watching trip in **Húsavík** (p240)

- Step gingerly through the hazy orange world at **Hverir** (p238), then crunch shattered lava underfoot around the turquoise lakes and gurgling mudpots at **Krafla** (p238)

- Savour thundering chutes, hypnotic rock forms and vast canyon gaps at **Jökulsárgljúfur** (p245) in the northern part of Vatnajökull National Park

- March to the end of the earth at **Langanes** (p251), passing wind-battered ruins and roaring bird colonies along the way

NORTHEAST ICELAND

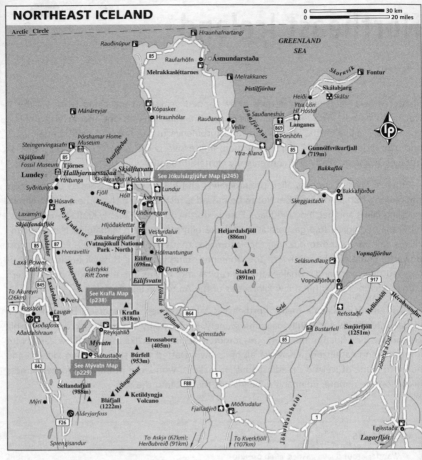

NORTHEAST ICELAND

MÝVATN REGION

Undisputed gem of the region, Lake Mývatn (*mee*-vawt) and the surrounding area are starkly beautiful, an otherworldly landscape of spluttering mudpots, weird lava formations, steaming fumaroles and volcanic craters. The Mývatn basin sits squarely on the Mid-Atlantic Ridge and the violent geological character of the area has produced an astonishing landscape unlike anywhere else in the country; this is the Iceland you've always imagined.

History & Geology

Ten thousand years ago the Mývatn basin was covered by an ice cap, which was destroyed by fierce volcanic eruptions that also obliterated the lake at its base. The explosions formed the symmetrical *móberg* peaks (flat-topped mountains formed by subglacial volcanic eruptions) south of today's lake, while volcanic activity to the east formed the Lúdent tephra (solid matter ejected into the air by an erupting volcano) complex.

Another cycle of violent activity over 6000 years later created the Ketildyngja volcano, 25km southeast of Mývatn. The lava from that crater flowed northwest along the Laxárdalur valley, and created a lava dam and a new, improved lake. After another millennium or so a volcanic explosion along the same fissure spewed out Hverfell (p234), the classic tephra crater that dominates the modern lake landscape. Over the next 200 years, activity escalated along the eastern shore and craters were thrown up across a wide region, providing a steady stream of molten material flowing toward Öxarfjörður. The lava dam formed during the end of this cycle created the present Mývatn shoreline.

Between 1724 and 1729 the Mývatnseldar eruptions began at Leirhnjúkur, close to Krafla (p238), northeast of the lake. This dramatic and sporadically active fissure erupted spectacularly in 1984, and by the early '90s the magma chamber had refilled, prompting experts to predict another big eruption. As yet this hasn't happened, but it's really only a matter of time.

In 1974 the area around Mývatn was set aside as the Mývatn-Laxá special conservation area, and the pseudocrater field at Skútustaðir, at the southern end of the lake, is preserved as a national natural monument.

Orientation

The lake is encircled by a 36km sealed road (Rtes 1 and 848), with the main settlement of Reykjahlíð (p231) on the northeast corner. A handy information centre is located here, as are several sleeping options for every budget category.

Most of the points of interest are linked by the lake's looping road, including the diverse lava formation in eastern Mývatn (p234), the cluster of pseudocraters near southern Mývatn (p235), and the bird-friendly marsh plains around western Mývatn (p236).

In northern Mývatn (p237), the Ring Road (Rte 1) veers east, away from Reykjahlíð, and takes you over the Námaskarð pass to the Hverir geothermal area. Then, a turn-off to the north (Rte 863) leads to cloudy Krafla, 14km from Reykjahlíð.

With your own vehicle this whole area can be explored in a single day, but if you're using the bus or a bicycle allow two days. If you want to hike and explore more distant mountains and lava fields, allow at least three.

Tours

Tourism reigns supreme at Reykjahlíð (p231) and for travellers without their own transport there are numerous tours around the area. Tours fill up fast during summer, so try to book at least a day before departure.

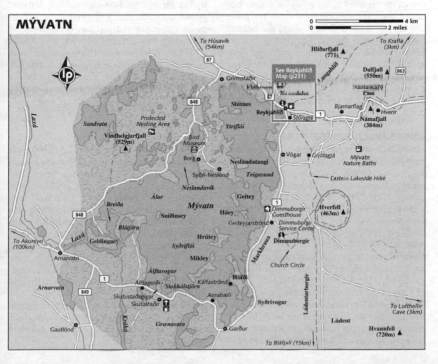

INTO THE MADDING SWARMS

Plague-like swarms of Mývatn's eponymous midges are a lasting memory for many visitors to the area in midsummer. As infuriating as they can be, these pesky intruders are a vital food source for wildlife. Their larvae are eaten by brown trout, and both the harlequin duck and Barrow's goldeneye subsist on them during the nesting season.

Unfortunately for humans, the midges are attracted to carbon dioxide, so every time you exhale, the little buggers gather around your face and invade your eyes, ears, nose and mouth. Mývatn has two types of midge: the small, skinny, mosquito-like *mýflugur* or *rikmý*, known to occasionally make kamikaze dives for your lungs; and the fatter, buzzing, hair-loving *bitmý* (blackfly).

The good news is that only one species bites, so wear a head net (which you can buy for around Ikr500 at the supermarket in Reykjahlíð), splash on the repellent and pray for a good wind to send the nasty little blighters diving for shelter amid the vegetation.

MÝVATN

For an abridged version of Mývatn's top sights, consider linking up with the 10-hour **SBA** (http://english.sba.is) tour. It starts in Akureyri (p216), but you can often hop aboard in Reykjahlíð.

LOFTHELLIR CAVE

The dramatic lava cave at Lofthellir is a stunning destination with magnificent natural ice sculptures dominating the interior. Although one of Mývatn's true highlights, the cave can only be accessed on a tour because the cave entrance (suitable only for the svelte) is hard to find along the barren landscape, and special equipment (headlamps, studded boots etc) is required. Ask at the Reykjahlíð information centre for the latest tour details – these trips only run by request from June to September. Figure around Ikr10,000 (minimum four people); dress for negative temperatures.

JÖKULSÁRGLJÚFUR (DETTIFOSS)

New roads and regular bus service makes it easy to pop up to Dettifoss and the surrounding national park. Super-Jeep tours can be arranged from the Reykjahlíð information centre (Ikr12,000), which take in Krafla, Gjástykki, Hafragilsfoss, Selfoss and Dettifoss on a seven-hour trip.

ASKJA

Mývatn Tours (☎ 464 1920; www.askjatours.is) runs long but rewarding day tours to the Askja caldera (p315) deep in the highlands. Tours (€120, 11 to 12 hours) depart from Hotel Reynihlíð in Reykjahlíð at 8am on Monday, Wednesday and Friday from late June to the end of August and daily from mid-July to mid-August. **Viking Travel** (☎ 894 5265;

www.vikingtravel@vikingtravel.is) offers a similar trip (Ikr17,000).

HORSE RIDING

Stop by the Reykjahlíð information centre to book horse-riding tours with nearby **Hestaleiga** (☎ 464 4103) and **Safaríhestar** (☎ 464 4203; Álftagerði 3) on the south side of the lake. Figure around Ikr5000 for two hours.

SIGHTSEEING CHARTER FLIGHTS

Mýflug Air (☎ 464 4400; www.myflug.is; Reykjahlíð airport) operates daily flight-seeing excursions (weather permitting, of course). A 20-minute trip around Mývatn and Krafla costs €60. A 'super tour' (€230) also includes Dettifoss, Jökulsárgljúfur, Ásbyrgi, Kverkfjöll, Herðubreið and Askja. You can also take a two-hour Arctic Circle tour to Grímsey for €175.

Getting There & Away

The Akureyri-to-Egilsstaðir bus (62/62a) stops at both Skútustaðir (Ikr2300, 1¼ hours) and Reykjahlíð (Ikr2800, 1¾ hours) year-round, with daily service from June to mid-September, and trips on Mondays, Wednesdays, Fridays and Sundays during the colder months. Travellers can also make Mývatn a day trip aboard SBA's bus 1 (Ikr9500), which departs from Akureyri at 8.30am, circles the lake, and heads back to Akureyri at 5.30pm. Bus 650/650a travels to/from Húsavík (Ikr2000, 40 minutes) twice daily from mid-June through to the end of August.

All buses pick-up/drop-off passengers at the tourist information centre in Reykjahlíð. Children under 12 years get a 50% discount on all bus fares.

Getting Around

There are wonderful hiking trails around Mývatn, but unfortunately they're not all connecting. Without a car or bicycle you may find getting around a bit frustrating, unless you don't mind long walks along the lakeshore road. You can roll the dice and stick out your thumb, although Mývatn isn't always the easiest place to hitch a ride.

You might consider renting a car in Akureyri if you're coming to northern Iceland without a private vehicle. During calmer weather, a good option for travellers without a car is to hire a mountain bike. In Reykjahlíð you can rent bikes from Bjarg campsite (p233) and Hlíð campsite (p233). The 36km ride around the lake can be easily done in a day, allowing time for sightseeing at all the major stops.

REYKJAHLÍÐ

pop 200

Reykjahlíð, on the northeastern shore of the lake, is the main village and the obvious base for trips around Mývatn. There's little to it beyond a collection of guest houses and ho-

tels, a supermarket, a petrol station and an information centre.

Information

The friendly **tourist information centre** (☎ 464 4390, 464 4460; www.visitmyvatn.is; ⏱ 8am-6pm Jun-Sep, 10am-5pm Oct-May), next to the Samkaup supermarket, has a display on the local geology as well as a large seating area perfect for waiting out bad weather. Pick up a free copy of the *Mývatn Lake* map – you'll have to pay for it at the info centre in Akureyri. See http://english.ust.is/National -Parks/Protectedareas/MyvatnandLaxa for additional details about the area.

The **post office** (Helluhraun) is on the street behind the supermarket. Inside is a 24-hour ATM.

Got a flat tyre from driving over one too many lava flows? You're in luck – Reykjahlíð has a **garage** (☎ 464 4117, emergency 848 2678; Múlavegur 1) at the corner of Rte 1 and Múlavegur.

Sights & Activities

After tackling the popular Eastern Lakeside hike (p235), there are some fantastic day hikes just north of Reykjahlíð – see p237 for details.

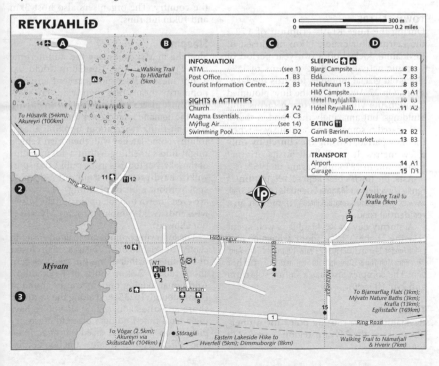

REYKJAHLÍÐ

INFORMATION	
ATM	(see 1)
Post Office	1 B3
Tourist Information Centre	2 B3

SIGHTS & ACTIVITIES	
Church	3 A2
Magma Essentials	4 C3
Myflug Air	(see 14)
Swimming Pool	5 D2

SLEEPING	
Bjarg Campsite	6 B3
Eldá	7 B3
Helluhraun 13	8 B3
Hlíð Campsite	9 A1
Hótel Reykjahlíð	10 B3
Hótel Reynihlíð	11 A2

EATING	
Gamli Bærinn	12 B2
Samkaup Supermarket	13 B3

TRANSPORT	
Airport	14 A1
Garage	15 D3

MARIMO BALLS

Marimo balls (*Cladophora aegagropila*) are bizarre little spheres of green algae that are thought to grow naturally in only two places in the world – Mývatn and Lake Akan in Japan. The spongy balls grow slowly, to about the size of a baseball, rising to the surface of the water in the morning to photosynthesise (when there's enough sunlight) and sinking to the bottom at night.

The name *marimo* is the Japanese word for 'algae ball' – around Mývatn, the locals call 'em *kúluskítur*, which literally means 'ball of shit'. Swing by the Bird Museum (p236) to check out these curious critters – they live in the small pool at the centre of the exhibition space. If no other tourists are around (and if you ask very politely) the friendly staff may let you hold one. There are also a few *marimo* balls living in a cloudy aquarium at the Sel-Hotel's restaurant (p236).

MÝVATN NATURE BATHS

Clouds of steam rise from the turquoise-blue waters at the **Mývatn Nature Baths** (Jarðbaðshólar; ☎ 464 4411; www.jardbodin.is; adult/8-16yr Ikr2000/1000, towel/swimsuit/bathrobe hire Ikr400/400/700; ☼ 9am-11pm Jun-Aug, noon-9.30pm Sep-May; ☎), 3km east of Reykjahlíð. This is northern Iceland's answer to the Blue Lagoon and, although smaller, it's a gorgeous place to ease aching muscles in the mineral-rich water. After a relaxing soak, try one of the three natural steam baths and a rich dessert at the large on-site restaurant.

TOWN CENTRE

During the huge Krafla eruption of 1727, the Leirhnjúkur crater, 11km northeast of Reykjahlíð, kicked off a two-year period of volcanic activity, sending streams of lava along old glacial moraines towards the lakeshore. On 27 August 1729 the flow ploughed through the village, destroying farms and buildings, but amazingly the wooden **church** was spared – some say miraculously – when the flow parted, missing the church by only a few metres. It was rebuilt on its original foundation in 1876, then again in 1962.

Ásta, the town's best-kept secret, pummels tense travellers at **Magma Essentials** (☎ 464 3740; www.magmaessentials.com; Birkihraun 11), hidden on a residential road.

A stormy day in Reykjahlíð is well spent relaxing at the 25m outdoor **swimming pool** (adult/under 14yr Ikr300/150; ☼ 9am-10pm mid-Jun–Aug, 9am-8pm Mon-Thu & 10am-4pm Sat Sep–mid-Jun) and hot tub. The complex also has a sauna, solarium and gym (Ikr550).

Tours

Reykjahlíð is the starting point for numerous tours of the Mývatn region – see p229 for details.

Festivals & Events

Held in March or April, **Orkugangan** is a popular cross-country skiing event in which participants swoosh from Krafla to Húsavík (60km).

The **Úrvadí Ur Mýflugur** festival (which idiomatically means 'making a mountain out of a molehill') is a family-friendly rock festival held in July in a barn between the town's two hotels.

In late May the annual **Mývatn marathon** (www.myvatn.is/marathon) follows a circuit around the lake, attracting hardy souls from across the country. The organisers also host 3km and 10km fun runs.

Sleeping

Sleeping in Mývatn during the summertime is, as *Project Runway*'s Tim Gunn would say, a 'hot mess'. The region's recent surge in popularity means that room rates are soaring (most places are [over]priced in euros), and the demand is far greater than the supply, so don't think twice about booking ahead! Johnny-come-latelies with their own vehicle might find something within a 40km radius of the lake, but tourists using public transport will be hard-pressed to scout out a sleeping spot without a bit of planning – campsites are even known to book up during the busier weekends (wild camping around Mývatn is not allowed).

The following options are located either in central Reykjahlíð or at Vógar, a small cluster of buildings further along the lake's eastern shore (about 2.5km south of Reykjahlíð). Additional lodging options can be found at Dimmuborgir (p235) and along the southern shore at Skútustaðir (p235). If you're having a hard time finding a place to crash, try picking up the pocket-sized *North Iceland; The Official Tourist Guide* – the booklet has a detailed list of accommodation in the region (sorted by type).

BUDGET & MIDRANGE

Hlíð campsite (Hlíð Ferðaþjónusta; ☎ 464 4103; www.simnet.is/hlid; Hraunbrún; sites per person Ikr1000, electricity Ikr500, sb/cabins Ikr4000/5000; 🖳 🛜) This large, well-maintained campsite has showers, toilets, drying sheds and, in summer, a kitchen tent. There's also a laundry service (Ikr500 per wash and Ikr500 to dry), mountain-bike rental (Ikr1200/1600 per afternoon/full day) and internet access (Ikr500 per hour/unlimited wi-fi). Sleeping-bag accommodation is available across the road in no-frills rooms with a large shared kitchen and bathroom. There are also six basic cabins sleeping two. The Hlíð is 300m uphill from the church.

Bjarg campsite (Ferðaþjónustan Bjarg; ☎ 464 4240; ferdabjarg@simnet.is; sites per person Ikr1100, sb/d Ikr2900/11,500; 🕑 mid-May–Sep; 🖳 🛜) This smaller site has a lovely location on the lake shore and features modern shower blocks, a kitchen tent, laundry service, summer boat rental (Ikr2000 for the first hour, Ikr1000 per hour thereafter), bike hire (Ikr2000 per day) and internet access (Ikr400/600 per half-hour/hour). Accommodation is also available in a couple of bright, freshly carpeted rooms in the main building.

Helluhraun 13 (☎ 464 4132, 846 7392; helluhraun13@gmail.com, www.helluhraun13.blogspot.com; Helluhraun 13; d Ikr12,500; 🕑 Jun-Sep) There are just three rooms and one bathroom at this small guest house, but they're spacious, bright and tastefully decorated, with wood floors and white linens. Breakfast is included in the price, as are the privileged views of the dramatic lava field out the kitchen window. Sleeping bags (Ikr3000) can be used in early June and late September.

Vógar (☎ 464 3800; www.vogafjos.net; Vógar; sites per person Ikr1000, sb dm/d €20/49, dm/d €30/68; 🕑 mid-May–mid-Sep) Sleeping-bag accommodation is located in utilitarian prefab huts, while made-up beds can be found in a cosy, honey-coloured farmhouse. Shared bathrooms throughout.

Eldá (☎ 464 4220; www.elda.is; Helluhraun 15; sb Ikr2900 Sep-May only, s/d Ikr9800/13,900; 🖳 🛜) This friendly family-run guest house operation owns four properties along Helluhraun and offers cosy accommodation in each one. There are guest kitchens and TV lounges, and an impressive buffet breakfast is included in the rates. All guests should check in at this location.

TOP END

Hótel Reykjahlíð (☎ 464 4142; www.reykjahlid.is; Reykjahlíð 2; Jun-Aug s/d Ikr20,000/25,500, Sep–May Ikr12,800/15,000; 🖳 🛜) Looking out over the lake, this small hotel with a relaxed attitude has a choice of bright, spacious rooms with contemporary, neutral furnishings and handy black-out blinds. The relaxed restaurant (open 7pm to 10pm) serves a good selection of traditional salmon, char and lamb dishes as well as more international chicken and vegetarian specialities (three courses Ikr4500 to Ikr5800). Reservations are a must.

Vogafjós Guesthouse (☎ 464 4399; www.vogahraun.is; Vógar; s/d incl €135/155) Fresh scents of pine and cedar fill the air in the Cowshed's ultra-cosy log cabins. Breakfast is served at the moo-filled cafe down the road (below).

Hótel Reynihlíð (☎ 464 4170; www.myvatnhotel.is; s/d €165/201; 🖳 🛜) The rude welcome we received hasn't deterred the scores of tour groups from shacking up at Mývatn's most upmarket (and overpriced) option. If you're gonna drop the big bucks then stick with a standard room. The superior rooms aren't a noticeable upgrade; they only have slightly better views. The in-house restaurant (two-/three-course dinner Ikr5900/6400) is the town's swankiest and features a long list of faves like smoked trout, *bacalao*, duck, fresh lamb and *skyr* with blueberries.

Eating & Drinking

The local food speciality is a moist, cake-like rye bread known as *hverabrauð*. It's slow-baked underground and served in every restaurant in town. Ask at the service centre in Dimmuborgir about watching the baking process. In addition to the following options, Reykjahlíð's upmarket hotels also have restaurants, as does the Mývatn Nature Baths down the road.

Vogafjós Café (The Cowshed; ☎ 464 4303, 464 3800; Vógar 1; snacks Ikr600-1000, mains Ikr2300-4000; 🕑 7.30-10am & 11am-11pm early May–early Oct & Dec) Located 2.5km south of Reykjahlíð, this bizarre but memorable cafe features large picture windows between the dining room and the dairy shed of a working farm. You can watch the cows being milked as you sip your coffee and tuck into the tasty selection of sandwiches, cakes, waffles, pancakes and smoked trout. The cows are milked daily at 7.30am and 6pm.

Gamli Bærinn (Old Farm Cafe; ☎ 464 4270; mains Ikr1500-2900; 🕑 10am-11pm) This busy pub-style restaurant beside Hótel Reynihlíð is a popular place for a bite. The menu features a wide selection of dishes, including traditional fish stew, pan-fried lamb, juicy burgers and a bumper selection of desserts. In the evening it becomes the local hangout – the opening hours are often extended during weekend revelry, but the kitchen closes promptly at 10pm.

The **Samkaup supermarket** (☾ 10am-8pm) at the N1 petrol station is well stocked and has a hot -dog grill.

EASTERN MÝVATN

If you're short on time, make this area your first stop. The sights along Mývatn's eastern lakeshore can be linked together on an enjoyable half-day hike (see the boxed text, opposite).

Stóragjá & Grjótagjá

About 100m beyond Reykjahlíð is **Stóragjá**, a rather eerie, watery fissure that was once a popular bathing spot. Cooling water temperatures (currently about 28°C) and the growth of potentially harmful algae mean it's no longer safe to swim in the cave, but it's an alluring spot with clear waters and a rock roof.

Further on at **Grjótagjá** there's another gaping fissure with a water-filled cave, this time at about 45°C – too hot to soak in, but you can get away with dipping your toes. It's a beautiful spot, particularly when the sun filters through the cracks in the roof and illuminates the interior.

Hverfell

Dominating the lava fields on the eastern edge of Mývatn is the classic tephra ring **Hverfell**. This near-symmetrical crater appeared 2500 years ago in a cataclysmic eruption of the existing Lúdentarhíð complex. Rising 463m from the ground and stretching 1040m across, it is a massive and awe-inspiring landmark in Mývatn.

The crater is composed of loose gravel, but an easy track leads from the northwestern end to the summit and offers stunning views of the crater itself and the surrounding landscape. From the rim of the crater the sheer magnitude of the explosion becomes apparent – a giant gaping hole reaching out across the mountain. A path runs along the western rim of the crater to a lookout at the southern end before descending steeply towards Dimmuborgir.

LÚDENTARBORGIR & BLÁFJALL

A second path on Hverfell leads southeast, away from the main lake area, to a region of forbidding mountains, deserts and rugged geological features. With plenty of time and determination, it makes challenging terrain for experienced hikers.

The **Lúdentarborgir** crater row (about 6km long) is part of the 8km **Þrengslaborgir** fissure. A marked path follows the astonishingly straight line of seismic divots. The trail ends at **Heilagsdalur** (20km south of Hverfell), where you can pitch a tent beside the abandoned house. The building here is owned by a tour operator based in Húsavík – be sure to ask permission at the info centre in Reykjahlíð if you plan to crash inside.

From Heilagsdalur, you can ascend the beautiful table mountain **Bláfjall** (1222m). The journey takes about 2½ hours; the hike is somewhat strenuous since there is no marked path to the summit. From the top, you'll be afforded breathtaking views of Herðubreið – Queen of the Mountains – and the crystal glaciers beyond.

Check out the *Útivist & afþreying #4* map for a visual plan of the journey. The trailhead is located near '15'; however, the path itself (heading south) does not have a number.

Dimmuborgir

The giant jagged lava field at **Dimmuborgir** (literally 'the Dark Castles') is one of the most fascinating flows in the country. And the story of Dimmuborgir's formation is almost as convoluted as its criss-crossing network of columnar lava. It's commonly believed that these strange pillars and crags were created about 2000 years ago when lava from the Þrengslaborgir and Lúdentarborgir crater rows flowed across older Hverfell lava fields. The new lava was dammed into a fiery lake in the Dimmuborgir basin and, as the surface of this lake cooled, a domed roof formed over the still-molten material below. The roof was supported by pillars of older igneous material, so when the dam finally broke, the molten lava drained and the odd pillars remained.

A series of colour-coded walking trails runs through Dimmuborgir's easily anthropomorphised landscape. The most popular path is the easy **Church Circle** (2.25km; also known as the Kirkjan route), which takes roughly one hour if you're a bit camera crazy like us. Travellers on a tighter schedule can try the **Small Circle**

EASTERN LAKESIDE HIKE

Although easily accessible by car, the sights along Mývatn's eastern lakeshore can also be tackled on a pleasant half-day hike in good weather. A well-marked track runs from Reykjahlíð to Hverfell (5km), passing intriguing Grjótagjá along the way. Then it's on to Dimmuborgir (another 2.5km) with its collection of ruin-like lava. If you start in the late afternoon and time your hike correctly, you'll finish the day with a hearty meal at Dimmuborgir while sunset shadows dance along the alien landscape. The Dimmuborgir Service Centre (below) offers **guided hikes** (three hours; around Ikr2000) along the aforementioned trail. The trip starts in Reykjahlíð and a shuttle ride back to town is included in the price.

If you are using the excellent *Útivist & afþreying* map series (available at most information centres in the region), this 8km hike is featured as Trail 16 on map #4.

(550m; 10 minutes) or the **Big Circle** (800m; 20 minutes) for a sampling of the lava field's gnarled turrets. Treacherous fissures abound – it's best to stick to the marked paths.

Be sure to visit the handy **Dimmuborgir Service Centre** (☎ 464 1144, 894 1470; www.visitdim muborgir.is; ⏰ 10am-10pm late May–early Sep, reduced hours early Sep–late May) at the top of the ridge (you can't miss it) – it's a tour office, souvenir shop, gallery and cafe all rolled into one. While Reykjahlíð hosts a bevy of tour options in the greater region, the staff at Dimmuborgir run a series of guided trips around Mývatn's eastern edge. At the time of research, free one-hour tours (daily at 11am and 5.30pm) looped the 'Church Circle' and focused on the local geology and culture. Other trips include a fascinating hike along the straight row of dramatic craters at Lúdentarborgir (opposite), and a four-day hike (80km) from the Víti crater at Krafla to scenic Ásbyrgi in Vatnajökull National Park. It's definitely worth checking in to see what new tour itineraries are being conjured up. The on-site restaurant (mains from Ikr1200) is a great place to enjoy a late dinner in summer. Grab a table on the outside terrace, nibble on the homemade *hverabraud*, and watch the sun dance its shadows across the jagged lava bursts and dimpled craters. Picnic lunches are available for busier schedules.

The aptly named **Dimmuborgir Guesthouse** (☎ 464 4210, 894 3042; www.dimmuborgir.is; Geiteyjarströnd 1; campsite/s/d/cottages €12/50/90/110-225) is the only accommodation in the area. Single and double rooms are tucked behind enormous picture windows in the main house (open all year, 20% discounts in June and September, 50% discounts during winter months) while the scatter of wooden cottages curve near the lake's edge in two neat rows (closed in the colder months) – No 9 is our favourite. It's worth swinging by if you're stuck without accommodation – the managers will often leave a small room available for stragglers. Oh, and don't miss the **smokehouse** hidden in the back – check out the rows of shiny orange salmon, and stock up on the finished product for tomorrow's picnic.

Höfði

One of the area's gentlest landscapes is on the forested lava headland at **Höfði**. Wildflowers, birch and spruce trees cover the bluffs, while the tiny islands and crystal-clear waters attract great northern divers and other migratory birds. Along the shore you'll see many small caves and stunning *klasar* (lava pillars), the most famous of which are at **Kálfaströnd** on the southern shore of the Höfði Peninsula. Here, the *klasar* rise from the water in dramatic clusters. Rambling footpaths lead across the headland and can easily fill an hour.

SOUTHERN MÝVATN

Eastern Mývatn may be the ultimate treasure trove of geological anomalies, but the south side of the lake lures the crowds with its epic cache of pseudocraters (p236). The most accessible swarm is located along a short path in **Skútustaðagígar**, just across from Skútustaðir (see below).

The nearby pond, **Stakhólstjörn**, and its surrounding area are havens for nesting waterfowl and were designated a national natural monument in 1973. The boggy marshland here is particularly delicate, so hikers are asked to stick to the marked trails.

Skútustaðir

The small village of Skútustaðir is the only 'major' settlement (and we use that term

NORTHEAST ICELAND

PSEUDOCRATERS

Like blasts on the landscape from some sinister alien spacecraft, the dramatic dimples along Mývatn's otherworldly terrain were formed when molten lava flowed into the lake, triggering a series of gas explosions. Known as 'pseudocraters', these hills came into being when trapped subsurface water boiled and popped, forming small scoria cones and craters. The largest clusters, which measure more than 300m across, are east of Vindbelgjarfjall (right) on the western shore of Mývatn. The smallest ones – the islets in the lake – are just a couple of metres wide and are best appreciated from the air.

lightly) around the lake apart from Reykjahlíð (p231). During Saga times, the area was owned by the notorious Vigaskúta, who was known for his ruthlessness and was marked for assassination by his neighbours. He was clever, though, and more often than not turned the tables on those who threatened him.

SLEEPING & EATING

Skútustaðir Farmhouse (☎ 464 4212; www.skutus tadir.com; d without/with bathroom Ikr10,000/13,000) This friendly guest house near the Sel-Hótel Mývatn has a selection of comfortable, homey rooms and offers sleeping-bag space (Ikr3500) in the low season.

Hótel Gígur (☎ 464 4455; www.keahotels.is; Skútustaðir; s/d Ikr14,600/18,500 Jun-Aug, Ikr11,400/14,500 Sep-May; 🖳 🛜) The lovely lakeside location here compensates for the extra-compact rooms at this business-style hotel. Popular with tour groups and often full, it's a comfortable place with tasteful but simple decor, en-suite bathrooms and free internet access for guests. The restaurant (mains Ikr2190 to Ikr4490) offers one of the best lake views in the whole area, with a lovely outdoor seating area and giant glass windows inside to protect you from the swarming midges as you watch the sunset over the lake.

Sel-Hótel Mývatn (☎ 464 4164; www.myvatn. is; s/d Jun-Aug €150/183, Sep-May €68/82; 🖳 🛜) Skútustaðir's top hotel is looking a bit faded, but its spacious, bright rooms are still comfy. There's a hot pot, sauna, lounge, cafeteria and souvenir shop. The restaurant (lunch/dinner buffet Ikr2100/4300) is home to a few *marimos*

(see the boxed text, p232) and offers an assortment of Icelandic oddities (rotten shark and the like) mixed in with a standard evening buffet. Ask about possible winter activities.

WESTERN MÝVATN

The clear and turbulent **Laxá** (Salmon River), one of the many Icelandic rivers so named, cuts the western division of Mývatn, rolling straight across the tundra towards Skjálfandi (Húsavík's whale-filled bay). The Laxá is one of the best – and most expensive – salmon-fishing spots in the country. More affordable brown-trout fishing is also available.

The easy climb up 529m-high **Vindbelgjarfjall**, further north along the western shore, offers one of the best views across the lake and its alien pseudocraters. The trail to the summit starts south of the peak on Rte 848. Reckon on about a half-hour to climb to the summit.

Birders unite! Western Mývatn offers some of the best birdwatching in the region, with over 115 species present – 45 nesting. Most species of Icelandic waterfowl are found here in great numbers – including nearly 10,000 breeding pairs of ducks. Three duck species – the scoter, the gadwall and the Barrow's goldeneye – breed nowhere else in Iceland. Other species frequenting the area include eider ducks, mallards, whooper swans, great northern divers, black-headed gulls, arctic terns, golden plovers, snipe and whimbrels. The area's bogs, marshes, ponds and wet tundra are a high-density waterfowl nesting zone. Off-road entry is restricted between 15 May and 20 July (when the chicks hatch), but overland travel on this soggy ground is challenging at any time.

For a bit of background, swing by the **Bird Museum** (☎ 464 4477; www.fuglasafn.is; Borg; adult/child & senior Ikr800/400; ☷ 11am-7pm mid-May–Aug, reduced hr Sep–mid-May), housed in a beautiful lakeside building that fuses modern design with the traditional turf house. Inside you'll find an impressive collection of taxidermic avians (more than 180 types from around the world) including every species of bird that calls Iceland home, except one – the grey phalarope. Designer lighting and detailed captions further enhance the experience. The menagerie of stuffed squawkers started as the private collection of a local named Sigurgeir Stefansson. Tragically, Sigurgeir drowned in the lake at the age of 37 – the museum was erected in his honour. The museum also houses a serene cafe and lends out high-tech telescopes to ornithological enthusiasts. Don't forget to take a look in the small water feature at the centre of the exhibition hall – see the boxed text (p232) for details on the spongy green surprise that lurks inside.

NORTHERN MÝVATN (MÝVATN TO KRAFLA)

As the lakeshore road circles back around towards Reykjahlíð, the marshes dry up and the terrain returns to its signature stretches of crispy lava. Travellers who continue along Rte 1 (Iceland's Ring Road) towards Krafla will discover a wicked world of orange sky and the gurgling remnants of ancient earthen cataclysms.

The lava field along Mývatn's northern lakeshore, **Eldhraun**, includes the flow that nearly engulfed the Reykjahlíð church. It was belched out of Leirhnjúkur during the Mývatnseldar in 1729, and flowed down the channel Eldá. With some slow scrambling, it can be explored on foot from Reykjahlíð.

If you are hiking directly to Krafla from Mývatn's northern crest, then you'll pass the prominent 771m-high rhyolite mountain **Hlíðarfjall** (also called Reykjahlíðarfjall), just before the halfway mark. Around 5km from Reykjahlíð, the mount can also be enjoyed as a pleasant day hike from the village, affording spectacular views over the lake on one side and over the Krafla lava fields on the other.

Along the Ring Road (Rte 1)

Northern Mývatn's collection of geological gems conveniently lie along the Ring Road (Rte 1) as it weaves through the harsh terrain between the north end of the lake and the turn-off to steaming Krafla. Car-less travellers will find plenty of paths for exploring the area on foot.

Bjarnarflag, 3km east of Reykjahlíð, is an active geothermal area where the earth hisses and bubbles, and steaming vents line the valley. Historically, the area has been home to a number of economic ventures attempting to harness the earth's powers. Early on, farmers tried growing potatoes here, but, unfortunately, these often emerged from the ground already boiled. In the late 1960s, 25 test holes were bored at Bjarnarflag to ascertain the feasibility of a proposed geothermal power station. One is 2300m deep and the steam still roars out of the pipe at a whopping 200°C.

Later a diatomite (microfossil) plant was set up and the skeletal remains of a type of single-cell algae were filtered and purified into filler for fertilisers, paints, toothpastes and plastics. All that remains of the processing plant today is the shimmering turquoise pond that the locals have dubbed the 'Blue Lagoon'. This inviting puddle is actually quite toxic and should not be confused with the luxurious **Mývatn Nature Baths** (p232) around the corner, which is sometimes called the 'Blue Lagoon of the North'.

The pastel-coloured **Námafjall** lies 3km further away (on the south side of the Ring Road). Produced by a fissure eruption, the ridge sits squarely on the spreading zone of the Mid-Atlantic Ridge and is dotted with steaming vents. A walking trail leads from the highway at Namaskarð pass to a view disc at the summit. This 30-minute climb provides a grand vista over the steamy surroundings. North of the pass is another ridge, **Dalfjall**, which sports a large and growing notch – dramatic evidence that the mountain is being torn in two by tectonic spreading.

THE YULE LADS

Most Christmases involve one fictitious Santa, but Iceland has 13. And they're all real.

Born to Gryla, a wicked trolless, the Yule Lads grew up in Lúdentarborgir. Tired of their mother's constant nagging, the bearded bachelors decided to find their own place, and chose the 'Dark Castles' of lava at Dimmuborgir nearby.

During the 13 days before Christmas, one Yule Lad leaves the rocky fortress each night to spread holiday cheer. Before bed, Icelandic children leave their shoes on the windowsill. Those who are well behaved will find a little gift inside when they wake up; troublemakers get potatoes (literally).

Sceptics can meet the Yule Lads in the flesh during their annual soak at the Mývatn Nature Baths on the first Saturday of December.

NORTHEAST ICELAND

As you tumble down the far side of Námafjall, you'll suddenly find yourself in the magical, ochre-toned world of **Hverir** – a lunar-like landscape of mud cauldrons, steaming vents, radiant mineral deposits and piping fumaroles. Belching mudflaps and stench of sulphur stew may sound as charming as a date with Homer Simpson, but Hverir's ethereal charm grips every passerby. Be careful though: the lingering stink of sulphur soaks the air, which means that a sudden change in wind direction can leave you shrouded in a juicy cloud of pungent steam. Safe pathways through the features have been roped off, and to avoid risk of serious injury and damage to the natural features, avoid any lighter-coloured soil and respect the ropes.

KRAFLA

More steaming vents, brightly coloured craters and aquamarine lakes await at Krafla, an active volcanic region 7km north of the Ring Road. Technically, Krafla is just an 818m-high mountain, but the name is now used for the entire area as well as a geother-

mal power station and the series of eruptions that created Iceland's most awesome lava field.

The heart of volcanic activity is known as the Krafla central volcano but, rather than a cone-shaped peak, Krafla is a largely level system of north–south trending fissures underlaid by a great magma chamber. Activity is normally characterised by fissuring and gradual surface swells followed by abrupt subsidence, which triggers eruptions. At present, the ground surface is rising, indicating possible activity in the future. The **Nordic Volcanological Center** (www.norvol.hi.is) tracks the most recent developments.

As the Krafla area is still considered active, a visit will naturally involve some risk. To be safe, avoid lighter-coloured soil (which indicates a live steam vent), mudpots, sharp lava chunks and scoria slopes. Stick to marked trails, and in winter be extremely wary of hidden fissures and avoid any melting snow, which may cover a hot spot.

Kröflustöð

The idea of constructing a geothermal power station at Krafla was conceived in 1973, and preliminary work commenced with the drilling of 24 test holes to determine project feasibility. In December 1975, however, after a rest of several hundred years, the Krafla fissure burst into activity with the first in a series of nine eruptions and 20 cases of surface subsidence. This considerably lowered the site's projected geothermal potential and nearly deactivated one of the primary steam sources, but the project went ahead and was completed in 1978. A second turbine unit and additional boreholes were added in 1996, and Krafla now operates at its intended capacity of 60 megawatts, using on average 15 to 17 boreholes at a time. The power plant's **visitor centre** (Gestastofa; admission free; ☉ 12.30-3.30pm Mon-Fri, 1-5pm Sat & Sun Jun-Aug) explains how it all works.

Stóra-Víti

The impressive dirt-brown crater of Stóra-Víti reveals a stunning secret when you reach its rim – a dark-blue pool of flood water at its heart. Surrounded by steaming vents, bubbling pools and desolate land, the vibrant colour makes a lasting impression as you track around the rim of the crater on a slippery walking trail.

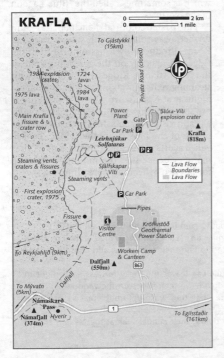

KRAFLA

0 ——————— 2 km
0 ——————— 1 mile

To Gjástykki (15km)

1980 explosion crater
1975 lava
1724 lava
1984 lava

Main Krafla fissure & crater row

Power Plant
Gate
Car Park

Stóra-Víti explosion crater

Krafla (818m)

Private Road (closed)

Leirhnjúkur Solfataras

Steaming vents, craters & fissures

Sjálfskapar Víti

Steaming vents

First explosion crater, 1975

Fissure

Car Park

Pipes

— Lava Flow Boundaries
— Lava Flow

To Reykjahlíð (9km)

Visitor Centre

Kröflustöð Geothermal Power Station

Workers Camp & Canteen

Dalfjall (550m)

863

To Mývatn (5km)

Dalfjall

To Egilsstaðir (161km)

Námaskarð Pass

1

Námafjall (374m)

Hverir

The 320m-wide explosion crater was created in 1724 during the destructive Mývatnseldar, and it's just one of many vents along the Krafla central volcano. Behind the crater are the 'twin lakes', boiling mud springs that spurted mud 10m into the air during the Mývatnseldar. They're now down to a mere simmer and Víti is considered inactive.

Leirhnjúkur & Krafla Caldera

Krafla's most impressive, and potentially most dangerous, attraction is the colourful Leirhnjúkur crater and its solfataras, which originally appeared in August 1727. It started out as a lava fountain and spouted molten material for two years before subsiding. After a minor burp in 1746, it became the menacing sulphur-encrusted mud hole that tourists love today.

From the rim above Leirhnjúkur you can look out across the Krafla caldera and the layers of lava that bisect it. The first of these lava flows was from the original Mývatnseldar, which was overlaid in places by lava from the 1975 eruptions, and again by 1984 lava.

The earth's crust here is extremely thin and in places the ground is ferociously hot. Steaming vents on the pastel-coloured rhyolite mountain to the west are the last vestiges of a series of explosions in 1975, when the small grass-filled crater on the western slope of the mountain south of Leirhnjúkur erupted as Kröflueldar, a continuation of Mývatnseldar.

A well-defined track leads northwest to Leirhnjúkur from the Krafla parking area; with all the volcanic activity, high temperatures, bubbling mudpots and steaming vents, you'd be well advised not to stray from the marked paths at any time.

Gjástykki

This remote rift zone at the northernmost end of the Krafla fissure swarm was the source of the first eruptions in 1724, and was activated when Leirhnjúkur went off in the 1975 eruptions. Between 1981 and 1984 the area was the main hot pot of activity in the Krafla central volcano, and the current Gjástykki lava fields date from this time. The area's best-known landmark is a red mountain that protrudes from dark fields of lava. Gjástykki is a very sensitive area and no private vehicles are allowed access. To visit you will need to join a tour; see p229.

Getting There & Away

From Reykjahlíð, a wonderful day hike leads to Hlíðarfjall and Leirhnjúkur along a marked path from near the airport. Another walking route leads from Namaskarð along the Dalfjall ridge to Leirhnjúkur.

In summer Krafla can be reached on the daily bus (Ikr1200, 15 minutes), which leaves at 8am and 11.30am from the information centre in Reykjahlíð and returns at 11.15am and 3.15pm. The Mývatn–Dettifoss excursion bus also runs via Krafla.

HÚSAVÍK REGION

HÚSAVÍK
pop 2340

Húsavík, Iceland's whale-watching capital, is a picturesque harbour town that has become a firm favourite on travellers' itineraries. With its colourful houses, unique museums and stunning snow-capped peaks across the bay, little Húsavík is undoubtedly the prettiest fishing town on the northeast coast.

History

Although the honours normally go to Reykjavík and Ingólfur Arnarson, Húsavík was the real site of the first Nordic settlement in Iceland. Garðar Svavarsson, a Swedish Viking who set off around 850 for the mysterious Thule or Snæland (Snowland), was actually responsible for the island's first permanent human settlement.

After a brief stop-off at Hornafjörður in the south, Garðar arrived at Skjálfandi on the north coast and built a settlement that he called Húsavík. Modestly renaming the country Garðarshólmur (Garðar's Island), he dug in for the winter. At the advent of spring he prepared to depart, but some of his slaves were left behind. Whether by accident or design, these castaways became Iceland's first real settlers, pioneering life in a new country and yet uncredited by the history books.

Information

The helpful **tourist information centre** (☎ 464 4300; www.husavik.is; Garðarsbraut 5; ⏰ 8.30am-7pm Jun-Aug) is notorious for changing locations each summer. At the time of research it was located beside the Kasko, opposite the Gentle Giant ticket booth. Plans are underway to move the info centre to the Whale Museum.

NORTHEAST ICELAND

HÚSAVÍK

INFORMATION
Hospital.....................................1 B1
Íslandsbanki...............................2 B2
Library....................................(see 5)
Police.....................................3 B1
Tourist Information Centre.........4 B2
Tourist Information Centre
(proposed)............................(see 6)

SIGHTS & ACTIVITIES
Húsavík Museum.........................5 B2
Húsavík Whale Museum..............6 A2
Húsavíkurkirkja..........................7 B2
Icelandic Phallological Museum....8 A1
North Sailing & Gentle Giants Ticket
Booths..................................9 B2
Swimming Pool.........................10 A1

SLEEPING
Árból.....................................11 B2
Baldursbrekka 17.....................12 A1
Baldursbrekka 20.....................13 A1
Campsite................................14 A1
Fosshótel Húsavík....................15 B2
Sigtún..................................16 B3
Vísir....................................17 B2

EATING
Gamli Baukur..........................18 A2
Gentle Café............................19 B2
Heimabakarí Konditori...............20 B2
Kasko Supermarket................(see 4)
Salka...................................21 A2
Skuld Café.............................22 A2
Vín Búð.................................23 B2

SHOPPING
Ískelda Galleri.........................24 B2

TRANSPORT
Bus Station..........................(see 27)
N1 Petrol Station.....................25 B1
Olis Petrol Station...................26 B3
Shell Petrol Station..................27 A1

Húsavík has a hospital, a post office and other facilities. The **Íslandsbanki bank** (Stórigarður 1) is opposite the church and has an ATM. There's internet access at the **library** (☎ 464 6165; Stórigarður 17; per 30min Ikr500; ☺ 10am-6pm Mon-Thu, to 5pm Fri).

Sights & Activities

Don't rush off after your whale-watching trip; Húsavík has a few surprises up its sleeve.

WHALE WATCHING

This is why you came to Húsavík. Over the last decade, the area has become Iceland's premier whale-watching destination, with up to 11 species coming here to feed in summer. The best time to see whales is between June and August. This is, of course, the height of tourist season, but you'll have almost a 100% chance of seeing a breaching beast. See the boxed text (p242) to learn more about Húsavík's whales.

Two whale-watching tours operate from Húsavík harbour. The original operator is **North Sailing** (Norður Sigling; ☎ 464 2350; www.north sailing.is; Gamli Baukur, Hafnarstétt), which has a fleet of beautiful old-school boats, including the

20-tonne oak schooner *Haukur*. Their popular 'Whales, Puffins & Sails' tour stops at beautiful Lundey (p244), and overnight trips to Grímsey (p225) are possible a few times during the summer. The other company is **Gentle Giants** (Hvalferðir; ☎ 464 1500; www.gentlegiants. is; Garðarsbraut 6), with their flotilla of lovingly restored fishing vessels. Gentle Giants also runs special trips to lovely Flatey (p244) – you'll most likely see whales along the way.

Don't stress too much over picking an operator; prices are standardised (adult/under 16yr €48/18) and services are comparable. Locals joke that the only differences between companies are the pastries served onboard – one offers cinnamon buns while the other serves *kleinur* (traditional twisty doughnuts). Trips depart throughout the day (June to August) from 8.30am to 8.30pm and large signs at the ticket booths advertise the next departure time. Boats also run in May, September and October with less frequency.

HÚSAVÍK WHALE MUSEUM

Best visited before you head out on a whale-watching trip, the excellent **Húsavík Whale**

Museum (Hvalamiðstöðin; ☎ 414 2800; www.whale museum.is; Hafnarstétt; adult/6-14yr Ikr900/450; ◷ 9am-7pm Jun-Aug, 10am-5pm May & Sep) will tell you all you ever needed to know about these gracious creatures. Housed in an old slaughterhouse at the harbour, the museum interprets the ecology and habits of whales, conservation and the history of whaling in Iceland through beautifully curated displays, including several huge skeletons soaring high above (they're real!).

The museum has a popular volunteer program – visit the website for details. You must apply by the end of February if you are interested in volunteering for the upcoming summer.

ICELANDIC PHALLOLOGICAL MUSEUM

Oh, the jokes are endless here. The unique **Icelandic Phallological Museum** (Hið Íslanska Reðasafn; ☎ 561 6663; www.phallus.is; Héðinsbraut 3a; adult/senior/under 15yr Ikr600/400/free; ◷ noon-6pm late May–mid-Sep) houses a bizarre collection of penises. From pickled pickles to petrified wood, there are over 300 different types of family jewels on display. New additions include contributions from a walrus, and the silver castings of each member of the Icelandic handball team. There are no actual human contributions though. But don't rush to volunteer – four donors-in-waiting have already promised to bequeath their manhood (signed contracts are mounted on the wall). Quirky sidenote: all displays are translated into Esperanto…

HÚSAVÍK MUSEUM

A folk, maritime and natural-history museum all rolled into one complex, the **Húsavík Museum** (Safnahúsið á Húsavík; ☎ 464 1860; www.husmus .is; Stórigarður 17; adult/under 16yr Ikr500/free; ◷ 10am-6pm Jun-Aug, to 4pm Mon-Fri Sep-May) is one of the best local museums you'll find in Iceland. The museums occupy the 1st and 3rd floors of the building (the library is on the 2nd floor), and an annexe nearby. The natural-history display has the usual array of stuffed animals, including arctic foxes, a frightening-looking hooded seal, and a stuffed polar bear, which was welcomed to Grímsey in 1969 with both barrels of a gun. The folk-history exhibits cover everything from a re-creation of an early farmhouse to a healthy collection of 16th-century weapons and historic books – including a copy of a Bible printed in 1584. There's also a carefully catalogued collection of 100,000 beer-bottle labels from around the world.

HÚSAVÍKURKIRKJA

Húsavík's lovely and unusual **church** is quite different to anything else seen in Iceland. Constructed in 1907 from Norwegian timber, the delicately proportioned red-and-white church would look more at home in the Alps.

DOUBLE DETOUR: ALDEYJARFOSS & THE LAXÁ POWER STATION

Several roads zip between Mývatn and Húsavík, yet very few people indulge in a detour. With a bit of extra time, you'll discover dozens of little-visited attractions – these are our two favourites.

Touring a power plant may sound tedious at first, but the **Laxá Power Station** has a secret – a delightful **sculpture museum** (◷ 1-5pm Mon-Fri, 1-6pm Sat & Sun) set among the compound's brassy levers and turbines. To reach this cleverly hidden exhibition space, follow the easy to find yellow signs for the turn-off to Laxávirkjun between Rte 845 and Rte 87.

Reaching otherworldly **Aldeyjarfoss** takes a bit more legwork. From Goðafoss, you'll have to follow Rte 842 for about 41km into the silent highlands. You'll pass a guest house at Kiðagil along the way, and just when you start to think that surely you're going the wrong way, you'll have to continue for another 10km. The dirt track comes to an end at Mýri, where you'll find a white gate leading straight ahead into the farmstead and a red gate (to your left) marked 'Sprengisandur'. Don't be shy – open the red gate – it's only two more kilometres to the waterfall. Although the road is marked 'F26', the 2km are doable in a 2WD. Soon, the sound of crashing water will confirm that you're in the right place. Park your dust-covered car at the A-frame huts and shuffle along the loose gravel until the stunning cascade suddenly emerges. Vast quantities of water burst forth, tumbling into the basalt-lined canyon below. As the waves smash against the stacks of honeycomb columns their echoes almost sound like the whispers of wandering trolls.

If you're keen on extending your detour (or the accommodation options in Húsavík and Mývatn are all booked up), there are plenty of charming B&Bs scattered throughout the area – check out the ubiquitous *Áning* and *The Ideal Holiday* farm-stay booklets for details.

THE WHALES OF HÚSAVÍK

After a riveting afternoon of whale watching (three humpbacks!), we grabbed a beer with Edda Elísabet Magnúsdóttir, a local PhD candidate in marine biology, to learn more about these gentle giants. The bay around Húsavík is an ideal place to study whales, and in 2007, the Húsavík Research Center (a branch of the University of Iceland) was established here, with a focus on marine mammal studies. Edda moved to Húsavík to work at the centre – her focus being underwater recordings and on-shore observations of the whales in the bay.

'Húsavík sits on a scenic bay known as Skjálfandi, which means 'the tremulous one' in Icelandic. The name is appropriate, since little earthquakes occur very frequently in the bay, usually without being noticed. These trembles are caused by the wrench fault in the earth's crust right beneath the bay. Skjálfandi's bowl-shaped topography and the infusion of freshwater from two river estuaries means that there is a great deal of nutrients collecting in the bay. The nutrient deposits accumulate during the winter months, and when early summer arrives – with its long sunlit days – the cool waters of Skjálfandi bay come alive with myriad plankton blooms.

'These rich deposits act like a beacon, attracting special types of mammals that are highly adapted to life in the cold subarctic waters. Every summer roughly nine to 11 species of whale are sighted in the bay, ranging from the tiny harbour porpoise (*Phocoena phocoena*) to the giant blue whale (*Balaenoptera musculus*), the biggest animal known to roam the earth. Plankton blooming kick-starts each year's feeding season; that's when the whales start appearing in greater numbers in the bay. The first creatures to arrive are the humpback whales (*Megaptera novaeangliae*) and the minke whales (*Balaenoptera acutorostrata*). The humpback whale is known for its curious nature, equanimity and spectacular surface displays, whereas the minke whale is famous for its elegant features: a streamlined and slender black body, and white striped pectoral fin. Although the average minke whale weighs the same amount as two or three grown elephants, they are known as the 'petite cousin' of the greater rorquals. The minke whale has the tendency to leap entirely out of the water and is likely the only rorqual capable of doing so. Several minke and

---

Inside its cruciform shape becomes apparent and is dominated by a depiction of the resurrection of Lazarus on the altarpiece. The carved font is also worth seeking out, as are the 17th-century murals and candlesticks.

OUTDOOR ACTIVITIES

After whale watching (p240), there are plenty of activities around town to keep the blood flowing. Hikers should ask at the information centre for details on local trails and hikes around the fossil-ridden Tjörnes Peninsula (p244) – pick up the *Útivist & afþreying* #3 map for details.

Short horse rides (one to three hours) and longer tours (five to nine days) are available at **Saltvík horse farm** (☎ 847 9515; www.skarpur.is/saltvik), 5km south of Húsavík.

The local **swimming pool** (☎ 464 1144; Laugarbrekka 2; ☀ 7am-9pm Mon-Fri, 10am-6pm Sat) has hot pots, and water slides for children.

Sleeping
BUDGET

Campsite (☎ 845 0705; sites per person Ikr900; ☀ May-Sep) Next to the sports ground at the north end of town, this popular campsite has such luxuries as heated toilets, washing machines and cooking facilities.

Baldursbrekka 20 (Aðalbjörg Birgisdóttir; ☎ 464 1005, 898 8325; onod@simnet.is; Baldursbrekka 20; sb/s/d Ikr2500/3500/7000; 🖳 ☎) You'll find a few basic but good-value rooms at this family home north of town. There's a guest kitchen and a warm welcome. Note: they don't take credit cards (shocking!).

Sigtún (☎ 464 1674, 846 9364; www.gsigtun.is; Túngata 13; s/d/tr incl breakfast from Ikr7000/11,000/14,500) A cut above most of the other guest houses, Sigtún offers prim and professional accommodation with sparkling common bathrooms and free laundry. There's another house on the south side of town at Laugarholt 7e. Despite being further away from town, we were quite fond of the second location. Check-in is from 4pm to 8pm.

Vísir (☎ 856 5750; dora@visirhf.is; Garðarsbraut 14; s/d Ikr7500/10,000; ☀ 1 Jun–25 Aug; 🖳 ☎) Located in a renovated office building, this prim option comes up trumps with its modern kitchen facilities, heaps of common space, free laundry and amazing views from the gigantic

humpback whales stay in the bay throughout the year, but most migrate south during the winter. The blue whale, undoubtedly the most exciting sight in Skjálfandi, is a recent summer visitor – they only started arriving around four years ago. They usually start coming in mid-June and stay until the middle of July. Watching these highly developed hydrodynamic giants in their natural environment is just spectacular. Other summer sightings in Skjálfandi include the orca, also known as the killer whale (*Orcinus orca*; some come to the bay to feed on fish, others come to hunt mammals), bottlenose whales (*Hyperoodon ampullatus*; a mysterious, deep-diving beaked whale), fin whales (*Balaenoptera physalus*), sei whales (*Balaenoptera borealis*), pilot whales (*Globicephala melas*) and sperm whales (*Physeter macrocephalus*).

'Whales only partly use their eyesight, relying much more heavily on their hearing. Toothed whales are known to be highly vocal. Many species – especially dolphins – use whistles and calls to communicate with each other. Most toothed whales use high-frequency echolocation to find prey, observe their surrounding environment and communicate with one another. Baleen whales – like blue whales, minke whales and humpback whales – produce sound at a much lower frequency, and it's solely used for communication. The blue-whale calls, for example, can travel thousands of kilometres underwater. In cooperation with several colleagues, I have discovered a special knocking sound (or 'click') that is likely produced by humpback whales when feeding.

'I also conduct shore-based observations from a lighthouse in Húsavík, where I survey the location and movement of individual whales. I use that information to better understand how each species negotiates the bay and am especially interested in seeing if the whale-watching boats affect the animals' behaviour. Whales are often curious about the vessels, but if the vessels drive up too fast, or come too close, the animals can get stressed. Ultimately, the overarching goal is to improve the knowledge about the biology of whales for the benefit of conservation and sustainable wildlife tourism.'

picture windows – it's the perfect place for groups. In winter, Vísir turns into a shared living space for Polish workers who spend the quieter months in Húsavík working at the local fish factory.

Baldursbrekka 17 (Emhild Olsen; ☎ 464 1618; Baldursbrekka 17; s/d Ikr8000/12,000; ⏲ Jun-Aug) Just opposite Aðalbjörg Birgisdóttir, and offering very similar facilities, is this well-priced guest house with comfortable rooms and friendly service.

MIDRANGE & TOP END

Árból (☎ 464 2220; www.simnet.is/arbol; Ásgarðsvegur 2; Jun–mid-Sep s/d incl breakfast €62/106, mid-Sep-May €55/79) Stuck in a decor time warp, this heritage house has spacious but old-fashioned rooms that are noticeably past their prime. Try to nab one of the cosier rooms in the pine-scented attic (Nos 7 and 8); a fossil-lined stairwell leads to the top.

Kaldbaks-Kot (☎ 464 1504; www.cottages.is; 2-4 person cabins €135-175; 💻 📶) Located 1.5km south of Húsavík (follow the turn-off to Kaldubakur) is this cluster of charming timber cottages that all feel exactly like grandpa's cabin in the woods. Enjoy breakfast (€10) on your porch or eat in the old cowshed, which has been transformed into an elegant dining room fit for Christmas dinner.

Fosshótel Húsavík (☎ 464 1220; www.fosshotel.is; Ketilsbraut 22; s/d incl breakfast from Ikr23,000/25,000 May-Sep, 50% off Oct-Apr; 💻 📶) Standard rooms (some wheelchair accessible) have predictable international-style decor, while superior options feature a few stylish touches – whale-themed knick-knacks abound. There's an on-site restaurant (mains Ikr900 to Ikr3500), which feels like you're eating on a cruise ship from the '70s; and the bar, Moby Dick, seems to be an accidental double-nod to both the town's whale obsession and phallus museum.

Eating

Skuld Café (☎ 464 2900; snacks Ikr250-1000; ⏲ 8.30am-10pm Jun-Sep) Set on the hill with a lovely outdoor deck overlooking the waterfront, this cosy summer cafe sells light meals and baked goods. Believe it or not, three families used to live in the teeny house all at once!

Gentle Café (snacks Ikr800-2000; ⏲ 8am-9pm Jun-Sep) This 'gourmet hut' just by Garðarsbraut offers

---

LUNDEY & FLATEY

As if there weren't enough Lundeys and Flateys in Iceland… these particular islands lie in the scenic Skjálfandi bay. Lundey (Puffin Island) dramatically emerges from the sea with a series of high, nest-covered cliffs. It's a popular breeding ground for several species of seabird including (yeah, you guessed it) puffins. Flatey (Flat Island) lives up to its name, rising only a couple of metres above the waves. Although abandoned during winter, the grassy island hosts a number of charming summer cottages. Popular tours to both islands are available with both of Húsavík's whale-watching operators – see p240.

---

local foods such as dried haddock, marinated herring, dried reindeer and smoked trout. The outdoor terrace has great views over the harbour.

Salka (☎ 464 2551; Garðarsbraut 6; mains Ikr1650-4300; ☺ 11.30am-10pm) Once home to Iceland's first cooperative, this historic building now houses a popular restaurant serving everything from smoked puffin to pizza. The real speciality here, though, is seafood, with excellent lobster, prawns (shrimp) and salt cod on offer.

our pick Gamli Baukur (☎ 464 2442; Hafnarstétt; mains Ikr1950 3500; ☺ 11.30am 9pm Sun Wed, to 1am Thu, 11am-3am Fri & Sat) Gamli Baukur is one of those rare places that manages to be both a favourite local hangout and a wonderfully friendly place for tourists. Owned by North Sailing, the lovely timber-framed restaurant-bar serves excellent food (juicy burgers, succulent fish soup and a zingy curry bouillabaisse) and flavourful coffee among shiny nautical relics. Live music and a sweeping terrace makes it the most happenin' place in northeast Iceland.

Both the N1 and Shell petrol stations have grills selling the usual fast-food fare, while the town bakery **Heimabakarí Konditori** (☎ 464 2900; Garðarsbraut 15; ☺ 8am-5pm) sells fresh bread, sandwiches and sugary cakes. **Kasko supermarket** (Garðarsbraut 5; ☺ 10am-6.30pm Sun-Thu, to 7pm Fri, to 6pm Sat) is in the centre of town, and there's a **Vín Búð** (cnr Garðarsbraut & Miðgarður).

Shopping
Up to your eyeballs in whale souvenirs and fluffy fleeces? Stop by **Ískelda Galleri** (Garðarsbraut;

☺ 10am-5pm Mon-Fri, 11am-2pm Sat) for something a bit different. Check out the artistic assortment of clothing and accessories (mostly for women) made from locally sourced wools and fish skins. There are no Christmas sweaters here – these are things you'd actually wear! Check out the studio in the back and don't forget to sign the wall on your way out.

Getting There & Away
There are four daily buses to Akureyri (Ikr2500, 1¼ hours) from June to August. In winter there are four daily buses during the week, two on Sunday and one on Saturday. From mid-June to August there are two daily buses to Reykjahlíð at Mývatn (Ikr2000, 40 minutes). See p248 for buses to Ásbyrgi and Þorshöfn. The bus terminal is at the N1 petrol station.

TJÖRNES PENINSULA
Heading north from Húsavík along Rte 85 you'll sweep along the coast of the stubby Tjörnes Peninsula, which separates Skjálfandi from Öxarfjörður.

Fossil-rich coastal cliffs flank the Hallbjarnarstaðaá river mouth 10km north of Húsavík. The cliffs are made up of alternating layers of fossil shells and lignite (a soft brown-black coal), with the oldest layers dating back about two million years. The fossils here are the shells of creatures that are now found only in waters of 12°C or warmer. The present water temperature along Iceland's Arctic Ocean coast is around 4°C, an indication that the sea here has cooled dramatically over the past two to three million years. You can get to the cliffs by turning off Rte 85 at Ytritunga farm. To put the fossils in context, it's worth visiting the **fossil museum** (☎ 464 1968; adult/under 14yr Ikr500/free; ☺ 10am-6pm Jun-Aug), about 2km further up Rte 85 at the farm Hallbjarnarstaðir.

For something a bit quirkier, continue another 10km up the road until you reach the **Þórshamar Home Museum** (☎ 464 1957; adult/under 14yr Ikr500/free; ☺ 9am-6pm Jun-Aug) at the tip of the peninsula. The eclectic collection contains Viking Age jewellery, as well as a variety of matchboxes, tobacco tins, old photographs and crockery.

KELDUHVERFI REGION
Giant cracks, fissures and grabens (depressions between geological faults) scar the

earth at low-lying Kelduhverfi, where the Mid-Atlantic Ridge enters the Arctic Ocean. Like Þingvellir (p121), the area reveals some of the most visible evidence that Iceland is being ripped apart from its core.

There are several comfy places to stay in the area. The modern guest house at **Keldunes** (☎ 465 2275; keldunes@isl.is; sb Ikr3000, s/d incl breakfast Ikr7900/13,900; ☎) has a great kitchen and TV lounge, a hot pot, varnished wooden floors, and large balconies for birdwatching. It's about 12km west of Ásbyrgi. Nearby, **Skúlagarður** (☎ 465 2280; skulagardur@simnet.is; sb Ikr2500, s/d incl breakfast Ikr6500/9300), a former boarding school, has a slew of bright functional rooms; and **Hóll** (☎ 465 2270; hrunda@is mennt.is; sb/d Ikr7800/13,500), a mere 7.5km from Ásbyrgi, is a farmstead with four simple rooms. Horse riding is available for Ikr3500 per hour.

JÖKULSÁRGLJÚFUR (VATNAJÖKULL NATIONAL PARK – NORTH)

In 2008 the Vatnajökull National Park – Europe's largest protected reserve – was formed when Jökulsárgljúfur merged with Skaftafell to the south. The idea was to protect the Vatnajökull glacier and all of its glacial run-off under one super-sized preserve. The Jökulsárgljúfur portion protects a unique subglacial eruptive ridge and a 30km gorge carved out by the formidable Jökulsá á Fjöllum (Iceland's second-longest river), which starts in the Vatnajökull ice cap and flows almost 200km to the Arctic Ocean at Öxarfjörður. *Jökulhlaups* (flooding from volcanic eruptions beneath the ice cap) formed the canyon and have carved out a chasm that averages 100m deep and 500m wide.

A wonderful two-day hike (see the boxed text, p247) weaves along the canyon, taking in all of the major sights en route. If you're not so keen on hiking, the big attractions, such as the waterfalls at the southern end of the park and horseshoe-shaped Ásbyrgi canyon at the northern end, are accessible by road in a leisurely day.

Orientation

Vatnajökull National Park's northern section can be roughly divided into three parts. The region's main information bureau is near the northern entry at Ásbyrgi, a verdant, forested plain enclosed by vertical canyon walls. Vesturdalur's caves and fascinating geological anomalies make up Jökulsárgljúfur's middle

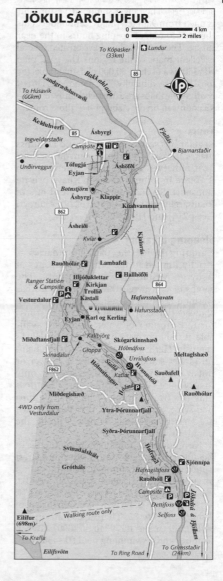

JÖKULSÁRGLJÚFUR

section. The mighty falls of Dettifoss anchor the park's southern entrance.

Information

The main tourist information point for Vatnajökull National Park (North) is the new visitor centre at **Gljúfrastofa–Ásbyrgi** (☎ 470 7100; www.vatnajokulsthjodgardur.is; 🕑 9am-9pm Sun-Thu, to 11pm Fri & Sat mid-Jun–mid-Aug, 10am-4pm May–mid-Jun & mid-Aug–Sep). The ranger station at Vesturdalur is open from 9am to 7pm. Recent budget cuts threaten to reduce opening hours in the near future. The park wardens have created several excellent maps of the region. The park map (Ikr350) is a useful 1:50,000 plan that ranks the local hikes by difficulty. The ubiquitous *Útivist & afþreying* maps are extremely handy as well – #3 zooms in on the Ásbyrgi–Dettifoss route.

Tours

Regular bus service to Ásbyrgi and Dettifoss makes it easy to tackle the canyon on your own. However, a tour can be a useful option if you're in a hurry and don't have private transport. Several companies offer tours of Jökulsárgljúfur from Mývatn (p229), Akureyri (see p216) and Húsavík.

Sleeping & Eating

Camping inside the park boundaries is strictly limited to the official campsites at Ásbyrgi, Vesturdalur and Dettifoss. The campsite at Ásbyrgi (Ikr850 per person) has washing facilities including well-maintained showers that cost Ikr300 (six x Ikr50 coins) for five minutes of water. Coins are available at the information centre. Vesturdalur's campsite (Ikr850 per person), near the helpful ranger station, has no electric power or hot water – well-kept toilets are the only luxury here. The free campsite at Detifoss only has two freshwater canisters; the limited water supply means that the grounds are strictly reserved for hikers doing the popular two-day hike.

Farmhouse accommodation is available in Kelduhverfi (see p244); otherwise, the nearest option is the basic summer accommodation at superfriendly **Lundur** (☎ 465 2247, 863 4311; www.lundurtravel.com; sites per person Ikr800, sb Ikr2700; 🕑 Jun–mid-Aug; 🖳 🛜 🛃), 5km northeast of Ásbyrgi on Rte 85. There's also an on-site restaurant (mains Ikr790 to Ikr2000), kitchen facilities and a swimming pool (Ikr450) with a hot pot.

The petrol station on Rte 85 near the info centre at Ásbyrgi has a decent selection of reasonably priced groceries; however, the food at the on-site grill isn't stellar. If you're hiking, it's best to purchase your supplies in Akureyri or Húsavík.

Getting There & Away

There are two north–south roads running parallel to one another on each side of the canyon. On the west side of the canyon, Rte F862 runs from Ásbyrgi to Dettifoss, but at the time of research only the stretch from Ásbyrgi to Vesturdalur could accommodate 2WD vehicles; 4WDs can make it all the way. There are big plans underway to create a long paved route running the length of the park's western side, connecting Rte 1 to Rte 85. An asphalted lane from the Ring Road to Dettisfoss will be ready in late 2010 – the rest of the way should be completed by 2012.

The road on the east side (Rte 864) is a poorly maintained gravel track beyond the park's boundaries. It's passable by 2WD vehicles, but its rutted and potholed surface will tire even the most patient of drivers. There are no plans to improve the road's conditions. Although the park is open all year, the east road is only open from late May/early June until sometime between early October and early November (weather dependant).

From late June to August, daily scheduled buses run from Akureyri and Húsavík to Ásbyrgi (Ikr4100), Hljóðaklettar (Ikr5000) and Dettifoss (Ikr6000). The leg from Ásbyrgi to Dettifoss costs Ikr2200. There's also a daily Mývatn–Dettifoss (Ikr2500, 1½ hours) bus via Krafla (Ikr1200, 15 minutes), leaving at 8am from the supermarket in Reykjahlíð and returning from Dettifoss at 2pm.

ÁSBYRGI

Driving off Rte 85 on to the flat, grassy plain at the northern end of the park, there's little to tell you you're standing on the edge of a massive horseshoe-shaped canyon. The lush **Ásbyrgi canyon** extends 3.5km from north to south and averages 1km in width, making it difficult to discern at its widest point. Near the centre of the canyon is the prominent outcrop **Eyjan**, and towards the south the sheer, dark walls rise up to 100m. The cliffs

ÁSBYRGI TO DETTIFOSS HIKE

The most popular hike in Vatnajökull National Park's Jökulsárgljúfur canyon is the two-day trip (34km) from Ásbyrgi to Dettifoss, which moves through birch forests, striking rock formations, lush valleys and commanding perpendicular cliffs while taking in all of the region's major sights. From Ásbyrgi you can follow the canyon's western rim or river's edge to Vesturdalur where you'll spend the night (camping is forbidden elsewhere). On the second day you'll continue on through to gushing Dettifoss, passing a dip at Hafragil along the way – the only part of the journey that is not categorised as 'easy'.

The hike can be done in both directions; however, the park rangers recommend starting in Ásbyrgi where you can pick up the required maps and brochures to annotate your journey. Also, the vistas reveal themselves more dramatically when travelling in a southerly direction. SBA runs a bus between Dettifoss and Ásbyrgi for those who need to return to their vehicle back north (see opposite). Adventurous types can tag on a second leg to Krafla. You'll want a GPS (there are no marked trails) and a copy of the *Útivist & afþreying* #3 map. Aim to spend a night on the west side of lake Eilífsvötn – it'll take one more day of hiking to reach the signature steaming fields.

protect a birch forest from harsh winds and hungry sheep, and the trees here grow up to 8m in height.

There are two stories about the creation of Ásbyrgi. The early Norse settlers believed that Óðinn's normally airborne horse, Slættur (known in literature as Sleipnir), accidentally touched down on earth and left one hell of a hoof print to prove it. The other theory, though more scientific, is also incredible. Geologists believe that the canyon was created by an enormous eruption of the Grímsvötn caldera beneath distant Vatnajökull. It released an immense *jökulhlaup*, which ploughed northward down the Jökulsá á Fjöllum and gouged out the canyon in a matter of days. The river then flowed through Ásbyrgi for about 100 years before shifting eastward to its present course.

From the car park near the end of the road, several short tracks lead through the forest to viewpoints of the canyon. Heading east the track leads to a spring near the canyon wall, while the western track climbs to a good view across the valley floor. The boardwalk leading straight ahead ends at a small lake (Botnstjörn) at the head of Ásbyrgi.

You can also climb to the summit of **Eyjan** (2km, 45 minutes return) or ascend the cliffs at **Tófugjá**. From there, a looping track leads around **Áshöfði** past the gorges. Alternatively, follow the rim right around to **Klappir**, above the canyon head, from where you can head south to Kvíar (or east to Kúahvammur) and return via the river (the route via Kvíar will take up to four hours return).

VESTURDALUR

Off the beaten track but home to diverse scenery, **Vesturdalur** is a favourite destination for hikers. A series of weaving trails leads from the scrub around the campsite to the cave-riddled pinnacles and rock formations of Hljóðaklettar, the Rauðhólar crater row, the ponds of Eyjan (not to be confused with the Eyjan at Ásbyrgi) and the canyon itself. Reckon on a full day or two to explore the area properly.

Hljóðaklettar

The bizarre swirls, spirals, rosettes, honeycombs and columns of basalt at **Hljóðaklettar** (Echoing Rocks) are a highlight of any hike around Vesturdalur and a puzzling place for amateur geologists. It's difficult to imagine what sort of volcanic activity produced the twisted rock forms here. Weird concertina formations and repeat patterns occur throughout, and the normally vertical basalt columns (formed by rapidly cooling lava) show up on the horizontal here. These strange forms and patterns create an acoustic effect that makes it impossible to determine the direction of the roaring river, a curiosity that gave the area its name.

A circular walking trail (2.4km) from the parking area takes less than an hour to explore. The best formations, which are also riddled with lava caves, are found along the river, northeast of the parking area. Look out for **Trollið**, with its honeycomb pattern, **Kirkjan**, a natural cave in a grassy pit, and **Kastali**, a huge basalt outcrop. Blueberries abound in late August.

Rauðhólar

The **Rauðhólar** crater row, immediately north of Vesturdalur, displays a vivid array of colours in the cinderlike gravel on the remaining cones. The craters can be explored on foot during an interesting 5km walk from the parking area.

Karl og Kerling

Two rock pillars, **Karl og Kerling** ('Old Man' and 'Old Woman'), believed to be petrified trolls, stand on a gravel bank west of the river, 2.5km from the Vesturdalur car park. Across the river is **Tröllahellir**, the largest cave in the gorge, but it's reached only on a 5km cross-country hike from Rte 864 on the eastern side.

Eyjan

From Karl og Kerling you can return to Vesturdalur in about three hours by walking around **Eyjan**, a mesalike 'island' covered with low, scrubby forests and small ponds. Follow the river south to Kallbjörg, then turn west along the track to the abandoned site of Svínadalur, where the canyon widens into a broad valley, and follow the western base of the Eyjan cliffs back to the Vesturdalur parking area.

Hólmatungur

Lush vegetation, tumbling waterfalls and an air of utter tranquillity make the **Hólmatungur** area one of the most beautiful in the park. Underground springs bubble up to form a series of short rivers that twist, turn and cascade their way to the canyon. The most popular walk here is the 3.5km loop from the parking area north along the Hólmá river to **Hólmáfoss**, where the harsh lines of the canyon soften and produce several pretty waterfalls. From here you head south again on the Jökulsá to its confluence with the Melbugsá river, where the river tumbles over a ledge, forming the **Urriðafoss** waterfall. To see the falls you need to walk 500m along the trail spur to Katlar. For the best overall view of Hólmatungur, walk to the hill Ytra-Þórunnarfjall, just 1km south of the car park.

Hólmatungur is only accessible by 4WD. If you are travelling by 2WD, you can park your vehicle at Vesturdalur and do a long round-trip day-hike. Camping is prohibited at Hólmatungur, but it's a great spot for a picnic lunch.

DETTIFOSS

The power of nature can be seen in all its glory at the mighty **Dettifoss**, the park's most famous attraction and one of Iceland's most impressive waterfalls. Although Dettifoss is only 44m high, a massive 193 cu metres of water thunders over its edge every second, creating a plume of spray that can be seen 1km away. With the greatest volume of any waterfall in Europe, this truly is nature at its most spectacular. On sunny days brilliant double rainbows form above the churning milky-grey glacial waters, and you'll have to jostle with the other visitors for the best views.

The falls can be seen from either side of the canyon, with a slightly broader vantage point on the western bank. See p246 for details on road access to the falls. Dettifoss is 31km from the Ring Road on the east side.

Selfoss

From the Dettifoss car park on the eastern bank it's a five-minute walk down to the canyon's edge. From there you can continue on for another 1.5km over the boulders to the falls at **Selfoss**. It's only 11m high but it's quite broad and very striking.

Hafragilsfoss

In one of the deepest parts of the canyon, 2km downstream from Dettifoss (in the direction of Vesturdalur), the 27m-high **Hafragilsfoss** cuts through the Rauðhóll crater row to expose the volcanic dyke that formed it. From the eastern bank, the best view is down the canyon from the small hill just north of the Hafragilsfoss parking area. In the same area are numerous red scoria cones and craters. The overlook on the western bank affords a marginal view of the falls, but the view down Jökulsárgljúfur is one of the best available.

NORTHEASTERN CIRCUIT

The wild, sparsely populated coastal route around Iceland's northeast peninsula is an engaging alternative to the direct road from Mývatn to Egilsstaðir.

Although unsealed in many places, Rte 85 around the coast has improved dramatically in recent years and is easily tackled in a 2WD vehicle. SBA runs a scheduled bus service from

Akureyri to Húsavík (p244), Ásbyrgi (p246; Ikr4100, 1¾ hours), Kópasker (Ikr5000, three hours), Raufarhöfn (Ikr6200, four hours) and Þórshöfn (Ikr7600, five hours) on weekdays all year round. There's currently no bus to or from Vopnafjörður.

KÓPASKER
pop 140

The tiny Kópasker, on the eastern shore of Öxarfjörður, is the first place you'll pass through before disappearing into the expansive wilds of Iceland's far northeast.

On 13 January 1976 Kópasker suffered a severe earthquake that destroyed several buildings and cracked the harbour wall. Today, there's a small **earthquake museum** (Skjálfta Setrið; ☎ 465 2105; earthquake@kopasker.is; admission free; ⊗ 1-5pm mid-Jun–mid-Aug), which investigates the quake and other tectonics in Iceland on a series of amateur storyboard posters.

If you'd like to stay, there's a free campsite, but your best bet is the professionally run **Kópasker HI Hostel** (☎ 465 2314; www.hostel. is; Akurgerði 7; sb member/nonmember Ikr2100/2500, s/d Ikr3800/5800; ⊗ May-Oct) across the street. Rooms and guest kitchens are spread across several buildings – everything is very well kept.

MELRAKKASLÉTTARNES

The low-lying flatlands, ponds and marshes of the bleak and little-visited Melrakkasléttarnes Peninsula feels more like the Australian Outback than the Icelandic wilderness. Large numbers of eider ducks, arctic terns, curlew and dunlin can be seen along the shingle beaches and boggy tundra.

About 18km north of Kópasker you can turn off Rte 85 and head north along a rough track to the extinct 73m crater Rauðinupur. Set on a wild headland with steep cliff faces, this remote finger of land feels like the end of the earth. Screeching gannets and a lonely lighthouse will be your only companions here, and as you look out to sea the power of nature and sense of dramatic isolation are immediately apparent.

Back on the main road and heading east through more fertile farmland, you approach the remote peninsula **Hraunhafnartangi**, the northernmost point of the Icelandic mainland. This desolate spot has narrowly missed being one of Iceland's biggest attractions – it's just 2.5km south of the Arctic Circle. If the headland was a little further north, there

could have been an interpretive centre, a tacky souvenir stall and a Christmas grotto. Instead it's a largely undiscovered headland that was a Saga Age landing site and is the burial place of saga hero Þorgeir Hávarsson, who killed 14 enemies before being struck down in battle. A marked trail leads along the gravel beach here to the brightly coloured lighthouse and the grave site.

The awkward left-side turn-off to the headland is marked with a small blue sign; look for the lonely lighthouse off in the distance. Camping is possible anywhere on the headland.

RAUFARHÖFN
pop 230

Like the setting of a Stephen King novel, distant Raufarhöfn (roy-ver-hup), Iceland's northernmost township, is an eerily quiet place with a prominently positioned graveyard. The port has functioned since the Saga Age, but the town's economic peak came early in the 20th century during the herring boom, when it was second to Siglufjörður in volume. Today, Raufarhöfn's rows of dull prefab housing give few clues to its illustrious past.

There are ambitious plans afoot to erect a massive stone circle on the hill just north of town. When completed, the **Arctic Henge** will be 54m in diameter with four gates (to represent the seasons) up to 7m in height. The plan is to use the stone henge as a finely tuned sundial to celebrate the solstices, view the midnight sun and explain the strong local beliefs in the mythological dwarves mentioned in the poem *Völuspá* (Wise Woman's Prophecy). The centrum might be completed by the time you read this.

If you didn't make it up to Grímsey, **Arctic Travel** (☎ 893 8386; www.arctictravel.is; Vogsholt 12; ⊗ mid-Jun–Sep) will take you to the Arctic Circle by boat – they'll even give you a little certificate. Sea-angling, sightseeing and midnight cruises are also on offer. Call for pricing details.

If you want to stay, there's a free campsite, but **Hótel Norðurljós** (Northern Lights; ☎ 465 1233; ebt@vortex.is; Aðalbraut 2; s/d incl breakfast Ikr9000/14,000; ⊗ mid-Jan–mid-Dec; ☎) is the town's only formal accommodation option. The exterior seems to have been battered by one too many storms, but the inside is quite cosy and rooms have tranquil harbour views.

our pick **Hótel Norðurljós restaurant** (2-course lunch/3-course dinner Ikr2200/3700) offers up some of the best home cooking you'll have during your Icelandic foray. The hotel owner moonlights as the chef, creating truly memorable dishes. Each meal incorporates an array of local ingredients; there's freshly caught fish, a surprising seaweed pesto, and even homemade *skyr* with handpicked berries. A terrace overlooks the harbour, and guests can borrow the owner's kayak or canoe to explore the nearby islands.

RAUÐANES

Heading south from Raufarhöfn, there's excellent hiking at Rauðanes, where marked trails lead to bizarre rock formations, natural arches, caves and secluded beaches. The small and scenic peninsula is edged by steep cliffs full of nesting birds, caves, offshore sea stacks and an exposed rock face, **Stakkatorfa**, where a great chunk of land collapsed into the sea. Pick up the *Útivist & afþreying* #5 map for a detailed look at the area.

The turn-off to Rauðanes is about 35km south of Raufarhöfn, but the track is only suitable for 4WD vehicles. All cars can park 1km from Rte 85, from where it's a 7km loop through the strange terrain.

ÞÓRSHÖFN & AROUND

pop 350

The town of Þórshöfn has served as a busy port since Saga times and saw its heyday when a herring-salting station was established here in the early 20th century. Today it's a modest place but makes a good base for visitors heading to the eerily remote Langanes Peninsula or on to Rauðanes. The rusty church at **Sauðaneshús** (☎ 468 1430; 11am-5pm mid-Jun–Aug), 7km north of town, provides excellent insights into how locals lived 100 years ago. It also sells traditional Icelandic pancakes. For tourist information, try the friendly staff at the **swimming pool** (☎ 468 1515; adult/child Ikr400/150; 8am-8pm Mon-Fri, 11am-5pm Sat & Sun Jun-Aug, 4-8pm Mon-Fri, 11am-2pm Sat & Sun Sep-May;) on the Langanes road.

Þórshöfn has a **campsite** (sites per person Ikr700) and two guest houses, but there's also the excellent **Ytra-Aland** (☎ 468 1290; www.ytra-aland. is; sb Ikr2800, s/d without bathroom Ikr7500/11,000, with bathroom Ikr8500/13,000), located 18km west of town. This friendly farm has adorable rooms in the main house and a new accommodation block with private bathrooms. The sweet

smell of pancakes and big smiles greet guests in the morning.

Dining options are slim. Try the unglamorous local haunt **Eyrin** (☎ 468 1250; Eyraveguri 3; mains Ikr880-3280; 10am-11pm Sun-Thu, to 1am Fri, to 3am Sat), serving a standard assortment of burgers and pasta; or you can self-cater at the **Samkaup supermarket** (10am-6pm Mon-Fri, to 2pm Sat) with a **Vín Búð** (5-6pm Mon-Thu, 4-6pm Fri) inside.

Getting There & Away

Air Iceland (☎ 570 3030; www.airiceland.is) operates flights to Þórshöfn from Akureyri once daily on weekdays from April to late October. The cheapest one-way fare is Ikr9500 (1¼ hours).

SBA runs a scheduled bus service from Þórshöfn to Raufarhöfn (Ikr1400, one hour), Kópasker (Ikr2600, 1¾ hours), Ásbyrgi (Ikr3500, 2¼ hours) and Húsavík (Ikr5100, 3¼ hours) on weekdays all year round.

LANGANES

Shaped like a goose with a very large head, foggy Langanes is one of the loneliest corners of Iceland. The peninsula's remarkably flat terrain, cushioned by mossy meadows and studded with crumbling remains, is an excellent place to break-in your hiking shoes – see the boxed text (opposite) for details.

Rte 869 ends only 17km along the 50km peninsula and, although it's possible to continue along the track to the tip at **Fontur** in a 4WD vehicle, parts of the road can be very difficult to navigate.

Before exploring the region, base yourself at the friendly **Ytra Lón HI Hostel** (☎ 468 1242; www.visitlanganes.com; sb member/nonmember Ikr2100/2600, sb s/d Ikr4200/6800, s/d Ikr12,000/16,000), 14km northeast of Þórshöfn and just off Rte 869. It's part of a working sheep farm run by a young family. In winters, the owners are happy for guests to help out on the farm when sheep come in from the pasture. The rooms are clean and bright, and there's a comfy common area, trampoline and hot pot. At the time of research, new cargo containers were being transformed into quirky studio summer cabins. Breakfast is available for Ikr1000 – you can also buy fresh lamb to cook in the well-equipped guest kitchen.

If you don't have your own vehicle, you can phone ahead to Ytra Lón and the owners will pick you up at the bus station in Þorsförn (Ikr1000 per person). Or you can hike from the bus station to Langanes using

HIKE TO THE END OF THE EARTH

Abandoned farms, lonely lighthouses and craggy windswept cliffs – there are few places in the world that feel as remote as Langanes (opposite). The following three-day itinerary makes for a rewarding journey with nary a hill or tourist in sight. If you plan on doing any part of this hike, it's worth picking up the handy *Útivist & afþreying #7* map (available for a nominal fee at Ytra Lón and local tourist information centres).

Start your journey at **Heiði**, an abandoned farmstead located 9km north of Ytra-Lón. Leave your car next to the weathered three-storey house and hike over the 'neck of the goose' (Trail 18 on the map) to **Hrollaugsstaðir**. Along the way you'll pass the remains of **H-2** (see p194) – there's barely anything there, but the site's history is pretty cool. If you need a bit of a head start (or you don't have your own car), the owners of Ytra Lón can shuttle you directly to Hrollaugsstaðir (Ikr3000 per vehicle; maximum four people). From here, it's a leisurely three-hour hike (Trail 16 on the map) to **Skálar** – keep an eye out for a barking colony of seals along the way. The abandoned fishing community of Skálar has a fascinating history (ask at Ytra-Lón for an informative booklet) and also makes a great place to camp for the night – there are maintained toilets, plenty of water and shelter, and an emergency cabin with medical supplies.

In the morning, leave your gear at Skálar and continue east as the peninsula begins to wane. White-washed **Fontur** lighthouse marks the very end of Langanes (and the end of Iceland for that matter!). Use a credit card to jiggle the front door open – skinny travellers can climb to the light for 360 degrees of panoramas. Before you leave, be sure to sign the guest book (kept in a water-tight box near the door) and check out the list of people who broke into the lighthouse before you (including us!). Leaving Fontur, follow the northern coast until you reach Skoruvík, then return south back to Skálar along the silent dirt track. You'll pass **Grafreitur**, a memorial to a group of fallen sailors, and the ruins of a small British base used to spy on the Nazis during WWII. The Skálar Loop (Trail 15) is approximately 25km.

The return to Heiði on the third day can be done in a number of ways. We recommend returning to the north side and following the coast (Trail 14) back to the abandoned farm (another 25km). On the way you'll pass the jaw-dropping bird cliffs at **Karl**. The cliffs are not marked, so you'll have to keep an eye out for the green-and-white house (it's the only building around). From the house, walk to the edge of the cliffs and look down to find several rocky outcroppings covered with an astonishing number of gannets. When the sea begins to swallow the hiking path and its surrounding boulders, it's only another 5km back to Heiði.

If you're short on time, the entire journey can be tackled in one day with a 4WD (ask at Ytra Lón about current road conditions before setting off). Days two and three can also be combined if you're an early riser and relatively fit.

---

the 'Back Road', which ends at Hóll. From there, follow the marked trail (Trail 10 on the *Útivist & afþreying* map) in a northeasterly direction (left) until you reach Ytra Lón. The hike takes just over three hours if you are travelling light.

VOPNAFJÖRÐUR & AROUND
pop 540

'Weapon fjord' was once the notorious home of a fearsome dragon that protected northeast Iceland from harm. Today's most prominent resident is the 1988 Miss World. As you can probably imagine, it's a sleepy kinda place.

The town's most significant building is the **Kaupvangur**, a restored customhouse. You'll find a small cafe and **tourist information centre** (☎ 473 1331, 862 1443; www.vopnafjordur.is; 🕑 10am-6pm Jun-Aug) on the ground floor. Pick up the handy *Útivist í Vopnafirði og á Út-Héraði* map (Ikr400) if you plan on hiking in the vicinity. Upstairs there's a well-curated exhibit about two locals – Jónas and Jón Muli – Iceland's version of the Gershwin brothers. Also on the second floor is a small display about east Iceland émigrés; down-on-their-luck locals purchased boat tickets to America from this very building.

The region's biggest attraction is the folk museum at **Bustarfell** (☎ 473 1466; adult/9-13yr Ikr500/100; 🕑 10am-6pm mid-Jun–mid-Sep), set in an 18th-century turf-roofed manor house 20km southwest of Vopnafjörður on Rte 85. The museum provides an interesting look at rural life two centuries ago and hosts a traditional festival on the second Sunday in July. There's a small cafe behind the turf house.

Hilariously positioned in the middle of nowhere, Vopnafjörður's **swimming pool** (☎ 473 1499) is located at Selásundlaug, 13km north of town along Rte 85 just south of the river Selá. It's definitely worth a stop, if only for a quick pop in the natural hot pot.

South of Vopnafjörður the truly spectacular mountain drive along Rte 917 takes you over **Hellisheiði** and down to the east coast. The road, which may be impassable in bad weather, climbs up a series of switchbacks and hairpin bends before dropping down to the striking glacial river deltas on the **Héraðssandur**. The views on both sides will be engrained in your memory forever.

Sleeping & Eating

Campsite (☎ 473 1423; sites per tent Ikr750, plus per person Ikr350) There's a good campsite on the outskirts of town with toilets and showers, and great views of the fjord and town below. Follow Miðbraut north and turn left at the school. A ranger comes by at 8am and 9pm to collect camping fees.

Refsstaður (Under The Mountain; ☎ 473 1562; twocats@ simnet.is; Refsstaður 2; s/d without bathroom Ikr2800/5000) Cathy, an American of Icelandic descent, has a special knack for hospitality. Her farmhouse, 9km south of town along Rte 819, feels incredibly homey and warm. She maintains the local emigration exhibit and provides an interesting perspective about life in rural Iceland.

Hótel Tangi (☎ 444 4000; Hafnarbyggð 17; sb Ikr3500, s/d without bathroom Ikr6500/8900, with bathroom Ikr10,900/14,900; ☼ May-Sep) A wonderful surprise hides behind the shockingly run-down exterior: modern sun-filled rooms! Really, these rooms are quite good – and the popular restaurant (mains Ikr1500 to Ikr3500) isn't half bad either.

The **Kauptún supermarket** (☼ 10am-12.15pm & 1-6pm Mon-Fri, noon-4pm Sat) shares a car park with the information centre; there's a **Vín Búð** (☼ 5-6pm Mon-Thu, 4-6pm Fri) inside.

Getting There & Away

Air Iceland (☎ 570 3030; www.airiceland.is) operates flights to Vopnafjörður from Akureyri once daily on weekdays from April to late October. The cheapest one-way fare on this route is Ikr9500 (40 minutes).

From Vopnafjörður it is 122km to Reykjahlíð and 92km to Egilsstaðir, so check fuel levels before you leave town. There is no bus service to Vopnafjörður.

NORTHEAST INTERIOR

Travelling between Mývatn and Egilsstaðir, the Ring Road takes a drastic short cut inland across the stark and barren highlands of the northeast interior. There's little to lure travellers off the road, but the loneliness can be an attraction in itself in this eerie and otherworldly place of endless vistas.

If you won't be travelling into the highlands proper (p307), you'll catch a glimpse of them here. Ostensibly barren, and to some unimaginably dull, the bleak landscape here is dotted with low hills, small lakes caused by melting snowfields, and streams and rivers wandering aimlessly before disappearing into gravel beds. For most of the year it's a stark grey landscape, but if you're visiting in spring you'll be treated to a carpet of wildflowers that somehow gain root in the gravelly volcanic surface.

It has always been a difficult place to eke out a living, and farms here are few and far between. Near the remote farm **Grímsstaðir**, close to the intersection of the Ring Road and Rte 864, 3km from the Jökulsá á Fjöllum, you can see an old **ferryman's hut**, built in 1880. Before the river was bridged it was crossed by ferry, and the former ferryman is said to haunt the run-down building. The hut is on the western bank of the river, 2km downstream from the Ring Road bridge.

Isolated **Möðrudalur**, an oasis in the barren desert amid an entanglement of streams, is the highest farm in Iceland at 469m. The bus between Egilsstaðir and Mývatn stops for half an hour at the charming highland cafe and guest house **Fjalladýrð** (☎ 471 1858, 865 1188; www.fjalladyrd.is; sites per person Ikr900, d sb/linen Ikr4900/7500, cottage Ikr13,900). It's worth spending the night if you're interested in tackling some of Iceland's icy interior. The busy owners are former highland wardens and run informative 4WD day trips to Askja and Kverkfjöll (Ikr17,900). Those who are simply passing through should try the succulent lamb dishes (soup Ikr1150, meat plate Ikr3500), which come from the local sheep farm.

ICELAND'S GREAT OUTDOORS

Iceland's breathtaking natural beauty and rarefied air put colour in your
cheeks, a spring in your step and passion in your soul. This unspoilt country
contains Europe's largest national park and the mightiest ice cap to be found
outside the poles; a sea full of whales and the world's biggest puffin colonies;
lonely mountains, hidden valleys and sinister canyons; and pristine lakes, rivers
and wiggling fjords. Launch yourself into this spectacular landscape with a
range of activities, many of which can be arranged as day trips from Reykjavík.

Walks & Hikes

To explore Iceland's glorious wilderness, strap on a backpack and head for the hills. Steaming geothermal pools, immense rivers of frozen ice, dusty craters, tumbling waterfalls, bleak bird cliffs and magical green valleys await. There's something for everyone, from easy coastal walks to multiday hikes through extreme and inhospitable terrain.

1 Landmannalaugar to Þórsmörk Hike

The four-day hike from Landmannalaugar (pictured left) to Þórsmörk is undoubtedly one of the world's greatest walks. The route (p288) passes through lava fields, over rainbow-coloured mountains and black obsidian ridges, down to enchanting Þórsmörk, hidden between two glaciers.

2 Skaftafell

Icelanders' favourite part of the Vatnajökull National Park, beautiful Skaftafell (p294) holds glinting glaciers and sparkling waterfalls in its cupped green hands, and is the base for multiday excursions into the surrounding rugged ridges.

3 Hekla

Here's your chance to walk to hell and back. Throughout the Middle Ages, this brooding volcano (p139) was considered to be the gateway to the devil's dimension – but the immense, immaculate mountain views from the top look pretty heavenly to us.

4 Hornstrandir Peninsula

One of Europe's last true wilderness areas, the dizzying sea cliffs, rugged mountains and toppling waterfalls of the uninhabited Hornstrandir Peninsula are only accessible by boat. The park ranger recommends wilderness hikers try the four- to five-day hike from Veiðileysufjörður to Hesteyri (p193).

5 Mývatn Eastern Lakeside Hike

Explore some of Iceland's weirdest volcanic features on this flat 'n' easy day-long walk (p235). Follow a split in the earth's crust, past steaming pools and the 1km-wide crater Hverfell, before losing yourself in a maze of black lava at Dimmuborgir.

6 Hellnar to Arnarstapi

A short but glorious little coastal path (p174) runs between the hamlets of Hellnar and Arnarstapi on the Snæfellsnes Peninsula. The cries of seabirds and the thunder of grey breakers accompany you past frozen lava flows and weather-worn caves.

7 Hvannadalshnúkur

For hardened hikers only, the route to the summit of Iceland's highest mountain, Hvannadalshnúkur (2119m; p298), is best attempted in April or May. Climbers should be well versed in glacier travel, as part of the route is over ice bridges.

8 Langanes Peninsula

If it's solitude you crave, take a three-day hike (p251) through the end-of-the-earth Langanes Peninsula. The walk starts from an abandoned farmstead, and takes in Cold War remnants, a deserted fishing village and the country's loneliest lighthouse.

Wildlife

Iceland's range of wildlife is small but bewitchingly beautiful and readily accessible. There are few better places for whale-watching, and the spectacular bird cliffs that fall the land's edge are a twitcher's dream. Iceland's docile horses are perfect for beginners, and the wild eyes of the Arctic fox will haunt you forever.

❶ Whale Watching

From June to August, you are almost assured of spotting one of these amazing creatures. Boats sail from Reykjavík harbour (p84), but Iceland's premiere whale-watching destination is Húsavík (p240), where up to 11 species visit the trembling waters of Skjálfandi bay.

❷ Horse Riding

With their peaceful temperaments and smooth running gait (the famous *tölt*), floppy-fringed Icelandic horses are ideal for all levels of rider. Arrange short horse-riding trips from Reykjavík (p84), or take a recommended hack into the highlands from Hella (p138).

❸ Puffin Colonies

These fascinating little birds, with their colourful beaks, complex burrows and endearing mating rituals, are found all over Iceland. The cliffs at Látrabjarg (p180), Vík (p147), Dyrhólaey (p146) and the islands off Reykjavík (p84) are good places to spot them, but the Vestmannaeyjar (p149) has around 10 million of them.

❹ Birdwatching

If you love seabirds, head for the huge cliff colonies at Látrabjarg (p180). The marshy surrounds of Lake Mývatn (p228) are perfect for migrating geese and all kinds of waders. And we heartily recommend a hay-cart ride to the nature reserve at Ingólfshöfði (p299).

❺ Arctic Foxes

The elusive Arctic fox, with its quick, quiet movements and haunting eyes, is one of Iceland's rarest animals. Why not increase your chances of seeing one by volunteering at the Arctic Fox Research Station (p188) in the Westfjords?

❻ Sheep!

OK, so the Icelandic sheep is pretty ubiquitous. But if you're a good horseperson, you can get closer to the Icelandic soul by helping farmers at the autumn *réttir* (p24), as they ride into the mountains to round up their sheep.

Watery Activities

Iceland is surrounded by a surging northern ocean, threaded with mighty rivers and bubbling with geothermal springs – so it's no wonder the country's adventure tourism often has a watery focus. Jump in for a swim and get to know the Icelanders' eternal passion for their pools and hot pots.

1 Swimming
From the world-famous Blue Lagoon (p117) to hot springs hidden in the mountains, Icelandic pools are on a higher plane. Most towns have an (outdoor) swimming pool – nothing beats lazing in hot water under a cold starry sky.

2 Boat Trips
A whole range of boat trips (p64) are on offer, from humble rowing boats on vast lakes to amphibious vehicles that bob around the icebergs of Jökulsárlón's film-set lagoon (p300) to tours of Iceland's most gorgeous fjords.

3 White-Water Rafting
Iceland's thundering chalky-blue glacial rivers make for an exhilarating white-water rafting experience, with the best trips on offer at Varmahlíð (p204) in northern Iceland.

4 Diving
It's a well-kept secret but the lakes and coastal waters of Iceland make for incredibly rewarding diving. The most popular site is Silfra at Þingvellir (p124), but you can also visit spectacular lava ravines, wrecks and thermal chimneys in northern Iceland and the Vestmannaeyjar (p152).

5 Kayaking
Sneak up on seals and seagulls in a kayak, where the only sound is the quiet 'splish' of your paddle. Iceland's deepest fjords are best for this most meditative of activities (p67), but you can also kayak near Reykjavík on the lagoon at Stokkseyri (p137).

Icy Explorations

Icelanders make the most of snowy winters with downhill ski slopes and cross-country ski marathons. The massive ice cap Vatnajökull and its attendant glaciers offer year-round snow and ice – burn across the permafrost on a snowmobile or let luminous blue swirls of frozen water entrance you on a glacier walk.

PAUL HARDING

❶ Snowmobiling

Iceland's ice caps become a playground when you bounce over the snow on a souped-up skidoo (p68) on Snæfellsjökull (p172), Langjökull, Mýrdalsjökull (p146) or (the daddy of them all) Vatnajökull (p302).

❷ Glacier Walks & Ice Climbing

The glowing blue of ancient ice, dazzling sunlight and the gush of meltwater create a dreamlike world halfway up a glacier. Strap on crampons or learn how to ice climb at lovely Skaftafell (p294).

❸ Skiing

The vertiginous mountain slopes surrounding many of Iceland's remote villages are ripe for downhill skiing, but the country's biggest ski area, Bláfjöll (p85), is handily parked just outside Reykjavík. Hardy souls can participate in one of the fantastically good-natured cross-country skiing events (p22).

❹ Dog Sledding

Tear over Mýrdalsjökull glacier on a sled pulled by a team of Greenland dogs (p146) – you get that top-of-the-world feeling without a snowmobile's noise and smell.

East Iceland

In 1728 a fire tore through central Copenhagen, charring everything in its path. But before it incinerated the precious library of Icelandic sagas, a quick-thinking bibliophile jumped inside to rescue the unique tomes. Almost all the sagas were saved from the blaze, but tragically the volume with east Iceland's ancient tales was lost, forever shrouding the region in mystery.

This air of intrigue and obscurity is still apt today. The region doesn't announce itself as loudly as other parts of the country, preferring subtle charms instead of big-ticket attractions.

The Eastfjords is the area's most delightful destination. On fine days there's nothing better than climbing a hillside, plonking yourself down in the heather and watching the cobalt blue waters as the fishing boats head home with their catch. The scenery is particularly dramatic around the northern fjord villages, backed by sheer-sided mountains covered in toppling streams and waterfalls. If the weather's fine, several days spent hiking or kayaking here may be some of your most memorable in Iceland.

Away from the coast, the country's longest lake, allegedly the home of a huge wormlike monster, stretches southwest from Egilsstaðir. On its eastern shore you'll find the country's largest forest – a source of great pride to tree-starved Icelanders. Head further inland and you'll come to the forgotten farms, fells and heathlands of the empty east.

Most people simply hit the accelerator and follow the overeager Ring Road as it ploughs through Egilsstaðir and out of the region. Thank those travellers for their urgency – it leaves a largely tourist-free corner of the country for more curious bods to explore.

HIGHLIGHTS

- Arrive in the country in style: sail up a lovely, long fjord to the bohemian village **Seyðisfjörður** (p272)

- Rummage through Petra Sveinsdóttir's massive mineral collection in **Stöðvarfjörður** (p280) then visit the mysterious spar mine in **Eskifjörður** (p277) to see where it all came from

- Chat with the hidden people, snap photos of puffin posses and daydream among the rhyolite cliffs in **Borgarfjörður Eystri** (p269)

- Learn the true definition of tranquil isolation in ruin-strewn **Mjóifjörður** (p275) or verdant **Skálanes** (p275)

- Drive through craggy mountain passes and skinny tunnels until you reach oddball **Neskaupstaður** (p278)

★ Borgarfjörður Eystri

Seyðisfjörður ★ ★ Skálanes
★ Mjóifjörður
Neskaupstaður ★
Eskifjörður ★

★ Stöðvarfjörður

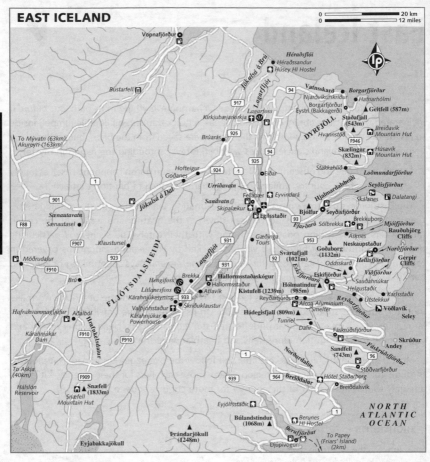

Getting There & Around

The East Iceland tourism website (www.east .is) is set to be uploaded with relevant transport information for the area during the life of this book.

AIR

In summer **Air Iceland** (Flugfélag Íslands; ☎ 471 1210; www.airiceland.is) flies about three times daily from Egilsstaðir to Reykjavík (Ikr7500 to Ikr15,700, one hour).

BUS

Egilsstaðir is a major crossroads on the Ring Road, so all buses pass through here. The main bus stop is located by the campsite and information centre.

From June to mid-September **SBA** (http://eng lish.sba.is) runs a daily bus between Akureyri and Egilsstaðir, calling at Mývatn en route. It departs from Akureyri at 8.30am, and from Egilsstaðir at 1.15pm. The journey takes 3¾ hours and costs Ikr6700 one way. Between mid-September and May a service runs on Monday, Wednesday, Friday and Sunday, departing at different times – see the latest schedule online.

For Egilsstaðir–Höfn buses, see p304.

Ferðaþjónusta Austurlands (☎ 472 1515) runs a minibus–post van between Egilsstaðir and Seyðisfjörður (Ikr1000, about 30 minutes). Between the beginning of June and mid-September it leaves Seyðisfjörður at 8.20am weekdays, with a second service at 1.30pm

Wednesday and Thursday. Between late June and early August there's also a weekend service, leaving at 1.30pm Saturday and 2.15pm Sunday. The rest of the year a bus runs at 4.30pm weekdays and at 6.20pm Sunday.

From early June to mid-September it leaves Egilsstaðir at around 9.15am weekdays, with a second service at 2.20pm on Wednesday and Thursday. Between late June and early August there's also a weekend service, leaving around 2.20pm on Saturday and Sunday. The rest of the year a bus runs at 5pm Monday to Friday and at 7pm Sunday.

Austfjarðaleið (East Iceland Bus Company; ☎ 477 1713; www.austfjardaleid.is) runs buses from Egilsstaðir to villages around the fjords. The Egilsstaðir–Norðfjörður (Ikr2000, 1¼ hours) service via Reyðarfjörður (30 minutes) and Eskifjörður (45 minutes) runs two morning buses daily from Monday to Saturday. There's also a bus that runs a 40-minute route around Fjarðabyggð (Neskaupstaður–Eskifjörður–Reyðarfjörður) on weekdays, at 7.40am and 5pm from Neskaupstaður, and back from Reyðarfjörður at 7.35am and 5.45pm. The Egilsstaðir-Breiðdalsvík (Ikr2200, 1½ hours) service, via Fáskrúðsfjörður (45 minutes) and Stöðvarfjörður (1¼ hours), runs on weekday mornings only. Jump online for the latest schedule details.

INLAND

EGILSSTAÐIR

pop 2270

However much you strain to discover some underlying charm, you'll find sprawling Egilsstaðir really isn't a ravishing beauty. It's the main regional transport hub, and a centre for commerce and industry. Sorry, it's about as enchanting as it sounds.

Thanks to the high-profile Kárahnjúkar hydroelectricity project (see p62) and its influx of workers, there has been feverish house building over the last few years. In time, no doubt, the town's entertainment facilities will catch up, but at present there's little to amuse visitors.

Egilsstaðir does have one saving grace – it's built on the banks of lovely **Lagarfljót**, Iceland's third-largest lake (p266). Since the time of the sagas, tales have been told of a monster, the Lagarfljótsormurinn, who lives in its depths. If you want to go and do some

beastie-hunting, or to explore the forest on the eastern bank of the lake, Egilsstaðir makes a very good base. Services include an excellent regional tourist office and some decent restaurants.

Orientation & Information

North past the airport and over the lake, you'll find Egilsstaðir's twin town. Fellabær has some pleasant accommodation options and a petrol station–bakery, but most services are in Egilsstaðir. The tourist office, petrol stations, bus terminal, banks (with ATMs), supermarkets and the campsite are all located on a large block just off the Ring Road. This is a good place to position yourself if you're hitching.

The regional **tourist information centre** (☎ 471 2320; www.east.is; ⏰ 9am-9pm daily Jun-Aug, 9am-5pm Mon-Fri, noon-4pm Sat & Sun Sep-May; ⌨), by the campsite and bus terminal, has enough free brochures to paper your living room. Maps and guides are plentiful – you'll find everything you need to explore the Eastfjords and beyond. It offers internet access as well (Ikr300 per 15 minutes); however, the town **library** (☎ 471 1546; Laufskógar 1; ⏰ 2-7pm Mon-Fri), upstairs in the same building as Minjasafn Austurlands, has free online access.

The post office is just up the hill on the corner of Selás and Fagradalsbraut.

Sights & Activities

Egilsstaðir's cultural museum **Minjasafn Austurlands** (East Iceland Heritage Museum; ☎ 471 1412; Laufskógar 1; adult/child Ikr400/200; ⏰ 11am-5pm daily Jun-Aug, 1-5pm Mon-Fri Sep-May) is quite a sweet little place. Its displays focus on the history of the region, and they include a reconstructed farmhouse and 10th-century grave goods. Much of the information is in Icelandic only.

The town's impressive **swimming pool** (☎ 470 0077; Tjarnarbraut; adult/child Ikr350/170; ⏰ 6am-9pm Mon, Wed & Fri, 6.30am-9pm Tue & Thu, 9.30am-7pm Sat & Sun Jun-Aug, reduced hours in winter), with its indoor and outdoor pools, saunas, hot pots and a gym, is at the top end of Tjarnarbraut, north of town.

In summer the boat *Lagarfljótsormurinn* pootles along pretty lake Lagarfljót. Unfortunately, although there's a terminus at the bridge in Fellabær, you can't actually catch a ride from there; passengers must set off from the Atlavík campsite, 30km southwest of town – see p267.

EAST ICELAND

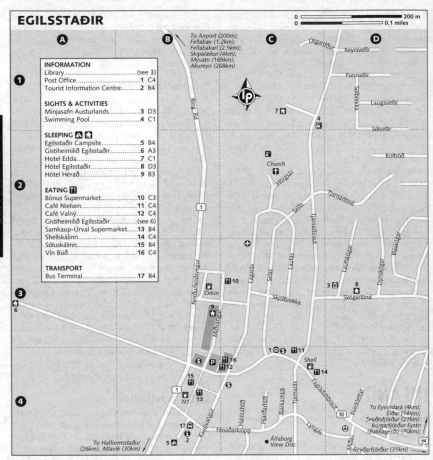

EGILSSTAÐIR

INFORMATION	
Library......................................(see 3)	
Post Office...................................1	C4
Tourist Information Centre.........2	B4
SIGHTS & ACTIVITIES	
Minjasafn Austurlands.................3	D3
Swimming Pool............................4	C1
SLEEPING	
Egilsstaðir Campsite......................5	B4
Gistiheimiliõ Egilsstaðir...............6	A3
Hotel Edda...................................7	C1
Hótel Egilsstaðir...........................8	D3
Hótel Hérað.................................9	B3
EATING	
Bónus Supermarket....................10	C3
Café Nielsen...............................11	C4
Café Valný..................................12	C4
Gistiheimiliõ Egilsstaðir............(see 6)	
Samkaup-Úrval Supermarket.....13	B4
Shellskálinn................................14	C4
Söluskálinn.................................15	B4
Vín Búð......................................16	C4
TRANSPORT	
Bus Terminal...............................17	B4

To Airport (200m);
Fellabær (1.2km);
Fellabakarí (2.5km);
Skipalækur (4km);
Mývatn (169km);
Akureyri (268km)

To Hallormsstaður
(26km); Atlavík (30km)

To Eyvindará (4km);
Eiðar (14km);
Seyðisfjörður (27km);
Borgarfjörður Eystri
(Bakkagerði) (70km);

Reyðarfjörður (31km)

Festivals & Events

If you are here in early November, stop by for the unusual 10-day **Dagar Myrkurs** (Days of Darkness), when the town perversely celebrates the failing light and the onset of winter with dark meals, dark dances, ghost stories, star walks, northern lights spotting, and torch-lit processions! When life gives you lemons…

Around the third weekend in June, Egilsstaðir's annual jazz festival **Djasshátíð Egilsstaða** (www.jea.is) takes place at various venues in the area.

The possible existence of the lake monster Lagarfljótsormurinn is a good excuse for a weeklong cultural festival, **Ormsteiti**, during late August.

Sleeping

Egilsstaðir campsite (☎ 471 2320; www.east.is; Kaupvangur 10; sites per person Ikr900; 🖳) Camping pitches are in utilitarian rows, but facilities are good – there's a kitchen and a washing machine (Ikr600). A dormitory building has sleeping-bag accommodation.

Skipalækur (☎ 471 1324; skipalaekur@simnet.is; sites per person Ikr650, sb/linen per person Ikr2300/4600, d with bathroom from Ikr12,000, chalet from Ikr9000 May-Sep, discounts rest of year) In Fellabær, across the river from Egilsstaðir, this farmhouse has accommodation to suit all purses. There's a small camping area, two fairly noisy prefab cabins with sleeping-bag accommodation, some rooms in a funny '70s-decorated house, and quirky, self-contained family-sized A-frame chalets lining the lake. All accommodation has access to showers, a kitchen, and a sitting room of some description.

Eyvindará (☎ 471 1200; eyvindara2@simnet.is; d with/ without bathroom Ikr16,000/13,000, cabin Ikr14,500; ☎) Set 4km away with good views back into town, serene Eyvindará is a lovely place to call home during your visit to east Iceland. A collection of prim country cabins and newly finished motel units sits hidden along a tree-lined escarpment dotted with fragrant blueberry blooms. Discounted sleeping-bag accommodation is available out of season. Breakfast is included.

Hotel Edda (☎ 444 4000; off Tjarnarbraut; www.hotel edda.is; s/d Ikr14,200/17,600; ☼ Jun–mid-Aug) Based in the school opposite the swimming pool, this is a typical Edda hotel. Rooms have private bathrooms, and there's a bar and restaurant with panoramic views.

Gistiheimilið Egilsstaðir (☎ 471 1114; www.egilss tadir.com; s/d Ikr13,700/18,200 May-Sep, Ikr8900/10,900 Oct-Apr; ☐ ☎) The town was named after this splendid heritage guest house and farm, on the banks of Lagarfljót, 300m west of the crossroads. Its sensitively renovated en-suite rooms retain a real sense of character, and are decorated with antique furniture – ask for one with a lake view. Breakfast (included) is in the lakeside dining room, which serves a splurge-worthy (€30) steak dinner nightly (right).

Hótel Hérað (☎ 471 1500; herad@icehotels.is; Miðvangur 5-7; s/d Ikr15,000/18,700 Jun-Aug, Ikr14,000/16,800 Sep-May; ☐ ☎) This three-star Icelandair hotel is the plushest in town. It's been hugely expanded since work began on the hydro-electricity project; a whole wing contains brand-new parquet-floored rooms, with satellite TV, bathrooms and buffet breakfast included. The stylish restaurant (open from 6pm to 9pm; mains cost from Ikr2600 to Ikr5900) is bathed in creamy whites and covered with hip Impressionist paintings – it's a good place to indulge. The house speciality is reindeer steak.

Hotel Egilsstaðir (☎ 471 2830; www.hringhotels. is; Skógarlönd 6; s/d incl breakfast €126/148 mid-May–Oct; ☐ ☎) Fresh touches are turning this expensive option into a more palatable choice than its previous incarnation. But with any luck you'll get one of the unrenovated rooms – it's like sleeping in the former Soviet Union!

Eating

Café Valný (☎ 471 2219; Miðvangur; ☼ 11am-6pm; ☎) This little coffee shop is a snug place in which to update your blog. Cartons of local tea and designer salad dressing are available for purchase in the back.

Café Nielsen (☎ 471 2626; Tjarnarbraut 1; lunch Ikr950-1550, dinner mains Ikr1850-4650; ☼ 11.30am-11.30pm Mon-Thu, to 2am Fri, 1pm-2am Sat, 1-11.30pm Sun) Occupying the midrange bracket between N1 eats and gourmet treats, the standard menu at Café Nielsen won't blow you away, but you'll probably end up eating here if you're spending any amount of time in town. In summer there's a pleasant leafy terrace and garden. The kitchen closes at 10pm sharp.

Gistiheimilið Egilsstaðir (☎ 471 1114; www.egilsstadir. com; mains Ikr2990-4900) Dried branches dangle over crisp white tablecloths and stripped wooden floors, giving the dining room an undeniable romantic appeal in the evening candlelight. The speciality here is the beef – Egilsstaðir raises its own cattle – though you can't go wrong with any of the well-prepared dishes.

Quick eats and an enormous sundae bar can be found at **Söluskálinn** (☎ 470 1230; burgers Ikr830, fish Ikr1690) at the N1 petrol station near the tourist office. Or try the **Shellskálinn** (Fagradalsbraut 13; mains from Ikr800; ☼ 10am-10pm) at the Shell petrol station at the top of town, which offers everything from pizza to Thai food.

Self-caterers have the well-stocked **Samkaup-Úrval supermarket** (☼ 9am-7pm Mon-Fri, 10am-6pm Sat, noon-6pm Sun) by the N1 petrol station, and the **Bónus supermarket** (☎ 471 2700; www.bonus.is; ☼ noon-6.30pm Mon-Thu, 10am-7.30pm Fri, 10am-6pm Sat, noon-6pm Sun) north of Fagradalsbraut. Samkaup-Úrval has a surprising assortment of Tupperware, plastic cutlery and thermoses – perfect if you're contemplating a camping trip.

The **Vín Búð** (☎ 471 2151; Miðvangi 2-4; ☼ 11am-6pm Mon-Thu, to 7pm Fri, to 4pm Sun Jun-Aug, noon-6pm Mon-Thu, 11am-7pm Fri, 11am-2pm Sat Sep-May) alcohol shop is on the ground floor of the office building diagonally across from the N1 station.

There's a small bakery, **Fellabakarí** (☎ 471 1800), open on weekdays, at the Ólís petrol station in Fellabær.

Getting There & Away

Egilsstaðir is the transport hub of east Iceland. There's an airport (1km north of town), and all bus services pass through (see p262).

The Ring Road steams through Egilsstaðir, but if you want to explore the Eastfjords you need to leave it here. Rte 94 takes you north to Borgarfjörður Eystri, Rte 93 goes east to Seyðisfjörður, and Rte 92 goes south to Reyðarfjörður and the rest of the fjord towns.

Getting Around

Avis (☎ 660 0623; www.avis.is), **Hertz** (☎ 522 4450; www.hertz.is), **Bílaleigur Akureyrar** (☎ 461 6070; www .holdur.is) and **Budget** (☎ 471 2022; www.budget.is) all have agents at the airport.

Bus connections with the Smyril Line ferry in Seyðisfjörður can be really inconvenient. If you get stuck, a **taxi** (☎ 898 2625) between Egilsstaðir and Seyðisfjörður costs around Ikr8000.

NORTH OF EGILSSTAÐIR

The region due north of Egilsstaðir is mostly water and grey sand. Few travellers visit, but if you've plenty of time, you might like to admire this landscape of dunes, basalt outcrops, marshes and river deltas (where the Lagarfljót and Jökulsá á Brú join the sea).

There's no regular public transport, but with your own vehicle you could do a loop drive along Rtes 94 and 925.

Eiðar

Eiðar, 14km north of Egilsstaðir on Rte 94, was the farm of Helgi Ásbjarnarson, grandson of Hrafnkell Freysgoði (see the boxed text, p268). The **church**, built in 1887, contains an interesting statue of Christ that washed up on the shore at Héraðssandur, near Húsey.

Spread across three dated schoolhouses just off the Egilsstaðir–Borgarfjörður road, **Hotel Edda** (☎ 444 4000; www.hoteledda.is; sb Ikr1700-2900, s/d Ikr6800/8500; ☼ mid-Jun–Aug) is a summer hotel with lots of sleeping-bag space, rooms with washbasins, a swimming pool and a surprisingly good restaurant dolled up with white tablecloths.

Kirkjubæjarkirkja

One of Iceland's oldest wooden churches, Kirkjubæjarkirkja (1851) is set in a peaceful deep-grassed graveyard, 3km west of Lagarfoss. It's a quaint little place, with a dusty harmonium, a sky-blue ceiling, creaking stairs up to a tiny gallery and the oldest pulpit in the country – a great 16th-century piece, carved with medieval-looking saints.

Húsey

The only reason to venture out to the isolated farm at Húsey, 60km north of Egilsstaðir near the shores of Héraðsflói, is to stay at the friendly **Húsey HI Hostel** (☎ 471 3010, 847 8229; www. husey.de; sb/linen €26/35). It has beautiful horses to ride (two-hour tours start at 10am and 5pm daily; €38) and there are curious seals cavorting in the riverine backdrop. The hostel has cooking facilities but there's nowhere to buy food, so bring supplies. Breakfast (€9) can be ordered. Book well in advance, and ask about pick-up options if you don't have your own vehicle.

SOUTH OF EGILSSTAÐIR
Lagarfljót

The grey-brown waters of the river-lake Lagarfljót are reputed to harbour a fearsome monster, **Lagarfljótsormurinn** (Lagarfljót Worm), which has allegedly been spotted since Viking times. The last 'sighting' was in 1987, when it was glimpsed coiled up in an inlet at Atlavík campsite. The poor old beast must be pretty chilly – Lagarfljót starts its journey in the Vatnajökull ice cap and its glacial waters flow north to the Arctic Ocean, widening into a 38km-long, 50m-deep lake, often called Lögurinn, south of Egilsstaðir.

Whether you see a monster or not, it's quite a lovely stretch of water, which can be circumnavigated by car. Rte 931, a mixture of sealed surfaces and gravel, runs all the way around the edge from Egilsstaðir–Fellabær – a distance of 56km. There's no public transport, and traffic is light on the western shore if you're planning to hitch.

The eastern shore is thick with birch and fir trees: Hallormsstaðaskógur (below) is Iceland's largest forest and a site of reverential pilgrimage for Icelanders. In summer you can take a pleasure cruise from the popular campsite there.

Hallormsstaðaskógur

The sequoia! The giant redwood! The mighty Scots pine! These are the trees you *won't* see in Iceland's biggest forest, Hallormsstaðaskógur. Although the country's coppices are comical to many foreigners (Q: What do you do if you get lost in an Icelandic forest? A: Stand up.), it's rude to snigger. Hallormsstaðaskógur is king of the woods and venerated by the arborically challenged nation.

SIGHTS & ACTIVITIES

Although the forest is small by most countries' standards, it's also quite cute – and a leafy reprieve after the stark, bare mountainsides to the north and south of Egilsstaðir. Common species include native dwarf birch and mountain ash, as well as 50 tree species gathered from around the world. Iceland's oldest larch colony, **Guttormslundur**, 2.5km south of Hótel Hallormsstaður, was planted in 1938; some of the trees are now 20m high!

Between mid-June and August, the 110-passenger cruise ship **Lagarfljótsormurinn** (☎ 471 2900; www.ormur.is; per person Ikr2000; ☾ 9pm daily) runs from Atlavík campsite to Egilsstaðir and back again.

You can arrange horse-riding tours at **Hestaleiga** (☎ 847 0063; ☾ 10am-7pm mid-Jun–Aug) at the hut by Hússtjórnarskólinn summer hotel. The same people also rent out pedal boats, rowing boats and canoes from Atlavík campsite.

SLEEPING

Atlavík campsite (☎ 849 1461; sites per person Ikr750) Down the hill, close to the lakeshore, is this beautiful and extremely popular campsite, named after the first settler in this area, Graut-Atli. It's often the scene of raucous parties on summer weekends. Showers cost Ikr200. The smaller, quieter Þurshofðavík campsite is just north of the petrol station.

Hótel Hallormsstaður (☎ 471 2400; www.hotel701. is; new bldg s/d Ikr14,200/19,900, red roofs s/d from Ikr9000/ 12,000, Glái Hundurinn s/d from Ikr9000/12,000) A veritable campus of buildings hidden amongst the trees, Hótel Hallormsstaður offers lodging options for most wallets. There's a brand-new reception building with inviting modern rooms, a schoolhouse enlivened with cartoon doodles, and the timber-framed Grey Dog (Glái Hundurinn) building further along. There's also a playground, bicycle rentals (Ikr3600 per day) and a **swimming pool** (☾ 10am-noon & 2-7pm mid-Jun–mid-Aug) right next door. Only the reception building is used as a hotel year-round.

Skriðuklaustur

The site of a 15th-century monastery, and the home of an Icelandic author feted by the Third Reich, **Skriðuklaustur** (☎ 471 2990; www. skriduklaustur.is; adult/under 16yr/student Ikr500/free/300; ☾ 10am-6pm Jun-Aug, noon-5pm May & early Sep) certainly has an interesting history. The unusual black-and-white turf-roofed building was built

in 1939 by Gunnar Gunnarsson (1889–1975), and now holds a cultural centre dedicated to him. This prolific writer achieved phenomenal popularity in Denmark and Germany – at the height of his fame only Goethe outsold him. He was nominated for the Nobel Prize three times, but his books have dated quite badly; the most readable is *Svartfugl* (translated into English as *The Black Cliffs*), about an infamous Icelandic murder.

The house also contains an interesting exhibition about the earlier Augustinian monastery, demolished during the Reformation of 1550. Archaeological finds include bones indicating that Skriðuklaustur was used as a hospice. Its most famous artefact is a carved statue of the Virgin Mary, found hidden in an old barn wall. Guided tours of the excavated site (around 30 minutes) depart from the reception every hour on the hour from 1pm to 5pm.

Downstairs, **Klausturkaffi** (Ikr1950; ☾ noon-2pm) serves a great lunch buffet made from local ingredients (wild mushrooms, reindeer meat, brambleberry puddings). More tantalising, however, is the brilliant all-you-can-eat cake buffet (Ikr1500), served between 2pm and 5.30pm.

Kárahnjúkasýning

Just up the road from Skriðuklaustur is the **visitor centre** (☎ 861 2195; ☾ 1-5pm) for the Kárahnjúkar hydroelectric project (see p62). There's free juice and coffee, and a 10-minute video offering a quick (though somewhat biased) overview of the project.

Hengifoss & Lítlanesfoss

Hengifoss is Iceland's second-highest waterfall. Once you've made the climb up and into the canyon you'll be blown away by the power of the water – after a rainstorm it sounds like a Boeing 747 taking off! The falls plummet 120m into a colourful brown-and-red-striped boulder-strewn gorge.

Getting to Hengifoss requires a return walk of about one hour. From the parking area on Rte 933, about 200m south of the bridge across the lake, a long stairwell leads up the hillside – Hengifoss is soon visible in the distance. It's a steep climb in places but flattens out as you enter the canyon. Halfway up is a smaller waterfall, **Lítlanesfoss**, which is surrounded by spectacular vertical basalt columns in a honeycomb formation.

EAST ICELAND

HRAFNKELL'S SORTA-SAGA

The saga of Hrafnkell is one of the most widely read Icelandic sagas, thanks to its short, succinct plot and memorable characters. The tale is particularly interesting because its premises seem to derail any modern notions of right, wrong and justice served. The only conclusions one can really draw are 'it's better to be alive than dead' and 'it's better to have the support of powerful chieftains than rely on any kind of god'.

The main character, Hrafnkell, is a religious fanatic who builds a temple to Freyr on the farm Aðalból in Hrafnkelsdalur (see opposite). Hrafnkell's prized stallion, Freyfaxi, is dedicated to the god, and Hrafnkell swears an oath to kill anyone who dares ride him without permission. As might be expected, someone does. The stallion himself tempts a young shepherd to leap onto his back and gallop off to find a herd of lost sheep. Discovering the outrage, Hrafnkell takes his axe to the errant youth.

When the boy's father, Þorbjörn, demands compensation for his son's death, Hrafnkell refuses to pay up, offering instead to look after Þorbjörn in his old age. Proudly, the man refuses, and the characters are launched into a court battle that ultimately leads to Hrafnkell being declared an outlaw. He chooses to ignore the sentence and returns home.

Before long, Þorbjörn's nephew Sámur Bjarnason arrives to uphold the family honour, stringing Hrafnkell up by his Achilles tendons until he agrees to hand over his farm and possessions. Sámur then offers him a choice: to live a life of subordination and dishonour, or to die on the spot; you might think a saga hero would go for death, but Hrafnkell chooses life.

Sámur moves into Aðalból, and makes a few home improvements. The pagan temple is destroyed, and the horse Freyfaxi weighted with stones, thrown over a cliff and drowned in the water below. Hrafnkell, by now convinced that his favourite god doesn't give two hoots about him, renounces his religious beliefs and sets up on a new farm, Hrafnkelsstaðir. He vows to change his vengeful nature and becomes a kind and simple farmer, becoming so well liked in his new neighbourhood that he gains even more wealth and power than before.

One day, Sámur and his brother Eyvindur pass by en route to Aðalból. Hrafnkell's maid sees them and goads her employer into taking revenge for his earlier humiliation. Hrafnkell abandons the Mr Nice Guy routine, sets out in pursuit of the troublesome brothers, kills Eyvindur, and offers Sámur the same choice that he was offered before – give up Aðalból and live in shame, or be put to death. Sámur also decides not to die. Hrafnkell thus regains his former estates and lives happily ever after at Aðalból.

WEST OF EGILSSTAÐIR

Snæfell

No one seems to know whether 1833m-high Snæfell is an extinct volcano, or if it's just having a rest. Iceland's highest peak outside the Vatnajökull massif is relatively accessible, making it popular with hikers and mountaineers. Snæfell looms over the southern end of Fljótsdalsheiði, an expanse of spongy tussocks of wet tundra, boulder fields, perennial snow patches and alpine lakes, stretching westwards from Lagarfljót into the highlands.

Work on the controversial Kárahnjúkar dam (p62) has brought improved roads around Snæfell, with the small-car-friendly Rte F910 from Fljótsdalur being the best way up. (It's still pretty vertical, though!) Along the way, watch for wild reindeer. At the base of the peak, at 800m elevation, is Ferðafélag Íslands' **Snæfell mountain hut** (N 64°48.250′, W 15°38.600′; per person Ikr2500), accommodating up to 62 people, with a kitchen, a camping area and showers.

Although climbing the mountain itself is not difficult for experienced, well-prepared hikers, the weather can be a concern and technical equipment is required. Discussing your route first with the hut warden is a good idea.

One of Iceland's most challenging and rewarding hikes takes you from Snæfell to the Lónsöræfi district (p304) in southeast Iceland. The five-day route begins at the Snæfell hut and heads across the glacier Eyjabakkajökull (an arm of Vatnajökull) to Geldingafell, Egilssel and Múlaskáli huts before dropping down to the coast at Stafafell.

This route should not be approached lightly – it's for experienced trekkers only. You'll need a GPS and, for the glacier crossing, you must be skilled at using a rope, crampons and an ice axe. If you're unsure of your skills, you'd be much wiser doing the trip commercially with **Ferðafélag Íslands** (☎ 568 2533; www.fi.is; Mörkin 6, IS-108 Reykjavík).

Jökulsá á Dal

A small stream, formed by rivulets from the hillsides, puddles through what was once a riverbed carved out by a more powerful river (now harnessed in the Hálslón reservoir). The part alongside the Ring Road is said to be haunted by mischievous leprechauns and bloodthirsty Norse deities.

The outcrop called **Goðanes**, about 3km west of the farm Hofteigur, was the site of an ancient pagan temple where some ruins are still visible. The iron-stained spring **Blóðkelda** (Blood Spring) carries an apocryphal legend that the blood of both human and animal sacrifices once flowed into it.

If travelling with kids, consider breaking up a long car journey at **Klaustursel** (☎ 471 1085; allis@centrum.is), 6km off the Ring Road along rough Rte 923 (the alarming little bridge you cross was once part of the American railway!). The farm has swans and geese, and you can pat the soft noses of the oh-so-pretty reindeer. Don't miss Olavia's unique accessories made from tanned hides.

Continuing along Rte 923 leads you to the valley of **Hrafnkelsdalur** (about 100km from Egilsstaðir), full of Saga Age sites relating to *Hrafnkell's Saga* (see the boxed text, opposite). The farm **Aðalból** (☎ 471 2788; www.simnet.is/samur; sites per person Ikr500, sb/linen Ikr2400/3500; ☽ Jun–mid-Sep) was the home of the saga's hero, Hrafnkell Freysgoði, and his burial mound is here. At the time of writing the occupier was marking a 10km-long saga trail, threading together places mentioned in the story; even if you're not a raving saga addict, it's an interesting walking area off the tourist trail.

There's simple accommodation available at Aðalból farm, and a petrol pump, but unless you preorder meals Egilsstaðir is the nearest place to buy food. The road becomes the F910 before you reach Aðalból, but it's easily driveable (if a bit skiddy) in a normal car. It's definitely 4WD only once you continue past Aðalból – an alternative route to Snæfell, or to the **Kárahnjúkar dam** (see p62).

The reconstructed turf farmhouse **Sænautasel** (☎ 471 1086; ☽ daily Jul & Aug), dating from 1843, really brings the past to life…plus it sells pancakes and coffee. This is one of several old farms on Jökuldalsheiði that were originally abandoned when Askja erupted in 1875. The building is beside the lake Sænautavatn, 32km west of Hofteigur and 4km south of the Ring Road via Rte 907. This area was a source of inspiration for Halldór Laxness' master work, *Independent People;* you may notice that many of the farm names here match those of the fictional farms in the book.

THE EASTFJORDS

Unlike the histrionic, wildly folding Westfjords, the Eastfjords wiggle more modestly around the coast. The difference is akin to an overtheatrical actor chewing up the scenery and an underemoting character in some Scandinavian art-house film.

Despite good surfaced roads and all the smelter-related activity, the Eastfjords still seems remote – a feeling enhanced by immense, dramatic mountainsides and the tiny working fishing villages that nestle under them.

The fjords are the true highlight of eastern Iceland. There are some lovely walks; you can kayak to far-off headlands; thousands of sea birds nest along the cliffs; and it's amazing how many dolphin pods you can spot if you choose a good vantage point and wait.

In a Finest Fjord competition it would be hard to pick a winner – Borgarfjörður has ethereal rhyolite cliffs, Seyðisfjörður fosters a cheery bohemian vibe, Mjóifjörður is riddled with waterfalls, and Norðfjörður hides amongst thick tufts of cottony fog. You'll just have to visit and choose your own favourite.

The following section is organised from north to south. For all information on public transport in the region, see p262.

BORGARFJÖRÐUR EYSTRI (BAKKAGERÐI)

pop 100

This village, the most northerly in the Eastfjords, is in a stunning location. It's framed by a backdrop of rugged rhyolite peaks on one side and the spectacular Dyrfjöll mountains on the other. There's very little in the village itself, although weird driftwood sculptures, hidden elves, crying sea birds and pounding waves exude a strange charm. (If anyone happened to watch the re-ality TV program *Rockstar Supernova*, this is where Magni is from!).

If you're looking for local information, check out www.borgarfjordureystri.is or try stopping by Álfheimar Gistihús (right) – it has several hiking brochures about the area, and sells an interesting CD of local legends retold by lively storytellers.

Sights & Activities

If you haven't seen any puffins during your Icelandic foray, now's your chance. The gigantic **puffin colony** on the islet **Hafnarhólmi** (connected to the mainland by a causeway 5km northeast of town), has more than 10,000 puffin couples, each with their own multi-room burrow. The free viewing platform is open in June and July and allows you to get up close and personal with these clumsy, cute creatures. The puffins arrive mid-April and on exactly 15 August they depart en masse – it's like they have a calendar! Back in the village there's a small hideout for **birdwatching** behind the general store.

Jóhannes Sveinsson Kjarval (1885–1972), Iceland's best-known artist, was brought up on the nearby farm Geitavík and took much of his inspiration from the rhyolite-studded surroundings at Borgarfjörður Eystri. The **Kjarvalsstofa** (☎ 862 6163; adult/child Ikr500/free; ☼ 1-5pm mid-Jun–Aug), inside the Fjarðarborg community centre, is the village's tribute to him, but we like his unusual altarpiece in the small church **Bakkagerðiskirkja** a lot more. It depicts the Sermon on the Mount and is directly aimed at his village of fishermen and farmers – Jesus is preaching from Álfaborg, with the mountain Dyrfjöll in the background. From the town's monument to the painter, it's a signposted half-hour walk to **Smalakofi Kjarvals**, the ruins of a stone shepherd's hut that Kjarval built as a child.

You can't miss the village's hairiest house... bright red **Lindarbakki** (1899) is completely cocooned by whiskery green grass, with only a few windows and a giant pair of antlers sticking out. It's a private home and not open to the public, but an interesting information board outside tells you more about its history. We particularly liked the estate agent's comments from 1979...

Álfaborg (Elf Rock), the small mound and nature reserve near the campsite, is the 'borg' that gave Borgarfjörður Eystri its name. From the 'view disc' on top there's a fabulous vista of the surrounding fields, which turn white in summer with blooming arctic cotton. Some locals believe that the queen of Icelandic elves lives here.

If you need a break from the kids, bring them to **Ævintýraland** (Adventure Land; admission Ikr300; ☼ 1-5pm Jun-Aug), where they can snuggle up with a colourful pillow and an iPod and listen to several reinterpretations of the local elf stories (there are 14 five-minute tales – eight have been translated into English). There's also a painting room (Ikr100 to Ikr500 per item), where the little ones can doodle on all sorts of items.

Festivals & Events

Held in an abandoned herring plant on the third weekend of July, **Bræðislan** is becoming one of the most famous summer concert festivals in all of Iceland. The event features three to five big-ticket bands and has included Emiliana Torrini (who used to spend her summer in isolated Borgarfjörður), Damien Rice, and Páll Óskar, who flitted across the stage in '09.

Sleeping

Campsite (☎ 472 9999; magnus@eldhorn.is; sites per person Ikr750) Beside the church, this quiet green site has a kitchen and free showers. The third night is free.

Borgarfjörður HI Hostel (Ásbyrgi; ☎ 472 9962, 866 3913; www.hostel.is; sb/linen Ikr2800/3400; ☼ May–mid-Sep) This small hostel offers sleeping-bag accommodation for up to 17 people. There's a guest kitchen and a washing machine.

Réttarholt (☎ 472 9913; helgim@mi.is; sb/linen Ikr2500/3500) This year-round guest house has three simple, brightly quilted rooms in the basement of a charming home. There's a cosy guest kitchen and the house is set in the most lovely garden, full of odd sculptures and pieces of lichen-covered wood.

Gistiheimilið Borg (☎ 472 9870, 894 4470; gisting borg@simnet.is; sb/linen Ikr2700/3900) Borg is a good bet for a bed, since the owner has a few houses in the village. Rooms are OK if old fashioned, with cooking and lounge facilities. Breakfast (Ikr900) is available in summer.

Álfheimar Gistihús (☎ 861 3677; www.borgarfjor dureystri.is; Merkisvegur; s/d Ikr11,000/14,000; ☐ ☎) The best place to stay in town by far, these brand-new rows of semidetached wooden cottages are simple yet stylish. There's an on-site restaurant that serves excellent local fare and the affable owners are a font of knowledge about the local area.

Eating

Álfa Café (☎ 897 2765, 470 2000; 🕙 11am-8pm) This is the main place to eat. Check out the 2250kg piece of raw jasper sitting on the front lawn (it's the biggest piece ever found in Iceland). Inside you'll find customers enjoying traditional light nibbles such as fish soup, flatbread with lamb sausage or smoked trout, while sitting at large stone-slab tables. Kitschy stone knick-knacks, such as cheese slicers, are also for sale.

Fjarðarborg community centre (☎ 472 9920; meals Ikr1000; 🕙 11-1am, late Jun-Aug) This joint's a bit dated but worth a try for barbecued burgers or other types of greasy eats. If you haven't secured any lodging, you can ask here about sleeping-bag space in various buildings nearby (around Ikr2700).

The tiny **Samkaup** (☎ 472 9940; 🕙 12.30-4.30pm Mon-Fri) by the pier sells groceries.

Getting There & Away

The only public transport to Borgarfjörður Eystri is the **postal van** (☎ 472 9805, 894 8305) from Egilsstaðir at noon on weekdays (Ikr2000/1000 per adult/child under 12). It returns at 8am, departing from Álfa Café and stopping at the Fjarðarborg community centre, too.

The village is 70km from Egilsstaðir along Rte 94, about half of which is sealed. It winds

---

PIT STOP!

Exactly halfway between Egilsstaðir and Borgarfjörður sits one of east Iceland's quirkier roadside wonders: a pistachio-coloured hut surrounded by miles and miles of nothingness. Built by a local eccentric who exclaimed 'people get thirsty when they take a drive!', the little structure is simply a solar-powered refrigerated drink dispenser. If the power is off, flick the 'on' switch (we're not kidding) and wait two minutes (you can sign the guest book while waiting). Then, voila: a refreshingly cold beverage.

We're not too sure who takes care of the little booth, but apparently someone swings by once a month to restock and turn the page on the calendar…

---

steeply up over the Vatnsskarð mountains before dropping down to the coast. There's a card-operated petrol pump by the Samkaup grocery store.

AROUND BORGARFJÖRÐUR EYSTRI

There are loads of trails criss-crossing the northeast – everything from easy two-hour strolls to serious mountain hiking for people with a head for heights! Watch your footing in nonvegetated areas – loose material makes for an experience akin to walking on thousands of tiny ball bearings.

The colourful rhyolite peak **Staðarfjall** (543m) rises 8km southeast of Borgarfjörður Eystri, and Geitfell (587m), just a bit north, makes a nice day walk (follow trails #19 and #20 if you are using the handy and widely available *Gönguleiðir á Austurlandi* #1 map). The best access to both hills is up the ridge near the Desjamýri farm, across the estuary from Borgarfjörður Eystri.

Check out the boxed text, p273, for a scenic multiday hike that connects Borgarfjörður to Seyðisfjörður.

Dyrfjöll

One of Iceland's most dramatic ranges, the Dyrfjöll mountains rise precipitously to an altitude of 1136m between the marshy Héraðssandur plains and Borgarfjörður Eystri. The name Dyrfjöll means Door Mountain and is due to the large and conspicuous notch in the highest peak – an Icelandic counterpart to Sweden's famous Lapporten. There are two walking tracks crossing the range, which allow for day hikes or longer routes from Borgarfjörður Eystri.

Stórurð, on the western flank of Dyrfjöll, is an extraordinary place scattered with huge rocks and small glacial ponds. To reach the site on a pleasant half-day hike, start at the red emergency hut along the main road and follow trail #9 then loop back along trail #8 (clearly marked on the *Gönguleiðir á Austurlandi* map series). The whole trip takes just over five hours.

Njarðvíkurskriður

A habitual site of accidents in ancient times, Njarðvíkurskriður is a dangerous scree slope on Rte 94 near Njarðvík. All the tragedies were blamed on a nuisance creature (half man, half beast), Naddi, who dwelt in a sea-level cave beneath the slope.

In the early 1300s Naddi was exorcised by the proper religious authorities, and in 1306 a **naddakross** (cross) was erected on the site bearing the inscription '*Effigiem Christi qui transis pronus honora, Anno MCCCVI*' – 'You who are hurrying past, honour the image of Christ – AD 1306'. The idea was that travellers would repeat a prayer when passing the danger zone and therefore be protected from malevolent powers. The cross has been replaced several times since, but the current one still bears the original inscription.

SEYÐISFJÖRÐUR
pop 700

If you visit only one town in the Eastfjords, this picturesque place should be it. Made up of multicoloured wooden houses, and surrounded by snowcapped mountains and cascading waterfalls, Seyðisfjörður is the most historically and architecturally interesting town in east Iceland. It's also a friendly place with a gregarious and bohemian community of artists, musicians and craftspeople.

Summer is the liveliest time to visit, particularly when the Smyril Line's ferry *Norröna* sails majestically up the 17km-long fjord to the town – a perfect way to arrive in Iceland.

The substance and soul of the village has traditionally been focused on the fishing industry. For a glimpse of what life here was like 40 years ago, we recommend the moving film *Kaldaljós* (Cold Light; 2004), partly filmed in Seyðisfjörður.

If the weather's good, the scenic Rte 93 from Egilsstaðir is a delight, climbing to a high pass then descending along the waterfall-filled river Fjarðará. If it's bad weather you probably won't see much more than the tail-lights of the car in front!

History

Seyðisfjörður started as a trading centre in 1848, but its later wealth came from the 'silver of the sea' – herring. Its long, sheltering fjord gave it an advantage over other fishing villages, and it grew into the largest and most prosperous town in east Iceland. Most of the beautiful and unique wooden buildings here were built by Norwegian merchants, attracted by the rich pickings of the herring industry.

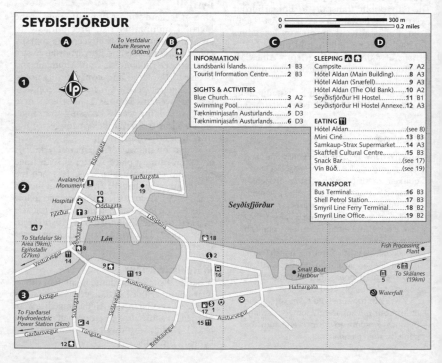

SEYÐISFJÖRÐUR

INFORMATION	
Landsbanki Íslands	1 B3
Tourist Information Centre	2 B3

SIGHTS & ACTIVITIES	
Blue Church	3 A2
Swimming Pool	4 A3
Tækniminjasafn Austurlands	5 D3
Tækniminjasafn Austurlands	6 D3

SLEEPING	
Campsite	7 A2
Hótel Aldan (Main Building)	8 A3
Hótel Aldan (Snæfell)	9 A3
Hótel Aldan (The Old Bank)	10 A2
Seyðisfjörður HI Hostel	11 B1
Seyðisfjörður HI Hostel Annexe	12 A3

EATING	
Hótel Aldan	(see 8)
Mini Ciné	13 B3
Samkaup-Strax Supermarket	14 A3
Skaftfell Cultural Centre	15 B3
Snack Bar	(see 17)
Vín Búð	(see 19)

TRANSPORT	
Bus Terminal	16 B3
Shell Petrol Station	17 B3
Smyril Line Ferry Terminal	18 B2
Smyril Line Office	19 B2

BORGARFJÖRÐUR TO SEYÐISFJÖRÐUR HIKE

Wildly wonderful and unexplored, the rugged nature between Borgarfjörður and Seyðisfjörður makes for one of the best multiday summer hikes in the region. To plan your journey, pick up the widely available *Gönguleiðir á Austurlandi* #1 map, or contact **Hafþor** (☎ 863 2320; groups Ikr20,000 per day) if you're looking for a guide.

On Day 1 start at Ölduhamar, just 2km outside the township of Borgarfjörður Eystri, and venture up into the mountains along the Brúnavíkurskarð pass (trail #19 on the map). Turn south (along trail #27) at emergency hut in Brúnavík, passing beautiful Kerlingfjall further on. After your six-to-seven-hour hike (15km), settle in for the night at the outfitted farmhouse/campsite in Breiðavík.

Day 2 features another stunning six or seven hours of hiking (13km along trail #30). You'll first walk through the grassy leas below Hvítafjall, then you'll link up with the 4WD track heading south to the Húsavík hut, where you'll spend the second night. The land between Breiðavík and Húsavík is infested with hidden people – the elf sheriff lives at Sólarfjall and the elf bishop lives at Blábjörg further south along the coast.

Another 13km of trails are tackled on Day 3 (six to seven hours along trail #37) as the path reunites with the sea at silent Loðmundarfjörður. The 4WD track ends at the new 'luxury hut' on the Norðdalsá river delta at the uppermost point of the fjord.

The last day, Day 4, links Loðmundarfjörður to Seyðisfjörður (trail #41). At the highest point of the mountain pass you'll find a log book signed by previous hikers. As you venture down into Seyðisfjörður you'll be treated to a watery fanfare of gushing chutes.

EAST ICELAND

During WWII Seyðisfjörður was a base for British and American forces. The only attack was on an oil tanker that was bombed by three German warplanes. The bombs missed their target, but one exploded so near that the ship sank to the bottom, where it remains today.

Seyðisfjörður's steep-sided valley has made it prone to avalanches. In 1885 an avalanche from Bjólfur killed 24 people and pushed several houses straight into the fjord. A more recent avalanche in 1996 flattened a local factory, but no lives were lost. The avalanche monument near the church is made from twisted girders from the factory, painted white and erected as they were found.

Information

The helpful **tourist information centre** (☎ 472 1551; 🕓 9am-5pm Mon-Fri May-Sep), in the modern ferry terminal building, sells bus passes and books onward accommodation. The centre also opens in conjunction with ferry arrivals throughout the year.

There's a **Landsbanki Íslands** (☎ 470 3040; Hafnargata 2) with an ATM, which can get crowded when the ferry arrives.

In summer there's free internet access at Skaftfell Cultural Centre (p274).

Sights

Seyðisfjörður is stuffed with 19th-century **timber buildings**, brought in kit form from Norway: read all about them in the brochure *Historic Seyðisfjörður*, available at the tourist office.

Several historical buildings have been transformed into cosy ateliers where local artisans work on various projects. Some studios sell knits, others sell art. A quick loop around town will reveal half a dozen places to drop some serious krónur. Also worth a look is the gallery space above the restaurant-cum-chill-out-spot at the Skaftfell Cultural Centre (p274). Exhibits change regularly – during our visit we saw a surprisingly intriguing installation of dirt collected from parks around the world.

For insight into the town's fishing and telecommunications history, there's a worthwhile technical museum, **Tækniminjasafn Austurlands** (☎ 472 1596; Hafnargata 44; adult/under 18yr Ikr500/free; 🕓 11am-5pm daily Jun–mid-Sep, 1-4pm Mon-Fri mid-Sep–May). It's housed in two buildings on Hafnargata: the impressive 1894 home of ship owner Otto Wathne, and a workshop from 1907. Seyðisfjörður was at the cutting edge of Icelandic technology in the 19th century – the first submarine telephone cable linking Iceland with Europe was brought ashore here in 1906. The museum charts this history with displays of old machinery, photographs, and a re-creation of the original telegraph station, foundry and machine shop.

The first high-voltage electricity in Iceland came from the **Fjarðarsel hydroelectric power** station (☎ 472 1122; www.fjardarsel.is), which opened in 1913. The power station, a 15-minute walk upriver from town, is still in operation; its small electricity museum opens on request.

Activities

The hills above Seyðisfjörður are the perfect spot for **hiking** neophytes. Start by walking up the road past the HI hostel to where a rough 4WD track takes off up the glacial valley to your left. The track peters out after a few hundred metres, but keep walking uphill, along the left side of the Vestdalsá river. After a couple of hours and several tiers of glorious waterfalls, you'll arrive at a small lake, Vestdalsvatn, which remains frozen most of the year. From the lake you can continue left over the tundra or return down the tiered rows of gushing waterfalls from where you came.

For an unearthly experience, stop by Hótel Aldan to sign up for a guided night **kayaking trip** (☎ 865 3741; www.iceland-tour.com; ☻ Jun-Aug) around the tranquil lagoon (two hours, Ikr2500) with Hlynur Oddssen, a Robert Redfort-esque character who spends his summers around town. Tailor-made tours are quite common – ask about daylong paddles (Ikr10,000) out to Skálanes. Hlynur also takes **mountain-bike tours** (Ikr2000 for a two-hour trip), including a four-hour trip out to the Brimnes lighthouse (Ikr4000). Or, you can hire bikes and take off on your own (Ikr1500/2000 per half/full day).

Seyðisfjörður's indoor **swimming pool** (☎ 472 1414; Suðurgata 5; adult/child Ikr300/150; ☻ 7-9am & 5-9pm Mon-Fri, noon-4pm Sat & Sun) has a sauna and hot pots.

In winter there's downhill and also cross-country **skiing** at the Stafdalur ski area, 9km from Seyðisfjörður on the road to Egilsstaðir – contact the tourist office for details.

Festivals & Events

Seyðisfjörður is highly regarded in east Iceland as an artistic centre. The town's cultural festival **Á Seyði** runs from mid-June to mid-August, offering plenty of exhibitions, workshops and music. An important part of the festival is the program of jazz, classical- and folk-music concerts, held on Wednesday evenings in the pretty **Blue Church** (Bláa Kirkjan; Ránargata) at 8.30pm from late June to mid-August. If you're leaving on the Thursday ferry, this is a great way to spend your final night in Iceland.

Sleeping

Campsite (☎ 861 3097; ferdamenning@sfk.is; Ránargata; sites per person Ikr600) This is a pleasant, sheltered, grassy site with big hedges and picnic benches. Note that camping isn't permitted in Vestdalur or anywhere along the roads.

Seyðisfjörður HI Hostel (Hafaldan; ☎ 472 1410; www. hostel.is; Ránargata 9; sb member/nonmember Ikr2300/2800, d member/nonmember Ikr6200/7200; ▢) Nothing puts a smile on our face more than a funky hostelry, but alas, we simply weren't impressed by Seyðisfjörður's contribution to the HI hostel chain. We were hoping for a backpacker bohemia, and although the comfy common space in the main building has pretty harbour views, we thought the staff curt and the bedrooms wholly underwhelming. The annexe at Suðurgata 8 is a bit more central and used to be the old hospital, but you'd never guess – Indian hangings and funky furniture make it less sterile.

our pick **Hótel Aldan** (☎ 472 1277; www.hotelaldan. com; Norðurgata 2) The wonderfully friendly hotel is shared across three old wooden buildings. Reception and the bar-restaurant (where breakfast is served) are at the Norðurgata location. The Snæfell location (in the old post office at Austurvegur 3) is a creaky, characterful three-storey place with the cheapest rooms (singles/doubles/triples Ikr11,900/ 15,900/17,900), fresh white paintwork, draped muslin curtains and Indian bedspreads to add a splash of colour. The Old Bank location (at Oddagata 6) houses a truly gorgeous boutique guest house with all mod-cons. Its luxurious rooms (singles/doubles/ triples Ikr13,900/18,900/22,900) are bright, spacious and furnished with antiques, and beds are snuggled under hand-embroidered bedspreads. The triple rooms have wicked little alcoves. Prices are reduced by Ikr2000 in winter.

Eating

Eating establishments open early on Wednesdays to accommodate ferry passengers.

Skaftfell Cultural Centre (☎ 472 1632; Austurvegur 42; mains Ikr1400-2800; ☻ noon-11pm summer, cultural events only winter; ▢ ☏) This arty bistro-bar is the kinda place where you can chill out and doodle in your journal while Groove Armada wafts through the air. There's free internet and you can choose from plenty of daily dish specials. If we lived in Seyðisfjörður, we'd probably come here everyday.

Hótel Aldan (☎ 472 1277; Norðurgata 2; mains Ikr3400-
4100; 7am-10pm mid-May–mid-Sep) Coffee and
light meals are served all day. In the evening,
damask tablecloths, crystal wine glasses and
flickering candles pretty-up the tables, and
the menu features traditional Icelandic ingredients (lamb, lobster, reindeer, fish) served
with contemporary salads and sauces. The
bar fairly buzzes when the boat comes in.
Reservations are advised.

Also worth a look is the **Mini Ciné** (☎ 845 4883;
Austurvegur; variable), which, as the name suggests, is a casual place to kick back and catch a
flick. When films aren't being shown you can
grab a coffee and a light meal. The **snack bar**
(☎ 472 1700; Hafnargata 2; noon-9pm) at the Shell
petrol station does hot dogs and sandwiches,
as well as cooked lunch/dinner mains
usually something filling and Icelandic, such
as fish soup or meatballs. The **Samkaup-Strax
supermarket** (☎ 472 1201; Vesturvegur 1; closed Sun)
is opposite the petrol station, and there's also a
Vín Búð (☎ 472 1191; Hafnargata 2a; 5-6pm Mon-Thu,
4-6pm Fri) alcohol shop.

Getting There & Away
The **Smyril Line car ferry** (☎ 472 1111; www.smyril-
line.com) *Norröna* sails year-round to
Seyðisfjörður from Denmark and the
Faeroes. From mid-June to August it sails
into town at 9am on Thursday, departing
for Scandinavia at 1pm the same afternoon;
from mid-April to mid-June (and for the
month of September as well) the boat pulls in
at 9am on Tuesday, leaving the following day
at 10pm. Check-In is at least one hour before
departure. See p336, or check the website
for more info.

See p262 for bus details.

AROUND SEYÐISFJÖRÐUR
The remote farm **Skálanes** (☎ 690 6966, 861 7008;
www.skalanes.com; mid-May–mid-Sep, by arrangement
rest of the yr), about 19km east of Seyðisfjörður, is
a wonderful nature reserve and heritage field
centre. The owner has an insatiable passion
for the outdoors and has lovingly restored the
once-abandoned farmstead into a veritable
Eden for amateur scientists, archaeologists
(remains from the Settlement Era have been
found), and tourists wishing to see pristine
bird cliffs (more than 40 avian species). Its
stunning isolation inspires nothing but relaxation and will undoubtedly appeal to your
inner hermit/naturalist.

A variety of stay-over packages are available
to travellers, from all-inclusive two-day visits
(Ikr31,500) and 4WD excursions (Ikr25,000
per day) to an in-depth five-day experience
geared towards true nature lovers (Ikr78,500).
B&B accommodation in beautifully refurbished rooms goes for Ikr6500 per night.

Getting to Skálanes is an adventure in itself.
You could walk all the way from Seyðisfjörður;
you could get there on a mountain bike; in a
normal car you can drive 13km along the
track until you get to the river, then walk
the last bit (which works out to be around
4km); in a 4WD you can drive the whole way
there (just be careful as you ford the river!);
or you can have the centre pick you up from
Seyðisfjörður (Ikr6000 per vehicle).

MJÓIFJÖRÐUR
pop 40
The next fjord south of Seyðisfjörður is
Mjóifjörður, flanked by spectacular cliffs and
rows of cascading waterfalls. The road leading
into the fjord (Rte 953) pushes the limits of
a 2WD (we blew a tyre here), but once you
make it in you'll be surrounded by lush hills
peppered with fascinating ruins and schools
of farmed fish leaping out of the frigid fjord
water. A rusted herring vessel sits beached –
like a giant ochre carcass – as you tumble
down into the fjord basin. A reminder of
the long-gone herring boom, the vessel was
responsible for hauling the unused bits of
herring to the dump in Neskaupstaður. Also
of interest are the rusting leftovers of the early-
20th-century Norwegian whaling station at
Asknes (accessible by 4WD only) and the
ruined Dalatangi light, Iceland's first lighthouse. The new lighthouse next door has wonderful art exhibitions during summer (open
from 1pm to 5pm Thursday to Sunday).

On the north side of the fjord at Brekkuþorp,
Sólbrekka (☎ 476 0020; mjoi@simnet.is; sb Ikr3000, cottages Ikr9000; closed Dec & Jan) is the one and only
place to stay around here and it's a welcome
sight for hikers. There's an old schoolhouse
near the sea, but the real treat lies up the hill –
two beautiful pine cottages built for four people each. There's also a little afternoon cafe
(1-5pm) open from July to mid-August. The
owners also offer fishing excursions (Ikr1500
per person).

There's some brilliant hiking around
Mjóifjörður. The folks at Sólbrekka can ferry
you across the fjord from where it's a beautiful

four-hour hike to Neskaupstaður, or you can climb over northern mountains to reach Seyðisfjörður on a six-hour trek. See p278 to reach Neskaupstaður by sea.

REYÐARFJÖRÐUR
pop 1090

In the Prettiest Fjord pageant Reyðarfjörður could never quite manage to take home the sash and crown. It's a relatively new settlement, which only came into existence – as a trading port – in the 20th century. More recently however, Reyðarfjörður did get the attention it had been looking for when Alcoa installed a giant 2km-long aluminium smelter just beyond the town along the fjord. Conservationists were up in arms, but the infusion of foreign workers has added a small splash of international flavour in Reyðarfjörður and the surrounding towns.

Sights & Activities

During WWII around 3000 Allied soldiers – about 10 times the local population – were based in Reyðarfjörður. At the top end of Heiðarvegur you'll find the **Icelandic Wartime Museum** (☎ 470 9063; www.fjardabyggd. is; Spítalakampur; adult/under 18yr Ikr500/free; ☼ 1-6pm Jun-Aug), which details these strange few years. The building is surrounded by mines, Jeeps and aeroplane propellers, and holds other war relics. Photographs and tableaux provide a good background to Iceland's wartime involvement. The museum is tucked behind a rusting set of army barracks, built as part of a hospital camp in 1943 but never used for that purpose. No Icelanders actually fought in World War II; however, many locals were killed at sea bringing large shipments of fish over to the UK.

Sleeping & Eating

Reyðarfjörður HI Hostel (Hjá Marlín; ☎ 474 1220, 892 0336; www.bakkagerdi.net; Vallagerði 9; sb s/d Ikr3500/6800, d Ikr9000; ☐ ☎) Budgetarians will love this hostel set in a lovely older home with green and grey aluminium siding. There's a fantastic bedroom-to-bathroom ratio, and you'll find a cosy restaurant (mains Ikr1000 to Ikr3200) on the 2nd floor, with imaginative pieces of modern art across the walls. In a second house down the street (not as attractive as the first, but still very comfy), there are simple rooms and a sauna (Ikr1000 per evening). HI members get a Ikr500 discount.

Fjarðahótel (☎ 474 1600; www.fjardarhotel.is; Búðareyri 6; s/d Ikr15,600/19,500; ☐ ☎) The only hotel in Reyðarfjörður, this comfortable business-style rooms (some with facilities for the disabled). An on-site 'steakhouse' (mains Ikr1100 to Ikr3500) gets good reviews.

There are burgers, pizzas and snacks at the Shell or Olís petrol stations, and a **Krónan supermarket** (☼ 9am-6pm Mon-Sat) lives inside the Molinn shopping centre.

ESKIFJÖRÐUR
pop 980

This friendly little town is stretched out along a dimple in the main fjord of Reyðarfjörður. Its setting is superb: it looks directly onto the mighty mountain Hólmatindur (985m), rising sheer from the shining blue water.

The surrounding hills are beautiful places for walking, particularly in autumn when their green sides are splattered with bright fungi and huge bog bilberries.

Orientation & Information

If you didn't buy walking maps in Egilsstaðir you can try stopping by Ferðaþjónustan Mjóeyri (opposite), located all the way at the very end of town on a charming little spit. The **Landsbanki Íslands** (☎ 410 4166; Strandgata 47) has an ATM and is located at the turn-off leading up to Neskaupstaður. Make a left when you arrive from Reyðarfjörður if you're looking for the brand new **swimming pool** (☼ 6.30am-9pm Mon-Fri, 10am-6pm Sat & Sun); the free campsite is straight ahead. For a bit of old-world charm, stop by **Bókabúðin Eskja** (☎ 476 1160; Útkaupstaðarbraut 1), the local bookstore.

Sights & Activities
MUSEUMS & HISTORIC SITES

The **East Iceland Maritime Museum** (Sjóminjasafn Austurlands; ☎ 470 9063, 470 9000; peturs@fjardabyggd.is; Strandgata 39b; adult/under 18yr Ikr500/free; ☼ 1-5pm Jun-Aug), in the black timber warehouse 'Gamla Buð' (dating from 1816), illustrates two centuries of the east coast's historic herring, shark, and whaling industry. More interesting is the **Old Boathouse** (☎ 477 1247, 698 6980; Strandgata; admission Ikr500; ☼ by appointment) down the street, which was largely abandoned until the owners of Mjóeyri took it over in 2009. When they entered the building they found that not a soul had been inside for the last 80 years. And they decided to leave it that way – when you enter the boathouse you're literally stepping back in time.

The remains of the world's largest spar quarry, **Helgustaðanáma**, can be found east of Eskifjörður, past Mjóeyri. Iceland spar (*silfurberg* in Icelandic) is a type of calcite crystal that is completely transparent and can split light into two parallel beams. It was a vital component in early microscopes, and large quantities were exported to some of Europe's top scientists starting from the 17th century until 1924, when the quarry closed. The largest specimen taken from Helgustaðanáma weighs 230kg and is displayed in the British Museum. Science aside, you can still see calcite sparkling in rocks around the quarry – very pretty – but you'll need a headlamp if venturing in on your own. The area is a national preserve, though, so you can't poke out pieces of crystal or take them away. Follow the rough dirt road 9km along the coastline until you get to an information panel; the quarry is then a 400m walk uphill.

Beyond the mine are the ruins at **Útstekkur**, which was once a bustling trade centre during Danish rule. In its heyday, more than 2400 people lived here, transporting goods from the rural Icelandic countryside onto Europe-bound freighters. Think of it as the old-school version of duty-free shopping at the airport. Trade centres were also set up at Vopnafjörður and Djúpivogur.

After the settlement ruins, the road turns into a rough dirt track for 4WDs, and leads to **Vöðlavík** – a huge black-sand beach that's perfect for families.

HIKING
The southern shore of the **Hólmanes Peninsula**, below the peak Hólmatindur, is a nature reserve. Hiking in the area offers superb maritime views – look out for pods of dolphins – and the chance to observe the protected vegetation and bird life. The Hólmaborgi hike, south of the main road, is a popular loop that takes but an hour or two.

There are also plenty of longer hiking routes up the nearby mountains: Kistufell (1239m), Goðaborg (1132m), Svartafjall (1021m) and Hádegisfjall (809m). Towards the end of the peninsula you may even see reindeer. If you summit any of the mountains during Walking Week (the last weekend in June) you'll find little stamps at the peak to fill your local hiking passport (Ikr500; available everywhere).

A popular multiday hike from Eskifjörður to Neskaupstaður starts at Karlsstaðir (you'll

need a 4WD to get there) and winds through mountainous Gerpir before linking up to the beautiful Barðnes Peninsula. Here you'll find a farmhouse to spend the night and a forest of petrified trees. You'll need a guide (ask at Mjóeyri, below) who knows the shifting tides along the way.

All of these routes are marked on the map *Gönguleiðir á Austurlandi II*, available from Egilsstaðir tourist office (p263) for a nominal fee.

SKIING
From Christmas to mid-April, skiing is possible on slopes near Oddsskarð, which is the pass leading over to Neskaupstaður. The longest run is 327m and is floodlit. There's also a basic ski hut, **Skíðaskáli** (☎ 476 1465; skidam@itn. is), where you can buy ski passes (Ikr1200/600 per day for adults/children under 16) and hire equipment (Ikr1500/1000 adult/child per day).

Sleeping & Eating
our pick **Ferðaþjónustan Mjóeyri** (☎ 477 1247, 698 6980; www.mjoeyri.is; Strandgata 120; sb Ikr3500, s/d Ikr5000/8000, cottage Ikr14,000; 🖳 🛜) Right at the eastern edge of town, this charming wooden house has unparalleled views – it literally sits in the middle of the waterway at the tip of a teeny peninsula. Tidy rooms off the super-comfy common space and adorable cottages out the back make Mjóeyri a great choice all around. The friendly owners have a couple of other projects as well – they offer tours of the spar mine, sustainable reindeer hunting, and they'll even let you take a look inside the antique-clad boathouse on the harbour. Breakfast (Ikr1000) can be requested, or you can hire a boat, catch your own fish and then barbecue it in the sheltered backyard!

Kaffihúsið (☎ 477 1064; www.kaffihusid.is; Strandgata 10; (s/d without bathroom Ikr5000/7000 Jun-Aug, Ikr4000/6000 Sep-May); 🖳 🛜) Primarily a restaurant (mains from Ikr1200; open from noon to 11pm) and hangout for the friendly Alcoa workers, Kaffihúsið also has a cluster of rooms in the back; they're simple affairs, but dolled up with good mattresses and plasma TVs. Don't leave without devouring the gut-busting 'super burger', but be sure to save room for dessert! The 'hot French cake' is divine – the effervescent owner calls it 'death by chocolate'. Ask here about possible tours of the Alcoa smelter.

Quick-eat options include a Shell petrol station with a **grill** (9am-10pm), and a **Samkaup-Strax supermarket** (☎ 476 1580; 10am-6pm Mon-Thu, to 7pm Fri, 11am-3pm Sat).

NESKAUPSTAÐUR (NORÐFJÖRÐUR)
pop 1410

Just getting to Neskaupstaður feels like a real odyssey. You travel via the highest highway pass (632m) in Iceland, through an alarming single-lane 630m-long tunnel, then drop from the skies like a falcon into town; attempt to drive further east and you simply run out of road. Although it's one of the largest of the fjord towns, this dramatic end-of-the-line location makes it feel very small and far away from the rest of the world.

As with most towns in the Eastfjords, Neskaupstaður began life as a 19th-century trading centre and prospered during the herring boom in the early 20th century. Its future was assured by the building of the biggest fish-processing and freezing plant in Iceland, Síldarvinnslan (SNV), at the head of the fjord.

Orientation & Information
Like other towns in the Eastfjords, Neskaupstaður is rather long and thin as it stretches out on the north side of the fjord. After passing Hótel Capitanó, you'll find most of the town's services (petrol station, bank etc) clustered along the fjord side of the road. Nesbær (opposite), the information point, is just beyond the bright-red Museum House; we found the staff at Frú Lú Lú (opposite) to be a font of local knowledge. If you're looking for the campsite, it's high above the town at the avalanche barriers (worth a visit for the great views).

Sights & Activities
MUSEUM HOUSE
Neskaupstaður's three small museums are clustered together in one bright-red warehouse, known as **Museum House** (☎ 470 9063, 470 9000; Egilsbraut 2; per museum adult/under 18yr Ikr500/free; 1-5pm Jun-Aug), by the harbour. Perhaps the most interesting part is the art gallery **Tryggvasafn**, which showcases a collection of striking paintings by prominent modern artist Tryggvi Ólafsson (1940–), who was born in Neskaupstaður. His colourful abstracts, some of which hang in national galleries in Reykjavík, Sweden and Denmark, depict Icelandic scenes and are visually quite striking.

The **East Iceland Museum of Natural History** has a big collection of local stones (including spar from the Helgustaðir mine), plus an array of stuffed animals, birds, fish and pinned insects. The **Jósafat Hinriksson Maritime Museum** is one man's collection of artefacts relating to the sea.

WALKING & HIKING
At the eastern end of town where the road runs out is the nature reserve **Folksvangur Neskaupstaðar** – perfect for short strolls. Various paths run through long grass, over tiny wooden bridges, and past boulders, peat pits, cliffs and the rushing sea. There are plenty of puffins to watch, as well as gulls and ravens.

For serious hikers, a rewarding route will take you up **Goðaborg** (1132m) from the farm Kirkjuból, 8km west of town. From the summit you can also descend into Mjóifjörður, the next fjord to the north; allow six hours and, due to late snows at higher altitudes, attempt it only at the height of summer.

A more difficult walk is from **Oddsskarð** along the ridges eastward to the lonely fjords Hellisfjörður and Viðfjörður. If you want to spend the night in Viðfjörður, you can test your wits by staying in the basement bunks at the abandoned farm at Nesbær – known to be one of the most haunted places in Iceland.

The dramatic Gerpir cliffs, Iceland's easternmost point, can be reached with difficulty; the only way to visit this beautiful place is on foot. To work out a route, use the small *Neskaupstaður Country* park brochure (available at Nesbær – opposite – for free) or the *Gönguleiðir á Fjarðalsóðum* (Ikr800 – you'll have to ask around for this one).

BOAT TRIPS
From June to mid-September **Fjarðaferðir** (☎ 477 1710; www.fjardafedir.is; adult/child Ikr1800/900) runs a scenic boat cruise to Mjóifjörður on Fridays and Mondays at 10.30am and 5pm (Mondays and Thursdays in winter pending interest). Often the guest house in Mjóifjörður serves white wine and shellfish on arrival. Sightseeing tours (two hours, Ikr4900) and fishing trips around Norðfjörður are also possible.

KAYAKING
There's no better way to explore the fjords than in a kayak. The friendly fellas at **Kaj Kayak Club** (Kayakklúbburinn Kaj; ☎ 863 9939; www.123.is/kaj; Kirkjufjara) offer guided two-hour trips (Ikr4000

per person) around Norðfjörður, exploring sea caves and resident bird life. Outings are on request; in midsummer ask about the midnight kayaking trip. The clubhouse is located across the street from Frú Lú Lú.

HORSE RIDING
You'll hear nothing but rave reviews about the horse stables at **Skorrahestar** (☎ 477 1736; www.123.is/skorrahestar; Skorrastaður), situated high in the bluffs.

Festivals & Events
A metal and punk mayhem festival, **Eistnaflug** (www.eistnaflug.is), which could be translated as 'Flight of Testicles', is held every summer in town on the second weekend in July. Every self-respecting rockin' band shows up, if not to play then to listen and drink!

Sleeping
Campsite (☎ 470 9000) This brand new site, with electricity and hot showers, overlooks the town and fjord from the Drangagil avalanche barrier. It's near the hospital – in case you get lost on the way (like we did).

Tónspil (☎ 477 1580; www.tonspil.is; Hafnarbraut 22; sb Ikr2800, s/d Ikr3900/6900) Like an extra in the film *High Fidelity*, you need to ask the dude in the music shop about the rooms above! Which are very, very simple (cork floor, white ply wardrobe, bed), but there's a handy TV room/kitchen area with microwave and hotplates. There's also a 'no smoking' sign posted, but we're pretty sure they're not talking about cigarettes… The music shop is open from 10am to 6pm Mondays to Saturdays.

Hótel Capitanó (☎ 477 1800; www.hotelcapitano.is; Hafnarbraut 50; sb/s/d Ikr3500/8900/12,900) The bright-blue corrugated iron building doesn't look like much, but all rooms have attached bathrooms and some of the doubles are spacious and well appointed. Modern art by celebrated local artist Tryggvi Ólafsson adorns the walls. An authentic Thai buffet (Ikr1750) is often served on weekend evenings. We recommend calling ahead – there was talk the hotel might be the next victim in the economic recession.

Hótel Edda (☎ 444 4860; www.hoteledda.is; Nesgata 40; s/d Ikr14,100/17,600; ☽ early Jun–mid-Aug) On the waterfront at the eastern end of town, this summer hotel has brilliant views but predictable, overpriced rooms. Although some may cringe at the chain name, Hótel Edda prides itself on providing top-notch cuisine, and the in-house

EASTER SEALS
The Paskahellir (Easter Cave) in Viðfjörður earns its name from an old local legend. In the Eastfjords it's commonly believed that at Easter all seals shed their skin and walk the earth as humans. One year, a lonely fisherman at Viðfjörður took a seal in as his wife while she roamed around in human form. He locked her skin in a coffin and hid it in the cave. After bearing seven children, she took the key to the coffin, retrieved her skin and returned to the sea where her seven seal children were waiting. The coffin now sits in Frú Lú Lú (below) and the cave can be seen on the Norðfjörður–Mjóifjörður cruise (opposite.)

restaurant is no exception. Dine on a short list of tasty fish while staring out over the fjord.

Eating
Nesbær (Litla Kaffihúsið; ☎ 477 1115; Egilsbraut 5; lunch Ikr850; ☽ 9am-6pm Mon-Wed & Fri, to 10.30pm Thu, 10am-6pm Sat, 1-5pm Sun; ☐) This cafe–bakery–knick-knack shop has a quintessential small-town vibe and offers yummy cakes, sandwiches and soup. Nesbær doubles as the town's information point, offering a few tattered brochures.

our pick **Frú Lú Lú** (☎ 865 5868; Egilsbraut 19; lunch Ikr990, tapas dinner Ikr1990; ☽ 11am-9pm Sun-Thu, to 3am Fri & Sat; ☞) We're stingy with our 'our pick' symbols – but this place deserves three. We ate here twice – the first time we came for an early lunch of organic soup and salad, and ended up chatting and dining with the staff and other customers until well past 11pm. Then, when we came back for seconds, we randomly had our fortune read by a celebrity psychic and savoured a buffet of Brazilian-inspired dishes. On a normal night (if there are any here) expect tailor-made tapas dinner specials and scrumptious double lattes served in oversized mugs. There's something bizarrely enchanting about this antique-clad joint, and it's well worth paying a visit to see what kind of magic unfolds for you…

Standard fast-food fare can be found at **Egilsbúð** (☎ 476 1313; Egilsbraut 1; ☽ 11am-midnight Mon-Thu, to 3am Fri & Sat) – the local community centre – or at the **Ólís petrol station** (☎ 477 1500; Hafnarbraut 19). **Samkaup-Úrval** (☎ 477 1301; Hafnarbraut 13; ☽ 10am-7pm Mon-Fri, noon-6pm Sat & Sun) and **Nesbakki supermarkets** (☎ 477 1609; Bakkavegur 3; ☽ 10am-7pm) are at the top of the hill near the campsite.

FÁSKRÚÐSFJÖRÐUR

pop 700

The rather insipid village of Fáskrúðsfjörður, sometimes known as Búðir, was originally settled by French seamen who came to fish the Icelandic coast between the late 1800s and 1914. In a gesture to the local Gallic heritage, street signs are in both Icelandic and French.

At the mouth of the fjord, the island **Skrúður** contains lots of bird life, as well as the world's biggest multiapartment 'puffin cave', formerly believed to have been a giant's home. Another little islet, **Andey** (Duck Island), has a large colony of eider.

Geologists may get a buzz from the laccolithic mountain **Sandfell** (743m), above the southern shore of Fáskrúðsfjörður, which was formed by molten rhyolite bursting through older lava layers. It's one of the world's finest examples of this sort of igneous intrusion (although Rio's Sugar Loaf Mountain is perhaps a mite more impressive). It's a two- to three-hour walk to the top.

The full story about the French seamen in Fáskrúðsfjörður can be found at **Fransmenn á Íslandi** (Les Français en Islande; ☎ 475 1525; www.fransmenn. net; Búðavegur 8; admission Ikr600; ☼ 10am-6pm Jun-Aug), up the hill. The museum uses photographs and paperwork to paint a detailed picture of the interactions between the French and the locals – Icelanders would trade salted fish and the French offered red wine in return (go figure).

The museum also has a quaint **cafe** (mains from Ikr500; ☼ 10am-6pm Jun-Aug). The owner bakes a wonderful pie made from fresh rhubarb plucked from just up the road; the other speciality here is quiche Lorraine.

Another option is **Café Sumarlina** (☎ 475 1575; Búðavegur 59; fish & lamb Ikr1100-2100, pizza Ikr2000; ☼ 10am-10pm Sun-Thu, to 3am Fri & Sat; ☞) down by the fjord basin. It's a friendly little place, in a creaking wooden house decorated with odd ornaments. Self-caterers can try **Samkaup-Strax** (☎ 475 1581; Skólavegur 59; ☼ 10am-6pm Mon-Thu, to 7pm Fri, 11am-3pm Sat) and **Vín Buð** (☎ 475 1530; Búðarvegur; ☼ 5-6pm Mon-Thu, 4-6pm Fri).

Besides the free **campsite** (☎ 470 9000) at the west end of the village, the only lodging option is the strange **Hótel Bjarg** (☎ 475 1466; www.hotel bjarg.is; Skólavegur 49; s/d 12,500/15,000), which feels like an orphanage for unwanted objets d'art. Even more bizarre is the stream that runs directly through the basement of the faded building (just look out of the window in the reception area). The owner can arrange a

bumpy boat ride (Ikr20,000) to the puffin island Skrúður during summer.

STÖÐVARFJÖRÐUR

pop 530

Even if geology makes you pass out from boredom, it's worth stopping in Stöðvarfjörður to see **Steinasafn Petru** (☎ 475 8834; www.steinapetra.com; Fjarðarbraut 21; adult/under 14yr Ikr700/free; ☼ 9am-6pm May-Sep, phone first Oct-Apr). This exceptional stone collection is octogenarian Petra Sveinsdóttir's lifelong labour of love. Inside the house, stones and minerals are piled from floor to ceiling – 70% of them are from the local area. They include unbelievably beautiful cubes of jasper, polished agate, purple amethyst, glowing creamy 'ghost stone', glittering quartz crystals…it's like opening a treasure chest. The garden is a wonderfully peaceful place, awash with more rocks, garden gnomes, and beach-combed flotsam and jetsam. Petra is now in a nursing home, but she visits once a week; her children and grandchildren are keeping her collection going.

Most people bolt from the town after seeing the stone show, but there are a few other distractions to keep you around. From 11am to 5pm during June, July and August you'll find a small **market** (Fjarðarbraut 40) at the 'Blue House', an abandoned fish factory. Here locals sell a variety of charming handmade products such as woollen sweaters, sweet jams, amateur art and salted fish. **Gallerí Snærós** (☎ 475 8931; Fjarðarbraut 42; ☼ noon-6pm May-Sep), one of the oldest galleries in rural Iceland, is the studio of two local artists who dabble in a variety of intriguing media.

Skip the free campsite just east of the village; you have to stay at **Kirkjubær** (☎ 892 3319, 846 0032; www.simnet.is/brigiral; Fjarðarbraut 37a; sb Ikr2500), one of the most memorable lodging options in the Eastfjords, if not the whole country. This tiny old church dates from 1925 but is now in private hands and has been renovated into a cute one-room hostel. The pulpit and altar are still there, and some of the pews are now part of the furniture. There's a full kitchen and bathroom, and the beds (mostly just mattresses) are on the upper mezzanine level. It supposedly sleeps 10, but that would be pretty cosy! The owners live in the yellow house just below the church at Skolúbraut 1 – pop in or you can call the number on the door and they'll tell you where to find the key. It's also worth asking about their boat/fishing trips out onto the fjord.

For other lodging options, check out the crowded corkboard at the entrance to **Brekkan**

(☎ 475 8939; Fjarðarbraut 44; snacks Ikr650-1950; ☺ 9am-10pm Mon-Fri, 10am-10pm Sat), the local chow house. It's the only sit-down place in town and makes absolutely no effort with the decor – but we have to admit the grease-laden pizza was pretty darn good. There's a stack of groceries in the back.

BREIÐDALSVÍK
pop 160

Fishing village Breiðdalsvík is beautifully sited at the end of Iceland's broadest valley, Breiðdalur. It's a very quiet place – more a base for walking in the nearby hills and fishing the rivers and lakes than an attraction in itself. The biggest excitement of the year is the **Austfjarðatröllið** strong-man competition in mid-August.

Located in the centre of 'town' (and we're using that term lightly here), **Hótel Bláfell** (☎ 475 6770; www.hotelblafell.is; Sólvellir 14; s/d incl breakfast Ikr9900/14,400 Jun–early Sep, discounts mid-Sep–May) has freshly furnished rooms and friendly new owners. Don't be put off by the cafeteria-style decor, the restaurant (mains from Ikr1200) here is quite good. Go for the local favourites – hearty meat- or fish-soup. The yummy fish stew is only served for lunch, but if you ask nicely they'll whip it up at dinner. Tighter budgets can pitch a tent at the free campsite out the back.

Outside Breiðdalsvík, on Rte 96 heading back towards Stöðvarfjörður, **Café Margret** (☎ 475 6625; s/d Ikr9900/15,900 Jun–mid-Sep, Ikr4900/7500 mid-Sep–May) is a beautiful boutique guest house built from Finnish pine. Its four precious rooms are stuffed with quaint antiques and quilts. The attached cafe (open 8am to 11pm June to mid-September, 10am to 5pm mid-September to May) is pricey, but it provides a welcome respite from hot dogs. All in all, the rooms get a '10', the food a '6' and the service gets a '3'.

BREIÐDALSVÍK TO DJÚPIVOGUR
Breiðdalur

As the Ring Road returns to the coast it passes through the lovely Breiðdalur valley, nestled beneath colourful rhyolite peaks. Near the head of the valley you may see reindeer. At the abandoned farm Jórvík a forestry reserve harbours native birch and aspen.

Once a school, **Hótel Staðarborg** (☎ 475 6760; www.stadarborg.is; s/d Ikr4500/12,500/28,000 May-Sep) has neat, modern rooms with proper shutters to keep out that midnight sun! Breakfast is included with made-up beds, and dinner (Ikr4500) is available on request. You can hire horses to explore Breiðdalur or fish in the neighbouring lake.

Staðarborg is 6km west of Breiðdalsvík on the Ring Road, near the turn-off to Rte 964.

Berufjörður

South of Breiðdalur along the Ring Road is Berufjörður, a longish, steep-sided fjord flanked by rhyolite peaks. The southwestern shore is dominated by the obtrusive, pyramid-shaped mountain **Búlandstindur**, which rises 1068m above the water. The westernmost ridge is known as Goðaborg or 'God's rock'. When Iceland officially converted to Christianity in 1000, locals are said to have carried their pagan images to the top of this mountain and thrown them off the cliff.

Around Berufjörður are several historical walking routes through the steeply rugged terrain. The best known of these climbs is from Berufjörður, the farm at the head of the fjord, and crosses the 700m Berufjarðarskarð into Breiðdalur.

our pick **Berunes HI Hostel** (☎ 478 8988, 869 7227; www.simnet.is/berunes; sites per person Ikr1000, sb Ikr2100-3000, s/d Ikr4100/5900, cottages from Ikr11,500; ☺ Apr-Sep; 🖳) is located on a 100-year-old farm with 'a good spirit', according to the owner. This wonderfully wobbly hostel/guest house is one of our all-time favourites. There's space for campers; delightful little rooms and alcoves; a kitchen and lounge with books in the old farmhouse; plus Berunes boasts two self-contained family apartments and a separate cottage. Join the owners in the bright dining room for breakfast (Ikr1000), which includes delicious homemade pancakes. Musicians are welcome to play the organ in the neighbouring 19th-century church. Nonmembers are charged Ikr500 extra, and linen costs Ikr800. The hostel is 25km along the Ring Road south of Breiðdalsvík.

If Berunes is full, try **Eyjólfsstaðir** (☎ 478 8137; sites per person Ikr500, sb Ikr2300) tucked 2km off the Ring Road in the secluded Fossá valley. There are kitchen facilities, a bathroom and a lounge in basic rooms, but the building feels rather threadbare.

DJÚPIVOGUR
pop 360

This friendly little fishing village, at the mouth of Berufjörður, gives summer visitors a flowery welcome. Its neat historic buildings, museum and small, colourful harbour are worth a look, and it has a couple of nice eating places; but the main reason to visit is to catch the boat to Papey island (p282).

Djúpivogur (*dyoo*-pi-vor) is actually the oldest port in the Eastfjords – it's been around since the 16th century when German merchants brought goods to trade. The last major excitement was in 162: pirates from North Africa rowed ashore, plundering the village and nearby farms, and carrying away dozens of slaves.

Information

The friendly **tourist information centre** (☎ 478 8220; langabud@langabud.is; ☒ 10am-6pm Jun–mid-Sep, to 4pm 15-31 May) is in the historic rust-coloured building, Langabúð, alongside the harbour.

The village also has a bank (there's an ATM in Við Voginn cafe), a post office and a swimming pool.

Sights & Activities

Some of the town's lovely **wooden buildings** date from the late 19th century. The oldest building, the long bright-red **Langabúð**, is a harbourside log warehouse dating from 1790, which now houses the tourist office, a coffee shop and an unusual local **museum** (☒ 10am-6pm Jun–mid-Sep, to 4pm mid-May–late May; adult/child Ikr500/300). Downstairs is a collection of works by renowned sculptor Ríkarður Jónsson (1888–1977). They range from lifelike busts of worthy Icelanders to mermaid-decorated mirrors and reliefs depicting saga characters. Ríkarður also championed the Icelandic woodcarving typeface, whose letters are possibly descended from runes – look out for this strangely illegible alphabet in his work. Upstairs, in the tar-smelling attic, is a collection of local-history artefacts.

The Djúpivogur Peninsula is compact and ideal for short hikes from town. A lovely walk is to **Álfkirkja** on the rock formation Rakkaberg, 500m north of town. The indoor **swimming pool** (☎ 4/8 8999; Varða 4; adult/child Ikr350/150; ☒ 7am-8.30pm Mon-Fri, 10am-6pm Sat & Sun Jun-Aug, 7am-8.30pm Mon-Fri, 11am-3pm Sat & Sun Sep-May), behind Hótel Framtíð, is a good place to unwind after hiking.

If you have a li'l extra time, it's worth giving Gusta a ring to see if you can swing by her studio, **Gusta Design** (☎ 863 1475; www.gustadesign.is). A local fashion designer, she creates unique accessories from reindeer skins and fish scales.

Sleeping & Eating

Campsite (☎ 478 8887; sites per person Ikr850) Situated just behind the Við Voginn shop, this site is run by Hótel Framtíð, so cough up your pennies at the reception there. The campsite has showers and cooking facilities.

Hótel Framtíð (☎ 478 8887; www.simnet.is/framtid; Vogaland 4; sb s/d Ikr3850/6800, s/d without bathroom Ikr8400/10,400, with bathroom Ikr13,400/17,100; ☎) This friendly hotel by the harbour is impressive for a village of this size. Although it's been around for a while (the building was brought in pieces from Copenhagen in 1905), a newer wing (built in 1999) adds modern fixtures to the mix. Four summer houses (Ikr17,000) are also available for rent. The menu at the in-house restaurant (mains cost Ikr3180 to Ikr4450; open from noon to 2pm and 6pm to 9pm) is short and sweet, and reads like a love poem to your tastebuds: succulent seafood soup and fresh-from-the-sea lobster. You can order a takeaway filter coffee if you need a quick buzz before tackling the next stretch of highway.

Langabúð Café (lunch Ikr1200; ☒ 10am-6pm Jun–mid-Sep, 10am-4pm mid-May–late May) A good option for lunch, this cafe has a suitably old-world atmosphere with views over the harbour, and serves cakes, soup and homemade bread. It can get very crowded with coach parties.

Við Voginn (☎ 478 8860; Vogaland 2; mains from Ikr950; ☒ 9am-10pm Mon-Fri, 10am-10pm Sat & Sun) A fast-food joint with an attached supermarket, Við Voginn is popular with locals and tourists on the run.

On the main road into town you'll find a **Samkaup-Strax supermarket** (Búland 2; ☒ 10am-6pm Mon-Fri, to 4pm Sat, noon-4pm Sun) with a **Vín Búð** (☒ 5-6pm Mon-Thu, 4-6pm Fri) attached.

AROUND DJÚPIVOGUR

The name of lovely offshore island **Papey** (Friars' Island) suggests it was once a hermitage for the Irish monks who may have briefly inhabited Iceland before fleeing upon the arrival of the Norse. This small and tranquil island was once a farm, but it's presently inhabited only by seals and nesting seabirds. Other highlights include the **Kastali**, home to the local hidden people; the **Hellisbjarg lighthouse**, which dates from 1922; Iceland's oldest and smallest **wooden church**, built in 1805; and the wind-battered ruins of an **apartment house** from the early 20th century. Camping is not allowed on the island.

From June to August **Papeyjarferðir** (☎ 478 8119, 659 1469; papey@djupivogur.is; adult/7-12yr Ikr6000/3000) runs four-hour tours to the island. Weather and numbers permitting (minimum four people), tours depart Djúpivogur harbour at 1pm daily, returning at 5pm. When things are really busy, there's also a 3pm tour. In fine weather this is a truly magical outing. Bring proper footwear – the island is boggy and wet year-round.

Southeast Iceland

Iceland's southeast is a kingdom made for trolls and ice giants, rather than creatures of warm flesh and blood. Mighty Vatnajökull, the largest ice cap outside the poles, dominates the region. Even casual visitors travelling along the Ring Road will be awestruck by its huge rivers of frozen ice pouring down steep-sided valleys towards the sea. The glacial lagoon Jökulsárlón, at the foot of the ice cap, is a photographer's paradise – wind and water sculpt its chilly-blue icebergs into fantastical shapes.

A terrible desert of dark glacial sand unrolls on the southern side of the Ring Road. The damage is caused by the Grímsvötn and Öræfi volcanoes, trapped beneath Vatnajökull. When they blow, huge areas of the ice cap melt, sending powerful rock-filled rivers smashing onto the coast. The most recent *jökulhlaup* (glacial flood) was only a decade or so ago.

Further inland is the epicentre of Iceland's worst eruption. In the late 18th century, the Lakagígar fissure erupted in a 30km-long sheet of flame and ash, blotting out the sun and causing famine across the northern hemisphere. Today such apocalyptic fire and darkness seem far away; the fragile lava craters are covered in soft green moss and the only sound is the wind. With desolation all around, it's not surprising that Skaftafell, the greenest part of Vatnajökull National Park, is a popular spot. This sheltered enclave between the glaciers and the dead grey sands throbs with life and colour.

Although part of the interior, we've included Fjallabak Nature Reserve and Landmannalaugar in this section. With a mesmerising landscape and superb hiking, this 'back road' between the southeast and southwest shouldn't be missed.

HIGHLIGHTS

- Admire the ever-changing ice sculptures at **Jökulsárlón** (p299), a bewitching glacial lagoon
- Bathe in steaming thermal pools at **Landmannalaugar** (p285), or rise to the challenge of the **Landmannalaugar to Þórsmörk hike** (p288) – one of the world's great walks
- Visit Iceland's favourite area of Vatnajökull National Park, **Skaftafell** (p294), an area of green and lovely life amid the vast dead sandar (sand deltas)
- Stride up **Laki** (p292) for views of three glaciers…and unbelievable volcanic devastation
- Feel like a mountaineer on an easy but exhilarating **glacier walk** (p298); make it real by scaling Iceland's highest peak, **Hvannadalshnúkur** (p298); or roar across the **Vatnajökull ice cap** (p302) on a snowmobile

SOUTHEAST ICELAND

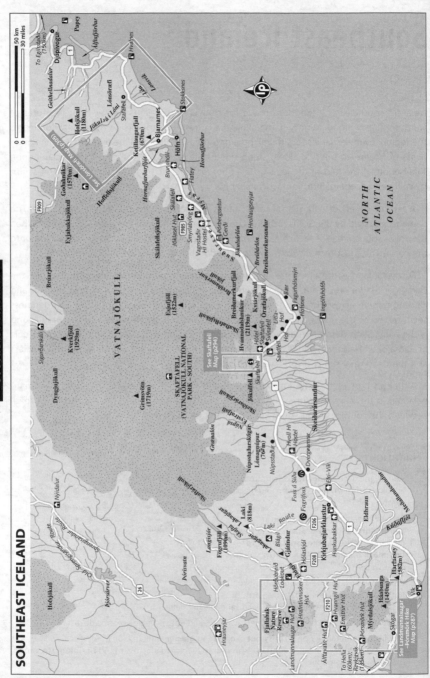

FJALLABAK NATURE RESERVE

FJALLABAK ROUTE

In summer, the Fjallabak Route (F208) makes a spectacular alternative to the coast road between Hella, in southwest Iceland, and Kirkjubæjarklaustur. Its name translates as 'Behind the Mountains', and that's exactly where it goes.

First, head north from Hella on Rte 26. The F208 begins near the Sigölduvirkjun power plant in the southwest on the Tungnaá river and passes through the scenic Fjallabak Nature Reserve to Landmannalaugar. From there, it continues east past the Kirkjufell marshes and enters Jökuldalur, then travels along a riverbed for 10km before climbing to the Hörðubreið lookout and descending to Eldgjá.

For the next 40km the road is fairly good, but there are a couple of river fords, so conventional vehicles going to Eldgjá from the east may have difficulties when the water is high. At Búland the route joins Rte 208 and emerges at the Ring Road southwest of Kirkjubæjarklaustur.

A non-4WD vehicle wouldn't have a hope of completing the through route. In summer, if the rivers are low, a conventional vehicle can reach Landmannalaugar from the west (F208 only). Note that rental-car companies prohibit taking 2WD vehicles on any F roads, so if something should go wrong on this route, your insurance will be void.

Since much of the Fjallabak Route is along rivers (or rather, in rivers!), it's not ideally suited to mountain bikes either. Lots of people attempt it, but it's not casual cycling by any stretch.

Getting There & Away

From mid-June to August there's a scheduled **Reykjavík Excursions** (☎ 580 5400; www.re.is) bus. It runs daily between Reykjavík and Skaftafell (via Selfoss, Hella, Landmannalaugar, Eldgjá and Kirkjubæjarklaustur), departing at 8.30am from either end. The 11-hour journey costs Ikr11,400 each way – unquestionably worth it.

The bus stops for two hours at lovely Landmannalaugar, but that's not really long enough for you to explore properly. Most travellers make a proper break here,

continuing the journey to Skaftafell at a later date. The section from Reykjavík to Landmannalaugar (5½ hours) costs Ikr6300 each way.

LANDMANNALAUGAR

Multicoloured mountains, soothing hot springs, rambling lava flows and clear blue lakes make Landmannalaugar unique. It's a favourite with Icelanders and visitors alike… as long as the weather cooperates! Allow several days to fully explore this area.

Landmannalaugar (600m above sea level) includes the largest geothermal field in Iceland outside the Grímsvötn caldera in Vatnajökull. Its weird peaks are made of rhyolite – a mineral-filled lava that cooled unusually slowly, causing those amazing colours.

Although Landmannalaugar gets quite chilly, the weather is generally more stable than in coastal areas, and when it does rain it's more of a wind-driven horizontal mist than a drenching downpour.

Information

The Landmannalaugar hut wardens can help with specific questions, including directions and advice on hiking routes. There are also two green buses, which are parked and opened up in summer as a tiny **information centre & shop** (☼ 11.30am-6pm late Jun-Aug) selling coffee, buns and plasters!

There's no petrol at Landmannalaugar. The nearest petrol pumps are 40km north at Hrauneyjar (close to the beginning of the F208), and 90km southeast at Kirkjubæjarklaustur, but to be on the safe side you should put in enough fuel to get you all the way back to Hella.

Activities

HOT SPRINGS

Just 200m from the Landmannalaugar hut, both hot and cold water flow out from beneath Laugahraun and combine in a natural pool to form the most ideal hot bath imaginable.

HORSE RIDING

Several companies offer horse treks to Landmannalaugar – see p138.

HIKING

Laugahraun, the convoluted lava field behind the Landmannalaugar hut, offers vast scope for exploration. Across it, the slopes of Iceland's most colourful mountain, rainbow-streaked **Brennisteinsalda**, are punctuated by steaming vents and sulphur deposits. Climb to the summit for a good view across the rugged and variegated landscape (it's a 7km round-trip from Landmannalaugar).

From Brennisteinsalda it's another 90 minutes along the Þórsmörk route to the impressive **Stórihver** geothermal field.

The blue lake **Frostastaðavatn** lies behind the rhyolite ridge immediately north of the Landmannalaugar hut. Walk over the ridge and you'll be rewarded with far-ranging views as well as close-ups of the interesting rock formations and moss-covered lava flows flanking the lake. If you walk at least one way on the road and spend some time exploring around the lake, the return trip takes two to three hours.

A fine day-hike from Landmannalaugar is to the ironically named **Ljótipollur** (Ugly Puddle), an incredible red crater filled with bright-blue water. Oddly enough, although it was formed by a volcanic explosion, its lake is rich in trout. That intense, fiery red comes from iron-ore deposits. You'll come across all kinds of scenery on the way to the Puddle, from tephra desert and lava flow to marsh and braided glacial valleys. To get there you can climb over the 786m-high peak **Norðurnámur** (well worthwhile) or just traverse its western base to emerge on the Ljótipollur road (a 10km to 12km return trip, depending on the route). A number of routes ascend to the crater rim, but the most interesting is the footpath that climbs its southernmost slope. If you walk all the way around the crater rim, it's an 18km hike that will take you the better part of a day.

Another good day walk from Landmannalaugar is around the peak **Tjörvafell** and the crater lake **Hnausapollur** (also known as Bláhylur).

Sleeping

Because the whole Fjallabak area is a protected nature reserve, wild camping is not allowed.

Landmannalaugar hut (☎ 863 1175; sb Ikr3300; ☾ Jul-Sep), run by Ferðafélag Íslands, accommodates 75 people, and books up quickly with tour groups and club members. Otherwise there's a **campsite** (sites per person Ikr900) with toilet and shower facilities.

LANDMANNALAUGAR TO ÞÓRSMÖRK

The harsh, otherworldly beauty of the Landmannalaugar to Þórsmörk route makes it one of the finest and most popular hikes in Iceland. See the boxed text, p288, for details of the walk.

Several huts along the Landmannalaugar–Þórsmörk route are owned and maintained by **Ferðafélag Íslands** (☎ 568 2533; www.fi.is). All have camping areas (per person Ikr900), although these tend to be exposed, and with sandy ground that can make it difficult to keep your tent pegged down. Book and pay for hut space well in advance (*at least* two or three months); otherwise bring a tent.

Hut etiquette requires travellers to clean up after themselves. You need to carry your rubbish out with you from the Hrafntinnusker and Emstrur huts. It's also a good idea to bring a pair of slippers with you so that you can leave your wet hiking boots outside and keep the huts clean!

The following huts are listed from north to south:

Landmannalaugar (☎ 863 1175; N 63°59.600', W 19°03.660'; per person Ikr3300; ☾ Jul-Sep) Holds 75 people. It has a kitchen, shower and a warden from July to September.

Hrafntinnusker (Höskuldsskáli; N 63°56.014', W 19°10.109'; per person Ikr3300) Holds 36 people. It has a kitchen, and a warden for July and August.

Álftavatn (N 63°51.470', W 19°13.640'; per person Ikr3300) Two huts holding 58 people. Each hut has a kitchen and shower, and a warden from June to August.

Hvanngil (N 64°50.026', W 19°12.507'; per person Ikr3300) This hut is on an alternative path, 5km south of Álftavatn. It holds 60 people, and has a kitchen and shower.

Emstrur (Botnar) (N 63°45.980', W 19°22.480'; per person Ikr3300) Two huts holding 40 people. There is a kitchen and shower, and warden from June to August.

Þórsmörk (Skagfjörðsskáli; ☎ mid-May–Sep 893 1191; N 63°40.960', W 19°30.890'; per person Ikr3300) Holds 75 people. It has a kitchen, shower and shop, and a warden from mid-May to September.

LANDMANNALAUGAR TO ELDGJÁ

East of Landmannalaugar, the F208 leaves Fjallabak Reserve and skirts the river Tungnaá as it flows past the Norðurnámshraun lava field.

After dropping into Jökuldalur the road deteriorates into a valley route along a riverbed and effectively becomes a 10km-long ford interspersed with jaunts across the odd sandbar or late snowfield. When it climbs

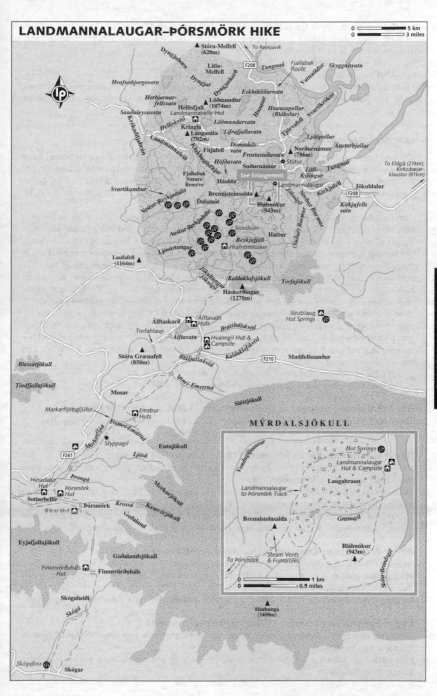

LANDMANNALAUGAR–ÞÓRSMÖRK HIKE

0 ————— 5 km
0 ————— 3 miles

out of the valley it ascends the tuff mountain **Hörðubreið**, from where there are superb views across the lowlands to the south.

Just west of the Herðubreið lookout, a rough 4WD road heads 25km northeast to the blue lake **Langisjór**. On the far side of the lake lie the astonishing green mountains of **Fögrufjöll** (1090m), and beyond them is the black-sand outwash plain of the glacial river Skaftá.

ELDGJÁ

Eldgjá (Fire Gorge) is a volcanic rift stretching 40km from Mýrdalsjökull to the peak

---

LANDMANNALAUGAR TO ÞÓRSMÖRK HIKE

The hike from Landmannalaugar to Þórsmörk – known as the Laugarvegurinn (Hot Spring Rd) – is one of the great walks of the world. The best map of the route is *Þórsmörk-Landmannalaugar* 1:100,000. In addition, there's a good booklet called *The Laugavegur Hiking Trail* by Leifur Þorsteinsson and Guðjón Magnússon (Ikr1900), which describes sights and side trips. It can be purchased from Ferðafélag Íslands (www.fi.is).

In high season the hike can be completed in four days by anyone in reasonable physical condition. Many people do it independently, but Útivist, Ferðafélag Íslands and the Icelandic Mountain Guides all offer organised trips (see p342), with the option of having your bags carried for you.

The track is usually passable for casual hikers from mid-July through to mid-September. Early in the season (early to mid-July) you may need an ice axe for assistance on steeper slopes. The track positively bustles in July and August, so consider walking it in early September, when you should have crisp weather and possibly a glimpse of the northern lights from near-empty huts. At that time of year, however, some snow bridges across ravines may have collapsed, necessitating detours.

At any time of year the Landmannalaugar to Þórsmörk hike is not to be undertaken lightly. It entails river crossings and requires all-weather gear, sturdy boots, and sufficient food and water. Most hikers walk from north to south to take advantage of the net altitude loss and the facilities at Þórsmörk. You can also continue along the Þórsmörk to Skógar track (see p143) and make a six-day trip of it.

See p286 for information about mountain huts along the route.

The following gives you a run-down of the walk's highlights:

Day 1: Landmannalaugar to Hrafntinnusker (12km, four to five hours)
Stórihver This sinister round hole, in an active geothermal zone, roars with boiling water.
Hrafntinnusker Fields of black obsidian glint in the sunlight.

Day 2: Hrafntinnusker to Álftavatn (12km, four to five hours)
Háskerðingur (side trip) Across the northern spur of the Kaldaklofsfjöll ice cap, the view from this 1278m summit is indescribable.
Álftavatn As you drop into the valley there are glorious views of Tindfjallajökull, Eyjafjallajökull and Mýrdalsjökull as well as many volcanic formations.
Torfahlaup (side trip) A 5km hike to where the mighty Markarfljót river is constricted and forced through a 15m-wide canyon. Looming above is the velvety peak of Stóra Grænafell.

Day 3: Álftavatn to Emstrur (16km, six to seven hours)
Hvanngil Take a well-earned rest in this pleasant green oasis.
Markarfljótsgljúfor (side trip) About 2km southwest of the Emstrur huts, this gaping green canyon will take your breath away.
Fording ice-cold streams Well, maybe not so much a highlight; more a memorable experience.

Day 4: Emstrur to Þórsmörk (15km, six to seven hours)
Ljósá The view from a footbridge down to the 'River of Light', as it squeezes through a 2m-wide fissure, is mesmerising.
Þórsmörk After barren mountains, it's a delight to walk among the twisting birch trees of this grassy green woodland.

Gjátindur. At its northeastern end Eldgjá is 200m deep and 600m across, with odd, reddish walls that recall the fire after which it's named. Although it's not as outwardly spectacular as you may expect, Eldgjá is quite intriguing and the name alone conjures up images of a malevolently mysterious and powerful place.

In the green and fertile **Hánípufit** area, 8km south of the Eldgjá turn-off, the river Skaftá widens into an entanglement of cascades and waterfalls measuring 500m across in places. It's unusual and quite beautiful.

At Lambaskarðshólar, west of the F208 road near Syðrifærá, 5km south of the Eldgjá turn-off, there's room for 69 people in the mountain-hut accommodation at **Hólaskjól** (☎ 865 7432, 855 5812; sites per person Ikr800, sb Ikr2700), which also offers hot showers and a campsite. It's a great place to hole up for a couple of days.

SOUTHERN VATNAJÖKULL

Vatnajökull is earth's largest ice cap outside the poles. At 8300 sq km, it's three times the size of Luxembourg, reaches a thickness of almost 1km, and, if you could find a pair of scales big enough, you'd discover it weighed an awesome 3000 billion tonnes! This mighty mass of ice holds Iceland's highest and lowest points – the 2119m mountain Hvannadalshnúkur, and a nameless trough underneath the ice cap, 300m below sea level.

Huge glaciers, pleated with crevasses, flow down from the centre of Vatnajökull. The best known is probably Skaftafellsjökull, a relatively small glacier that ends within 1.5km of the campsite at Skaftafell. Another famous beauty is Breiðamerkurjökull, which crumbles into icebergs at the breathtaking Jökulsárlón lagoon.

The drive from Kirkjubæjarklaustur to Höfn is truly mind-blowing. Rte 1 takes you across vast deltas of grey glacial sand, past lost-looking farms, around the toes of craggy mountains, and by glacier tongues and ice-filled lagoons. The only thing you won't pass is a town.

In June 2008, **Vatnajökull National Park** (www .vatnajokulsthjodgardur.is) was founded, joining the ice cap and the former Skaftafell and Jökulsárgljúfur National Parks to form one 12,000 sq km megapark – 11% of the entire country. In practice, not much has changed on the ground (although four new visitor centres at Skríðuklaustur, Höfn, Mývatn and Kirkjubæjarklaustur are being built over the next few years). The park's creation is predominantly a political move to draw attention to the alarming speed at which the ice is melting.

KIRKJUBÆJARKLAUSTUR
pop 120

Many a foreign tongue has been tied in knots by trying to say Kirkjubæjarklaustur. It might help if you break it into bits: *Kirkju* (church), *bæjar* (farm) and *klaustur* (convent). Otherwise, do as the locals do and call it 'Klaustur' (pronounced more or less like 'cloister').

Klaustur is tiny, even by Icelandic standards – a few houses and farms scattered on a backdrop of brilliant green. It's a major crossroads to several dramatic spots in the interior – Fjallabak, Landmannalaugar and Laki. Klaustur is also the only real service town between Vík and Höfn: there's a petrol station and a good cafe.

History

According to the *Landnámabók*, this tranquil village situated between the cliffs and the river Skaftá was first settled by Irish monks *(papar)* before the Vikings arrived. Originally, it was known as Kirkjubær; the 'klaustur' bit was added in 1186 when a convent of Benedictine nuns was founded (near the modern-day church).

During the devastating Laki eruptions of the late 18th century, this area suffered greatly and, west of Kirkjubæjarklaustur, you can see ruins of farms abandoned or destroyed by the lava stream. The lava field, Eldhraun, averages 12m thick. It contains over 12 cu km of lava and covers an area of 565 sq km, making it the largest recorded lava flow from a single eruption.

Information

The **tourist office** (☎ 487 4620; ⊙ 9am-7pm Mon-Fri, 10am-5pm Sat, 1-5pm Sun mid-Jun–mid-Aug, 9am-5pm Mon-Fri, 10am-5pm Sat, 1-5pm Sun mid–end-Aug) was last seen skulking in the basement of the building opposite the church in 2009.

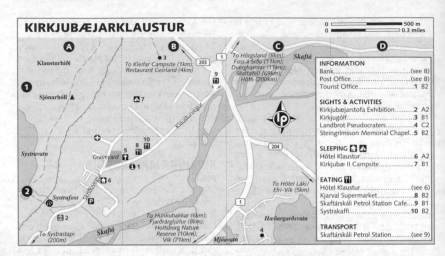

SOUTHEAST ICELAND

Sights & Activities

The regular basalt columns of **Kirkjugólf**, smoothed down and cemented with moss, were once mistaken for an old church floor rather than a work of nature, and it's easy to see why. The 80-sq-metre honeycomb lies in a field about 400m northwest of the petrol station (a path leads to it from by the information board, or drive down Rte 203, where there's another gate).

Religious connections are particularly strong in this area. The prominent rock pillar **Systrastapi** (Sisters' Pillar), near the line of cliffs west of town, marks the spot where two nuns were reputedly executed and buried for sleeping with the devil and such other no-nos.

At the western end of the village a lovely double-raced waterfall, **Systrafoss**, tumbles down the cliffs via the Bæjargil ravine. The lake **Systravatn**, a short and pleasant saunter up the cliffs above the falls, was once a bathing place for nuns.

Steingrímsson Memorial Chapel, the triangular, distinctly atypical wood-and-stone chapel on Klausturvegur, was consecrated in 1974. It commemorates Jón Steingrímsson's Eldmessa (Fire Sermon), which 'saved' the town from lava on 20 July 1783 (see the boxed text, opposite).

Ongoing archaeological digs have unearthed 14th- and 15th-century convent houses (at the northeast corner of the old churchyard). If you want to know more, visit the small **Kirkjubæjarstofa exhibition** (☎ 487 4645;

Klausturvegur 2; admission Ikr500; ⏰ 9-11am & 2-6pm Tue-Fri, 2-6pm Sat & Sun Jun-Aug).

South of the Ring Road is a vast pseudocrater field known as **Landbrot**. It was formed during the Laki eruptions of 1783, when lava poured over marshland and fast-evaporating steam exploded through to make these barrowlike mounds.

Tours

Based at Hörgsland (see opposite), the **Jeppaferðir Ehf** (☎ 487 6655; www.horgsland.is; Hörgsland 1) company does tailor-made 4WD tours to surrounding areas, including Lakagígar. Contact it for prices.

Sleeping & Eating

Kirkjubæ II campsite (☎ /fax 487 4612; sites per person Ikr750; ⏰ Jun-Aug) This neat green site with sheltering hedges is right in town. It has pretty good facilities, including a kitchen, hot showers (Ikr200 per five minutes) and a laundry (Ikr800 minimum).

Kleifar campsite (☎ 487 4675; sites per person Ikr750; ⏰ Jun-Aug) There's a second, more simple campsite 1.5km along Rte 203 (signposted towards Geirland).

Hótel Klaustur (☎ 487 4900; www.icehotels.is; Klausturvegur 6; s/d Ikr18,300/21,800) One of the Icelandair chain, the 57-room Klaustur looks like a Soviet-bloc hotel but contains a three-star interior with businesslike rooms and a spa/sauna. The restaurant has an à la carte menu with typical Icelandic mains and some unusual starters – snails, anyone? Breakfast costs Ikr1400.

Systrakaffi (☎ 487 4848; Klausturvegur 13; light meals Ikr900-1800, mains Ikr1800-3600; ☺ noon-10pm daily mid-May–Aug, 6-10pm daily Sep) The most atmospheric place for a meal is this characterful little cafe bar. It has a varied menu, which offers everything from sandwiches and burgers to big tilting bowls of salad, local trout and smoked-lamb mains using produce from nearby farms.

For freshly made fast-food snacks, there's the **Skaftárskáli petrol station cafe** (☎ 487 4628). Self-caterers have the **Kjarval supermarket** (☎ 487 4616; Klausturvegur; ☺ 9am-8pm Jun-Aug, shorter hours Sep-May).

Getting There & Away

The Reykjavík–Höfn bus service runs daily from June to mid-September, and on Tuesday, Friday and Sunday the rest of the year.

Summer buses depart at 8.30am from Reykjavík and at 11am from Höfn (winter buses set off from Reykjavík/Höfn later in the day), and stop at Hótel Klaustur or the petrol station in Kirkjubæjarklaustur. Eastbound from Reykjavík, the bus passes Kirkjubæjarklaustur at 2.30pm (Ikr6600), continuing to Skaftafell and Jökulsárlón. Westbound from Höfn, it passes Kirkjubæjarklaustur at 1.45pm (Ikr5200), continuing on to Reykjavík.

The Fjallabak bus between Reykjavík and Skaftafell passes at around 6.15pm eastbound and at 9.30am westbound daily from mid-June to 31 August. The entire route costs Ikr9000.

AROUND KIRKJUBÆJARKLAUSTUR
Sights
FJARÐRÁRGLJÚFUR

This peculiar and darkly picturesque canyon, carved out by the river Fjarðrá, is a humbling two million years old. A walking track follows its southern edge for a couple of kilometres, and there are plenty of places to gaze down into its rocky, writhing depths. The canyon is 3.5km north of the Ring Road; you can walk there across lava fields or drive along the Laki road (Rte 206; you'll reach the canyon before it becomes an F road).

Around the nearby Holt farm is the small **Holtsborg Nature Reserve**. This is the only place in Iceland where wild roses grow naturally.

FOSS Á SIÐU & DVERGHAMRAR

Foss á Siðu, 11km east of Kirkjubæjarklaustur, is an attractive **waterfall** that normally tumbles down from the cliffs. During especially strong sea winds, however, it actually goes straight up! Opposite the falls is the outcrop Dverghamrar, which contains some classic **basalt columns**.

Sleeping & Eating

There's quite a bit of farmhouse accommodation in the area immediately around Kirkjubæjarklaustur.

Hörgsland (☎ 487 6655; www.horgsland.is; sb/linen/cottages from Ikr3000/4000/9000) This place, a readers' favourite on the Ring Road about 8km northeast of Kirkjubæjarklaustur, is like a minivillage of very spacious and comfortable self-contained cottages. The two-bedroom timber cabins sleep at least six and each have a kitchen, lounge and verandah. There are a couple of outdoor hot pots here, as well as a shop, a cafe and a petrol station, and you can arrange fishing permits and 4WD tours.

Hótel Láki/Efri-Vík (☎ 487 4694; www.efrivik.is; s/d cottage Ikr10,000/13,000, hotel Ikr14,000/18,500) This farm, 5km south of Kirkjubæjarklaustur on Rte 204, is a good choice. As well as beds in comfortable cottages, it has just opened a new hotel wing with large, stylish double rooms; a further extension is under construction. There's also a nine-hole golf course, boat rental, a sauna, hot tub and lake fishing, and in 2009 the owners were building a spa.

Hunkubakkar (☎ 487 4681; hunku@simnet.is; s/d Ikr12,000/16,000) This farmhouse, 7km west of

---

HELLFIRE & BRIMSTONE

The 18th-century eruptions of the volcano Laki brought death and devastation to much of southeastern Iceland, especially Kirkjubæjarklaustur. On 20 July 1783, a particularly fast-moving river of molten lava threatened to engulf the town.

The pastor Jón Steingrímsson, convinced it was due to the wickedness of his flock, gathered the terrified parishioners in the church. There he delivered a passionate hellfire-and-brimstone sermon while the appropriate special effects steamed and smoked outside. By the time the oratory ended, the flow had stopped at a rock promontory – now called Eldmessutangi (Fire Sermon Point) – just short of the town. The grateful residents credited their good reverend with some particularly effective string-pulling on their behalf.

Klaustur along Rtes 1 and 206, has simple parquet-floored rooms in the main building and cottages to rent in the grounds. Other facilities include a restaurant and horse hire. You'll have to book in advance for stays between October and May.

Restaurant Geirland (☎ 487 4677; geirland@centrum. is; Geirland; mains Ikr1900-3200; ⏰ 7-11pm Jun-Aug) This new restaurant is part of the farmhouse accommodation at Geirland, about 4km from Kirkjubæjarklaustur along Rte 203. Mains make use of fresh local produce – sea trout, lamb steak – plus there's always a vegie course. Their ham(lamb)burger was recently voted the region's best burger!

LAKAGÍGAR

It's almost impossible to comprehend the immensity of the Laki eruptions, one of the most catastrophic volcanic events in human history.

In the spring of 1783, a vast set of fissures opened, forming around 135 craters that took it in turns to fountain molten rock up to 1km into the air. These Skaftáreldar (River Skaftá Fires) lasted for eight months, spewing out more than 30 billion tonnes of lava, which covered an area of 500 sq km in a layer up to 19km thick. Fifty farms in the region were wiped out.

Far more devastating were the hundreds of millions of tonnes of ash and sulphuric acid that poured from the fissures. The sun was blotted out, the grass died off, and around two-thirds of Iceland's livestock died from starvation and poisoning. Some 9000 people – a fifth of the country – were killed and the remainder faced the Móðuharðindi (Haze Famine) that followed.

The damage wasn't limited to Iceland, either. All across the northern hemisphere clouds of ash blocked out the sun. Temperatures dropped and acid rain fell from the sky, causing devastating crop failures in Japan, Alaska and Europe (possibly even helping to spark the French Revolution).

The whole Lakagígar area is contained within the boundaries of Vatnajökull National Park. Wardens will occasionally pop out of the wilderness with brochure-maps of the area for sale. You should stick to the paths in this ecologically sensitive region.

Camping is forbidden within the Laki reserve. The nearest campsite, with a toilet and fresh water, is at Blágil, about 11km from Laki. There were also plans, on hold due to the economic troubles, to build an information centre and cabins at Galti.

GETTING THERE & AWAY

If you want to drive, Rte F206 (just west of Kirkjubæjarklaustur) is generally passable from July to early September. It's a long 50km to the Lakagígar crater row. The road is unsuitable for 2WD cars, as there are several rivers to ford. Even low-clearance 4WD vehicles may not be suitable in the spring thaw or after rain, when the rivers tend to run deep.

From July to August you can get to the Lakagígar area on the worthwhile **Reykjavík Excursions bus** (☎ 580 5400; www.re.is). The 10-hour tour (with a jumpy CD guide) allows around 3½ hours' walking in the crater area. It departs daily, at 8.30am from Skaftafell (Ikr10,500) and at 9.30am from the petrol station at Kirkjubæjarklaustur (Ikr7600). Bring a packed lunch.

Laki

Although Laki (818m) is extinct, it has loaned its name to the still-volatile, 25km-long Lakagígar crater row, which stretches northeastward and southwestward from its base. Laki can be climbed in about 40 minutes from the parking area, and we highly recommend it. From the top there are boundless 360-degree views of the active fissure, vast lava fields and glinting ice-white glaciers in the distance.

Lakagígar Crater Row

The Lakagígar crater row is fascinating to explore. The entire area is riddled with black sand dunes and lava tubes, many of which contain tiny stalactites. Down at the foot of Laki, marked walking paths lead you in and out of the two nearest craters, including an interesting lava tunnel – bring a torch. Another cave, two hours' walk south of the Laki parking area, shelters a mysterious lake.

Nowadays the lava field belies the apocalypse that spawned it more than 220 years ago. Its black, twisted lava formations are overgrown with soft green moss.

Fagrifoss

Fagrifoss (Beautiful Falls) is certainly not a misnomer: this **waterfall** must be one of

HOW TO AVOID BEING SKUA-ED

The great sandar regions on Iceland's southern coast are the world's largest breeding ground for great skuas (*Stercorarius skua* in Latin, *skúmur* in Icelandic). These large, meaty, dirty-brown birds with white-patched wings tend to build their nests among grassy tufts in the ashy sand. You'll often see them harassing gulls into disgorging their dinner, killing and eating puffins and other little birds, or swooping down on YOU if you get too close to their nests.

Thankfully (unlike feather-brained arctic terns), skuas will stop plaguing you if you run away from the area they're trying to defend. You can also avoid aerial strikes by wearing a hat or carrying a stick above your head. Occasionally ravens or groups of smaller birds will get together to mob a skua and drive it off: these aerial battles are interesting to watch.

Iceland's most bewitching, with rivulets of water pouring over a massive black rock. You'll come to the turnoff on the way to Laki, about 22km along the F206.

THE SANDAR

Another area of devastation are the sandar, soul-destroyingly flat and empty regions sprawling along Iceland's southeastern coast. High in the mountains, glaciers scrape up silt, sand and gravel that is then carried by glacial rivers or (more dramatically) by glacial bursts down to the coast and dumped in huge desertlike plains. The sandar here are so impressively huge and awful that the Icelandic word is used internationally to describe this topographic phenomenon.

Skeiðarársandur is the most visible and dramatic, stretching some 40km between ice cap and coast from Núpsstaður to Öræfi. Here you'll encounter a flat expanse of grey-black sands, fierce scouring winds (a cyclist's nightmare) and fast-flowing grey-brown glacial rivers.

In July and August, the **Icelandic Mountain Guides** (☎ 587 9999; www.mountainguide.is) run a guided four-day (60km) hike through Núpsstaðarskógar, over to Grænalón lagoon, across the glacier Skeiðarárjökull and then into Morsárdalur in Skaftafell. The trip costs Ikr79,000 with food, camping gear, glacier equipment and transport from Skaftafell included. There's a supplement to pay if the walking group has fewer than five people.

Iceland's third-largest hostel, **Hvoll HI Hostel** (☎ 487 4785; hvoll@hostel.is; dm Ikr2100, s/d Ikr4000/5800; ⌚ Feb-Oct), is on the edge of Skeiðarársandur (3km south off the Ring Road via a gravel road) and feels very remote despite its size. It's very much like the Reykjavík hostel in its clean new design and busy atmosphere; facilities include several kitchens, a TV room,

a laundry, bookshelves full of Mickey Spillane, and a payphone. It makes an excellent base for exploring Skaftafell, Núpsstaðarskógar and the surrounding sandar.

Meðallandssandur

This region spreads across the Meðalland district south of Eldhraun and east of the river Kúðafljót. The sandy desert is so flat and featureless that a number of ships have run aground on its coast, apparently unaware they were nearing land. Shipwrecked sailors have died in quicksand while trying to get ashore. There are now several small lighthouses along the coast.

Skeiðarársandur

Skeiðarársandur, the largest sandar in the world, covers a 1000-sq-km area and was formed by the mighty Skeiðarárjökull. Since the Settlement Era, Skeiðarársandur has swallowed a considerable amount of farmland and it continues to grow. The area was relatively well populated (for Iceland, anyway), but in 1362 the volcano Öræfi beneath Öræfajökull erupted and the subsequent *jökulhlaup* laid waste the entire district.

The section of Rte 1 that passes across Skeiðarársandur was the last bit of the national highway to be constructed – as recently as 1974 (until then, Höfnites had to drive to Reykjavík via Akureyri). Long gravel dykes have been strategically positioned to channel flood waters away from this highly susceptible artery. They did little good, however, when in late 1996 three Ring Road bridges were washed away like matchsticks by the massive *jökulhlaup* released by the Grímsvötn (or Gjálp) eruption (see the boxed text, p295). There's a memorial of twisted bridge girders and an information board along the Ring Road just west of Skaftafell National Park.

SOUTHEAST ICELAND

The sands are a major breeding area for great skuas (see the boxed text, p293) – particularly appropriate birds for such a harsh region.

Núpsstaður & Núpsstaðarskógar

Bizarrely eroded cliffs and pinnacles tower over the old **turf-roofed farm** and church at Núpsstaður. The farm buildings date back as far as the early 19th century, and the church, which is dedicated to St Nicholas, was mentioned as early as 1200. It was renovated in 1957 by Einar Jónsson and is one of the last turf churches in Iceland.

Inland is Núpsstaðarskógar, a beautiful **woodland area** on the slopes of the mountain Eystrafjall. Since it's no longer possible to cross the Núpsá river by raft, this area is best explored on a tour run by the Icelandic Mountain Guides (see p293).

Grænalón

From the southern end of Núpsstaðarskógar a good two-day hike will take you over the ridges and valleys west of immense Skeiðarárjökull to Grænalón. This ice-dammed **lake** has the ability to drain like a bathtub. The 'plug' is the western edge of Skeiðarárjökull; when the water pressure builds to breaking point, the glacier is lifted and the lake lets go. It has been known to release up to 2.7 million cu metres of water at 5000 cu metres per second in a single burst.

To get there you'll have to join the Icelandic Mountain Guides' Núpsstaðarskógar tour (see p293), as it's impossible to cross the Núpsá and Súlaá rivers on foot (the IMG have special equipment, including a big 4WD). The topo sheet to use is *Lómagnúpur* 1:100,000 (1986).

SKAFTAFELL (VATNAJÖKULL NATIONAL PARK – SOUTH)

Skaftafell, now part of Vatnajökull National Park (Europe's largest at 12,000 sq km), encompasses a breathtaking collection of peaks and glaciers. It's the country's favourite wilderness: 160,000 visitors per year come to marvel at thundering waterfalls, twisted birch woods, the tangled web of rivers threading across the sandar, and brilliant blue-white Vatnajökull with its lurching tongues of ice.

Skaftafell deserves its reputation, and few Icelanders – even those who usually shun the great outdoors – can resist it. On long summer weekends all of Reykjavík (includ-ing the city's raucous all-night parties) may seem to descend on it. However, if you're prepared to get out on the more remote trails and take advantage of the fabulous hiking on the heath and beyond, you'll leave the crowds far behind.

There's very little accommodation close to the park, so you'll need either a tent or

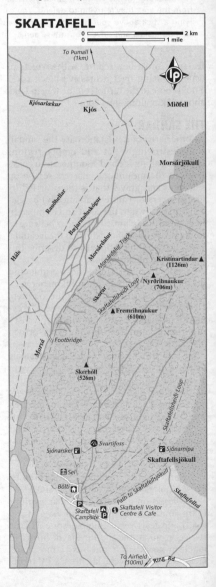

JÖKULHLAUP!

In late 1996 the devastating Grímsvötn eruption – Iceland's fourth-largest of the 20th century, after Katla in 1918, Hekla in 1947 and Surtsey in 1963 – shook southeast Iceland and caused an awesome *jökulhlaup* (glacial flood) across Skeiðarársandur. The events leading up to it are a sobering reminder of the power of Iceland's volatile fire-and-ice combination.

On the morning of 29 September 1996, a magnitude 5.0 earthquake shook the Vatnajökull ice cap. Magma from a new volcano, in the Grímsvötn region beneath Vatnajökull, had made its way through the earth's crust and into the ice, causing the eruption of a 4km-long subsurface fissure known as Gjálp. The following day the eruption burst through the surface, ejecting a column of steam that rose 10km into the sky.

Scientists became concerned as the subglacial lake in the Grímsvötn caldera began to fill with water from ice melted by the eruption. Initial predictions on 3 October were that the Ice would lift and the lake would spill out across Skeiðarársandur, threatening the Ring Road and its bridges. In the hope of diverting floodwaters away from the bridges, massive dyke-building projects were organised on Skeiðarársandur.

On 5 November, over a month after the eruption started, the ice *did* lift and the Grímsvötn reservoir drained in a massive *jökulhlaup*, releasing up to 3000 billion litres of water within a few hours. The floodwaters – dragging along icebergs the size of three-storey buildings – destroyed the 375m-long Gígjukvísl Bridge and the 900m-long Skeiðará Bridge, both on the Skeiðarársandur. See video footage of the eruption and enormous multitonne blocks of ice being hurled across Skeiðarársandur at the Skaftafell visitor centre.

Some other of Grímsvötn's creations include the Ásbyrgi canyon (see p246), gouged out by a cataclysmic flood over just a few days. In 1934 an eruption released a *jökulhlaup* of 40,000 cu metres per second, which swelled the river Skeiðará to 9km in width and laid waste large areas of farmland.

Grímsvötn erupted again in December 1998, and most recently in November 2004, when a five-day eruption threw steam and ash 12km into the atmosphere, disrupting air traffic. There was no *jökulhlaup* on either occasion.

a firm hotel booking if you want to explore the park properly.

History

The historical Skaftafell was a large farm at the foot of the hills west of the present campsite. Shifting glacial sands slowly buried the fields and forced the farm to be moved to a more suitable site, on the heath 100m above the sandar. The district came to be known as Hérað Milli Sandur (Land Between the Sands), but after all the farms were annihilated by the 1362 eruptions, the district became the 'land under the sands' and was renamed Öræfi (Wasteland). Once the vegetation returned, however, the Skaftafell farm was rebuilt in its former location.

Skaftafell National Park was founded in 1967 by the Icelandic government and the WWF. In June 2008, it was merged with the Jökulsárgljúfur (p245) National Park to form the massive wilderness area of Vatnajökull National Park.

Information

The newly renovated, helpful **visitor centre** (☎ 478 1627; www.vatnajokulsthjodgardur.is; ✆ 8am-9pm mid-Jun–mid-Aug, 9am-7pm early Jun & late Aug, 10am-4pm Apr, May & Sep; ▣) has an information desk with free brochures and maps for sale, good informative displays on the Öræfi area, a fascinating film about the 1996 Grímsvötn *jökulhlaup* (shown in peak season only), exhibitions, a cafe and internet access (per 20/40/60 minutes Ikr400/700/1000). The staff here really know their stuff.

The Icelandic Mountain Guides and the Glacier Guides both have summer-opening huts (open from around 8.30am to 8pm, April to August) in the car park at Skaftafell visitor centre, where you can talk to knowledgeable experts and get kitted out for glacier walks – see Tours (p297) for details.

All flora, fauna and natural features of the park are protected, open fires are prohibited and rubbish must be carried out. In the busy area around Skaftafellsheiði, stick to the tracks to avoiding damaging delicate plant life.

Don't get too close to glaciers or climb on them without the proper equipment and training – the average ice-block calving off Skaftafellsjökull would crush anyone within a few metres of the face.

Although it's not the best map in the world, the thematic map of Skaftafell published by **Ferðakort** (☎ 562 3376; www.ferdakort .is) shows the nonglacial area of the park at 1:25,000 and the Öræfi district at 1:100,000 (2002). It's available at the visitor centre (Ikr1230) and in bookshops and tourist offices elsewhere in Iceland.

Sights

The traditional turf-roofed farmhouse **Sel** (admission free), built in Burstir style in 1912, is worth a glance. There's not much inside, but it's always open and the hill just above offers a good photo opportunity of the farmhouse and the grey sandar stretching out to the coast.

Activities

Skaftafell is ideal for day hikes and also offers longer hikes through its wilderness regions. Most of Skaftafell's visitors keep to the popular routes on Skaftafellsheiði. Hiking in other accessible areas, such as upper Morsárdalur and Kjós, requires more time, motivation and effort.

Wild camping is not allowed in the park. Compulsory camping permits (Ikr850) for Kjós are available from the information centre. Also inquire about river crossings along your intended route.

SVARTIFOSS

Star of a hundred postcards, Svartifoss is a gloomy **waterfall** flanked by black basalt columns. It's reached by an easy track leading up from the campsite (about 1½ hours return). However, due to immense pressure in this area of the park, rangers are encouraging visitors to explore elsewhere. If you do go to Svartifoss, it's worth continuing west up the short track to **Sjónarsker**, where there's a view disc and an unforgettable view across Skeiðarársandur.

SKAFTAFELLSJÖKULL

Another popular and less sensitive trail is the easy one-hour return walk to Skaftafellsjökull. The (wheelchair-accessible) sealed track begins at the visitor centre and leads to the **glacier**

face, where you can witness the bumps and groans of the ice – although the glacier is pretty grey and gritty here. The glacier has been receding in recent years and over the past 50 years has lost nearly 1km of its length.

SKAFTAFELLSHEIÐI LOOP

On a fine day, the five- to six-hour walk around Skaftafellsheiði is a hiker's dream. It begins by climbing from the campsite past Svartifoss and Sjónarsker, continuing across the moor to 610m-high **Fremrihnaukur**. From there it follows the edge of the plateau to the next rise, **Nyðrihnaukur** (706m), which affords a superb view of Morsárdalur, Morsárjökull and the iceberg-choked lagoon at its base. At this point the track turns southeast to an outlook point on the cliff above Skaftafellsjökull (Gláma).

For the best view of Skaftafellsjökull, Morsárdalur and the Skeiðarársandur, it's worth scaling the summit of **Kristínartindar** (1126m). The easiest way follows a wellmarked route up the prominent valley southeast of the Nyðrihnaukur lookout.

MORSÁRDALUR & BÆJARSTAÐARSKÓGUR

The seven-hour hike from the campsite to the glacial lake in Morsárdalur is fairly ordinary but enjoyable. There's a footbridge across the lake outlet, and from there you can continue to **Kjós**. Alternatively, cross the Morsá on the footbridge near the point where the Kambgil ravine comes down from Skaftafellsheiði and make your way across the gravel riverbed to the birch woods at **Bæjarstaðarskógur**. The trees here reach a whopping (for Iceland) 12m, and 80°C springs flow into the tiny but heavenly Heitulækir to the west in Vestragil. The return walk to Bæjarstaðarskógur takes about six hours; add on an extra hour to visit Heitulækir.

OTHER HIKES

Other possibilities include the long day trip beyond Bæjarstaðarskógur into the rugged Skaftafellsfjöll. A recommended destination is the 965m-high summit of the **Jökulfell ridge**, which affords a commanding view of the vast expanses of Skeiðarárjökull. Even better is a three-day excursion into the Kjós region. When you reach Kjós, a very difficult hike leads to the base of Þumall (Thumb), then west along the glacier edge, around the valley rim and south down to your starting point.

Tours

The **Icelandic Mountain Guides** (☎ Reykjavík office 587 9999, Skaftafell 894 2959, 478 2559; www.mountainguide.is) is the country's mountain-rescue squad, so you can feel pretty safe on the excellent organised hikes. It has staffed information desks at the Skaftafell visitor centre between April and mid-September, where you can book a place on a hike in person.

The mountain guides lead a range of walks, including glacier walks on Sólheimajökull (p146) and Svínafellsjökull (p298); guided hikes up Iceland's highest peak (p298); and longer backpack hikes including the challenging four-day route from Núpsstaðarskógar to Skaftafell (p294), and an epic nine-day hike from Laki to Skaftafell (Ikr145,000). See the website for more suggestions.

Also based at Skaftafell in the summer, relative newcomers the **Glacier Guides** (☎ 659 7000; www.glacierguides.is; ☻ Jun-Aug) offer slightly cheaper glacier walks on two nearby glaciers. Their easiest walk is a 1½ hour stroll up Virkisjökull (per person Ikr4990, minimum age 8 years), a 15-minute drive away, with trips departing from Skaftafell at 9.15am, 11am, 1pm and 3.15pm daily. A tougher four-hour walk up Fjallsjökull (per person Ikr9990, minimum age 15 years) includes a stop at Jökulsárlón (p299) on the way back to Skaftafell.

There are **sightseeing flights** (☎ 478 2406, 899 2532; www.atf.is) from the tiny airfield just outside the national park over Vatnajökull, Grímsvötn, the Lakagígar crater row or the glaciers. Prices start at €130 for 30 minutes.

Sleeping & Eating

Visitor centre campsite (☎ 478 1627; sites per person Ikr850) Since Skaftafell is a national park, most people bring a tent to this large, gravelly campsite (with laundry facilities). It gets very busy and loud in summer. The only other place you're allowed to camp is at the Kjós campsite (per person Ikr850) – buy a permit from the visitor centre before you set off.

Bölti (☎ 478 1626; fax 478 2426; Skaftafellsheiði; sb in 6-person hut Ikr3000, sb d 7800; ☻ Mar-Oct) This farm, on the hill above the western end of the Skaftafell campsite, is in a superb location with dizzying views out over the sandur. There's sleeping-bag accommodation on bunk beds in six-person huts; tiny kitchen areas include a kettle and two electric rings. Book ahead in summer.

Food in the park is limited to the new (and very busy!) cafe inside the visitor centre, which sells coffee, soup, sandwiches and a tiny selection of groceries.

The nearest hotel, Hótel Skaftafell, is at Freysnes (see p298), 5km east of the national park entrance, and there's farmhouse accommodation (sleeping-bag space and cabins) at the Hof and Litla-Hof farms, 23km away.

Getting There & Away

The Reykjavík–Höfn bus service runs daily from June to mid-September, and on Tuesday, Friday and Sunday the rest of the year.

Summer buses depart at 8.30am from Reykjavík and at 11am from Höfn (winter buses set off from Reykjavík/Höfn later in the day), stopping at the Skaftafell visitor centre at 3.45pm eastbound (Ikr8200) and at 1pm westbound (Ikr3600).

From mid-June to August there's another bus from Reykjavík to Skaftafell via the scenic Fjallabak inland route through Landmannalaugar and Eldgjá, departing daily from Reykjavík at 8.30am and arriving at Skaftafell at 7.30pm (Ikr9000). Westbound it departs from Skaftafell at 8.30am.

SKAFTAFELL TO HÖFN

Glittering glaciers and brooding mountains line the 130km stretch between Skaftafell and Höfn. In clear weather the unfolding landscape makes it difficult to keep your eyes on the road. The premier tourist stop is the iceberg-filled lagoon Jökulsárlón. Other attractions include exhilarating glacier walks, 4WD and snowmobile tours on the Vatnajökull ice cap, puffin-spotting at Ingólfshöfði and horse riding.

Freysnes, Svínafell & Svínafellsjökull

The farm **Svínafell**, 8km southeast of Skaftafell, was the home of Flosi Þórðarson, the character who burned Njál and his family to death in *Njál's Saga*. It was also the site where Flosi and Njál's family were finally reconciled, thus ending one of the bloodiest feuds in Icelandic history (see p141). There's not much to this tiny settlement now, but you can go swimming at **Flosalaug** (☎ 478 1765; adult/child 7-14yr Ikr500/250; ☻ 1-10pm Jun-Aug), a complex with a shallow round pool, hot pots, showers and a campsite.

In the 17th century, the glacier **Svínafellsjökull** nearly engulfed the farm, but it has since retreated. On the northern side of the glacier (towards Skaftafell), a dirt road leads 2km to a car park, from where it's a short walk to the snout.

ACTIVITIES

From mid-May to mid-September you can enjoy daily walks up Svínafellsjökull with the **Icelandic Mountain Guides** (☎ Reykjavík office 587 9999, Skaftafell 894 2959; www.mountainguide.is). It's utterly liberating to strap on crampons and suddenly be able to stride up a glacier, and there's so much to see on the ice. Waterfalls, ice caves, glacial mice and different-coloured ash from ancient explosions are just some of the glacier's slightly hallucinatory joys. There's a 2½-hour walk (adult/child 10 to 15 years Ikr5500/3900, minimum age 10 years) for beginners, but we'd recommend the longer four-hour 'Glacier Adventure' (Ikr8200 per person, minimum age 16 years), or even a full-day walk. Ice-climbing is also available. The only equipment you need to bring is warm clothes and hiking boots.

In the winter, local company **Öræfaferðir** (☎ 894 0894; www.oraefaferdir.is), based at the farm Hofsnes, offers similar tours for similar prices.

SLEEPING & EATING

Flosi (☎ 478 1765; www.svinafell.com; sites per person Ikr850, sb Ikr3000) At the Svínafell swimming pool, this place has a campsite and six basic cabins, each with four bunks, and a simple amenities block. If you have your own vehicle, it's an alternative to the campsite at Skaftafell.

Hótel Skaftafell (☎ 478 1945; www.hotelskaftafell. is; Freysnes; s/d €170/190, d with glacier view €210; ☷ Mar-Oct) Recently acquired by the Fosshotel chain, this is the closest hotel to the Skaftafell visitor centre, 5km east at Freysnes. Its 63 rooms (all with bathroom and TV) are functional rather than luxurious, but staff are helpful, and even the rooms in the prefabricated buildings at the back have great glacial views. There's a good restaurant (mains Ikr2500 to Ikr3500) serving 'Sean Connery salad', fresh char, puffin, lamb and lobster, and a recommended rhubarb and cardamom mousse. A pleasant walking trail leads to Svínafellsjökull from behind the building.

The petrol station opposite Hótel Skaftafell has a shop selling hot dogs, and a summer canteen serving traditional Icelandic food such as *plokkfiskur* (fish stew).

Öræfajökull & Hvannadalshnúkur

Iceland's highest **mountain**, Hvannadalshnúkur (2119m), pokes out from the ice cap Öræfajökull, an offshoot of Vatnajökull. This lofty peak is actually the northwestern edge of an immense 5km-wide crater – the biggest active volcano in Europe after Mt Etna. It erupted in 1362, firing out the largest amount of tephra in Iceland's recorded history: nearby glaciers are liberally spattered with bits of compressed yellow ash from the explosion. The region was utterly devastated – hence its name, Öræfi (Wasteland).

The best access for climbing Hvannadalshnúkur is from Sandfellsheiði, above the abandoned farm Sandfell, about 12km southeast of Skaftafell. Climbers should be well versed in glacier travel, and, although most guided expeditions manage the trip in a very long and taxing day (see below), independent climbers should carry enough supplies and gear for several days. The best time for climbing the mountain is April or May, before the ice bridges melt.

TOURS

The **Icelandic Mountain Guides** (☎ Reykjavík office 587 9999, Skaftafell 894 2959; www.mountainguide .is) run guided 10- to 15-hour ascents of Hvannadalshnúkur. The trip costs Ikr19,900 per person (minimum of two people), including transport and use of equipment. If you're looking for a challenge, this is one of the best deals in Iceland. Trips run on request between April and mid-September. Book in advance, and allow yourself extra days in case the weather causes a cancellation.

There's a briefing the evening before, and the trip begins at 5am the next day. Transport is provided up to the snow line, where you transfer to snowshoes for the ascent to the 1820m-high crater rim. After walking across the crater, you make the final summit ascent of almost 300m with crampons and an ice axe. You need to bring warm clothing and your own food and water.

Note that each year the ice bridges that make the hike possible are melting earlier and faster, so the season for climbing the mountain is becoming shorter and shorter. Although trips are theoretically possible until mid-September, in 2009 there were prohibitive restrictions on the trips by late July: prices rose to Ikr39,800 per person (as one guide per four people was deemed necessary), and only experienced mountaineers were allowed on the trips.

Glacier Guides (☎ 659 7000; www.glacierguides.is; Jun-Aug) offer the same trip for the same price. Local company **Öræfaferðir** (☎ 894 0894; www.oraefaferdir.is) also leads climbs up the mountain (generally in early spring, as they focus on birdwatching trips in late spring and summer). The owner holds the world record for ascents of Hvannadalshnúkur.

Hof & Bær

At Hof farm is a picturesque wood-and-peat **church**, built on the foundations of a previous 14th-century building, and a **Viking temple** dedicated to Þór. It was reconstructed in 1883 and now sits pleasantly in a thicket of birch and ash with flowers growing on the grassy roof.

About 6km further east, **Bær** is a farm that was buried by ash in the 1362 Öræfi eruption. The walls are surprisingly intact, but visitors are asked not to trample all over them since the ruins are both protected and part of an ongoing archaeological excavation.

At the Hof farm, and beautifully situated beneath the Öræfajökull glacier, the **Frost & Fire Guesthouse** (☎ 478 2260; www.frostogfuni.is; s/d Ikr10,500/13,500, d with bathroom Ikr14,800; late May-early Sep) offers two different types of rooms (neither with the panache of its sister establishment in Hveragerði, p133). The majority are in cottages with shared bathrooms; the better option are those in the main farmhouse, which are en suite and roomy. Prices include breakfast, and there's a new sauna and hot pot. This is a good base for glacier tours to Öræfajökull. Nearby is another farm, **Lítla-Hof** (☎ 478 1670), with similarly priced rooms.

Ingólfshöfði

The 76m-high Ingólfshöfði promontory rises from the flatlands like a strange dream. In spring and summer, this beautiful, isolated **nature reserve** is overrun with nesting puffins, skuas and other sea birds, and you'll often see seals and whales offshore. It's also of great historical importance – it was here that Ingólfur Arnarson, Iceland's first settler, stayed the winter on his original foray to the country in AD 871. The reserve is open to visitors, but the 9km drive across the shallow tidal lagoon isn't something you should attempt, even in a 4WD.

Luckily, you can get here by hay wagon. The local farm gets out its trusty tractor between May and August and runs **tours** (adult/child 6-16yr Ikr3500/1000; noon Mon-Sat May-Aug) to the reserve. The half-hour ride across the sands is followed by an interesting two-hour guided walk round the headland, with an emphasis on birdwatching. You can book through **Öræfaferðir** (☎ 894 0894; www.oraefaferdir.is), or simply turn up outside the farm at Hofsnes (signposted, just off the Ring Road) 10 minutes before the tour is due to start.

Breiðamerkursandur

The easternmost of the large sandar, Breiðamerkursandur is one of the main breeding grounds for Iceland's great skuas (see the boxed text, p293). Thanks to rising numbers of these ground-nesting birds, there's also a growing population of arctic foxes. Historically, Breiðamerkursandur also figures in *Njál's Saga*, which ends with Kári Sölmundarson arriving in this idyllic spot to 'live happily ever after' – which has to be some kind of miracle in a saga.

The sandar is backed by a sweeping panorama of glacier-capped mountains, some of which are fronted by deep lagoons. **Kvíárjökull glacier** snakes down to the Kvíár river and is easily accessible from the Ring Road. Leave your car in the small car park just off Rte 1 (you can't drive any further) and follow the walking path into the valley. It's quite an uncanny place: boulders line the huge western moraine like sentinels, the mossy grass is full of fairy rings, and a powerful glacial wind frequently surges down from the ice above.

The 742m-high **Breiðamerkurfjall** was once a nunatak enclosed by Breiðamerkurjökull and Fjallsjökull, but the glaciers have since retreated and freed it.

At the foot of the peak is the glacial lagoon **Breiðárlón**, where icebergs calve from Fjallsjökull before sailing out to sea. Although it's not as dramatic as Jökulsárlón, in some ways it's more satisfying, thanks to the lack of people. It's set back from the Ring Road and not immediately obvious, plus the (very rough) dirt road is extremely off-putting. It's possible to get here in a car (but don't blame us if you get stuck), or else it's a 25-minute walk from Rte 1.

Jökulsárlón

A host of spectacular, luminous-blue icebergs drift through Jökulsárlón **lagoon**, right beside the Ring Road between Höfn and Skaftafell.

SOUTHEAST ICELAND

Even when you're expecting this surreal scene, it's still a mighty surprise – just count how many shocked drivers slam on the brakes and skid across the road, and make sure you don't do the same thing yourself. It's worth spending a couple of hours here, admiring the wondrous ice sculptures, looking for seals or taking a trip in an amphibious boat.

The icebergs calve from Breiðamerkurjökull, an offshoot of Vatnajökull, crashing down into the water and drifting inexorably towards the sea. They can spend up to five years floating in the 17-sq-km, 600m-deep lagoon, melting, refreezing and occasionally toppling over with a mighty splash, startling the birds.

Although it looks as though it's been here since the last ice age, the lagoon is only about 75 years old. Until 1932 Breiðamerkurjökull reached the Ring Road; it's now retreating rapidly, and the lagoon is consequently growing at a rate of knots.

Jökulsárlón is a natural film set. It starred briefly in *Lara Croft: Tomb Raider* (2001), pretending to be Siberia – the amphibious tourist-carrying boats were even painted grey and used as Russian ships. You might also have seen it in the James Bond film *Die Another Day* (2002), for which the lagoon was specially frozen and six Aston Martins were destroyed on the ice!

ACTIVITIES
Between mid-May and mid-September you can take a 35-minute trip on the lagoon in brilliant **amphibious boats** (☎ 478 2222; info@jokul sarlon.is; per person Ikr2600), which trundle along the shore like buses before driving into the water. Guides hop on board to tell you interesting factoids about the lagoon, and you get to taste 1000-year-old ice. Trips set off around every half-hour between 10am and 5pm daily.

If you're short of time or money, you can get just as close to those cool-blue masterpieces by walking along the shore, and you can taste ancient ice by hauling it out of the water.

SLEEPING & EATING
The **Jökulsárlón cafe** (☎ 478 2122; 9am-7pm Jun–mid-Aug, 10am-5pm late May & early Sep) beside the lagoon is a good pit stop for information and some of southeast Iceland's best seafood soup.

If you have a campervan with toilet, it's OK to stay in the car park. Otherwise camping by the lagoon isn't really condoned (par-

ticularly not on the eastern side, where there are lots of nesting birds).

Suðursveit & Mýrar
Between Jökulsárlón and Höfn the Ring Road passes several small farms, backed by mountains and yet more glaciers.

SIGHTS & ACTIVITIES
The museum **Þórbergssetur** (☎ 478 1078, 867 2900; Hali í Suðursveit; admission Ikr700; 9am-9pm May-Sep, noon-5pm Tue-Sun Oct-Apr) pays tribute to the most famous son of this sparsely populated region – writer Þórbergur Þórðarson (1888–1974), who was born at Hali in Suðursveit. The exhibition contains full-sized models of the farmhouse where he grew up and his study in Reykjavík, illustrated by quotes from his work. Þórbergur was a real maverick (with interests spanning yoga, Esperanto, astronomy, archaeology and geology), and his first book *Bréf til Láru (Letter to Laura)* caused huge controversy because of its radical socialist content. Þórbergssetur also functions as a kind of cultural centre, with changing art exhibitions, and a popular restaurant.

As for glaciers, if you want to get up onto **Vatnajökull**, the daddy of them all, for a snowmobile, skiing or 4WD tour (see the boxed text, p302), then this area is where you branch vertically off into the mountains. Rte F985, which leads up to the **Jöklasel hut**, is about 35km east of Jökulsárlón.

Staying on the Ring Road, you'll cross the lovely **Mýrar**, a region of wetlands surrounding the deltas of Hornafjarðarfljót and Kolgrímaá, home to lots of **water birds**.

The prominent and colourful mountain **Ketillaugarfjall** rises 670m above the Hornafjarðarfljót delta near Bjarnarnes. Its name derives from a legend about a woman named Ketillaug, who carried a pot of gold into the mountain and never returned. A brilliantly coloured alluvial fan at its base is visible from the road.

SLEEPING & EATING
Vagnsstaðir HI Hostel (☎ 478 1048; glacierjeeps@simnet.is; sites per person Ikr850, sb dm Ikr2100; May–mid-Oct) As the home of the Glacier Jeeps outfit (see p302), this is the obvious place to stay the night before or after a tour onto the Vatnajökull ice cap. The hostel itself, by the Ring Road 50km west of Höfn, is simple and purpose-built in the shadow of some imposing mountains.

Smyrlabjörg (☎ 478 1074; smyrlabjorq@eldhorn.is; s/d €110/144; ☷ closed late Dec; ☜) This friendly country hotel has 45 simply furnished rooms, all with satellite TV and attached bathroom. There's a restaurant serving an Icelandic buffet for dinner in summer, and a bar. It's a great place if you're after mod-cons but still want geese in the yard, mountain views, and utter peace and quiet.

Skálafell (☎ 478 1041; skalafell@simnet.is; sb Ikr3200, d Ikr14,700-18,600) At the foot of the Skálafell glacier, this friendly working farm has a couple of rooms in the quaint family farmhouse and three two-bedroom cabins. There are no cooking facilities, but breakfast and dinner are available. The owners have set up a marked walking trail from the farm to Skálafellsjökull, complete with little information boards about local lore and legends.

Brunnhóll (☎ 478 1029; brunnholl@brunnholl. is; s without bathroom Ikr8,300, s/d with bathroom from Ikr10,300/16,500; ☷ Apr-Oct; ☜) A gorgeous farm property 30km from Höfn on the southern side of the Ring Road, Brunnhóll has a cosy guest house and a bright, glassed-in dining room where breakfast is served. Rooms with glacier views cost around Ikr2000 extra. The good folk at Brunnhóll are also the makers of Jöklaís (Glacier Icecream), which you can buy at the farm.

Café Hali (☎ 867 2900; www.hali.is; Hali í Suðursveit; mains around Ikr2900; ☷ cafe open from 9am daily, dinner 7-9pm Jun-early Sep) The Þórbergssetur museum and cultural centre contains this tremendously civilised cafe-restaurant, where you can linger over a latte, or try local specialities such as lamb soup and freshly-caught trout.

HÖFN
pop 1640

Although it's no bigger than many European villages, the southeast's main town feels like a sprawling metropolis after driving through the wastelands on either side. Its setting is stunning; on a clear day wander down to the waterside, find a quiet bench and just gaze at Vatnajökull and its brotherhood of glaciers.

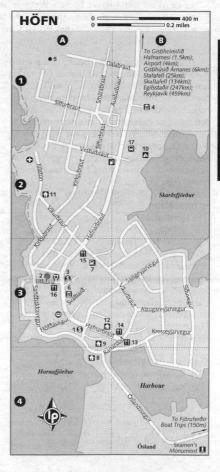

SOUTHEAST ICELAND

RIDING ON THE VATNAJÖKULL ICE CAP

Although the Vatnajökull ice cap and its attendant glaciers look spectacular from the Ring Road, most travellers will be seized by a wild desire to get even closer.

However, access to Vatnajökull is limited to commercial tours…unless you happen to be set up for a serious polar-style expedition. The ice cap is riven with deep crevasses, which are made invisible by coverings of fresh snow, and there are often sudden, violent blizzards. But don't be disheartened! It's a mind-blowing experience just to get near the glacier, and you can travel way up into the whiteness on organised snowmobile and 4WD tours.

The easiest route up to Vatnajökull is the F985 4WD track (about 40km east of Jökulsárlón, 55km west of Höfn) to the broad glacial spur Skálafellsjökull. The 16km-long road is practically vertical in places, with iced-over sections in winter. Please don't even think of attempting it in a 2WD car – you'll end up with a huge rescue bill.

At the top, 840m above sea-level, is the **Jöklasel hut** (☎ 11.15am-5pm Jun–mid-Sep) with a cafe that must have the most epic views in Iceland. On a clear day you can see 10km across the ice cap to towering snowcapped peaks and south towards the ocean – it's like being on top of the world.

From here, the most popular tour option is the one-hour **skidoo ride** (per person Ikr10,500). You get kitted out with overalls, boots and gloves, then play follow-the-leader along a fixed trail. It's great fun, and, although it only gives you the briefest introduction to glacier travel, an hour of noisy bouncing about with the stink of petrol in your nostrils is probably enough for most people!

'Höfn' simply means 'harbour', and is pronounced like an unexpected hiccup (if you're not prone to hiccups, just say 'hup' while inhaling). It's an apt name – this modern town still relies heavily on fishing and fish processing, and is famous for its lobster (there's even an annual lobster festival). Bus travellers will have to stay overnight here, and most other travellers stop to use the town's many services, so it pays to book accommodation in summer. Höfn makes a very handy base for trips to the glacier.

Information

The **tourist office** (☎ 478 1500; www.visitvatnajokull.is; Hafnarbraut 30; ☼ 10am-6pm Jun-Aug, 1-6pm May & Sep, 1-4pm Mon-Fri Oct-Apr) is also the ticket desk for the glacier exhibition (see below). Internet access at the **library** (☎ 470 8050; Litlabrú; ☼ 10am-4pm Mon-Fri summer, 9am-5pm Mon-Thu, 11am-5pm Fri & 11am-2pm Sat winter), in the community centre opposite the supermarket, costs Ikr400 per hour.

Landsbanki Íslands and **Sparisjóðurinn**, both on Hafnarbraut, handle foreign exchange. You'll find an ATM just inside the shopping centre.

Sights & Activities

The **Jöklasýning Glacier Exhibition** (www.joklasyn ing.is; Hafnarbraut 30; adult/child under 16yr Ikr1000/free; ☼ 10am-6pm Jun-Aug, 1-6pm May & Sep, 1-4pm Mon-Fri Oct-Apr) explains the history and geology of Vatnajökull and southeastern Iceland in great detail. For a break from all the reading, there are a couple of films – an excellent 10-minute video of the 1996 Grímsvötn eruption, plus clips from James Bond movies made in the region. There's also a small collection of exhibits relating to glacier exploration, some altogether-too-strange glacial mice, a baffling plastic 'ice cave', and a good natural-history room. You can check that the glacier's still there from the viewing platform on the roof.

Birdwatching and a boat ride, ATVing and a history lesson – trips run by **Fjöruferðir** (☎ 840 0541; www.fjoruferdir.is; Ikr8500) are a cornucopia of experiences. Boats leave from Ósland (see below) at 10am, noon, 2pm, 4pm, 6pm and 8pm in summer, taking you to the black-sand Suðurfjörur beach. Here you transfer to quad bikes, driving along the shore to view WWII remains.

The regional folk museum **Byggðasafnið Gamlabúð** (☎ 478 1833; Hafnarbraut; admission free; ☼ 1-5pm mid-May–mid-Sep), near the campsite, is housed in an 1864 trade warehouse that was moved to Höfn from Papaós, further east. It has agricultural displays as well as small natural-history and marine-life exhibits.

Höfn is blessed with amazing glacier views. There are a couple of short **water-side paths** where you can amble and gape – one by Hótel Höfn, and another round the marshes and lagoons at the end of the promontory Ósland (about 1km beyond the harbour – head for the **seamen's monument** on the rise). The latter path is great for watching **sea birds**, though if you walk to it during nesting season

Prices are per person, with two people to a skidoo – there's Ikr6500 extra to pay if you want a skidoo to yourself. You can also take a more sedate **super-Jeep** ride up onto the ice. It's also possible to do longer trips to Breiðamerkurjökull, Grímsvötn, Kverkfjöll, Öræfajökull and Snæfell, as well as cross-country skiing tours (Ikr25,000 per person).

If you don't have your own 4WD transport, from June to August two glacier companies can drive you up to the Jöklasel hut:

Glacier Jeeps (☎ 478 1000; www.glacierjeeps.is) At 9.30am and 2pm daily this company collects people in a super-Jeep from the little parking area at the start of the F985. You're then driven up to Jöklasel, where you can go on a skidoo ride (Ikr11,500) or 4WD tour (Ikr11,500) on Vatnajökull – prices include transport from the F985.

Vatnajökull Travel (☎ 894 1616; www.vatnajokull.is) This friendly outfit will pick you up from Höfn (8.30am), or from the F985 parking area (9.30am), take you up to Jöklasel, where you can do the skidoo or 4WD thing, and then drive you to Jökulsárlón for a lagoon boat trip. Prices vary according to what you select; for example, a pick-up from Höfn plus skidoo ride and lagoon boat-trip costs €255; or you can even fly from Reykjavík to indulge in skidoo and boat trips (€510).

Coming from Höfn or Skaftafell, scheduled buses can drop you at the F985 parking area, from where you can link up with tours. In summer, there's also a daily bus from Höfn (departing 8.30am) that goes up to Jöklasel and back, then on to Jökulsárlón, then straight back to Höfn.

you will be attacked in Hitchcock style by zillions of arctic terns on the causeway road.

Höfn has just been blessed with a brand-new outdoor **swimming pool** (☎ 470 8477; Víkurbraut 9; adult/child 6-16yr Ikr350/150; ⏱ 6.45am-9pm Mon-Fri, 10am-7pm Sat & Sun), with three shining waterslides, three hot pools and a steam bath.

Höfn has a nine-hole **golf course** at the end of Dalabraut at the northern end of town.

Tours

A visit to this region wouldn't be complete without a pilgrimage to Vatnajökull – see the boxed text, opposite.

Festivals & Events

Every year in early July, Höfn's annual **Humarhátíð** (Lobster Festival) honours this crunchy crustacean, which is a renowned local catch. There's usually a fun fair, flea markets, dancing, music, ice-sculpture competitions, lots of alcohol and even a few lobsters.

Sleeping

Höfn campsite (☎ 478 1606; camping@simnet.is; Hafnarbraut 52; sites per person Ikr850, sb Ikr2500, 6-person cabins Ikr8500; ⏱ mid-May–mid-Sep) Lots of travellers stay at the hilly campsite on the main road into town. There are also 16 good-value log cabins here, with two double and two single beds, and kitchens (but limited cooking equipment).

Nýibær HI Hostel (☎ 478 1736; hofn@hostel.is; Hafnarbraut 8; sb dm/tw Ikr2500/5800) At the harbour

end of town, Höfn's best budget option is a medium-sized place that's usually bustling with travellers in summer (it's open all year). It's in an old but cosy house with a kitchen, and a dining room that doubles as the common area (where many a glacier tour and long-distance hike has been dissected!). There are also laundry facilities.

Gistiheimilið Hvammur (☎ 478 1503; hvammur3@simnet.is; Ránarslóð 2; sb Ikr3000, s/d Ikr8500/10,400) Run by the same couple that runs the hostel, Hvammur is the pick of the guest houses for its 30 simple rooms, all with washbasins and satellite TV. Some overlook the boat-filled harbour.

Gistihúsið Árnanes (☎ 478 1550; www.arnanes.is; sb Ikr4700, s/d without bathroom Ikr13,400/16,700, with bathroom Ikr16,700/20,900; ⌨) On the Ring Road 6km west of Höfn, this rural place is an excellent choice for its cottages and guest-house rooms (some with balconies). Prices include breakfast. The sleeping-bag accommodation is disappointing, though – with mountain views all around, it seems a shame to be underground! There's an agreeable dining room–art gallery, with set meat and fish courses (from Ikr2000); it's open in summer only, and then only if there are enough diners.

Gistiheimilið Ásgarður (☎ 478 1365; asgardur@eldhorn.is; Ránarslóð 3; s/d/tr Ikr11,000/15,000/19,000; ⌨ 🛜) Harbourside Ásgarður is more like a hotel than a guest house. All rooms have a bathroom and a small TV, and some have glacier views. They're a bit boxy, but the guest

SOUTHEAST ICELAND

house is in a good location and the people are very friendly. Breakfast is included.

Gistiheimilið Hafnarnesi (☎ 426 7515, 844 6175; www .hafnarnes.is; s/d Ikr6500/8500; 🛜) Owner Kristín is a hospitable host, warmly welcoming guests to her house. There's a sitting room and fully equipped kitchen, and the simple rooms on the upper floor have glacier views. Hafnarnesi is perched on a hillock on the edge of town.

Hótel Höfn (☎ 478 1240; www.hotelhofn.is; Vikurbraut; s/d from Ikr19,250/26,500; 🖥) Höfn's business-class hotel is often busy with tour groups in summer. All rooms have a bathroom and TV, and breakfast is included. The rooms are a bit frayed around the edges – even the deluxe ones aren't particularly flash – but perhaps you won't notice the decor if you get one with glacier views. There's a decent restaurant, and discounts are available out of season.

As the southeast's only megalopolis, Höfn often fills up quickly in summer. **Hótel Edda Nesjum** (☎ 444 4850; Nesjaskóli; s/d from Ikr8000/10,000; 🗓 Jun–mid-Sep), 8km down the road at Nesjaskóli, is a possible accommodation option when all else is full. There's an on-site restaurant and a petrol station and grill opposite, but all other facilities are in Höfn. You'll really need a car, although the glacier tour companies may pick you up from the hotel with advance arrangement.

Eating & Drinking

Café Tulinius (☎ 869 9340; snacks Ikr650-1390; 🗓 from 11am Mon-Fri summer) Down by the harbour, this new summer-only cafe serves fancy coffees, traditional Icelandic snacks (flatbread with smoked lamb, rye-bread sandwiches) and creamy cakes. It's named after the merchant Otto Tulinius, Höfn's first settler, who built it as his home in 1897, and still retains its refined, old-world atmosphere.

Kaffi Hornið (☎ 478 2600; Hafnarbraut 42; 🗓 11am-11pm Sun-Thu, to midnight Fri & Sat; light meals Ikr990-1900, mains Ikr1900-4200; 🛜) This log-cabin affair is an unpretentious bar-restaurant, decorated with changing art exhibitions. The food comes in stomach-stretching portions. Choose from burgers, pasta, fish and lamb mains, a salad bar, a couple of vegie options and Höfn speciality roasted lobster in a creamy sauce (Ikr4950).

Ósinn (☎ 478 1240; www.hotelhofn.is; Vikurbraut; mains Ikr2900-4900; 🗓 9am-10pm) The family restaurant on the ground floor of Hótel Höfn has a good choice of snacky meals (burgers, pizzas etc), and some of the tastiest fish,

meat and pasta mains in town. Go for local fish dishes including Höfn's famous lobster – as an á la carte dish or on a pizza.

Humarhöfnin (☎ 478 1200; www.humarhofnin.is; Hafnarbraut 4; mains Ikr3000-5000; 🗓 noon-10pm mid-May–Sep) Located in another historic building (which was once the town's co-operative store), this rustic-style restaurant opened during the 2007 Lobster Festival. Humarhöfnin specialises in cooking up pincer-waving little critters, and it also has a relaxed bar area perfect for an early-evening drink.

There's a **Nettó supermarket** (☎ 478 1800; Hafnarbraut; 🗓 10am-7pm Mon-Fri, 10am-6pm Sat, noon-6pm Sun) and a **bakery** (☎ 478 2161; 🗓 8am-5pm Mon-Fri, 9am-4pm Sat) in the Miðbær shopping centre near the library.

Getting There & Away
AIR
Höfn's airport is about 4km northwest of town. **Eagle Air** (☎ 562 2640; www.eagleair.is) flies year-round between Reykjavík and Höfn (from Ikr12,400 one way), Sunday to Friday.

BUS
Buses arrive at and depart from the campsite, which is a 10-minute walk from the town centre. The daily Reykjavík–Höfn bus (Ikr11,200) runs from 1 June to 15 September. It leaves from Reykjavík at 8.30am and from Höfn at 11am, and takes 8½ hours. At other times of year the bus runs on Tuesdays, Fridays and Sundays only, and departs later in the day.

From mid-May to August a bus runs daily from Höfn (at 8.30am) up to the Jöklasel hut, on the edge of the Vatnajökull ice cap. It stays there for 2½ hours (giving you time to go snowmobiling) before heading to Jökulsárlón, where it stays for two hours, before returning to Höfn.

Höfn–Egilsstaðir buses run daily from 1 June to 15 September. Buses leave from Höfn at 8.30am, calling at Djúpivogur and Berunes. Buses return from Egilsstaðir at 1.30pm.

LÓNSÖRÆFI

If you're in Iceland to get in touch with your inner hermit, the nature reserve Lónsöræfi should be on your list. This protected area, east of Höfn, contains some spectacularly colourful rhyolite mountains, as well as the Stafafellsfjöll peaks, and at 320 sq km is one of Iceland's largest conservation areas. There are countless hiking opportunities, from day walks to the long-distance route taking you north to Snæfell.

You can camp at sites in the reserve, and there are mountain huts along the Lónsöræfi–Snæfell hike, which begins at the Illikambur parking area. The only road in the reserve is the rough 4WD track that ends at Illikambur. There's nowhere to eat or buy food; bring supplies from Höfn or Djúpivogur.

SIGHTS & ACTIVITIES
Stafafell

In the absolute middle of nowhere, Stafafell is a lonely farm, lost under the mountains. It's a

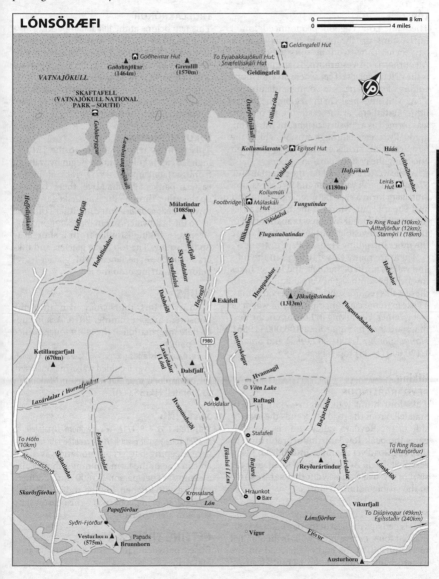

LÓNSÖRÆFI

0 — 8 km
0 — 4 miles

SOUTHEAST ICELAND

great hiking base for exploring Lónsöræfi; you can arrange tours and hikers' transport here, and the farmer Bergsveinn knows everything about the area. Stafafell functioned as a remote parsonage until 1920. The present church contains some lovely artefacts, including an original altarpiece. You can stay the night in the farmhouse at the campsite (right).

Lón

The name Lón (Lagoon; pronounced 'lone') fairly sums up the nature of this shallow bay enclosed by two long spits between the Austurhorn and Vesturhorn. To the northwest is the delta of **Jökulsá í Lóni**, where an enormous colony of swans nests in spring and autumn.

As with other peaks in the region, the batholithic **Austurhorn**, at the eastern end of Lón, was formed as a subsurface igneous intrusion, gradually revealed through erosion. This is the best access for strolls on the Fjörur sand spit enclosing the eastern portion of Lón.

At the western end of Lón, the commanding 575m-high peak **Vesturhorn** and its companion **Brunnhorn** form a cape between Skarðsfjörður and Papafjörður. Ruins of the fishing settlement Syðri-Fjórður, which was abandoned in 1899, are still visible, and just south of it are the more intriguing ruins of Papatóttir.

There are many easy day hikes in the hills and valleys north of Stafafell, and longer hikes towards the southeast of Vatnajökull. Some of these walks require substantial river crossings, so use extreme caution, especially in warm or wet weather. For hiking in Lónsöræfi, the best maps are the *Hornafjörður* 1:100,000 (1986), *Hamarsfjörður* 1:100,000 (1987) and *Snæfell* 1:100,000 (1988) topo sheets.

Hiking

REYÐARÁRTINDUR

This four-hour walk begins 7km east of Stafafell. From the road, it ascends the eastern side of the Reyðará valley and circumnavigates the peak Reyðarártindur, returning to the Ring Road via the valley **Össurárdalur**, 11km east of Stafafell. Across the Ring Road near the start of this walk is a **view disc** that names some of the visible natural features.

HVANNAGIL

This is perhaps the best of the day hikes, a well-marked four- or five-hour walk from Stafafell to Hvannagil, at the end of the road on the eastern bank of the Jökulsá í Lóni. Head up

this dramatic rhyolite valley and, after less than 1km, you'll see a sheep track climbing the ridge on your right. At the top of this ridge you'll have a view down Seldalur. Keep to the left side of this valley until you pass the side valley, **Raftagil**, which descends back to the Jökulsá í Lóni. You can pick your way down Raftagil or follow the ridge above the eastern side of Seldalur.

TRÖLLAKRÓKUR

This trip begins at the **Illikambur** parking area (about 20km north of Stafafell), accessible along 4WD Rte F980. From there, it's five or six hours to Egilssel hut at Tröllakrókur, an area of bizarre wind-eroded pinnacles. Above, you can see the tongue of **Öxárfellsjökull**, the eastern extreme of the Vatnajökull ice cap. Allow two days for the return trip.

JÖKULGILSTINDAR

This two-day trip climbs up to the 1313m-high ice cap Jökulgilstindar. Begin by walking from Stafafell up the 4WD track along the eastern bank of **Jökulsá í Lóni**, then continue up the valley through the Austurskógar woods toward **Hnappadalur**. You can either continue up to the headwaters of Hnappadalur or climb steeply to Jökulgilstindar from a short way up the valley. The top has a glacier, and hikers should be experienced with glacier travel before venturing onto the ice.

TOURS

Mountain bus tours may run into the Lónsöræfi area in summer 2010. Ask for up-to-date information at the Höfn tourist office (see p302).

Ferðafélag Íslands (☎ 568 2533; www.fi.is; Mörkin 6, Reykjavík) have several guided walks in Lónsöræfi, for example, a four-day trip from Múladalur to Stafafell (Ikr35,000).

SLEEPING

Stafafell (☎ 478 1717; www.eldhorn.is/stafafell; sb Ikr2500, cottages per night Ikr7000, reduced rate for longer stays) Sleeping-bag accommodation is available in one of the farm buildings; there's also a campsite (per person Ikr600) and cottages for hire with kitchen, lounge and TV. There's no food, so bring your own – the nearest shop is 25km away in Höfn.

GETTING THERE & AWAY

Buses between Höfn and Egilsstaðir pass Stafafell.

The Highlands

Wandering through Iceland's highlands will give you a new understanding of the word 'desolation'. You may have travelled the Ring Road thinking that Iceland is light on towns; that sheep seem to outnumber people; that you haven't run across a McDonald's for many a mile. Well, you ain't seen nothing yet. Here there are practically no services, accommodation, hot-dog stands, bridges, mobile-phone signals or guarantees if something goes wrong. Gazing across the expanses, you could imagine yourself in Mongolia or the Australian Outback or, as many people have noted, on the moon. And those aren't overactive imaginations at work – the *Apollo* astronauts actually trained here before their lunar landing!

This isolation, in essence, is the reason that people visit. Although some travellers are disappointed by the interior's ultrableakness, others are humbled by the sublime sight of nature in its rawest, barest form. The solitude is exhilarating, the views are vast, and it's immensely tough but equally rewarding to hike or bike these cross-country routes.

Historically, people used the trails as summer short cuts between north and south, if with heavy hearts. Myths of ghosts and fearsome outlaws spurred travellers along the tracks with all speed. Today it's probably wiser to worry about the weather. Conditions can be fickle and snow isn't uncommon, even in mid-summer. Good warm clothing, and face and eye protection from gritty, wind-driven sand are particularly important. Road-opening dates given in this chapter depend on weather conditions – check www.vegagerdin.is for the latest information.

THE HIGHLANDS

HIGHLIGHTS

- Hike across the Oreo-cookie-like lava field at blustery **Askja** (p315), then take a dip in the tepid turquoise waters of the Víti crater nearby
- Marvel at icy sculptures hidden in the geothermal caves at **Kverkfjöll** (p317)
- Pay homage to the Queen of the Mountains, **Herðubreið** (p314)
- Pity the melancholy ghosts and outlaws on Iceland's longest, loneliest north–south track, the godforsaken **Sprengisandur route** (p310)
- Spice up the endless vistas of desolation with stops at hot springs and climbable crags along the notorious **Kjölur route** (p309)

THE HIGHLANDS

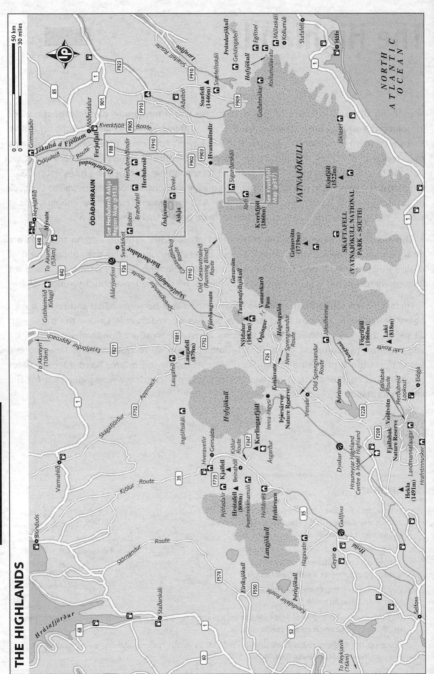

Sleeping

Almost all mountain huts in Iceland are operated by **Ferðafélag Íslands** (Iceland's Touring Association; Map pp72-3; ☎ 568 2533; www.fi.is; Mörkin 6, IS-108 Reykjavík). **Ferðafélag Akureyrar** (Touring Club of Akureyri; Map p214; ☎ 462 2720; www.ffa.est.is; Strandgata 23, Akureyri) operates all the mountain huts and most campsites along the Askja Way. It's wise to reserve accommodation in advance, as huts are usually booked out in summer. For more details about mountain-hut accommodation, see p324.

Getting Around

Before you embark on your journey through the highlands it is important to take note of a few items. Most of the routes described in this chapter are strictly for high-clearance 4WD vehicles, as jagged terrain and treacherous river crossings are not uncommon (see p68 for more info). It's recommended that vehicles travel in pairs, so if one gets bogged or breaks down, the other can drag it out, fetch help or transport all passengers to shelter. There are very few petrol stations in the highlands – you should fill up on petrol and supplies whenever you find one.

KJÖLUR ROUTE (KJALVEGUR)

If you want to sample Iceland's central deserts but don't like the idea of dangerous ford crossings, the 200km Kjölur route has had all its rivers bridged. In summer there's even a scheduled bus that uses it as a 'shortcut' between Reykjavík and Akureyri. The bus may be an appealing option at first; however, we've received comments from several readers that while the first hour of Outback desolation is riveting, the other nine hours can be snooze-inducing if you aren't planning to disembark anywhere along the way.

Rte F35 starts just past Gullfoss (p127), passing between two glaciers before emerging near Blönduós on the northwest coast. It reaches its highest point (700m) between the Langjökull and Hofsjökull ice caps, near the mountain Kjalfell.

The Kjölur route usually opens in early June.

SLEEPING

Ferðafélag Íslands (☎ 568 2533; www.fi.is) maintains 38 cottages across Iceland including all of the huts along the Kjölur route, except for those at Hveravellir, which are run by **Hveravellafélag**

(www.hveravellir.is). Kerlingarfjöll (p310) also has a privately run 'resort'. The following huts have toilets and a kitchen (no utensils though), and most have running water. Always take your garbage with you. They are listed from south to north here:

Hagavatn (N 64°27.760', W 20°14.700'; sb Ikr2000) Small, 12-person hut near the southern end of Langjökull, about 15km off the Kjölur route by 4WD track. No running water.

Hvítárnes (N 64°37.007', W 19°45.394'; sb Ikr2500) Has a volunteer warden for most of July and August; hut sleeps 30. Toilet in separate building.

Þverbrekknamúli (N 64°43.100', W 19°36.860'; sb Ikr2500) About 4km southeast of the mini–ice cap Hrútafell. Sleeps 20. Latrine available year-round.

Þjófadalir (N 64°48.900', W 19°42.510'; sb Ikr2000) Sleeps 12. Located at the foot of Mt Raudkollur.

Hveravellir (sb around Ikr2500) Two huts with a total of 53 sleeping-bag spaces.

GETTING THERE & AWAY

Daily from mid-June to early September scheduled buses travel along the Kjölur route between Reykjavík and Akureyri. Both **SBA-Norðurleið** (☎ 550 0770; www.sba.is) and **TREX** (☎ 551 1166; www.bogf.is) offer this service, which costs Ikr9900 and takes between nine and 10 hours. SBA has a 40-minute rest at Hveravellir, while TREX stops for 1½ hours at Kerlingarfjöll. Buses leave around 8am from both ends, stopping briefly at a few destinations including Geysir, Gullfoss and Varmahlíð.

Drivers with 4WD vehicles will have no problems on the Kjölur route. You won't find a car-rental agency that provides insurance to those with plans of taking a 2WD through – while physically possible, it is not advised.

Of all the interior routes, Kjölur is probably the best for cycling and hiking. For a humorous account of a bike trip on the Kjölur route, read Tim Moore's *Frost on My Moustache* (see p20 for details). It's an extra Ikr1200 if you bring your bike on the bus.

Hvítárvatn

The pale-blue lake Hvítárvatn, 45km northeast of Gullfoss, is the source of the glacial river Hvítá – a popular destination for Reykjavík-based white-water rafting operators. A glacier tongue of Iceland's second-largest ice cap, Langjökull, carves into the lake and creates icebergs, adding to the beauty of this spot.

In the marshy grasslands northeast of Hvítárvatn is Ferðafélag Íslands' oldest hut, Hvítárnes, built in 1930. The hut is believed to

---

KJÖLURVEGUR HIKE

A good preparation for more challenging interior hiking routes is the easy and scenic Kjölurvegur hike from Hvítárvatn to Hveravellir. The trail follows the original horseback Kjölur route (west of the present road), via the Hvítárnes, Þverbrekknamúli and Þjófadalir mountain huts.

From the Hvítárvatn turn-off it's 8km along the 4WD track to Hvítárnes hut. From there you follow the Fúlakvisl river (14km) to Þverbrekknamúli hut. Continue between the river and Kjalhraun lava field to Þjófadalir hut (14km). The final day is a 12km walk to Hveravellir, where you can soak in the local hot springs. Overall, the marked route is easy to follow and huts are four to six hours apart.

The route can be done in three days at a leisurely pace. Access is by the Kjölur bus (see p309), but remember to reserve a seat for the day you want to be picked up.

---

be haunted by the spirit of a young woman. If a female camper sleeps in one particular bed (the bunk on the west wall past the kitchen), it is said she will dream of the ghost carrying two pails of water. From the Kjölur road, where the bus will drop you, it's an 8km walk along the 4WD track to the hut.

Kerlingarfjöll

Until the 1850s Icelanders believed that this mountain range (12km southeast of Rte 35 on Rte F347) harboured the vilest outlaws. It was thought they lived deep in the heart of the 150-sq-km range in an isolated Shangri-la-type valley. So strong was this belief that it was only in the mid-19th century that anyone ventured into Kerlingarfjöll, and it was only in 1941 that the range was properly explored by Ferðafélag Íslands. Today, the TREX bus stops here for 1½ hours during its regular jaunt (the SBA bus does not).

It's certainly dramatic. The colourful landscape is broken up into jagged peaks and ridges, the highest of which is Snækollur (1477m), and it's scattered with hot springs.

At **Kerlingarfjöll** (☎ winter 894 2132, summer 664 7878; www.kerlingarfjoll.is; sites per tent €7, sb €25-33, linen €60, chalet €250; ☼ mid-Jun–Sep) there are a handful of huts and houses with a total space for around 90 in sleeping bags. There's also a large campsite, a restaurant and hot tubs. Check the website for a detailed list of local hikes and tours.

Hrútafell

This relatively tiny 10-sq-km ice cap rises 800m above the surrounding landscape. It sits on top of Hrútafell mountain, which is a *móberg* peak – shaped like a birthday cake due to subglacial volcanic eruptions. From the Kjölur route, as soon as Hrútafell comes into

view, look on the eastern side of the road for a cairn shaped exactly like a Hershey's Kiss!

Hveravellir

Hveravellir is a popular and enticing geothermal area of fumaroles and multicoloured hot springs (it's important to stay on the boardwalks to avoid damaging this sensitive area). Located 30km north of the Kerlingarfjöll turn-off (and 93km north of Gullfoss), Hveravellir is the 'hub' of the Kjölur route and the finishing point of the Kjölurvegur hike (see the boxed text, above).

Among its warm pools are the brilliant-blue Bláhver; Öskurhólshver, which emits a constant stream of hissing steam; and a luscious human-made bathing pool. Another hot spring, Eyvindurhver, is named after the outlaw Fjalla-Eyvindur (see the boxed text, p312). Hveravellir is reputedly one of the many hideouts of this renegade, who spent much of his life hiding from his enemies in the highlands. On a small mound near the geothermal area are the ruins of a shelter where he's believed to have holed up with his wife, Halla, during one 18th-century winter.

In summer, a petrol station is open at Hveravellir – the only one along the Kjölur route. The SBA bus stops here for 40 minutes. Visit www.hveravellir.is for detailed information about activities and hikes in the area.

Hofsjökull

Hofsjökull, east of the Kjölur Pass, is the third-largest ice cap in the country, measuring 995 sq km. A massive volcanic crater lies underneath the ice.

SPRENGISANDUR ROUTE

To Icelanders, the name Sprengisandur conjures up images of outlaws, ghosts and long sheep drives across the barren wastes. The Sprengisandur route (F26) is the longest north–south trail and crosses bleak desert moors that can induce a shudder even today in a 4WD!

Sprengisandur offers some wonderful views of Vatnajökull, Tungnafellsjökull and Hofsjökull, as well as Askja and Herðubreið from the western perspective. An older route, now abandoned, lies a few kilometres west of the current one.

The Sprengisandur route proper begins at Rte 842 near Goðafoss in northwest Iceland. You'll pass through a red metal gate as the road turns into F26. There's a billboard-esque poster explaining the sights and finer points of the route, and 2km later you'll happen upon one of Iceland's most photogenic waterfalls, **Aldeyjarfoss**. Churning water bursts over the cliff's edge as it splashes through a narrow canyon lined with the signature honeycomb columns of basalt (see the boxed text, p241, for more info).

After the falls, the Sprengisandur route continues southwest through 240km of inhospitable territory all the way to Þjórsárdalur. There are two other ways to approach Sprengisandur, both of which link up to the main road about halfway through.

A cheery notice at a nearby campsite toilet block reads:

Iceland is a harsh land and does not suffer fools. Rugged terrain and ever-changing weather have led many to their graves.

GETTING THERE & AWAY
From early July to early September, Reykjavík Excursions runs the 14/14a bus along the Sprengisandur route from Landmannalaugar to Mývatn at 8.30am on Sunday, Tuesday and Thursday (10 hours). In the other direction, they depart from Mývatn at 8.30am on Monday, Wednesday and Friday. Although it's a scheduled bus, it's used as a 'tour', with extended pauses at Hrauneyjar, Nýidalur, Aldeyjarfoss and Goðafoss. This route is included in the 'Highlights Passport', which starts at Ikr33,500.

Drivers should note that there's no fuel along the way. The nearest petrol stations are at Akureyri if you come in on the Eyjafjörður approach; at Varmahlíð if you're driving the Skagafjörður approach; at Fosshóll, near Goðafoss, if you're coming from the north along the main route through Bárðardalur; and at Hrauneyjar if you're driving from the south.

Eyjafjörður Approach
From the north the F821 from southern Eyjafjörður (south of Akureyri) connects to the Skagafjörður approach at Laugafell. This route is very pleasant, with few tourists, but it's a more difficult drive.

Skagafjörður Approach
From the northwest the 81km-long F752 connects southern Skagafjörður (the nearest town is Varmahlíð on the Ring Road) to the Sprengisandur route. The roads join near the lake Fjórðungsvatn, 20km east of Hofsjökull.

Laugafell
The main site of interest on the Skagafjörður is **Laugafell**, an 879m-high mountain with some nice hot springs bubbling on its northwestern slopes. You can stay nearby at the Ferðafélag Akureyrar **hut** (☎ 462 2670; N 65°01.630′, W 18°19.950′; per person Ikr2000; ☺ Jul & Aug), with 35 beds, a kitchen and a beautiful geothermally heated pool. Some stone ruins near the springs are reputed to have housed escapees from the Black Death.

OF BLIZZARDS & BONES
The spookily named Beinahóll (Bone Hill), 4km west of the road near Kjalfell, is the cue for a tragic tale. Although they realised it might be difficult so late in the season, in late October 1780, five farmers decided to return with their new flock of sheep to Skagafjörður along the Kjölur route. When a blizzard set in, they holed up and waited for it to pass, but the storm raged for three weeks without stopping, and all five men perished. Eerily, although the victims' bodies were discovered, when authorities arrived later to collect them, two had disappeared.

Today, sheep and horse bones still lie across the macabre hillock, and a memorial stone has been raised by the men's descendants. Icelanders believe that Beinahóll is haunted by the victims of this sad incident, and that to remove any of the bones or disturb the site is to invite permanent bad luck.

THE BADLANDS

Historically in Iceland, once a person had been convicted of outlawry they were beyond society's protection and aggrieved enemies could kill them at will. Many outlaws, or *útilegumenn*, such as the renowned Eiríkur Rauðe (Erik the Red), voluntarily took exile abroad. Others escaped revenge-killing by fleeing into the mountains, valleys and broad expanses of the harsh Icelandic interior, where few dared pursue them.

Undoubtedly, anyone who could live year-round in these bitter, barren deserts must have been extraordinary. Icelandic outlaws were naturally credited with all sorts of fearsome feats, and the general populace came to fear the vast badlands, which they considered to be the haunt of superhuman evil. The *útilegumenn* thereby joined the ranks of giants and trolls, and provided the themes for popular tales, such as the fantastic *Grettir's Saga*.

One particular outlaw has become the subject of countless Icelandic folk tales. Fjalla-Eyvindur, a charming but incurable 18th-century kleptomaniac, fled into the highlands with his wife, and continued to make enemies by rustling sheep to keep them alive. Throughout the highlands you'll see shelters and hideouts attributed to him and hear tales of his ability to survive in impossible conditions while always staying one jump ahead of his pursuers. One of Iceland's best-known folk songs describes how his wife, Halla, threw their newborn child into a waterfall when food was scarce during a harsh winter.

Nýidalur

Nýidalur (known as Jökuldalur), the range just south of the Tungnafellsjökull ice cap, was discovered by a lost traveller in 1845. With a campsite, two Ferðafélag Íslands **huts** (☎ summer 854 1194; N 64°44.130′, W 18°04.350′; sb Ikr2000; ✆ Jul-Aug) and lots of hiking possibilities, it makes a great break in a Sprengisandur journey. The huts have kitchen facilities, showers and a summer warden. Nights are particularly chilly here – something to do with the 800m elevation – so bring good warm gear.

Petrol isn't available here. There are two rivers – the one 500m from the hut may be difficult to cross (even for a 4WD). Ask locally for advice on conditions.

Although there aren't any hiking tracks per se, the hiking is great. Soft options include strolling up the relatively lush **Nýidalur valley** or wandering up the 150m-high hill east of the huts for a wide view across the desert expanses. A more challenging day hike will take you up to the colourful pass at **Vonarskarð**, a broad, 1000m-high saddle between Vatnajökull, Tungnafellsjökull and the green Ógöngur hills. This route also passes some active geothermal fields.

Þórisvatn

Before water was diverted from Kaldakvísl into Þórisvatn from the Tungnaá hydro-electric scheme in southwest Iceland, it had a surface area of only 70 sq km. Now it's Iceland's second-largest lake at 82 sq km. It lies 11km northeast of the junction between Rte F26 and the Fjallabak route.

Hrauneyjar

Somewhat unexpectedly, in the bleakest position imaginable (west of Þórisvatn in the Hrauneyjar region), you'll find a guest house and shiny new hotel – the only one in the highlands! **Hrauneyjar Highland Centre & Hótel Highland** (☎ 487 7782; www.hrauneyjar.is, www.hotel highland.is;guest house sb s/d €50/61, s/d bathroom €99/111, hotel s/d from €174/215; ✆ guest house year-round, hotel mid-Jun–mid-Sep; 🔊) lies at the crossroads of the Sprengisandur route (F26) and the F208 to Landmannalaugar, so it's very handy for lots of highland attractions. The simple guest-house rooms have shared bathrooms. If you want luxuries – comfy rooms, a restaurant, a sauna…and a helicopter pad – head for the hotel, 1.4km away.

Staff can arrange excursions to sites of interest, including the beautiful **Dynkur waterfall**, which is a worthwhile 4WD excursion about 20km north.

Petrol and diesel are available.

Veiðivötn

This beautiful area just northeast of Landmannalaugar is an entanglement of small desert lakes in a volcanic basin, a continuation of the same fissure that produced Laugahraun in the Fjallabak Nature Reserve. This is a wonderful place for wandering, and you can spend quite a lot of time following 4WD tracks that wind across the tephra sands between the numerous lakes. On the hill to the northeast is a **view disc** pointing out the various lakes and peaks.

Veiðivötn lies 27km off the southern end of the Sprengisandur road south of Þórisvatn, via the F228 4WD road. Access from Landmannalaugar is thwarted by the substantial river Tungnaá, so you'll need private transport to get to Veiðivötn. At Tjaldvatn, below Miðmorgunsalda (650m), is a campsite with huts.

ÖSKJULEIÐ ROUTE (ASKJA WAY)

The Öskjuleið route runs across the highlands to Herðubreið, the Icelanders' beloved 'Queen of Mountains'; and to the desert's most popular marvel, the immense Askja caldera. The usual access road is Rte F88, which leaves the Ring Road 32km east of Mývatn, but Askja is also accessible further east from Rte F910.

For much of the way it's a flat journey, following the western bank of the Jökulsá á Fjöllum, meandering across tephra wasteland and winding circuitously through rough, tyre-abusing sections of the aptly named 5000-sq-km lava flow Ódáðahraun (Evil Deeds Lava).

If you are following Rte F88 you will encounter two river crossings. There are detailed signs at the river's edge explaining the proper method of fording the river. Along Rte 910 you'll be crossing the glacial rivers by bridge before encountering two clean river crossings. The water here does not swell in summer (unlike many other rivers in the highlands) and these crossings are smaller than the ones along Rte F88.

After a long journey through the lava- and flood-battered plains, things perk up at the lovely oasis of Herðubreiðarlindir, at the foot of Herðubreið. The route then wanders westwards through dunes and lava flows past the Dreki huts and up the hill toward Askja, where you'll have to leave your car at the Öskjuop car park and walk the remaining 2.5km to the caldera.

If you took F88 into Askja, try leaving along F910 so you don't have to retrace all of your steps. Other options from Askja include heading east towards Egilsstaðir, or west on the Gæsavatnaleið route (p316) to Sprengisandur.

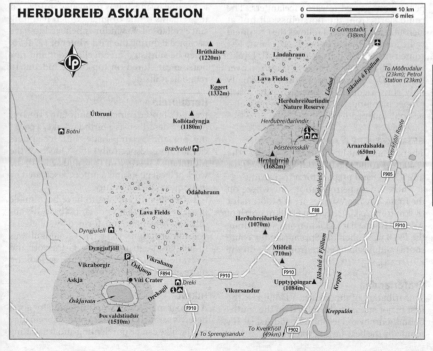

HERÐUBREIÐ ASKJA REGION

THE HIGHLANDS

To reach Kverkfjöll, head east on the F910 for 22km, then south on the F902 to reach the ice caves (see p317).

Öskjuleið is definitely for 4WD vehicles only. Even mountain buses have been known to get bogged in treacherous sinking sands. The route usually opens in early July.

TOURS

There are several operators that run tours out of Reykjahlíð (see p230) in the Mývatn region. These tours run between late July and the end of August (naturally when the routes to Askja are open!). Scenic flights from Mývatn over Askja are also possible (see p230). Super-Jeep tours from Varmahlíð (see p205) take in the caldera as well. Another possibility is to link up with the tours from the farm at Möðrudalur (p252). Elisabet, the owner and guide, was a park warden in the area for many years and knows more about the region than most tour leaders. Most operators can give day-trippers the opportunity to spend the night at Askja camp, and they can be picked up at the end of the following day trip. **Ferðafélag Akureyrar** (☎ 462 2720; www.ffa.is) organises hut-to-hut hiking tours (Ikr49,000 per person) geared towards Icelanders. The route starts from the Þorsteinsskáli hut at Herðubreiðarlindir and follows the Öskjuleið route to Svartárkot in upper Bárðardalur. The route runs via the huts at Bræðrafell, Dreki, Dyngjufell and Botni. The tour takes you over the vast Ódáðahraun lava flow and usually only runs a couple of times in July. With proper planning, this five-day trip may also be done independently.

GETTING THERE & AWAY

There's no public transport along the Öskjuleið route. Take a tour (see above), or hire a 4WD and prepare for a rocky ride.

There are no petrol stations anywhere on the route. The nearest ones are at Möðrudalur (87km from Askja), Mývatn (100km north of Askja), Hrauneyjar (235km from Askja along the F910 west, then the Sprengisandur route south) and Aðalból (90km from Askja on the F910 east).

Grafarlandaá

This tributary of the Jökulsá á Fjöllum is the first major stream to be forded on the southbound journey to Herðubreið and Askja. It's reputedly the best-tasting water in Iceland, so

fill your bottles here! The banks also make a pleasant picnic spot.

A short walk from the road takes you to a dramatic canyon being formed by Jökulsá á Fjöllum. The stunning set of waterfalls makes it feel like a mini Jökulsárgljúfur in the making.

Herðubreiðarlindir

The oasis Herðubreiðarlindir, a nature reserve thick with green moss, angelica and the pinky-purple flower of the arctic riverbeauty (*Epilobium latifolium*), was created by springs flowing from beneath the Ódáðahraun lava. You get a superb close-up view of Herðubreið from here (unless, of course, you're greeted by dense fog and/or a wall of blowing sand, as is usually the case).

The mini-tourist complex has a nature-reserve information office, a **campsite** (sites per tent Ikr900) and the Ferðafélag Akureyrar 30-bed **Þorsteinsskáli hut** (N 65°11.544', W 16°13.360'; sb from Ikr2000; ☼ mid-Jun–early Sep), a pretty cushy lodge with showers, a kitchen and a summer warden.

Behind the hut is another Fjalla-Eyvindur 'convict hole'; this one is scarcely large enough to breathe inside. It was renovated in 1922 on the remains of the original, which had long since collapsed. Eyvindur is believed to have occupied it during the hard winter of 1774–75, when he subsisted on angelica root and raw horse meat stored on top of the hideout to retain heat inside.

Herðubreið

Iceland's most distinctive mountain (1682m) has been described as a birthday cake, a cooking pot and a lampshade, but Icelanders call it (more respectfully) the 'Queen of the Mountains'. It crops up time and again in the work of local poets and painters, fascinated by its unquestionable beauty.

If Herðubreið appears to have been made in a jelly mould, that's not far off base. It's another *móberg* mountain, formed by subglacial volcanic eruptions. In fact, if Vatnajökull was to suddenly be stripped of ice, Grímsvötn and Kverkfjöll would probably emerge looking more or less like Herðubreið.

HIKING

A topographic sheet won't do you any good here. As serenely beautiful as Herðubreið may be, the hike can be unrelenting and frustrating if you are not properly prepared. In the spring, as the weather warms slightly, there are a lot of falling rocks, which can alter paths and topography. Clouds often shroud the mountain, which makes it difficult to find your way, especially if you are near the summit – there is only one way down the mountain! A GPS is a must. The wardens highly advise having a helmet as well.

From the Þórsteinsskáli hut a marked trail runs to Herðubreið and you can then hike all the way around it in a day. The mountain looks the same from all sides, so disorientation is a possibility, but on clear days you'll see Kollótadyngja to the west–northwest and Herðubreiðarlindir to the east–northeast, so it shouldn't be too much of a problem.

Herðubreið was once thought to be unclimbable, but it was eventually scaled in 1908. Under optimum conditions you can climb the mountain in summer over one very long day. The route to the top ascends the western slope. We don't want you to get the wrong idea, however; this climb is difficult, and the threat of snow, rock falls, landslides or bad weather makes it impossible to tackle without the proper mountaineering gear. Don't go alone, prepare for the foulest weather imaginable, and remember to inform the attendant at Herðubreiðarlindir or Askja of your intentions.

Kollótadyngja

The peak Kollótadyngja (1180m), 10km northwest of Herðubreið, is a textbook example of a shield volcano. Its broad, shieldlike cone oozed lava gently rather than exploding violently. At its base is the Ferðafélag Akureyrar **Bræðrafell hut** (N 65°11.310', W 16°32.290'; sb Ikr2000), which accommodates 12 people and has a coal stove but no running water. The best access is the trail leading west from the Herðubreið circuit.

Drekagil

The name of the gorge Drekagil, 35km southwest of Herðubreið, means 'Dragon Canyon', after the form of a dragon in the craggy rock formations that tower over it. The canyon behind the Ferðafélag Akureyrar **Dreki huts** (Askja Camp; ☎ 853 2541; N 65°02.503', W 16°35.690'; sb new/old hut Ikr3300/2800; late Jun-early Sep) resembles something out of Arizona or the Sinai; bitter winds and freezing temperatures just don't suit this desert landscape!

The Dreki huts are an ideal base for a day or two of exploring the area. Not only does the dramatic Drekagil ravine offer an easy stroll up to an impressive waterfall, but you can also walk 9km up the road and marked trail to Askja. There is also a marked trail to the Bræðrafell hut. The huts sleep a total of 60, and there are showers, a kitchen, an information centre and a summertime warden. Camping (Ikr900 per tent) is also permitted (you'll probably see rows of white tents set up for a local touring group), but the wind and cold can become oppressive.

At Dreki the Gæsavatnaleið route (F910) turns off the Öskjuleið to cross some intimidating expanses and connect with the Sprengisandur route at Nýidalur.

Dyngjufjöll

The stark Dyngjufjöll range, which shelters the Askja caldera and the Drekagil gorge, is what remains of a volcanic system that collapsed into its magma chamber. **Þorvaldstindur**, the highest point along its southern rim, rises to 1510m.

This inhospitable territory may be intriguing, but it isn't terribly inviting to the casual hiker. If you want to explore beyond the tracks and footpaths, make careful preparations and take due precautions.

You'll find overnight accommodation at the remote and basic **Dyngjufell hut** (N 65°07.480', W 16°55.280'; sb Ikr2000), also maintained by Ferðafélag Akureyrar, northwest of the caldera.

Askja

Perversely, the cold, windy and utterly desolate Askja caldera is the main destination for all tours in this part of the highlands. As bleak and terrible as it may be, this immense 50-sq-km caldera shouldn't be missed. It's difficult to imagine the sorts of forces that created it – pondering the landscape will naturally produce boggling thoughts about the power of nature and the insignificance of us puny humans.

The cataclysm that formed the lake in the Askja caldera (and the Víti crater) happened relatively recently (in 1875, to be exact) when 2 cu km of tephra was ejected from the Askja volcano. The force was so strong that bits of debris actually landed in Continental Europe. Ash from the eruption poisoned large numbers of cattle in northern Iceland, sparking

THE HIGHLANDS

a wave of emigration to America. It's quite daunting to realise that such cataclysmic events could be replayed at any time.

After the initial eruption, a magma chamber collapsed and created a craterous 11-sq-km hole, 300m below the rim of the original explosion crater. This new depression subsequently filled with water and became the sapphire-blue lake **Öskjuvatn**, the deepest in Iceland at 220m.

In 1907, German researchers Max Rudloff and Walther von Knebel were rowing on the lake when they completely vanished; their bodies were never found. It was suggested that the lake may have hazardous quirks, possibly cold currents or whirlpools; but a rickety canvas boat and icy water could easily explain their deaths. There's a stone cairn and memorial to the men on the rim of the caldera (with a guest book tucked inside – look for our name!).

In the 1875 eruption a vent near the northeastern corner of the lake exploded and formed the tephra crater **Víti**, which contains geothermal water. Although a bit on the chilly side if you're expecting a soothing swim (temperatures range between 22°C and 30°C), a dip in this turquoise-blue pool is one of the highlights of any Askja adventure. As always, the Icelandic way is to strip down and bathe in the nude; if you're shy (or afraid of 'shrinkage'), then bring a swimsuit. The route down is slippery but not as steep as it looks.

Askja's convoluted creation and unique geology is actually quite fascinating – it's well worth doing a bit of rock research online before your visit. A simple online search will yield dozens of informative sites.

GÆSAVATNALEIÐ ROUTE

The 120km-long Gæsavatnaleið route (F910), also known as the Austurleið (it doesn't pass anywhere near its namesake Gæsavötn), connects the Sprengisandur route and the Öskjuleið. There's little traffic and the scenery is excellent. The road crosses vast lava fields and sandy stretches, and there are always high ice caps in the background. It's not nearly as treacherous as it once was, since a new road has been built north of the old one and the largest river is now bridged. However, it's still difficult to drive and you should only attempt this route if you have a lot of 4WD experience. It is important that you contact the warden at Askja before attempting this route. They will be able to provide you with the most up-

to-date info on weather patterns and 'road' conditions. This trip involves a river crossing – avoid travel in the evening as the water level is always higher and you greatly increase your chances of getting stuck and sinking.

The route from Askja to Dragon Canyon opens before F910. Once this road opens up, you are advised to tackle it in one long day (it's slow goin' over the lava fields), as camping along the route is forbidden.

Old Gæsavatnaleið

If anyone tells you the Gæsavatnaleið is impossible, they're speaking of the old southern route best known as the road followed by the escaping hero, Alan Stewart, in Desmond Bagley's thriller *Running Blind*. It's not really impossible, but as yet no tour company is willing to brave it and, when the new Gæsavatnaleið route opened, this route stopped being maintained. As a result, this is one of Iceland's roughest journeys, notorious for floods and deep sand drifts. It should only be tackled with at least two hardy 4WDs – it's also imperative that you ask for advice before venturing out.

KVERKFJÖLL ROUTE

As its name suggests, this 108km-long route creeps southwards to the amazing Kverkfjöll ice caves. It connects Möðrudalur (65km east of Mývatn, off the Ring Road) with the Sigurðarskáli hut, 3km from the lower caves, via the F905, F910 and F902. The petrol station at Möðrudalur is the last place to fill up.

Along the way are several sites of interest, including the twin pyramid-shaped Upptyppingar hills near the Jökulsá á Fjöllum bridge, and the Hvannalindir oasis where there is – you guessed it – another of good ol' Fjalla-Eyvindur's winter hide-outs! He even built a rather hi-tech sheepfold at this one, so the animals could visit the stream without having to face the elements. Hvannalindir lies about 20km north of the Sigurðarskáli hut.

After visiting Askja (see p315), you can follow up with a trip to Kverkfjöll by driving south on Rte F902.

The large **Sigurðarskáli hut** (Kverkfjöll Hut; ☎ 863 9236; N 64°44.850', W 16°37.890'; sb Ikr3000, sites per person Ikr900, service fee Ikr400) has comfortable sleeping accommodation in a new hut and a well-maintained campsite.

The road to Kverkfjöll usually opens around 19 June, which is much earlier than the route to Askja. If you are planning to visit

Kverkfjöll, it's good to get there early because there's a higher chance of accessing the caves (warmer weather = tumbling ice blocks and bouts of glacial melting). Ask the warden first about cave conditions and for recommendations for a successful exploration of the area.

Kverkfjöll

Kverkfjöll is actually a mountain spur capped by the ice of Kverkjökull, a northern tongue of Vatnajökull. Over time, it's also come to refer to the hot-spring-filled ice caves that often form beneath the eastern margin of the Dyngjujökull ice.

The glacier water at Kverkfjöll is actually quite clean compared to other glacial runoff in Iceland. At spots it can be a tad silty, so you may want to carry a bit of your own water as well. If you are travelling at the beginning or end of summer the glacial water will be completely frozen over.

SIGHTS & ACTIVITIES
Lower Kverkfjöll Ice Caves

Besides being the source of the roiling Jökulsá á Fjöllum, central Iceland's greatest river,

Kverkfjöll is also one of the world's largest geothermal areas. The lower Kverkfjöll ice caves lie between 2km and 3km from the Sigurðarskáli hut, a 15-minute walk in each direction from the 4WD track's end.

Here the hot river flows beneath the cold glacier ice, clouds of steam swirl over the river and melt shimmering patterns on the ice walls, and there you have it – a spectacular tourist attraction. Perhaps this was the source of the overworked fire-and-ice cliché that pervades almost everything ever written about Iceland. Huge blocks of ice frequently crash down from the roof – don't enter the ice caves or you risk being caught in their heated combat. Also, the giant blocks of ice can alter the entrance to the cave – it's best to ask where the safest access point is currently located (there's only one point of entry, and it's not an issue if you are on a tour). There can be a danger of sulphur inhalation further inside the cave.

Upper Kverkfjöll Ice Cave & Hut

From the lower ice caves, the tours continue up onto the glacier itself. Guided tours hike through the gap between glacial fingers and stop at a nunatak called **Chocolate Hill** for a pause. Chocolate Hill earned its name because British explorers would eat chocolate bars to boost their energy for the climb and would leave their wrappers behind. It is extremely dangerous to mount the icy tongues before Chocolate Hill – wardens have not marked a path here as the topography is always changing.

From here it's a stiff three-hour hike climbing up and looping back down around **Langafönn** to reach the upper ice cave and geothermal area, where sulphur and rhyolite silt combine with the steam heat to create some of the gooiest mud imaginable. The cave has many entry points and is larger than the lower ones, but unfortunately you cannot explore here as the wardens have deemed it too dangerous to go in (which is just as well since the cave is considered less impressive than the ones below). Never walk up to the geothermal area alone.

It's then a 40-minute climb to the Icelandic Glaciological Society's six-bunk **Jörfi Hut**, at 1720m. There's no water or heating, but it makes a viable ice-cap base. Nearby is the beautiful lagoon **Gengissig**, which was formed in a small volcanic eruption in 1961. Bring your towel – this is a great spot for a bath

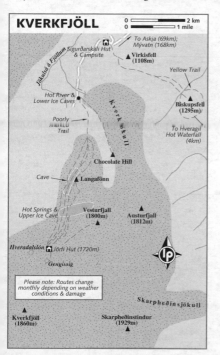

KVERKFJÖLL

0 ———— 2 km
0 ———— 1 mile

To Askja (69km);
Mývatn (168km)

Sigurðarskáli Hut
& Campsite

▲ Virkisfell
(1108m)

Yellow Trail

Hot River &
Lower Ice Caves

▲ Biskupsfell
(1295m)

Poorly
Marked
Trail

To Hveragil
Hot Waterfall
(4km)

■ Chocolate Hill

Cave ——— ▲ Langafönn

Hot Springs &
Upper Ice Cave

▲ Vesturfjall
(1800m)

▲ Austurfjall
(1812m)

Hveradalslón ⌂ Jörfi Hut (1720m)

Gengissig

Please note: Routes change
monthly depending on weather
conditions & damage

Skarphéðinsjökull

▲ Kverkfjöll
(1860m)

Skarphéðinstindur
(1929m) ▲

(Icelanders usually skinny dip). Another hour beyond the hut will take you to the highest peak of western **Kverkfjöll** (1860m), with a fine view over the *kverk* (gap) through which the Kverkfjöll glacier passes.

Hiking

A one-hour marked hike from behind Sigurðarskáli hut will take you up **Virkisfell** (1108m). At the top you'll have a spectacular view over Kverkfjöll and the headwaters of the Jökulsá á Fjöllum.

If you want to reach the hot waterfall and 30°C river in **Hveragil** you will need to have a lengthy debriefing with the warden and bring along a GPS. It is a difficult 12-hour return trip.

TOURS

Without a robust 4WD vehicle the only way to visit Kverkfjöll is on a tour. If you do have your own vehicle you can park and walk up to the ice caves – anywhere further is strictly ill-advised. The park rangers offer trips from the base hut on all days with good weather. It's a four-hour trip to the glacier with crampons (Ikr3000) and an eight- to nine-hour trip to the geothermal area (Ikr7000). You must wear walking boots that cover the ankle; otherwise your crampons will not fit properly. Runners simply won't work. Call ☎ 863 9236 for tour details. Besides the warden-led tours, the only other way to get the full picture of Kverkfjöll and have the possibility to mount the glacial crown is to join a tour from Möðrudalur (p252). The most convenient option, however, is the popular three-day **Askja–Kverkfjöll–Vatnajökull tour** (☎ Akureyri 550 0700, Reykjavík 550 0770; www. sba.is), run by SBA-Norðurleið. It leaves on Monday from early July to mid-August from Akureyri (Ikr25,000, 8.30am) and Mývatn (Ikr24,000, 11am).

For all of these trips you must bring your own food and organise your own accommodation (either book a hut or bring a tent). Hiking boots or other strong footwear, a sleeping bag and warm clothing are essential.

Gateway to Greenland & the Faeroes

CONTENTS

For many visitors Iceland provides a stepping stone to the wild, mysterious lands of Greenland and the Faeroes. Both are easily accessible and, although the journey may poke a hole in your wallet, it's more cost effective than planning a separate trip, especially since you've already come this far. Air Iceland's regular summer flights to Kulusuk, Constable Point, Nuuk, Ilulissat and Narsarsuaq make it easy to tag on a trip to Greenland, while regular flights (or extended ferry layovers) to the Faeroes allow you to easily discover these little-visited islands once used as a stopping point for Viking explorers.

GETTING THERE & AWAY

Air

GREENLAND

Iceland's main domestic carrier, **Air Iceland** (Flugfélag Íslands; ☎ in Iceland 570 3030; www.airiceland.is), flies from the domestic airport in downtown Reykjavík (REK) to a variety of destinations in Greenland, including Kulusuk (two hours, Monday to Saturday May to mid-September), Constable Point (two hours, once or twice weekly), Narsarsuaq (three hours, twice weekly late May to mid-September), Nuuk (three hours, four times weekly June to August, twice weekly May and early September) and Ilulissat (three hours 15 minutes, twice weekly mid-June to August). Due to the immense popularity of these Greenland tours, the roster of flights and destinations continues to grow with each passing season.

Air Greenland (☎ 299 34 34 34; www.airgreenland.com) code-shares with Air Iceland, offering continuing helicopter service on the east coast from Kulusuk and Constable Point to the secluded settlements of Ammassalik and Ittoqqortoormiit respectively. A network of intra-Greenland flights links an assortment of additional west-coast destinations like tangled shoestrings. There are also direct flights from Nuuk and Sisimiut to Kulusuk and Narsarsuq. See website for more details.

FAEROES

In summer, Air Iceland code-shares with the Faeroese airline **Atlantic Airways** (☎ 298 34 10 00; www.atlantic.fo), offering direct service from the domestic airport in downtown Reykjavík (REK) to Vágar (FAE) in the Faeroes.

In the warmer months (between 30 June and 18 September) there are two or three flights a week – there's always a Friday flight and the other flight(s) run on weekdays. During the off-season (from 29 March to 29 June, and 19 September to 24 October) there is a flight on Monday and Friday. With a bit of planning, you can nab a one-way ticket for Dkr495 (Ikr12,000), which is comparable to Iceland's domestic airfares.

Atlantic Airways also offers air service to London (Stansted), Stavanger, Copenhagen, Aalborg and Billund, making the Faeroes an intriguing layover option if you are flying between Iceland and any of these destinations.

Due to the jagged topography and thick tufts of fog, it is sometimes difficult to land at Vágar. If the plane cannot land, it will be rerouted to Norway or back to Iceland where you'll spend the night (paid for by the airline, of course) and try again the following day. Inclement weather can also delay take-offs, so plan accordingly if you have travel connections. This is usually only an inconvenience in July.

Sea

Smyril Line (☎ 298 34 59 00; www.smyril-line.com) car ferries link Iceland to Denmark, stopping at Tórshavn in the Faeroes along the way. See p336 for details.

GATEWAY TO GREENLAND & THE FAEROES

TOURS

To get the most out of a short trip to Greenland you may wish to join an organised tour. If you're visiting Greenland from Iceland, then consider joining one of the well-liked Air Iceland tours. A popular option is the day trip to Kulusuk (see the boxed text, below); however, Greenland's ultimate beauty unfurls during lengthier stays. Air Iceland's longer-stay trips include an eight-day fishing trip to Kuussuaq, a five-day stay in Nuuk, the capital, and a three-day culture-focused visit to Ammassalik, where first contact with the local Inuit was made a mere 95 years ago.

Greenland's tourism board has a hands-on website featuring a detailed list of the preferred tour operators and travel agencies offering trips through the island. Check out www.greenland.com/content/english/press_agents/greenland_travel_planner/travel_agencies for regularly updated details — operators are sorted by country. The website also features a handy travel planner for those who prefer to design their own journey. This is starting to become a viable option as the local tourism infrastructure continues to develop.

Like Greenland, the Faeroes tourism website (www.visitfaroeislands.com) has a drop-down list of accredited tour operators and cruises sorted by nation. The leading travel agency in the Faeroes is **GreenGate Incoming** (☎ 298 35 05 20; www.greengate.fo; Jónas Broncksgøta 35, FO-100 Tórshavn). All-inclusive package trips are widely available, however the Faeroes' small size makes it quite easy to base yourself in Tórshavn and arrange a variety of day trips (see opposite for ideas).

GREENLAND

As remote, wild and exotic as Iceland may seem to first-time visitors, it's positively pedestrian when compared to the splendours of Greenland. Nothing quite prepares you for the raw power of nature and the majestic scenery of this incredible place. Four times the size of France but with a population of just 57,600, it's a truly wild and humbling country. The sheer vastness of the ice cap, the size of the icebergs, the tenacity of the wildlife and the stoic attitude of the wonderful people will stay with you for life.

Travel here requires a combination of plane and helicopter flights and ferries through iceberg-strewn bays. Once at your destination you can choose to hike, ski, dog sled or kayak around the local area to see the towering peaks on the east coast, the gargantuan icebergs in Disko Bay or the surprisingly green fields of the south. Independent travel is easy to arrange, but there are plenty of all-inclusive packages if you'd rather let someone else do the planning.

For more information on Greenland, contact **Greenland Tourism** (www.greenland.com); Nuuk (☎ 299 34 28 20; PO Box 1615 DK-3900 Nuuk); Copenhagen (☎ 45 3283 3880; PO Box 1139, Strandgade 91, DK-1010 Copenhagen).

A DAY IN GREENLAND

A convenient halfway-point between Europe and North America, Reykjavík has developed quite the reputation as a trendy layover destination. Tourists who are tight on time tend to use the capital as a base for scenic day trips. Glacial lagoons, geysers, lava fields and windswept islands can be tackled before nightfall, but few people realise that a trip to Greenland can easily fit into the itinerary. In summer, Air Iceland offers regular tours to the faraway community of Kulusuk in east Greenland. Hidden in an endless tapestry of icy whites and cool blues, Kulusuk represents the ultimate frontier.

With only 360 inhabitants (and no flushing toilets), the little village slowly reveals itself to day-trippers during the stunning walk over from the airport. The distant mirage of brightly coloured wood-box houses suddenly becomes a reality as cameras click furiously. Although the traditional Greenlandic drum-dance demo is a tad kitsch, the rest of the experience is like one giant dream sequence. At the end of the tour you have the option of returning to the airport by sea or by land. The boat ride (an extra €25) puts you face-to-face with the popcorn-like ice chunks floating in the bay, while the hike gives visitors one last chance to take in the dramatic scenery of snow-strewn crags.

Prices start at €428 – OK, so it's pricey, but how many people can say that they have a 'Kalaallit Nunaat' stamp in their passport?

See p319 for more details.

FAEROE FORAY

Biweekly flights and ferries give Arctic adventurers three or four days to explore these truly magical islands. A half-week is just enough time to check the following highlights off your to-do list:

- **Tórshavn** The first thing you'll notice are the striking turf roofs adorning almost every bright-coloured building in the marina. The quaintness is palpable, yet you still know that you're in a capital. Although light on sights, Tórshavn makes a great base if you're planning a series of day trips. While mild summer evenings illicit thoughts of Mediterranean fishing villages or Caribbean outposts, the faint howl of distant winds confirms that the Faeroes are indeed children of the Arctic.

- **Gjógv** Perhaps the most adorable village in the entire world, Gjógv (jaykf) may be hard to pronounce, but it's oh-so easy to love. Tiny turf-roofed cottages sit clustered around a naturally formed harbour tucked within a gorge, which looks as though a lightning bolt has ripped straight through the terrain creating a sheltered cove. There's good hiking here, and an adorable inn should you want to spend the night.

- **Mykines** Marking the western limits of the island chain, Mykines (*mee*-chi-ness) is where the local landscapes come to a dramatic climax – innumerable bird colonies (puffins!), haunting basalt sea-stacks and silent solitary cliffs. Although considered quite remote by Faeroese standards (there are only 11 inhabitants!), the island is connected to Vágar by helicopter and ferry services. It's well worth visiting. Just make sure you plan your visit at the beginning of your trip – harsh winds and dense fog can delay your return.

- **Vestmanna Cliffs** You'll find plenty of bird cliffs in Iceland and the Faeroes, but these special crags are so visually striking that visitors often fail to notice the legions of swooping avians. In summer, there are three boat trips per day (DKr225, 2½ hours) departing from the village of Vestmanna, in northern Streymoy.

- **Hestir** Like a resting horse pausing for a quenching sip of seawater, little Hestir rears just south of Streymoy. The island is best known for its hollow grottoes carved into the cliffs by the pounding waves. On Thursday evenings you can take a boat into the caves and listen to soothing saxophone jazz as it bounces off the stone walls. See www.tutl.com for more info.

FAEROES

At the end of 2007, National Geographic proclaimed the Faeroes as the most 'authentic and unspoilt' island destination in the entire world – we were not surprised. Flung out into the North Atlantic, halfway between Norway and Iceland, these enchanting islets seem almost to lie on the edge of the earth, and their remote location and low profile lend them a genuine air of mystery.

In many ways the fiercely independent residents of these 18 wind-scoured islands remain closer to their Viking roots than any of their neighbours. Their ancestors can be traced back to the first seafaring explorers who set out from southern Norway in the 9th century and claimed Orkney, the Shetland Islands, Iceland and Greenland – and maybe even America. Today most people earn a living from farm-ing or fishing, and the laid-back atmosphere of the cosy villages is more reminiscent of the Scottish islands than Iceland. The landscape, too, resembles the Scottish highlands, with Munro-like peaks and towering grass-topped sea cliffs, mobbed by nesting sea birds.

These marvellous islands can easily be tackled on a three-day layover between flights or ferries (see the boxed text, above). Boats dock in central Tórshavn, the capital, while planes land on Vágar, an island further west. A brilliant network of paved roads, tunnels and car ferries link the various islands, providing access to remote fjord-side villages and humbling ocean landscapes.

For more information on the Faeroes, contact the **Faroe Islands Tourist Board** (☎ 298 30 61 00; www.visitfaroeislands.com; Bryggjubakka 12, FO-110 Tórshavn, Faroe Islands), or see www.faroeislands.com.

Directory

CONTENTS

ACCOMMODATION

There's no shortage of accommodation in Iceland; there's a huge range, from luxury hotels to mountain huts, campsites, hostels, homely farmhouses, guest houses and summer hotels set in rural schools. It must be said, however, that accommodation is often of a lower standard than you might expect from a developed European destination. Although rooms are generally spotless, they are usually small, with thin walls and limited facilities – this can come as a shock to those who are accustomed to a certain amount of space and comfort on their travels.

Iceland's best-kept secret is the sleeping-bag option (designated 'sb' in this guide) offered by numerous guest houses and some

WARNING: POSTCRASH PRICES

Iceland's horrific economic problems (see p34) mean that the króna is extremely vulnerable and prices are unstable. Many Icelandic companies have begun listing prices in euros only, as it's a more stable currency. Where this is the case, we have followed suit rather than attempting to convert using ever-fluctuating exchange rates.

Throughout this book, we have given prices being used in summer 2009, but the tremendous financial uncertainty means that nothing is set in stone. Prices may look very different by the time you get here.

hotels. For a fraction of the normal cost you'll get a bed without a duvet or blanket; just bring your own sleeping bag and you can keep costs down substantially.

In this guide accommodation reviews are listed according to price: for a double room with linen and bathroom, budget accommodation costs up to Ikr12,000, mid-range Ikr12,000 to Ikr22,000 and top-end more than Ikr22,000. Many hotels and guest houses close during the winter; where this is the case, opening times are shown in the review. If no opening times are shown, accommodation is open all year. We've given summer prices throughout; in winter most guest houses and hotels offer discounts of between 20% and 45%. Between June and mid-August it's a good idea to book all accommodation in advance.

Camping

Tjaldsvæði (organised campsites) are found in almost every town, at farmhouses in rural areas and along major hiking trails. The best sites have washing machines, cooking facilities and hot showers, but others just have a cold-water tap and a toilet block.

Wild camping is possible in some areas but in practice it is often discouraged. In national parks and nature reserves you must camp in marked campsites, and you need to get permission before camping on fenced land in all other places. Icelandic weather is notoriously fickle, though, and if you intend to camp it's wise to invest in a good-quality tent.

When camping the usual rules apply: leave sites as you find them, use biodegradable soaps, carry out your rubbish and bury your toilet waste away from water sources. Campfires are not allowed, so bring a stove. Butane cartridges and petroleum fuels are available in petrol stations and hardware shops. Blue Campingaz cartridges are not readily found in Iceland; the grey Coleman cartridges are more common. You can often pick up partly used canisters left behind by departing campers at the campsites in Reykjavík and Keflavík.

Camping with a tent or campervan/ caravan usually costs between Ikr800 and Ikr1000 per person, with most campsites open from June to August or early September only. The free directory *Tjaldsvæði Íslands* (available from tourist offices) lists many of Iceland's campsites.

Emergency Huts

ICE-SAR (Icelandic Association for Search & Rescue; ☎ 570 5900; www.icesar.is) and **Félag Íslenskra Bifeiðaeigenda** (Icelandic Automobile Association; ☎ 562 9999; www.fib.is) maintain bright-orange survival huts on high mountain passes and along remote coastlines. The huts are stocked with food, fuel and blankets and should only be used in an emergency. Users should sign the hut guest book and state which items they have used, so they may be replaced for future users.

BOOK YOUR STAY ONLINE

For more accommodation reviews and recommendations by Lonely Planet authors, check out the online booking service at www.lonelyplanet.com/hotels. You'll find the true, insider low-down on the best places to stay. Reviews are thorough and independent. Best of all, you can book online.

Farmhouses

Throughout Iceland accommodation is available in rural farmhouses, many of which offer camping and sleeping-bag spaces as well as made-up beds and summer cabins. Most either provide meals or have a guest kitchen, some have outdoor hot pots (hot tubs) or a geothermal swimming pool, and many provide horse riding. Roadside signs signal which farmhouses provide accommodation and what facilities they offer. Rates are similar to guest houses in towns, with sleeping-bag accommodation costing Ikr2500 to Ikr3500 and made-up beds from Ikr4000 to Ikr7000 per person. Breakfast costs about Ikr1000, while an evening meal (usually served at a set time) costs Ikr2200 to Ikr3500.

Approximately 140 farmhouses are members of **Ferðaþjónusta Bænda** (Icelandic Farm Holidays; Map pp72-3; ☎ 570 2700; www.farmholidays.is; Síðumúli 2, IS-108 Reykjavík), which publishes an annual members' guide. Twenty-five are wheelchair accessible – see the website for details.

DIRECTORY

PRACTICALITIES

- Iceland uses the metric system – distances are in kilometres and weights are in kilograms.
- The electrical current is 220V AC 50Hz (cycles); North American electrical devices will require voltage converters.
- Most electrical plugs are of the European two-pin type.
- Iceland uses the PAL video system, like Britain and Germany, and falls within DVD zone 2.
- The daily paper *Morgunblaðið* is in Icelandic but features cinema listings in English.
- For tourist-oriented articles about Iceland in English, check out the glossy quarterly magazine **Iceland Review** (www.icelandreview.is).
- Iceland's two TV stations show Icelandic programs during the day and American imports in the evening.
- Radio station RUV (Icelandic National Broadcasting Service; FM 92.4/93.5) has news in English at 7.30am Monday to Friday from June to August.
- Most hostels and hotels have satellite TV featuring other European channels.

DIRECTORY

Guest Houses

The Icelandic term *gistiheimilið* (guest house) covers a wide variety of properties from family homes renting out a few rooms to custom-built minihotels. These places can vary enormously in character from stylish, contemporary options to those overwhelmed by net curtains and chintzy decor. Most include a buffet-style breakfast in the price (expect to pay about Ikr1000 if not), and some also offer sleeping-bag accommodation and have guest kitchens.

As a general guide, sleeping-bag accommodation costs Ikr2500 to Ikr4000 (not including breakfast), double rooms from Ikr10,000 to Ikr14,000 and self-contained units from Ikr11,000 per night.

Some Icelandic guest houses open only from June to August; others take in students in the winter months – especially in Reykjavík.

Hostels

Iceland has 33 excellent youth hostels, administered by the **Bandalag Íslenskra Farfugla** (Icelandic Youth Hostel Association; Map pp72-3; ☎ 553 8110; www.hostel.is; Sundlaugavegur 34, IS-105 Reykjavík). All hostels offer hot showers, cooking facilities, luggage storage and sleeping-bag accommodation, and most offer private rooms. If you don't have a sleeping bag, you can hire sheets and blankets for Ikr800 per stay. Many hostels close for the winter, so check reviews in this book or online for information on opening times.

Members of **Hostelling International** (HI; www.hihostels.com) pay Ikr1900 to Ikr2200 for a dorm bed; nonmembers pay roughly Ikr500 extra per night. Single/double rooms cost roughly Ikr3800/6000. Children aged five to 12 years pay half price. To become a member you should apply in your home country before travelling.

Hotels

Every major city and town has at least one business-style hotel, usually featuring comfortable but innocuous rooms with private bathroom, phone, TV and sometimes minibar. The hotels also have decent restaurants serving international/Icelandic food. Summer prices for singles/doubles start at around Ikr13,000/18,000 and include a buffet breakfast. Prices drop substantially outside peak season (June to mid-September), and many hotels offer cheaper rates if you make your booking on the internet.

Two of the largest local chains are **Fosshótels** (☎ 562 4000; www.fosshotel.is), and **Icelandair Hotels** (☎ 444 4000; www.icehotels.is), which also runs the Edda chain (see below).

SUMMER HOTELS

Once the school holidays begin, many schools, colleges and conference centres become summer hotels offering simple accommodation. Summer hotels open from early June to late August and are run by local town or village councils or by **Edda Hótels** (☎ 444 4000; www.hoteledda.is). All 13 Edda hotels have their own restaurant, and many have geothermal swimming pools. The four Edda PLUS hotels are three-star places where all rooms have private bathroom, TV and phone. Expect to pay Ikr2500 to Ikr3200 for sleeping-bag accommodation, Ikr8000/10,000 for a single/double with washbasin and Ikr14,600/18,300 for a single/double at an Edda PLUS.

Mountain Huts

Private walking clubs and touring organisations maintain *sæluhús* (mountain huts) on many of the popular hiking tracks around the country. The huts are open to anyone and offer sleeping-bag space in basic dormitories. Some also have cooking facilities, campsites and a warden. The huts at Landmannalaugar and Þórsmörk are accessible by 4WD, and you can get to the huts in Hornstrandir by boat, but most are only accessible on foot. Even so, it's a really good idea to book with the relevant organisation as places fill up quickly.

The main organisation providing mountain huts is **Ferðafélag Íslands** (Icelandic Touring Association; Map pp72-3; ☎ 568 2533; www.fi.is; Mörkin 6, IS-108 Reykjavík), which owns 38 huts around Iceland, some maintained by local walking clubs. The best huts have showers, kitchens, wardens and potable water; they cost Ikr3300 for nonmembers. Simpler huts cost nonmembers Ikr2000 and usually just have bed space, toilet and a basic cooking area. Camping is available at some huts for around Ikr900 per person. GPS coordinates for huts are included in the destination chapters.

The following also provide huts:

Ferðafélag Akureyrar (Touring Club of Akureyri; Map p214; ☎ 462 2720; www.ffa.is; Strandgata 23) Runs huts and most campsites in the northeast, including the Askja Way.

Hostelling International Iceland (☎ 553 8110; www.hostel.is) At Húsadalur in Þórsmörk.

Útivist (Map pp72-3; ☎ 562 1000; www.utivist.is; Laugavegur 178, IS-105 Reykjavík) Runs huts at Básar and Fimmvörðuháls Pass in Þórsmörk.

ACTIVITIES

Iceland's dramatic scenery, vast tracts of wilderness and otherworldly atmosphere make it a superb playground for outdoor enthusiasts. The rugged highlands and scenic coastline offer some fantastic opportunities for hiking (p65) – Þórsmörk, Landmannalaugar and Hornstrandir are very popular destinations – as well as horse riding (p65). Sea kayaking (p67) through dramatic fjordland scenery is a favourite in many towns along the coast, and sea angling (p66) is gaining a following. With Iceland's light traffic, cycling (p64) is a fantastic way to travel around. The majestic ice caps offer stunning scenery for ice trekking (p66), snowmobiling (p68) and ice climbing (p66), while the meltwater forms mighty rivers that provide plenty of white-water rafting (p69) opportunities. During the winter months skiing (downhill and cross-country; p67) and snowboarding (p68) are big activities, and a range of newer activities such as diving (p64), potholing and snowkiting (p68) are beginning to take off. For something more leisurely, almost every town has a geothermal swimming pool and a golf course, and many coastal areas offer brilliant opportunities for birdwatching (p64) and whale watching (p69).

BUSINESS HOURS

Reviews throughout this book do not mention opening hours unless they differ from the standard opening hours below:

Banks 9am to 4pm Monday to Friday.
Cafe-bars 10am to 1am Sunday to Thursday and 10am to between 3am and 6am Friday and Saturday.
Cafes 10am to 6pm.
Offices 9am to 5pm Monday to Friday.
Off-licences (liquor stores) Variable; many outside Reykjavík only open for a couple of hours per day.
Petrol stations 8am to 11pm.
Post offices 8.30am or 9am to 4.30pm or 5pm Monday to Friday.
Restaurants 11.30am to 2.30pm and 6pm to 10pm.
Shops 10am to 6pm Monday to Friday, 10am to noon or 4pm Saturday.
Supermarkets 10am to 11pm.

CHILDREN

Iceland is a fairly easy place to travel with children, and although there aren't many activi-

ties especially aimed at younger travellers, the dramatic scenery, abundance of swimming pools and the friendliness of the locals help to keep things running smoothly.

Practicalities

Children are warmly welcomed in Iceland and a range of discounts on transport and admission fees reflects this. On internal flights and tours with Air Iceland, children aged from two to 11 years pay half-fare and infants under two fly free. Most bus and tour companies offer a 50% reduction for children aged from four to 11 years; Reykjavík Excursion tours are free for under 11s (see p86). Admission to museums and swimming pools varies from 50% off to free.

The changeable weather and frequent cold and rain may put you off camping as a family, but children aged from two to 12 are usually charged half-price for farmhouse and some other accommodation. Under twos can usually stay for free. The larger hotels often have cots and children's menus available, but you'll rarely find these in guest houses. Many restaurants in Reykjavík and larger towns offer discounted children's meals, and most have high chairs.

Toilets at museums and other public institutions usually have dedicated nappy-changing facilities; elsewhere, you'll have to improvise. Attitudes to breast feeding in public are generally relaxed. Formula, nappies and other essentials are available everywhere, but it's hard to find child-care facilities. Best bet is to ask at the tourist office.

All the international car-hire companies offer child seats for an extra cost (these should be booked in advance), but you may want to bring your own to be safe. All cars in Iceland have front and rear seatbelts, including taxis. Buses sometimes have belts, but these are not compatible with child seats.

Sights & Activities

Once you've decided on a family holiday in Iceland one of the biggest considerations will be what to see and where to go, as distances can be long between attractions. It may be a good idea to limit yourself to one part of the island to avoid boredom-induced tantrums and frequent bouts of carsickness.

Reykjavík is the most child-friendly place in Iceland simply because it has the greatest variety of attractions and facilities. The family fun park and zoo (p84) are popular attractions, and local children can be seen feeding the birds on Tjörnin (p83), the city's lake, every day. The most suitable museums for older children are the open-air Árbæjarsafn (p77) and the dramatic Saga Museum (p76) – the latter's realistic-looking figures may scare younger kids.

Almost every town in Iceland has a geothermal swimming pool, often with a children's play pool, water slides, and hot pots where adults can relax while the children play.

Another activity ideal for children is whale watching – the best spot in the country to see them is at Húsavík (p240), and there are regular summer trips from Reykjavík's harbour (p84).

The short, mild-mannered Icelandic horses appear to have been specifically bred with children in mind, and horse farms all over the country offer riding by the hour from Ikr4000 – see p65.

Children will also enjoy some of the more lively geothermal areas, such as Geysir (p126), where the Strokkur geyser erupts at six-minute intervals, and Mývatn (p228), where the abundance of odd features, lava fields and steaming vents can provide several days of entertainment for families. If you're driving long distances, the waterfalls just off Rte 1 in southwest Iceland are worthwhile detours to keep children amused, and the glaciers Sólheimajökull (p146) and Vatnajökull (p289) are also right next to the main road. Adults and children alike find the icebergs at Jökulsárlón (p299) fascinating.

CLIMATE CHARTS

Icelandic weather is unpredictable at the best of times, with bright, sunny days reverting to cold, wet and miserable conditions within a matter of hours. Rainfall in Iceland is fairly consistent throughout the year, but, because temperatures plummet in winter, it often falls as snow from September to May. The south and west coasts are usually the wettest parts of the country, with the north and east enjoying generally drier but colder conditions in winter. Areas with geothermal activity are often noticeably warmer than surrounding areas. Temperatures drop considerably as you go up into the mountains, particularly around the ice caps. For more information on weather in Iceland and the best time to travel, see p17.

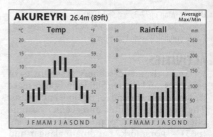

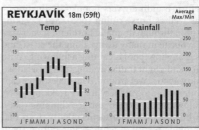

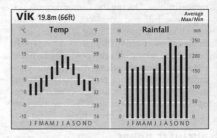

CUSTOMS REGULATIONS

Iceland has quite strict import restrictions. Duty-free allowances for travellers over 20 years of age are 1L of spirits (21% to 79% alcohol) and 1L of wine (less than 21%); or 1L of spirits and 6L of foreign beer; or 1.5L of wine and 6L of beer; or 3L of wine. People over 18 can bring in 200 cigarettes or 250g of other tobacco products. You can also import up to 3kg of food (except raw eggs, meat or dairy products), provided it doesn't cost more than Ikr18,500. This may help self-caterers to reduce costs.

To prevent contamination, recreational fishing and horse-riding clothes require a veterinarian's certificate stating that they have been disinfected. Otherwise officials will charge you for disinfecting clothing when you arrive. It is illegal to bring used horse-riding equipment (saddles, bridles etc) into the country.

Many people bring their cars on the ferry from Europe – special duty-waiver conditions apply for students and visitors staying up to one year. Vehicles cannot be sold without payment of duty.

Permits must be obtained in advance to import firearms, drugs, plants, radio transmitters and telephones (one personal GSM mobile phone per person is permitted). Contact the **Directorate of Customs** (☎ 560 0300; www.tollur.is; Tryggvagötu 19, IS-101 Reykjavík). Animals can only be brought in with the permission of the authorities and must be quarantined. Plants, animals (including bird eggs and eggshells) and 'natural objects' (particularly stalagmites and stalactites) may not be taken out of Iceland.

For a full list of customs regulations, see www.tollur.is.

DANGERS & ANNOYANCES

Iceland has a very low crime rate and in general any risks you'll face while travelling here are related to the unpredictable weather and the geological conditions.

Whether travelling in summer or winter, visitors need to be prepared for inclement conditions. The weather can change without warning, and it's essential for hikers to get a reliable forecast before setting off – call ☎ 902 0600, extension 44, or visit www.vedur.is/english for a daily forecast in English. Extreme cold can be dangerous when walking around glaciers and throughout the country in winter, so proper clothing is essential. Those driving in winter should carry food, water and blankets in their car. Emergency huts are provided in places where travellers run the risk of getting caught in severe weather, and car-hire companies can provide snow tyres or chains in winter.

When hiking, river crossings can be dangerous, with glacial run-off transforming trickling streams into raging torrents on warm summer days. See p68 for more information on how to cross rivers safely. High winds can create vicious sandstorms in areas where there is loose volcanic sand. It's also worth noting that hiking paths in coastal areas are often only accessible at low tide, so be sure to seek local advice and obtain the relevant tide tables (known as *sjávarfallatöflur*). Consult the hydrographic department of the **Icelandic Coast Guard** (☎ 545 2000; www.lhg.is; Skógarhlíð 14, IS-105 Reykjavík) for further information.

When visiting geothermal areas, stick to boardwalks or obviously solid ground, avoiding thin crusts of lighter-coloured soil around steaming fissures and mudpots. You also need to be careful of the water in hot springs and mudpots – it often emerges out of the ground at 100°C. Always get local advice before hiking around live volcanoes. In glacial areas beware of dangerous quicksand at the end of glaciers, and never venture out onto the ice without crampons and ice axes (even then, watch out for crevasses).

One risk most travellers must face is dangerous driving on Iceland's roads. Locals universally ignore the speed limit, cut corners and weave out of their lanes. For more information on driving in Iceland, see p339.

DISCOUNT CARDS

Students and the elderly qualify for discounts on internal flights, some bus fares, tours and museum entry fees, but you'll need to show proof of student status or age.

Seniors (67 years and older) qualify for significant discounts on internal flights and ferry fares – any proof of age should suffice.

TAX-FREE SHOPPING

Any purchases you make in Iceland over Ikr4000 (at a single point of sale) may be eligible for a 15% VAT refund. Shops offering VAT refunds display a special 'tax-free shopping' sign in the window. You'll need to ask for a form in the shop, fill it in, then present it at Keflavík airport; on the Smyril Line ferry two hours before departure; at the information desks in the Kringlan and Smáralind shopping centres, Reykjavík; at the main Reykjavík tourist office; or (again in Reykjavík) at the Forex foreign-exchange desk inside the Icelandic Travel Market private tourist office on Bankastræti before you leave in order to collect your rebate. Goods must be taken out of the country within three months of purchase. If any individual rebate exceeds Ikr5000, you will also need to show your goods to Customs before leaving the country. See www.is.eurorefund.com for details of the scheme.

The **International Student Identity Card** (ISIC; www.isic.org) is the most widely recognised form of student identification. Cardholders who are under 26 get substantial discounts (up to 50%) on internal flights, ferries, museum admissions and some bus fares. Some restaurants and bars also offer student discounts. All young people under 26 with proof of age can get special stand-by fares on internal flights.

EMBASSIES & CONSULATES

Up-to-date details of embassies and consulates within Iceland and overseas can be found (in English) on the Icelandic Ministry of Foreign Affairs website www.mfa.is.

Although many countries have some kind of representation in Iceland, this is often merely just a trade representative working for an Icelandic company. A handful of countries do have formal embassies in Reykjavík:

Canada (Map pp78-9; ☎ 575 6500; rkjvk@international.gc.ca; Túngata 14)

Denmark (Map pp78-9; ☎ 575 0300; rekamb@um.dk; Hverfisgata 29)

Finland (Map pp72-3; ☎ 510 0100; www.finland.is; Túngata 30)

France (Map pp78-9; ☎ 575 9600; www.ambafrance.is; Túngata 22)

Germany (Map pp78-9; ☎ 530 1100; www.reykjavik.diplo.de; Laufásvegur 31)

Japan (Map pp72-3; ☎ 510 8600; japan@itn.is; 6th fl, Laugavegur 182)

Norway (Map pp78-9; ☎ 520 0700; www.noregur.is; Fjólugata 17)

Sweden (Map pp72-3; ☎ 520 1230; www.sweden abroad.com/reykjavik; Lágmúli 7)

UK (Map pp78-9; ☎ 550 5100; http://ukiniceland.fco.gov.uk/en; Laufásvegur 31)

USA (Map pp78-9; ☎ 562 9100; www.usa.is; Laufásvegur 21)

FOOD

Despite the country's economic troubles, and the consequently good exchange rates for foreign visitors, eating is still one of the main expenses of a trip to Iceland. For the purposes of this book, restaurants with average main courses costing under Ikr1500 are classified as budget; those from Ikr1500 to Ikr3500 are midrange and those with main courses above Ikr3500 are top end.

You can keep your costs down by cooking for yourself. Most places offering hostel beds or sleeping-bag spaces have guest kitchens, and supermarket prices are reasonable. If you're camping, it's worth noting that most supermarkets also have a microwave where you can heat up purchases, and some also serve free coffee. The next cheapest option is to eat at the fast-food grills and snack bars found in most villages (usually at the petrol station), where you can pick up a burger, chips and a drink for about Ikr700 – but bear in mind the food is unhealthy and quickly becomes tedious. At formal restaurants, expect to pay Ikr1800 to Ikr4000 for main courses. Pizza restaurants are a cheaper bet, with main courses costing around Ikr1500. Otherwise, opt for the good-value lunch buffets and eat a smaller meal in the evening. Even in the best restaurants, tipping the staff is not expected; service is always included in the bill.

You'll find more information on food and special dishes in the Food & Drink chapter, p49.

For cafe and restaurant standard opening hours, see p325.

GAY & LESBIAN TRAVELLERS

Icelanders have a fairly open attitude towards homosexuality, though the gay scene is quite low-key, even in Reykjavík (see p87). Aggression against gays and lesbians is rare. The main gay and lesbian organisation is **Samtökin '78** (Map pp78-9; ☎ 552 7878; www.samtokin78.is; 4th fl, Laugavegur 3, IS-101 Reykjavík; ☺ office 1-5pm Mon-Fri), which doubles as an informal gay community centre with a drop-in cafe (open from 8pm to 11pm Mondays and Thursdays year-round, sometimes also from 1pm to 5pm Saturdays in late July and in August). For a useful source of information on news, events and entertainment venues, see www.gayice.is.

HOLIDAYS

Icelandic public holidays are usually an excuse for a family gathering or, when they occur at weekends, a reason to rush to the countryside and go camping. If you're planning to travel during holiday periods, particularly the August holiday, you should book camping areas, mountain huts and transport well in advance, particularly in popular areas such as Þórsmörk. Icelandic hotels and guest houses generally shut down from Christmas Eve to New Year's Day.

Public Holidays

National public holidays in Iceland:
New Year's Day 1 January
Easter March or April (Maundy Thursday and Good Friday to Easter Monday; changes annually)
First Day of Summer First Thursday after 18 April
Labour Day 1 May
Ascension Day May or June (changes annually)
Whit Sunday and Whit Monday May or June (changes annually)
Independence Day 17 June
Shop & Office Workers' Holiday First Monday in August
Christmas 24 to 26 December
New Year's Eve 31 December

School Holidays

The main school summer holiday runs from June to August, which is when most of the Edda and summer hotels open up. There are big student parties when school breaks up and when school restarts, so popular camping areas may be packed out. Þórsmörk is the venue for a huge student bash in July, which is either a reason to come or a reason to stay away. The winter school holiday is a two- to three-week break over the Christmas period (December to January).

INSURANCE

Although Iceland is a very safe place to travel, theft does occasionally happen, and of course illness and accidents are always a possibility. A travel-insurance policy to cover theft, loss and medical problems is strongly recommended. Always check the small print to see if the policy covers any potentially dangerous sporting activities, such as hiking, rock climbing, horse riding, skiing or snowmobiling. For more information on the health aspects of travel in Iceland, including insurance, see p344. For information on motor insurance, see p341.

INTERNET ACCESS

You'll find public internet access available in most Icelandic libraries, even in small towns. These are by far the best and cheapest places to check your mail, with most offering internet access for about Ikr200 to Ikr400 per hour – a fraction of the cost at hotels. Reykjavík has a private internet cafe, and most top-end hotels, youth hostels and tourist offices have internet terminals with fast and reliable connections.

Wi-fi access is common in Iceland: with a wireless-enabled laptop, you can pick up a signal in most cafes, bars and hotels in central

---

ARE YOU OLD ENOUGH?

Iceland has legal minimum ages for many activities:
Voting 18 years.
Driving 18 years (20 to 25 years for car hire, depending on the company).
Drinking 20 years.

Reykjavík, and in many farm properties, guest houses and hotels across the rest of the country. We have used the symbol '🛜' throughout the chapters in this book to show where wi-fi is available to guests/customers.

For information on useful websites about Iceland, see p20.

LEGAL MATTERS

Icelandic police are generally low-key and there's very little reason for you to end up in their hands. It's worth knowing, however, that drink driving laws are very strict – one drink can put you over the legal limit of 0.05% blood-alcohol content. The penalty is loss of your licence plus a large fine. If you are involved in any other traffic offences – speeding, driving without due care and attention etc – you may be asked to go to the station to pay the fines immediately.

Drunk and disorderly behaviour may land you in a police cell for a night, but you will usually be released the following morning. Take note, however, that the penalties for possession, use or trafficking of illegal drugs are strict; these activities usually incur long prison sentences and heavy fines.

If you are arrested by the police, they can notify your embassy or consulate, or anyone else you specify, on your behalf. Lawyers are not provided by the state in Iceland, but the police can arrange a lawyer for you at your own expense. You can generally be held for 24 hours without being charged. You can only be searched if you give consent, unless they have reason to be suspicious.

MAPS

In general, maps of Iceland are not fantastic – many are based on prewar land surveys. Most Icelandic maps are now published by Ferðakort. The largest selection of road maps and hiking maps can be found in Reykjavík's bookshops, or from the specialist Ferðakort map department at **Iðnú bookshop** (Map pp72-3;

☎ 562 3376; www.ferdakort.is; Brautarholt 8; ☽ 10am-5pm Mon-Thu, to 4pm Fri). UK readers could contact **Dick Phillips** (☎ 01434 381 440; Whitehall House, Nenthead, Alston, Cumbria, CA9 3PS), which stocks more than 200 Icelandic maps.

The best map for general driving around Iceland, the 1:500,000 *Ferðakort Touring Map* (Ikr1545) includes all the larger villages and roads, and many small farms and B&Bs. The more in-depth 1:200,000 *Road Atlas* (Ikr3530) has full mapping plus details of accommodation, museums, swimming pools and golf courses.

More detailed maps include the 1:250,000 maps of Westfjords and north Iceland, west and south Iceland, and northeast and east Iceland (Ikr1985 each); and 1:100,000 hikers' maps for Hornstrandir, Skaftafell, Húsavík/Lake Mývatn, and Þórsmörk/Landmannalaugar (Ikr1230 each).

Serious walkers should get their hands on sheet maps from the 1;50,000 American series, based on surveys completed by the US military, which cover much of the country in detail. Sheets cost Ikr1115 each.

The tourist offices of the various regions produce useful maps showing sites of tourist interest and they stock the free tourist booklet *Around Iceland,* which has bags of information and town plans.

MONEY

Iceland is an almost cashless society where the credit card is king. Icelanders use plastic for even small purchases. As long as you're carrying a valid card, you'll have little need for travellers cheques and will need to withdraw only a limited amount of cash from ATMs.

For information on costs, see p18.

ATMs

Almost every town in Iceland has a bank with an ATM, where you can withdraw cash using MasterCard, Visa, Maestro or Cirrus cards. Íslandsbanki ATMs additionally allow withdrawals using a Diners Club card. You'll also find ATMs at larger petrol stations and in shopping centres.

Cash

The Icelandic unit of currency is the króna (Ikr). Coins come in denominations of one, five, 10, 50 and 100 krónur. Notes come in 500-, 1000-, 2000- and 5000-króna denomi-

nations. In July 2009 the Icelandic parliament applied for EU membership. Iceland is expected to join the EU in 2011, at which time the currency will probably change over to the euro.

For exchange rates, see the inside front cover, or online at www.xe.com.

Credit & Debit Cards

Icelanders use credit and debit cards for nearly all purchases, and major cards such as Visa, MasterCard, Maestro and Cirrus – and to a lesser extent Amex, Diners and JCB – are accepted in most shops, restaurants and hotels. You can also pay for the Flybus from the international airport to Reykjavík using plastic – handy if you've just arrived in the country. If you intend to stay in rural farmhouse accommodation or visit isolated villages, however, it's a good idea to carry enough cash to tide you over.

Moneychangers

The Icelandic love of plastic makes changing foreign currency almost unnecessary. Nevertheless, if you prefer more traditional methods of carrying cash then foreign-denomination travellers cheques and banknotes can be exchanged for Icelandic currency at all major banks. Most banks charge a small commission fee for the transaction, but Landsbanki Íslands offers the service free of charge. Out of normal banking hours, you will have to rely on the poor rates and high charges of commercial exchange offices, or hope that your hotel or guest house can help you out.

Tipping

As service and VAT are always included in prices, tipping isn't required in Iceland.

Travellers Cheques

Travellers cheques in major currencies such as euros, US dollars, UK pounds and Danish krone are accepted by all banks and by the commission-hungry private exchange offices.

POST

The **Icelandic postal service** (Pósturinn; www.postur.is) is reliable and efficient, and rates are comparable to those in other Western European countries. An airmail letter or postcard to Europe costs economy/priority Ikr110/120;

to places outside Europe it costs Ikr120/160. You'll find a full list of postal rates for letters and parcels online.

The best place to receive poste restante is the central post office in Reykjavík – tell potential correspondents to capitalise your surname and address mail to Poste Restante, Central Post Office, Pósthússtræti 5, IS-101 Reykjavík, Iceland. The service costs Ikr580 per month.

SHOPPING

Icelandic souvenir shops are filled with generic mugs, T-shirts and key rings plastered with images of trolls or the Icelandic flag, but you'll also find more upmarket gifts. Woollen hats, gloves and sweaters hand-knitted to traditional designs are popular, along with warm, hard-wearing outdoorwear from companies such as 66° North. CDs of Icelandic music are a good buy. More unusual gifts include silver jewellery inspired by Icelandic runes, dried fish, chocolate-coated liquorice, and high-quality ceramics (sold in the boutiques and galleries on Skólavörðustígur in Reykjavík).

If you're making any purchases over Ikr4000 it's worth claiming back the permitted 15% VAT refund. For more details of the scheme, see p327.

For standard opening hours for shops, see p325.

SMOKING

Smoking has been illegal in enclosed public spaces since June 2007, including in cafes, bars, clubs, restaurants and on public transport. You may still come across some hotel rooms where smoking is permitted, but it's not common.

SOLO TRAVELLERS

There's no difficulty in travelling alone in Iceland, but if you fancy hooking up with other travellers, the Reykjavík youth hostels are an excellent place to start. The more backpackery Laugavegur branch in particular, with its large communal areas, is the starting point for many a shared trip and new friendship.

Another place you may be able to find travel companions is Lonely Planet's **Thorn Tree** (www.lonelyplanet.com/thorntree) – post a message on the forum's Scandinavia branch and see if any other travellers are going to be in Iceland when you are. Failing all that, you may

---

> **EMERGENCY NUMBERS**
>
> For police, ambulance and fire services in Iceland, dial ☎ 112.

want to join an organised adventure tour – see p342 for listings of tour companies operating in Iceland.

TELEPHONE & FAX

Iceland Telecom **Síminn** (www.siminn.is) provides most phone, mobile phone and internet services in the country, with Vodafone covering the remainder. Public payphones can usually be found at post offices and public places such as bus or petrol stations, and most now accept credit cards as well as coins. Public fax services are provided at most post offices.

The telephone directory and *Yellow Pages* are in Icelandic, but directory-enquiries operators usually speak English. Telephone directories are alphabetised by first name, so Guðrun Halldórsdóttir would be listed before Jón Einarsson. There's an online version of the phone book at www.simaskra.is.

Service numbers:

Directory enquiries (local) ☎ 118
Directory enquiries (international) & collect calls
☎ 1811
Operator assistance ☎ 115

Mobile Phones

Iceland has the highest per capita mobile phone (cell phone) use in the world and uses the GSM network in populated areas. The NMT network covers the interior and other remote regions; to have coverage in these areas you'll need to hire an NMT phone locally. Visitors with GSM or multiband phones will be able to make roaming calls, providing the service has been activated   contact your local phone company for more information. (Mobile phones from North America will probably not work, as they tend to use a different standard.)

If you're going to be in Iceland for a while it may be worth buying a local prepaid SIM card (Ikr2500 including Ikr2000 of free call credit) that will allow you to make calls at local rates. You can buy prepaid cards and further top-ups at grocery stores, newsagents and petrol stations. You'll need an unlocked phone for this to work.

DIRECTORY

Phone Codes

There are no area codes in Iceland, so you can dial the seven-digit number from anywhere in the country for the same price. For international calling, first dial the international access code ☎ 00, then the country code (listed in telephone directories), the area or city code, and the telephone number. International call rates are the same around the clock. To phone Iceland from abroad, dial the local international access code, the country code (☎ 354) and the seven-digit phone number. Toll-free numbers in Iceland begin with ☎ 800, and most seven-digit mobile phone numbers start with ☎ 8 (some start with ☎ 6).

Phonecards

The smallest denomination phonecard (for use in public telephone boxes) costs Ikr500, and can be bought from grocery shops, newsagents, post offices and Síminn telephone offices. Low-cost international phonecards are also available in many shops and youth hostels.

TIME

Iceland's time zone is the same as GMT/UTC (London), but there is no daylight-saving time. So from late October to late March Iceland is on the same time as London, five hours ahead of New York and 11 hours behind Sydney. In the northern hemisphere summer, it's one hour behind London, four hours ahead of New York and 10 hours behind Sydney.

TOURIST INFORMATION

Icelandic tourist-information offices are helpful, friendly and well informed and can be invaluable in assisting you to find accommodation, book tours or see the best an area has to offer. Employees usually speak several European languages including English.

Most tourist offices provide the useful booklets *Around Iceland* (a general tourist guide), *Iceland on Your Own* (a public-transport guide) and *Áning* (a guide to accommodation). All are free and published annually. If you plan to stay in farmhouse B&Bs, pick up a copy of *The Ideal Holiday*, a guide to farmhouse accommodation.

The **Icelandic Tourist Board** (Map pp78-9; ☎ 535 5500; www.icetourist.is; Geirsgata 9, IS-101 Reykjavík) is the umbrella organisation in charge of tourism.

There are tourist offices at **Keflavík International Airport** (☎ 425 0330; www.reykjanes.is)

and in Reykjavík at the **Main Tourist Office** (Upplýsingamiðstöð Ferðamanna; Map pp78-9; ☎ 590 1550; www.visitreykjavik.is; Aðalstræti 2). Reykjavík also has several private tourist-information offices, and there are council-run information offices in towns and villages around the country.

The main regional tourist information offices:

East & southeast Iceland (Map p264; ☎ 471 2320; www.east.is; Kaupvangur 10, IS-700 Egilsstaðir)
North Iceland (Map p214; ☎ 553 5999; www.northiceland.is, www.visitakureyri.is; Hafnarstræti 82, IS-600 Akureyri)
South & southwest Iceland (Map p131; ☎ 483 4601; www.southiceland.is, www.south.is; Sunnumörk 2-4, IS-810 Hveragerði)
West Iceland (☎ 437 2214; www.west.is; Sólbakki 2, IS-310 Borgarnes)
Westfjords (Map p186; ☎ 450 8060; www.westfjords.is; Aðalstræti 7, IS-400 Ísafjörður)

Icelandic Tourist Board offices overseas:
Denmark (☎ 32 833 741; www.visiticeland.com; Islands Turistråd Skandinavia, Strandgade 89, 1401 København K)
Germany (☎ 30 5050 4200; www.icetourist.de; Isländisches Fremdenverkehrsamt, Rauchstrasse 1, D-10787 Berlin)
USA (☎ 212-885 9700; www.goiceland.org; 655 Third Ave, New York, NY 10017)

If you arrive in a town after the tourist office has closed, the local petrol station is often a good bet for information on the area.

TRAVELLERS WITH DISABILITIES

Iceland is trickier than many places in northern Europe when it comes to access for travellers with disabilities. International and internal flights can accommodate most disabilities, but some flights use small aircraft that may be unsuitable for the mobility impaired. Air Iceland and Smyril Line offer discounts for travellers with disabilities on flights and ferries. The car ferries *Baldur* and *Herjólfur* have facilities for wheelchairs.

Most of the newer buses on Reykjavík's city bus routes have a 'kneeling' function so that wheelchairs can be lifted onto the bus; elsewhere, however, public buses generally have awkward steps.

In Reykjavík **Hertz** (☎ 505 0600; www.hertz.is; Flugvallarvegur) has a wheelchair-accessible minivan for hire. The company **All Iceland Tours** (www.allicelandtours.is; jmg16@mac.com) offers tailor-made trips around the country in adapted super-Jeeps.

The website www.whenwetravel.com lists which hotels in Iceland are wheelchair accessible. Once you've clicked on the destination, then on hotels, a Wheelchair Accessible option appears in the menu.

There are reduced admission fees for most museums, galleries and tourist attractions.

For more details on facilities for people with disabilities, contact the tourist office in Reykjavík or get in touch with **Sjálfsbjörg** (☎ 550 0360; www.sjalfsbjorg.is; Hátún 12, IS-105 Reykjavík).

The UK-based website **Door-to-Door** (www.dptac.gov.uk/door-to-door) is a good starting point when planning overseas travel, and has a helpful section on air travel and getting to and from UK airports. In the USA you'll get similar, valuable information from the **Society for Accessible Travel & Hospitality** (☎ 212-447 7284; www.sath.org; 347 5th Ave, Suite 605, New York, NY 10016) or **Accessible Journeys** (☎ 610-521 0339; www.disabilitytravel.com; 35 West Sellers Ave, Ridley Park, PA 19078). **Access Able Travel** (www.access-able.com) has a worldwide travel forum where you can post questions about disabled travel.

VISAS

Citizens of Schengen nations (Austria, Belgium, Denmark, Finland, France, Germany, Greece, Italy, Luxembourg, the Netherlands, Norway, Portugal, Spain and Sweden) can enter Iceland as tourists for up to three months with a valid identity card. Citizens of the European Economic Area (EEA), including Ireland and Britain, can visit for up to three months on a passport that is valid for at least three months from their date of arrival. To stay longer you must apply for a residence permit, which is only available from Icelandic embassies or consulates overseas. See www.utl.is or www.mfa.is for more information.

Citizens from Australia, New Zealand, Japan, Canada and the US can travel without a visa for up to three months within any six-month period; this period is deemed to begin on the first entry to any Schengen nation.

Other nationalities should check www.utl.is to see whether they need to apply for a visa from an Icelandic consulate before arriving. The fee varies depending on nationality, and the visa typically allows a three-month stay. Officials will usually request proof that you have sufficient funds for your visit and an onward plane or boat ticket.

VOLUNTEERING

A volunteering holiday is a good (and relatively cheap) way of getting intimately involved with Iceland's people and landscape. For an overview of possible projects in Iceland, try **Volunteer Abroad** (www.volunteerabroad.com).

Iceland's Environment Agency **Umhverfisstofnun** (UST; http://english.ust.is/of-interest/ConservationVolunteers) recruits more than 200 volunteers each summer for work on practical short-term conservation projects around the country, mainly creating or maintaining trails in Vatnajökull National Park (incorporating Skaftafell and Jökulsárgljúfur), and in the Mývatn and Fjallabak nature reserves. Its programs are often run in conjunction with volunteer organisations from abroad:

British Trust for Conservation Volunteers (BTCV; ☎ UK 01302 388 883; www.btcv.org; Sedum House, Mallard Way, Doncaster, DN4 8DB, UK) Volunteers pay BTCV a fee for accommodation and food costs and must pay for their own transport to a designated pick-up point. Over 18s only.

Iceland Volunteer Trail Teams A home-grown conservation group, set up by the Environment Agency, which works on 11-week summer projects in Skaftafell. Over 20s only.

Working Abroad (UK ☎ 01935 864 458; www.workingabroad.com; The Old School House, Pendomer, Yeovil, Somerset, BA22 9PH, UK) Three-week conservation projects (£450 fee includes food and camping) in the national parks. Volunteers must be between 20 and 40 years old.

Icelandic-based **SEEDS** (SEE beyonD borders; ☎ 845 6178; www.seedsiceland.org; Klapparstígur 16, Reykjavík) organises work camps and volunteering holidays – from helping rangers in the national parks to putting on travelling art exhibitions.

You should also consider contacting organisations directly; for example, the **Arctic Fox Research Station** (p188) and the **Húsavík Whale Museum** (p240) need volunteers to help monitor wildlife.

Two international organisations arrange cultural and conservation projects. **Service Civil International** (www.sciint.org) is a network of voluntary organisations facilitating participation in short-term volunteering projects working with local community groups; projects include conservation, tree planting, trail building, eco-villages, and archaeological and festival work. Volunteers pay a membership and administration fee to their local branch and make their own way to a project, but once they're there all food and accommodation is provided free of charge. **United Planet** (www.unitedplanet.org)

runs long-term (six- to 12-month) projects including humanitarian service, language and intercultural training, cultural-learning activities and exploration. Costs cover housing, insurance and a language course.

WOMEN TRAVELLERS

Women travelling alone in Iceland should encounter few problems, though common-sense precautions apply – walking around city streets alone after dark and hitching alone are not really recommended. When out on the town in Reykjavík be prepared for the advances of Icelandic men – if you think they're being too forward, just make this clear and they will leave you be. In rural areas pubs and restaurants are often combined and attract mainly couples during the week, so single women should have few problems.

In Reykjavík, rape-crisis advice is available from the women's counselling and information centre for survivors of sexual violence, **Stígamót** (☎ 562 6868; www.stigamot.is).

WORK

Citizens of EEA countries do not require a work permit to apply for jobs in Iceland; all other citizens must secure a job offer and work permit before arriving. Work permits are generally only granted to fill seasonal job shortages or for highly skilled professions that are underrepresented in Iceland. For information on residence permits, visit the **Icelandic Directorate of Immigration** (www.utl.is).

In a bankrupt country, where unemployment rose from about 1.6% just before the 2008 crash to almost 8% by 2009, work is hard to come by for all. Companies are reluctant and/or unable to hire foreigners, especially those looking for something better than cleaning, waiting tables or seasonal farm work.

The website of **Vinnumalastofnun** (Directorate of Labour; ☎ 515 4800; www.vinnumalastofnun.is) is a good source of information on living and working in Iceland and has links to the Eures job-search facility (www.eures.is/english), which lists public-employment jobs online.

If you're interested in doing farm work, **Nínukot** (☎ 561 2700; www.ninukot.is; PO-Box 12015, 132-Reykjavík) is an employment agency specialising in farm placements.

See p333 if you wish to do voluntary work in Iceland.

Transport

GETTING THERE & AWAY

Iceland has become far more accessible in recent years with a greater variety of flights and destinations available. Ferry transport is also possible and makes a good alternative for European travellers wishing to take their own car into the country. Flights, tours and rail tickets can be booked online at www.lonelyplanet.com/travelservices.

ENTERING THE COUNTRY

As long as you are in possession of the right documentation, immigration control should be a quick formality at the air- or ferry port where you arrive. Citizens of Schengen nations, the European Economic Area (EEA), the US, Australia, New Zealand, Japan, Canada, Israel and several Latin American nations can travel in Iceland without a visa for up to three months. Other nationalities require a visa; for more information, see p333.

AIR
Airports & Airlines

Iceland's main international airport is **Keflavík International Airport** (KEF; ☎ 425 0600, 425 6000; www.kefairport.is), 48km southwest of Reykjavík. Internal flights and those to Greenland and the Faeroes use the small **Reykjavík Domestic Airport** (REK; www.reykjavik

airport.is) in central Reykjavík. A couple of international flights (usually to/from London and Copenhagen) land at tiny **Akureyri Airport** (AEY; www.flugstodir.is) – see p221 – in Iceland's 'second city' in the north.

AIRLINES FLYING TO/FROM ICELAND

Only a handful of airlines fly to Iceland; all have great safety records.

Air Iceland (NY; ☎ 570 3030; www.airiceland.is)

Atlantic Airways (RC; ☎ Faeroes 34 10 10; www.atlantic.fo)

Iceland Express (HW; ☎ 550 0600; www.icelandexpress.is; Efstaland 26, Grímsbæ, IS-108 Reykjavík)

Icelandair (FI; ☎ 505 0100; www.icelandair.is; Reykjavík Domestic Airport, IS-101 Reykjavík)

SAS (SK; ☎ 577 6420; www.flysas.is; Laugavegur 170, IS-101 Reykjavík)

Australia & New Zealand

To get to Iceland from Australia or New Zealand, you will need to connect through Europe or the USA on a separate carrier.

Continental Europe

Icelandair has regular flights between Keflavík and Copenhagen, Oslo, Stockholm, Paris, Frankfurt, Helsinki and Amsterdam.

Icelandair also has seasonal flights between Keflavík and Barcelona, Bergen, Berlin, Düsseldorf, Madrid, Milan, Munich and Stavanger.

In summer, Iceland Express flies to Alicante (three times weekly), Basel (twice weekly), Berlin (three times a week), Billund (twice weekly), Copenhagen (nine times weekly),

TRANSPORT

THINGS CHANGE...

The information in this chapter is particularly vulnerable to change. Check directly with the airline or a travel agent to make sure you understand how a fare (and ticket you may buy) works and be aware of the security requirements for international travel. Shop carefully. The details given in this chapter should be regarded as pointers and are not a substitute for your own careful, up-to-date research.

TRANSPORT

CLIMATE CHANGE & TRAVEL

Climate change is a serious threat to the ecosystems that humans rely upon, and air travel is the fastest-growing contributor to the problem. Lonely Planet regards travel, overall, as a global benefit, but believes we all have a responsibility to limit our personal impact on global warming.

Flying & Climate Change

Pretty much every form of motor travel generates carbon dioxide (the main cause of human-induced climate change) but planes are far and away the worst offenders, not just because of the sheer distances they allow us to travel, but because they release greenhouse gases high into the atmosphere. The statistics are frightening: two people taking a return flight between Europe and the US will contribute as much to climate change as an average household's gas and electricity consumption over a whole year.

Carbon Offset Schemes

Climatecare.org and other websites use 'carbon calculators' that allow jetsetters to offset the greenhouse gases they are responsible for with contributions to energy-saving projects and other climate-friendly initiatives in the developing world – including projects in India, Honduras, Kazakhstan and Uganda.

Lonely Planet, together with Rough Guides and other concerned partners in the travel industry, supports the carbon offset scheme run by climatecare.org. Lonely Planet offsets all of its staff and author travel.

For more information check out our website: lonelyplanet.com.

Frankfurt (twice weekly), Gothenburg (twice weekly), Luxembourg (twice weekly), New York Newark (four times weekly), Oslo (twice weekly) and Warsaw (twice weekly), with one flight a week to Aalborg, Barcelona, Bologna, Birmingham, Geneva, Kraków, Milan, Paris and Rotterdam. From September to May, the flight schedule is reduced to Alicante (twice weekly), Berlin (twice weekly), Copenhagen (seven times a week) and Warsaw (once a week).

SAS operates direct flights from Keflavík to Oslo (2¾ hours) three times a week.

UK

Icelandair (☎ 0870 7874020; www.icelandair.net) has flights to Keflavík from London Heathrow (three hours) at least twice daily, and regular service throughout the year to Glasgow (two hours) and Manchester (2½ hours).

Iceland Express (☎ 550 0600; www.icelandexpress.com) flies nine times daily (seven in winter) from London Gatwick to Keflavík (three hours) and twice weekly to Akureyri (three hours) in summer. Two weekly flights from London Stansted also fly to Keflavík in winter.

USA & Canada

In summer, Icelandair flies daily from Keflavík to Boston, Minneapolis, New York

and Toronto, with additional services from Keflavík to Orlando, Halifax and Seattle. In winter daily flights continue to/from Boston and New York, with several flights per week to/from Toronto. You can also include Iceland as a free three-day stopover on the way to Britain or continental Europe.

SEA

Smyril Line (Seyðisfjörður ☎ 472 1111; www.smyril-line.com) has a car ferry from Hanstholm or Esbjerg (Denmark) through Tórshavn (Faeroes) to Seyðisfjörður in east Iceland. Boats run all year, but Iceland is only part of the itinerary from mid-April until the end of September. Between October and early April the ferry only travels between Denmark and the Faeroes.

Passengers have a choice of couchettes (bed-seats) or one- to four-berth cabins. From Hanstholm to Seyðisfjörður, the one-way couchette fare for a car and two passengers is €445/286 in high/mid-season. A cabin with two lower berths and no window costs an additional €323/115. High season runs from the end of June to the end of August, mid-season from May to mid-June and late August to mid-September. Children, seniors and students qualify for reduced rates year-round.

If you are travelling from Denmark to Iceland and would like to have a stopover in the Faeroes, you will have to disembark and board the next ferry (the following week). Contact the Smyril Line or see p321 for information about trip packages.

GETTING AROUND

AIR

Iceland has an extensive network of domestic flights, which locals use almost like buses. In winter a flight can be the only way to get between destinations, but weather at this time of year can play havoc with schedules.

See the Iceland Airline & Ferry Routes map (p338) for the current routes operating in Iceland.

Air Iceland (☎ 570 3030; www.airiceland.is) operates flights from Reykjavík to Akureyri (45 minutes, minimum five flights daily), Egilsstaðir (one hour, minimum two daily), Ísafjörður (40 minutes, minimum two daily) and Vestmannaeyjar (25 minutes, twice daily). One-way prices start at Ikr4990 for all domestic flights. See p221 for flights from Akureyri's airport.

Eagle Air (☎ 562 4200; www.ernir.is; Reykjavík Domestic Airport, IS-101 Reykjavík) operates flights to smaller airstrips, including Sauðárkrókur, Hornafjörður (Höfn), Bildudalur and Gjögur. Flights cost €115 one way.

Flugfélag Vestmannaeyja (☎ 481 3255; www.eyja flug.is; IS-900 Vestmannaeyjar) runs flights over to Vestmannaeyjar from Selfoss and tiny Bakki airport, south of Hvolsvöllur. At the time of writing, however, a new harbour was being built at Bakki, with the Vestmannaeyjar ferry due to sail from there from July 2010. This may affect flights so check for the latest info.

Air Passes

Air Iceland offers a couple of air passes, which must be purchased either outside Iceland or in Icelandic travel agencies catering for foreign visitors. The Air Iceland Pass is available with four/five/six sectors for €388/390/450 in high season (mid-June to mid-August). Fly As You Please gives 12 consecutive days of unlimited flights in Iceland for €466, excluding airport taxes. Children under 12 pay half-rates.

Air Charters

Flugfélag Vestmannaeyja (☎ 481 3255; www.eyjaflug. is) runs charter flights over to Vestmannaeyjar

from tiny Bakki airport, about 20km south of Hvolsvöllur.

Other charter airlines include **Eagle Air** (☎ 562 4200; www.ernir.is), at Reykjavík airport, and **Mýflug** (☎ 464 4400; www.myflug.is), at Mývatn.

BICYCLE

Cycling through Iceland's dramatic landscape is a fantastic way to see the country, but you should be prepared for some harsh conditions along the way. Gale-force winds, driving rain, sandstorms, sleet and sudden flurries of snow are all possible at any time of year.

It's essential to know how to do your own basic repairs and to bring several puncture-repair kits and spares, as supplies are hard to come by outside the city. Reykjavík has several well-stocked bike shops. Two of the best include **Örninn** (☎ 588 9890; Skeifan 11d, IS-108 Reykjavík) and **Markið** (☎ 553 5320; Ármúli 40, IS-108 Reykjavík).

If you want to tackle the interior, the Kjölur route has bridges over all major rivers, making it fairly accessible to cyclists. A less challenging route is the F249 to Þórsmörk. The Westfjords also offers some wonderful cycling terrain, though the winding roads and steep passes can make for slow progress.

Transporting Bicycles

Most airlines will carry your bike in the hold if you pack it correctly. You should remove the pedals, lower the saddle, turn the handlebars parallel to the frame and deflate the tyres. Buses charge between Ikr1000 and Ikr2000, but space may be a problem.

If you have brought your own bicycle along you can store your bike box at the

---

ESSENTIAL WEB RESOURCES

Two websites every traveller should know about:

- www.semferda.net – Handy car-sharing site that helps drivers and passengers to link up around the country. A savvy alternative to hitching. Passengers often foot the petrol bill.

- www.vegagerdin.is – Iceland's road administration site details road openings and closings around the country. Vital if you plan to explore Iceland's little-visited corners.

TRANSPORT

TRANSPORT

ICELAND AIRLINE & FERRY ROUTES

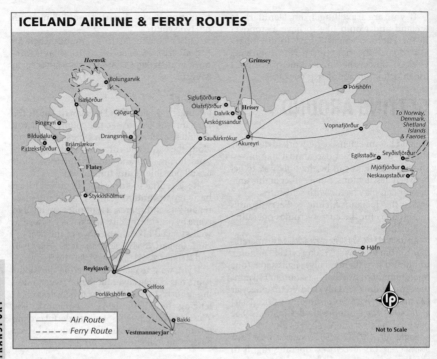

campsite in Keflavík for free for the duration of your visit.

Hire

Various places around Iceland rent out mountain bikes, but these are generally intended for local use only and aren't up to long-haul travel. If you intend to go touring, bring your bike from home or purchase one when you arrive.

BOAT

Several ferries operate in Iceland. The car ferry *Herjólfur* sails between Þorlákshöfn and Vestmannaeyjar, and the *Baldur* sails between Stykkishólmur, Flatey and Brjánslækur – at the time of writing both run year-round. From July 2010, however, a new harbour terminal for the Vestmannaeyjar ferry is set to open at Bakki, about 20km south of Hvolsvöllur (see the boxed text, p155); contact any tourist centre, or the ferry company **Eimskip** (☎ 481 2800; www.eimskip.com) and the **BSÍ bus station** (☎ 562 1011; www.bsi.is) to check the latest transport details. Passenger ferries include the *Sævar* between Arskógssandur and Hrísey, the

Sæfari between Dalvík and Hrísey or Grímsey, and the *Anný* between Neskaupstaður and Mjóifjörður. Small summer-only ferries run from Reykjavík's Sundahöfn harbour to the island of Viðey, and from Ísafjörður and Drangsnes to stops at Hornstrandir in the Westfjords.

BUS

Iceland has an extensive network of bus routes with services operated by a number of bus companies. All are members of the consortium **BSÍ** (Bifreiðastöð Íslands; Map pp72-3; ☎ 562 1011; www.bsi.is; Vatnsmýrarvegur 10), based in the BSÍ bus terminal in Reykjavík. The booking desk sells tickets and distributes the free *Ísland á Eigin Vegum* (Iceland on Your Own) brochure, which contains timetables. From June to August there are regular buses to most places on the Ring Road, and to larger towns in the Westfjords and on the Reykjanes and Snæfellsnes Peninsulas. During the rest of the year services range from daily to nonexistent. In small towns and villages, buses stop at the main petrol station.

Main bus companies:

Reykjavík Excursions (Map pp72-3; ☎ 580 5400; www.re.is; BSÍ bus terminal, Vatnsmýrarvegur 10, Reykjavík) South and southwest Iceland.

SBA-Norðurleið (☎ 550 0700, 550 0770; www.sba.is) Northeast Iceland.

Stjörnubílar (☎ 456 5518; www.stjornubilar.is) Westfjords.

TREX (Bílar og Fólk; ☎ 551 1166; www.bogf.is) South, west and north Iceland.

Bus Passes

Iceland's bus operators are coming out with new and improved bus passes every year to make public transport around the island as easy as possible. Nevertheless, it's still significantly more convenient to hire your own vehicle. Consider teaming up with other travellers to reduce your rental costs.

Visit www.bsi.is and www.bogf.is for a longer list of passports. Some options:

Beautiful South Passport (from €104) Valid from mid-June to August for 11 consecutive days (extra days available). Unlimited travel along the south coast and to Þórsmörk and Lakagígar.

Full-Circle Passport (from €183) Valid from June to August for one circuit of the Ring Road in one direction, stopping wherever you like.

Highland Circle Passport (from €192) Valid from July to August for one circular route to the north of Iceland via the Sprengisandur and Kjölur routes.

Snæfellsnes Passport (from €84) Valid from mid-June to August for one circuit of Snæfellsnes Peninsula, starting and ending in Reykjavík.

West Iceland & Westfjords (from €128) Valid from June to August for one circuit of the Westfjords, to/from Reykjavík via Snæfellsnes Peninsula and Staðarskáli.

CAR & MOTORCYCLE

Driving in Iceland gives you unparalleled freedom to discover the country and, thanks to good roads and light traffic, it's all fairly straightforward. The Ring Road (Rte 1) circles the country and is mostly paved. Beyond this major route fingers of pavement or gravel stretch out to most communities. Outside the Ring Road you are likely to pass no more than a handful of cars each day, even in high season.

In coastal areas driving can be spectacularly scenic, and incredibly slow as you weave up and down over unpaved mountain passes and in and out of long fjords. Even so, a 2WD vehicle will get you almost everywhere in summer.

In winter heavy snow can cause many roads to close and mountain roads generally remain closed until the end of June. Some mountain roads start closing as early as September after the warm summer months. For up-to-date information on road and weather conditions, visit www.vegagerdin.is.

Bring Your Own Vehicle

Car hire in Iceland is shockingly expensive, so taking your own vehicle to the country may not be as daft as it sounds. For temporary duty-free importation, drivers must carry the vehicle's registration documents, proof of valid insurance (a 'green card') and a driving licence. Import duty is initially waived for one month, so you must either re-export the vehicle within this period or apply for an extension, which is valid for an additional two months. Permission for duty-free importation is granted at the point of arrival and is contingent upon agreeing to not lend or sell your vehicle. For more information, contact the **Directorate of Customs** (☎ 560 0300; www.tollur.is; Tryggvagata 19, IS-150 Reykjavík) or the **Internal Revenue Office** (☎ 563 1100; rsk@rsk.is; Laugavegur 166, IS-150 Reykjavík).

Driving Licence

You can drive in Iceland with a driving licence from the US, Canada, Australia, New Zealand and most European countries. If you have a licence from anywhere

---

DRIVE SAFELY

Road Rules

- Drive on the right
- Front and rear seat belts are compulsory
- Dipped headlights must be on at all times
- Blood alcohol limit is 0.05%
- Mobile-phone use is prohibited except with a hands-free kit
- Children under six must use a car seat

Speed Limits

- Built-up areas 50km/h
- Unsealed roads 80km/h
- Sealed roads 90km/h

TRANSPORT

TRANSPORT

else you may need to get an international driving licence, which is normally issued by the local automobile association in your home country.

Fuel & Spare Parts

There are regularly spaced petrol stations around Iceland, but in the highlands you should check fuel levels and the distance to the next station before setting off on a long journey. Unleaded petrol costs about Ikr184 to Ikr189 per litre, diesel about Ikr174 to Ikr179 per litre. Leaded petrol isn't available. Most smaller petrol stations are unstaffed; swipe your credit card in the machine, enter the maximum amount you wish to spend and fill up. You will only be charged for the cost of the fuel put into your vehicle. It's a good idea to check that your card will work by visiting a staffed station while it is open, just in case you have any problems (American credit cards do not have a pin and thus might not work).

Icelandic roads can be pretty lonely, so carry a jack, a spare tyre and jump leads just in case. Although the Icelandic motoring association **Félag Íslenskra Bifreiðaeigenda** (FÍB; ☎ 414

9999; www.fib.is; Borgartún 33, Reykjavík) is only open to residents of Iceland, if you have breakdown cover with an automobile association affiliated with ARC Europe you may be covered by the FÍB – check with your home association.

Hire

Travelling by car is often the only way to get to parts of Iceland. Although hire-car rates are expensive by international standards, they compare favourably against bus or internal air travel within the country. The cheapest cars on offer, usually a Toyota Yaris or similar, cost around Ikr20,000 per day. Figure on paying around Ikr45,000 for a 4WD. Rates include unlimited mileage and VAT. You'd think that with such high prices it would be easy to find a car. Think again. In the height of summer many dealerships completely run out of rentals.

To rent a car you must be 20 years old (25 years for a 4WD) and you will need to show a valid licence. Be sure to check the small print, as additional costs such as extra insurance, airport pick-up charges and one-way rental fees can really rack up.

ROAD DISTANCES (KM)

	Akureyri	Borgarnes	Egilsstaðir	Höfn	Ísafjörður	Reykjavík	Selfoss	Seyðisfjörður	Stykkishólmur	Vík
Akureyri	---									
Borgarnes	315	---								
Egilsstaðir	265	580	---							
Höfn	512	519	247	---						
Ísafjörður	567	384	832	902	---					
Reykjavík	389	74	698	459	457	---				
Selfoss	432	117	640	402	500	57	---			
Seyðisfjörður	292	607	27	274	859	680	667	---		
Stykkishólmur	364	99	629	618	391	173	216	656	---	
Vík	561	246	511	273	630	187	129	538	345	---

F ROADS

We can think of a few choice F words for these bumpy, almost nonexistent tracts of land, but in reality the 'F' stands for *fjall* – the Icelandic word for mountain. Most F roads only support 4WDs and, while some of them may almost blend into the surrounding nature, off-road driving is strictly prohibited everywhere in Iceland. Before tackling any F road you should educate yourself as to what lies ahead (river crossings, boulders etc) and whether or not the entire route is open. See www.vegagerdin.is for road closure details.

There are more than 50 registered car-hire companies in Iceland. If you are arriving in Iceland without any prior rental-car arrangements, it's worth looking around and asking at your accommodation if they have any discounts. The following options are based in the Reykjavík and Keflavík areas (this list is not exhaustive) – agencies in other locations around the country can be found within the relevant destination chapters. Passengers entering Iceland via Seyðisfjörður will find car-hire agencies in nearby Egilsstaðir (see p266).

ALP (☎ 562 6060; www.alp.is; Dugguvogur 10, IS-104 Reykjavík)

Átak (☎ 554 6040; www.atak.is; Smiðjuvegur 1, IS-200 Kópavogur)

Avis (☎ 591 4000; www.avis.is; Knarrarvogi 2, IS-104 Reykjavík) Also located at Reykjavík Domestic Airport and Keflavík International Airport.

Bílaleiga Akureyrar/Höldur – National (☎ 568 6915, 425 0300; www.holdur.is/en; Skeifan 9, IS-109 Reykjavík) Also at Keflavík International Airport.

Budget (☎ 551 7570, 562 6060, 421 5551; www.budget.is; Vatnsmýrarvegur 10, IS-101 Reykjavík) Also at Reykjavík Domestic Airport and Keflavík International Airport.

Dalfoss (☎ 561 3553; www.dalfoss.is; Sóleyjargata 31, IS-101 Reykjavík)

Hasso (☎ 555 3330, 421-6277; www.hasso.is; Smiðjuvegur 34, IS-200 Kópavogur) Also based at Iðavellir 8, IS-230 Reykjanesbær.

Hekla (☎ 590 5000; www.hekla.is; Laugavegur 170-174, IS-105 Reykjavík)

Hertz (☎ 522 4420, 522 4430; www.hertz.is) Branches at Reykjavík Domestic Airport and Keflavík International Airport.

Saga (☎ 421 3737; www.sagacarrental.is) Keflavík International Airport.

Insurance

If you are bringing your own vehicle into Iceland you'll need a 'green card', which proves that you are insured to drive while in Iceland. Green cards are issued by insurance companies in your home country. Contact your existing insurer for details.

When hiring a car, check the small print carefully; most vehicles come with third-party insurance only so you'll need to take out additional Collision Damage Waiver (CDW) to cover you for damage to the hire car. Also check the excess (the initial amount you will be liable to pay in the event of an accident) as this can be surprisingly high.

Hire vehicles are not covered for damage to the tyres, headlights and windscreen, or damage caused to the underside of the vehicle by driving on dirt roads, through water or in sandstorms. Some policies also prohibit 'off-road driving'. This usually only refers to mountain roads (F roads) and 4WD tracks, but check with the car-hire company to be sure. Car-hire agreements also do not cover damage to the hire car caused by collisions with animals.

Parking

Other than in central Reykjavík parking in Iceland is easy to find and free of charge. It should be noted, however, that Akureyri has a bizarre system of plastic clocks that you must follow otherwise you will be fined – see p222 for details. For information on parking in the capital, see p104.

Road Conditions & Hazards

Good road surfaces and light traffic make driving in Iceland relatively easy, but there are some specific hazards that drivers will encounter. Not all roads are sealed, and the transition from sealed to gravel roads is marked with the warning sign *Malbik Endar* – slow down to avoid skidding when you hit the gravel. In most cases roads have two lanes with steeply cambered sides and no hard shoulder; be prepared for oncoming traffic in the centre of the road, and slow down and stay to the right when approaching blind rises, marked as *Blindhæð* on road signs. You'll also need to be prepared to give way when approaching single-lane bridges – marked as *Einbreið Brú*.

Most accidents involving foreign drivers in Iceland are caused by the use of excessive speed on unsurfaced roads. If your car does

TRANSPORT

TRANSPORT

begin to skid, take your foot off the accelerator and gently turn the car in the direction you want the front wheels to go. Do not brake. In other areas severe sandstorms can strip paint off cars, blister your windows and even topple over your vehicle; at-risk areas are marked with orange warning signs.

In winter make sure your hire car is fitted with snow tyres or chains; be sure to carry blankets, food and water; and take extra care when driving on compacted snow.

Roads suitable for 4WD vehicles only are F-numbered (see the boxed text, p341, for more on F roads). Always travel in tandem on these roads and carry emergency supplies and a full tool and repair kit. Always let someone know where you are going and when you expect to be back. River crossings can be extremely dangerous, as few interior roads are bridged. Fords are marked on maps with a 'V', but you'll need to check the depth and speed of the river by wading into it – do not attempt this without a life jacket and lifeline. To cross the river use a low gear in 4WD mode and cross slowly and steadily without stopping or changing gear.

You'll find useful information and a video on driving in Iceland at www.umferdar stofa.is/id/2693.

HITCHING

Hitching anywhere in the world is never fully without risk. Nevertheless, we met scores of tourists that were hitching their way around the country (we even picked up a few) and most of them had very positive reports. Single female travellers and couples tend to get a lift the quickest – sorry guys, best find a woman to travel with. Of course when it comes to hitching, patience is a prerequisite, and logic is important too – be savvy about where you position yourself. Don't stand in the middle of a long straight stretch of highway because drivers will zoom right by before they even notice you. Try standing at junctions, near petrol stations or even by Bónus supermarkets. When you arrive at your accommodation for the night it doesn't hurt to let everyone else know where you're trying to get to the next day. Chances are there's another traveller going that way who can give you a ride.

Summer is by far the best time to hitch a ride and you'll find that both locals and tourists are up for helping hitchers out. You'll get picked up in the winter out of pity – but there aren't too many people driving around at that time of year.

If the idea of hitching makes you uncomfortable, check out www.semferda.net, a handy car-sharing site.

LOCAL TRANSPORT
Bicycle
You can hire bicycles for local riding from some tourist offices, hotels, hostels and guest houses. The standard daily charge is about Ikr2000 to Ikr2500 per day, plus a deposit (a credit-card imprint will usually suffice). Helmets are a legal requirement for all children aged under 15.

Bus
Reykjavík has an extensive network of local buses connecting all the suburbs, and running all the way to Akranes, Borgarnes, Hveragerði, Selfoss and Hvalfjarðarsveit. See www.straeto. is for information on timetables, schedules and routes.

Free local bus networks operate in Akureyri (☎ 462 4020) and Ísafjörður (☎ 893 1058), and the Reykjanesbær area (www.sbk.is) has a municipal service as well.

Taxi
There are around 600 taxis in Iceland, of which almost 500 operate in the Reykjavík area. You'll be hard-pressed to find a taxi driver in Reykjavík or Akureyri that doesn't speak English. Cabbies offer sightseeing tours of the city and nearby attractions. See the destination chapters for more information.

Taxis are metered and – like all other transport in Iceland – they can be quite pricey. Tipping is not expected.

TOURS
Although joining a bunch of other travellers on an organised tour may not be your idea of an independent holiday, Iceland's rugged terrain and high costs can make it an appealing option. Tours can save you time and money and can get you into some stunning but isolated locations where your hire car will never go. Many tours are by bus, others by 4WD or super-Jeep, and some by snowmobile or light aircraft. Most tours give you the option of tacking on adventure activities such as whitewater rafting, kayaking, snowmobiling, horse riding and ice trekking.

There are usually substantial discounts for children and for making bookings online, so shop around before making any decisions. The following is a list of some of the best companies around; you'll find other specific tours and tour operators covered in the destination chapters.

Activity Group (☎ 580 9900; www.activity.is) This group of adventure-tour companies offers activities all over Iceland, including snowmobile tours, white-water rafting, dog sledding and quad-bike (ATV) rides. It has a base at the Húsafell recreation centre in west Iceland.

Air Iceland (☎ 570 3030; www.airiceland.is; Reykjavík Domestic Airport, IS-101 Reykjavík) Iceland's largest domestic airline runs a wide range of combination air, bus, hiking, rafting, horse-riding, whale-watching and glacier day tours around Iceland from Reykjavík and Akureyri. It also runs day tours to Greenland and the Faeroes from Reykjavík.

Dick Phillips (☎ 01434-381440; www.icelandic-travel .com; Whitehall House, Nenthead, Alston, Cumbria, CA9 3PS, UK) British-based Dick Phillips runs a specialist Icelandic travel service, and has decades of experience leading wild hiking, cycling and skiing trips.

Explore Adventures (☎ 562 7000; Laugavegur 11, IS-101 Reykjavík) Adventure-tour company offering glacial hiking, snorkelling, kayaking, caving, canyoning, ice climbing, climbing, hiking and cycling day tours from Reykjavík.

Ferðafélag Íslands (Icelandic Touring Association; Map pp72-3; ☎ 568 2533; www.fi.is; Mörkin 6, IS-108 Reykjavík) Leads summer hikes in Hornstrandir, Landmannalaugar and Þórsmörk, and also runs some bus tours and cross-country skiing trips.

Guðmundur Jónasson Travel (Map pp72-3; ☎ 511 1515; www.gjtravel.is; Borgartún 34, IS-105 Reykjavík) This ever-popular company offers multiday bus tours with light hiking each day. It's an excellent option for active people who'd rather not make their own arrangements.

Highlanders (Map pp72-3; ☎ 568 3030; www.hl.is; Suðurlandsbraut 10, IS-108 Reykjavík) This super-Jeep operator offers tours up to Landmannalaugar, Hekla, Langjökull and along the south coast. It also offers rafting on the Þjórsá river in southwest Iceland.

Iceland Excursions (Gray Line Iceland; Map pp78-9; ☎ 540 1313; www.grayline.is; Hafnarstræti 20) A bustour operator with comprehensive day trips plus horse riding, whale watching, underground explorations, diving, and self-drive holidays. Book online for the best prices.

Iceland Rovers (☎ 567 1720; www.icelandrovers.is; PO Box 8950, Reykjavík) Runs a range of adventure day tours

to Hekla and Landmannalaugar, northern lights tours, and history and geology tours.

Ísafold Travel (☎ 544 8866; www.isafoldtravel.is; Suðurhraun 2b, IS-210 Garðabær) Tailor-made tours for small groups and individuals, including angling, geology, hiking, photography, wellness and women-only tours.

Mountain Guides (☎ 587 9999; www.mountainguide. is; Vagnhöfði 7, IS-110 Reykjavík) This adventurous company offers a wide range of hiking and climbing tours, including day trips to Heiðmörk (near Reykjavík), Hengill and Sólheimajökull, and a series of ice-climbing and trekking tours around Skaftafell. It also provides equipment rental and private guiding for more serious climbers.

Mountain Taxi (☎ 544 5252; www.mountain-taxi.com) This company runs year-round 4WD tours covering popular tourist sites such as the Golden Circle, Landmannalaugar, Hekla volcano, Mýrdalsjökull and Fjallabak as well as multiday and winter 4WD tours.

Mountaineers of Iceland (☎ 581 3800; www. mountaineers.is; Krókhála 5a, IS-110 Reykjavík) Specialises in adventure tours, including day trips to the Golden Circle and Hengill, multiday super-Jeep expeditions, snowmobile and photographic tours, glacier tours, white-water rafting, kayaking, canyoning and horse riding.

Reykjavík Excursions (Kynnisferðir; Map pp72-3; ☎ 580 5400; www.re.is; BSÍ bus terminal, Vatnsmýrarvegur 10, Reykjavík) Reykjavík's most popular day-tour agency, with a comprehensive range of year-round tours.

Touris (☎ 897 6196; www.tour.is; Frostaskjól 105, IS-107 Reykjavík) This super-Jeep operator offers Golden Circle tours with an off-road highland drive, and 4WD tours to Langjökull, Þórsmörk and Landmannalaugar.

Útivist (Map pp72-3; ☎ 562 1000; www.utivist.is; Laugavegur 178, IS-105 Reykjavík) This recommended organisation runs friendly informal hiking trips and covers just about every corner of Iceland. It also runs one of the mountain huts at Þórsmörk.

Vestfjarðaleið (☎ 562 9950; www.vesttravel.is; Hesthálsi 10, IS-110 Reykjavík) This friendly company runs day trips to Þórsmörk, Landmannalaugar, Snæfellsnes and the Golden Circle, as well as a five-day hiking trip from Landmannalaugar and Þórsmörk and four-day hikes from Hengill to Þingvellir.

Youth Hostel Travel Service (Map pp72-3; ☎ 553 8110; www.hostel.is; Sundlaugavegur 34, IS-105 Reykjavík) In conjunction with other companies, the hostel association organises a wide range of tours, including sightseeing, horse riding, glacier trips, rafting, hiking and whale watching.

TRANSPORT

Health

CONTENTS

Travel health depends on your predeparture preparations, your daily health care while travelling and how you handle any medical problem that does develop. If you do fall ill while in Iceland, you will be very well looked after, as health care is excellent.

BEFORE YOU GO

Prevention is the key to staying healthy while abroad. A little planning before departure, particularly for pre-existing illnesses, will save trouble later – see your dentist before a long trip, carry a spare pair of contact lenses and glasses, and take your optical prescription with you. Bring medications in their original, clearly labelled containers. A signed and dated letter from your physician describing your medical conditions and medications, including generic names, is also a good idea. If carrying syringes or needles, be sure to have a physician's letter documenting their medical necessity.

INSURANCE

If you're a citizen of the EU, a European Health Insurance Card (EHIC) entitles you to reduced-cost emergency medical treatment in Iceland. It doesn't cover nonemergency medical treatment, dental treatment, ambulance travel or emergency repatriation home. The EHIC has replaced the old E111 form,

CHECK BEFORE YOU GO

It's usually a good idea to consult your government's travel-health website (if available) before departure:
Australia www.smartraveller.gov.au
Canada www.travelhealth.gc.ca
UK www.fco.gov.uk/en/travel-and-living-abroad
USA wwwnc.cdc.gov/travel

which ceased to be valid in January 2006. The easiest way to apply for an EHIC is online – check your country's Department of Health website for details; in the UK, you can also pick up a postal application form from some post offices.

Citizens from other countries should find out if there is a reciprocal arrangement for free medical care between their country and Iceland. If you do need health insurance, strongly consider a policy that covers you for the worst possible scenario, such as an accident requiring an emergency flight home. Find out in advance if your insurance plan will make payments directly to providers or reimburse you later for overseas health expenditures. The former option is generally preferable, as it doesn't require you to pay out of pocket in a foreign country.

RECOMMENDED VACCINATIONS

The World Health Organization (WHO) recommends that all travellers should be covered for diphtheria, tetanus, measles, mumps, rubella and polio, regardless of their destination. Since most vaccines don't produce immunity until at least two weeks after they're given, visit a physician at least six weeks before departure.

INTERNET RESOURCES

The WHO's publication *International Travel and Health* is revised annually and is available online at www.who.int/ith. Other useful websites include www.mdtravelhealth. com (travel-health recommendations for every country, updated daily), www.fitfor travel.scot.nhs.uk (general travel advice), www.ageconcern.org.uk (advice on travel for the elderly) and www.mariestopes.org.uk (information on women's health and contraception).

IN TRANSIT

DEEP VEIN THROMBOSIS (DVT)

Blood clots may form in the legs during plane flights, chiefly because of prolonged immobility – the longer the flight, the greater the risk of developing a clot. The chief symptom of DVT is swelling or pain of the foot, ankle or calf, usually but not always on just one side. When a blood clot travels to the lungs, it may cause chest pain and breathing difficulties. Travellers experiencing any of these symptoms should immediately seek medical attention.

To prevent DVT on long flights you should walk about the cabin, contract leg muscles and wiggle your ankles and toes while sitting, drink plenty of fluids, and avoid alcohol and tobacco.

JET LAG & MOTION SICKNESS

To avoid jet lag (common when crossing more than five time zones) try drinking plenty of nonalcoholic fluids and eating light meals. Upon arrival, get exposure to natural sunlight and readjust your schedule (for meals, sleep and so on) as soon as possible.

Antihistamines such as dimenhydrinate (Dramamine) and meclizine (Antivert, Bonine) are usually the first choice for treating motion sickness. A herbal alternative is ginger.

IN ICELAND

AVAILABILITY & COST OF HEALTH CARE

High-quality health care is readily available, and for minor, self-limiting illnesses, pharmacists can dispense valuable advice and over-the-counter medication. They can also advise when more specialised help is required. Doctor's appointments cost Ikr2600 for European visitors, with a 25% reduction for children under the age of 16, and Ikr8000 for visitors from outside Europe.

The standard of dental care is usually good; however, it's sensible to have a dental check-up before a long trip.

TRAVELLER'S DIARRHOEA

It's very unlikely that you will suffer diarrhoea in Iceland. The tap water is absolutely safe to drink and is probably less contaminated than bottled water, since it generally flows straight from the nearest glacier.

If you are susceptible to upset stomachs, do what you would do at home: avoid dairy products that contain unpasteurised milk, make sure your food is served piping hot throughout and avoid buffet-style meals.

If you are unlucky enough to develop diarrhoea, be sure to drink plenty of fluids, preferably an oral rehydration solution (eg dioralyte). If diarrhoea is bloody, persists for more than 72 hours or is accompanied by fever, shaking, chills or severe abdominal pain, you should seek medical attention.

ENVIRONMENTAL HAZARDS
Giardia

Giardia is an intestinal parasite that lives in the faeces of humans and animals and is normally contracted through drinking water. Problems can start several weeks after you've been exposed to the parasite, and symptoms may sometimes remit for a few days and then return; this can go on for several weeks or even longer. The first signs are a swelling of the stomach, followed by pale faeces, diarrhoea, frequent gas and possibly headache, nausea and depression. If you exhibit these symptoms you should visit a doctor for treatment.

Although most unpopulated areas in Iceland serve as sheep pastures, there seems to be very little giardia; however, while most people have no problems drinking untreated water from streams and rivers, there's still a possibility of contracting it. If you are unsure, purify your drinking water by boiling it for 10 minutes or use a chemical treatment such as iodine.

Hypothermia & Frostbite

Proper preparation will reduce the risks of getting hypothermia. Even on a hot day in the mountains, the weather can change rapidly – carry waterproof garments and warm layers, and inform others of your route.

Acute hypothermia follows a sudden drop of temperature over a short time. Chronic hypothermia is caused by a gradual loss of temperature over hours.

HEALTH

Hypothermia starts with shivering, loss of judgment and clumsiness. Unless rewarming occurs, the sufferer deteriorates into apathy, confusion and coma. Prevent further heat loss by seeking shelter, wearing warm, dry clothing, drinking hot, sweet drinks and sharing body warmth.

Frostbite is caused by freezing and the subsequent damage to bodily extremities. It is dependent on wind-chill, temperature and the length of exposure. Frostbite starts as frostnip (white, numb areas of skin), from which complete recovery is expected with rewarming. As frostbite develops, however, the skin blisters and becomes black. Loss of damaged tissue eventually occurs. You should wear adequate clothing, stay dry, keep well hydrated and ensure you have adequate calorie intake to prevent frostbite. Treatment involves rapid rewarming. Avoid refreezing and rubbing the affected areas.

Insect Bites & Stings

Mosquitoes are found even in Iceland, although rarely. They're not as ferocious as their southern cousins and may not carry malaria, but they can cause irritation and infected bites. Use a DEET-based insect repellent if necessary.

Bees and wasps cause real problems only to those with a severe allergy (anaphylaxis). If you have such an allergy, carry EpiPen or similar adrenalin injections.

Seasickness

The sea around Iceland is an unpredictable beast. Things can sometimes get rough aboard whale-watching trips, or on the little ferries that run to islands off the coast of Iceland (eg to the Vestmannaeyjar or to Grímsey).

If you're feeling queasy, fresh air and watching the horizon may help, as this balances the sensations in the inner ear and the visual information received by the eyes. If possible, move to the centre of the boat where the rocking is least pronounced, and try lying down and closing your eyes or sucking on crystallised ginger. If you are vomiting a lot, be sure to rehydrate with liquids.

It's usual to take seasickness medication half an hour before you sail. Bring your preferred brand from home, or buy over-the-counter medications such as Dramamine from a pharmacist before your journey. Seasickness medication is not available on board any of the Icelandic boat services.

TRAVELLING WITH CHILDREN

All travellers with children should know how to treat minor ailments and when to seek medical treatment. Make sure the children are up to date with routine vaccinations, and discuss any possible travel vaccines with your doctor well before departure, as some vaccines are not suitable for children under 12 months.

Remember to avoid contaminated food and water. If your child is vomiting or has diarrhoea, lost fluid and salts must be replaced. It may be helpful to take rehydration powders for reconstituting with boiled water.

For more information on travelling with little ones, see Lonely Planet's *Travel with Children*.

SEXUAL HEALTH

Condoms are widely available, and can be found most easily at *apótek* (pharmacies) and supermarkets. When buying condoms, look for a European CE mark, which means they have been rigorously tested, and then keep them in a cool, dry place or they may crack and perish.

Emergency contraception is most effective if taken within 24 hours after unprotected sex. It's available from the national hospital in Reykjavík, and at other hospitals around Iceland.

HEALTH

Language

CONTENTS

Icelandic belongs to the Germanic language family, which includes German, English, Dutch and all the Scandinavian languages except Finnish. It's the nearest thing in existence to Old Norse, the language spoken by the Vikings. In fact, modern Icelandic has changed so little since the Settlement that present-day speakers can read the language of the 12th- and 13th-century sagas without difficulty. Interestingly, Icelandic still retains the ancient letters 'eth' (ð) and 'thorn' (þ), which existed in Old English but have disappeared from modern English.

Icelanders are proud of their literary heritage, and they are particularly keen to stick to their language when it comes to the written word. To avoid having to adopt foreign words for new concepts, neologisms (new words) are created – *útvarp* (radio), *sjónvarp* (television), *tölva* (computer) and *þota* (jet) are just a few that have become part of the Icelandic vocabulary.

Icelanders are rather informal, and a person is rarely addressed by title or surname. They use the ancient patronymic system, where *son* (son) or *dóttir* (daughter) is attached to the father's or, less commonly, the mother's first name. The telephone book entries are listed according to first names.

Most Icelanders speak English and often several other languages too, so you'll have no problems if you can't muster any Icelandic. However, any attempts you do make to speak the lingo will certainly be much appreciated. If you'd like a more in-depth guide to Icelandic, pick up a copy of Lonely Planet's *Scandinavian Phrasebook* or *Small Talk: Northern Europe*. For a food and drink glossary, see p54.

Be aware, especially when you're trying to read bus timetables or road signs, that place names can be spelled in several different ways due to Icelandic grammar rules. For example, the sign that welcomes visitors to the town of Höfn in the southeast reads *Velkomin til Hafnar* (Hafnar is the grammatically correct form of Höfn in the context of this sentence).

ALPHABET & PRONUNCIATION

Many letters are pronounced as in English; the exceptions are listed below. Stress generally falls on the first syllable in a word.

If you're searching for words in an Icelandic dictionary, index or telephone book, be aware that ð, þ, æ and ö have their own separate places in the alphabet: ð comes after d, and the other three letters appear at the very end of the alphabet.

Vowels

á	as the 'ow' in 'cow'
au	as the word 'furry' without 'f' or 'rr'
é	as the 'ye' in 'yet'
ei	as the 'ay' in 'say'
i, y	as the 'i' in 'hit'
í, ý	as the 'ee' in 'see'
ó	as in 'note'
ú	as the 'oo' in 'cool'
Æ æ	as the 'ai' in 'aisle'
ö	as the 'u' in 'nurse'

Consonants

dj	as the 'j' in 'juice'
Ð ð	as the 'th' in 'rather'
f	as the 'f' in 'farm'; between vowels or at the end of a word, as the 'v' in 'van'; before l or n, as the 'b' in 'big'
g	as the 'g' in 'go'; between vowels, as the 'y' in 'yes'; before r or ð or at the end of a word, as the 'ch' in Scottish 'loch'
hv	as 'kv'
j	as the 'y' in 'yes'
ll	as the 'ttl' in 'kettle'
p	as in 'pit'; before s or t, as the 'f' in 'fit'
r	always trilled
Þ þ	as the 'th' in 'thin'

LANGUAGE

ACCOMMODATION

Where is a ... hotel?	Hvar er ... hótel?
cheap	ódýrt
nearby	nálægt
camping ground	tjaldstæði
guest house	gistiheimili
motel	gistihús
youth hostel	farfuglaheimili
Do you have any rooms available?	Eru herbergi laus?
May I see it?	Má ég sjá það?
I'd like (a) ...	Gæti ég fengið ...
bed	rúm
double room	tveggjamannherbergi
single room	einstklingsherbergi

CONVERSATION & ESSENTIALS

Hello.	Halló.
Good morning/ afternoon.	Góðan daginn.
Good evening.	Gott kvöld.
Good night.	Góða nótt.
Goodbye.	Bless.
Excuse me.	Afsakið.
Sorry.	Fyrirgefðu.
Thank you.	Takk fyrir.
You're welcome.	Það var ekkert.
Yes./No.	Já./Nei.
How are you?	Hvað segir þú gott?
Fine. And you?	Allt fínt. En þú?
What's your name?	Hvað heitir þú?
My name is ...	Ég heiti ...
Where are you from?	Hvaðan kemur þú?
I'm from ...	Ég er frá ...
Do you speak English?	Talar þú ensku?
I (don't) understand.	Ég skil (ekki).
What does ... mean?	Hvað þýðir ...?
What's the weather like?	Hvernig er veðrið?
It's ...	Það er ...
cold	kalt
hot	hlýtt
raining	rigning
snowing	snjókoma

DIRECTIONS

Where is ...?	Hvar er ...?
Could you write the address, please?	Gætir þú skrifað niður heimilisfangið?
How do I get to ...?	Hvernig kemst ég til ...?

EMERGENCIES

Help!	Hjálp!
I'm lost.	Ég er villtur/villt. (m/f)
I'm sick.	Ég er veikur.
Go away!	Farðu!
Where is the toilet?	Hvar er snyrtingin?
Call ...!	Hringdu á ...!
a doctor	lækni
an ambulance	sjúkrabíl
the police	lögregluna

Is it far from here?	Er það langt héðan?
Can you show me (on the map)?	Geturðú sýnt mér (á kortinu)?
Go straight ahead.	Farðu beint áfram.
Turn left.	Beygðu til vinstri.
Turn right.	Beygðu til hægri.
far	langt í burtu
near	nálægt

EATING OUT

I'd like ..., please.	Get ég fengið ..., takk.
a table for (four)	borð fyrir (fjóra)
the nonsmoking section	reyklaust borð
I'd like (the) ..., please.	Get ég fengið ..., takk.
bill	reikninginn
drink list	vínseðillinn
menu	matseðillinn
that dish	þennan rétt
Do you have vegetarian food?	Hafið þið grænmetisrétti?
What would you recommend?	Hverju mælir þú með?
Would you like a drink?	Má bjóða þér eitthvað að drekka?
Cheers!	Skál!

HEALTH

Where is a ...?	Hvar er ...?
chemist	apótek
dentist	tannlæknir
doctor	læknir
hospital	sjúkrahús
antibiotics	fúkalyf
condoms	smokkar
contraceptive	getnaðarvörn
tampons	vatttappar/tampónar

NUMBERS

1	*einn*
2	*tveir*
3	*þrír*
4	*fjórir*
5	*fimm*
6	*sex*
7	*sjö*
8	*átta*
9	*níu*
10	*tíu*
11	*ellefu*
12	*tólf*
13	*þrettán*
14	*fjórtán*
15	*fimmtán*
16	*sextán*
17	*sautján*
18	*átján*
19	*nítján*
20	*tuttugu*
21	*tuttugu og einn*
30	*þrjátíu*
40	*fjörutíu*
50	*fimmtíu*
60	*sextíu*
70	*sjötíu*
80	*áttatíu*
90	*níutíu*
100	*eitt hundrað*
1000	*eitt þúsund*

SHOPPING & SERVICES

I'm looking for a/the ...	*Ég er að leita að ...*
bank	*banka*
city centre	*miðbænum*
market	*markaðum*
police	*lögreglunni*
post office	*pósthúslnu*
public toilet	*almenningssalerni*
telephone centre	*símstöðinni*
tourist office	*upplýsingaþjónustu fyrir ferðafólk*

What time does it open/close?	*Hvenær opnar/lokar?*
I'd like to buy ...	*Mig langar að kaupa ...*
How much is it?	*Hvað kostar þetta?*
There's a mistake in the bill.	*Það er villa í reikningnum.*
Where can I get internet access?	*Hvar get ég fengið að nota internetið?*
I'd like to send an email.	*Mig langar til að senda tölvupóst.*

TIME & DATES

Monday	*mánudagur*
Tuesday	*þriðjudagur*
Wednesday	*miðvikudagur*
Thursday	*fimmtudagur*
Friday	*föstudagur*
Saturday	*laugardagur*
Sunday	*sunnudagur*

What time is it?	*Hvað er klukkan?*
today	*í dag*
tomorrow	*á morgun*

TRANSPORT

Where can I buy a ticket?	*Hvar kaupi ég miða?*
Can we get there by public transport?	*Er hægt að taka rútu þangað?*

What time does the ... leave/arrive?	*Hvenær fer/kemur ...?*
boat	*báturinn*
bus	*vagninn*
plane	*flugvélin*

One ... ticket (to Reykjavík), please.	*Einn miða ... (til Reykjavíkur), takk.*
one-way	*aðra leiðina*
return	*fram og til baka*

first	*fyrst*
last	*síðast*
next	*næst*

I'd like a taxi ...	*Get ég fengið leigubíl ...*
at (9am)	*klukkan (níu fyrir hádegi)*
tomorrow	*á morgun*

How much is it to ...?	*Hvað kostar til ... ?*
Please take me to (this address).	*Viltu aka mér til (þessa staðar).*
Please stop here.	*Stoppaðu hér, takk.*

Also available from Lonely Planet:
Scandinavian Phrasebook

Glossary

See p49 in the Food & Drink chapter for useful words and phrases dealing with food and dining. See the Language chapter (p347) for other useful words and phrases.

á – river (as in Laxá, or Salmon River)
álfar – elves
álfhóll – 'elf hillock'; small wooden house for elves, often seen in Icelandic gardens
Alþingi – Icelandic parliament

basalt – hard volcanic rock that often solidifies into hexagonal columns
bíó – cinema
brennivín – local schnapps
bær – farm

caldera – crater created by the collapse of a volcanic cone

dalur – valley

eddas – ancient Norse books
ey – island

fjörður – fjord
foss – waterfall
fumarole – vents in the earth releasing volcanic gas

gata – street
geyser – spouting hot spring
gistiheimilið – guest house
gjá – fissure, rift
glíma – Icelandic wrestling
goðar – chieftain

hákarl – putrid shark meat
hestur – horse
hot pot – outdoor hot tub or spa pool, found at swimming baths and some accommodation
hraun – lava field
huldufólk – hidden people
hver – hot spring
höfn – harbour

ice cap – permanently frozen glacier or mountain top
Íslands – Iceland

jökulhlaup – glacial flooding caused by volcano erupting beneath an ice cap
jökull – glacier, ice cap

kirkja – church

Landnámabók – comprehensive historical text recording the Norse settlement of Iceland
laug – hot spring
lava tube – underground tunnel created by liquid lava flowing under a solid crust
lón – lagoon

mudpot – bubbling pool of superheated mud
mörk – woods or forest

nes – headland
nunatak – hill or mountain surrounded by a glacier

puffling – baby puffin

reykur – smoke, as in Reykjavík (literally 'Smoky Bay')
runtur – 'round tour'; Icelandic pub crawl or aimless driving around town

sagas – Icelandic legends
sandur – glacial sand plain
scoria – glassy volcanic lava
shield volcano – gently sloped volcano built up by fluid lava flows
skáli – hut; snack bar
stræti – street
sundlaug – heated swimming pool

tephra – rock/material blasted out from a volcano
tjörn – pond, lake
torg – town square

vatn – lake (as in Mývatn, or Midge Lake)
vegur – road
vents – natural clefts where hot steam emerges from the ground
vík – bay
vogur – cove, bay

The Authors

FRAN PARNELL
Coordinating Author, Reykjavík, Southwest Iceland, Southeast Iceland

Fran's passion for Scandinavia began while studying for a masters degree in Anglo-Saxon, Norse and Celtic. A strange university slide show featuring sublime Icelandic mountains and a matter-of-fact man who'd literally dug his own grave awakened a fascination that has kept on growing. Deserted valleys and blasted mountain tops are her chosen lurking places, and Hekla is her favourite volcano. Fran returns to Iceland as often as possible and, when not there, can read, think and dream of little else. Fran has also worked on Lonely Planet's guides to Scandinavian Europe, Sweden and Reykjavík. For this edition she also wrote Destination Iceland, Getting Started, Events Calendar, Itineraries, History, The Culture, Iceland's Great Outdoors and Directory.

BRANDON PRESSER
West Iceland, The Westfjords, Northwest Iceland, Northeast Iceland, East Iceland, The Highlands

Growing up in northern Canada, Brandon was all too familiar with sweeping desolate terrain and shiver-worthy landscapes. But no snowdrift was big enough to prepare him for the sheer awesomeness of the remote Icelandic countryside. It was a simple transcontinental layover that turned harmless curiosity into full-blown infatuation and now, several years later, he's checked off almost every fjord head and mountain pass from his to-do list. He's even received compliments on his Icelandic pronunciation! (His grammar, however, is improving at glacial speeds.) Brandon spends most of the year writing his way across the globe – he's authored a dozen Lonely Planet guides and explored more than 50 countries. Which one is his favourite? You're reading about it right now. Brandon also wrote Food & Drink, Environment, Activities, Gateway to Greenland & the Faeroes and Transport.

Behind the Scenes

THIS BOOK

This 7th edition of *Iceland* was researched and written by Fran Parnell and Brandon Presser. The 1st edition was written by Deanna Swaney, who also updated the 2nd edition. The 3rd edition was updated by Graeme Cornwalls and Deanna Swaney, and Graeme updated the 4th edition on his own. We sent Paul Harding and Joe Bindloss on the road to update the 5th edition, while Fran Parnell and Etain O'Carroll wrote and updated the 6th edition.

Commissioning Editor Jo Potts
Coordinating Editor Susan Paterson
Coordinating Cartographer Amanda Sierp
Coordinating Layout Designer Kerrianne Southway
Managing Editor Laura Stansfeld
Managing Cartographers Adrian Persoglia, Herman So
Managing Layout Designer Sally Darmody
Assisting Editors Susie Ashworth, David Carroll, Nigel Chin, Justin Flynn, Averil Robertson
Assisting Layout Designer Nicholas Colicchia
Cover Research Naomi Parker, lonelyplanet.images.com
Internal Image Research Aude Vauconsant, lonely planetimages.com
Project Managers Rachel Imeson, Glenn van der Knijff
Language Content Branislava Vladisavljevic

Thanks to Lucy Birchley, Matthew Cashmore, Owen Eszeki, Ryan Evans, Annelies Mertens, Lucy Monie, Wayne Murphy, Trent Paton, Lyahna Spencer

THANKS
FRAN PARNELL

A huge thank you to everyone who helped during research and writing. This includes tourist-office, museum and library staff, particularly Ásta at Reykjavík; Þorbjörg at Þorbergssetur; Anna at Útivist; Kári at Heimaey library; and everyone at Hafnarfjörður library. It's always fun catching up with Jón Trausti Sigurðarson at Grapevine. Thanks too to Guðni; Alice Olivia Clarke for insights on Reykjanes; Kristín and sister at Höfn for trusting me with their home; Lonely Planet readers (especially Sara Meese); and Kurt Leuthold and family for sheer gallantry. Brandon, it was a genuine pleasure to work with someone with such a passion for Iceland (and Arctic foxes!). Thanks to Lonely Planet's Jo Potts for her calm, kind presence throughout; and the coordinating team who kept the show on the road: Imogen Bannister, Herman So, Rachel Imeson, Amanda Sierp and Susan Paterson, and editors Averil and Susie.

BRANDON PRESSER

My research trip was unforgettable – a million *takk fyrirs* are owed. First, thanks to Jo Potts for commis-

THE LONELY PLANET STORY

Fresh from an epic journey across Europe, Asia and Australia in 1972, Tony and Maureen Wheeler sat at their kitchen table stapling together notes. The first Lonely Planet guidebook, *Across Asia on the Cheap,* was born.

Travellers snapped up the guides. Inspired by their success, the Wheelers began publishing books to Southeast Asia, India and beyond. Demand was prodigious, and the Wheelers expanded the business rapidly to keep up. Over the years, Lonely Planet extended its coverage to every country and into the virtual world via lonelyplanet.com and the Thorn Tree message board.

As Lonely Planet became a globally loved brand, Tony and Maureen received several offers for the company. But it wasn't until 2007 that they found a partner whom they trusted to remain true to the company's principles of travelling widely, treading lightly and giving sustainably. In October of that year, BBC Worldwide acquired a 75% share in the company, pledging to uphold Lonely Planet's commitment to independent travel, trustworthy advice and editorial independence.

Today, Lonely Planet has offices in Melbourne, London and Oakland, with over 500 staff members and 300 authors. Tony and Maureen are still actively involved with Lonely Planet. They're travelling more often than ever, and they're devoting their spare time to charitable projects. And the company is still driven by the philosophy of *Across Asia on the Cheap*: 'All you've got to do is decide to go and the hardest part is over. So go!'

sioning the title and for your support throughout the project. To Fran – it was such a treat working with you! Thanks also to Susan, Susie and the rest of Lonely Planet's all-star production team. In Iceland, thanks to Kjartan for always checking in; Ásta for your pearls of wisdom; Siggy and Ester for letting me tag along in Hornstrandir; Tanja and Astrid for your hospitality; Manny for your positive energy; Nanna for being Nanna; Vilborg for being too damn good at your job; and everyone at Air Iceland and Icelandair for sharing your passion for Iceland and its sagas with me. Additional thanks to Jón Páll, Sirrý, Arngrimur Vidar, Cosima, Þorgeir, Valdimar, Cathy, and Ásbjörn. Thanks also to Justine and Abby for pointing out my unhealthy *skyr* obsession. To Eli for once again opening your Rolodex of quirky contacts. Finally, to my chorus of local voices (Sigurstreinn, Edda, Erlendur, James, Jón, Friðrik & Adda, and Aggi), thank you for sharing your experiences – this new edition is much richer as a result.

OUR READERS
Many thanks to the travellers who used the last edition and wrote to us with helpful hints, useful advice and interesting anecdotes:

Melissa Addey, Aaron Alamo, Reinier Bakels, Katharine Barnes, William Barnes, Lydia Beall, Kristiina Bernhardt, Marije Boks, Abigail Borchert, Agnes Brá Birgisdóttir, Alix Branch, Jan Burmeister, Sally Burnett, Daniel and Rachel Century, Joe Chan, Mette Holst Christensen, Margo Coffey, Steve Davies, Kathryn Davison, Richard Denny, Sanne Emborg, Elli Faherty, Caroline Fink, Marta Font, Zoe Fortune, Chris Fox, Omar Gardner, Stephen Grange, Diane Graves, Fernando Gurtubay, Frank Haanebrink, Anna Hamer, Brendan Hanratty, Mark Hebden, Jasmin Heinz, Börkur Hrólfsson, Jennifer Huang, Chris Hutchinson, Harpa Ingolfsdottir, Christina Jaki, Anna Sigridur Jóhannsdóttir, Cathy Josephson, Walter G Kealey III, Richard Kottle, Barry Landesman, Patrick Lee, Audrey Leuba, Ursula Lindgren, Anna Maceachern, Magdalena Malinowska, Kathryn Malmgren, Kelvin McKerracher,

Clemens Metz, Margie Mikliechuk, Charline Nennig, David Nurenberg, Nicolle Oneill, Juka A Órden, Paul Ormrod, Stacy Orr, Gavin Parnaby, Robin Pater, Laurent Pouvreau, Anna Ptaszynska, Nic Rouquette, Liz Ruddick, Francesco Segoni, Jennifer Smith, Vic Sofras, Milo Stoessel, Carol Sweetenham, Ryan Taylor, Kate Tench, Stefan Thorgrimsson, Kate Underwood, Juha Valimaki, Loes Van Breugel, Axel Vetter, Stefan Vogel, Konstantin Willmann, Trish Wright, Shak Yousaf, Ásdís Þula Þorláksdóttir.

ACKNOWLEDGMENTS
Many thanks to the following for the use of their content:

Globe on title page ©Mountain High Maps 1993 Digital Wisdom, Inc.

BEHIND THE SCENES

Index

INDEX

000 Map pages
000 Photograph pages

000 Map pages
000 Photograph pages

INDEX

MAP LEGEND
ROUTES

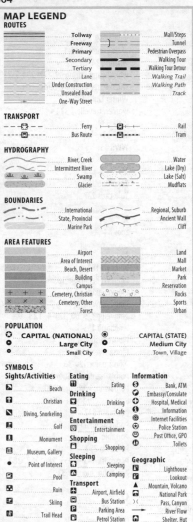

Tollway	Mall/Steps
Freeway	Tunnel
Primary	Pedestrian Overpass
Secondary	Walking Tour
Tertiary	Walking Tour Detour
Lane	Walking Trail
Under Construction	Walking Path
Unsealed Road	Track
One-Way Street	

TRANSPORT

Ferry	Rail
Bus Route	Tram

HYDROGRAPHY

River, Creek	Water
Intermittent River	Lake (Dry)
Swamp	Lake (Salt)
Glacier	Mudflats

BOUNDARIES

International	Regional, Suburb
State, Provincial	Ancient Wall
Marine Park	Cliff

AREA FEATURES

Airport	Land
Area of Interest	Mall
Beach, Desert	Market
Building	Park
Campus	Reservation
Cemetery, Christian	Rocks
Cemetery, Other	Sports
Forest	Urban

POPULATION

✪ CAPITAL (NATIONAL)	● CAPITAL (STATE)
● Large City	● Medium City
○ Small City	● Town, Village

SYMBOLS

Sights/Activities
- Beach
- Christian
- Diving, Snorkeling
- Golf
- Monument
- Museum, Gallery
- Point of Interest
- Pool
- Ruin
- Skiing
- Trail Head
- Zoo, Bird Sanctuary

Eating
- Eating

Drinking
- Drinking
- Cafe

Entertainment
- Entertainment

Shopping
- Shopping

Sleeping
- Sleeping
- Camping

Transport
- Airport, Airfield
- Bus Station
- Parking Area
- Petrol Station
- Taxi Rank

Information
- Bank, ATM
- Embassy/Consulate
- Hospital, Medical
- Information
- Internet Facilities
- Police Station
- Post Office, GPO
- Toilets

Geographic
- Lighthouse
- Lookout
- Mountain, Volcano
- National Park
- Pass, Canyon
- River Flow
- Shelter, Hut
- Waterfall

LONELY PLANET OFFICES

Australia (Head Office)
Locked Bag 1, Footscray, Victoria 3011
☎ 03 8379 8000, fax 03 8379 8111
talk2us@lonelyplanet.com.au

USA
150 Linden St, Oakland, CA 94607
☎ 510 250 6400, toll free 800 275 8555
fax 510 893 8572
info@lonelyplanet.com

UK
2nd fl, 186 City Rd,
London EC1V 2NT
☎ 020 7106 2100, fax 020 7106 2101
go@lonelyplanet.co.uk

Published by Lonely Planet
ABN 36 005 607 983

© Lonely Planet 2010

© photographers as indicated 2010

Cover photograph: Northern lights, Iceland, Torleif Svensson/Corbis.
Many of the images in this guide are available for licensing from
Lonely Planet Images: lonelyplanetimages.com.

Printed by China Translation and Printing Services Ltd
Printed in China.

Although the authors and Lonely Planet have taken
all reasonable care in preparing this book, we make
no warranty about the accuracy or completeness of
its content and, to the maximum extent permitted,
disclaim all liability arising from its use.